INTERGROUP ACCOMMODATION IN PLURAL SOCIETIES

INTERGROUP ACCOMMODATION IN PLURAL SOCIETIES

A selection of conference papers with special reference to the Republic of South Africa

Edited by
Nic Rhoodie
Head, Department of Sociology, and Director, Institute for Plural Societies, University of Pretoria

Winifred Crum Ewing
Assistant to the Editor

Palgrave Macmillan

© Nic Rhoodie 1978

Softcover reprint of the hardcover 1st edition 1978

All rights reserved. No part of this publication may be reproduced or transmitted, in any form or by any means, without permission

First published 1978 by
THE MACMILLAN PRESS LTD
London and Basingstoke
Associated companies in Delhi
Dublin Hong Kong Johannesburg Lagos
Melbourne New York Singapore Tokyo

British Library Cataloguing in Publication Data

Intergroup accommodation in plural societies
1. Pluralism (social sciences)—Congresses
I. Rhoodie, Nic   II. Ewing, Winifred Crum
III. University of Pretoria. Institute for Plural Societies
301.45   HM131

ISBN 978-1-349-04316-3   ISBN 978-1-349-04314-9 (eBook)
DOI 10.1007/978-1-349-04314-9

This book is sold subject to the standard conditions of the Net Book Agreement

Contents

Preface	xiii
Notes on the Contributors	xv

INTRODUCTION   Nic Rhoodie   1

1 LIMITS OF GOVERNMENT IN THE THIRD WORLD
   Ernest W. Lefever   13
    I   Limits of Politics in the Third World   15
    II   The Rule of Law and Justice   19
    III   Kinds of Authoritarian Regimes   21
    IV   Pluralism and the Internal Colony   23
    V   A Postscript on South Africa   24

2 MAJORITY RULE VERSUS DEMOCRACY IN DEEPLY DIVIDED SOCIETIES   *Arend Lijphart*   27
    I   Majoritarian Democracy and the British Paradigm   28
    II   The Plural Societies Paradigm   31
    III   Consociational versus Majoritarian Democracy   33
    IV   A Comparison of the Viability of the two Models   35
    V   Drawbacks of the Consociational Model   38
    VI   Conclusion: Determinism versus Free Choice   40

3 A MODEL OF A MULTINATIONAL SOCIETY AS DEVELOPED IN AUSTRIA-HUNGARY BEFORE 1918
   Friedrich Prinz   44
    I   Nationalism Today   45
    II   The Nationality Question in Austria-Hungary   46
    III   Personal Autonomy or the Principle of Personality   46
    IV   Renner's Ideas and South Africa Today   48
    V   Strong and weak points of Personal Autonomy   50
    VI   Summary and Conclusion   51

4	**ETHNO-NATIONAL VERSUS OTHER FORMS OF GROUP IDENTITY: THE PROBLEM OF TERMINOLOGY** *Walker Connor*	53
	I Ethnicity	64
	II Primordialism	67
	III Pluralism	71
	IV Tribalism	72
	V Regionalism	73
	VI Communalism	75
	VII Parochialism	76
	VIII Subnationalism	77
	IX Accurate Terminology	77
5	**THE RIGHT TO SELF-DETERMINATION: DEFINITION, REALITY AND IDEAL POLICY** *Raymond D. Gastil*	84
	I The Definition and Contexts of Subnationalism	86
	II Adjustive Reactions to Demands for Self-determination	90
	III Self-determination in International Law	96
	IV Basic Principles for Examining Claims to Self-determination	99
	V The Theoretical Argument for Self-determination	100
	VI The Rights to Self-Determination of Territorial Minorities	105
	VII Balancing Self-determination and Other Values in Future Policy	108
6	**ISLAMIC-ARABISM VERSUS PLURALISM: THE FAILURE OF INTERGROUP ACCOMMODATION IN THE MIDDLE EAST** *Moshe Ma'oz*	115
	I Introduction	115
	A. The Islamic Era	116
	B. The Modern Era	117
	II The Fertile Crescent versus Egypt	118
	A. Arab-Jewish Conflicts	120
	B. The Arab-Kurdish Conflict	121
	III Muslim-Christian Conflict in Lebanon	122
	IV The case of Syria	125
	A. The role of the French Mandate	126
	B. Integration of Minority Groups in Political Life	127
	C. 'Alawis Seize Power	130
	D. The Mechanism of the 'Alawi Elite in Power: Jadid Compared to Asad	131
	E. The Regime's Civilian and Popular Cast	133

Contents vii

	F. Opposition to Jadid's 'Alawi Regime (1966–1970)	134
	G. Asad's New Policies regarding Intergroup Accommodation	135
V	Conclusions	137

7 PATTERNS OF INTERGROUP ACCOMMODATION IN SOUTHEAST ASIA: IS DEMOCRATIC PLURALISM POSSIBLE? *Justus M. van der Kroef* 143
    I   The Communist Party of Malaya: An Example of Accommodation 143
    II The Chinese in Sarawak and Malaysia Generally 145
    III The Chinese in Thailand 148
    IV Indonesia: the Chinese and other Ethnic Groups 149
    V   The Socialist Republic of Vietnam 152
    VI The Union of Burma 154
    VII The Southern Philippines 156
    VIII National Ideology: 'Civil Religion' 159
    IX The Marxist-Leninist (Maoist) Route to Accommodation 163
    X   The Social Consequences of Economic Activity 164
    XI Conclusions: Attitudes to Democratic Pluralism 167

8 THE PUBLIC SERVICES IN A PLURAL SOCIETY
William Gutteridge 174
    I   A Community of Diverse Ethnic Groups 174
    II Organisation of the Public Services 175
    III Composition of the Public Services, particularly the Police and the Army 177
    IV Some Constructive Approaches 178

9 PRESCRIPTIONS FOR THE PLURAL SOCIETY: THEORY AND PRACTICE IN THE SOUTH AFRICAN CONTEXT
Alvin Rabushka 179
    I   A Paradigm of Politics in the Plural Society 181
    II Race and Politics in South Africa 182
    III Prescriptions for the Plural Society: the Case of South Africa 186
    IV Theory of Racial Harmony 190

10 SOME EDUCATIONAL IMPERATIVES REGARDING THE PEACEFUL PURSUIT OF INTERGROUP ACCOMMODATION IN A PLURAL SOCIETY *Edward Fort* 197
    I   Background Overview 197
    II The Challenge of Cultural Pluralism 199

III	Black Americans, a Rise of Neo-ethnicity, Absence of Total Assimilation	202
IV	Racism and Education and the Challenge Internationally	206
V	Black Students in a White University Setting	213
VI	Barriers to Black Equal Opportunity on White Campuses	215
	A. Insensitivity of College Administrators and Staff	215
	B. The Academicians' Assault on Open Admissions in Higher Education	216
	C. Assault on Black Studies	219
	D. Slowness of True Affirmative Action	220
VII	Conclusion on the Higher Education Scene	222
VIII	Organisational Imperatives for Dropping the Barriers to Equal Educational Opportunities for Black and Other Minority Students in Pluralistic Societies	222
	A. The Pre-Higher Education Scene	222
	B. The Higher Education Scene	225
IX	Conclusion	228

11 THE SPECIAL ROLE OF THE MASS NEWS MEDIA IN A PLURAL SOCIETY *Leonard R. Sussman* 231

I	American Minorities	232
II	How Well Did the News Media Explain the Black and White Groups to One Another?	234
III	Changes in the Role of the Press	239
IV	The Importance of Press Credibility in Coverage of Civil Disorders	241
V	The Development of Press Guidelines for the Coverage of Civil Disorders	243
VI	Attempts by the Third World to Create a Universal Standard of Government-imposed Press Guidelines and Implementation	244
VII	The Special Role of the Mass News Media	246

12 THE PROBLEMS OF INTERGROUP ACCOMMODATION AND PLURALISM IN THE POLITICS OF PAKISTAN
Khalil A. Nasir 249

I	Politics of Pluralism in the Formative Years of Pakistan	249
II	The Problems of Pluralism in the Constitution-making Process	254
III	The Politics of Regional Pluralism: the Failure of Consolidation and the Emergence of Bangladesh	257

IV	The Role of Religious Pluralism in Pakistani Politics	264
V	The Political Dynamics of Cultural Diversities in Pakistan	272
VI	Conclusion	280

13 THE PROTECTION OF MINORITY RIGHTS IN AFRICA
W. J. Breytenbach   285

I	The Problem of Minority Protection	285
II	The International Pattern	286
III	Minorities and Factors Responsible for Minority Situations	288
IV	Factors Responsible for the Violation of Minority Rights	290
V	How Minorities could be Protected and/or are indeed Protected in some Cases	294
VI	Evaluation	297

14 WHAT IS THE LESSON OF SWISS SOLUTIONS TO PLURALIST PROBLEMS FOR SOUTH AFRICA?
Christopher Hughes   299

I	Style and Form of Government	299
II	Religion	300
III	Language	301
IV	Language and Religion Combined	301
V	The Lesson	303
VI	Since 1970	303
VII	Conclusion	304

15 PLURAL SOCIETIES AND THE APPLICATION OF DEMOCRACY   *Mburumba Kerina*   305

I	Introduction	305
II	Intergroup Conflict and Accommodation in Plural Societies	306
III	Complex Political Structures for Plural Societies	308
IV	Ethnicity and Democracy	310
V	The Proposed Formula for Namibia	311
VI	The Turnhalle Constitutional Conference and the Craft of Diplomacy: Politics of Realism versus Politics of Frustration	312
	POSTSCRIPT UNITY IS NAMIBIA'S PRESSING NEED	318

16	A COMPARATIVE PERSPECTIVE ON METROPOLITAN AREAS AS LABORATORIES FOR COMMUNITY-ORIENTED LOCAL GOVERNMENT REORGANISATION IN SOUTH AFRICA *W. B. Vosloo*	322
	I The Scope of Metropolitanisation	323
	II Metropolitan Problem and Approaches to Metropolitan Reform	323
	III The Characteristics of the South African Metropolis	327
	IV Governmental Organisation in Metropolitan Areas	329
	V The Challenge of Metropolitan Reorganisation in South Africa	331
	VI Conclusion	333
17	PLURAL ACCOMMODATION IN SOUTH AFRICA: PROBLEMS, PERSPECTIVES AND SOLUTIONS *G. C. Olivier*	335
	I The Failure of Liberal Constitutionalism in South Africa	337
	II The Failure of Apartheid	338
	III South Africa as a Transitional Society	338
	IV South Africa as a Plural Society	341
	V Patterns and Directions of Change in South Africa	343
	VI A Strategy for Change: Some Practical Suggestions	346
18	DERIVING POLICY FOR SOUTH AFRICA *Anthony de Crespigny*	348
	I Factual Assumptions	349
	II Value Assumptions	361
	III Policy Derivations	362
19	SOUTH AFRICA – A BLACK VIEWPOINT *Percy Qoboza*	368
	I Separate Development Unacceptable and Unworkable	368
	II Consultation Essential for Deriving New Policies	368
	III Homelands, Townships and Black Leaders	369
	IV Some Questions and Answers	370
	V Black and White Love for Our Country: Hopes for the Future	372
20	THE RESTORATION OF HUMAN RIGHTS: A MEANS TOWARDS ACHIEVING SOCIAL JUSTICE IN SOUTH AFRICA *B. G. Ranchod*	374
	I Aim 1: Eliminate Racial Discrimination (Statutory)	375
	II Restoration of Fundamental Human Rights	378

Contents xi

21 THE DEVOLUTION OF POWER IN SOUTH AFRICA:
PROBLEMS AND PROSPECTS *Lawrence Schlemmer* 381
   I   Plural Devolution of Power 381
   II   Reform within the Institutions of the Common Society 383
   III   Plural Devolution on the Basis of Race and Privilege 385
   IV   Consociational Accommodation 387
   V   Alternatives to Devolution of Power 391

22 SOUTH AFRICA'S DOMESTIC POLITICS: KEY
QUESTIONS AND OPTIONS *W. J. de Klerk* 397
   I   Multinationalism 397
   II   Aggressive Heterogeneity 399
   III   Multinationalism and International Politics 400
   IV   Four Options 401
   V   Conclusion 409

23 INDIVIDUAL ECONOMIC RESPONSIBILITY: A NECESSARY CONDITION FOR A STABLE ORDER IN SOUTH AFRICA *J. A. Lombard and P. J. van der Merwe* 411
   I   South Africa on the Threshold 411
   II   The Socio-economic Dimensions 413
   III   The Way Ahead 417

24 INTERNAL SECURITY AND EXTERNAL SUPPORT - THE
SOUTH AFRICAN DILEMMA *Peter Janke* 421
   I   USSR and Mozambique 422
   II   USSR and Angola 423
   III   USSR and the Liberation Movements 425
   IV   Can the Soviet Threat be Contained? 428

25 CITIZENSHIP AND INTERGROUP ACCOMMODATION
IN PLURAL SOCIETIES *Marinus Wiechers* 430
   I   Citizenship and Distribution of Power 430
   II   Nationality and National and International Law 431
   III   International Human Rights 433
   IV   The Position in South Africa 435
   V   Different Citizenship Status 437
   VI   Political Realities in South Africa 439

26 THE STRUCTURING OF POLITICAL CHANGE IN
SOUTH AFRICA   *C. F. Nieuwoudt*   443
    I   Change and Development   443
   II   Political Institutions   445
  III   Developments in South Africa   447
  IV   Problems Inherent in Development   451
   V   Institutional Framework   453
  VI   Conclusion   455

27 CLEAVAGE AND CONFLICT IN MODERN TYPE
SOCIETIES   *Talcott Parsons*   456
    I   The Theoretical Paradigm as applied to Society as a Whole   456
   II   The South African Situation   461

28 THE PROBLEMS OF PLURAL SOCIETIES WITH
SPECIAL REFERENCE TO THE URBAN BLACKS OF
SOUTH AFRICA   *M. T. Moerane*   467
    I   Historical Background   467
   II   Dr Verwoerd's Homeland Plan   469
  III   Shared Homeland for all South Africans   469
  IV   Present Structure of Power   470
   V   Need for an Inclusive South Africanism   471
  VI   The Way to a Truly National Government   472
 VII   Creating the Right Atmosphere for Progress   475

Index   477

Preface

This book is the outcome of an international conference on intergroup accommodation in plural societies held in Cape Town from 24 to 26 May 1977. The organising body and principal sponsor was the Institute for Plural Societies of the University of Pretoria. Twenty-three chapters of the book are papers read at the conference. Chapter 27, by Professor Talcott Parsons, a general commentary on societal cleavages in South Africa, was written shortly after the conference. Chapters 2, 22, and 26 (by Lijphart, De Klerk and Nieuwoudt) are papers presented at the annual conference of the Political Science Association of South Africa from 29 to 30 September 1977 at the Rand Afrikaans University in Johannesburg. The concluding chapter was written by Manasse Moerane, a former Black editor of South Africa's largest circulation Black daily newspaper, *The World*.

That this publication was produced at all is entirely due to the outstanding teamwork of a small group of dedicated people. In the first instance, a vote of thanks goes to those staff members of the Department of Sociology of the University of Pretoria who selflessly gave their very best services to ensure the success of the Cape Town conference. In particular, I would like to mention Dr Kobus Oosthuizen and Miss Elna van Niekerk. I would also like to record my appreciation of the sterling effort of Miss Hester Lampbrecht, public relations officer of the Pretoria-based Foreign Affairs Association, and Mrs Sandra Joubert, secretary of IPSO. The latter, in particular, put in many hours of hard work to meet the demands of a conference of this nature. Next, a word of thanks to the 55 conferees whose enthusiastic and constructive participation in the proceedings made of the conference the success it undoubtedly was. In particular, I would like to convey a special word of thanks to the 22 guests from abroad. IPSO is also much indebted to the Foreign Affairs Association (FAA) in Pretoria and the Chicago-based Foundation for Foreign Affairs, which acted as co-sponsors of the conference. We are equally indebted to Dr the Hon

P. G. Koornhof who, in his capacity as Minister of National Education, formally opened the conference, and to Dr Hilgard Muller, Chancellor of the University of Pretoria and former Minister of Foreign Affairs of the Republic of South Africa, who at a reception on 24 May formally welcomed the conferees on behalf of the University of Pretoria.

Finally, our cordial thanks to Mrs Winifred Crum Ewing who edited the various contributions, read the proofs and compiled the index for this publication.

NIC RHOODIE

Pretoria
November 1977

Notes on the Contributors

DR W. J. BREYTENBACH is Chief Researcher at the African Institute of South Africa in Pretoria. Before joining the research staff of the Africa Institute in 1970, he lectured in Anthropology and Applied Anthropology at the University of Pretoria. He has published seven books and numerous articles on government and politics in African states, especially on Southern African states, and also on labour matters in Southern Africa.

Dr Breytenbach obtained the following degrees from the University of Pretoria: BA (African Studies); BA Hons (Anthropology); BA Hons (Applied Anthropology); and MA (Anthropology). He obtained his doctorate in Development Administration and African Politics from the University of South Africa with a thesis on the Kingdom of Lesotho. He was awarded a Lester Martin Fellowship by the Harry S. Truman Institute of the Hebrew University of Jerusalem in 1977. During his research in Jerusalem he concentrated mainly on the concept of self-determination in African politics. He is also a member of the Foundation for the Study of Plural Societies, The Hague, the Society for International Development, Washington, and the South African Institute for International Affairs, Johannesburg. He is an Associate of *To the Point* and contributes the editorial 'Focus' to the magazine *Bantu*.

DR WALKER CONNOR is a Professor of Political Science and Faculty Exchange Scholar at the State University of New York at Brockport. He is a member of the Board of Editors of *Ethnicity*, *World Affairs* and the *Journal of Asian Affairs*. His many achievements include that of Research Associate, Center for International Affairs, Harvard University, 1973-74; Fellow, Woodrow Wilson International Center for Scholars, 1975-76; Rhodes Fellow and Visiting Fellow of Race Relations, St Antony's College, Oxford, 1977-78. He is currently completing two manuscripts entitled *The National Question in Marxist Theory and Strategy* and *The Ethnic Strain in World Politics*.

PROFESSOR ANTHONY DE CRESPIGNY is Head of the Department of Political Science at the University of Cape Town. In the course of the last twenty years he has had experience as Lecturer at the Witwatersrand and Natal Universities; Senior Lecturer at Monash University, Australia; Chairman of Political Science Department, Case Western Reserve University, Cleveland, Ohio.

His publications include three major works co-authored and co-edited: *Contemporary Political Theory* (Aldine-Atherton, USA; Nelson, London); *Contemporary Political Philosophies* (Dodd, Mead, USA; Methuen, London); *Ideologies of Politics* (Oxford University Press). He has published many articles in international journals, mainly in the field of political philosophy.

DR WILLEM J. DE KLERK has been trained in philosophy, psychology and theology. He has a doctor's degree in pastoral theology, a master's degree in psychology and an honours degree in philosophy. For many years he was professor at the Potchefstroom University for Christian Higher Education, where he was awarded his doctorate in theology after several overseas research projects. Before that he was a minister of the Dutch Reformed (*Gereformeerde*) Church. In 1973 he was appointed editor-in-chief of *Die Transvaler*, an Afrikaans newspaper in Johannesburg. Before that he had become well-known as a political writer, contributing to many publications, and had won acclaim as a public speaker. Since 1973 he has declined several offers from universities and other institutions in order to make his career in journalism. Today, his speciality is writing and speaking on political issues of the moment. Apart from his daily contributions to his own newspaper and political columns in weekly papers, he regularly publishes articles in other journals, usually on the South African political situation. He has also made a valuable contribution to the promotion of culture, both as author and speaker.

DR EDWARD B. FORT is Chancellor of the University of Wisconsin Center System and a leader in the movement to improve and desegregate the US educational system. He received the degree of Bachelor of History from Wayne State University in 1954. Since then he has been continuously engaged in teaching and in working to improve the educational process. After military service in the Office of Education, US Army, West Berlin, he taught in Michigan (1956–60 and 1964–71) and in California (1960–64 and 1971–74). In 1974 he took up his present appointment.

He received his Doctorate in Educational Administration from the

University of California at Berkeley in 1964 and he has held Visiting Professorships at the Universities of Michigan, Detroit and Michigan State. He has served as consultant to numerous educational institutions, including the President's National Conference on Education of the Disadvantaged, 1966; Center for Urban Education, New York City; Center for Inner-City Studies, Northeastern Illinois University, Chicago; Rockefeller Foundation, 1970–71: Humanities and Social Science Division (Minorities Administrative Internship Program; Superintendency Training Consultant). He has participated in a dozen professional organisations and task forces and he has written a number of articles and monographs relating to the educational system, based on his personal experience and observation in this field.

DR R. D. GASTIL is a social anthropologist. He received his basic academic training – both undergraduate and graduate – at Harvard. His speciality in the area of anthropology is the situation of dependent peoples in many cultures. He worked extensively in Iran, Afghanistan and the Middle East.

He is the author of a number of books on recent political issues such as the Vietnam War. His latest book deals with regionalism in the United States. He was, amongst others, consultant to the Hudson Institute in New York and later to the Pattell Research Institute. For the past five years he has been a Director of Freedom House for Comparative Survey of Freedom, in New York.

PROFESSOR WILLIAM FRANK GUTTERIDGE was born in England in 1919. During the Second World War he served in the Manchester Regiment and as DAAG of the 2nd British Division in India and Burma, being appointed MBE in 1946. After reading Modern History at Hertford College, Oxford, of which he is an MA, he joined the teaching staff at the Royal Military Academy, Sandhurst, in 1949. He was a senior lecturer there in Commonwealth History and Government until 1963, a background against which he started to develop his research into the performance of military regimes in Africa. He was the recipient of a Nuffield Foundation Travelling Fellowship in 1960/61, which he spent largely in Africa. In 1963 he went to Lanchester Polytechnic, Coventry, as Head of the Department of Languages and Modern Studies and then, in 1971, to the University of Aston in Birmingham, as Director of Complementary Studies, a position he still holds. In 1976 he was appointed to a personal chair in International Studies.

He is the author of four books: *Armed Forces in New States* (1962),

Military Institutions and Power in the New States (1965), *The Military in Africa Politics* (1969), and most recently *Military Regimes in Africa* (1975), as well as articles on similar themes and monographs entitled *The Coming Confrontation in Southern Africa* (1971) and *Africa's Military Rulers: an Assessment* (1975).

PROFESSOR CHRISTOPHER HUGHES graduated from Oxford immediately before the outbreak of war in 1939, and returned after the war to take a postgraduate degree there, and was subsequently a student of Nuffield College, Oxford. He was recently awarded the Oxford DLitt. After four years at the University of Glasgow, during which he went to Berne for a year as Carnegie Fellow, he spent a time at Goettingen in the German section of the Foreign Office, and then came to the University of Leicester in 1957 as Lecturer, and from 1962 to 1974 as Professor and Head of the Department of Politics: he is now Professor of Politics there. In 1972 he spent a semester in the Federal Technical University in Zurich as Professor of History.

Professor Hughes' publications include three books on Switzerland: *The Federal Constitution of Switzerland* (Oxford, 1954), *The Parliament of Switzerland* (London, 1962), and *Switzerland* (Nations of the Modern World) (Benn, London, 1975).

DR PETER JANKE read modern history at Magdalen College, Oxford, and received his doctorate in 1973 for researching into the growth of constitutional government in Spain and Portugal. He has taught at the University of Navarre and in Madrid, and is at present Senior Researcher at the Institute for the Study of Conflict in London. His publications on Africa include: *Southern Africa: End of Empire* (ISC, London, 1974) and *Southern Africa: New Horizons* (ISC, London, 1976). He is a regular contributor to the *British Army Journal*, the *Police Journal*, *Soviet Analyst* and *Brassey's Annual* (RUSI, London), and lectures at the National Police College, the Royal Naval College, Greenwich, the Royal Military College of Science and the Royal United Services Institute for Defence Studies. He is a member of the International Institute for Strategic Studies and of the Royal Institute of International Affairs (Chatham House).

PROFESSOR MBURUMBA KERINA was born in Namibia, then known as South West Africa. He received his initial education in South West Africa and in South Africa before going overseas, first to the USA and then to Indonesia, where he received his doctorate. He has played a prominent part in the evolution of Namibia from its status as a trustee territory, administered by South Africa. He laid the first petition from his people before the United Nations. He was also instrumental in having South Africa taken to the International Court of Justice by Liberia and Ethiopia.

He was a co-founder of the South West Africa Peoples Organisation (SWAPO). He was very active in its early development but when he became aware how many of his fellow-members were determined to use violence he resigned in order to devote his energies to work for a peaceful transition to independence for SWA/Namibia. It was on his initiative the name 'Namibia' was adopted for his homeland. Professor Kerina became the Director of Information and Communications in the Namibia Foundation, and in this office he was very closely concerned with the Turnhalle Constitutional Conference and the formation of the Democratic Turnhalle Alliance. Recently he became the President of the Namibia Patriotic Coalition.

PROFESSOR ERNEST W. LEFEVER is Director of the Ethics and Public Policy Program at Georgetown University in Washington, DC. He is a senior research scholar at the Kennedy Institute, a professorial lecturer in international relations in the Department of Government, and a senior staff associate of the Center for Strategic and International Studies, all of Georgetown University.

From 1964 to 1976 Professor Lefever was on the senior foreign policy studies staff of the Brookings Institution where he focused on US foreign and military policy toward the Third World. His most recent study dealt with the acquisition of nuclear weapons in Asia, Africa and Latin America.

He received an AB from Elizabethtown College and a BD and PhD from Yale University. He serves on the advisory council of the US Institute for the Study of Conflict and is a member of the International Institute for Strategic Studies (London), the Washington Institute of Foreign Affairs, and the Johns Hopkins University of Scholars. He serves on the editorial boards of *World Affairs* and Foreign Policy Papers, a monograph series.

Professor Lefever has written or edited nine books: *Ethics and United States Foreign Policy* (1957); *Profile of American Politics* (co-author, 1960); *Arms and Arms Control* (1962); *Crisis in the Congo* (1965); *Uncertain Mandate: Politics of the U.N. Congo Operation* (1967); *Spear and Scepter: Army, Police and Politics in Tropical Africa* (1970); *Ethics and World Politics* (1972); and *TV and National Defense* (1974).

He has written for many American journals and newspapers, including the *New York Times, Wall Street Journal, Washington Post, Detroit News, Boston Globe,* and *TV Guide.*

AREND LIJPHART has been Professor of International Relations at the University of Leiden in the Netherlands since 1968. He received his PhD from Yale University in 1963, and he taught at the University of California in Berkeley from 1963 to 1968. He has also been a Visiting Professor at Harvard University and a Visiting Research Fellow at the Institute of Advanced Studies of the Australian National University in Canberra and at the Netherlands Institute for Advanced Study in Wassenaar. He is the author of *The Trauma of Decolonization: The Dutch and West New Guinea* (New Haven: Yale University Press, 1966), *The Politics of Accommodation: Pluralism and Democracy in the Netherlands* (Berkeley: University of California Press, 1968; 2nd ed., 1975), and *Democracy in Plural Societies: A Comparative Exploration* (New Haven: Yale University Press, 1977). He was the editor of the *European Journal of Political Research* from 1971 to 1975, and he has also edited *World Politics* (Boston: Allyn & Bacon, 1966; 2nd ed., 1971) and *Politics in Europe: Comparisons and Interpretations* (Englewood Cliffs: Prentice-Hall, 1969). In addition, he has published articles on comparative politics and international relations in the *American Political Science Review,* the *British Journal of Political Science,* the *Canadian Journal of Political Science, World Politics, Comparative Political Studies,* the *European Journal of Political Research,* the *International Social Science Journal,* the *International Studies Quarterly, Acta Politica,* and other journals.

PROFESSOR J. A. LOMBARD is head of the Department of Economics of the University of Pretoria and member of the Planning Advisory Council of the Prime Minister and of the Commission on the Monetary System and Monetary Policy. He has written or edited several textbooks and articles on the economic sciences, particularly in the field of economic politics, government finances and international economic co-operation.

After gaining a BA degree at the University of Pretoria in 1947, he joined the staff of the Economic Planning Council of that time. He graduated MA in 1950 and in the following year he went abroad to further his studies in London and Washington. In 1954 he graduated PhD from the London School of Economics. After his return to South Africa he joined the Civil Service, later becoming an economist in the Treasury and Deputy Economic Adviser to the Prime Minister. After-

Notes on the Contributors   xxi

wards he also served as member of the Commission of Enquiry into Fiscal and Monetary Policy and the Bantu Affairs Commission. Today he is also a director of Santam Bank.

MOSHE MA'OZ, born in Tel-Aviv in 1935, is the Academic Director of the Harry S. Truman Research Institute, The Hebrew University of Jerusalem. As a student at the Hebrew University he studied History of the Muslim Lands and Arabic Language and Literature, obtaining his BA in 1958. In a further period he studied History of the Middle East, International Relations, Turkish and French, obtaining his MA in 1961. After two years in the Prime Minister's Office, Jerusalem, as Assistant Adviser on Arab Affairs in Israel, he went to St Antony's College, Oxford, and obtained his PhD in 1966. He then took up an appointment at Tel-Aviv University as Lecturer in History of the Middle East and Senior Research Fellow, the Shiloah Research Centre. Returning to the Hebrew University in Jerusalem, he became Chairman of the Department of History of the Muslim Lands, Chairman of the Institute of Asian and African Studies, and Director for the Centre of Research on Palestinian Arabs and the Arab Israeli Conflict, Harry S. Truman Research Institute.

Over a period of ten years he has been invited to present papers at more than a dozen scholarly conferences in the USA, Europe and Israel. He has contributed many articles to eminent journals, such as *Bulletin of the School of Oriental and African Studies*, University of London, *Middle East Journal*, Washington, and *Jerusalem Papers on Peace Problems*. Professor Ma'oz has published four books: *Ottoman Reform in Syria and Palestine 1840–61* (Clarendon Press, Oxford, 1968); *Modern Syria* (Tel-Aviv, 1964 (in Hebrew)); *Studies on Palestine during the Ottoman Period* (ed.) (The Magnes Press, Jerusalem, 1975); *Palestinian Arab Politics* (ed.) (The Harry S. Truman Institute, Jerusalem, 1975).

M. T. MOERANE was born of Basotho educational pioneering stock in the Mt Fletcher district of Transkei. He graduated as BA from the University College of Fort Hare, BA Hons (Psychology) from the University of Natal and B Econ. from the University of South Africa. For more than twenty years he played an active part in education, mainly as principal teacher in primary, high and technical schools, both in urban and rural areas. For eleven years until 1974 he was also editor of the largest Black newspaper in South Africa, *The World*, which was banned on 19 October 1977.

Mr Moerane has also been closely involved with various Black educational, social and political organisations. *Inter alia*, he was President of the Natal African Teachers Union; President of the African Teachers Association of South Africa; President of the Association for Educational and Cultural Advancement of the African People, until it was banned in October 1977. He presided over the launching of the Black People's Convention, the premier Black political organisation until it was banned. At present he is President of the Soweto Resident's Council. Mr Moerane has travelled widely through Africa, Europe, the US and Canada and has contributed several monographs, mainly on the urban Blacks of South Africa, to various publications.

KHALIL AHMAD NASIR was born in 1917 in the northern part of prepartitioned India, the areas of present-day Pakistan.

After receiving his BA degree in 1936 from the Punjab University, he entered the Ahmadiyya Muslim seminary in Qadian, India. On the completion of his religious studies, he went to the United States in 1946 to serve as a minister of the Ahmadiyya Movement in Islam. From 1948 to 1959, he was director of the American Fazl Mosque in Washington, DC and editor of the *Muslim Sunrise Quarterly*.

During his period of service with the Ahmadiyya Movement, he continued his graduate studies. He received his MA in Political Science in 1948 from Northwestern University and his PhD in 1957 from American University, Washington, DC, specialising in international relations and organization. In 1954, he became a naturalised American citizen.

Professor Nasir joined the faculty of the Political Science Department of C. W. Post Center, Long Island University, in 1960 where he has been teaching both undergraduate and graduate courses in area studies, international relations and international law. In 1967, he was a Visiting Professor of International Relations at Iowa Wesleyan College and later at Chung-ang University in Seoul, Korea.

Dr Nasir is the author of several publications. He has travelled extensively around the world as a lecturer and delegate to various conferences. He has participated in the World Religions Congress in Japan and the World Conference on Religion for Peace in Louvain, Belgium. From 1968 to 1971, he lectured at the Foreign Service Institute of the Department of State, Washington, DC.

In 1975, he was appointed as Director of the International Studies Program at C. W. Post Center, a position that he still holds.

PROFESSOR C. F. NIEUWOUDT is dean of the Faculty of Economic and Political Science at the University of Pretoria, head of the Department of Political Science and International Politics, and chairman of the Institute of Strategic Studies at the same university. He is also president of the Political Association of South Africa, member of the Council of the South African Institute of Public Administration and of the Suid-Afrikaanse Akademie vir Wetenskap en Kuns (South African Academy of Science and Art).

Professor Nieuwoudt graduated BA, MA and DPhil from the University of Pretoria, and, except for a short period in Europe, his entire academic career has been associated with this university. In 1963 he was appointed lecturer in political science and international politics and in 1966 he became professor and head of the department. He enrolled for one year at the London School of Economics and in 1969 undertook a study tour through Europe and Britain. He has published numerous articles in several magazines, mostly on subjects related to political science.

PROFESSOR G. C. OLIVIER is associate professor of political science and international politics at the University of Pretoria, member of the Institute for International Affairs, member of the Council of the Political Association of South Africa and editor of the journal *Politikon*. For many years his speciality has been foreign policy and political development in underdeveloped areas.

He graduated BA in 1963, BA Hons (political science) in 1964 and MA (political science) in 1968. Later, he was awarded the degree of DPhil on a thesis entitled 'The bases of South Africa's foreign policy'. In 1972 he spent three months at the London School of Economics studying the theory of foreign policy and international politics, and for three months during 1975 he was visiting lecturer at the University of Tübingen as guest of the West-German government.

His first academic appointment in South Africa was head of the Department of Political Science at the University College of Zululand. In 1966 he joined the Department of Political Science of the University of Pretoria and, after a year as senior lecturer at the Randse Afrikaanse Universiteit, he returned to the University of Pretoria in 1971.

PROFESSOR TALCOTT PARSONS is Emeritus Professor of Sociology at Harvard University. He has held numerous academic appointments in recognition of his exceptionally wide experience in the field of sociology and political science. These include Fellow of the American Academy of Arts and Sciences (President 1967-71); member of the American Philosophical Society; Fellow of the Ford Center for Advanced Study in the Behavioral Sciences, 1957/58. He has received honorary doctorates from the Universities of Cologne, Chicago, the Hebrew University in Jerusalem, the University of Pennsylvania, and from Boston College and Stonehill College.

Professor Parsons is the author of *Protestant Ethic and Spirit of Capitalism* (translation of Max Weber, 1930); *Structure of Social Action* (1937); *Toward a General Theory of Action* (1951); *The Social System* (1951); *Essays in Sociological Theory* (revised 1954); *Structure and Process in Modern Society* (1960); *Societies: Evolutionary and Comparative Perspectives* (1966); *Sociological Theory and Modern Society* (1967); *American Sociology* (1968 (editor)); *Politics and Social Structure* (1969); *The System of Modern Societies* (1971); *Social Systems and the Evolution of Action Theory*, 1977. He is co-author of *Working Papers in the Theory of Action* (1953); *Family, Socialization and Interaction Process* (1955); *Economy and Society* (1956); *Theories of Society* (1961); *Social Structure and Personality* (1964); *Readings on Premodern Societies* (1972); *The American University* (1973); Contributor to the *American Sociological Review, American Journal of Sociology, Social Forces, Psychiatry, Journal of History of Ideas, Social Research, Social Science Quarterly, Harvard Educational Review, American Political Science Review*, and others.

PROFESSOR FRIEDRICH EGON PRINZ specialises in Medieval History, Social History, and the History of Bavaria and the Danube Area. He is Professor of Medieval History and Comparative Provincial History at the University of Munich, and Director of the Institute for Bavarian History there.

He is a committee member of the J. G. Herder Research Council, and co-editor of the Journal for East European Research (*Zeitschrift für Ostforschung*). He made six tours of the United States and Canada between 1967 and 1977, lecturing at seven leading universities. He also made a thorough study of American university affairs.

Included in the seven books he has published are *Prague and Vienna 1848: Problems of the National Revolution* (Munich, 1968), *Clergy and War in the Early Middle Ages* (Stuttgart, 1971), *Wenzel Jaksch – Edward Beneš: Letters and Documents from the Exile in London (1939–1943)* (Cologne, 1973), *Monasticism and Society in the Early Middle Ages* (Darmstadt, 1976). Professor Prinz has also made some major contributions to historical textbooks and contributed some seventy articles to scientific journals.

PERCY QOBOZA was born in 1938 in Sofiatown, Johannesburg. He was educated at Pax College, Pietersburg (South Africa), where he matriculated. He then attended the Roma University Seminary in Lesotho for two years, where he followed a theology course. Then he obtained employment as a clerk in the Johannesburg City Council for a year, and then became an organiser for the Progressive Party of South Africa. He started his career as a journalist in 1964 when he became a reporter for *The World*, the Black newspaper with the largest circulation in South Africa. He had two years' experience as a court reporter, two as a municipal and one as a general reporter, then six years as news editor until in 1974 he was appointed Editor. He held this post until *The World* was banned in October 1977. From August 1975 to July 1976 he held a Fellowship at the Nieman Foundation at Harvard University.

PROFESSOR ALVIN RABUSHKA received BA, MA, and PhD in Political Science from Washington University (St. Louis). He taught at the University of Rochester between 1968 and 1976 and is now a Senior Fellow of the Hoover Institution of Stanford University. Professor Rabushka is author of seven books and numerous articles. The books are: *Politics in Plural Societies* (Charles E. Merrill, 1972); *Race and Politics in Urban Malaya* (Hoover Institution Press, 1973); *The Changing Face of Hong Kong* (American Enterprise Institute, 1973); *A Theory of Racial Harmony* (University of South Carolina Press, 1974); *The Urban Elderly Poor* (Heath, 1975); *Value for Money: The Hong Kong Budgetary Process* (Hoover Institution Press, 1976); *How Tenants See Public Housing* (Hoover Institution Press, 1977).

PROFESSOR B. G. RANCHOD was born in Port Elizabeth in May 1944. After matriculation, he proceeded to study law at the University of Cape Town. Whilst there he served on the Day Student's Council, the Law Students Council and on several student committees. He was awarded a Bachelor of Arts degree in 1965 and two years later the Bachelor of Laws degree. During the final year of his studies he read in Chambers and was subsequently admitted to the Cape Bar. He was then awarded a scholarship to read for the *doctorandus iuris* degree in law at Leiden. He obtained this degree in June 1969, with Roman Dutch Law and Private International Law as his main subjects. Shortly thereafter he was awarded a bursary by the Norwegian government to do a diploma course in Scandinavian politics at the University of Oslo. On the basis of the results attained in the Masters examinations the Dutch Ministry of Education awarded him a fellowship to do a doctorate in law. His researches took him to Lund in Sweden and to Cambridge University.

His doctoral thesis, 'The Foundations of the South African Law of Defamation', was defended in public on 21 June 1972 and the degree of Doctor of Laws of the University of Leiden conferred on him. This thesis has been published by the Leyden University Press – the first South African legal thesis published by that press.

Shortly thereafter Professor Ranchod was appointed as senior lecturer in law (July 1972) at the University of Durban-Westville and promoted to Professor and Head of the Department of Private Law as from 1 January 1974. He has been Dean of the Faculty of Law since January 1976.

NIC RHOODIE is a graduate of Pretoria University (MA and PhD *cum laude*), where he is at present Professor and Head of the Department of Sociology. A founder member and former President of the South African Sociological Association and the Association for Sociologists in Southern Africa, he specialises in social stratification, race and minority problems. Professor Rhoodie is Director of the Institute for Plural Societies at Pretoria University and Chief Editor of the *South African Journal of Sociology*. He visited the United Kingdom as a British Government guest in 1967, followed by a visit to the United States as a State Department guest in 1969. He has written extensively on various aspects of intergroup problems. His major works are *Apartheid and Racial Partnership in Southern Africa* (Academica, Pretoria, 1969); *Social Demography* (with Dr C. F. Swart: Academica, Pretoria, 1973); and *Social Stratification and Coloured Status* (McGraw-Hill, Johannesburg, 1977 – in Afrikaans). He edited *South African Dialogue. Contrasts in South African Thinking on Basic Race Issues* (McGraw-Hill, Johannesburg, 1972) and co-edited the five-volume *Case Studies on Human Rights and Fundamental Freedoms. A World Survey* (Martinus Nijhoff, The Hague, 1975–76).

PROFESSOR LAWRENCE SCHLEMMER joined the Institute for Social Research at the University of Natal in 1964 as Senior Research Fellow and became Director of the Institute for Social Research in 1972.

In 1976 the Institute for Social Research changed its status to become the Centre for Applied Social Sciences, offering a graduate Diploma in Applied Social Sciences as well as conducting basic and Applied Social Research. Professor Schlemmer is currently Director and Professor at the Centre.

He has more than 65 publications to his credit – books, journal

Notes on the Contributors xxvii

articles, research reports and chapters in books. These publications cover the field of Political Sociology, the Sociology of Pluralism, Industrial Sociology and the Sociology of Planning. Publications include the works *Privilege, Prejudice and Parties* (South African Institute of Race Relations), *Employment Opportunity and Race in South Africa* (Studies in Race and Nations Series, University of Denver Press, USA) and *Change, Reform and the Economy in South Africa* (Ravan Press, forthcoming).

On several occasions Professor Schlemmer has been invited to deliver papers at conferences abroad, including an international conference on Race Relations held at Lake Como, Italy (organised by the University of Denver, Colorado); a conference on Regional Politics in Southern Africa held at Dalhousie University, Canada; a conference on Change in Contemporary South Africa convened by Yale University, held in New York, and at the 1976 Annual Congress of the African Affairs Association, held in Boston, USA.

Professor Schlemmer is Vice-President of the South African Institute of Race Relations, a member of the Association for Sociology in Southern Africa, a member of the Natal Regional Committee of the Urban Foundation and a member of the Planning Advisory Committee to the KwaZulu Government.

LEONARD R. SUSSMAN has been Executive Director of Freedom House for the past ten years. This non-governmental organisation in its thirty-sixth year endeavours to strengthen free institutions in the United States and abroad. It conducts research, convenes academic meetings, publishes advisories and a bimonthly, *Freedom at Issue*, on public issues in the foreign and domestic fields. It is known worldwide for its *Comparative Survey of Freedom*, an analysis of the level of political and civil rights in every nation and dependency.

Mr Sussman edits *Freedom at Issue* and has directed the seven-year study of the US mass news media, to be published in July. It is entitled, *Big Story: How the American Press and Television Reported and Interpreted the Crisis of Tet 1968 in Vietnam and Washington*, by Peter Braestrup, with public opinion analyses by Burns W. Roper. Mr Sussman has written the introduction.

He also contributed the chapter on 'Scholars and the Press' in *The Idea of a Modern University*, edited by Sidney Hook *et al.* Mr Sussman has written extensively on the current Third World challenge to the Western news media, his articles having appeared in *Quadrant* (Australia), *The New Lugano Review* (Switzerland) and in the United States.

His book on the subject will soon appear under the auspices of the Center for Strategic and International Studies, Georgetown University, Washington, DC.

He was also co-organiser of the International Council on the Future of the University, a group of 200 scholars from fifteen countries working to preserve academic freedom and the integrity of scholarship. He has been a journalist with United Press, cable editor of a daily newspaper, and news editor of a New York radio station. Mr Sussman holds an MS from Columbia University and a BA from New York University.

DR JUSTUS M. VAN DER KROEF is Charles Anderson Dana Professor of Political Science and Chairman of the Department of Political Science in the Universty of Bridgeport, Connecticut. He was born in Jakarta, Indonesia, and holds a PhD from Columbia University, New York. He has been a Senior Fellow in the Research Institute on Communist Affairs, Columbia University and a Post-Doctoral Research Fellow in the University of Queensland, Brisbane, Australia. He has been Visiting Professor of Asian Studies at Nanyang University, Singapore, the University of the Philippines, Quezon City, Philippines, and Sri Vidyodhaya University, Nugegoda, Colombo, Sri Lanka. He has served as consultant on Southeast Asian affairs to the Special Operations Research Office in Washington, DC, the Center for Strategic and International Studies of Georgetown University, Washington, DC, and to the Foreign Policy Research Institute, Philadelphia.

He contributes frequently to such journals as *Pacific Affairs, Asian Survey* and *Orbis*. He is a member of the editorial advisory board of the *Journal of Asian Affairs* and of the *World Affairs Quarterly*, and is book review editor for Southeast Asia of *Asian Thought and Society*. He has published six books, the latest of which is *Indonesia After Sukarno* (University of British Columbia Press, 1972). He is a Director of the American-Asian Educational Exchange (New York).

PROFESSOR P. J. VAN DER MERWE, having matriculated in 1946, started a career in the Government service during which time he obtained BComm and BA degrees as well as a THED by means of extramural study. After being appointed as a lecturer in the Department of Economics at the University of Pretoria, he continued his studies, obtaining the degrees BEcon (Hons) and MA (Econ) and in 1971 his doctorate, with a thesis entitled 'The Bantu Labour Market in South Africa'.

Professor van der Merwe has served on many commissions and is at present a member of the Economic Committee of the Bantu Affairs

Commission, and the Commission of Enquiry into Labour Legislation. He has also undertaken various research projects concerning labour matters for institutions such as the Human Sciences Research Council, the Bureau for Economic Research re Bantu Development, the SA Federated Chamber of Industries, the Bureau for Economic Policy and Analysis, The Economic Advisory Council, etc. He is generally considered one of South Africa's leading writers and authorities on economic aspects of labour problems.

PROFESSOR W. B. VOSLOO is head of the Department of Political Science and Public Administration at the University of Stellenbosch, council member of the South African Institute of Public Administration and associate member of the Suid-Afrikaanse Akademie vir Wetenskap en Kuns (South African Academy for Science and Art).

Professor Vosloo graduated MA *cum laude* (Political Science) from the University of Pretoria in 1960 and in 1965 was awarded the degree PhD by Cornell University in the US. While studying at Cornell he was appointed teaching assistant in the Department of Government and later research assistant in the School of Business and Public Administration of the same university. He joined the University of Stellenbosch in 1966. During the past few years he has served as member of the Commission of Enquiry into matters affecting the Coloured People and the Commission of Enquiry into Administrative Training for the Civil Service.

He has undertaken several study tours abroad. In 1969, for instance, he was the guest of both the British Foreign and Commonwealth Office and the West German government. He has published numerous articles in many journals, mostly on political matters.

MARINUS WIECHERS was born in 1937 in Pretoria where he matriculated in 1954 at the Afrikaans Boys' High School; in 1958 he obtained the BA (law) and in 1960 the LL B degree at the University of Pretoria. In the same year he was appointed lecturer at the University of South Africa. In 1965 he obtained the degree of doctor of laws at the University of Pretoria after having studied at the University of Paris during 1962–3. In 1966 he was promoted to professor of law at the University of South Africa and at present he is head of the Department of Constitutional and Public International Law at the same University.

He has studied in France and Germany and in 1968 he was awarded a Carnegie travel grant to visit the United States of America; in 1973 he again visited the United States, this time as an exchangee under the

United States – South Africa Leader Exchange; in 1974 he studied in Heidelberg, Germany, as an Alexander von Humboldt stipendiary. In 1970–71 he was a legal representative of the SA government at the International Court in the SWA cases; during 1974–5 he acted as legal adviser to the Theron Commission on Matters relating to the Coloured Population Group; during 1976–7 he acted as legal adviser to the Damara and Tswana delegations at the Turnhalle constitutional conference. He is the author of a textbook on South African Administrative Law, the author of a second revised edition of Constitutional Law and the writer of several articles on international, constitutional and administrative law.

Introduction

Nic Rhoodie

This Introduction is based on Professor Rhoodie's welcoming address delivered on the first day of the International Conference on Intergroup Accommodation in Plural Societies, Cape Town, 24 May 1977.

I don't think I have to labour the point that the twin problems of human rights and policy options for intergroup accommodation are today as important an international issue as the struggle for politico-economic ascendancy between the superpowers. In fact, in contemporary socio-scientific thinking these two issues are usually bracketed together as closely related dimensions of international behaviour. In virtually every country, human rights and policy options for intergroup accommodation are intimately tied up with the ideological cleavages that play such a vital role in the current international power struggle. In this context, it is self-evident that the theme of this conference is certainly germane to the special position of the Third World in the present world order.

In saying this, I am not in any way suggesting that the problems of intergroup accommodation in plural societies are socio-political phenomena peculiar to modern times. Unquestionably, we are dealing with a problem syndrome as old as mankind itself. In terms of language, race, religion and ethnicity, the empires of the Accadians, Assyrians, Chaldeans, Babylonians, Greeks and Romans were anything but homogeneous and, in their domestic intergroup relations, a far cry from the relatively stable intergroup accommodation found in many modern Western countries. Be that as it may, for reasons well known to all with a modicum of education, mankind today is more preoccupied with and involved in issues related to human rights and intergroup accommodation in plural societies than in any previous period of its history. A corollary of this preoccupation is the proliferation of socio-scientific literature and research on these issues – a fairly accurate measure of their growing importance in the affairs of mankind.

In terms of real human misery, there is much similarity between the deprivation experienced by millions of people in plural societies throughout the contemporary world and that suffered by the Accadians, Assyrians and the rest as a result of group interaction at their time. In one major respect, however, we have a distinct advantage over our ancient forebears. Today we have at our disposal the scientific apparatus and sophisticated terminology to research and identify these problems. They are analysed and described in terms such as institutionalised violence; alienation; social stratification (including the various forms of social inequality subsumed under this general concept, e.g. class, caste, racial and cultural minorities, etc.); segregation and separatism; relative deprivation; opportunity and reward systems; life chances; power-sharing and consensual decision-making; counter-culture; intergroup mobility; democratic, geopolitical, institutional and structural pluralism – to mention but a few examples selected at random.

It is generally accepted that the emergence during the past 25 years of about 100 new nation states has not significantly reduced the world's intergroup problems. On the contrary, the process of emancipation has spawned many new problem situations no less perplexing in their diversity and complexity than those that faced the erstwhile Western colonial powers. The groups involved in these conflict relationships were not created by the new states: the vast majority have existed as identifiable groups for centuries. The transformation of the Western colonial system into the Third World of today only served to concentrate these problem situations within the geopolitical confines of smaller nation states, none of which can claim to be socio-culturally homogeneous. In fact, only very few of them have the political and socio-cultural structure usually necessary to avoid serious latent and/or overt group conflicts.

A general inventory of the human condition supports the viewpoint that the concept of the plural society has become almost synonymous with intergroup competition. In real-life situations, this competition is manifested in many forms. Researchers are ever amazed by the vast number of conflict situations bedevilling human relations in scores of countries in the world today. In the Sudan, Moslem Arabs are competing with non-Moslem Blacks; Uganda's problems are well known even to the marginally literate; in Ethiopia, the Eritreans are fighting a civil war for independence; the Tutsi-Hutu confrontation in Rwanda and Burundi has led to human slaughter on a massive scale; the recessionist movements in Biafra and Katanga are still fresh in our minds; the group problems of my own country are aired, dissected, debated and 'resolved' every day in hundreds of newspapers and conference rooms around the world; the independence struggle of the Kurds in Iraq is still very much alive; in India and Pakistan, several ethnic groups are involved in separatist movements; the Nagas of India and the Tamil speakers of Sri Lanka are demanding more meaningful ethnic autonomy; in the Mediterranean, Greek and Turkish Cypriots are still at daggers drawn along the so-called Atilla line; Basque belligerence in Spain is the consequence of their quest for autonomy; the devolution of power to the Scots and Welsh is certainly relevant to our conference theme – so is the Walloon-Flemish cleavage in Belgium. In addition, the position of many ethnic minorities in the Soviet Union is well documented; aboriginal communities in Australasia are clamouring for a greater measure of self-determination; in South-East Asia, several Chinese minority communities are struggling to preserve their identities; Japan's ethnic minorities claim that they are being short-changed by the dominant Japanese society; Muslim separatism in the Philippines is a fact; the French Canadian separatist movement underscores the problems of Canada's plural society; over the past two decades a resurgence of ethnic consciousness has created many intergroup problems in the US, involving among others Blacks, Indian communities, Puerto Rican and Mexican-Americans; further south, the plural societies of Latin America are also suffering the trials and tribulations of human diversity. And so we can go on quoting many more similar problem situations emanating from intergroup competition in plural societies.

A global assessment of the problem syndrome under discussion reveals that we are quite well informed on both the symptoms and causes of these problems. Social scientists have no difficulty at all in identifying problem areas, the actors involved and, to a lesser extent, the underlying why's and wherefore's. Identifying symptoms and causes is one thing; finding equitable and viable solutions to these problems is altogether a different matter. The latter requires systematic socio-political engineering and it is precisely in this area that the record of the international community has been least impressive. There has been very little progress and even less common ground among the nations. The success of any solution designed for any one plural society will depend to a large extent on the share in the reward and opportunity system claimed by each of the various groups involved. In Uganda, for instance, the current power elite will no doubt claim that their country is very successful in resolving local intergroup problems!

When it comes to the resolution of conflict in plural nation states, I believe there is general agreement that if, in a plural society anywhere in the world, civilized people have to choose between compulsory assimilation of the melting-pot winner-take-all type, on the one hand, and, on the other, a pluralist accommodation guaranteeing group rights and consensual decision-making across group boundaries, they will naturally opt for the latter, on condition, of course, that accommodation is based on genuine democratic pluralism. In most countries where the melting-pot system has been applied, the winner-take-all approach has exacerbated domestic intergroup problems, in several instances to the point of partial or selective genocide, e.g. Burundi, Uganda and Cambodia. Who would dispute that a winner-take-all assimilationist approach would cause civil war in countries such as India, Pakistan, Sri Lanka, the Philippines, Cyprus, Yugoslavia, Malaysia, the Sudan, Nigeria, Lebanon and even in some Western countries, such as Belgium, Spain and Canada?

These days one often hears the argument that pluralism is fast losing its salience because, inevitably, universalistic values and needs will erode the cultural and historical differences between groups. In the long term this may very well be the case, but governments of plural states are concerned with the situational realities of here and now and there is no evidence to suggest that the historical, socio-cultural and political forces sustaining and perpetuating pluralism will in the foreseeable future be eroded to the extent that intergroup accommodation may be based primarily on universalistic values and needs. In any country with a plural national society, therefore, the government will have to take into account human rights of both a universalistic and particularistic nature. We all know that, at least in theory, it is far easier for a government to run a homogeneous than a heterogeneous society. In plural national societies, however, the various established groups comprising the national population cannot be wished away or discarded like so much redundant junk in an attic. This applies particularly to numerically strong ethnic or subnational groups with firm historical bases. Cultural and subnational cleavages will not disappear simply because they are a nuisance to certain dominant power groups. In this context, I wish to quote from Crawford Young's seminal work,

The Politics of Cultural Pluralism.

No African leader would be found today to endorse the view put forward by Sekou Toure of Guinea, who at the time of independence declared: 'In three or four years, no one will remember the tribal, ethnic or religious rivalries which, in the recent past, caused so much damage to our country and its population.' Nor is any Asian leader likely to follow the secular faith of a Jawaharlal Nehru in the integrative effect of nationalism and modernisation; although a profound student of history, he was taken wholly by surprise by the magnitude of the communal violence which accompanied Indian partition in 1947. A year later, he made the equally saddening discovery of the force of linguistic solidarity when he listened to the evidence submitted to the Linguistic Provinces Committee in 1948. 'The work of sixty years of the Indian National Congress was standing before us, face to face with centuries-old India of narrow loyalties, petty jealousies and ignorant prejudices engaged in mortal conflict and we were simply horrified to see how thin was the ice upon which we were skating. Some of the ablest men in the country came before us and confidently and emphatically stated that language in the country stood for and represented culture, race, history, individuality and finally a sub-nation.' (1976, pp. 6–7)

Glazer and Moynihan conclude:

> ... in the welter of contemporary forms of group expression and group conflict there is both something new and something common: there has been a pronounced and sudden increase in tendencies by people in many countries and in many circumstances to insist on the significance of their group distinctiveness and identity and on new rights that derive from this group character. ... formerly seen as survivals from an earlier age, to be treated variously with annoyance, toleration, or mild celebration, we now have a growing sense that they may be forms of social life that are capable of renewing and transforming themselves. As such, perhaps, the hope of doing without ethnicity in a society as its subgroups assimilate to the majority group may be as utopian and as questionable an enterprise as the hope of doing without social classes in a society. (1975, pp. 3, 4–5)

Cultures and subnational communities are not founded or floated, dissolved or liquidated like clubs or business corporations. And individuals will continue to articulate their needs from a communal point of reference as long as their cultures survive. For instance, after five decades the USSR is still a multi-ethnic national society despite relentless efforts to create a universal socialist commonwealth under Russian-Communist domination.

David and Audrey Smock emphasise that

> the politicisation of plural subgroups ... [has] caught many social scientists unprepared. ... communal attachments do not quietly wither away with exposure to modernising influences. Quite the contrary, modernisation often creates the very conditions necessary for the incubation of strong communal identities and sets the stage for communal competition ... by endowing societies with new opportunities and resources. (1975, pp. 3, 4)

At the present time, subnational communities conceptualised in terms of ethnicity constitute the main socio-political elements of the plural nation state. Of the 150 member states of the UN, only 12 are non-plural in the ethnic sense. In roughly one half of these states at least five clearly distinctive ethnic groups can be identified. Said and Simmons (1976, p. 16) point out that out of an estimated 164 disturbances of significant violence involving states between 1958 and 1966,

> a mere 15 were military conflicts involving two or more states. The most significant violence after 1945 has found its *casus belli* in ethnic, tribal, and racial disputes that have often exerted a spillover effect in international politics.

Traditional concepts of international ideological cleavages do not adequately explain the rash of post-war intergroup belligerence. As Greeley has concluded:

> The conflicts that have occupied most men over the past two or three decades and which have led to the most horrendous outpouring of blood have had precious little to do with this ideological division. ... In a world of the jet engine, nuclear energy, the computer, and the regionalized organization, the principal conflicts are not ideological but tribal. Those differences among men which were supposed to be swept away by science and technology and political revolution are as destructive as ever. (1971, p. 343)

For example, the ethnic factor has been a major determinant of the geopolitical structuring of Europe since the beginning of the nineteenth century. Connor has observed that 'in the period from 1815 to the end of World War II, Portugal, Spain and Switzerland were the only European states not to have been either created or to have undergone territorial alterations as the result of ethnic aspirations.' (1976, p. 113)

Socio-scientific thinking on the 'plural society' has become much more sophisticated since Furnivall's formal introduction of the concept in 1948. (See among others Smith, 1960, 1965, 1969(a), 1969(b), 1969(c); Dahl, 1967; Kuper, 1969(a), 1969(b), 1970, 1974; Schermerhorn, 1970, and Van den Berghe, 1969, 1973.) Schlemmer (1977, p. 4) points out that as a conceptual framework this initial concept, 'intended as a heuristic device to analyse exploitative colonial relationships', had a limited applicability because it did not allow sufficiently for the influence of class conflict. Schlemmer continues:

> Kuper (1971) and Van den Berghe (1969) take us a long way towards filling the theoretical lacuna; the latter author including as forms of pluralism types of stratification and differentiation based on race, caste, estate or class. 'To the extent that classes are corporate groups they will develop subcultural differences and some class specific institutional structures' (Van den Berghe, 1969, p. 68).

Today it is generally accepted that pluralism has a multidimensional social structure, the three major dimensions being corporate social organisation, culture (encompassing, in the broad sense of the term, cultural differentials such as ethnicity, language, religion, historicity, etc.), and somatic norm image (as an index or criterion of racial 'status'). Despite the continuous refinement of the terms 'plural society' and 'pluralism', they have not yet reached the degree of precision which would permit social scientists to utilise them as operational concepts with fairly general validity. There is still a great deal of confusion with regard to the concept 'pluralism' as indicative of a specific form of socio-political organisation within the geographical framework of the nation state. Thus, social and political scientists working in this area are trying to arrive at greater conceptual refinement by qualifying the term 'pluralism' in some way or another, e.g. 'democratic pluralism', 'open', 'spontaneous' and 'voluntary pluralism' (more or less equivalent to Gordon's 'liberal pluralism'), as opposed to 'geopolitical', 'structured' and 'institutional pluralism' (which in broad terms may be subsumed under what Gordon terms 'corporate pluralism') (1975, pp. 105-6).

The fundamental problem facing any government wishing to introduce democratic pluralism centres on the question: how to reconcile the basic human rights of the individual with the basic rights of the group. The constitutional systems of most Western countries allow a clear distinction between fundamental rights applicable to the individual, and those applicable to a group with a distinctive corporate and legal personality of its own. An analysis of this most important legal differentiation in many plural states between individual and group rights clearly shows that in countries whose populations are segmented in a complex manner, such as Belgium, Cyprus, Canada, Lebanon, Spain, India and the Republic of South Africa, individual and group rights can be reconciled by way of a pluralistic socio-political system.

Fundamental human rights which are usually considered to be the inalienable birthright of the individual are, for instance, equality before the law, freedom of association and movement, freedom of speech and religion, the right to life and the right to certain opportunities to satisfy fundamental material and spiritual needs, e.g. the opportunity to receive education and to follow a chosen occupation. But there is also another dimension to human rights, namely those related to the survival and preservation of the cultural identities, life-styles and basic social institutions of historically established groups. In states with plurally structured populations there is, as far as this second and most important dimension of rights is concerned, an agreement between the state and the various groups which collectively comprise the state's national society – and not between the state and each individual member of each group. As far as the first dimension of human rights is concerned, i.e. those pertaining to the individual (such as equality before the law, the right to life, etc.), the agreement is between the state and the individual, regardless of the latter's group affiliation. Since the state regulates and determines the rights of the various groups, no individual member of any particular group may demand that the state deal with him directly. As far as group rights are concerned, the individual member has an equal say within his own group, i.e. he has an equal opportunity to participate in decision-making within his own group. Once a certain group has accepted a certain dispensation, an individual member opposed to the majority decision of that group can hardly demand that the state enter into a special agreement with him in his individual capacity.

In my view this two-dimensional approach to human rights provides the only basis for an ongoing reconciliation of the rights of the individual with those of the group. An individual has two basic relationships – to his group and to the state. Therefore, in plural states, individual human rights are universalistic in certain respects and, in others, particularistic. Universalistic are those fundamental human rights which are independent of group affiliation, and particularistic are those which usually pertain to the individual in terms of his association with a particular group. For instance, a Flemish-speaking Belgian may claim not only universalistic rights, such as the right to life, freedom of speech, religion, etc., but also, at the same time, certain particularistic rights, such as the right to have his children educated in the medium of Flemish, and the right to participate in political processes designed to ensure the survival of his Flemish cultural and historical identity.

In no debate on intergroup accommodation in plural societies may the crucial issue of human rights be ignored. These rights are easy to define but difficult to implement. If the entire world were populated by individuals sharing roughly the same life-style, subscribing more or less to the same code of ethics and values and using the same normative criteria to assess human activities, it would certainly not have been an impossible task to institutionalise a generally acceptable system of human rights. But there is no such commonality in the world of today. Hence, it is hardly surprising that the concept of human rights is as relative as it is. Considering the sharply differing levels of human evolution in the technological and economic sense, the vast disparities in ideological orientation and the unique historical and socio-political structures of each individual country, it seems highly improbable that within the foreseeable future the international community will be able to adopt and impartially implement a universally recognised and universally enforceable code of human rights. If the International Commission of Jurists were to draw up such a code today, how many nations would be prepared to apply it? How many would be able to enforce it? Obviously, a country's position in the human rights rankings should be determined by its *actual performance*. Consequently, as an Afrikaner, I cannot resist the temptation to point out that in the field of human rights South Africa is performing not nearly as badly as some would have us believe. A recent assessment of actual performance published by the New York-based Freedom House organisation revealed that while South Africa certainly did not figure in the top twenty nations, it certainly outranked the bottom 100 (Gastil, 1977, pp. 5–15).

The South African government has committed itself, both at home and abroad, to the elimination of discrimination based on race and colour. It is imperative that White South Africans stop splitting hairs on the question whether or not in the past they had *intended* to discriminate against non-Whites. Instead, they should proceed to implement the government's declared commitment in this field. I believe that the rapid phasing-out of all discriminatory practices should receive the highest priority if the Whites are to succeed in normalising intergroup relations. The only basis on which the Republic of South Africa will succeed in creating a socio-political system with which all the peoples of the country can identify is a broad democratic South Africanism transcending narrow sectional interests. To this end, it should initiate institutional adjustments geared to the demands of such a common South Africanism. Our adaptive responses to these demands should crystallise in institutions which can safeguard genuine group interests and simultaneously provide for joint and consensual decision-making in the highest power organs of the state. All institutions for community interests should enjoy parity in legislative and executive competence. The highest decision-making institutions should be structured in such a way that the legislative and executive process will exclude matters likely to split the incumbents into racial or ethnic blocs.

By decentralising its decision-making institutions, South Africa can ensure that the conflict potential inherent in its plural society is spread so thin that all partisan or group issues will be local instead of national questions. Institutionalised safeguards against group domination and institutionalised access to and participation in the top decision-making functions by all the country's subnational units are prerequisites for a viable plural democracy in South Africa. This process will demand a high degree of constitutional innovation and political imagination from all the parties involved. In particular, the White power elite will have to programme the process of nation-building within a socio-political framework sufficiently open-ended to allow for constructive and functional adaptive responses to both the common and group-particularistic needs of South Africa's diverse peoples.

Mindful of the special problems posed by intergroup accommodation in plural polities, I conclude by once again quoting Crawford Young:

> The tensions built into this process are obvious. But nation-building can only move forward through ongoing consociational bargaining and compromise. There is simply no escape from the existing state system as the political frame within which mankind must seek a

better life. Conflict, some argue, is creative; that may well be, yet endemic civil strife along lines of cultural cleavage is surely not a pathway to either peace or prosperity. There is no single prescription; each plural polity has its own unique configuration of diversity. The sensitive application of wisdom accumulated in the observation of the politics of cultural pluralism is not beyond the reach of statesmanship. There is, of course, no other choice. (1976, pp. 527-8)

There are no instant, *ersatz* solutions to the complex problems of modern plural states. The smaller national societies that fall into this category should be neither regarded as pawns in the international power struggle nor treated as ideological outcasts that have to be rehabilitated and converted (even by proxy) to the norms and standards of their stronger neighbours simply because it would serve the latter's own national interests.

REFERENCES

Connor, Walker, 1976. 'The Political Significance of Ethnonationalism within Western Europe', in Said and Simmons (q.v.).
Dahl, R., 1967. *Pluralist Democracy in the United States* (Chicago: Rand McNally & Co.).
Furnivall, J. S., 1939. *Netherlands India* (Cambridge: The University Press).
Gastil, Raymond D., 1977. 'The Comparative Survey of Freedom', *Freedom at Issue*, No. 39, Jan-Feb 1977.
Glazer, Nathan, and Moynihan, Daniel P. (eds), 1975. *Ethnicity. Theory and Experience* (Cambridge, Mass.: Harvard University Press).
Gordon, Milton M., 1975. 'Toward a General Theory of Racial and Ethnic Group Relations', in Glazer, Nathan, and Moynihan, Daniel P. (q.v.).
Greeley, Andrew, 'The Rediscovery of Diversity', *The Antioch Review*, Fall 1971.
Kuper Leo, 1969(a). 'Plural societies: perspectives and problems', pp. 7-26 in Kuper, Leo, and Smith, M. G. (eds), *Pluralism in Africa* (Berkeley and Los Angeles: University of California Press).
Kuper, Leo, 1969(b). 'Ethnic and racial pluralism: some aspects of polarization and depluralization', pp. 459-487 in Kuper, Leo and Smith, M.G. (q.v.).
Kuper, Leo, 1970. 'Stratification in plural societies: focus on White settler societies in Africa', pp. 77-93 in Plotnicov, Leonard, and Tuden, Arthur (eds) *Essays in Comparative Social Stratification* (Pittsburgh, Penn.: Pittsburgh University Press).
Kuper, Leo, 1974. 'Conclusion: a personal statement on evolutionary change in race relations' in Kuper, Leo, *Race, Class and Power* (London: Gerald Duckworth and Co.).
Said, Abdul A., and Simmons, Luis R., 1976 (eds). *Ethnicity in an International Context* (New Brunswick, New Jersey: Transaction Books).

Schermerhorn, R. A., 1970. *Comparative Ethnic Relations* (New York: Random House).
Schlemmer, Lawrence, 'Theories of the Plural Society and Change in South Africa', *Social Dynamics* 3(1) 1977, pp. 3-16.
Smith, M. G., 1965. *The Plural Society in the British West Indies* (California: University of California Press).
Smith, M. G., 1969(a). 'Institutional and political conditions of pluralism', pp. 27-66 in Kuper, Leo, and Smith, M. G. (q.v.).
Smith, M. G., 1969(b). 'Some developments in the analytic framework of pluralism', pp. 415-58 in Kuper, Leo, and Smith, M. G. (q.v.).
Smith, M. G., 1969(c). 'Pluralism in precolonial African societies', pp. 91-152 in Kuper, Leo, and Smith, M. G. (q.v.).
Smock, David R., and Smock, Audrey C., 1975. *The Politics of Pluralism: A Comparative Study of Lebanon and Ghana* (New York: Oxford; and Amsterdam: Elsevier Scientific Publishing Co. Inc.).
Van den Berghe, Pierre L., 1969. 'Pluralism and the polity: a theoretical exploration', pp. 62-81 in Kuper, Leo, and Smith, M. G. (q.v.).
Van den Berghe, Pierre L., 1973. 'Pluralism', pp. 959-77 in Honigmann, John J. (ed). *Handbook of Social and Cultural Anthropology* (Chicago: Rand McNally).
Young, Crawford, 1976. *The Politics of Cultural Pluralism* (Madison: The University of Wisconsin Press).

1 Limits of Government in the Third World

Ernest W. Lefever
Professorial Lecturer in International Relations in the Department of Government and Director of the Ethics and Public Policy Program at Georgetown University, Washington, DC.

The term Third World is a delightfully ambiguous phrase which embraces both the diversity and common characteristics of the less-developed states of Asia, Africa, and Latin America. The realities of the Third World - often little understood - determine the possibilities of both domestic and foreign policy.

The foreign policy of the industrial powers toward Asian, African, and Latin American states must necessarily be in response to an assessment of threats, challenges, and opportunities in these areas. If the perception of the United States, for example, is clouded by ignorance, illusion, or excessive expectation, bad policy is the inevitable result.

A major purpose of my paper is to dispel certain persistent illusions about the possibilities of democratic self-government in the Third World by pointing to the limits of politics in traditional and transitional societies. The age-old question of how men should be governed - especially in complex and plural societies - is vastly complicated in our time by demands for broadly based consent; rising self-consciousness among ethnic and religious groups; and instant, vivid, and universal communications which let virtually everyone look over everyone else's shoulder.

Despite vast differences in climate, culture, economic organisation, and religious outlook, all men everywhere face the same essential political questions: How shall our society be ordered? What should be the relationship between the governors and the governed, between central authority and citizen consent, between the responsibilities of the state and the rights of individuals? Differences in cultural heritage do not alter the fundamental political question, but they do substantially influence the nature of the response and the viability of the various models of government which emerge.

The modalities of government have changed over time, but the essential functions of the state remain the same. Fifteen hundred years ago, St Augustine defined the purpose of government succinctly and with a touch of humour. If it were not for the state, he said, men would devour one another as fishes. A thousand years later Martin Luther said the function of the state was to restrain evildoers. With these views John Calvin was in full accord.

Good and humane government has three tasks. The first is to *govern*, to maintain order and security throughout its domain. The second task of government is to govern *justly*, to uphold the rule of law. The third task of government is to govern *democratically*, to be responsive to the will of the governed.

Few governments of the world perform all three tasks well. In fact, most governments barely govern, much less govern justly or democratically.

The central thesis of this paper is that Western democracy has failed to take root in the Third World and is not likely to do so in the near future because these societies have not developed the fundamental concepts, values, and traditions essential to government based on broad citizen participation. One would be hard pressed to point to a single Third World state that operates along British or American lines, even though its constitution may so specify.

The prerequisites for democracy on the Anglo-American model are exacting and rarely duplicated. Our cherished Western institutions of authority and consent are the culmination of a five-thousand-year heritage which embraces the Judaeo-Christian ethic and its respect for the dignity of the human person, Greek democracy and political theory, Roman law and organisation, and the Magna Carta, with its implicit guarantee of rights for every citizen. Our political system depends upon the operation of competing political parties secure in the concept of a 'loyal opposition' and undergirded by a free press, freedom of speech, and widespread respect for the rule of law – all of which must rest on the foundation of a broad moral and political consensus.

The Western political ethos which emerged from this rich heritage remains a vital force in the West, though even there it is challenged – from within by a failure of will and moral confusion and from without by the new barbarians who rule by coercion rather than consent, who have substituted the will of a self-anointed elite for the rule of law, and who insist that the 'good society' can emerge only from class conflict.

It is hardly surprising, therefore, that in the Third World, where the Western political ethic is an alien concept known only by reputation, it is understood by few and practised by almost none. Consequently, US policies based on the demand for liberal and democratic governments are almost bound to fail.

I LIMITS OF POLITICS IN THE THIRD WORLD

The hundred or so Third World countries vary widely in size, power, natural resources, economic achievement, history, culture, ethnic diversity, ideology, and political experience. Yet all of them face the same fundamental task – establishing an effective structure of authority, order, and consent. And most of them confront five major problems in their effort to develop a viable and humane political system.

1. Most such countries are in a state of uncertainty and flux, as they attempt to move from a traditional culture to a more complex, industrialised society. There are few agreed-upon procedures and rules for guiding social and political change.
2. Virtually all Third World states are characterised by ethnic, linguistic, and religious diversity rather than by national cohesion.
3. The orientation of many of the politically active elites tend to be vaguely Marxist, collectivist, and authoritarian, rather than democratic.
4. Most Third World economies are underdeveloped and heavily dependent upon the industrialised states.
5. In their foreign policy, most Third World governments attempt to augment their material resources and enhance their bargaining position by playing off the West against the Communist bloc.

These five characteristics, which largely determine the character of Third World regimes, deserve brief elaboration.

1. *Transitional Societies.* Many of the countries of Asia, Africa, and Latin America are confronted by chaos and uncertainty spawned by their transition from traditional ways of thinking and doing things to more 'modern' ways. Traditional cultures are essentially tribal. The extended family-language group not only defines the mores, customs,

and daily routines but more important, it circumscribes the worldview of its members. This is especially pronounced in tropical Africa where the most serious barrier to state-wide cohesion and to an effective central government is the dogged persistence of tribal identity.

A study of Ghana in 1965 pointed to

> the persistence of elements of traditional social structure even within the most 'modern' sectors of Ghanaian society. Ethnic background, kinship affiliation, and traditional residence patterns still play a role even within the urban context and indeed may provide the basis for organizations which appear at first sight to be essentially Western.[1]

This is another way of saying that the colonial experience in most instances has resulted in only a thin veneer of Western concepts and values, even among the so-called Westernised elite. It could hardly have been otherwise, given the brevity and superficiality of the Western contact compared with the length and depth of the tribal experience.

The persistence of tribalism and traditional worldviews is not widely understood in the United States, where a short decade and a half ago there were great expectations that instant decolonisation would spawn a score of new democracies in Africa.

2. *Ethnic Diversity.* The hard facts of ethnic diversity in most Third World countries has often been overlooked or downplayed in the West because of the lingering illusion that tribalism is politically and morally obsolete and that modern communication would succeed in replacing kinship loyalties and tribalism with a larger national consciousness, if not with a sense of universal identity. Here, as in other areas, the idealists and believers in inevitable progress were profoundly wrong.

For more than a decade I have been proclaiming, with increasing acceptance I might add, that ethnic particularism – far from fading away – is on the rise. There are two chief reasons for this – both flying in the face of earlier predictions. One is decolonisation itself. When the political cohesion and coherence imposed by the European powers was withdrawn, often abruptly and without preparation for self-government, the endemic forces of tribe, language, and region reasserted themselves. These atavistic forces have often proved stronger than the fragile authority of the new state, resulting in mutinies, assassinations, coups, countercoups, and civil wars.

The second reason for the resurgence of ethnic identity is the new technology of instant and vivid communication. Ironically, radio and television, which were supposed to bring mankind together, may be having precisely the opposite effect among those in the Third World who count most politically – the literate or semi-literate city-dwellers with access to radio, TV, and movies.

An Ibo in Nigeria, for example, who feels his tribe is being discriminated against by authorities may have his tribal consciousness further raised by seeing or hearing reports of minority groups in the United States or the Middle East demonstrating against existing conditions. By learning more about how other 'downtrodden' groups are acting, he may identify emotionally with their cause and be stimulated to take similar action to better his condition. In short, the contagion of discontent spread by mass communication magnifies rather than obliterates diversity.

This growing ethnic self-consciousness is a worldwide phenomenon – flourishing among the Blacks and Indians in the United States, the French in Canada, the Indians in some Latin American countries, the Catholics in Northern Ireland, the Basques in Spain, the Turks in Cyprus, and various tribes in Asia, to say nothing of the many groups in tropical and southern Africa.

Ethnic politics is a worldwide reality and it will remain so for a long time. Consider these statistics. According to one study of 132 states of the world, only 12 (9.1 per cent) were found to be composed of only one ethnic group.[2] (Of these, only one is in Africa – Somalia.) About a third of them lacked any single dominant group. Of the 132 states:
25 had a dominant ethnic group comprising 90 per cent or more of the population;
25 had a dominant group representing 75–89 per cent of the population;
31 had a significant group comprising 50–74 per cent of the population;
39 (the largest bloc) had no single group comprising half the population.
It is estimated that in 53 states the population is divided into five or more significant ethnic groups. Of these, of course, the Republic of South Africa is the most complex. It should be noted, however, that it is not the sheer number of groups – there are dozens in the United States – but rather the size and difference among such groups that constitute the problem. It was relatively easy for America to 'absorb' a million Northern Europeans, but it would be impossible for sophisticated, industrialised White South Africa to integrate culturally and

politically ten million largely illiterate Bantu without catastrophic consequences for the economy and political stability.

In the West, as Raymond Aron has pointed out, ethnic conflict has replaced class conflict as the chief cause of internal conflict. But the ethnic factor is often exacerbated by real or perceived class differences. And for psychological and political reasons, ethnic conflict is inclined to spill across international borders.

According to one tabulation of 164 significant violent conflicts involving governments between 1958 and May 1966, only 15 were military clashes of two or more states. In the remaining 149 internal conflicts, ethnic, tribal, and racial factors played a major or even primary role.

3. *Political Orientation of Elite.* The intellectual and political leaders of the Third World tend to be vaguely Marxist in ideology and authoritarian in method. The authoritarianism emerges naturally from traditional practices of political control. The collectivist-class struggle ideology was imported during the latter decades of the colonial experience in Asia and Africa, reflecting the most articulate social critique in Britain and France during that period.

Since World War II, some of the rising leaders in the already independent Latin American states also adopted a semi-Marxist interpretation of colonialism, imperialism, and poverty as they sought to wrest power from the more conservative rulers. Hence, Marxist ideology with its condemnation of the West and its panoply of pejorative code words directed against the real and alleged sins of the erstwhile colonial powers is the prevailing ideology in the Third World.

As Daniel Patrick Moynihan has pointed out, Third World invective is directed primarily against 'neocolonialism', often a euphemism for US foreign and economic policy.[3] The United States is simultaneously admired, envied, and hated because of its power, success, and influence. Professor Moynihan rightly notes that anti-Americanism has become the cement of Third World ideology.

4. *Dependence on the Developed World.* Most Third World countries are heavily dependent upon the industrial world for technology, as well as for productive and managerial skills. Though they need trade and investment for economic growth, many of their leaders denounce the operation of multinational corporations which, as a matter of hard fact, have been and are the chief engines of modernisation in their societies. They blame 'colonialism' for their backwardness and are reluctant to acknowledge a basic fact pointed out by Gunnar Myrdal in his *Asian Drama* – Third World countries are underdeveloped not

because of external exploitation, but because of a lack of internal technical and organisational skills and the paucity of disciplined work habits. The economic problem is further exacerbated by a welfare state ideology imported from Europe which emphasises distribution over production.

5. *Foreign Policy.* For these and other reasons, the foreign policy of many Third World regimes, at least at the declaratory level, consists largely of hurling inflammatory symbols against the West and at the same time demanding reparations for the alleged past sins of the industrial powers and their multinational enterprises. This stance is aided and abetted by the Soviet Union and other Marxist-Leninist regimes. The demands for a 'new international economic order' by Third World leaders exploit and seek to increase the sense of guilt in the West and are often underscored by a thinly disguised threat to join forces with Moscow or Peking if the 'neocolonialists' fail to pay conscience money. Professor P. T. Bauer, emphasising the role of guilt feelings in the developed world, quotes W. B. Yeats: 'Come, fix upon me that accusing eye. I thirst for accusation.'[4]

II THE RULE OF LAW AND JUSTICE

Most Third World states are governed by small, authoritarian elites who emphasise order over freedom in the political sphere and distribution over production in the economic sphere.

To enhance their authority, Third World regimes generally co-opt the influential elites – the military, leading families, banks, businesses, intellectuals, and sometimes labour leaders. Opposition groups – whether press, political parties, or student organisations – may be tolerated if they are small and weak, but usually they are closely watched. When an opposition group or leader transgresses the ill-defined limits of permissible activity, swift corrective action is taken by the regime. The very concept of a 'loyal opposition' is almost completely lacking among the rulers and dissenting groups. The opposition is often seen as disloyal or subversive because it has traditionally behaved in that way.

Authoritarian regimes, arbitrary rule, capricious decrees, and a less-than-loyal opposition in Asia, Africa, and Latin America are all reflections of a fundamental defect as seen from the Western democratic perspective – the absence of the most precious achievement of the Western political tradition, the rule of law coextensive with the state.

Tribes and other groups may have a rule of law for their own members, but this falls far short of a rule of law for all individuals, of whatever group or class, within one sovereign jurisdiction. Equal justice under law, orderly and competitive politics, wide participation in public affairs, and democracy itself are not possible without the rule of law, the codification of a moral and customary consensus developed over generations.

The concept of each individual being equal under the law is a unique achievement of the West. As Adda B. Bozeman points out:

> This has not been the case in either Africa or Asia where human groupings have been held together effectively in comprehensive orders dominated by respect for religion, etiquette, the stabilizing function of war and conflict, or perhaps the superior wisdom regularly imputed to selected men. In short, law is not recognized everywhere as a distinct idea or a paramount reference.[5]

In the West, adds Professor Bozeman,

> the supremacy of law is linked explicitly with schemes of social and political organization ... whether ... the city, the kingdom, the empire, the nation-state, or the international society ... since European law has been associated from its beginnings with the need felt on the one hand to isolate and protect individual rights, and on the other to define the responsibilities of citizenship, government has been viewed preferentially as a compact or contract between men. That is to say, in this civilization in which the individual human being has been disengaged from the group, it is possible to assume that men, be they governors or governed, are capable of entering into binding obligations.[6]

Professor Bozeman concludes that neither the Western concept of law nor the norms or values on which it rests 'can be presumed to exist in other systems of public order'. This may appear to be an exaggeration, but I believe it is dramatically true in Black Africa where oral tradition, tribal kinship loyalties, and ascribed authority to hereditary rulers or selected elders form the basis of order and justice.

The oral tradition also imposes other constraints on the quality of the political order because of its limited comprehension of time and space. Exclusive reliance on oral discourse seriously limits future-oriented thought and planning essential to building an orderly structure of law and political authority. For instance, when the disposition of a case brought before a tribal chief is not codified, except by oral tradition, it is of limited utility ten years hence. Further, even an accurate memory of one chief's judicial decisions will avail little when another chief with a different outlook takes his place.

Oral tradition also limits the possibilities of spatial and territorial order for essentially the same reasons. When there are no written treaties or land deeds, small ethnically defined areas or even large political territories created by conquest tend to disintegrate as a result of migration or the death of the principals. Consequently, references to precolonial African 'states' and 'empires' are often misleading.

This evidence suggests the validity of my central thesis: that Western-style democracy has failed to take root in the Third World and is unlikely to succeed in the near future. Hence, the folly of US threats to diminish or withhold support of allies for their inability to conform to our democratic model. As diplomatist George F. Kennan said: 'It is difficult to see any promise in an American policy which sets out to correct and improve the political habits of large parts of the world's population,' adding that authoritarian and often brutal government 'has been the common condition of most of mankind' for millenia and will remain so 'for long into the future, no matter how valiantly Americans insist on tilting against the windmills.'[7]

III KINDS OF AUTHORITARIAN REGIMES

Despite their written constitutions, which are almost always based on Western democratic models, most Third World regimes are authoritarian. The three customary branches of government, if they are permitted to remain, usually blur into one. The courts and the parliament tend to be extensions of executive authority and preference. In many Third World states, for example, the courts rarely find against the executive, at least on significant issues.

The varieties of authoritarian rule run from simple one-man dictatorships, such as that in Uganda, to military or civilian regimes which permit, within limits, an 'independent' judiciary, a parliament, some opposition political activity, and an opposition press. Often these limits are circumscribed by emergency decrees which may be approved by a rubber-stamp legislature.

Most such regimes have come to power by military coups, the majority bloodless. Others evolved incrementally by invoking one emergency power after another in the name of preserving the security of the state against subversion. Virtually all authoritarian rulers promise to return to 'normal' democratic and constitutional procedures, including free elections, when the security of the country permits it.

The vast majority of the people in the Third World are disenfranchised. They live under minority ruling elites who were not elected and who cannot be voted out of office. In Asia, Africa, and Latin America a *coup d'état*, not an election, is the 'normal' way to change governments. Bullets, whether fired or held in reserve, have been more potent than ballots.

The composition of an authoritarian elite, whether hereditary, 'elected', or installed by a *coup*, has some bearing on the quality of order and justice possible. A one-man regime tends to be arbitrary and often brutal. President Idi Amin of Uganda is an example *par excellence*. Two striking exceptions, the one-man rule of Ethiopia's late Haile Selassie and Iran's Shah have been constructive and largely benign, though hardly democratic. Both the Emperor and the Shah broadened the base of their inherited authority by soliciting the advice and participation of various influential groups in their societies. This fell far short of a popular mandate, but it involved wider consent than that of most Black African states where central power and authority are more narrowly based.

In terms of order, justice, and the opportunity for civil and political rights, it is important to emphasise the salient distinction between authoritarian regimes and totalitarian regimes. An authoritarian government, however harsh, permits a significantly greater degree of political, economic, social, cultural, educational, religious, and artistic diversity than a totalitarian state.

In a totalitarian state, the one-party regime not only determines the political structure, but makes or attempts to make all significant legal, economic, social, and educational decisions. There are no oases of freedom or human choice because the elite has virtually usurped the role of the family, church, and school. The State claims the attributes of God by asserting its omniscience and it buttresses this assertion by attempting to be omnipotent and omnipresent.

There is a profound moral difference between a totalitarian North Korea and an authoritarian South Korea in terms of human rights and the possibilities of change toward greater political participation. The South Koreans enjoy economic and religious freedom, but certain civil and political rights as we know them in the West have been suspended. Likewise, Chile enjoys many more civil and political rights under the present junta than Cuba does under Castro. In Africa, there is also a great difference between Zambia and Zaire on the one hand and Angola and Mozambique on the other, though the two former Portuguese territories are not and may never become full-fledged totalitarian states.

IV PLURALISM AND THE INTERNAL COLONY

As noted earlier, only a handful of states in the contemporary world are characterised by ethnic homogeneity. This has always been the case. City states and empire states of the ancient world all embraced tribal or ethnic groups, some of which were more populous than the ruling group. Ancient Rome at its zenith, for example, ruled over many diverse peoples in the Mediterranean world and beyond. Even within the imperial city only a select few were Roman citizens with full rights and privileges. Rome, like every great empire before or since, has had both external and internal colonies.

External colonies are easier to understand and manage than internal colonies. In 1897, Rudyard Kipling referred to the peoples of the British Empire's overseas territories as 'lesser breeds without the Law'. This was a blunt and somewhat old-fashioned way of saying that the colonial peoples were British subjects, but not British citizens. They were under British law, but subjects were not granted the same rights as citizens.

During the decolonisation period of the past two decades, Western governments have found it easier to deal with their overseas territories than with 'colonies' inside their own home states. An internal colony may be defined as any significant group of persons within a state who are denied full civil or political rights, whether on the basis of race, sex, language, literacy, property, or previous condition of servitude. In both Britain and America it took many years before all adult citizens enjoyed full citizenship rights. In the United States half the population was denied the right to vote until 26 August, 1920, when the Nineteenth Amendment to the Constitution granted women the right to vote. In the early days of the American Republic, there were also property and literacy requirements for voting. And after the Civil War there were other legal and extra-legal barriers to Negro voting in some parts of the country. In short, America's internal colonies have included women, the Indians, and the Blacks.

An internal colony may be even more broadly defined to include any significant group that for reasons other than legal restrictions does not, in fact, participate fully in the mainstream of political, economic, or cultural life. Examples, past and present, abound: the rural Indians of many Latin American countries; French-speaking Canadians; Arabs in Israel; Jews, Estonians, and Mongolians in the Soviet Union; Sudeten Germans in Czechoslovakia; Sikhs in India; Chinese in Indonesia; Muslims in the Philippines; Ibos in Nigeria; and the Baluba in Zaire.

In the modern state, with few exceptions, all such groups have full citizenship rights on paper, but in practice many of them do not. This is particularly true in Third World authoritarian states where for economic and communication reasons alone many of the remote rural and tribal peoples are actually if not legally disenfranchised.

In tropical Africa, constitutional guarantees notwithstanding, the majority of citizens are disenfranchised and denied full civil rights because they are ruled by small unelected elites. These disenfranchised citizens can be considered an internal colony. But in a deeper and more discriminatory sense, certain tribal groups suffer more than others. This is dramatically the case in Uganda. And it was, and may still be, the case in Ethiopia where the Amhara tended to monopolise both political and ecclesiastical power. In these and other cases, the 'lesser breeds' were relegated to the status of an internal colony.

The principal point is this. Most states are pluralistic, and in this ethnic diversity some groups tend to be closer to the locus of power than others. When certain groups continue to be disadvantaged over a considerable period, they can be properly called internal colonies, though the extent of discrimination against such groups varies widely. Usually Third World governments deal with their internal ethnic colonies, which have legal equality with the dominant group, by manipulative policies of appeasement, promises, and threats; or by playing them off against other groups. Such policies fall short of affording them equal protection under the law or equal participation in the political process. Again, it is important to recognise that frequently economic circumstances virtually dictate such discrimination by the political system.

V A POSTSCRIPT ON SOUTH AFRICA

Perhaps no state past or present has faced an internal colony situation as complex and as agonising as that of the Republic of South Africa today. I do not intend to define this situation in detail, much less

prescribe a remedy. But let me note several things as a kind of postscript.
1. *First* (and this is only for the ill-informed), South Africa is a modern state rooted in the rule of law with a democratic government based on a limited electorate. The three branches of government have juridical and actual independence and competitive politics flourishes within the electorate.
2. *Second*, within South Africa there are two internal colonies. One consists of the Bantu nations in the rural countryside and the other consists of the Bantu, Coloureds, and the Asians living in 'White country', or urban areas. Unlike the situation in most other states, the status of these 'national' groups is legally defined and circumscribed. The members of these two colonies live under the rule of law, but they are denied certain civil and political rights enjoyed by the electorate, notably the right to vote in state-wide elections and the right to become permanent residents in 'White country', except when conferred by special legislation. They are more like subjects than full citizens.
3. *Third*, in its policy of a restricted franchise, South Africa is practising substantially what the United States did in the early days of the Republic, though the size and character of the ethnic groups differ vastly.
4. *Fourth*, in actual practice a larger percentage of the total population of South Africa participates in politics than in the great majority of Black African states. More persons in South Africa benefit from the rule of law as well as from greater economic and educational opportunity, than in most of the Black-ruled African states.
5. *Fifth*, if one thinks of the Bantu homelands as internal colonies, the South African government has done and is doing more toward preparing them for self-government – in terms of administrative training, education, and economic assistance – than any of the former European colonial powers did for their African territories.
6. *Sixth*, the problem of dealing with the Bantu homelands in moral, legal, economic, and political terms is not as difficult as the problem of increasing the rights and political participation of the presently unenfranchised groups within 'White country'.
7. My *seventh* and final point. The problems of relating political authority and consent in South Africa are the responsibility of the government and peoples of South Africa, not of outsiders, however well-intentioned they may be.

We Americans sometimes are tempted to meddle in other people's affairs. We have enough internal problems of our own. We have heavy foreign policy responsibilities around the globe. We have security and alliance commitments to keep.

If friendly governments request our assistance or advice, we should provide help that serves our mutual interests in peace and development. But we should not force our views on our friends, much less attempt to embarrass governments that stand with us in the struggle against the totalitarians. We should extend a friendly hand to all governments that pursue a constructive and peaceful foreign policy, even if their domestic institutions and practices do not fully measure up to our standards.

After all, some of these countries, such as South Korea, the Republic of China, and the Republic of South Africa, are under siege. They need understanding as they grapple with the problems of external security and internal justice.

Perfection is always the enemy of the good. By demanding impossible changes, we may be playing into the hands of the totalitarians. We should keep our sense of perspective. As Leopold Tyrmand has said: civilised people should 'not burden each other' with their 'excessive humanity'. Columnist Michael Novak recently warned his fellow Americans: 'One of the best ways to create an immoral foreign policy is to try too hard for a moral one.'

NOTES

1. Philip J. Foster, *Education and Social Change in Ghana* (Routledge & Kegan Paul, 1965) p. 301.
2. Abdul Said and Luiz R. Simmons, *Ethnicity in an International Context* (Transaction Books, New Brunswick, New Jersey, 1976).
3. 'The United States in Opposition', *Commentary*, March 1975, pp. 31-44.
4. P. T. Bauer, 'Western Guilt and Third World Poverty', *Commentary*, January 1976, p. 31.
5. Adda B. Bozeman, *The Future of Law in a Multicultural World* (Princeton University Press, 1971) p. xi.
6. Ibid., pp. xii and xiii.
7. George F. Kennan, '"Democracy" as a World Cause', *Washington Post*, 11 July 1977.

2 Majority Rule versus Democracy in Deeply Divided Societies

Arend Lijphart

Professor of International Relations at the University of Leiden, Holland. The paper was read at the Congress of the Political Science Association of South Africa, 30 September 1977, and subsequently published in Politikon, *official journal of PSASA.*

INTRODUCTION

Two widely accepted – but nevertheless quite erroneous – theoretical notions appear to dominate contemporary scholarly thinking and writing about the politics, in culturally, ethnically, and racially divided societies: the equation of democracy with majority rule, and the proposition that democracy is not a viable form of government for such deeply divided societies. These ideas are both so basic and so prevalent in political science that they may be compared to 'paradigms' in Thomas S. Kuhn's sense of the term.[1]

In this paper, I shall try to disprove these paradigmatic notions. My argument will be, in the first place, that there are two principal types of democracy: in addition to majoritarian democracy there is a distinctly different alternative type that I have labelled 'consociational' democracy, following the examples of the Dutch Calvinist political theorist Johannes Althusius (1563–1638) and, more recently, of David E. Apter.[2] Instead of majority rule, consociationalism stresses consensual decision-making, proportionality, and minority rights. Secondly, I shall argue that democracy is not inevitably destined to fail in deeply divided societies: if a democratic government belongs to the consociational type or if it incorporates consociational elements to a significant degree, it should have a good chance to be viable and effective. Thirdly, I shall try to show that in societies with extremely deep cultural, ethnic, and racial cleavages, consociational democracy is not just a preferable alternative to majoritarian democracy but that it is the *only* realistic possibility. In other words, democracy and majority rule are incompatible in deeply divided societies: hence it is, as the title of this paper emphasises, a question of majority rule *versus* democracy.

I should like to make two additional introductory remarks. The first is that, although theory and practice are often only tenuously connected with each other, this is not the case here. The confusion of majority rule with democracy and the pessimism about democracy in divided societies are widespread among both theorists and practitioners. These errors are therefore not merely of academic interest but may have serious practical consequences. Secondly, the pessimistic view of the chances of democracy entails the special danger that it may become a self-fulfilling prediction: if politicians and their political advisers accept the proposition that democracy cannot succeed in deeply divided societies, they will not even *try* to introduce it or to make it succeed. Like all self-fulfilling predictions, this proposition is not intrinsically valid but it may turn out to be true because political actors believe it to be true and, acting on this assumption, make it true.

I MAJORITARIAN DEMOCRACY AND THE BRITISH PARADIGM

What are the reasons for the prevalent indentification of democracy with majority rule? One reason appears to be the recognition that the only logical alternative to majority rule is minority rule (or at least a minority veto). Unanimity or broad agreement among all citizens is more democractic than simple majority rule, but in the absence of a strong consensus, it seems more democratic that decisions are made by majorities instead of by minorities. As Willmoore Kendall has shown, even John Locke with his passionate concern for minority rights was forced to admit that majority decision-making was the logical rule of last resort.[3] In practice, however, most democratic systems have tried to avoid pushing this principle too far. Especially with regard to the most fundamental and sensitive questions, such as constitutional amendments, extraordinary majorities are often required. Accordingly,

Majority Rule versus Democracy

Jean-Jacques Rousseau, in spite of being much more majoritarian-minded than Locke, advised that the more grave and important the questions discussed, the nearer should the opinion that is to prevail approach unanimity.'[4]

The major democratically governed country in which majority rule is applied even to constitutional questions is, significantly, the United Kingdom.[5] It is my contention that the most important reason for the equation of democracy with majority rule is that the British model of democracy – or what is often referred to as the 'Westminster model' – has long been accepted as the normative democratic paradigm for the rest of the world.

This British model is thoroughly majoritarian in five main respects: (1) The cabinet is composed of members of the majority party, and the minority is completely excluded; in parliament, there is a confrontation between government and opposition, but the government has majority support and can get its proposals enacted even against strenuous objections by the minority. (2) The electoral system is the single-member district plurality method in which the candidate with the majority vote (or, if there is no majority, with the largest minority vote) wins, and the other candidates are excluded. (3) This electoral method encourages and tends to maintain a two-party system in which the two parties are of approximately equal size; the winning party therefore represents no more than a narrow majority, and the minority opposition is relatively large. (4) The majority is not only able to form a one-party cabinet but also captures the other 'spoils' of office according to the winner-take-all principle. (5) The system of government is unitary and centralised, and there are no restricted geographical or functional areas from which the parliamentary majority is barred.

It is surprising that the British paradigm has had such influence as a normative ideal type, because the government-versus-opposition pattern of democracy, the first characteristic of the Westminster model mentioned above, may be interpreted as an undemocratic principle: it is a principle of exclusion. As Sir Arthur Lewis has forcefully pointed out, the primary rule of democracy should be that citizens have the opportunity to participate, either directly or indirectly, in making decisions. The second meaning of democracy, that the will of the majority must prevail, violates the primary rule if the representatives are divided into a government and an opposition: it excludes the minority from the decision-making process for an extended period. However, the exclusion of the minority is mitigated if majorities and minorities alternate in government – in other words, if today's minority can become the majority in the next election instead of being condemned to being in opposition permanently. Hence the government-versus-opposition pattern can be regarded as democratic only if the vital condition of alternation in government is fulfilled. In deeply divided societies, where the lines of cleavage are sharply drawn and correspond closely to political preferences, the necessary flexibility to achieve such alternation is absent. Lewis argues therefore that the majority rule in deeply divided societies is 'totally immoral, inconsistent with the primary meaning of democracy, and destructive of any prospect of building a nation in which different peoples might live together in harmony'.[6]

A second reason why the strength of the Westminster model is remarkable is that in practice many deviations from it can be observed but that these deviations have not affected the faith in its value as a normative paradigm. Even the United Kingdom itself is not run according to the British model! It is customary, for instance, that the leader of the opposition in the House of Commons is consulted by the government on questions that are especially important or sensitive. This is very different from the imposition of the majority will on a reluctant minority. Moreover, there have been frequent deviations from a pure two-party system and one-party cabinets. In other countries, too, the principles of the British paradigm may be accepted in theory while they are being violated in practice. Writing in 1974, before the end of the Labour Party's domination of Israeli politics, Emanuel Gutmann notes that

> it is quite surprising to what extent adherence to the classical parliamentary pattern of government-opposition confrontation is taken as the norm in a country in which no change of government has yet occurred.[7]

But we should not be surprised about such discrepancies between theory and practice. As Kuhn points out, it is in the nature of a paradigm that it is not easily shaken by counter-instances: even 'persistent and recognised anomaly does not always induce crisis' and will not necessarily lead to the rejection of a paradigm.[8]

The normative influence of the British majoritarian paradigm has been felt both in the Western world and, often with disastrous consequences, in the divided societies of the non-Western world. It is interesting to notice that, when Woodrow Wilson proposed the introduction in the United States of a strong cabinet based on majority support in Congress, he did so in the following words: 'Congress must be organized in conformity with what is now the prevailing legislative practice of the world. *English precedent and the world's fashion* must be followed.'[9] With regard to the Third World, Edward Shils comments: 'There are no new states in Asia or Africa . . . in which the elites who demanded independence did not, at the moment just prior to their success, believe that self-government and democratic government were identical.' And they often also believed that democratic government meant British-style democracy including, among other things, 'a legislative body *under the dominance of the majority party.*'[10] Lewis even compares the bias imposed by the Westminster model to brainwashing, and he suggests that Third World leaders 'will need much unbrainwashing before they grasp their problems in true perspective'.[11]

II THE PLURAL SOCIETIES PARADIGM

The second paradigm differs from the first, or British, paradigm in that it is a statement of an empirical relationship, whereas the first paradigm is a definitional statement. On the other hand, the two paradigms are closely related since in the second paradigm's proposition that democracy cannot work in deeply divided societies, the definition of democracy is supplied by the first paradigm.

The idea that deep social cleavages and democracy are incompatible has dominated political theorising for a long time. An early example is John Stuart Mill's gloomy view of the chances of representative democracy in deeply divided societies:

> Free institutions are next to impossible in a country made up of different nationalities. Among a people without fellow-feeling, especially if they read and speak different languages, the united public opinion, necessary to the working of representative government, cannot exist.[12]

It is also implicit in the work of J. S. Furnivall who coined the term 'plural society' for a society deeply divided by religious, cultural, linguistic, ethnic, and racial cleavages – a term that I shall also use from here on. In a plural society, Furnivall states, 'each group holds by its own religion, its own culture and language, its own ideas and ways,' and the different groups live 'side by side, but separately, within the same political unit'.[13] Furnivall used the concept of plural society in his analysis of colonial dependencies and he argued that their political cohesion could only be maintained by the non-democratic method of colonial control.

This plural-societies paradigm can also be discerned in more recent writings on the politics of both the Western and the non-Western world. It underlies Gabriel A. Almond's distinction between the homogeneous political cultures of the 'Anglo-American political systems' and the fragmented political cultures of the 'Continental European systems'. The Continental European countries – primarily France, Italy, and Weimar Germany – are culturally and ideologically plural societies that may be governed democratically, but their democracy can only be weak and unstable.[14] Plural societies are characterised by mutually reinforcing cleavages whereas more homogeneous societies have multiple cross-cutting affiliations. Seymour M. Lipset links this factor to the possibility of democracy in the following words: 'the chances for stable democracy are enhanced to the extent that groups and individuals have a number of cross-cutting, politically relevant affiliations.'[15] Especially with regard to the Third World, the plural-societies paradigm is stated in its starkest form by M. G. Smith. Domination by one segment is part of his definition of plural society, because he believes that there is no other way to maintain political order in such societies: 'Cultural diversity or pluralism automatically imposes the structural necessity for domination by one of the cultural sections. It . . . necessitates nondemocratic regulation of group relationships.' In accordance with this theory, he predicts that 'many of the newly independent states may either dissolve into separate cultural sections, or maintain their identity, but only under conditions of domination and subordination in the relationships between groups.'[16]

Political practitioners who base their decisions on the plural-societies paradigm are likely to commit two kinds of error: in their quest for democracy they may attempt to make the plural society less plural and more homogeneous, or, accepting the plural nature of a society as an unalterable fact, they may turn to non-democratic forms of government. The plural character of a society may be reduced by assimilation or partition. Assimilation is the remedy prescribed by Furnivall: 'The functions of the Government are to create a common social will as the basis for a Government that shall represent the people as a whole. . . . The transformation of society is a prerequisite of changes in the form of Government.'[17] Although the replacement of separate segmental loyalties by a common national feeling seems to be a logical solution to the problems of a plural society, it is not a practical solution. Especially in the short run, it is unlikely to be effective, and it may even stimulate a defensive reaction on the part of the separate segments and encourage inter-segmental hostility and violence.[18]

An alternative solution is to divide a plural society into two or more homogeneous societies by partition or secession. Contemporary statesmen and political scientists tend to treat this possibility with less favour than it deserves. Samuel P. Huntington states: 'The twentieth century bias against political divorce, that is, secession, is just about as strong as the nineteenth century bias against marital divorce. Where secession is possible, contemporary statesmen might do well to view it with greater tolerance.'[19] Huntington's condition that partition should be feasible is, of course, a crucial one; the difficulties in the case of a plural society with geographically interspersed segments may be insuperable.[20] What seems to me to be even more important is that partition may not be necessary as a method of creating the preconditions for democracy. The possibilities of consociational democracy should be seriously considered before the drastic solution of partition is attempted.

Politicians who accept the deep divisions of a plural society as an unalterable given are also likely to make grave and unnecessary mistakes as a result of the plural societies paradigm. Even basically prodemocratic political leaders in plural societies who, erroneously, regard democracy as a total impossibility in their countries, are logically tempted to insist on the continuation of oligarchical or minority rule or to opt for a non-democratic form of 'majority rule.'[21]

III CONSOCIATIONAL VERSUS MAJORITARIAN DEMOCRACY

The concept of consociational democracy challenges the two paradigms discussed above.[22] My contention is that the British majoritarian paradigm of democracy is too restrictive, that the concept of democracy should be broadened to include the consociational model as well, and that this broader democratic concept invalidates the plural societies paradigm.

Consociational democracy is characterised by four principles: grand coalition government, mutual veto, proportionality, and segmental autonomy. All four principles deviate from majority rule. First, government by grand coalition means that the political leaders of all significant segments of the plural society cooperate in governing the country. It may be contrasted with the government-versus-opposition pattern of the Westminster model. Majority rule is replaced by joint consensual rule. Grand coalitions can take the form of a grand coalition cabinet in parliamentary systems, of 'grand' councils with important coordinating or advisory functions, or of a grand coalition of a president and other top office-holders in presidential systems.

Secondly, the mutual or minority veto gives each segment the guarantee that it will not be outvoted by the majority when its vital interests are at stake. Majority rule is here replaced by negative minority rule. The mutual veto is synonymous with John C. Calhoun's 'concurrent majority' principle. In Calhoun's words, this minority veto gives each segment 'the power of protecting itself, and places the rights and safety of each where only they can be securely placed, under its own guardianship. Without this there can be no systematic, peaceful, or effective resistance to the natural tendency of each to come into conflict with others.'[23]

Thirdly, proportionality is the basic standard of political representation, civil service appointments, and allocation of public funds. It contrasts sharply with the winner-take-all character of majority rule. With regard to political representation, there are two further extensions of the proportionality principle which entail even greater deviations from majority rule: the over-representation of small segments and parity of representation. These are both principles of *dis*proportionality in favour of minorities. Parity is attained when the minority or minorities are over-represented to such an extent that they reach a level of equality with the majority or the largest group. In practice, the effect of the majority rule in the Westminster model is to exaggerate the representation and power of the majority. Minority over-representation and parity have the opposite effect of giving disproportional influence and security to small segments. They are especially useful alternatives to proportionality when a plural society is divided into segments of highly unequal size. In federal theory and practice, these two principles are often applied to the composition of the upper house.

Fourthly, consociational democracy delegates as much decision-making authority as possible to the separate segments. This segmental autonomy is the final deviation from majority rule. It may be characterised as minority rule over the minority itself in a specified area of the minority's exclusive concern. It compliments the grand coalition principle: on all issues of common interest, the decisions should be made jointly by the segments with approximately proportional degrees of influence; on all other issues, decision-making should be left to each segment. A special form of segmental autonomy that is especially suitable for plural societies, is federalism.

The consociational model described in terms of these four characteristics is not just a theoretical construction. There are several empirical examples of consociational democracy in various parts of the world. In Europe, where the phenomenon of consociationalism first attracted scholarly attention, the examples are Austria during the period of Catholic-Socialist grand coalitions from 1945 to 1966, Belgium since the First World War and, as far as the linguistic problem is concerned, especially since 1970, the Netherlands in the 1917-67 period, and Switzerland from 1943 on. Empirical cases of consociational democracy in the Third World are Lebanon from 1943 to 1975, Malaysia in the 1955-69 period, Cyprus during the few years from its independence in 1960 until 1963, Surinam from 1958 to 1973, and the Netherlands Antilles since 1950. In addition, there are two cases of what I have labelled 'semi-consociational' democracy: Israel since its independence in 1948, and Canada – both the contemporary Canadian system and, even more clearly, the pre-democratic United Province of Canada from 1840 to 1867. These two countries have had a number of consociational elements, but they cannot be regarded as fully consociational.

IV A COMPARISON OF THE VIABILITY OF THE TWO MODELS

What are the lessons that can be drawn from these empirical examples of consociational democracy? In particular, do they offer sufficient evidence of the success of consociationalism to justify the prescription of consociational democracy as a normative model for policy-makers?

It is my conviction that consociational engineering can indeed be recommended with reasonable confidence, but there are two reasons why it is wise to exercise caution in this respect. In the first place, not all of the empirical cases listed above are clearly successful cases. For instance, Cyprus probably has to be counted as a clear failure of an attempt at consociational engineering. On the other hand, the termination of consociationalism must not be equated with its failure. Austria, for example, shifted from grand coalition governments to one-party majority cabinets in 1966, but this was not because consociational cooperation had failed but because it had been so successful in alleviating the tensions between the religious-ideological groups that further consociational measures had become superfluous. Moreover, not all of the cases that appear to be 'failures' represent failures of consociational democracy. For instance, the outbreak of civil war in Lebanon in 1975 can be attributed largely to the intrusion of external forces – although the inflexible institutionalisation of some of Lebanon's consociational devices must also share part of the blame. All of the evidence cannot be reviewed in the limited space of this paper, but we can conclude that the application of the consociational model is not a *sufficient* condition for the success of democracy in plural societies.

A second reservation that I should state is that the empirical cases represent a wide spectrum of degrees of pluralism, and that the success of consociational democracy in only religiously and ideologically plural societies like Austria and the Netherlands is not directly relevant to plural societies with much deeper cleavages. On the other hand, the intensity of the cleavages in only mildly plural Austria should not be underestimated: they were sufficiently strong to cause a civil war in the Austrian First Republic during the interwar years. Moreover, the empirical cases of consociational democracy do include instances of extremely deep ethnic and racial cleavages like Malaysia and Surinam. It is nevertheless necessary to conclude that the chances for consociational democracy decrease as the degree of pluralism of plural societies increases.

There is also a positive conclusion that can be drawn from an examination of the set of consociational cases: the consociational model offers better chances for stable democracy than the majoritarian model. It is important to note that there are no unambiguous cases of successful majoritarian democracy in deeply plural societies. The main counter-example appears to be India, but it is doubtful that Indian democracy can be regarded as fully majoritarian: the Congress party that dominated Indian politics until recently has been a broadly aggregative party led by an intra-party grand coalition of politicians of diverse ethnic origin, and the federal system has provided a high degree of autonomy for the linguistic segments.

These conclusions are graphically portrayed in Figure 2.1. The horizontal axis represents the degree to which a society is plural, from complete homogeneity (0 per cent pluralism) to the most extreme plural society (100 per cent pluralism). Needless to say, the measurement along this dimension reflects impressionistic judgements and is not based on a rigorously operationalised index. The vertical axis, representing the probabilities of success of democracy, uses an equally rough and non-operationalised index. The curves PSC and QSTD represent the chances of success of the majoritarian and consociational

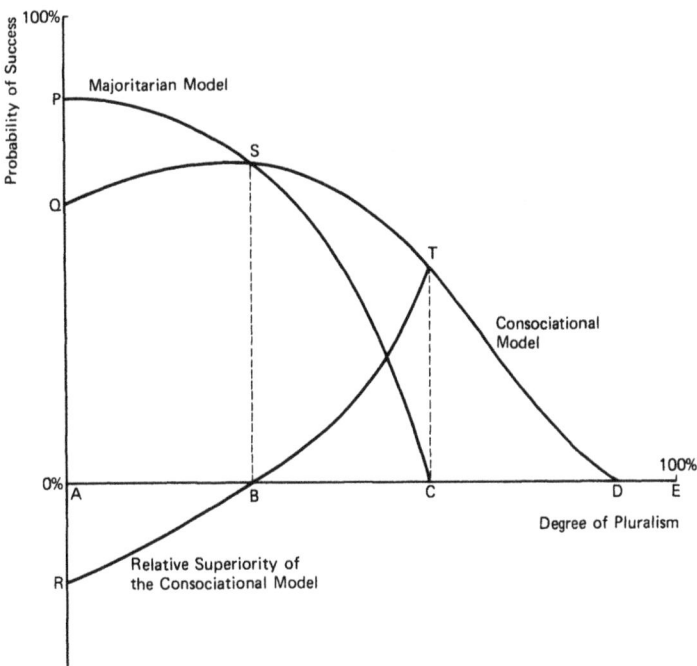

FIG. 2.1 Probabilities of Success of the Consociational and Majoritarian Models of Democracy

models respectively. Whether or not democracy succeeds obviously depends not only on the democratic model that is chosen and on the degree of pluralism, but also on a number of other factors – which I shall briefly discuss later in this paper. Figure 2.1 is therefore based on a *ceteris paribus* assumption. One further assumption is made in the figure: I conservatively assumed that in the most extreme cases of pluralism (the area between D and E on the horizontal axis) democracy, even consociational democracy, may be completely impossible.

At the other end of the continuum, the chances of both types of democracy are good, but, of course, they do not reach 100 per cent: even in the most homogeneous societies, there is no guarantee that democracy will work. In homogeneous societies (A-B on the horizontal axis), I estimate the possibilities of success of consociational democracy to be slightly less good than those of the majoritarian type. The reason is that such societies may become oppressively homogeneous and conformist unless there is a vigorously adversarial opposition challenging a majority-based government. I shall not elaborate on this question because it falls outside the scope of this paper.

The area on the horizontal axis that is of special interest for our purposes lies between points B and D. As the degree of pluralism increases from B on, the probability of success of both types of democracy decreases, but much more rapidly for the majoritarian than for the consociational model. Between B and C, the two models do not offer a sufficient condition for viable democracy, nor are they necessary methods: the choice of either model may result in successful democracy. It should be noted, however, that the *relative* prospects of the consociational model improve compared with those of the majoritarian model. The curve RBT represents the difference between the probabilities of the two models. From R to B the consociational model is inferior to the majoritarian model, but from B to T it is increasingly superior.

In the area from C to D, the chances of the consociational model continue to decline but those of the majoritarian model have been reduced to nil. This means that here the consociational model does become a *necessary* method for the achievement of viable democracy. As I stated at the beginning of this paper, in plural societies with very deep cleavages, democracy and majority rule are incompatible: the realistic choice is not between the majoritarian and consociational democratic models, but between consociational democracy and no democracy at all.

V DRAWBACKS OF THE CONSOCIATIONAL MODEL

If consociational engineering is seriously contemplated, it is important to examine not only the strength but also the potential weaknesses of consociational democracy. Its critics have stressed two problems: the question of democratic quality and the question of political effectiveness. The first criticism is that a strong opposition is a necessary ingredient of democracy and that the consociational model is qualitatively deficient in this respect. This objection is based on a majoritarian bias: consociational democracy is faulted because it differs on this vital point from the majority rule principle. Moreover, the objection fails to take into account that a government-versus-opposition pattern of politics in plural societies is likely to lead to the minority's permanent exclusion from power. Democracy without adequate opportunities for participation in decision-making can hardly be considered superior to democracy without strong political opposition.

Another criticism of the quality of consociational democracy is that it can only achieve peaceful coexistence among the segments of a plural society instead of the classical democratic ideal of 'fraternity' among all citizens. In the terminology of peace research, consociational democracy's primary aim is 'negative' rather than 'positive' peace.[24] On the other hand, peaceful coexistence is a precondition for and may be a first step toward the development of fraternal feelings. And since in a plural society true brotherhood is not a realistic short-term objective, democratic peaceful coexistence is a perfectly honourable goal in itself: it is vastly preferable both to non-democratic peace and to strife-torn democracy.

The second set of criticisms, which focus on the problems of effectiveness, must be considered to be the more serious ones. Several of the characteristics of consociational democracy may entail indecisiveness and inefficiency. Decision-making will inevitably be slower in a grand coalition than in a small coalition or a one-party government, and the veto power raises the further danger that decision-making will become immobilised completely. There are some countervailing advantages, however. The principle of proportionality is a convenient and time-saving method for allocating appointments and public resources, and it removes a host of divisive issues from the decision-making process. Segmental autonomy offers similar advantages: in Jürg Steiner's words, it allows political demands to be 'split up among different political levels', which contributes to a 'relatively small input of demands' at the highest level of decision-making where grand coalitions and vetoes operate, and thus reduces the danger of immobilism.[25] Also, the greater speed and decisiveness of majoritarian government are more apparent than real in a plural society. They may give better results in the short run but at the expense of increasing frustration and hostility on the part of the excluded minority. Short-term effectiveness is therefore likely to lead to grave crises in the long run. Conversely, consociationalism may appear slow and ponderous in the short run but can be much more effective over long periods of time.

The conclusion must be that consociational democracy does have drawbacks but that these should not be exaggerated. Moreover, especially when there is no realistic alternative, it would be very unwise to reject consociationalism on the grounds of these drawbacks. A more prudent and constructive policy would be to accept consociational democracy but in its implementation to try to minimise its potential weaknesses as much as possible.

CONCLUSION: DETERMINATION VERSUS FREE CHOICE

As indicated earlier, Figure 2.1 is based on a *ceteris paribus* assumption. Of course, all other factors are never equal in real life. In my research on plural societies, I have therefore tried to determine the conditions that are conductive to the establishment and maintenance of consociational democracy. Several favourable conditions can in fact be identified: a multiple balance of power among the segments of a plural society in which no segment has a majority and the segments are of approximately equal size, a relatively small total population, external threats that are perceived as a common danger by the different segments, the presence of some society-wide loyalties, the absence of extreme socio-economic inequalities among the segments, the relative isolation of the segments from each other, and prior traditions of political accommodation that predispose to decision-making by the grand coalition method.[26]

These factors cannot be discussed in detail here, but what I want to emphasise is that they are neither necessary nor sufficient conditions. Most of the consociational cases that I have examined show a mixture of favourable and unfavourable background conditions, but the two cases of semi-consociational democracy are unusually valuable in demonstrating that these factors should not be credited with decisive influence. In spite of consistently optimal background factors, Israel has not developed a fully consociational democracy. Conversely, in spite of overwhelmingly unfavourable conditions in Canada, strongly consociational practices have developed in that country, especially during the period of the United Province. This means that consociational engineering may be attempted even when the conditions for it do not appear promising at all.

It may be particularly important to stress that historical traditions should not be regarded as ineluctable constraints on the freedom of political decision-makers. Hans Daalder has forcefully called attention to the fact that pre-democratic historical tendencies toward moderation and compromise in the Netherlands and Switzerland have made a great positive contribution to the development of consociational democracy in these countries.[27] On the other hand, there are several significant examples of the establishment of consociational institutions and practices in spite of strong majoritarian traditions. For some of its colonial dependencies, the British government encouraged and endorsed consociational arrangements that clearly violated its own tradi-

Majority Rule versus Democracy 41

tions of majority rule: the thoroughly consociational constitution for independent Cyprus and the formation of the Alliance of ethnic parties as a means of consociational cooperation in Malaysia. Perhaps an even better example is the British resort to such decidedly un-British political devices as 'power-sharing' - another term for grand coalition - and proportional representation in order to try to solve the problems of the plural society in Northern Ireland.

As Gabriel Almond and Robert Mundt write, 'choices in politics are constrained but indeterminate.' This conclusion may be disappointing for 'political *science*, but for political problem solving there may be cause for satisfaction.' Consociational theory belongs to what Almond and Mundt call the '*political* science literature that stresses room for manoeuver, ranges of freedom, the place for risk-taking'.[28] Faith in democracy combined with a realistic assessment of the needs of a plural society may well enable political leaders to overcome adverse political traditions and other unfavourable background conditions and to fashion creative solutions along consociational lines.

NOTES

Many of the ideas contained in this article were drawn from, and are elaborated in greater detail in, my book *Democracy in Plural Societies: A Comparative Exploration* (New Haven and London: Yale University Press, 1977).
1. Thomas S. Kuhn, *The Structure of Scientific Revolutions* (Chicago: University of Chicago Press, 1962).
2. Johannes Althusius's *Politica Methodice Digesta* was first published in 1603. David E. Apter was the first modern author to use the term 'consociational', and his main example of this type of regime was newly independent Nigeria; see his *The Political Kingdom in Uganda: A Study in Bureaucratic Nationalism* (Princeton: Princeton University Press, 1961), esp. pp. 24-5. In my own writings on democracy in divided societies, I originally used the term 'politics of accommodation' see my *The Politics of Accommodation: Pluralism and Democracy in the Netherlands* (Berkeley: University of California Press, 1968; 2nd ed., 1975). I adopted the term 'consociational' in my articles 'Typologies of Democratic Systems', *Comparative Political Studies*, vol. 1, no. 1 (Apr 1968), pp. 3-44, and 'Consociational Democracy', *World Politics*, vol. 21, no. 2 (Jan 1969) pp. 207-25.
3. Willmoore Kendall, *John Locke and the Doctrine of Majority Rule* (Urbana: University of Illinois Press, 1965).
4. Jean-Jacques Rousseau, *The Social Contract*, trans. by G. D. H. Cole (New York: Dutton, 1950) p. 107.
5. Another example is Israel, which is still without a full-fledged written constitution and where the Knesset possesses legislative sovereignty. It may also be argued that the French Fifth Republic belongs to the same category, because the 1962 referendum on the direct election of the presi-

dent established the principle that the constitution can be changed by a simple – popular rather than parliamentary – majority vote.
6. W. Arthur Lewis, *Politics in West Africa* (London: Allen & Unwin, 1965) pp. 64–6.
7. Emanuel Gutmann, 'Religion and National Integration in Israel', paper presented at the Round Table on Political Integration of the International Political Science Association, Jerusalem, 1974, p. 25.
8. Kuhn, p. 81.
9. Woodrow Wilson, 'Committee or Cabinet Government', *Overland Monthly* (Jan 1884), quoted by Walter Lippmann in his Introduction to Woodrow Wilson, *Congressional Government: A Study in American Politics* (New York: Meridian Books, 1956) p. 13 (emphasis added).
10. Edward Shils, 'The Fortunes of Constitutional Government in the Political Development of the New States', in John H. Hallowell (ed.), *Development: For What?* (Durham: Duke University Press, 1964) p. 103 (emphasis added).
11. Lewis, p. 55.
12. John Stuart Mill, *Considerations on Representative Government* (New York: Liberal Arts Press, 1958) p. 230.
13. J. S. Furnivall, *Colonial Policy and Practice: A Comparative Study of Burma and Netherlands India* (Cambridge: Cambridge University Press, 1948) p. 304.
14. Gabriel A. Almond, 'Comparative Political Systems', *Journal of Politics*, vol. 18, no. 3 (Aug 1956), pp. 391–409, reprinted in Almond, *Political Development: Essays in Heuristic Theory* (Boston: Little, Brown, 1970) ch. 1.
15. Seymour Martin Lipset, *Political Man: The Social Bases of Politics* (Garden City, N.Y.: Doubleday, 1960) pp. 88–9.
16. The quotations are from Leo Kuper's summary of Smith's theory in 'Plural Societies: Perspectives and Problems', in Leo Kuper and M. G. Smith (eds), *Pluralism in Africa* (Berkeley: University of California Press, 1969) p. 14.
17. Furnivall, pp. 489–90.
18. See Eric A. Nordlinger, *Conflict Regulation in Divided Societies*, Occasional Papers in International Affairs, no. 29 (Cambridge, Mass.: Harvard University, Center for International Affairs, 1972) pp. 36–9.
19. Samuel P. Huntington, Foreword to Nordlinger, *Conflict Regulation in Divided Societies*, p. vii.
20. D. J. Kriek discusses these practical problems posed by the South African policy of separate development, which he, significantly, calls a 'paradigm' in the Kuhnian sense (and which may be regarded as a derivative of the plural-societies paradigm) in 'Politieke alternatiewe vir Suid-Afrika op soek na 'n nuwe paradigma', *Politikon*, vol. 3, no. 1 (June 1976) pp. 57–89.
21. Conway W. Henderson calls this the 'apologist' position which should be replaced by a more democratically optimistic 'revisionist' outlook. See his 'Underdevelopment and Political Rights: A Revisionist Challenge', *Government and Opposition*, vol. 12, no. 3 (summer 1977), esp. pp. 278–83.
22. There is an extensive literature on consociational democracy, although different authors often use different terms to describe the concept. See

Val R. Lorwin, 'Segmented Pluralism: Ideological Cleavages and Political Cohesion in the Smaller European Democracies', *Comparative Politics*, vol. 3, no. 2 (Jan 1971) pp. 141–75; Gerhard Lehmbruch, *Proporzdemokratie: Politisches System und politische Kultur in der Schweiz und in Osterreich* (Tübingen: Mohr, 1967); Kenneth McRae (ed.), *Consociational Democracy: Political Accommodation in Segmented Societies* (Toronto: McClelland & Stewart, 1974); and Nordlinger, *Conflict Regulation in Divided Societies*. For reviews of this literature, see Hans Daalder, 'The Consociational Democracy Theme', *World Politics*, vol. 26, no. 4 (July 1974) pp. 604–21; Brian Barry, 'Political Accommodation and Consociational Democracy', *British Journal of Political Science*, vol. 5, no. 4 (Oct 1975) pp. 477–505; and Jeffrey Obler, Jürg Steiner and Guido Dierickx, *Decision-Making in Smaller Democracies: The Consociational 'Burden'*, Sage Professional Papers in Comparative Politics, vol. 6, no. 01-064 (Beverley Hills: Sage, 1977). For a discussion of consociationalism in the context of the South African political situation, see W. B. Vosloo, 'Pluralisme as teoretiese perspektief vir veelvolkige naasbestaan in Suid-Afrika', *Politikon*, vol. 1, no. 1 (June 1974) pp. 4–14.
23. John C. Calhoun, *A Disquisition on Government* (New York: Liberal Arts Press, 1953) p. 28.
24. See Johan Galtung, 'Violence, Peace, and Peace Research', *Journal of Peace Research*, vol. 6, no. 3 (1969) pp. 183–6.
25. Jürg Steiner, 'The Principles of Majority and Proportionality', *British Journal of Political Science*, vol. 1, no. 1 (Jan 1971) p. 69.
26. See Lijphart, *Democracy in Plural Societies: A Comparative Exploration* (New Haven: Yale University Press, 1977) ch. 3. John Seiler analyses these conditions in South Africa and Namibia in 'Consociational Authoritarianism: Incentives and Hindrances toward Power Sharing and Devolution in South Africa and Namibia', paper delivered at the Annual Meeting of the American Political Science Association, September 1977.
27. Hans Daalder, 'On Building Consociational Nations: The Cases of the Netherlands and Switzerland', *International Social Science Journal*, vol. 23, no. 3 (1971) pp. 367–8.
28. Gabriel A. Almond and Robert J. Mundt, 'Crisis, Choice and Change: Some Tentative Conclusions', in Gabriel A. Almond, Scott C. Flanagan and Robert J. Mundt (eds), *Crisis, Choice and Change: Historical Studies of Political Development* (Boston: Little, Brown, 1973) p. 649.

3 A Model of a Multinational Society as Developed in Austria-Hungary before 1918

Friedrich Prinz
Professor of Medieval History and Comparative Provincial History, University of Munich, Bavaria

Austria-Hungary, though destroyed by the Peace Treaties of 1918/19, was at the beginning of our century one of the most important states in the world. It had nationality problems which it tried to overcome by a new means of internal political organisation. This leads me to believe that the experiences of the Habsburg Monarchy may have a contribution to make to the solution of ethnic problems with which we are confronted today. It is true there are great and decisive differences between the Austrian nationality problems and the ethnic problems of a multiracial society like South Africa, but there are also comparable and crucial items. These are worth scrutinising to see how they could be helpful in the situation which exists here and which is under pressure from communist-guided nationalism.

I NATIONALISM TODAY

The themes of 'national confrontation' and 'mass expulsion' are of evident significance for the twentieth century. This is an atrocious trend in modern society and nobody can predict whether or not it will cease within the next decade. What are the reasons for this outburst of aggressive nationalism? Is it true that, as communist propaganda stresses again and again, nationalism today is nothing but an ideological form of class warfare? There is no doubt of the importance of the interaction between 'social' problems on the one hand and 'national' or 'racial' problems on the other. It would however seem to be an oversimplification to try to explain by reference to one single pattern the various markedly different situations in the changing world of the seventies. To use exclusively the class-warfare pattern in order to explain nationalism is in some way to surrender to communist ideology from the very beginning. Let me therefore try to define and to extrapolate some essential factors of nationalism today and of the consequences for the future.

It is significant for modern mass-nationalism that both its self-interpretation and its practical political aims are closely connected with national territorialism. More specifically there underlies modern mass-nationalism a conviction that every nation, every people or 'ethnic unity' has a right or even the duty to build up a territory of its own and that within the borderlines of a certain territory or state there should be only one people of one ethnic homogeneous nation. State and nation should be as far as possible identical.

The consequences of this political ideology were and are terrible all over the world, because in pursuance thereof every nation tries to homogenise its territory and thereby to purify the country from other races or ethnic groups. This has resulted in some cases in a more or less forced assimilation of the minorities within the territory of a nation. That was and remains a very common approach to the solution in human terms of nationality problems. In contrast is the practice of the expulsion of minorities, very often millions of people. This began after World War I with the mass transfer of millions of Greeks from Turkey, continued with the expulsion of millions of Germans after 1945, and you do not need me to tell you that a similar process is going on in Angola and Mozambique.

The main reason for this development is the historical and typically European connection of modern nationalism and national self-consciousness with the idea of territorialism culminating with the slogan 'One Nation – One State'.

I need not explain why Lenin's concept of using modern mass-nationalism was and is one of the most successful weapons for preparing a pure communist revolution. Taking this for granted it is clear that all means which can help to reduce national tension and national or racial confrontation are also remedies against communist infiltration. Reducing national and racial antagonism is at the same time an essential element in cutting the dangerous linkage between nationalism and social revolution which together form, I think, the most explosive ideological mixture in our century.

II THE NATIONALITY QUESTION IN AUSTRIA-HUNGARY

If we accept that this is the case there would seem to be some value in searching out and testing models and patterns of multinational and multiracial societies which have, in the course of history, faced nationalism much as we do in the last quarter of the twentieth century. It may be true that history cannot offer simple solutions for contemporary problems, but on the other hand historical experience may and should help to sharpen our eyes for similar problems and probably to identify and adapt solutions which have been tried in the past.

Some three years ago Professor Kurt Glaser published an interesting paper on 'Development Problems of Multi-Ethnic Societies'.[1] In this article he dealt with the experiences of a multinational empire containing nationalist ideologies and centrifugal trends which led at the end of World War I to the dissolution of its Habsburg monarchy. In his paper Professor Glaser mentioned 'the most original proposal' for the solution of nationality problems developed in 1903 by Karl Renner, who after World War II became the *Bundespräsedent* of the Republic of Austria. I would like to address myself to Professor Glaser's brief remarks because the model elaborated by Karl Renner is of some interest for the solution of the problems in South Africa.

III PERSONAL AUTONOMY OR THE PRINCIPLE OF PERSONALITY

What is the core, the essential point of Renner's ideas?

He took account of the fact that the Empire's nationalities were not settled in compact blocks or areas but were widely scattered and intermingled in most parts of Austria-Hungary. He therefore invented the concept of 'personal autonomy' or the 'principle of personality' and he did so in deliberate opposition to those working towards modernising the Dual Monarchy by trying to solve its problems on the basis of the 'territorial principle'. The partisans of the latter endeavoured to divide the Habsburg monarchy into definite political territories based either on the so-called historical rights and historical borders of the 'crownlands' or on the ethnic borderlines of the nations within the Empire. The distinct territorial governments so to be formed should thereafter be combined into a kind of confederation. The principle of personality advocated by Renner was a rejection of such a concept of distinct national states within the monarchy because in so much of the Empire the population was ethnically mixed. Thus every proposed national territory would have within it, and would need to tolerate, substantial ethnic minorities. Renner's idea was not to establish a distinct German, Czech, Polish, Magyar or Croat state inside the monarchy and along practically undefinable ethnic borderlines, but to try to give to the monarchy as a whole an organisation of an international or, better still, a supranational character. Just as two generations previously Louis Kossuth, the Hungarian leader of the 1848 Revolution, among the plans formed during his life in exile had cherished the idea of solving the nationality problems of Hungary on the basis of religious autonomy and freedom so in 1903 Karl Renner adduced an analogous scheme.[2] He based his scheme on the concept that, just as the religious controversies could not be solved on a territorial basis because the principle of *Cujus Regio, Ejus Religio* led to incessant warfare, so nationality problems could not be answered by a territorial dismemberment of the old state. The same principle of personality should be introduced here too. What he proposed could be called 'two-track federalism'.

The main task which Renner set himself in his famous book *Das Selbstbestimmungsrecht der Nationen*[3] or 'The Nations' Right of Self-Determination' has been described as

> ... to explore and to present this internal state order and supranational order of law, which should replace the political struggle of the nationalities for power with the orderly procedure of court and parliamentary transaction ... to materialise the legal concept of the nation first within the narrow frame of the nationality state, and thus to present an example for the future national order of mankind.[4]

This sounds in some way rather utopian and indeed Renner's programme has often been criticised for its impracticability, for instance by Dr Edvard Beneš, the co-founder of the Czechoslovak Republic.[5]

My own belief that Renner's ideas were neither impracticable nor unrealistic is supported by the fact that his pattern or model for solving nationality problems and ethnic confrontations found tangible expression in the so-called Moravian Settlement of 1905 (*Der Mahrischer Ausgleich*) between the Czechs and the Germans.[6] Only the breakup of Austria-Hungary at the end of World War I stopped the further modernisation of the monarchy along the lines of Renner's ideas.

IV RENNER'S IDEAS AND SOUTH AFRICA TODAY

Now, what exactly were Renner's ideas and what is their practical relevance to the problems with which South Africa is confronted today? In accordance with the principle of personal autonomy the members of each of the nations making up the Austro-Hungarian empire were to be entitled to form 'national unities' otherwise termed 'national curias' or '*National-Kurien*'. These were to take the form of associations, local, intermediate and central. In them would be vested the jurisdiction of the state on all matters relating to cultural life and the educational system. The essential point was that they were to be organised on an Empire-wide basis, disregarding its territorial subdivisions. Such a system needs no exact boundaries between ethnic groups and creates no problem of minorities because no nationality has a special claim to a fixed territory. In this manner, so Renner planned, all the nations of the monarchy, the Germans, the Czechs, the Poles and all the others, could each become united from its own national or ethnic point of view without the creation of ethnically based political divisions within the Empire. The decisive point of such a new representative system is that autonomy takes a form in which autonomous status applies to the individual and not to a territory. Renner's views on this point have been summarised as follows:

> Everywhere the territory of the state appears divided according to a simple plan into provinces ... districts ... and townships. Yet we must organise the country according to two principles. We must put a double network on the map, an economic and an ethnic one. We

must cut across the functions of the state. We must separate national and political affairs, we must organise the population twice, once nationally and once according to administrative requirements (*staatlich*). In either case the territory units will be different. This means a new constitutional and administrative institution ... It means a political and legal task which we Austrians have to face bravely and determinedly.[7]

According to Renner's programme there were to be established eight national governments. All would be based in Vienna, the administrative capital of the Empire, but as national governments they would have as their exclusive concern cultural and national affairs. They were to be organised according to the principle of personal autonomy at all levels, from the national down to that of individual communities.

These national governments, the *Curias*, were to be one column of the new constitutional structure which Renner planned for Austria and they were to be balanced by eight administrative Governments which were to be styled *Gubernia*. These were to be organised primarily on the basis of socio-economic needs and interests. Through them was to be handled the administration of the state, using the term administration in a very precise sense; that is to say it covered all matters except 'national' affairs. To Renner the terms 'national' and 'cultural' were almost interchangeable. The *Gubernia* would replace the outdated structure of the seventeen existing 'crownlands', each of which still had its own constitution containing many elements characteristic of a medieval estate. Renner's further proposals for bringing the two elements together in the form of a supreme Federal power united under the Emperor were extremely complex and I need not pursue them.

One aspect however should be mentioned because it reflects a problem with which South Africa today is also confronted. This is the problem of migratory workers. There were in Austria some hundreds of thousands of these, mainly agricultural workers as compared with the mine workers whom you have in South Africa. Territorial autonomy is of no value to those who are driven, in pursuit of work, to move away from the home area of their national language and ethnic background. 'Horizontal mobility' causes grave problems in our industrialised society. Is there not an opportunity to solve such problems by way of the concept of personal autonomy, which leads in turn to a widely available educational system based on national and ethnic principles? As a way to escape national and social confrontation it may certainly be a difficult one but it is also one which is viable.

V STRONG AND WEAK POINTS OF PERSONAL AUTONOMY

Before I apply myself to analysing the strong and weak points in Renner's line of argument may I first quote the brilliant criticism of Renner's pattern of personal autonomy which Oscar Jaszi formulated in 1929:

> In a period which heated national consciousness of the Germans, the Magyars, the Czechs, the Poles and others almost to boiling point, when the idea of a nation was no longer a simple cultural and ethnographic connection but an effort to unite the traditional national settlements into an independent state, the imagination of Renner was manifestly too schematic and too bloodless in the eyes of the fighting nations. These nations would perhaps have been inclined to combine their independent states with the others in a confederation, but they refused to accept the competency of a superstate even in matters which they felt were not strictly national.[8]

This may be entirely correct, but since all the peoples whom Jaszi mentions, other than German Austrians, are now under Soviet domination, one may be permitted to ask whether the goals of extreme nationalism are really the only thinkable values for mankind in our day? Indeed they are under Soviet domination mainly because of their own terrible nationalism during the two World Wars!

I myself believe that the weak points in Renner's pattern of a multinational or multiracial society are much more to be found in his concept that one can strictly cut off national (that is to say cultural) affairs from their socio-economic context. This is in fact impossible and Renner attracted much contemporary criticism on this crucial point. I need explain neither the strong interaction between economic matters on the one hand and national or ethnic self-consciousness on the other, nor that it is much more difficult to build up ethnic unities (which are subsequently to be brought to cooperate with each other) when such unities are of different levels of economic development and not all enjoy a Western standard of life. Nevertheless the creation of different national and ethnic bodies and unities, based on the principle of personality, seems to have some advantages, notwithstanding the difficulties that arise from the double structure of state and society already mentioned.

VI SUMMARY AND CONCLUSION

May I now summarise my views on the suggestion that Karl Renner's concept of personal autonomy and the principle of personality can be of constructive interest to us in our present problems?

1. Where, as especially in Africa, there are artificial borderlines, deriving from nineteenth-century colonialism and still continuing to divide the older and more natural geographic tribal formations or the historical structure of the country as formed by settlers from Europe, then political bodies and representative institutions formed from ethnic unities may provide a long-term solution. Both the artificial and the natural types of frontier mentioned above have their indivisible historical rights, both can and should be preserved or restored by the new superstructure of ethnic bodies on the principle of personality, personal representation and self-government.

2. All over the world we find ourselves faced with national and ethnic animosities. Confrontation becomes a reality not least because of the intermingling of such animosities with the worldwide Marxist pattern of class warfare, thereby jeopardising the whole of our existing structure. But it seems to me that ethnic confrontation could be reduced or even avoided if non-territorial political bodies and unities, built up on the basis of general elections in national sections, were prepared to solve their problems through negotiation at the highest possible administrative level. Such negotiating structure would thus become a continuing institution and not just a means of managing actual crises.

3. The third and as I believe the most important point is the historical political lesson to be derived from the nationality conflicts in Austria-Hungary. It is the majority/minority problem or, more exactly, the problem of the relationship between the two elements especially when the relative proportions are fixed on hard and fast national or ethnic lines. Experience teaches us that majority rule only remains legal and democratic so long as the minority has a real chance to become the majority one day. In ethnically homogeneous societies this system of political change does work but, as history shows, it has never worked really well in multinational societies. To protect democratic principles therefore an elaborate system to protect the minority is and must be a vital element. Political bodies deriving from the principle and practice of personality are essential in the creation of a new model constitution to prevent a majority rule which would be in reality a racial rule.

4. The crucial point in order to bring about a stable compromise is, in the case of South Africa for instance, the readiness of the white people

to make large-scale economic concessions. South Africans have an additional opportunity to transform the present system step by step from one based on the old concept of territorial nationalism, so typical of Europe in the nineteenth century, and to form a new type of multiracial society, a society which is not stuck with pseudo-territorial borderlines between its ethnic groups. By working out a new political system like this South Africa can and will give an example and model for a worldwide industrial society with large-scale horizontal mobility. This would seem to me absolutely clearly to be an opportunity for the application of Arnold Toynbee's formula of 'challenge and response' as the motor for the development of mankind.

5. This leads me to my last point, which derives from Karl Renner's deep conviction that the trend of history is towards multiracial political systems. As Karl Deutsch has pointed out this applies not only in respect of economic matters and not only because of modern means of communication; multinational systems and societies are more adequate to the needs of our world than the classic type of national state, one with a more or less homogeneous population. South Africa has the unique chance of developing a modern multiracial society as a model for the future of the whole world.

NOTES

1. In *Accelerated Development in South Africa* (London, 1974).
2. O. Jaszi, *The Dissolution of the Hapsburg Monarchy* (Chicago, 1929; 2nd ed. 1964) p. 177.
3. Karl Renner, *Das Selbstbestimmungsrecht der Nationen in besonderer Anwendung auf Osterreich*, Part I: *Nation und Staat* (Vienna, 1918). This book is a completely revised edition of his earlier book *Der Kampf der Osterreichischen Nationen um den Staat* (Leipzig – Vienna, 1903).
4. R. A. Kann, *The Multi-National Empire: Nationalism and National Reform in the Hapsburg Monarchy, 1848–1918*, 2 vols (New York, 1950) II, pp. 157ff.
5. E. Beneš, *Le Problème Autrichien et la Question Tchèque* (Thèse), Dijon, 1906, pp. 279ff. Compare F. Prinz, *Beneš, Jaksch und die Sudetendeutschen* (Stuttgart, 1975) p. 15.
6. H. Glassl, *Der Mährische Ausgleich* (Munich, 1967).
7. Quotation after R. A. Kann, *Multi-National Empire*, p. 159.
8. O. Jaszi, *Dissolution*, p. 180.

4 Ethno-national versus Other Forms of Group Identity: The Problem of Terminology

Walker Connor
Professor of Political Science and Faculty Exchange Scholar at the State University of New York

Events of the past decade have by now impressed upon even the more casual observer of world politics that ethno-nationalism constitutes a major and growing threat to the political stability of most states. Rather than witnessing an evolution of stable state- or suprastate-communities, the observer of global politics has viewed a succession of situations involving competing allegiances in which people have illustrated that an intuitive bond felt toward an informal and unstructured subdivision of mankind is far more profound and potent than are the ties that bind them to the formal and legalistic state structure in which they find themselves. Present or recent large-scale violence within such Third World states as Burma, Burundi, Chad, Ethiopia, Guyana, India, Iraq, Kenya, Malaysia, Nigeria, Pakistan, the Philippines, the Sudan, Thailand, Turkey, and Uganda (to mention but a few of the afflicted states) amply testifies to the widespread failure of governments to induce a substantial segment of their citizenry to transfer their primary loyalty from a human grouping to the state.[1] Nor have the older, more technologically integrated states of the First World proved to be immune. Austria, Belgium, Canada, Denmark, France, Italy, the Netherlands, Switzerland, and the United Kingdom have all experienced ethnically motivated unrest.[2] And though

Marxist-Leninist states of the Second World officially claim that, by faithfully carrying out Lenin's prescriptions for devitalising nationalism at home, they have successfully solved what they call their national question, the restiveness of national groups constitutes a major element in the internal and external political affairs of the Soviet Union, China, Czechoslovakia, Laos, Romania, Vietnam, and Yugoslavia.[3]

Few indeed are the scholars who can claim to have anticipated even the possibility of such a trend. The conventional wisdom of the first two post-World War II decades held (1) that the newly emerging Third World states would win the battle of loyalties over 'tribal' allegiance; (2) that World War II had taught the peoples of Western Europe that nationalism was too parochial a focus for the modern age and that, as a result, a supranational and suprastate consciousness of being European was rapidly becoming the primary identity of the region's inhabitants; and (3) that the highly centralised, 'monolithic' Marxist-Leninist structure(s), combined with the effective indoctrination of its people in the tenets of Marxist-Leninist ideology, made consideration of forces such as ethno-nationalism simply irrelevant.

There are numerous reasons why so many scholars failed to anticipate the resistance that state-integration has in fact encountered. Elsewhere, this writer has listed twelve overlapping and reinforcing contributing elements,[4] and unquestionably the list could be enlarged. But the theme of this paper is that the most significant factor accounting for the divergence between scholarly expectations and actuality has been a basic misunderstanding concerning the nature of nationalism.

The most fundamental error involved in scholarly approaches to nationalism has been a tendency to equate nationalism with a feeling of loyalty to the state rather than with loyalty to the nation. This confusion has led scholars to assume that the relationship of nationalism to state-integration is functional and supportive rather than dysfunctional and defeatist. And since there is general agreement that nationalism remains a compelling and dominant motivational force, the linking of nationalism to the state has been viewed as all but guaranteeing the victory of the latter against all competitors for the loyalty of its inhabitants.

The error of improperly equating nationalism with loyalty to the state is the consequence of a much broader terminological disease that plagues the study of global politics. It would be difficult to name four words more essential to global politics than are state, nation, nation-state, and nationalism. But despite their centrality, all four terms are shrouded in ambiguity due to their imprecise, inconsistent, and often totally erroneous usage. In 1939 a study of nationalism undertaken by the Royal Institute of International Affairs noted that 'among other difficulties which impede the study of *nationalism*, that of language holds a leading place.'[5] In the four decades that have subsequently elapsed, the linguistic jungle that encapsulates the concept of nationalism has only grown more dense.

It is particularly paradoxical that the widespread misuse of the most elemental terms should be tolerated during a period in which so many authorities within the discipline are emphasising the need for a more precise and scientific vocabulary. Karl Deutsch has praised the great strides already made in this direction:

> In science, including social science, a word is only a kind of noise unless we sooner or later use it to lead to a procedure that will tell us whether or not a certain event or fact belongs under the word. The meaning of a word is defined by its limits, by knowing what does not belong under it as clearly as what does. Any word that could include everything and anything has no place in science. . . . Today when someone speaks about *natives*, the immediate questions are, 'How do you define "native"?' 'How do you know who is a native?' The same questions arise when we speak of *workers*, *patriots*, or any general social classification of this sort. Such terms can no longer be taken casually.[6]

Yet despite this tribute to terminological precision, the same work by Professor Deutsch is honeycombed with illustrations of improper and contradictory usage of the four terms we have described as pivotal.[7] Professor Deutsch is *not* singled out here because he has been unusually uncircumspect in this regard, but rather in order to illustrate the breadth of the problem. That even an acknowledged scholar of nationalism and one who espouses the cause of vocabular precision should improperly and inconsistently utilise these fundamental terms indicates how acceptable such malpractice has become.

One of the most common manifestations of terminological licence is the interutilisation of the words *state* and *nation*. This tendency is perplexing because at one level of consciousness most scholars are clearly well aware of the vital distinctions between the two concepts. The state is the major political subdivision of the globe. As such, it is readily defined and, what is of greater moment to the present discussion, is easily conceptualised in quantitative terms. Peru, for illustration, can be defined in an easily conceptualised manner as the territorial-political unit consisting of the sixteen million inhabitants of the 514,060 square miles located on the west coast of South America between 69 degrees and 80 degrees West and 2 degrees and 18 degrees 21 minutes South.

Defining and conceptualising the nation is much more difficult because the essence of a nation is intangible. This essence is a psychological bond that joins a people and differentiates it, in the subconscious conviction of its members, from all other people in a most vital way. The nature of that bond and its wellspring remain shadowy and elusive, and the consequent difficulty of defining the nation is usually acknowledged by those who attempt this task. Thus, a popular dictionary of International Relations defines a nation as follows:

> A social group which shares a common ideology, common institutions and customs, and a *sense* of homogeneity. 'Nation' is difficult to define so precisely as to differentiate the term from such other groups as religious sects, which exhibit some of the same characteristics. In the nation, however, there is also present a strong group *sense* of belonging associated with a particular territory considered to be peculiarly its own.[8]

Whereas the key word in this particular definition is *sense*, other authorities may substitute *feeling* or *intuition*, but proper appreciation of the abstract essence of the nation is customary *in definitions*. But after focusing attention upon that essential psychological bond, little probing of its nature follows. Indeed, having defined the nation as an essentially psychological phenomenon, authorities, as we have noted, then regularly proceed to treat it as fully synonymous with the very different and totally tangible concept of the state.

Even when one restricts *nation* to its proper, non-political meaning of a human collectivity, the ambiguity surrounding its nature is not thereby evaporated. How does one differentiate the nation from other human collectivities? The above-cited definition spoke of 'a sense of homogeneity'. Others speak of a feeling of sameness, of oneness, of belonging, or of consciousness of kind. But all such definitions appear a bit timid, and thereby fail to distinguish the nation from numerous other types of group. Thus, one can conceive of the Amish, the Appalachian hill people, or 'down Mainers' as all fitting rather neatly within any of the preceding standards.

With but very few exceptions, authorities have shied away from describing the nation as a kinship group and have usually explicitly denied that the notion of shared blood is a factor. Such denials are supported by data illustrating that most groups claiming nationhood do in fact incorporate several genetic strains. But such an approach ignores the wisdom of the old saw that when analysing sociopolitical situations, what ultimately matters is not *what is* but *what people believe is*. And a subconscious belief in the group's separate origin and evolution is an important ingredient of national psychology. When one avers that he is Chinese, he is identifying himself not just with the Chinese people and culture of today, but with the Chinese people and their activities throughout time. The Chinese Communist Party was appealing to just such a sense of separate origin and evolution in 1937:

> We know that in order to transform the glorious future into a new China, independent, free, and happy, all our fellow countrymen, every single, zealous descendent of Huang-ti [the legendary first Emperor of China] must determinedly and relentlessly participate in the concerted struggle. . . . Our great Chinese nation, with its long history, is unconquerable.[9]

Bismark's famous exhortation to the German people, over the heads of their particular political leaders, to 'think with your blood' was a similar attempt to activate a mass psychological vibration predicted upon an intuitive sense of consanguinity. An unstated presumption of a Chinese (or German) nation is that there existed in some hazy, prerecorded era a Chinese (or German) Adam and Eve, and that the couple's progeny has evolved in essentially unadulterated form down to the present.

Since the nation is a self-defined rather than an other-defined grouping, the broadly held conviction concerning the group's singular origin need not and seldom will accord with factual data. Thus, the anthropologist may prove to his own satisfaction that there are several genetic strains within the Pushtun people who populate the Afghani-Pakistani border-region and conclude therefrom that the group represents the variegated offspring of several peoples who have moved through the region. The important fact, however, is that the Pushtuns themselves are convinced that all Pushtuns are evolved from a single source and have remained essentially unadulterated. This is a matter which is *known* intuitively and unquestionably, a matter of attitude and not of fact. It is a matter the underlying conviction of which is not apt to be disturbed substantially even by the rational acceptance of anthropological or other evidence to the contrary. Depending upon the sophistication of the treatise, this type of sensory knowledge may be described as *a priori* 'an emotional rather than rational conviction', 'primordial', 'thinking with the heart (or with the blood) rather than with the mind', or 'a *gut* or *knee-jerk* response'. Regardless of the nomenclature, it is an extremely important adjunct of the national idea.[10] It is the intuitive conviction which can give to nations a psychological dimension approximating that of the extended family, i.e., a feeling of common blood lineage.

The word *nation* comes from the Latin and, when first coined, clearly conveyed the idea of common blood ties. It was derived from the past participle of the verb *nasci*, meaning to be born, and the Latin noun *natio* connoted *breed* or *race*. Unfortunately, terms used to describe human collectivities (terms such as race and class) invite an unusual degree of literary licence, and *nation* certainly proved to be no exception.[11] Thus, at some medieval universities, a student's *natio* designated the sector of the country from whence he came. But when introduced into the English language in the late thirteenth century, it was with its primary connotation of a blood-related group. One etymologist notes, however, that by the early seventeenth century, *nation* was also being used to describe the inhabitants of a country, regardless of that population's ethnonational composition, thereby becoming a substitute for less specific human categories such as *the people* or *the citizenry*.[12] This infelicitous practice continues to the present day, and accounts for often-encountered references to the American citizenry as the American nation. Whatever the American people are (and they may well be *sui generis*), they are not a nation in the pristine sense of the word. However, the unfortunate habit of calling them a nation, and thus verbally equating American with German, Chinese, English, and the like, has seduced scholars into erroneous analogies. Indeed, while proud of being 'a nation of immigrants' with a 'melting pot' tradition, the absence of a sense of common origin may well make it more difficult, and conceivably impossible, for the American to appreciate instinctively the idea of the nation in the same dimension and with the same poignant clarity as do the Japanese, the Bengali, or the Kikuyu. It is difficult for an American to appreciate what it means for a German to be German or for a Frenchman to be French, because the psychological effect of being American is not precisely equatable. Some of the associations are missing and others may be quite different.

Far more detrimental to the study of nationalism, however, has been the propensity to employ the term nation as a substitute for that territorial juridical unit, the state. How this practice developed is unclear, though it seems to have become a relatively common practice in the late seventeenth century. Two possible explanations for this development present themselves. One involves the rapid spread of the doctrine of popular sovereignty that was precipitated about this time by the writings of men such as Locke. In identifying *the people* as the fount of all political power, this revolutionary doctrine made the people and the state near-synonyms. *L'état c'est moi* became *l'état c'est le peuple*. And therefore the nation and the state had become near-synonyms, for we have already noted the tendency to equate nation with the entire people or citizenry. Thus, the French *Declaration of Rights of Man and Citizen* would proclaim that 'the source of all sovereignty resides essentially in the nation: no group, no individual may exercise authority not emanating expressly therefrom.' Though the drafters of the Declaration may not have been aware, 'the nation' to which they referred contained Alsations, Basques, Bretons, Catalans, Corsicans, Flemings, and Occitanians, as well as Frenchmen.

It is also probable that the habit of interutilising *nation* and *state* developed as alternative abbreviations for the expression *nation-state*. The very coining of this hyphenate illustrated an appreciation of the vital differences between *nation* and *state*. It was designed to describe a territorial-political unit (a state) whose borders coincided or nearly coincided with the territorial distribution of a national group. More concisely, it described a situation in which a nation had its own state. Unfortunately, however, *nation-state* has come to be applied indiscriminately to all states. Thus one authority has stated that 'a prime fact about the world is that it is largely composed of nation-states.'[13] The statement should read that 'a prime fact about the world is that it is *not* largely composed of nation-states.' A survey of the 132 entities generally considered to be states as of 1971 produced the following breakdown:

(1) Only 12 states (9.1 per cent) can justifiably be described as nation-states.
(2) Twenty-five (18.9 per cent) contain a nation or potential nation accounting for more than 90 per cent of the state's total population but also contain an important minority.[14]
(3) Another 25 (18.9 per cent) contain a nation of potential nation accounting for between 75 per cent and 89 per cent of the population.

(4) In 31 (23.5 per cent), the largest ethnic element accounts for 50 per cent to 74 per cent of the population.
(5) In 39 (29.5 per cent), the largest nation or potential nation accounts for less than half of the population.

Were all states nation-states, no great harm would result from referring to them as nations, and people who insisted that the distinction between *nation* and *state* be maintained could be dismissed as linguistic purists or semantic nitpickers. Where *nation* and *state* essentially coincide, their verbal interutilisation is inconsequential because the two are indistinguishably merged in popular perception. The state is perceived as the political extension of the nation, and appeals to one trigger the identical, positive psychological responses as appeals to the other. To ask a Japanese *kamikaze* pilot of a *banzai*-charge participant whether he was about to die for *Nippon* or for the Nipponese people would be an incomprehensible query since the two blurred into an inseparable whole. Hitler could variously make his appeals to the German people in the name of state (Deutsches Reich), nation (Volksdeutsch), or homeland (Deutschland), because all triggered the same emotional associations. Similar responses can be elicited from members of a nation that is clearly predominant within a state. But the invoking of such symbols has quite a different impact upon minorities. Thus, 'Mother Russia' evokes one type of response from a Russian and something quite different from a Ukrainian. De Gaulle's emotional evocations of *La France* met quite different audiences within the Ile de France and within Brittany or Corsica.

Whatever the original reason for the interutilisation of *nation* and *state*, even the briefest reflection suffices to establish the all-pervasive effect that this careless use of terminology has had upon the intellectual-cultural milieu within which the study of nationalism is perforce conducted. The League of Nations and the United Nations are obvious misnomers. The discipline called International Relations should be designated *Interstate* Relations.[15] One listing of contemporary organisations contains sixty-six entries beginning with the word *International* (e.g., the International Court of Justice and the International Monetary Fund), none of which, either in its membership or in its function, reflects any relationship to nations. International Law and International Organisation are still other significant illustrations of the common but improper tendency to equate state and nation. National income, national wealth, national interest, and the like, refer in fact to statal concerns. A recently coined malapropism, *transnational* (and even *transnationalism*) is used to describe interstate, extragovernmental relations. Nationalisation is still another of the numerous misnomers that muddy understanding of the national phenomenon.

With the concepts of the nation and the state thus hopelessly confused, it is perhaps not too surprising that *nationalism* should come to mean identification with the state rather than loyalty to the nation. Even the same International Relations Dictionary whose definition of the *nation* we cited for its proper appreciation of the psychological essence of the nation makes this error. After carefully noting that 'a nation may comprise part of a state, or extend beyond the borders of a single state', it elsewhere says of *nationalism* that 'it makes the state the ultimate focus of the individual's loyalty.'[16] It also says of nationalism that 'as a mass emotion it is the most powerful political force operative in the world.'[17] Few would disagree with this assessment of the power of nationalism, *and this is precisely the problem. Impressed with the force of nationalism, and assuming it to be in the service of the state, the scholar of political development has been preprogrammed to assume that the new states of Africa and Asia would naturally become the foci of their inhabitants' loyalties.* Nationalism, here as elsewhere, would prove irresistible, and alternative foci of loyalty would therefore lose the competition to that political structure variously called the nation, the state, or the nation-state. This syndrome of assumptions and terminological confusion which has generally characterised the political development school is reflected in the early self-description of its endeavours as 'nation-building'. Contrary to its nomenclature, the 'nation-building' school has in fact been dedicated to building viable states. And with a very few exceptions, the greatest barrier to state unity has been the fact that the states each contain more than one nation, and sometimes hundreds. Yet a review of the literature will uncover little reflection on how the psychological bonds that presently tie segments of the state's population are to be destroyed. One searches the literature in vain for techniques by which group-ties predicated upon such things as a sense of separate origin, development, and destiny are to be supplanted by loyalty to a state-structure, whose population has never shared such common feelings. The nature and power of those abstract ties that identify the true nation remain unmentioned, to say nothing of unprobed. The assumption that the powerful force called nationalism is in the service of the state makes the difficult investigation of such abstractions unnecessary.

As in the case of substituting the word *nation* for *state*, it is difficult to pinpoint the origin of the tendency to equate nationalism with loyalty to the state. It is unquestionably a very recent development, for the word *nationalism* is itself of very recent creation. G. de Bertier de Sauvigny believes it first appeared in 1798 and did not reappear until 1830. Moreover, its absence from lexicographies until the late nineteenth and early twentieth centuries suggests that its use was not extensive until much more recently. Furthermore, all of the examples of its early use convey the idea of identification not with the state, but with the nation as properly understood.[18] While unable to pinpoint nationalism's subsequent association with the state, it indubitably followed and flowed from the tendency to equate state and nation. It also unquestionably received a strong impetus from the great body of literature occasioned by the growth of militant nationalism in Germany and Japan during the 1930s and early 1940s.

As outstanding illustrations of the fanatical responses that nationalism can engender, German and Japanese nationalism of this period have come to occupy an important place in all subsequent scholarship on nationalism. And, unfortunately, these manifestations of extreme nationalism have been firmly identified with loyalty to the state. The most common word applied to them has been *fascism*, a doctrine postulating unswerving obedience to an organic, corporate state. The most popular alternative descriptive phrase, *totalitarianism*, perhaps even more strongly conveys the idea of the complete (total) identification of the individual with the state.

The linking of the state to these examples *par excellence* of extreme nationalism suggests the likelihood that the other states will also become the object of mass devotion. If some states could elicit such fanatical devotion, why not others? Granted that few would wish to see such extreme and perverted dedication to the state arise elsewhere. But if the concept of a Japanese state could, during World War II, motivate *banzai*-charges, *kamikaze* missions, and numerous decisions of suicide rather than surrender (as well as the many post-war illustrations of people enduring for years an animal-like existence in caves on Pacific islands) because of a loyalty to the Japanese state that was so unassailable as to place that state's defeat beyond comprehension, then surely the states of the Third World should at least be able to evoke a sufficiently strong loyalty from their inhabitants as to prevail against any competing group-allegiances. If a loyalty to a German state could motivate Germans to carry on a war long after it became evident that the cause was hopeless and that perseverance could only entail more deprivation, destruction, and death, then surely other states could at least elicit a sense of common cause and identity from their populations that would prove more powerful than any counter-tendencies to draw distinctions among segments of the populace. If the German and Japanese experiences were pertinent elsewhere, then optimism concerning the stability of present state structures would be justified. But what has been too readily ignored is the fact that Germany and Japan were among that handful of states that clearly qualify as nation-states. As earlier noted, in such cases the state and the nation are indistinguishably linked in popular perception. Japan to the Japanese, just as Germany to the Germans, was something far more personal and profound than a territorial-political structure termed a state; it was an embodiment of the nation-idea and therefore an extension of self. As postulated by fascist doctrine, these states were indeed popularly conceived as corporate organisms, for they were equated with the Japanese and German nations. As Hitler wrote in *Mein Kampf*:

> We, as Aryans, are therefore able to imagine a State only to be the living organism of a nationality which not only safeguards the preservation of that nationality, but which, by a further training of its spiritual and ideal abilities, leads it to its highest freedom.[19]

But could such an emotion-laden conception of the state take root where the nation and the state were not popularly equated? The single rubric of fascism was applied to Hitler's Germany, Tojo's Japan, Mussolini's Italy, Franco's Spain, and Peron's Argentina. It is evident, however, that appeals in the name of Spain have not elicited any great emotion from the Basques, Catalans, and Galicians. In polygenic Argentina, Peron's message was not a unifying appeal to all Argentinians, but was in fact a divisive call in the name of socio-economic class. Within Italy, a sense of loyalty to the state proved woefully and surprisingly inadequate in the face of its first major test, the invasion by Allied forces. The reason appears to be that the concept of a single people (national awareness) had not yet permeated the subconsciousness of the Italians to the same measure as a similar concept had permeated the German and Japanese people.[20] In equating nationalism with loyalty to the state, scholars had failed to inquire how many cases there have been where fanatical devotion to a state has arisen in the absence of a popular conception of the state as the state of one's particular nation. Rather than suggesting certain victory on the part of new states in the competition for loyalty, the experiences of Germany and Japan exemplify the potential strength of those emotional ties to one's nation with which the multi-ethnic state must contend. German and Japanese nationalism were more prophetic auguries of the growth of concepts such as, *inter alia*, Ibo, Bengali, Kikuyu, Naga, Karen, Lao, Bahutu, Kurd, and Baganda, than they were auguries of the growth of concepts such as Nigeria, Pakistan, Kenya, India, Burma, Thailand, Rwanda, Iraq and Uganda.

Mistakenly equating nationalism with loyalty to the state has further contributed to terminological confusion by leading to the introduction of still other confusing terms. With nationalism pre-empted, authorities have had difficulty agreeing on a term to describe the loyalty of segments of a state's population to their particular nation. Ethnicity, primordialism, pluralism, tribalism, regionalism, communalism, and parochialism are among the most commonly encountered. This varied vocabulary further impedes an understanding of nationalism by creating the impression that each is describing a separate phenomenon. Moreover, reserving nationalism to convey loyalty to the state (or, more commonly, to the word *nation* when the latter is improperly substituted for state), while using words with different roots and fundamentally different connotations to refer to loyalty to the nation, adds immeasurably to the confusion. Each of the above terms has exercised its own particular negative impact upon the study of nationalism.

I ETHNICITY

Ethnicity (identity with one's ethnic group) is, if anything, more definitionally chameleonic than *nation*. It is derived from *ethnos*, the Greek word for *nation* in the latter's pristine sense of a group characterised by common descent. Consonant with this derivation, there developed a general agreement that an ethnic group referred to a basic human category (i.e., not a subgroup). Unfortunately, however, American sociologists came to employ *ethnic group* to refer to 'a group with a common cultural tradition and a sense of identity which exists as a subgroup of a larger society'.[21] This definition makes ethnic group synonymous with minority, and, indeed, with regard to group relations within the United States, it has been used in reference to nearly any discernible minority, religious, linguistic, or otherwise.

The definition of ethnic group by American sociologists violates its original meaning with regard to at least two important particulars. In the traditional sense of an ancestrally related unit, it is evident that an ethnic group need not be a subordinate part of a larger political society but may be the dominant element within a state (the Chinese, English, or French, for example) or may extend across several states, as do the Arabs. Secondly, the indiscriminate application of ethnic group to numerous types of groups obscures vital distinctions between various forms of identity. In a stimulating and often cited introduction to a volume entitled *Ethnicity*, Nathan Glazer and Daniel Patrick Moynihan, while rejecting the notion that ethnicity refers only to minorities, defended the incorporation of several forms of identity under this single rubric.

Thus, there is some legitimacy to finding that forms of identification based on social realities as different as religion, language, and national origin all have something in common, such that a new term is coined to refer to all of them – 'ethnicity.' What they have in common is that they have all become effective foci for group mobilization for concrete political ends . . .[22]

However, despite the usefulness that such a categorisation possesses for the study of the politics of special interest groups, there is little question but that it has exerted a damaging influence upon the study of nationalism. One result is that the researcher, when struggling through thousands of entries in catalogues, indices to periodicals, and the like cannot be sure whether a so-called ethnic study will prove germane to the study of nationalism. Sometimes the unit under examination does constitute a national or potential national group. Other times it is a transnational (inter- or intrastate) group such as the Amerindians. And, in most instances, it is a group related only marginally, if at all, to the nation, as properly understood (e.g., Polish Americans or the Catholic community within the Netherlands). Moreover, a review of the indices and bibliographies found in those ethnic studies that do deal with a national or potential national group illustrate all too often that the author is unaware of the relationship of his work to nationalism. The student of nationalism and the student of ethnicity seldom cross-fertilise. The American journal *Ethnicity* and the *Canadian Review of Studies in Nationalism*, for example, are remarkably free of overlap with regard to (1) the academic background of their contributors and (2) footnoted materials.

Even if the author uses the term *ethnicity* solely in relation to national groups, his equating of nationalism with loyalty to the state will predispose him to underestimate the comparative magnetism of the former.[23] But the much more common practice of employing ethnicity as a cloak for several different types of identity exerts a more baneful effect. Such a single grouping presumes that all of the identities are of the same order. We shall reserve further comment on the adverse consequences of this presumption to a later discussion of *primordialism* and pluralism, noting here only that this presumption circumvents raising the key question as to which of a person's several identities is apt to win out in a test of loyalties.

Anthropologists, ethnologists, and scholars concerned with global comparisons have been more prone to use *ethnicity* and *ethnic group* in their pristine sense of involving a sense of common ancestry.[24] Max Weber, for example, noted:

> We shall call 'ethnic groups' those human groups that entertain a subjective belief in their common descent . . . , this belief must be important for the propagation of group formation; conversely, it does not matter whether or not an objective blood relationship exists. Ethnic membership (*Gemeinsamkeit*) differs from the kinship group precisely by being a presumed identity . . .[25]

This definition would appear to equate *ethnic group* and *nation* and, as earlier noted, Weber did indeed link the two notions.[26] However, elsewhere Weber made an important and useful distinction between the two:

> The idea of the nation is apt to include the notions of common descent and of an essential though frequently indefinite, homogeneity. The 'nation' has these notions in common with the sentiment of solidarity of ethnic communities, which is also nourished from various sources, as we have seen before [ch. V:4]. *But the sentiment of ethnic solidarity does not by itself make a 'nation.'* Undoubtedly even the White Russians in the face of the Great Russians have always had a sentiment of ethnic solidarity, yet even at the present time they would hardly claim to qualify as a separate 'nation.' The Poles of Upper Silesia, until recently, had hardly any feeling of solidarity with the 'Polish nation.' They felt themselves to be a separate ethnic group in the face of the Germans, but for the rest they were Prussian subjects and nothing else.[27]

Weber is here clearly speaking of pre-national peoples or, what we termed earlier, potential nations.[28] His illustrations are of peoples not yet cognisant of belonging to a larger ethnic element. The group consciousness to which he refers – that rather low level of ethnic solidarity that a segment of the ethnic element feels when confronted with a foreign element – is not very important politically and comes closer to xenophobia than to nationalism. To the degree that it represents a step in the process of nation-formation, it testifies that a group of people must know ethnically what they *are not* before they know what they *are*. Thus, to Weber's illustrations, we can add the Slovaks, Croats, and Slovenes who, under the Habsburg Empire, were aware that they were neither German nor Magyar, long before they possessed positive opinions concerning their ethnic or national identity. In such cases, meaningful identity of a positive nature remains limited to locale, region, clan, or tribe. Thus, members need not be conscious of belonging to the ethnic group. Ernest Barker made this same point with regard to all peoples prior to the nineteenth century:

> The self-consciousness of nations is a product of the nineteenth century. This is a matter of the first importance. Nations were already there; they had indeed been there for centuries. But it is not the things which are simply 'there' that matter in human life. What really and finally matters is the thing which is apprehended as an idea, and, as an idea, is vested with emotion until it becomes a cause and a spring of action. In the world of action apprehended ideas are alone electrical; and a nation must be an idea as well as a fact before it can become a dynamic force.[29]

To refine Barker's wording only slightly, and his meaning not at all, a nation is a self-aware ethnic group. An ethnic group may be readily discerned by an anthropologist or other outside observer, but until the members are themselves aware of the group's uniqueness, it is merely an ethnic group and not a nation. While an ethnic group *may*, therefore, be other-defined, the nation *must* be self-defined.[30] Employing ethnic group or ethnicity in relationship to several types of identities therefore beclouds the relationship between the *ethnic group* and the *nation* and also deprives scholarship of an excellent term for referring to both nations and potential nations.

II PRIMORDIALISM

Primordialism, another common substitute for nationalism, is usually associated with Clifford Geertz, although Professor Geertz has acknowledged his debt in this matter to Edward Shils.[31] Moreover,

Geertz did not in fact write of primordialism but of primordial sentiments. The use of the plural was not accidental, for Geertz does not conceive the matter of competing loyalty dichotomously as loyalty to the state versus loyalty to the nation. Rather, he perceives 'primordial sentiments' or 'primordial attachments' as a number of distinct and only sometimes overlapping phenomena. Psychological ties stemming from a common linguistic, racial, tribal, regional, or religious background are treated by Geertz as totally separable, though often reinforcing, fundamental identities.

As noted in our comments concerning ethnicity, Geertz is certainly not alone in treating fundamental ties as multi-natured. Thus the conflict between Walloon and Fleming is described by a number of writers as essentially linguistic, since there is no religious or other easily discerned division present; the problem in Northern Ireland is, by contrast, regularly identified as religious since there is no language or racial problem present; the problem in Singapore is often described as racial because there are visible distinctions that can be made between the typical Malay and Chinese; Indonesia's problems of identity are often described as regional because the islandic character of its geography is readily perceived; Taiwanese self-identity is apt to be referred to as ethnic only because there is no tangible difference between the Taiwanese and the mainland Han. The question, however, is whether each of these examples does in fact constitute a separate species, or whether their description as essentially religious, linguistic, etc., is not the result of mistaking the tangible manifestations of the nation for its psychological essence.

Any nation, of course, has tangible characteristics and, once recognised, can therefore be described in tangible terms. The German nation can be described in terms of its numbers, its religious composition, its language, its location, and a number of other concrete factors. But none of these elements is, of necessity, essential to the German nation. The essence of the nation, as earlier noted, is a matter of self-awareness or self-consciousness. Many of the problems associated with defining a nation are attributable precisely to the fact that it is a self-defining group. That is why scholars such as Ernest Barker, Rupert Emerson, Carleton Hayes, and Hans Kohn have consistently used terms such as *self*-awareness and *self*-consciousness when analysing and describing the nation. It is this group-notion of kinship and uniqueness that is the essence of the nation, and tangible characteristics such as religion and language are significant to the nation only to the degree to which they contribute to this notion or sense of the group's self-identity and uniqueness. And it is worth noting that a nation can lose or alter any or all of its outward characteristics without losing its sense of vital uniqueness which makes it a nation. Thus, the Irish and the Scots could lose their language without losing their conviction of a separate national identity. Similarly, Jews can sever their affiliation with Judaism, while remaining very consciously tied to the Jewish nation. Indeed, in a period in which the traditional costumes, ceremonies, and other customs that formerly helped the outsider to identify distinctive nations are giving way to increasing global conformity, nationalism, in its proper sense, is obviously on the rise. Tangible characteristics, therefore, do not constitute the essential factor, and all of the above situations, although identified as essentially linguistic, religious, racial, etc., are in fact all of the same genus, ultimately being predicated upon divergent national identities.

There are several reasons accounting for the propensity to mistake the tangible manifestations of the nation for its psychological essence. One factor is that tangible elements are the most readily seen and easily conceptualised. Moreover, for the television commentator, the news reporter, and even the scholar, tangible considerations are not only more easily perceived, but are also more easily transmitted in understandable terms to one's audience. The new scholarly emphasis on quantification is also involved, as researchers have overly concentrated their efforts on the search for quantifiable determinants of nationalism.[32]

The problem, however, cannot be totally blamed upon the outsider. Those most involved in a conflict of national identity can also contribute to this emphasis on the more visible elements in at least three ways. A specific characteristic of a nation often becomes the rallying point in a national struggle and, in such event, is described as indivisible from the nation itself. The Ukrainians, the Franco-Canadians, and several national groups within India and Pakistan thus insist that their particular language must be preserved or their national identity will disappear. The 'primordial' imperative in these cases is thus described as linguistic. We have noted, however, that several nations have lost their language without losing the national consciousness. It is particularly pertinent to note that Irish nationalists of the nineteenth and early twentieth centuries made the same assertion concerning the linkage of language and national uniqueness, but post-independence attempts to resurrect Gaelic have been spurned by the majority of the Irish people, who have none the less clearly retained their national identity.[33] A second contributing element is that people of one nation, as a shorthand method of describing a more complex set of standards by which they distinguish another group, have a tendency to grasp upon a single attribute. Thus to the people of Scottish and English extraction in Northern Ireland, the Irish are 'Catholics'. The reverse of the process produces 'the Prods'. The observer is therefore easily lulled into believing that the issue can be reduced to a religious struggle, although the real issue involved differences in fundamental national identity.[34] A third and more difficult consideration to document is essentially psychological. People involved in a conflict of national identities appear to experience a need to express or explain their emotional responses to the other group in more 'logical' and concrete form. The *sense* or *feeling* of uniqueness that creates the gulf between them must be translated into more tangible form, such as into differences of religion, customs, or dialect. A clearly related phenomenon is the apparently widely felt compulsion to 'justify' one's prejudices (i.e., the emotional responses to foreign stimuli) by ascribing readily perceived (or readily misperceived) distinguishing attributes to the other group.

Quite apart from obscuring the root cause and psychological depth of the particular issue, the practice of describing such situations as, for example, essentially linguistic, racial, or religious, involves the same danger that we noted with regard to the use of multiple terms such as ethnicity: there is the risk of concluding that each term is describing a separate phenomenon. Analyses that emphasise a tangible element are often interspersed with expressions such as 'cultural nationalism', religious nationalism' or 'linguistic nationalism'. Though such terms have the merit of noting that nationalism is present, they give the impression that it is but one of several different species and that it could not survive the disappearance of tangible factors.

The use of *primordialism* is therefore at least preferable to 'primordial sentiments' in that it does not further fractionalise the national concept. The major criticism of primordialism is that its suggestion of primitiveness, as in the case of *tribalism*, implies that it will wither away as modernisation progresses. There is a strong hint that it does not affect 'modern' societies. But a listing of the European states that have recently experienced national friction illustrates that national consciousness is not limited to the Third World. The Soviet Union, Romania, Cyprus, Czechoslovakia, Yugoslavia, Italy, France, Spain, Switzerland, Belgium, and the United Kingdom have all recently known problems stemming from growing national consciousness on the part of segments of their populations. 'Black Nationalism' in the United States and Franco-Canadian unrest in Canada offer further testimony that industrialisation, intensive communication systems, high ratings on a global educational index, and impressive Gross National Products do not constitute safeguards against frictions arising from growing national consciousness.

III PLURALISM

The origin of *pluralism* is customarily linked to the anthropologist, J. S. Furnivall. Furnivall was particularly interested in colonial milieus in which indigenes, colonials, and non-indigenous peoples who had been imported by the colonials lived side by side. Such a unit he called a *plural society*:

> It is in the strictest sense a medley, for they mix but do not combine. Each group holds by its own religion, its own culture and language, its own ideas and ways. As individuals they meet, but only in the market-place, in buying and selling. There is a plural society, with different sections of the community living side by side, but separately, within the same political unit.[35]

Though Furnivall was describing a very particular form of society, and one now largely *passé*, his terminology was soon applied by others to describe any society containing heterogeneous characteristics. Thus, the third edition of *Webster's New International Dictionary* (1971) contains the following definition of *pluralism*, no counterpart of which had appeared in the previous edition: 'a state or condition of society in which members of diverse ethnic, racial, religious, or social groups maintain an autonomous participation in and development of their traditional culture or special interest within the confines of a common civilization.'

The inclusion of social groups makes *pluralism* an even more inclusive term than *ethnicity*, for the latter excluded socioeconomic class. Pluralism therefore encompasses seemingly all forms of group-identity that are less than state-wide, and the adjective, *cultural*, which customarily precedes it, does little to mitigate its catch-all nature.[36] This lack of discrimination implies that all group identities are of the same order. And when linked to pluralism's *a priori* acceptance of the society as an enduring given, it lends itself to the Madisonian concept of the balancing of cross-cutting interests. Since the regional, economic, social, religious, ethno-national, racial, and other identities of the individual do not perfectly coincide with one another, this theory postulates that the competing interests arising from all identities will tend to check the fissiparous tendency of any particular one, thus guaranteeing the continued viability of the state. But such a prognostication ignores the evidence offered by several ethnonational separatist movements, that the wellsprings of national identity are more profound than are those associated with religion, class, and the like, and may, therefore, *not* be susceptible to sufficient amelioration, because of other shared interests, to preserve the state. That the individual partakes of several group identities simultaneously is beyond dispute. But that these identities are not of the same order was the basis for Rupert Emerson's sage description of the nation as 'the largest community which, when the chips are down, effectively commands men's loyalty, overriding the claims both of lesser communities within it and those which cut across it or potentially enfold it within a still greater society.'[37]

IV TRIBALISM

As currently applied, the words *tribe* and *tribalism* are usually associated with non-Arab Africa where they have added a special dimension to the obscurity surrounding the study of nationalism. Though the term tribe is far from precise and its meaning a matter of contention among anthropologists, it has traditionally been employed to describe an ethnically homogeneous sociopolitical unit, but one which forms *only part of* a larger interrelated grouping. This concept of the tribe as an ethnically subordinate unit is usually honoured outside of Africa; thus, the key sociopolitical units that comprise such Asian peoples as the Azerbaijani, Kurds, and Pushtuns are called tribes, thereby conveying that in each case there exists a single ethnic group which embraces all of the tribal units. In non-Arab Africa, on the other hand, the preponderant number of human categories to which the *term* tribe is most commonly affixed constitute separate nations or potential nations in and by themselves. Well-known examples include the Ashanti, Kongo, Hausa, Ibo, Xhosa, and Zulu. There is liable to be as much difference – psychologically as well as tangibly – between two African 'tribes' as there is between Frenchman and German. In referring to them as tribes rather than as nations or potential nations, scholars have been lulled into badly underestimating the emotional magnetism that these collectives exert upon individuals. Calling this magnetism *tribalism*, while reserving *nationalism* to describe attachment to the new states, both reflects and strengthens a presumption that the loyalty of the individual will assuredly over time be transferred from the part (which is actually the nation but called the tribe) to the whole (actually the state but called the nation).

This presumption is reinforced because 'tribe', in addition to conveying the idea of subethnic status, also popularly connotes a primitive, evolutionary stage in human organisation. Thus, the Celtic and Germanic tribes were ultimately absorbed in a trans-tribal, national unit. By analogy, it can be assumed that the 'tribes' of Africa will be absorbed in, for example, 'the Nigerian nation'. Time is thus perceived as clearly on the side of the states, and they and not the tribes are viewed as the wave of the future.

There is a final problem concerning the meaning of tribe as applied to non-Arab Africa. Most of the distinctive ethnic groups, though called tribes, are themselves organised on a multi-tribal basis. As a result, parent and subordinate groups are often identically described. This dual use of the term makes it very dangerous to generalise concerning the probability of *all so-called tribes* becoming absorbed in a larger identity. Increased contacts should cause ethnically subordinate units to become increasingly aware of what they have in common, thus giving rise to the nation-concept. But increased contacts between different ethnic groups cannot be presumed to have any such effect.

V REGIONALISM

Much that has been said concerning tribalism pertains also to the use of the word *regionalism* as a substitute for nationalism. Part of the confusion is due to the fact that regionalism in today's parlance has two quite incompatible meanings, one involving a trans-state identity and the other an intrastate identity. Thus, the trans-state integration of a segment of the globe is called, for example, European *regionalism*; and structures such as NATO, SEATO, the EEC, and the Arab League are called *regional* organisations. On the other hand, regionalism is used to describe intrastate divisions based upon sentimental ties to the locale. It is in the second sense, that of sectionalism, that nationalism is often improperly referred to as regionalism.

To an even greater degree than primordialism and tribalism, regionalism simply does not convey the same sense of emotional commitment as does nationalism, so the mere use of the former reflects and reinforces a conviction that it will not prove a worthy competitor for man's most fundamental allegiance.³⁸ Moreover, the equating of regionalism with nationalism is confusing because regionalism, as properly used, often coexists with true nationalism. German nationalism, for example, has not precluded differences in regional attitudes among Prussians, Rhinelanders, Bavarians, etc. The important fact, however, is that in any test of loyalties, those factors which all members of the German nation feel they have in common are deemed more important than are regional distinctions.

There are, to be sure, a number of cases in which the national 'idea' (national consciousness) has not yet fully coalesced, and in which regional identity therefore remains a true competitor with nationalism for people's loyalty. Thus, the concept of the Arab West (al-magrib al Arabi) still exerts a substantial impact upon the identity of Arabs to the west of Libya. While Arab nationalism is penetrating the area, some of the inhabitants still sense that there are vital differences between Arabs of western and eastern Arabdom, which outweigh in importance their common Arabness.³⁹ However, it is generally conceded that sectionalism wanes with increased contacts among the various parts of an ethnically homogeneous population. Developments in a series of situations support the proposition that more intensive contacts among parts of a population that has some foundation for a sense of common origin will increase that consciousness. Today's nations were once composed of segmented peoples whose fundamental sense of identity did not extend beyond the family, village, clan, or tribe. Moreover, once a sense of national consciousness is established, further increases in interregional contacts clearly tend to homogenise the population's customs, tastes, and attitudes. But where one is dealing not with a single potential nation, but with groups whose customs and beliefs bespeak, on balance, not a common history but distinctive origins and development, increased contacts tend to have the opposite effect. Rather than strengthening the appeal of those traits held in common, there is a tendency to emphasise the traits which divide. The great increase in tensions which a multitude of multi-ethnic states have been experiencing underlines this dichotomy. Expanded contacts have made the Kurds, Lao, Luo, Flemings, Welsh, and Franco-Canadians more nationally conscious, but it has also made them more opposed to, respectively, the Arab and Turk, Thai, Kikuyu, Walloon, English, and Anglophone.

Increased communications and transportation within a state thus has one impact among members of the same nation or potential nation, but has quite another among members of separate nations. The error of referring to nationalism as regionalism has thus led authorities to assume that the variations in identity with which they are dealing will disappear with modernisation. But the body of actual evidence points in the opposite direction.

VI COMMUNALISM

As still another substitute for true nationalism, *communalism* also raises a number of problems. Depending upon the intention of the user, this term can have such diverse meanings as (1) a system of government in which the major political units (communes) are local, self-governing communities; (2) a synonym for communism; (3) a derogatory Soviet reference to Mao's scheme for restructuring society at the time of the Great Leap Forward; or (4) the currently faddish belief in or practice of communal living. It might be said that a term that can offer something positive to (1) John Birchers, (2) Marxist-Leninists, (3) the Taiwan regime, and (4) alienated moderns can't be all bad. But it can also be asked whether a word that means so many different things to so many different peoples could have any impact, other than obscurantist, upon the study of nationalism.

Communalism entered recent literature involving nationalism with respect to political developments in South Asia. Communalism became a popular way of describing the tendency of South Asian people to divide along an Islamic-Hindu breakdown. In the period prior to the British withdrawal from India, communalism there came to mean the growing tendency of people to stress the importance of an identity linked to religion rather than to stress what was commonly, but erroneously, called an 'Indian nationalism'. In this region, then, communalism came to be viewed as a competitor with what was termed 'nationalism' (i.e., what, in fact, was what we have termed state loyalty), but it was not used (as primordialism, tribalism, and regionalism have been used elsewhere) as synonymous with what we have identified as 'true nationalism'. Rather, communalism, by postulating a fundamental identity along religious lines that would both incorporate several nations and sever others, repudiated the importance that we have ascribed to the nation-concept.

Support for this contention was offered by the pre-independence ferment for dividing India into two states, one of which openly aspired to be identified as an Islamic republic; by a number of plebiscites in which nations were divided along religious lines in their affinity toward

Pakistan; and by the bloodletting perpetuated by religious groups upon one another both at the time of British withdrawal and at periodic intervals since then. It is clear, however, that growing national consciousness has characterised the peoples of the area. The fact that the multinational union of India is still territorially intact is not without significance, but the price of continued union has been a series of concessions to various nations concerning India's internal boundaries, acceptable levels of group autonomy, etc. In some cases, for example among the Kashmiri, Mizos, and Nagas, such concessions have not even sufficed to gain passivity. And in Pakistan, separatist agitation among the Sindi and Pushtuns seriously questions the power of religious over national sentiment. But clearly the most serious rebuttal of the paramountcy of communalism over the nation-idea has been occasioned by the Bengali. It is not just their secession from Pakistan that is most noteworthy, but rather the many illustrations, particularly poignant during the secession struggle, that the common Bengali bond straddles both the Hindu-Islamic division and the Pakistani-Indian division of the Bengali people.[40]

While communalism has been treated as a competitor with the nation-concept in literature on South Asia, there is a growing tendency to equate the two elsewhere.[41] The term, therefore, has the remarkable versatility to connote a number of concepts that are in no way related to nationalism; or to signify a religious identity that contests the validity of nationalism; or to be synonymous with nationalism while never being identified as such. As a sower of confusion, it has few equals.

VII PAROCHIALISM

If *primordialism* and *tribalism* suggest something of a patronising view of nationalism in the Third World as a quaint echo of something Europeans had shed before the end of 'the Dark Ages', the connotation that the word *parochialism* has acquired within American intellectual circles causes its equation with nationalism to result in an accusing finger being pointed at anyone who recognises a bond of loyalty to his nation. The third edition of Webster's *New International Dictionary* defines parochialism as 'the quality or state of being parochial; esp: selfish pettiness or narrowness (as of interests, opinions, or views).' The use of such judgemental terms tells us more about the author's emotional biases concerning, among other things, the state-nation competition than it does about the national phenomenon.[42] It also suggests that dispassionate analysis and evaluation of the national bond are not apt to follow.

VIII SUBNATIONALISM

It is fitting that we should conclude this list of improper substitutes for nationalism with that of *subnationalism*.[43] Granted, the users of this term at least indicate an awareness that they are confronting some approximation of nationalism. However, in its clear presumption that nationalism is in the employ of the state and in its relegation of loyalty to the ethno-national group to a subordinate order of phenomena, *subnationalism* has no peer. In and of itself, it is an affirmation of the ultimate victory of state-loyalty over ethnic loyalty.

IX ACCURATE TERMINOLOGY

Where today is the study of nationalism? In this Alice-in-Wonderland world in which nation usually means state, in which nation-state usually means multi-nation state, in which nationalism usually means loyalty to the state, and in which ethnicity, primordialism, tribalism, regionalism, communalism, parochialism and subnationalism usually mean loyalty to the nation, it should come as no surprise that the nature of nationalism remains essentially unprobed. Indeed, careless vocabulary has even precluded a realistic assessment of the magnitude of nationalism's revolutionary potentiality. Unidentified as such, nationalism has tended to be either ignored or misunderstood in the literature on political development. When identified under an improper appellation, it has been dismissed as something that will wither away as modernisation progresses or as something too distasteful to be countenanced. So long as nationalism remains unrecognised and multi-titled, its implications are apt to remain unappreciated. And if both it and its implications are unrecognised, then greater understanding of the nature of nationalism is not apt to follow.

But while it is a major contributing element to the ambiguity surrounding nationalism, careless terminology is also a reflection of nationalism's intangible nature. As philosophers are well aware, terminological carelessness finds fertile soil in the area of abstraction. The abstract, illusive quality of the national bond in itself impedes scholarly investigation. It may well be, therefore, that knowledge of the quintessence of nationalism will continue to evade man. In a most thought-provoking article, Ladis Kristof has suggested that the scientific form of inquiry may be inappropriate for phenomena of this type.[44] Dissection and logic, even in concert, may prove not only inadequate but misleading when applied to the study of sensory loyalties. Rupert Emerson, whose scholarly dedication and sensitive insight into nationalism has benefited all who have pondered his works, has expressed essentially the same sentiment in a few prefacing words to an impressive investigation of the elements that most commonly accompany nationalism:

> The simplest statement that can be made about a nation is that it is a body of people who feel that they are a nation; and it may be that when all the fine-spun analysis is concluded this will be the ultimate statement as well. To advance beyond it, it is necessary to attempt to take the nation apart and to isolate for separate examination the forces and elements which appear to have been the most influential in bringing about the sense of common identity which lies at its roots, the sense of the existence of a singularly important national 'we' which is distinguished from all others who make up an alien 'they'. This is necessarily an overly mechanical process, for nationalism, like other profound emotions such as love and hate, is more than the sum of the parts which are susceptible of cold and rational analysis.[45]

Emerson's comments suggest that the basic prerequisite for greater understanding of nationalism may be a measure of humility. Some doubt concerning one's ability to penetrate its innermost core may prove more appropriate than confidence for gaining insight into the national phenomenon. An acknowledgement that total understanding might continue to evade best ensures that one will maintain a proper appreciation for the complexity of the subject and will not, as so often has been the case, confuse the most apparent manifestations with essence. Acknowledging that one cannot explain the quintessence of nationalism need not preclude advances in understanding. Even in a totally physical area, men of medicine have made great strides in learning about the symptoms and responses to stimuli of melanomic cancer, while remaining ignorant of its basic cause and nature. But it was first necessary that melanoma be identified and distinguished from other phenomena. Similarly, the prerequisites to greater understanding of nationalism are (1) that it be recognised and (2) that it and only it be identified as such.

NOTES

1. For a more complete listing and additional details concerning the states of Asia, see this writer's 'An Overview of the Ethnic Composition and Problems of Non Arab Asia', *Journal of Asian Affairs*, I (spring 1976) 9–25, and, for the states of Africa, this writer's 'Nation-Building or Nation-Destroying?', *World Politics*, XXIV (Apr 1972), particularly pp. 352–4.
2. For details, see this writer's 'The Political Significance of Ethnonationalism within Western Europe', in Abdul Said and Luiz Simmons (eds), *Ethnicity in an International Context* (Edison, N.J.: Transaction Books, Inc., 1976), pp. 110–33, and 'Ethnonationalism in the First World: The Present in Historical Perspective', in Milton Esman (ed.), *Ethnic Pluralism and Conflict in the Western World* (Ithaca, N.Y.: Cornell University Press, 1977) pp. 19–45.
3. For details, see this writer's forthcoming *The National Question in Marxist Theory and Strategy* (Princeton, N.J.: Princeton University Press).
4. 'Nation-Building or Nation-Destroying?' *World Politics*, XXIV (Apr 1972), particularly pp. 332–55.
5. *Nationalism: A Report by a Study Group of Members of the Royal Institute of International Affairs* (London: Oxford University Press, 1939) p. xvi.
6. *Nationalism and Its Alternatives* (New York: Alfred A. Knopf, 1969) p. 138.
7. Nation, for example, is used to denote (*a*) the total population of a country, regardless of its ethnonational composition (pp. 23, 33); (*b*) only the assimilated part of the country's population (pp. 40, 43); the state (pp. 32, 33, 79); and specific multinational states such as Belgium and Switzerland (p. 70). Nation-state is first correctly defined as 'a state that has become largely identical with one people' (p. 19) and then is employed indiscriminately to describe all states (pp. 32, 33, 35, 49, 60, 61, 63, 112, 113, 114, 120, 125, 171, 172, and 176), specifically including such multinational states as Czechoslovakia, Romania, and Yugoslavia (p. 62); it is also used to connote a unitary in contradistinction to a federal state (p. 120). Nationality refers to an ethnonational identity (pp. 54, 68) or to citizenship (p. 125). Nationalism refers to 'concern for fellow nationals, for countrymen' (p. 25), regardless of ethnonational differences, and yet the author can speak of the nationalism of minorities (p. 53).
8. Jack C. Plano and Roy Olton, *The International Relations Dictionary* (New York: Holt, Rinehart and Winston, Inc., 1969) p. 119. Emphasis added.
9. Conrad Brandt, Benjamin Schwartz and John Fairbank, *A Documentary History of Chinese Communism* (London: George Allen & Unwin Ltd., 1952), p. 245. Parenthetical material added.

10. Max Weber [Economy and Society, vol. I, edited by Guenther Roth and Claus Wittich (New York: Bedminster Press, 1968) p. 395] notes that 'the concept of *nationality* [or *nation*] shares with that of the *people* (Volk) – in the *ethnic* sense – the vague connotation that whatever is felt to be distinctively common must derive from common descent.' An old European definition of a nation, though intended to be humorous and derisive and which Karl Deutsch cites as such, hit almost the same mark: 'A nation is a group of people united by a common error about their ancestry and a common dislike of their neighbours' (*Nationalism and Its Alternatives*, op. cit., p. 3).
11. A recent example of the loose manner in which nation may be used is a work, published in the United States, entitled *Lesbian Nation*.
12. Raymond Williams, *Keywords: A Vocabulary of Culture and Society* (New York: Oxford University Press, 1976) p. 178.
13. Louis J. Halle, *Civilization and Foreign Policy* (New York: Harper & Row, 1952) p. 10. For another example of this practice of referring to states as nation-states, see Dankwart Rustow, *A World of Nations* (Washington: Brookings, 1967) p. 30, for a reference to the United Kingdom and the Soviet Union as nation-states. Note also Rustow's concluding remarks (p. 282): 'More than 130 *nations*, real or so-called, will each make its contribution to the history of the late twentieth century ....' For other illustrations, see this writer's 'Ethnonationalism in the First World: The Present in Historical Perspective,' op. cit., particularly pp. 20–1.
14. By a potential nation is meant a group of people who appear to have all of the necessary prerequisites for nationhood, but who have not as yet developed a consciousness of their sameness and commonality, nor a conviction that their destinies are intertwined. They are usually referred to by anthropologists as ethnolinguistic groups. Such peoples' sense of fundamental identity is still restricted to the locale, extended family, clan, or tribe. The Andean states and south-western Asia offer several illustrations of such pre-national people.
15. A random survey of books published within the United States and designed for college courses in global politics will provide ample documentation of the impact this misuse of terminology has exerted upon the discipline. In addition to the host of titles consisting of or containing the expressions *International Relations* or *International Politics* are such well-known examples as *Politics Among Nations, The Might of Nations, Nations and Men, The Insecurity of Nations, How Nations Behave,* and *Games Nations Play*. Another illustration is offered by the American professional organisation called the International Studies Association. Its official raison d'être, as set forth in the early issues of its *Quarterly*, notes that the organisation 'is devoted to the orderly growth of knowledge concerning the impact of nation upon nation'.
16. Plano and Olton, op. cit., pp. 119, 120.
17. Ibid., p. 120.
18. See G. de Bertier de Sauvigny, 'Liberalism, Nationalism, and Socialism: The Birth of Three Words', *The Review of Politics*, vol. 32 (Apr 1970), particularly pp. 155–61.
19. *Mein Kampf* (New York: Reynal & Hitchcock, 1940) p. 595.

20. For details, see this writer's 'The Political Significance of Ethnonationalism within Western Europe', op. cit., particularly pp. 126–30.
21. George Theodorson and Achilles Theodorson, *A Modern Dictionary of Sociology* (New York: Thomas Crowell & Co., 1969) p. 135. For a similar definition, see H. S. Morris' selection on 'Ethnic Groups' in *The International Encyclopedia of the Social Sciences* (New York: Macmillan & Co., and The Free Press, 1968).
22. Nathan Glazer and Daniel P. Moynihan, *Ethnicity: Theory and Experience* (Cambridge, Mass.: Harvard University Press, 1975) p. 18.
23. See, for example, Peter Busch, *Legitimacy and Ethnicity* (Lexington, Mass.: D. C. Heath & Co., 1974), in which ethnicity refers to the breakdown of the population of Singapore into Chinese, Malay, and other such components, and in which nationalism refers to identity with the Singaporean state.
24. See, for example, Tomotshu Shibutani and Kian Kwan, *Ethnic Stratification: A Comparative Approach* (New York: Macmillan & Co., 1965) p. 47, where an ethnic group is defined as composed of 'those who conceive of themselves as being alike by virtue of their common ancestry, real or fictitious, and who are so regarded by others.'
25. *Economy and Society*, op. cit., p. 389.
26. See above, note 10.
27. Weber, op. cit., p. 923.
28. See above, p. 65.
29. Ernest Barker, *National Character and the Factors in Its Formation* (London: Methuen, 1927) p. 173.
30. As Charles Winick, *Dictionary of Anthropology* (New York: Philosophical Library, 1956) p. 193, has observed with regard to an *ethnos*: 'A group of people, linked by both nationality and race. These bonds are usually unconsciously accepted by members of the group, but outsiders observe the homogeneity.'
31. Clifford Geertz, 'The Integrative Revolution: Primordial Sentiments and Civil Politics in the New States' in Clifford Geertz (ed.), *Old Societies and New States* (New York: The Free Press, 1963), particularly p. 109.
32. For a rather unusual claim concerning the degree to which nationalism has already succumbed to modern analysis, see the *New York Times*, 16 March 1971, for a prepublication review of the study by Karl Deutsch, John Platt, and Diter Senghaas, which lists what the authors consider to be 'the 62 major accomplishments in the behavioral and social sciences since 1900.' Among them is listed 'Quantitative models of nationalism and integration (mathematical study of nationalistic response)'. The contributors are listed as K. Deutsch, B. Russett, and R. L. Merritt, and the time of the accomplishment is placed between 1942 and 1967.
33. Still another interesting example is that of the Basques. Though their level of nationalism is obviously very high, they are the *least* interested of all non-Castilian speaking groups within Spain in requiring education in their language. This attitude is reflected in a poll cited in Milton da Silva, *The Basque Nationalist Movement: A Case Study in Ethnic Nationalism* (unpublished dissertation, University of Massachusetts, 1972).
34. Contrary to most analyses, both sides in the conflict do not consider

themselves Irish. A poll indicates that less than 50 per cent do. For more details, see 'Nation-Building or Nation-Destroying?', op. cit., pp. 339–41, and 'Ethnonationalism in the First World', op. cit., pp. 40–1.
35. J. S. Furnivall, *Colonial Policy and Practice* (Cambridge: Cambridge University Press, 1948) p. 305.
36. For example, the multi-volume *Case Studies on Human Rights and Fundamental Freedoms* produced by the Foundation for the Study of Plural Societies (The Hague: Martinus Nijhoff), as well as the Foundation's journal, *Plural Societies*, contain articles dealing with such diverse groups and topics as, *inter alia*, national minorities, religious groups, sex-discrimination, castes, and races.
37. *From Empire to Nation* (Boston: Beacon Press, 1960) pp. 95–6.
38. For an article grouping ethnonational movements (such as those in Brittany, Corsica, Scotland, and Wales) with localism (such as that evidenced within a number of German Länder) under the single rubric of 'subnational regionalism', see Werner Feld, 'Subnational Regionalism and the European Community', *Orbis*, 18 (winter 1975) pp. 1176–92. The result is a confusing comparison of different phenomena. For a description of Scottish nationalism as regionalism (and a corresponding under-evaluation of its potency), see John Schwartz, 'The Scottish National Party', *World Politics*, XXII (July 1970) pp. 496–517, and particularly p. 515,, where the author speaks of a 'regional identity'. See also Jack Haywood, *The One and Indivisible French Republic* (New York: Norton, 1973), pp. 38 and 56, where the movement within Brittany is referred to as regionalism. No reference to ethnonationalism is made, nor are there any references to France's other ethnic minorities. Since the term *region* implies a larger whole, the indivisibility of France (as indicated by the title) is assured. The propensity to refer to ethno-national movements within France and Italy as regionalism has probably been heightened in recent years by 'regionalisation' plans to decentralise authority. In both cases, the borders of the new regions often closely correspond with the distribution of ethnic groups.
39. One manifestation of a separate regional identity is found in a comparison of constitutions. While the constitutions of most Arab states contain statements that their populations are part of an 'Arab nation', the constitutions of Morocco and Tunisia each omit this expression and emphasise that their state is part of 'the Greater Maghrib'. Still another manifestation of regionalism is the progressive lessening of emotionalism sparked by the Arab's 'arch enemy', Israel, as one moves toward the Arab West. President Bourguiba of Tunisia was able many years ago to recommend that Arab states recognise Israel without raising much domestic furore. A similar position would be foolhardy for a leader in the Levant.
40. For details, see Connor, 'An Overview of the Ethnic Composition and Problems of Non-Arab Asia', op. cit.
41. See, for example, Robert Melson and Howard Wolpe, 'Modernization and the Politics of Communalism: A Theoretical Perspective', *American Political Science Review*, LXIV (Dec 1970) pp. 1112–30. See too F. H. H. King, *The New Malayan Nation: A Study of Communalism and Nationalism* (New York: Institute of Pacific Relations, 1957).

42. While less innately prejudicial, other often-encountered terms, such as particularism, suggest this same pro-state bias on the part of the author.
43. See, for example, Victor Olorunsola (ed.), *The Politics of Cultural Sub-Nationalism in Africa* (Garden City, New York: Doubleday & Co., 1972). See also 'Subnational Regionalism and the European Community', op. cit.
44. Ladis Kristof, 'The State-Idea, the National Idea and the Image of the Fatherland', *Orbis*, vol. 11 (spring 1967) p. 255.
45. Emerson, op. cit., p. 102.

5 The Right to Self-determination: Definition, Reality and Ideal Policy

Raymond D. Gastil

Director of Freedom House for Comparative Survey of Freedom in New York

INTRODUCTION

At the end of World War II Alfred Cobban succinctly summed up the history and prospects of the doctrine of self-determination.[1] To Cobban the idea of self-determination had arisen as a concomitant of the idea of democracy, and its justification lay in its rationale as a further extension of individual liberties. However, Cobban felt that by the 1940s it had been carried to such extremes, and twisted to support so many undemocratic regimes, that the idea was as much a threat to individual liberties as it was a guarantee. When he wrote Cobban was concerned with the weakness of small states, and he hoped for controls over fissiparous and anarchic nationalisms through new mechanisms of international order. With these concerns, Cobban proposed that independence be the primary goal of self-determination only when a sovereign state fails to grant the legitimate rights of peoples to their own way of life through regional or other alternatives.

In the decades since World War II many have hoped that the cosmopolitan force of economic and educational development would gradually reduce interest in local nationalisms through the growth of more universalistic societies. However, as Walker Connor points out, there is now a growing lack of faith that education, modernisation, and enhanced communication will lead to the assimilation of communal groups into 'new nations'.[2] If we define assimilation as loss of a popular sense of separate group identity, at least in this century, 'No examples of significant assimilation are offered which have taken place since the advent of the age of nationalism and the principle of the self-determination of nations.'[3] This suggests that the world faces continuing upheavals fuelled by an unending chain of peoples rising to self-consciousness. In Connor's reckoning, of 132 states only 12 are ethnically homogeneous, while in 25 the largest ethnic group accounts for more than 90 per cent of the population, in 25 between 75 and 89 per cent, in 31 for 50 to 74 per cent, and in 39 the largest ethnic group accounts for less than 50 per cent.

With this degree of heterogeneity the dilemma faced by advocates of freedom is a very real one. When a territorial minority, such as the Welsh or Quebecois, claims that the state it finds itself in does not allow it a sufficient right to govern itself, then for the members of this group political freedom might be argued to exist only to the extent that this group is a self-governing unit. The fact that there is seldom a compelling case for the boundaries of any political unit other than the vagaries of history casts doubt on the degree to which political rights exist for anyone who would desire a different state identity. The fact that so many tiny islands have opted for independence – and many island groups continue to face threats of further fragmentation – suggests that there is no territorial dimension or degree of ethnic homogeneity that may be counted on to limit the centrifugal effects of the desire for self-determination. Once people perceive the opportunity to perfect their political freedoms by reducing the size of the unit in which they live, and thus increasing their personal chance for participation and influence, they are likely to demand their right. Economic advantage or defence requirements may delay fragmentation, but in the long run they are likely to do no more than retard centrifugal demands.

Since, therefore, the assertion of rights to self-determination is likely to be with us for a very long time, it is desirable that we carefully consider the present state of the international acceptance of this right, as well as the basic principles upon which the right is asserted. While many recent discussions point to the kinds of symbols of separateness that might be employed by a people, and to the characteristics of demands for self-determination that receive widespread support,[4] few go further and inquire seriously into the boundaries and conditions of legitimate demands for self-determination. In this paper I will attempt to fill part of this gap. After making some distinctions and definitions in the area of self-determination, considering the present range of pragmatic or adjustive responses that are given to demands for self-determination, and summarising the present position of self-determination in International Law, I will suggest a new adaptation of Cobban's principles for considering claims to self-determination, and relate these principles to other policy values.

I THE DEFINITION AND CONTEXTS OF SUBNATIONALISM

Walker Connor has persuasively argued that an important cause of confusion in discussions of the right of self-determination has been the contradictory use of the words 'nation' and 'nationalism' as both synonymous with and distinct from 'state' and 'statism'.[5] Serious political scientists have within one paper warned against the confusion of terms and then proceeded to confuse them. Connor particularly points out that one result of the confusion is that 'nation-building' is generally used in the literature to describe what is in fact the destruction of the existing peoples or nations in an area and their replacement by a new 'nation' coterminous with the state (whose dimensions may be no more than an accident of colonial history).

The confusion, however, goes deeper, for 'nationalism' has frequently been invoked to overcome or disregard internal communal conflicts through establishing a powerful we – they distinction across an actual or potential state boundary. As Connor himself points out, the American and French revolutions established the principle that a people has a right to determine who will rule it, the principle upon which 'national self-determination was later to be based'.[6] American, French, and British nationalisms have always had as one of their objectives the overcoming of internal ethnic cleavages, just as Bukharan nationalism in the early twentieth century had as its goal overcoming the opposition of Turkish and Persian ethnic units and tribal groups within the Bukharan Emirate.[7] Analysts cannot dismiss the use of expressions such as 'Nigerian nationalism' when they are long acquainted with the integrative meaning of American, Canadian, Belgian, or Swiss nationalisms.

For this discussion the solution we have devised is to speak of nationality and nationalism only when referring to feelings of loyalty, pride, or partially engendered in a people defined by the boundary of an independent state (or in some cases a territorially distinct colony). We will refer to *subnationality* and *subnationalism* when discussing a group that presently or potentially strives for enhanced self-determination with purposes and feelings analogous to those of state nationalities, and often with political independence as a conceivable goal.[8] Given this distinction, nation-building can be 'people destroying' (that is, destructive of present or potential subnationalisms) without the contradiction that Connor finds.

For the denial of group rights to exist must there be a definable group of people that feel they are a group? Do subnational rights exist separately from this consciousness? This is a serious question because external perceptions of subnationality often lead to actions that eventually create a group consciousness that did not previously exist. Yet for many purposes analysts and administrators wish to prepare ahead of events for expressions of subnationalism that are likely to occur with modernisation and democratisation. Moreover, it seems a requirement of justice that we take cognisance of those groups that would make subnationalist demands were they not encapsulated within totalitarian or other anti-communal systems.

But the problems of anticipatory definition are manifold. One of the reasons statistical samples comparing cultures cannot be relied on in anthropology is the impossibility of deciding on the appropriate units. What one text may define as one cultural unit, the next may divide into four groups. Should we, for example, speak of European culture, American culture, or Texan culture? Similarly, for the purposes of political analysis the concept of 'a people' is frequently evanescent and shifting. Repeatedly, those who have moved from the level of broad generalisation to consider ethnic conflicts in detail find that the peoples thought to exist in a particular country do not have a substantial existence in the minds of the inhabitants themselves, exist only in certain narrow contexts, or have come to have psychological reality only in the last few years.[9]

Historically, self-identification that we label subnationalism develops only when there is a confrontation of peoples that requires a change in the traditional forms of identification. For the average peasant villager or primitive tribesman, the only meaningful contacts are with the inhabitants of his immediate vicinity. For him the 'peoples' of interest are defined by village boundaries or lineage distinctions, or a cluster of these. Yet, except for a few peoples fortunate enough to find themselves on small islands, such micro-units are not what is usually taken seriously in discussions of subnationalisms. However, we are logically forced to suggest that this dismissal is too hasty; the micro-units that the people themselves understand must be taken seriously wherever they exist if we are really concerned with the question of self-determination.

Beyond this simplest level subnationality grows out of contact, usually competitive contact, in political or economic spheres. Such contact is especially aroused by common experiences such as invasions, slave raids, or migrations, but in recent years is primarily traced to the mixing of peoples from different backgrounds in cities. Under these conditions, as a self-defence mechanism in a search for allies, individuals who formerly identified themselves only in local terms are willing to take on a broader communal identification or ethnicity – often one created for or labelled for them by others.

It is not surprising that the most common source of politically relevant group identity is based on identification with a political unit of the past. Thus, studies have shown that in Zaire it was the Kongo people of the lower Congo who could identify with a medieval kingdom, while in Uganda it was the Ganda that had an operating kingdom up to the 1960s that had the most developed sense of their identities as separate peoples. If there has never been a previous political unit, then language, racial, religious, or other marks of difference may become politically salient.[10]

However, in these latter cases we must be careful to consider (1) how significant the assumed group identity is to the people concerned, and (2) why it has become a salient issue. The reason for our concern is that outsiders – colonisers or others – have often found it useful for their own reasons to label groups on the flimsiest of evidence as though they constituted tribes, nations, religious communities, etc. If actions are then taken on this basis – for example, setting up special provinces for the people, translating the bible into 'their language' (thereby necessarily abstracting a subnational language from a variety of dialects), or signing a treaty with 'them', then the outsiders may unintentionally have created the basis for a new subnational consciousness. Extreme examples are the creation of the 'Ngala' in the confines of Leopoldville from an amalgam of up-river peoples, or of the Teso of Uganda from the centralising and organisational actions of British administrators. 'Visayan' was a linguist's term for a variety of related dialects in the Philippines, yet when speakers of these dialects go to other parts of the Philippines they now refer to themselves as Visayans.[11] In conflict with others new labels help the members of an incipient group to achieve their individual needs, and reduce the isolation attendant upon a more mobile life. The new communal attachment gives the individual a fairer chance to achieve his just share of goods and respect in a new world made up of others who already rely on such identification.

Finally we must note the extent to which subnationalism is exploited by both internal and external forces. The British colonialists were often accused of divide-and-rule tactics. For whatever reason, they often did encourage ethnic identification and division, sharpening such identities in order to combine indirect rule with administrative responsibility. More recently, conflicts such as that in Cyprus have seen a variety of outside pressures push the local peoples further apart. Muslim intransigence in the Philippines, and Pathan intransigence in Pakistan have certainly been partially defined by external support. It is not to deny the legitimacy of any subnationalist movement to point out that it may be considerably more than a natural welling up of sentiment for eternal group values.[12]

Given these caveats, let us then define a *people* as a group of persons with generational continuity that is objectively distinguishable from other groups in terms of features such as language, religion, customs, special history, or residential territory. Generally such a group is not a caste, a social class, or a lineage grouping (such as, for example, the tribes of Somalia or Arabia), but it may be based on a political (including tribal) division even within the same ethnic group (as in Botswana). A *self-conscious people* exists when some members of a people label and identify the people to which they belong as a separate group. If in the name of this people, these members then ask for official acknowledgement of their people's special rights at any level, then we may speak of a *subnation* within a state or within a nation where it is identified with a state.

There are, of course, peoples within peoples within peoples. Thus Evans-Pritchard's segmentary analysis of the Nuer in the Sudan[13] is applicable to many systems, including Switzerland where the people of one commune may hate those of the next, join with them collectively in hatred of the people in the next canton, join with people of the next canton *vis-à-vis* other Swiss of other religious or language groups, and identify with the peoples of all cantons as Swiss nationals against the world. One person may also belong to several different peoples in non-segmentary form, for example, as a person who is both a good nationalist American *and* a good nationalist Irishman with special interests in the future of the Irish in Ireland. The non-exclusiveness of nationalism is generally not confusing when we direct our attention only to those nationalistic peoples, of whatever variety or interrelationship, that are interested in political self-determination as a group, or we have reason to believe may come to be so interested.

After a detailed study Crawford Young has suggested that heterogeneous states be distinguished as follows:
1. Single dominant group with minorities, such as Rwanda and Sri Lanka,
2. Core culture with peripheral cultures, such as Peru or Ethiopia,
3. Bipolar polity, such as Cyprus or Belgium,
4. Multipolar without dominance, such as most sub-Saharan African states,
5. Multiplicity of cultures with cross-cutting allegiances, such as India, Nigeria, Indonesia, and Uganda.[14]

This is a very useful classification for describing the complexity of the situation, but it fails to emphasise those distinctions most relevant to an evaluation of the claims to self-determination of a particular group. In these terms the most important distinction is between heterogeneous societies in which the peoples represented are territorially distinct, and those in which they are essentially intermixed. Employing by analogy the concepts of English grammar we might distinguish between *compound states* consisting of territorially distinct peoples and *complex states* characterised by a variety of intermixed peoples. Some states such as the USSR are, of course, compound and complex. Compound states may, then, be either *communal* in which subnational peoples are officially recognised as the building blocks of society, or *non-communal* in which national political organisation and symbols are meant to be separate from and eventually supersede those of any particular communal group. Either communal or non-communal states may include peoples that currently or potentially demand a larger degree of self-determination. Non-communal, compound states such as Cameroon or Zaire are typically made up of many ethnic groups, with the top leaders either from a variety of groups, or the key leader from one of the less important groups. In such states peoples that have reached a conscious level of subnationalism may be absent, or nearly so. In some cases, however, they include one or more highly articulate subnationalities, such as the Ganda of Uganda.

II ADJUSTIVE REACTIONS TO DEMANDS FOR SELF-DETERMINATION

The United Nations Charter refers to a right of self-determination for all peoples, and later declarations and covenants have confirmed this right.[15] Yet, paradoxically, an operative right of secession exists in no state in the world. The right was granted to certain peoples in Soviet constitutions, but was most certainly denied in practice.[16] It has been pointed out that almost every state founded in the recent past on a plea of self-determination has immediately denied the same right to those peoples who happened to lie within its newly-won borders. United Nations declarations and Secretary-General U Thant have supported these denials in spite of the organisation's abstract support of self-determination.[17]

Since there have been no generally accepted definitions of 'a people' or of a group that has a legitimate right to call itself a nation, informed opinion on the justice of the multitudinous present and potential issues of national justice around the world are casually swayed by the fads and accidents of communication. In spite of continuing rhetoric the time is long past when overseas colonialism was the main obstacle to self-determination. The traditional division of the world into independent countries and non-self-governing territories is useful only for historical reasons or the satisfaction of United Nations delegates.[18] On the one hand, the overwhelming number of units described as colonies are small French, British, or ANZUS island communities. Most of their peoples have either expressed through democratic procedures their desire to remain colonies, or recently have voted in favour of independence and are well on their way to obtaining it. People in these societies live far freer and more democratic lives than most peoples in the world. On the other hand, there are much larger communities with long historical traditions of distinct cultural and political heritage within states such as the USSR, China, Uganda or Iraq that are denied self-determination and do not have access to democratic forms. Yet these peoples are conventionally regarded as neither colonial peoples nor non-self-governing. Yet where are the limits? Surely not all peoples with some claim to identity have a moral right to independence. And even within one country, such as the USSR, would not the most utopian idealist sooner or later discover peoples with so few members that he could not recommend independence?

In international law every state is granted a right of self-defence. Since international law regulates relations among states, this right applies to all states as independent systems of control over particular territories. Then, if a challenge comes from within that would diminish a state's territory, it has a right to defend itself against this threat as surely as against an external threat.[19] What established its territory as its own was the state's previous ability to control it. But why, then, did the informed public applaud anti-colonialist revolts in Africa, but not those of the Biafrans and Bugandans? Apparently it is control at a distance that is discountenanced. But international opinion is more upset by the control of Rhodesia by the whites than of Burundi by the minority Tutsi. Evidently control by 'outsiders' disturbs modern consciences. But why don't liberal Euro-Americans raise money for liberation movements among Georgians or Uzbeks in the USSR? The relative lack of publicity might be the answer, yet the well-known case of the Kurds of Iraq, who have fought year after year for their independence, has also elicited little international sympathy. Apparently, according to world opinion, everything else being equal, a people at a distance from their rulers has a much more acceptable right to independence than one living contiguously to them.

At first glance it appears inexplicable that the United Nations or the media should differentiate between the rights to self-determination of contiguous and non-contiguous groups. This is particularly so if we consider that in President Wilson's day self-determination had primarily to do with contiguous peoples. But this position becomes understandable when we reflect that while most UN states do not have overseas colonies, most states do include areas with dissatisfied or potentially dissatisfied peoples. Therefore, it is in the interest of most statesmen to note selectively the unfulfilled desires for self-determination of those ruled by outsiders at a distance, while ignoring demands for self-determination by contiguous peoples.

Parenthetically, in raising issues of self-determination, we do not attempt to deal with the fact that a people may control its own state, but this state may, in turn, be controlled to some extent by other states. Less powerful states, and their peoples, are, in theory, less able to act freely on a world scale than the more powerful. However, as long as there is not direct physical intervention and imposition of control, the people controlling a state will be regarded as self-determining for our purposes. The only exceptions might be states such as Czechoslovakia and Mongolia where outside pressure appears overwhelming. Otherwise, the claim that the economic or military power of the wealthier states greatly reduces the self-determination of peoples in smaller or less wealthy states is not generally substantiated in the modern world. Taking population size alone into account, there may be a gain in per capita political power as we move from larger to smaller states – although not, of course, in military power. As to wealth, the ability of weak states to enforce 200-mile claims to ocean frontiers, or of small banana-producing states successfully to fight the great fruit companies in recent years, or of even the poorest states to expropriate the multinationals should put to rest this claim as a general proposition. By and large the multinationals have more reliable power in their home countries than they do in even the poorest foreign countries.

However, weakly developed political systems may be highly susceptible to corporate bribery or the actions of clandestine agencies such as the CIA or KGB.[20] This influence is primarily due to the willingness of local political leaders and publicists to work for foreign governments, and reflects more the weakness of some nationalisms than the strength of wealthy or powerful foreigners.[21] For this reason such 'control' is highly unreliable and transitory. Even with the massive scale of our presence in Vietnam, we could not reliably influence the behaviour of Thieu and Ky.[22] The man we helped set up as ruler in Guyana has now turned away from both capitalism and Pro-Americanism, for he needs us no longer. Even though in the Dominican intervention the United States went far beyond the use of the CIA, the results of our actions could have been quietly and quickly reversed in any year since our intervention without the US being able to make an effective counter. Perhaps better than any other example, the Bay of Pigs adventure showed how feeble the American ability to control small states is whenever determined opposition is encountered.

Interstate self-determination, then, is thriving in most of the world, but only in special situations will intrastate self-determination receive worldwide support now that the era of European colonialism is ended. What is the nature of these situations? In a paper on the drive of the East Bengalis for self-determination, Nanda suggests six bases for their unusual success, or for the world's acceptance of it.[23] These were: physical separation, the impressive size of the population of East Bengal, the cultural gulf between Bengalis and other Pakistanis, the apparent exploitation of the East by the West, the West's refusal to accept the electoral victory of the East's autonomists, and the brutal suppression of their resulting revolt. Of course, as important as any of Nanda's reasons for success was the willingness of the Indian government to drive out the West Pakistanis; this intervention, in turn, was influenced by India's perennial desire to reduce Pakistan's size, importance, and consequent threat. India, in turn, was supported by a USSR desirous of expanding contacts in the area, and interested in weakening the China-Pakistan alliance. The unwillingness of the United States or China to counter effectively in support of Islamabad was due to both our internal weakness and the location of the struggle. But it was also due to the reasons that Nanda lists. For these reasons American and Chinese leaders could not win points in the arenas of domestic or international opinion by opposing the Indian invasion – in spite of the dangerous precedents that it set.

Moving beyond Nanda, let us consider the full range of commonsense criteria that world elites consider in attempting to adjust political action to current or prospective claims to self-determination. These are:

1. *Symbolic differentiation of the group.* To attract attention peoples or subnationalities must be distinguished by badges of separateness, such as race, language (or dialect), religion (or sect), civilisation, and historical experience. Self-consciousness as a group is generally regarded as a prerequisite for world concern, yet most groups have only a small elite with such consciousness. One of the most dynamic aspects of the problem is the fact that a group's sense of difference changes over time, with education often increasing its manifestation.

2. *Size of population.* The group demanding self-determination must be of reasonable size relative to the rest of the state. While a few thousand may be sufficient in a world of small islands (for example, Anguilla under St Kitts) or in very unpopulated areas, hundreds of thousands might be ignored in large countries (such as non-Bengalis in East Bengal).

3. *Size and distinctiveness of territory.* Again, islands are obvious units, but peoples in large territories on the map, even when very few in number such as Eskimos, are more often given attention than much larger populations in smaller areas, such as the Spanish in northern New Mexico. Generally, a distinct home territory makes self-determination more feasible, but some degree of self-determination is possible even without a territorial base (see below).

4. *Expected growth or decline in the demand.* Some subnationalities have for reasons of state educational policy, population growth differentials, or longer historical trends, grown or declined in size or distinctiveness relative to other peoples, and particularly in regard to their state's dominant people (*Staatsvolk*). Equally important is growth or decline in the people's interest in self-determination. Karl Deutsch has shown from examples in India and Finland how increasing literacy has led to a rise in the consciousness of vernacular peoples that leads to demands to either displace the previous Staatsvolk in the state, or for increasing autonomy and separation.[24] Everything else being equal, evidence cited above indicates the likelihood of increasing interest in self-determination by a people as it develops.

5. *Recency of separate existence.* Historically, Burke's doctrine of

'prescription' has been the basis of establishing right through passage of time.[25] South China was originally not Chinese, but no one would today propose *on this basis* that there is a good case for the self-determination of the South Chinese. However, the Soviet Union finally extinguished Bukharan independence only in the 1920s. This is a perilously short time. Still, Soviet rule of Bukhara is based on a better temporal claim than that of most newly independent states over their minority peoples. It is not only time, however, but the nature of the previous situation. In particular, a people may be more likely to have its claim listened to if historically it was a *Staatsvolk* of a now defunct state than if it was only a minority in a previous state, or previously without complex political forms.

6. *The crimes of the past.* The doctrine of prescription was often countered by the claim that wrong could never be righted by time.[26] This seems particularly true if the wrongs are overwhelming and pernicious. It is on this basis that non-Jewish liberals have supported the ancient claims of the Jews of Palestine in the twentieth century, in spite of the inordinate passage of time. After the persecution of Jews reached its climax in Europe, recompense was in order (though unfortunately for Christian consciences Nazis were not Palestinian Arabs).

7. *The status of self-government.* The support of the outside public for the autonomy of a subnationality within a democratic state is influenced by how large a vote they can muster for their cause. There is less persistent support for independence where the people involved have voted against independence, as in Puerto Rico and Northern Ireland (taken as a whole). In the latter case the demand of the majority is not for independence but for local control – a situation repeated and for many of the same reasons in the case of Belize (British Honduras).[27] If a people votes for self-determination and is then denied it, it will generally receive strong support in Euro-America. On the other hand, if a people is incorporated in a non-democratic state with little authentic means of expression, support in Euro-America will occur only if there is a strong outside interest group associated with its cause (as is the case for Soviet Jews).

8. *Level of public awareness of movement.* Obviously, if the informed public does not know about a self-determination movement, there will be no generation of public opinion in its favour. The elite pushing the cause of an ethnic or territorial group must be able to make it an issue and keep it an issue before it will be able to influence public interests or consciences.

9. *Likelihood of success.* Independence movements generally receive

little recognition if they face strong and implacable governments. As one analysis points out, it is a matter of historic record that no totalitarian regime has been overthrown in this century save through defeat in war.²⁸ Therefore, short of war, what good would it do to support Tibetans under present conditions? To encourage their efforts today might be to go against the just war doctrine that it is wrong to fight without a reasonable expectation of success.²⁹ Fruitless death and suffering have few defenders. At the opposite extreme, it has been eminently practical to support the causes of Turks in Cyprus, or Bengalis in East Pakistan, because of the likelihood that they could receive strong outside support.

10. *Non-threatening to other interests.* As has been pointed out, Western publics find it in their interest to recognise the rights of suppressed people that are far away, and battling for self-determination against an isolated state that is unlikely to cause trouble to others, or to call in friends. Lack of interest in the rights of self-determination of subnationalities in communist states rests in part on the fear that interest in them would lead to dangerous counteractions. It is safer to support Rhodesian blacks or Amazon natives.

III SELF-DETERMINATION IN INTERNATIONAL LAW

Vernon van Dyke relates the relative inattention of the United Nations Charter and the Universal Declaration of Human Rights to group rights, such as self-determination or minority rights, to the individualistic conception of man in both communist and non-communist intellectual traditions.³⁰ Individuals are expected to have responsibilities to, and rights from, the state (or humanity), and not be submerged in less universalistic groupings. He points to this attitude as the basis for the argument before the International Court of Justice that territories such as Namibia or Rhodesia should not be considered in any other terms than those of one man/one vote unitary states. A recent and extreme expression of this position is found in a lengthy article in the *American Journal of International Law* asserting that states have no right to differentiate between citizens and non-citizens, for such discrimination goes against the 'newly emerged general norm of non-discrimination which seeks to forbid all generic differentiation among people in access to value shaping and sharing for reasons irrelevant to individual capabilities and contributions.³¹ Discrimination in favour of citizens, they assert, is scarcely worse than discrimination on the basis of race, sex, or religion. The implication that political rights of people in non-universal states are ultimately illegitimate would probably not be denied by the authors.

Van Dyke points out that in spite of the regnant universalising assumptions, in many modern societies special group rights have been granted. Beginning with the distinctions accorded to citizenship, he goes on to consider ethnic decentralisations such as those in Canada, India, and the USSR. He points out that by law many countries must be ruled by persons in certain groups – from Scandinavia's requirement of Lutheran kings to Islamic state requirements of Muslim rulers, often of particular sects. In Fiji most of the land is reserved to people of Fijian ancestry (now in the minority), and in many areas of Malaysia land can only be acquired by Malays. Aaland Islanders in Finland, and the peoples of Northern Nigeria can deny land to outsiders, while in the Americas special lands have been set aside for the exclusive use of particular aboriginal peoples. In Israel Arabs are excluded from the army. There are generally good historical reasons for such special rights or disabilities, but whatever the reasons the individuals involved are not treated simply as individuals in the eyes of the law.

Van Dyke also points out that there are many countries that legally or customarily enforce political or civil service quotas, and recently such quotas have again become common in education – from Kenya to the USA. Many countries have given special economic rights to particular peoples, generally their own ruling *Staatsvolk*, as in Malaysia or many black African states. In these terms it might be said that the special ethnic plans and regulations of the Rhodesians and South Africans have an implicit basis in the group rights concepts as accepted in practice in international law – however, the acceptability of the specifics of these group rights is, of course, another matter.

In spite of the general inattention to group rights, Rigo Sureda argues that the UN has developed a new body of international law specifying the right of self-determination.[32] Briefly, the right is that of a former overseas European colony to full independence from the colonial power. The state subsequently created should, in this body of law, be the same unit as was formerly administered as a unit by the colonial power. It is on this basis that Indonesia was able successfully to advance its claim to West Irian, while Katanga and Biafra failed to find acceptance under UN 'law'. The UN position was spelled out most clearly in its rejection of the Belgian attempt to have the international organisation extend the definition of non-self-governing territories to 'subordinate peoples' within a metropolitan state, and in its acceptance of Resolution 1541 that specified that the right applied only to non-contiguous territories. This position can be seen as little more than an extension of the Aaland decision in the early twenties. In this case the League of Nations found that although the Aaland Islands were inhabited mostly by Swedes, previous administration from what had become Finland made the Swedish claim inadmissible. Too many states had too many analogous enclaves. However, it is important to note that the League added stipulations that would guarantee self-determination by the people of the Aaland Islands within the Finnish state. Specifically, Finland was enjoined from the too common practice of changing the ethnic composition of the islands to cement its claim.[33] This concept is in accord with the idea of the 'minorities regime' developed after World War I, a concept that unfortunately does not interest the anti-colonialist UN.

The United Nations has, therefore, enunciated a theoretical or abstract right of all peoples (a term it has itself defined very broadly)[34] to self-determination, while creating through a body of legislative decisions international law that narrowly restricts the application of the right to the context of a struggle against Western imperialism. It seems clear that for an American or West European the law produced in this manner does not exhaust the issue.

While preferring total independence, the United Nations has accepted three definitions of self-determination: independence, free association with another state, and integration with another state.[35] In both the second and third cases the UN has been careful to note the people's right later to choose complete independence. This seems to imply that all peoples should have political and civil rights, for how else could they be said to choose? In the case of the Fiji Islands the General Assembly has insisted that rule should be on the basis of one man, one vote (in spite of the fact that most UN states do not have free voting systems).[36] The United States has suggested that such rights be placed at the core of the definition rather than on the periphery by proposing to the General Assembly:

> The existence of a sovereign and independent state possessing an independent government, effectively functioning as such to all distinct peoples within its territory is presumed to satisfy the principle of equal rights and self-determination as regards those peoples.[37]

In considering this American concept it is well to remember that to Woodrow Wilson self-government and self-determination were essentially synonymous; to Wilson they both meant the democratic governance by a people of its own affairs.[38]

IV BASIC PRINCIPLES FOR EXAMINING CLAIMS TO SELF-DETERMINATION

DEFINITIONS

Although the American proposal may have gone too far in identifying self-determination with constitutional democracy, it does offer a way around the theoretical UN position that would promote unlimited subdivision if taken seriously. Borrowing from the individualistic American approach, but accepting the balancing legitimacy of group rights, I propose that self-determination be specified as follows: Self-determination may be (*a*) verified (plebiscitary) or (*b*) unverified. It can be expressed through independence, regional federalism, or democratically contingent acceptance of a centralised system of control. These forms of self-determination are defined as follows:

(*a*) 1. Verified self-determination is only possible where general political and civil rights exist. Where verified self-determination is achieved, the legitimacy of demands to convert a right to regional self-determination to a right to complete independence is greatly diminished, although not extinguished.

(*a*) 2. Contingent self-determination exists where a people has by democratic means accepted centralised rule by a state it does not rule, and remains able by the same means to reject such rule.

(*b*) Unverified self-determination is assumed where the effective power in the government ruling over a people is in the hands of people identified as belonging to that people.

In defining self-determination we should remember that no people (or person) is completely self-determining. States and the people that control them vary widely in their ability to determine their own fate. Therefore, for a people to put forward a claim for self-determination means that it demands an increase in its power to influence its future. It cannot demand an annulment of the power relationships and contextual determinations that exist in the world independently of this demand.

Given these definitions, the claims of subnationalisms should generally be supported by those wishing to enhance political rights. But we should distinguish between those cases in which the aspiring people has a *prima facie* right to decide its fate separately from those around it and those in which this right is more questionable. I believe we can say that a subnation with a *prima facie* right to self-determination may either be the *Staatsvolk* (ruling nationality) of an existing state (as the Poles in Poland), or a conquered people that was formerly the *Staatsvolk* of an internationally recognised state (as are the Lithuanians). If a subnation has been forced out of an original home territory into a foreign state, it may wish to determine the state to which it belongs and/or the degree of its dependence on a particular state's laws. A *Staatsvolk* may also want a smaller, more homogeneous state than the one it inherited (for example, the Turkish leaders in the Ottoman Empire after World War I wanted to exclude most areas inhabited by non-Turks from their new nation).

Returning to definitions, let us define a *homogeneous* state as one in which there are no subnationalisms or potential subnationalisms. *Heterogeneous* states may be pluralist, imperial, or non-communal. A *pluralist* state contains several subnationalities with rights to self-determination, all of which are met in some degree within a federal framework. An *imperial* state contains several subnationalities, generally including some with *prima facie* claims, but only one of which has had its claim fulfilled as the *Staatsvolk* of ruling nation (for example, the USSR). A *non-communal* state has been defined above as a compound state in which no people is granted group rights. In terms of our specifications homogeneous and pluralist states are generally acceptable responses to demands for enhanced self-determination, as could be non-communal states as provisional political solutions.[39]

V THE THEORETICAL ARGUMENT FOR SELF-DETERMINATION

In order to get a better feeling for where injustice lies in those cases in which the right of self-determination is questionable, it is necessary to consider more carefully the theoretical underpinning of this right. The discussion must begin by considering the generally accepted right of states to preserve their territorial integrity. It will be recalled that the UN has also accepted the international law that all states have the right to self-defence, including that of defence against internal rights of secession. Paradoxically, in accepting this position the UN is accepting a tradition of the colonialist era that rights to territory are confirmed by effective occupation and control over a period of time.[40] In speaking of Britain's rights to India, Burke tells us:

> There is a sacred veil to be drawn over the beginnings of all governments. Ours, in India, had an origin like those which time has sanctified by obscurity... But, whatever necessity might hide or excuse, or palliate in the acquisition of power, a wise nation, when it has once made a revolution upon its own principles and for its own ends, rests there... By conquest, which is a more immediate designation of the hand of God, the conqueror succeeds to all the painful duties and subordination of the power of God, which belonged to the sovereign whom he has displaced.[41]

Burke tells us, then, that however a state may attain control, control implies responsibility. It is impossible for governments to meet all demands for self-determination, if they are responsibly to ensure the safety and well-being of all the people in a given territory. The UK could grant self-determination to the peoples of Northern Ireland tomorrow, but in their present relationship the results could be even more tragic than the events of the last decade. Thus, unless they find a formula satisfactory to the major disputants, the British may stay and be vilified by all.

This is the right and duty of states in the colonialist, pre-populist era from which we have emerged. However, since Burke's legitimisation of imperialism is not acceptable today, it must be limited by the doctrine of self-determination. This, in turn, is based on the tradition exemplified by John Stuart Mill's classic statement of the rights of peoples to govern themselves:

> A portion of mankind may be said to constitute a nationality if they are united among themselves by common sympathies which do not exist between them and others – which make them cooperate with each other more willingly than with other people, desire to be under the same government, and desire that it should be government by themselves or a portion of themselves exclusively.
>
> Where the sentiment of nationality exists in any force, there is a *prima facie* case for uniting all the members of the nationality under the same government, and a government to themselves apart. This is merely saying that the question of government ought to be decided by the governed. One hardly knows what any division of the

human race should be free to do if not to determine with which of the various collective bodies they choose to associate themselves.[42]

This seems to be an extreme doctrine. However, Mill goes on to qualify freedom in terms of utilitarianism and a scaling of peoples according to their presumed social evolution. On this basis his subsequent discussion modifies the requirements of self-determination. He argues, for example, that since the right to self-determination of a superior, more advanced people, whether majority or minority, is superior to that of a less advanced, it is advantageous for the Basques and Welsh to become assimilated to the French and English peoples, rather than that they emphasise their distinctiveness. However, Mill thought that the British in India had a responsibility to raise the Indian people to a level at which they could determine their own affairs, and as long as the British were engaged in so raising the Indians, this responsibility was prior to that of the Indian desire for self-determination. For Mill the rights of small communities, such as Gibraltar, were nullified by the defence requirements of the large state that controls them. The right of self-determination through independence or federal arrangement is, then, limited through the utilitarian calculus to that of large communities of an equivalent level of civilisation and capable of free democratic government.[43]

What makes Mill's position seem stark today is that his justifications for exceptions to principle are so out of harmony with modern liberal thinking that they are ignored. Mill's patronising of dependent peoples (reminiscent of the Soviet or Chinese elder brother attitude) is no longer officially acceptable in our culture. Although I would personally argue that the right to self-determination of a people not led democractically is a contradiction in terms, and that the rights of certain small communities might be sacrificed to the demands for defence of more inclusive democratic systems, neither of these views is commonly held in the liberal community. Mill's argument comes to our generation, then, without its qualifications.

In these terms the rights of the government of a homogeneous state are only those that the people have freely granted. The government is the mechanism that a particular people has chosen to express its collective desires. If this is so, then the rights of the governments of heterogeneous states are restricted to those granted by the affirmation of their policies by the individuals of their subnationalities both separately and collectively. *Vis-à-vis* its peoples the legitimacy of a homogeneous or heterogeneous state is, then, contingent upon the continued relative satisfaction of the peoples involved (and thus by definition the imperial state is generally illegitimate). A state's rule must bring more benefit than harm over a period of time to all of its constituent peoples, or they will have no reason but fear of repression to remain within. Therefore, a state can legitimately preserve itself only when its constituent peoples want it to, and to the extent they do. It is, in this view, a contradiction for a government to attempt to preserve jurisdiction over a people that does not want its jurisdiction. It has no right to prevent escape from its rule (except for particular crimes) of persons not wanting its control, just as it has no right to control peoples living in territory it took possession of by force, or that it forced on to its territory.

But how do we know what a particular subnationality wants in a heterogeneous state? We can distinguish three types of situation. In the first, there is tight state control over the territory and people and a lack of reasonably democratic procedures. In this case, for any people that is not dominant in the government of the state a small disaffected elite may temporarily be regarded as representing the desires of the people. Outside observers have no reliable way of knowing what the people desire, but they do know that the people in the name of which its disaffected speak have not been given any substantial opportunity to know what it wants. The second situation is one where there are, or have been, democratic procedures that give us a good idea that a people wishes enhanced self-determination. Finally, there are situations, such as that of Puerto Rico, where the majority has repeatedly expressed disinterest in further self-determination, but the world continues to hear from a disaffected minority. Outside support for enhanced self-determination in this case is inappropriate until such time as its advocates change the judgement of their own people.

There is, of course, a principled argument against supporting demands for enhanced self-determination. The balance of recent thinking by political scientists and economists has been integrative, planning-oriented, and thus hostile to the fragmentation that would often result from attempts to meet subnational demands. From this viewpoint small countries are seen as unfortunate anachronisms, and federal systems as inefficient compromises with political reality. In recent years this professional consensus has weakened somewhat,[44] but it persists in the face of evidence that small countries are by no means less likely to offer their citizens economic development, justice, or political and civil rights than larger states. It is true that everything else being equal small states are weaker militarily than larger states, but for most of the world such weakness remains inconsequential (except perhaps in Western Europe where continued political division results in unnecessary weakness).

It is my suspicion that the desire to construct or maintain large unitary states in most of the world is not well-advised. In particular, this centralising, state-forming trend has not allowed for the natural evolution of democratic polities. It is not simply chance that European democracy developed in small states and thrives best in either small states or federal unions today. Too often, placing an arbitrary, originally foreign structure over a variety of competing groups has led to an appeal to force, and thus to administration by the least common denominator. For example, in Uganda the most advanced and ordered part of the pre-independence colony, the Kingdom of Buganda, was forced through the process of national integration to submit to increasingly harsh rule by outsiders with which its people had little in common.[45] One recent student of Benin suggests that instead of the solution of imposed dictatorship that eventually resulted, even this relatively small country should have been made into a loose confederation of three states. He believes that this would have been more meaningful to the largely illiterate peasantry, and that it might have prevented the imposition of military rule that resulted from the attempt at centralisation that resulted from adhering to the French model.[46] In part, Burmese democracy was choked by the military dominance of a society eternally at war with its non-Burmese periphery. Similarly, managing the enterprise of Indonesia has required the suppression of small subnational groups with no noticeable gain to the majority.

In supporting self-determination as an ideal, it should be repeated that this does not imply that a balancing of the rights of states and their peoples will always lead to advocacy of complete independence. Echoing the Aaland Islands decision of the League, and the official American position, if a state meets its obligations to a people in terms of economic, cultural, and political equality under democracy, other factors may place a legitimate limit on the potential demand for self-determination, or as Cobban puts it:

> Although in (some) cases independent statehood may be out of the question, all nations or subnations should exercise self-determination within the limits of what is practicable, in the form of regional autonomy.[47]

VI THE RIGHTS TO SELF-DETERMINATION OF TERRITORIAL MINORITIES

A right to self-determination may exist in a complex union for a people that is not the majority population in any particular area. Two arguments support this right. First, many peoples have been overrun by others, and in some cases it has been deliberate state policy to change population balances by bringing in outside or *Staatsvolk* colonists (for example, in China, the USSR, and Israel). While no definition of a people's rights can undo history, their definition should at least not encourage deliberate attempts to change population balances of a particular people in an area. Secondly, some peoples, such as Gypsies, Jews, Parsees, Chinese in some countries and Armenians in others, have a strong ethnic pattern combined with a tendency to diffused 'micro-' rather than 'macro-territoriality'. More recently the same pattern has developed for the American Negroes as a result of their urbanisation. Mill's dictum of the rights of groups to self-rule should apply to such groups to the extent that there are practical ways to express this desire that do not seriously infringe on the rights of other peoples.

For non-majority peoples that have been overrun, the self-determination demand will legitimately include the right to carve out a territorial base that can achieve the desired level of self-government. This must, of course, be done without violence to the rights of other peoples. For while in Millsian terms conquering states do not acquire rights over conquered peoples, the new peoples that follow on the heels of conquest soon acquire rights equivalent to the rights of those they dispossess – in spite of the historical injustice. How soon the successor people achieves such 'squatter rights' is, of course, a critical issue. However, the general rule is that all peoples are groups of individuals and, as individuals, they are as historically determined into their present situation as all other peoples, including those they may have dispossessed. The solution may be for the peoples concerned to establish a non-communal state in which the several peoples cooperate on the basis of equality until such time as a new resolution is demanded.

For a people that has never had a territorial majority in a country, such as the Jews in most of the world, such a resolution might be achieved through a state structure modelled on that suggested by Renner and Bauer for the Austro-Hungarian Empire, and more recently by Uri Ra'anan.[48] The concept is that subnationalities should be granted special voting rolls, taxation systems, and personal laws such as was done in the millet system of the Ottoman Empire where law was the separate responsibility of each religious community. Often, of course, the millet system worked because of a highly developed micro-territoriality (ghettos), and such territories might be the basis for non-territorial systems. In the Renner-Bauer form, rights to self-determination would remain imperfect, and could not lead to complete independence. However, at least in a pluralist state formed on what is in effect a people's pact, a system of this kind might offer the highest degree of group freedom that is available in a complex state. Before we dismiss this alternative the reader should reflect that in medieval Europe territory was only one among several bases upon which legal boundaries among peoples were drawn.

If the rights to self-determination of a minority people without a macro-territorial base are limited on practical grounds, so may be those of very small peoples. Recently a few thousand Haida Indians in British Columbia have laid claim to the Queen Charlotte Islands, their ancient homeland.[49] They are said to wish independence. The two most salient reactions are to accept the Haida claim as a logical development of principle, or simply to rule it out on the grounds of practicality and the larger interests of Canadian society. A compromise between these positions would be to grant internal autonomy without rights of secession or control of foreign affairs to the Haidas – this would be analogous to the British relation to the Channel Islands or the Isle of Man. It could be argued that to go beyond this would lead ultimately to a multitude of independencies that would harm the interests of all Canadians. The Haidas would not be granted complete independence because this could be achieved only at the risk of the dissolution of Canada and consequent loss to all its peoples. But I would not want to prove such an argument for Queen Charlotte Island. The desire for complete micro-independence might practically be controlled by making clear that, once independent, a people such as the Haida would not have the right to call on their former state for financial or other help. In general, however, economic arguments against small states are not conclusive.[50] And practical arguments against establishing small states become weaker as we consider peoples numbering over 100,000, and certainly cease before one million, for already we are in the size-domain of many self-sustaining members of the United Nations.

Another example of theoretical interest is the recent absorption of the Kingdom of Sikkim by the Indian state.[51] The historical background is a common one of the succession of peoples. In the seventeenth century the Bhutias left Tibet and conquered the Lepchas of Sikkim, and today the two peoples are closely aligned. However, in the nineteenth century the British encouraged the immigration of Nepalese. By 1970 the Bhutia-Lepcha people upon which the king depended for support were greatly outnumbered by the Hindu Nepalese, whose more natural allegiance was to an Indian state. Therefore, in spite of the irregularities of the process, the Indian intervention in the early 1970s was probably a gain for self-determination, as well as for democracy. Yet the rights of the Bhutia-Lepcha, now a minority in their own country, should be considered. These rights might have been preserved by preventing the immigration of non-Buddhist peoples in the past (as in the Aaland Islands decision). In the future they might be preserved by establishing an autonomous area under the old Bhutia system, or through a non-territorial alternative.

The case of Sikkim raises the more general problem that if we are to recognise rights to self-determination, then we must also recognise the right of a people to prevent large-scale movement of other peoples into the land. Academics have always contemptuously denigrated the activities of 'Know-nothings' and other exclusionists in the United States. Yet recent studies suggest that as a result of immigration, WASPs may have become a minority in the United States they supposedly dominate.[52] Certainly, when a foreigner visits New York today, he does not visit a WASP city, no matter what power Edith Wharton's aristocracy may retain. Perhaps the resulting American mosaic is what most WASPs of the nineteenth century, if given a choice, would have wanted. But if not, then they were justified in supporting exclusionary laws. Similarly, the friends of self-determination must not carelessly condemn recent attempts to restrict non-white immigration to England, or the 'Uberfremdungsinitiativen' in Switzerland.[53] For there is a great deal of difference between the prejudice that unfairly ascribes evil to another group and the considered judgement that their customs and traditions are sufficiently different that one group should not allow the other to take away through demographic movement its right to determine its own fate.

This point of view should be especially appealing to those who, like myself, feel that democracy is easier to achieve and maintain in small homogeneous states than in larger ones. George Kennan, for example, sees democracy as largely restricted to countries of 'small size and cultural cohesion'.[54] It is true that one study concludes that small homogeneous states have less conflict partly because such states more easily suppress dissent.[55] However, the relation between conflict and the subsequent suppression of dissent, and ultimately the loss of rights, seems more obvious when we look at the full range of states.

VII BALANCING SELF-DETERMINATION AND OTHER VALUES IN FUTURE POLICY

Looking toward the future it may be predicted that the self-determination of peoples defined by previous colonial boundaries, or the natural boundaries of islands, will proceed toward general realisation almost everywhere. This will be a verifiable self-determination in all those countries in which democratic institutions are well established through local traditions or massive outside influence. For example, although few inhabitants are of European background, the people of tiny Anguilla have apparently both the formal and informal traditions necessary for a democractic polity.[56] In many cases a verifiable initial phase of self-determination can occur in such instances even when the prior situation is not supportive of democratic forms. For example, the UN investigations in Bahrain that established the desire of the people to be free of both Arab and Iranian outside rule appears to have been a recent model of independent verification of the desires of a people.[57]

However, the outlook for subnationalities within organised states is much poorer. Their demands will fester, for most states will not grant rights of self-determination until both internal and external pressures become very high. Exceptions may be found in those instances such as Belgium where the competing peoples make up most of the population and there is no defined *Staatsvolk* or strong national ideology. Another exception may be found in the case of Canada, where a federal system, the strength of the French minority in Quebec, weak Canadian nationalism, and the commitment of the *Staatsvolk* to liberal democratic principles make it impossible for the state to ignore the demands, however far they may eventually be pushed. India has shown itself willing and able to grant important autonomy within a federal framework to a variety of peoples, but the precariousness of the position of the Hindi *Staatsvolk* makes it unwilling to countenance secession – indeed India's tendency has been to accrete peoples and territories at the margin into its system. In the long term this is both morally and practically an insufficient response, but it is possible that the Indian state can prove itself to its constituent peoples, so that they may with greater self-awareness continue to accept membership in the pluralist state. An obstacle to general acceptance of self-determination in many democracies is that they lack experience in decentralising power to constituent peoples. Another obstacle is the current socio-economic planning ideology that sees populations organised primarily in economic relationships, and regards even present international boundaries as artificial. Given this ideology, it has been hard to accept the reasonableness of Scottish or Welsh aspirations for self-determination even within a liberal British society closely attuned to the legitimacy of a wide variety of demands for other human rights at home and abroad. But movement is occurring here, while it is not in states such as the Soviet Union of Yugoslavia where the goal of the state remains the eventual assimilation of all peoples to one, secular, mass society with a more or less set ideological schema. Self-determination in these states has been promoted primarily as a transitory means of mobilising the population.[58]

Where democracy persists, the liberal beliefs of elites will ultimately force acceptance of demands of constituent peoples upon reluctant centralisers. However, in some liberal states a further recognition and acceptance of people-related regionalism may be able to preserve the general state structure as well as a sense of state-nationalism transcending lesser affiliations. In imperial states, self-determination, if and when it comes, will probably mean complete breakdown of central state authority, together with rejection of the state nationalism that formerly went with it. In these states change is unlikely to be easy, or without violence.

Given this prospect, how does a well-intentioned public develop a principled rather than merely adjustive policy toward subnational demands? In a recent paper Alois Riklin suggested four goals for a less nationalistic Swiss foreign policy: peace, independence, individual rights, and equality (justice).[59] In Riklin's view all four goals must be balanced, for no one goal can have an absolute claim on Swiss attention. From our perspective Riklin's 'independence' may be thought of as self-determination, or more generally 'group rights', while equality or justice would seem to imply both justice between individuals and between groups. At first sight it would appear that to promote self-determination as supported or subordinated by concern for peace, individual rights, and justice should become the legitimate goal of the liberal state and its supporting public wherever these are found. But what guidance does this offer?

Given our policy definitions of self-determination, only if a state is democratic, and its peoples have accepted its rule by democratic procedures, do its leaders have a legitimate right to speak for its peoples. Thus, our interest in the right of self-determination extends also to the *Staatsvolk* or ruling people of a non-democratic state. Mill's point was that rights of individuals and groups to political freedom were closely related. In this sense the lesser peoples of an imperial state have a double claim on our attention, for they are deprived of both freedom as individuals and freedom as members of those groups with which they identify.

Yet we know that policy support of demands for greater self-determination, including independence, may be dangerous to peace, increase inequalities, and reduce individual rights. We are concerned here especially with the latter. That achieving group self-determination may end in losing individual rights is no idle worry is suggested by the fact that for half of the former European colonies individuals have less freedom today than immediately before independence. Certainly self-determination for the American South in the nineteenth century might have meant less individual freedom. Theoretically a study comparing large with small democracies suggests that the larger offer more individual freedom, for people with different ideas than the majority are more able to find allies in the larger societies.[60] The balance betwen individual and group rights, then, would seem to lie in regarding group self-determination as one among many political and civil rights. As such it is a right with relatively little claim on our attention when there is a strong case that other rights are likely to be lost in its pursuit.

With the foregoing exception, we conclude that as principled policy the informed public should support subnationalisms wherever they occur, and expect and welcome the development of new subnationalisms. This support should not, however, go so far as to identify independence as a necessary or desirable goal for all subnationalisms, particularly those in democracies where the majority of a people has expressed itself against independence. Subnational demands are especially worthy of support in the absence of political rights and civil liberties, and particularly suspect where it appears that granting such demands would reduce these rights and liberties. Before supporting a self-determination movement the public should inquire as closely as possible into the actual size of the group making the demand, or at least self-conscious of its existence as a group. These principles should not lead us to oppose 'nation-building' in highly fragmented societies, for we realise that all nations and subnations are to some extent artificial. However, they should lead us to oppose all nation-building that relies on the suppression of subnationalities or other group identifications. Communal states, or non-communal states supportive of lesser identifications, may be more difficult to rule, but then all expression of rights and liberties is likely to complicate the lives of our governors.

After examining the current state of self-determination, and developing some conceptual tools, this paper examined the implications of the Millsian belief that the most basic right of both individuals and groups is the right to decide what state should administer their government. Carrying this view to its logical conclusion has raised many issues of application and conflicting rights. These may not be resolved without ultimately restricting the extent of our concern with the rights of peoples, nations, or nationalities considered separately from those of individuals *qua* individuals.[61] We cannot judge other people only as individuals and remain very concerned with the rights of peoples; nor can we be interested in the rights of peoples and condemn their desire to treat individuals at times as members of groups rather than as individuals. In this paper we have not pretended to resolve these dilemmas, but we do hope that we have suggested some of the implications of taking seriously a belief in the right of all peoples to self-determination.

NOTES

1. Alfred Cobban, *National Self-determination* (London: Oxford University Press, 1945).
2. Walker Connor, 'Nation-building or Nation-Destroying', *World Politics*, 24 (Apr 1972) pp. 319–55.
3. Ibid., p. 350.
4. For example, Walker Connor, 'The Politics of Ethnonationalism', *Journal of International Affairs*, 27 (1973) pp. 1–21. Also Rupert Emerson, 'Self-Determination', *American Journal of International Law*, 65 (1971) pp. 459–75.
5. Connor, 'Nation-Building or Nation-Destroying', pp. 332–5. See also Uri Ra'anan, 'The Multi-Ethnic State: Some Concepts of Conflict Resolution', unpublished paper, 1974.
6. Connor, 'The Politics of Ethnonationalism', especially pp. 5–6.
7. See Edward Allworth (ed.), *The Nationality Question in Soviet Central Asia* (New York: Praeger, 1973); Teresa Rakowska-Harmstone, *Russia and Nationalism in Central Asia: The Case of Tadzhikistan* (Baltimore: Johns Hopkins University Press, 1970).
8. For a recent usage of 'subnationalism' compare Crawford Young, *The*

Politics of Cultural Pluralism (Madison: University of Wisconsin Press, 1976) p. 231.
9. Ibid.
10. Ibid., pp. 163–215, 216–73.
11. Ibid., pp. 171–3, 229–30, 346–7.
12. See especially Stephanie Neuman (ed.), *Small States and Segmented Societies* (New York: Praeger, 1976).
13. E. E. Evans-Pritchard, *The Nuer* (London: Oxford University Press, 1940) pp. 139–91.
14. Young, *Politics of Cultural Pluralism*, pp. 95–7, 506.
15. See Emerson, 'Self-Determination'. The right is spelled out most clearly in the *International Covenant on Economic, Social and Cultural Rights*, Part 1, passed in 1966 by the General Assembly and repeated in the *International Covenant on Civil and Political Rights*.
16. See Richard Pipes, *The Formation of the Soviet Union* (New York: 1968); also Laszlo Revesz, 'Sowjetische Streiflichter: Juden und andete Minderheiten', *Schweizer Monatshefte*, 54 (1974) pp. 10–14.
17. See Walker Connor, 'Self-Determination: The New Phase', *World Politics*, 20 (1967) pp. 30–53. For a full account of the UN position see A. Rigo Sureda, *The Evolution of the Right of Self-Determination: A Study of United Nations Practice* (Leiden: A. W. Sijthoff, 1973).
18. See the discussion in R. D. Gastil, 'Comparative Survey of Freedom V', *Freedom at Issue*, no. 29 (Jan/Feb 1975) pp. 3–9.
19. Cf. Robert Osgood and Robert Tucker, *Force, Order and Justice* (Baltimore: Johns Hopkins, 1967) pp. 273–7; D. P. O'Connell, *International Law*, 2nd. ed. (London: Stevens & Sons, 1950) pp. 316–20.
20. Cf. Philip Agee, *Inside the Company: CIA Diary* (New York: Stonehill/Bantam, 1975–76); John Barron, *KGB* (New York: Readers Digest Press/Bantam, 1974).
21. This is characteristic of 'praetorian societies'. See Samuel Huntington, *Political Order in Changing Societies* (New Haven: Yale University Press, 1968).
22. Cf. Allen Goodman, *Politics in War* (Cambridge, Mass.: Harvard University Press, 1973).
23. Ved P. Nanda, 'Self-Determination in International Law: The Tragic Tale of Two Cities – Islamabad (West Pakistan) and Dacca (East Pakistan)', *American Journal of International Law*, 66 (Apr 1972) pp. 321–36.
24. See Karl Deutsch, *Nationalism and Social Communication* (Cambridge, Mass.: MIT Press, 1953).
25. O'Connell, *International Law*, pp. 422–8.
26. See Paul Lucas, 'Edmund Burke's Doctrine of Prescription', *The Historial Journal*, XI, 1 (1968) pp. 35–63.
27. Cf. *Latin America*, 19 Oct 1973, p. 336, and 21 June 1974, p. 189. The government of Belize does not wish complete independence before it is confident that it will not be absorbed by Guatemala, a nation dominated by different races and cultures.
28. Osgood and Tucker, *Force, Order and Justice*, p. 231, note 16. The authors appear to define totalitarian narrowly to include only authentic fascist and communist states.

29. See Paul Ramsey, *War and the Christian Conscience* (Durham: Duke University Press, 1961; also his *The Just War* (New York: Scribners, 1968) pp. 356–7. According to the doctrine it is wrong to commit suicide, or to cause the death of another, unless there is a reasonable chance of achieving a justifiable goal.
30. Vernon van Dyke, *Human Rights, the United States and the World Community* (New York: Oxford, 1970) pp. 77–102, and his 'Human Rights and the Rights of Groups', *American Journal of Political Science*, 18, 4 (Nov 1974) pp. 725–42.
31. M. McDougall, H. Lasswell, and Lung-chu Chen, 'The Protection of Aliens from Discrimination and World Public Order', *American Journal of International Law*, 70, 3 (1976) pp. 432–69 (432–3).
32. Sureda, *The Evolution of the Right to Self-Determination*; also van Dyke, *Human Rights, the United States, and the World Community*.
33. Ibid., pp. 32–4, 111–18.
34. Ibid., p. 100.
35. Emerson, 'Self-Determination', especially p. 470.
36. Sureda, *Evolution of the Right of Self-Determination*, p. 180.
37. Ibid., quoted p. 468.
38. Michla Pomerance, 'The United States and Self-Determination: Perspectives on the Wilsonian Conception', *American Journal of International Law* 70, 1 (1976) pp. 1–28.
39. Homogeneity and heterogeneity are, of course, in terms of 'peoples', and not in the degree of structural differentiation as in the famous distinctions of Tönnies and Durkheim. In the modern language of anthropology or sociology the preferable terms might be 'monistic' versus 'pluralistic'. In the special language of M. G. Smith the imperial society is referred to as a plural society with 'differential incorporation', a pluralist society as one of 'consociation', and apparently a homogeneous society as one of 'uniform incorporation'. See Pierre van den Berge, 'Pluralism', in J. J. Honigmann (ed.), *Handbook of Social and Cultural Anthropology* (Chicago: Rand McNally, 1973) pp. 959–78. Consociation as 'consociational democracy' has received a good deal of attention in the recent political science literature, for example, Arend Lijphart, 'Consociational Democracy', *World Politics*, 21 (Jan 1969) pp. 207–75, and James A. Dunn, 'Consociational Democracy and Language Conflict', *Comparative Political Studies*, 5 (Apr 1972) pp. 3–39.
40. O'Connell, *International Law*, pp. 403–44.
41. Edward Burke, *Works* VII (London: George Bell, 1890) pp. 60, 100.
42. John Stuart Mill, *Representative Government*, in Everyman edition; J. S. Mill, *Utilitarianism, Liberty, and Representative Government* (New York: Dutton, 1951). See also the discussion in Rupert Emerson, *From Empire to Nation* (Cambridge, Mass.: Harvard University Press, 1960) pp. 218–19.
43. Mill, *Representative Government*, pp. 487–94, 508–32.
44. For the range of positions in the current professional discussion see David and Audrey Smock, *The Politics of Pluralism* (New York: Elsevier, 1975) pp. 1–23.
45. Young, *Politics of Cultural Pluralism*, pp. 216–73.
46. Dov Ronen, *Dahomey: Between Tradition and Modernity* (Ithaca: Cornell

University Press, 1975), expecially pp. 244-5.
47. Cobban, *National Self-Determination*, p. 174.
48. Ra'anan. 'The Multi-Ethnic State'; also Emerson, *From Empire to Nation*, p. 111.
49. *Seattle Times*, 28 Aug 1974.
50. A reasoned discussion of the problems and possibilities is J. J. Spengler, 'Small Island Economies: Some Limitations', *South Atlantic Quarterly*, 70 (1971) pp. 48-61. See also William J. Brisk, *The Dilemma of the Ministate: Anguilla* (Columbia: University of South Carolina Press, 1969), and Burton Benedict (ed.), *Problems of Small Territories* (London: University of London, 1967).
51. *Keesing's Contemporary Archives*, 1973, p. 25909; 1974, pp. 26555, 26636; *New York Times*, 5 Sep 1974.
52. See Andrew Greeley, 'The Demography of Ethnic Identification', unpublished paper, NORC, March 1973 (especially Table 16).
53. See Benjamin Barber, *The Death of Communal Liberty* (Princeton: Princeton University Press, 1974) pp. 252-7.
54. See George Urban, 'From Containment to ... Self-Containment: A conversation with George F. Kennan', *Encounter* (Sep 1976) pp. 10-43 (22).
55. Robert Dahl and Edward Tufte, *Size and Democracy* (Stanford: Stanford University Press, 1973).
56. Cf. Brisk, *The Dilemma of a Ministate*, pp. 63-78. See also *Keesing's Contemporary Archives*, 25 Mar, 1977, pp. 28267-8.
57. See Rouhollah Ramazani, *The Persian Gulf: Iran's Role* (Charlottesville: University of Virginia Press, 1972).
58. Cf. Roman Szporluk, 'Nationalities and the Russian Problem in the USSR: An Historical Review', *Journal of International Affairs*, 27, 1 (1973) pp. 22-40; also Allworth, *The Nationality Question in Central Asia*, and Lyman Legters, 'Ideology and Integration, Marxism in Yugoslavia', in Neuman, *Small States and Segmented Societies*, pp. 139-53.
59. Alois Riklin, 'Schweizerische Unabhängigkeit heute', *Schweizer Monatschefte*, 54, 3 (June 1974) pp. 163-173.
60. Dahl and Tufte, *Size and Democracy*.
61. This was also van Dyke's conclusion (*Human Rights, the United States, and the World Community*, pp. 101-2.

6 Islamic-Arabism versus Pluralism: The Failure of Intergroup Accommodation in the Middle East

Moshe Ma'oz
Academic Director, the Harry S. Truman Research Institute, The Hebrew University of Jerusalem

I INTRODUCTION

Several parallel developments have combined to make the Middle East a region populated by many religious and ethnic groups: it is the cradle of the three monotheistic religions and their offshoots, it has been periodically conquered by outside forces which have left their imprint on the area, and it has been swept by waves of immigration throughout its history.

The religious and ethnic groups in the area can be divided into three categories: (*a*) the majority group (75 per cent), which is at once Arab and Muslim – i.e. possesses an Arab national-cultural identity, and professes the Sunni (Orthodox) Muslim faith; (*b*) religious groups which are non-Sunni Muslim but are Arabic-speaking, first the various Christian communities – Greek Orthodox, Greek Catholic, Copts, Maronites, Latins and Protestants; and secondly the various heterodox-Islami groups – Shi'is, 'Alawis, Druzes and Ismailis; (*c*) non-Arab ethnic groups, several of which are Sunni Muslims – Kurds,

Turkomans and Circassians; and others which are neither Arab nor Muslims, i.e. Jews, Armenians, Assyrians, and others.[1]

In view of this division the central question that arises is: does this heterogeneous population constitute a plural society marked by a pattern of coexistence and accommodation between the various groups? The answer must be essentially negative; and in this paper an attempt will be made to explain why and to examine the resultant conflicts between the various groups.

The main source of this conflict has for generations been characterised by the struggle between forces representing religious and national superiority or homogeneity on the one hand, and those standing for autonomy or pluralism, on the other. The forces of Orthodox (Sunni) Islamism and pan-Arabism which represent the religious and national beliefs of the majority of the population, have successively imposed Islamic and Arab uniformity and, conversely denied the non-Muslim and non-Arab minority groups the full rights of political equality or self-determination.

A. THE ISLAMIC ERA

For centuries under the domination of Islamic empires one section of the non-Muslim group in the Middle East – the Christian and Jewish communities – were given limited autonomy under the *millet* (religious community) system and were allowed to manage only their religious and educational affairs and matters of personal status. In all other matters, however, they were treated by the state and by the majority population as inferior subjects: they were discriminated against in public institutions, denied full freedom of worship, periodically persecuted and even forced to embrace Islam.[2] In particular, Christians and Jews were denied equal rights in the political community even during the nineteenth century when they were officially granted equality under the *Tanzimat* reforms of the Ottoman empire.[3] Christian groups in various places who insisted on emancipation were subject to pogroms and massacres by their Muslim neighbours.[4]

As for the other non-Sunni Muslim groups, the heterodox sects of Shi'is, Ismailis, 'Alawis and Druzes, they were regarded by the Islamic state and population as deviators or heretics and consequently were periodically persecuted, Islamised by force and occasionally were even faced with annihilation. Yet, unlike most Christians and Jews, the heterodox-Islamic groups were by and large armed and resided in remote or impassable areas, and thus were able to resist Orthodox-Muslim subjection and to protect their political and religious autonomy.[5] Those heterodox populations, however, who were unable to defend themselves in Sunni Muslim areas chose to adopt the old *Taqiyya* method – i.e. to act and behave outwardly as Sunni Muslims in order to avoid persecution.[6]

During that long Islamic period, up to the present century, Muslim hegemony and attempted-homogeneity in the Middle East was supplemented by the force of Arabism, i.e. Arab culture, notably the Arabic language. This was not only the speech of Allah, the Koran and the Muslim religious leaders (*'ulama*), but also the language of the majority population and of large sections of the administrative and judicial systems. Consequently, many members of the non-Arab ethnic-linguistic groups in the region – Kurds, Circassians, Copts, Armenians, Assyrians and Jews – were bound to adopt the Arabic language and in the process partly became culturally Arabised.

B. THE MODERN ERA

In the course of the current century, the dual forces of Islam and Arabism continued jointly to forge their supremacy *vis-à-vis* the non-Muslim and non-Arab groups. But the relative strength of these forces mutually interchanged, while their conflict with the minority groups took new forms and produced different results in the various parts of the region – all of this, under changing political circumstances and fresh ideological developments.

The religious sentiments of both the Islamic majority and non-Islamic minority groups were on the wane for several generations although remaining strong among the masses; the main factor underlying this development was the impact of the modern ideas of nationalism which had been imported from the West. Under the impact of such ideas various nationalist movements have emerged since the beginning of the present century. Among those the most powerful ideological-political force in the Middle East has been the pan-Arab movement. It has striven to bring about Arab political hegemony and cultural unity throughout the region, and in this process it has clashed with the newly emerging non-Arab national movements: The Maronite-Lebanese, the Jewish-Zionist, and Kurdish-Iraqi and the south Sudanese.

It should be indicated that the new conflict between the national movements of the majority population and of the minority groups has a significant correlation with the old conflict between the Orthodox-Muslim majority and the non-Muslim religious groups. For, essentially, the Arab national movement in both its phases – the pan-Arab and the regional – has placed Islam as a cornerstone in both its ideology and policy.[7] And although Christian Arabs were among the pioneers and ideologists of Arab-nationalism[8] they have neither been able to weaken its Islamic character nor to set up a secular or non-religious foundation for the Arab states of the Middle East. Indeed, although Christian and other non-Muslim Arab-speaking groups in the Arab states have been in theory full and equal members in their respective political communities, in practice they have been treated by and large as second-class citizens. The fact that most Arab states declare Islam as the official religion in their respective constitutions shows this point, and serves as a clear indication of the Islamic tendencies of Arab nationalism.

These Islamic tendencies have been particularly noticeable in the conflict between Arab nationalism and the national movements which are neither Arab nor Muslim, i.e. the Zionist movement in Palestine-Israel, being Jewish; the South-Sudanese movement, being Christian and pagan; and the Maronite-Lebanese movement which is Catholic Christian and has also certain non-Arab ethnic features. It can thus be concluded that the conflict between the majority population and the minority groups in the Middle East during the last few generations has operated on two levels: the major conflict is of a national ethnic nature between the Arab and non-Arab populations, sometimes intensified by religious factors, namely Islamic versus non-Islamic conceptions. Coinciding with this was the old prolonged religious-communal conflict between the Muslim Sunni and non-Muslim groups, both Christian and heterodox. Those two conflicts have occurred throughout the Middle East in the countries of the region, and have taken different courses in the various Arab countries.

II. THE FERTILE CRESCENT VERSUS EGYPT

In Egypt – the biggest Arab country – the large Muslim Arab majority (36 million out of some 40 million today) aided by the centralised character of the regime, has been able to sustain its hegemony without interruption and to maintain Arab Islamic uniformity for generations. The non-Muslim and non-Arab minority groups – Copts, Armenians,

Jews and others – were too few or too weak to make a significant impact on the political community and on the character of the state. Most members of the groups contented themselves with the religious-communal arrangements and the economic opportunities accorded to them; many have even undergone a process of Arabisation. But those who have tried to keep their own identity have suffered discrimination in the judicial and public administration and have occasionally been subject to Muslim ill-treatment.[9] Some have actively participated in the mainstream of the national movement while others refused to accept the dictates of the majority and chose to emigrate.

Unlike Egypt, which has small non-Arab non-Muslim minority groups (10 per cent), the Fertile Crescent region as a whole (some 24 million) consisted for generations of relatively large and fairly powerful non-Arab and/or non-Sunni Muslim groups, totalling some 60 per cent of the population. This phenomenon, which stemmed from historical and political developments and was backed by geographical and topographical factors, has contributed to weakening the Arab Muslim homogeneity of the Fertile Crescent. As a result this area has acquired a character of a multinational or multireligious region.

Reflecting this phenomenon, three of the non-Arab and/or non-Muslim groups in this region have developed during the modern era into viable national movements in their respective homelands. Two of these movements – the Christian Maronite in Lebanon and the Jewish-Zionist in Palestine (Eretz-Israel) – emerged in the nineteenth century and were at least partly nurtured on their respective religious faiths; both were drawn from societies with high cultural standards and have been supported by their fellow communities abroad. The third movement – Kurdish nationalism in Iraq – lagged behind the former movements both in its pace of development and its degree of cohesion. This was partly due to the tribal structure of the Kurdish people, partly because the Kurdish homeland is landlocked, and partly owing to the fact that the Kurds profess the Sunni Muslim faith – the religion of the Arab majority in Iraq.

Nevertheless, Kurdish nationalism and certainly the Maronite and Jewish national movements have striven to transform their respective people from ethnic religious groups into viable national communities, and to establish independent states in their historic homelands. But these three movements were confronted and attacked in their respective regions by forces of Arabism and/or Islam, and periodically were also blocked or exploited by the Mandatory powers Britain and France, which had divided the Fertile Crescent into several countries according to their imperial interests and not along ethnic-national lines. Thus these three national movements which experienced separate development, and conducted their struggles under different circumstances, achieved varied results in their conflict against Arabism and/or Islam.

A. ARAB–JEWISH CONFLICTS

The Jewish national movement, which had been granted by Great Britain in 1917 a national home in Palestine (Eretz-Israel), started its struggle against Arabism and Islam as a small minority in Mandated Palestine. And although Great Britain transferred during the Mandate period its support from the Jewish national movement to Arab nationalism, the Jewish-Zionist community grew in numbers and established its autonomous national organs in Palestine. And in 1948 the Jewish Yishuv succeeded in establishing a sovereign state in part of its ancient land, through a fierce struggle against the formidable forces of pan-Arabism.

But even though the Jewish nation in Israel was able to realise its national and political sovereignty it has not ceased to be in conflict with the Arab people both within the borders of Israel and outside these borders.

Externally Israel is still engaged in a fierce struggle against the attempts of pan-Arabism to do away with the Jewish national entity and to reduce it to the status of a religious community under Arab domination. Internally the Jewish state is confronted with an Arab minority group which comprises two sections: Israeli citizens (12 per cent of the population) and the Palestinian Arabs in the West Bank and the Gaza Strip (some 35 per cent of the Israeli population). Both sections have strong Palestinian Arab identity and regard themselves as part of the all-Arab majority in the Middle East. Thus in certain respects the political and ideological conflict between Arabs and Jews in Israel and the West Bank is an extension of the Arab Israeli confrontation in the Middle East. Yet despite this bi-dimensional conflict the Jewish national community has been so far the only non-Arab non-Muslim group in the Middle East which has realised its distinct national-cultural aspirations, thus partly foiling Arab Muslim attempts at national and cultural uniformity in the area.

In contrast the two other national movements in the Fertile Crescent – the Kurdish movement in Iraq and the Maronite national community in Lebanon – have been unable to attain achievements

Islamic-Arabism versus Pluralism

similar to those of the Jewish people in Israel.

B. THE ARAB-KURDISH CONFLICT

The Kurdish national movement emerged at the beginning of the present century in a struggle against the regime of the young Turks. At the Sèvres conference in 1920 the Kurds were promised, by the victorious powers, an autonomous status in large sections of historical Kurdistan, and were also given an option for political independence in these areas. But these pledges were never fulfilled; and following the Lausanne treaty of 1923 Ottoman Kurdistan was divided between Turkey and the newly founded states of Iraq and Syria, whereas Iranian Kurdistan remained a part of the Persian state. The Kurds of Iraq numbering 18 per cent to 20 per cent of the total population were recognised by various regimes in Iraq since 1918 as a nation or a national minority; and were promised political and cultural autonomy in their regions. But these promises remained by and large dead letters, and were never fully implemented. As a result a series of Kurdish rebellions broke out in the last fifty years, directed against the Iraqi Arab regimes and aimed at establishing an autonomous or independent Kurdistan in north Iraq.

Under the British Mandate the Kurds of Iraq were promised in 1922 the right to establish a Kurdish government in areas where they constituted an absolute majority.[10] But until the end of the Mandate in 1932 these promises were not fulfilled; instead the British were periodically engaged in quelling Kurdish insurrections and disturbances led by the Sheikhs Mahmud Barazani and Ahmad Barazani.[11] The independent Iraqi monarchy issued in 1932 and 1944 pledges granting cultural autonomy and a share in the administration to the Kurds of Kurdistan. In fact however the Iraqi government tried gradually to Arabise the Kurdish areas, thus provoking a fresh series of disorders and uprisings, particularly between 1943 and 1946, led by Mustafa Barazani. A new chapter in Arab-Kurdish relations seemed to have opened in 1958 when General Qassem liquidated the Iraqi monarchy in a military coup and established a republican regime in Baghdad. The provisional constitution of the new regime stated that 'Arabs and Kurds are equal partners in this nation and state, and the constitution guarantees the national rights of the Kurds within the Iraqi national entity.'[12] In effect, Qassem was not prepared to grant the Kurdish people political-national autonomy within Iraq, but intended to integrate the Kurds into the Iraqi people. The Kurds revolted again in 1961 under Mustafa Barazani and were able to establish by 1962 a *de facto* autonomous government in the Kurdish mountains; they managed also to defeat formidable expeditions despatched by the Iraqi army against their strongholds.

Further political negotiations and military engagements were conducted between the Kurdish rebels and the various Arab-Iraqi regimes during the period 1963–6, but produced no political solution to the conflict. In 1966 the Iraqi premier Abd al-Rahman al-Bazzaz declared a ceasefire and suggested that autonomous rights should be granted to the Kurds within a new countrywide decentralisation system. The negotiations which followed, however, were not concluded although the ceasefire continued until 1969. Not until 1970 was a political settlement finally reached between the two sides to the conflict, and this was essentially based on Bazzaz's programme. The 1970 agreement provided for autonomous political and cultural rights for the Kurds in their region and for Arab-Kurdish cooperation and brotherhood in the Iraqi state and government.[13] But once again the Arab-Iraqi regime did not fully keep the agreement and worked systematically to undermine Kurdish autonomy, weaken Kurdish strength and morale and create friction and conflicts within the people. The Kurdish national movement revolted again in 1974, but following an Iraqi-Iranian agreement in March 1975 the Kurds lost the vital support of Iran. The Iraqi army was then able to crush the Kurdish rebellion with great brutality, and seized control of the entire Kurdish region. Many Kurds were executed or deported and a measure of Arabisation has been fully enforced on the Kurdish nation of Iraq.

III MUSLIM-CHRISTIAN CONFLICT IN LEBANON

The intergroup conflict in the western part of the Fertile Crescent – in Lebanon – was of a different nature from that in Iraq or Palestine and accordingly has taken another form. Already in 1861 the Christian Maronites had succeeded in establishing an autonomous political entity in Mount Lebanon after a long and bloody struggle against the Druzes over the domination in that area.[14] But in 1920 the Maronite political predominance and numerical majority – some 80 per cent of the population – were drastically reduced with the creation of Great Lebanon by the French Mandatory government, for the districts which were then annexed to Mount Lebanon were mostly populated by Sunni

Islamic-Arabism versus Pluralism

Muslims (Beirut and Tripoli), Shi'i Muslims (southern and eastern districts), and some Greek Orthodox. Consequently, according to the 1932 Lebanese census, the Maronite majority group consisted of only 29 per cent of the total population, although together with other Christian groups – Greek Orthodox (10 per cent), Greek Catholics (6 per cent), Armenian (6 per cent) and others – The Christians held a slim majority of 54 per cent. The Muslim population was divided into several groups: Sunnis (some 21 per cent), Shi'is (some 18 per cent) and Druzes (some 6 per cent). These demographic changes not only served to weaken the position of the Maronites but also interfered with the process of founding a national Lebanese state based on the local Christian population. Yet, during the time of the French Mandate, the basic political, social and economic hegemony of the Christian Maronites was preserved both because of their marginal numerical majority and high socio-cultural standard, and owing to the strong backing they received from the French authorities. But when the French mandate terminated Christian Maronite leaders reached the conclusion that the preservation of the territorial unity and political independence of Lebanon required the inclusion in the government of non-Christian sects and the formation of a Lebanese multi-communal state where Christians would hold a dominant position. In 1943 the various leaders of the Lebanese groups came to an unofficial 'gentleman's agreement' known as the 'National Pact' which provided for the division of governmental authority according to a 'communal key' whereby the President would be a Christian Maronite, the Prime Minister a Sunni Muslim, the President of Parliament a Shi'ite-Muslim, etc. It also fixed a proportional representational system within the Parliament and government administration, with a ratio of six Christians to five Muslims. Thus for about a generation many Lebanese tended to comply with these arrangements and a measure of intergroup accommodation was achieved, and was seen as a model of Muslim-Christian coexistence in the Middle East.[15] This situation however, did not last long, as Arab nationalist and radical groups, for the last two or three decades, have demanded the abolition of the confessional regime, or to change the allocation of power in favour of the Muslim groups, while some even advocated the inclusion of Lebanon in a wider Arab state (Greater Syria).

These demands and tendencies were encouraged and promoted by pan-Arab groups and organs and by Arab nationalist regimes in Syria and Egypt. They reached a peak in 1958 with the union between Egypt and Syria under the leadership of Gamal Abdul Nasser, when Arab nationalist and radical leaders and groups in Lebanon organised a 'National Front' and vigorously demanded that their country should join the united Arab Republic. The 'National Front' called in May 1958 for a general strike which developed into virtually an armed rebellion, soon turning into a civil war between pan-Arab Muslims and pro-Lebanon Christians. At the end of this war, during which US forces landed in Lebanon, a compromise was reached whereby the Muslim elements gained strength in Lebanese power politics. This started simultaneously a process of gradual decline in Christian predominance, a process which abated after the Israel victory in the 1967 war. It revived and intensified later with the growing involvement of the Palestinian armed organisations in Lebanese affairs after the September 1970 events in Jordan. Following the 1973 Arab-Israeli war, Muslim and Arab nationalist pressures grew at a rapid pace, forcing the Christians to turn over some of their positions to the Muslims. Radical leftist elements and Palestinian rejectionist groups exploited the weakness of the Christians' establishment and on several occasions in February and again April 1975 used force against both government troops and against Maronite phalangist headquarters. These violent means provoked a fierce Maronite retaliation, setting off a second and more brutal Muslim-Christian Lebanese civil war in less than two decades. The civil war, which lasted some twenty months, resulted in tens of thousands of dead and wounded and hundreds of thousands of emigrants (mainly Christians), as well as the collapse of both the Lebanese economy and its government machinery.[16]

In the course of the war it became clear that the Christian Maronites were fighting no longer for their dominant position in Lebanon, but rather for their own lives and for the fate of their community. They were struggling not only against Muslim and radical groups within Lebanon but against several non-Lebanese Arab forces such as the Palestinian Fatah fighters, units of the 'Palestine Liberation Army' dispatched by Egypt and Syria, 'Sa'iqa' semi-regular forces partly staffed by Syrians, and the 'rejectionist' organisations which included Iraqi as well as other non-Lebanese guerrillas. But apart from military attacks the Maronites were also subject to political pressure by most Arab countries, which demanded a Muslim-Arab predominance in Lebanon. Arab-Muslim leaders were not satisfied with an equal sharing of power between Christians and Muslims as Syria had suggested. The prominent rector of Al-Azhar (the Muslim University in Cairo) declared that such an arrangement represented a plot against Islam and the Arabs, while Junior Muslim leaders in Lebanon called for a *Jihad* (holy war) against their Christian fellow-countrymen. Thus by February 1976 the various Arab Muslim and radical forces took control of some 70 per cent of the Lebanese territory, besieging the Christians in Mount Lebanon and in certain enclaves in Beirut. Syria – which had been helping the Arab Muslim and radical forces since the beginning of the war – intervened at that stage as she became worried lest Lebanon should be controlled by her ultra-radical rival – Iraq. Syrian leaders tried then to impose a political settlement whereby the Muslims and Christians of Lebanon would equally share the government, which – as expected by Syria – would be controlled from Damascus. But when this settlement was opposed by the Lebanese radicals and Palestinian guerrillas, Syria in June 1976 dispatched her regular troops into Lebanon; and for several months the Syrian soldiers, with the help of Maronite forces – fought the Palestinians and the radicals, and eventually were able to impose a 'Pax Syriana' on Lebanon. Thus for the last six months Lebanon has become virtually a Syrian protectorate wherein Lebanese Muslims and Christians equally share nominal authority. The Maronites in Mount Lebanon, however, have managed so far to maintain their autonomous position and even to set up their own machinery of government. Yet there should be no doubt that the Maronites – who are at the mercy of Damascus – have lost their dominant role in Lebanon alongside with the loss of Lebanese independence. Lebanon is from now on expected to undergo a process of radical change in her identity, namely a transformation from a predominantly Christian Western-oriented political community into a Syrian-patterned Muslim-oriented Arab polity. Indeed this process is likely to be influenced by, or adapted to, the Syrian experience of forging her various religious and ethnic groups into one national community.

IV. THE CASE OF SYRIA

Religious and ethnic intergroup conflict shaped socio-political life in Syria for generations. As early as the beginning of the 1870s a British resident observer in Damascus described the intergroup conflict in Syria as follows: 'They hate one another. The Sunnites excommunicate the Shiahs and both hate the Druzes, all detest the Ansariyyehs ('Alawites), the Maronites do not love anybody but themselves and are duly abhorred by all, the Greek Orthodox abominate the Greek Catholics and the Latins; all despise the Jews.'[17]

The Sunni Muslim majority was actually at the focus of the intergroup relationship. Not only did the Sunnis oppress or persecute the various minority groups; they also played off these groups one against the other. They would for example occasionally mobilise heterodox sects to attack Christians, or would join Christians who persecuted Jews. On other occasions Sunni Arab notables or the Sunni Turkish governors would employ or provoke ethnic groups of the Sunni Muslim faith – such as Kurds and Circassians – to fight against the heterodox sects, Druzes, 'Alawis and Shi'is.[18]

A. THE ROLE OF THE FRENCH MANDATE

The French Mandatory power which in 1920 succeeded Ottoman Turkish government in Syria tried in its own way to settle the intergroup tensions and conflicts, by encouraging local autonomy and separate development for various minority groups. They separated the Druze and the 'Alawi regions from Sunni Muslim Syria, granting them political autonomy and encouraging their communal education, jurisdiction, etc. Likewise, the Mandatory power placed the Christian-Kurdish-Arab region of the Jazira under special administration, divorced from the control of the Sunni Arab government in Damascus. The French also promoted and fostered the religious and cultural autonomy of various Christian groups, notably the Catholic and non-Arab communities.[19] These measures obviously strengthened isolationist or separatist tendencies among the various religions and ethnic groups, and conversely angered the Sunni Arab majority group and deepened its suspicion and animosity towards the minority groups. The tensions between the majority and minority groups were further strengthened as the French recruited soldiers from the minority groups and employed them periodically to crush Sunni Arab demonstrations and uprisings.

It is true that the Arab national movement in Mandated Syria aimed at doing away with the intercommunal cleavages and conflicts, and integrating all groups of the population into one Arab nation. It issued guidelines and slogans advocating religious tolerance, equal rights and patriotic brotherhood; and it even placed among its leadership several Christian personalities, mainly Greek Orthodox and Protestant. However the bulk of the Muslim and Christian population was not geared to coexist in one national community. The Muslim rank and file in the national movement, and certainly the Muslim masses, continued to express their objection to intergroup accommodation and equality through acts of violence against their Christian and heterodox fellow-countrymen. The Christians for their part, like the heterodox groups, continued mostly to fear or suspect the Muslims, and consequently to strengthen their political or/and cultural autonomy with French encouragement.[20]

But when the French Mandate terminated and Syria became an independent republic in 1946, the Syrian Arab government adopted a series of measures aiming at integrating the minority groups into an Arab Syrian nation state.

B. INTEGRATION OF MINORITY GROUPS IN POLITICAL LIFE

One of the first steps taken by the Syrian government after independence was to reduce or abolish communal representation in parliament, as part of the trend towards integration. Between 1947 and 1949, the parliamentary representation of the Christian communities was reduced from nineteen to fourteen delegates, the 'Alawis from seven to four, and the Druze from five to three delegates. The Jewish representation – one delegate – was abolished; and the Kurds, Turkomans and Circassians no longer had separate representation, but were included in the Arab Sunni majority. Under the Syrian dictator Adib Shishakli (1949–54) communal representation was further reduced, and in 1953 a bill completely abrogating the communal system in parliament was passed. Further legislation abolished the separate jurisdictional rights in matters of personal status which the French had granted the 'Alawis and the Druze. These communities, like the Shi'is and Ismailis, were now subject to Syrian law, though the Druze were granted some separate rights, similar to those enjoyed by their brethren in Lebanon. Shishakli also forbade the existence of communal clubs or associations, as well as regional and racial organisations – all of which were ordered to adopt Arabic names and hold all proceedings in Arabic (which also became the exclusive language in the state schools).

In addition to his Arabisation policy, Shishakli also fostered the Islamic character of the country and its public institutions. At least half of the members on every board of directors of every association in Syria had to be Muslims; and in a draft constitution prepared under Shishakli's supervision in 1950 Islam was established as the state religion – in contrast to the 1930 Mandatory constitution, in which Islam was merely the president's religion.

This series of orders and regulations sparked agitation among the minority groups. The various Christian minorities resented and vehemently protested against this infringement of their parliamentary representation and the intention to declare Islam the official religion. As a result, and following pressure by Christian and other members of parliament, the 1950 constitution – and later also the 1953 constitution – declared that Islam was the president's religion. Some Armenians, on the other hand, who were also hurt by the Arabisation of the educational system, preferred to emigrate from Syria, while the Kurdish tribes of Jazira (which also had suffered from Shishakli's anti-tribal policy) showed signs of restlessness and agitation. But whereas these minorities were not strong enough to resist or endanger the central government, the Druze and 'Alawis had military power and favourable topographical conditions which enabled them to sustain their autonomy, although not for long.

The Syrian authorities, immediately after independence, made great efforts to destroy the military and political strength of the Druze and 'Alawis and to impose the central government's authority. In the summer of 1946, for example, the government sent a large force to Jabal Ansariyya to fight an 'Alawi uprising: the rebels were defeated and their leader was sentenced to death and executed.

In 1952, another 'Alawi uprising was quickly subdued, and their region became completely subject to government control.

In contrast, the Syrian government initially feared to challenge the Druze on the battlefield and preferred to weaken them by fostering a rivalry between two Druze factions. Subsequently military forces were sent to Jabal Druze to enforce conscription and disarm and subdue the inhabitants. The Druze reacted by participating energetically in the coup against the government. Shishakli continued the anti-Druze campaign and ordered the arrest of Druze leaders for taking part in an alleged pro-Hashemite plot and in a conspiracy with foreign elements against the regime. As a result, a big uprising broke out at the beginning of 1954 in Jabal Druze, but was soon crushed by the Syrian army using tanks and aircraft.

The crushing of the Druze revolt in 1954 became a turning-point in the balance of power between the communities. The Arab-Sunni government for the first time achieved decisive military superiority over these centrifugal forces through the use of sophisticated weapons and a big and well-trained army; the seclusion and political autonomy of these elements was terminated. From then on, the heterodox communities began to take an increasing part in political life and in the struggles for power which took place in the country, both within the parties – mainly the Ba'th party – and through the army. They thus became involved in a process of integration which had begun some time before with other minority groups, mainly Orthodox and Protestant-Christians and Kurdish urban elements.[21]

For example, in the 1954 elections, sixteen Christians were elected to the Syrian parliament; some of these and others held leading positions on the political scene of the 1950s as party leaders, ministers, and prime ministers. Personalities of Kurdish origin too played important roles in Syrian politics of that period.

Similarly, Druze and 'Alawi personalities began to participate in the political life of Syria within the framework of the military groups and the political parties. 'Alawi officers, for instance, commanded the Syrian air force; in the early 1950s Druze officers were actively involved in the military coups which occurred at that period, while Druze leaders served in senior government positions.

It must, however, be emphasised that a considerable number of these politicians and officers, especially the Druze and 'Alawis, still possessed strong communal solidarity and a close attachment to their communities. They tended to appoint members of their groups as assistants or bodyguards and army officers, and some even gave preference to communal interests when they were at odds with those of the state. The communities themselves, on the other hand, had strong sentiments of identification with their representatives in the army and the government, and many youngsters joined the armed forces and the new dynamic Ba'th party. These trends paved the way for the ascent of young members of the minority groups, notably 'Alawis, to the centre of power of present-day Syria: the Ba'th military regime.

The Arab Socialist Resurrection (Ba'th) party, which was originally established at the end of 1953, consisted of members with a heterogeneous social background, and communal affiliation. On the one hand, its members were drawn from the new middle class, the intelligentsia, and the young bourgeoisie: most came from the big cities, especially Damascus, and in part they were Sunni Muslims and in part Christian Orthodox, Protestant, and others. On the other hand, the party absorbed Sunni peasants and workers of the Syrian lowlands, as well as 'Alawi, Druze, and Ismaili youngsters who had joined the party during the 1950s. In spite of the growing number of Ba'th members from the lower strata, the party was mainly run by members of the urban middle class, pioneers in the struggle against the traditional ruling elite. But the Ba'th activists among the urban intelligentsia were worn out in the political struggle of 1954–8 and lost their power during the period of the union with Egypt, 1958–61, whereas the rural minority elements within the party gained strength through the central focus of power in the state – the army. Young people from the minorities were drawn to the army in increasing numbers, hoping to improve their social and economic status. Some of these young men were sent to officers' courses or promoted by senior Ba'th officers who were seeking to strengthen their influence by increasing the number of their followers – members of their community or party – in the officers' cadre. These new and young officers, many of them 'Alawis or Druze, quickly rose in the military hierarchy, while the veteran officers' cadre, mostly Sunni Muslims, was shattered following the military coup of 1949–54, the struggle for power in the army during 1954–8, and the big purges in the officers' cadre during the union with Egypt and in 1961–62.

C. 'ALAWIS SEIZE POWER

Those young officers of minority origin were the backbone of the March 1963 Ba'th revolution. They established a new regime in the name of the Ba'th, since most of them were party members or sympathisers and considered themselves bound by its mission – though in many ways they deviated from the original course of the Ba'th. They used the party to legitimise their regime but did not allow any real power to the veteran leadership. At the end of 1964, they completely excluded the veteran leadership from the political life of Syria: while Amin al-Hafiz, leader of the young officers, established himself as ruler of Syria.

But then a fierce struggle took place in the top ranks of the new regime. This struggle has continued up to the present, with climaxes in February 1966 and November 1970 taking place between communal groups and personalities, as well as military and civilian factions.

Thus in 1965, a power struggle occurred between General Amin al-Hafiz, the strong man, and General Salah Jadid, the chief of staff and former ally of al-Hafiz in their joint struggle against the veteran civilian leadership. Salah Jadid (an 'Alawi) surrounded himself with officers of 'Alawi and Druze origin and strove to seize power whereas al-Hafiz, a Sunni Muslim, relied upon his former rivals, members of the civilian leadership, who were mostly Sunni Muslims. The Jadid faction, however, controlled the centres of power in the army, air force, armoured corps and commandos, and in February 1966 they seized power and unseated their rivals by means of a *coup d'état*.

Following the coup, the temporary and unprecedented cooperation between 'Alawi and Druze officers was terminated. The 'Alawi officers' cadre, led by Salah Jadid and Hafiz al-Asad, commander of the air force, enjoyed a clear numerical and tactical superiority in the army command and the party leadership. They overcame the Druze faction and removed it from key positions.

Further dismissals and purges carried out among the regime's top ranks were also of a communal nature. For example, three members of the Jundi family, of Ismaili origin, which had controlled sensitive key positions, were discharged. Following the 1967 war, a Sunni faction within the regime were also dismissed for their reservations concerning the strengthening of the 'Alawi element in the government.

However, communal affiliation was not the only factor in the struggle for power among the Syrian top ranks in the 1960s. Other factors at times overcame communal loyalty, e.g. personal and factional interests, one manifestation of which was the continuous struggle for power between Salah Jadid and Hafiz al-Asad, heads of the ruling 'Alawi faction. This contest, which began behind the scenes in 1966, erupted in September 1969 and was concluded with Asad's victory in November 1970. This rivalry between the 'Alawi leaders obviously also had political aspects: they disagreed on foreign policy and security issues, or on economic and other domestic matters.

Yet both 'Alawi leaders were confronted with a major dilemma, namely: how to sustain their regime *vis-à-vis* the Sunni Muslim majority which regarded it as a minority 'Alawi rule, or what should be done in order to achieve an intergroup accommodation in Ba'thi Syria without endangering the 'Alawi regime.

The two 'Alawi leaders adopted different politics in an attempt to solve this dilemma; but neither of them could afford to give up the 'Alawi military basis on which their regimes had rested since their ascendancy.

D. THE MECHANISM OF THE 'ALAWI ELITE IN POWER:
  JADID COMPARED TO ASAD

Both the governments of Salah Jadid (1966–70) and Hafiz Asad (1970–) enjoyed the 'Alawi military support upon which the Ba'th regime has depended since the coup of February 1966.

Salah Jadid had been gradually building this support since the Ba'th officers seized power in 1963. Following the coup, Jadid was appointed Army Chief of Personnel, and by the end of the year he had become Army Chief of Staff. In both capacities Jadid followed a policy of discharging officers who had been in the opposition camp from important or sensitive positions. Simultaneously, officers loyal to him were appointed, particularly those of his own community. He urged 'Alawi reserve officers to join the army, sent them to the Military Academy, and assigned them to staff positions. These 'Alawi officers, both veterans and newcomers, occupied senior or sensitive positions in such select army units as the armoured corps, commandos, air force, and artillery.[22]

Hafiz Asad, who overthrew his fellow 'Alawi, Salah Jadid, continued to rely upon the 'Alawi officer cadre. He strengthened and upgraded it and entrenched it in key posts in the various branches of the armed forces, particularly in select fighting units. Following his predecessor's practice, Asad placed his brother Rifat in command of an elite unit of the armoured forces in charge of the security of vital centres in the Damascus area.

Most of the 'Alawi officers who had been loyal to Jadid apparently transferred their support to Hafiz Asad once it became clear that he was in control of the government. The 'Alawi officer cadre has recognised that its fate is tied to that of Asad, that under his leadership it has a guarantee of security and advancement. But it can anticipate extinction if Asad is overthrown.

Nevertheless, it should be stressed that not all senior and sensitive posts in Syria are monopolised by 'Alawi officers. Many positions, including some of the most important, are filled by officers with Sunni Muslim or other communal affiliation. These individuals may be grouped into three categories: professional officers who are not involved in politics, officers of the Ba'th affiliation who identify with the government and do not view it as an 'Alawi regime, and others who hope to further their military careers by exploiting the government's need for their professional skill. Among these officers there seem to be a noticeable number of members of other minority groups – Christian, Druze, and Ismaili. Hafiz Asad has apparently sought to gain the friendship of the minority groups in order to build an intergroup alliance for his government. He possibly also recognised that the minorities, in contrast to the Sunnis, would not pose a threat to 'Alawi dominance in the armed forces. Simultaneously Asad has tried also to foster loyalty to his regime among the Sunni Muslim majority group, soldiers and civilians alike.

As far as the Sunni soldiers are concerned, the military framework enables Asad to educate the officers and soldiers in a uniform, systematic manner, and thus to forge the army into a loyal, stable base of support for the regime and a melting-pot for the new Syrian political community. The major challenge for the regime, however, has been to overcome the opposition of the Sunni Muslim majority population to the rule of a minority group in the country.

E. THE REGIME'S CIVILIAN AND POPULAR CAST

Indeed, the 'Alawi officers who seized power in February 1966 faced a double dilemma. In order to legitimise their government, they had to prove that it was not a military but a civilian regime, and that it was not 'Alawi-dominated, but represented the entire population. Thus, immediately after the coup, the leaders of the new government disbanded the National Council of the Revolutionary Command which had exercised supreme authority since March 1963. In its place they formed a civilian government which rested chiefly upon the left-wing faction of the Ba'th party, which was identified with the regional (Syrian) Ba'th leadership.

Most of the posts in this Ba'th government, including the presidency, premiership and many of the cabinet ministries, were filled by civilians rather than military men – the great majority by Sunni Muslims. Only two of the three military men in the Cabinet were 'Alawis, the senior being Hafiz Asad who served as Minister of Defence. Salah Jadid himself did not have a ministerial position, and controlled the regime through his party function – Assistant Secretary-General.

By so doing the 'Alawi governing group has tried to avoid projecting the image of a military-communal clique ruling the country by force. While the 'Alawis wanted to safeguard their dominance in the armed forces, they have also sought to de-emphasise their group origin and make it appear irrelevant to political and social life. For as long as they are identified as members of a heterodox minority community, the difference between them and the majority Sunni Muslim population could not be ignored. Therefore, apart from the civilian Sunni cabinet they formed, the 'Alawi rulers have presented themselves, and want others to view them, as Syrian Arabs in every respect, participating with their fellow-citizens belonging to other groups, in a supra-group society. In order to build this image, the leaders of the Ba'th regime have endeavoured to establish a new political community in Syria, founded upon values shared by the great majority of the population.[23] An effort has been made to nurture the most important common conception – the Arab national and cultural identity which is deeply rooted within the consciousness of about 85 per cent of the population (excluding the Kurds, Armenians, Turcomans and other non-Arab ethnic groups).

Another concept shared by many is the sense of local (Syrian) patriotism which both Jadid and Asad sought to reinforce, by endeavouring to turn Syria into a factor of importance in the Arab world and the international community. A related, if negative, concept also shared by the majority of the Syrians is the ideology of anti-Zionism and opposition to the existence of the State of Israel. The government has done much to glorify this ideology and express it in practical terms.

Undoubtedly the promotion of these concepts has helped create a new Syrian national community in which the 'Alawis can participate as equal members. But that has not been sufficient. The Syrian population, composed mainly of Sunni Muslims, has a long tradition of Sunni identification and dominance together with an attitude of superiority, suspicion and antagonism towards the heterodox minority groups. This is especially so regarding the 'Alawis, who for centuries have been considered religious deviants, if not heretics, and as socially inferior.

In order to uproot these traditional prejudices and integrate the Sunni Muslim population into a national community encompassing all communities it is most important to erase the entrenched religious communal basis of Syrian political and social life. In other words, the heads of the 'Alawi Ba'th regime have had to try and blur religious-communal differences, by separating religion from the state, and/or by secularising public life. This issue has been indeed a major challenge and indeed the main obstacle in the 'Alawi attempt at establishing an intergroup accommodation within a new Syrian national community.

F. OPPOSITION TO JADID'S 'ALAWI REGIME (1966–70)

Despite the civilian character of the Ba'th government, its far-reaching socio-economic reforms, and extreme anti-West and anti-Israel policies, Jadid's regime was not popular among large segments of the population. Except for the small, though cohesive, group of Ba'th supporters – party members and sympathisers, radical-left intellectuals, and some farmer and labour elements – the regime encountered strong and widespread opposition. It came not only from members of the upper and middle classes, mostly Sunni Muslims who were hard hit by the government's nationalisation policies and rigid socialist reforms. In particular, the masses of orthodox Sunni Muslims headed by their religious leaders, the 'Ulama, opposed Jadid's secularist policies which sought to separate the state and Islam and to circumscribe the influence of Muslim leaders. The Christian communities also protested against the government's interference in their religious communal affairs, particularly the restrictions placed upon Christian religious studies, and the nationalisation of the Christian schools (carried out in September 1967). In addition broad groups within the Muslim, Christian and even Druze populations were angered by what they regarded as an 'Alawi domination over the government being carried out by controlling the military centres of power.

This resentment found sharp expression even among the veteran leaders of the Ba'th who were opposed to a military government that allegedly lacked the support of the party and the masses. For example, the former Secretary-General of the party called the Ba'th regime a ruthless military clique without precedent in Syrian history and denounced the 'sectarian grouping' of the 'Alawis in the officers' cadre under the Salah Jadid.[24]

The reaction of the Sunni Muslims was even fiercer and indeed violent. In May 1967 general strikes and demonstrations broke out in the major Syrian cities against the 'Alawi 'atheist' regime. Some of these demonstrations were led jointly by Muslim 'Ulama and Christian clergymen – a unique event in Syrian history.

The sharp unrest within the Syrian population increased after the war of June 1967 following rumours that the military leaders had sent Sunni units into battle against Israel while keeping the 'Alawi units around Damascus to protect the regime.

Despite the growing unrest there was no organised group in Syria capable of overthrowing the government and seizing control. This was mainly due to the unopposed dominance of the 'Alawi officer cadre in the army, which constitute the solid although narrow foundation of the minority Ba'th regime.

G. ASAD'S NEW POLICIES REGARDING INTERGROUP ACCOMMODATION

Yet it became apparent during the late 1960s that a growing number of 'Alawi officers – led by Hafiz Asad, then number two in the 'Alawi hierarchy – were pleased neither with the character of their regime, nor with its domestic policies regarding intergroup relations. They evidently feared that the increasing unpopularity of the government and its public identification with the 'Alawi minority group could eventually lead to the complete discrediting of the 'Alawis in the armed forces and in Syrian society. In the long run it might even endanger their very physical existence. These considerations, together with Asad's appetite for power, apparently exacerbated his struggle with Jadid which ended in November 1970 with the victory of Asad and his military supporters.

After taking control, Asad worked methodically to create a more positive image of the new Ba'th government, and in the first place he displayed sensitivity concerning intergroup relations among the population.

Asad's efforts were directed mainly toward the majority Sunni Muslim group, and some of his measures were especially geared to conciliate conservative Muslim sectors. Thus, for example, in June 1971 he restored to the Syrian Constitution the old Islamic format of the presidential oath, 'I swear by Allah Akbar,' which had been deleted by Jadid from the 1969 provisional Constitution. In February 1973 he added to the Constitution a clause providing that the President of the country must be a Muslim. This clause had initially been abolished by Jadid in 1969, and did not appear in the draft of the permanent Constitution of 1973.[25]

Asad also sought to strengthen his own image as a loyal Muslim: since assuming office, he has participated in prayers and religious ceremonies in various mosques, and also made a 'Little Hajj' (pilgrimage to Mecca) in February 1974, when he visited King Faisal of Saudi Arabia. That same month he participated in the Islamic Conference in Pakistan. On the domestic scene he made favourable gestures to Islamic religious leaders by distributing honours to them, promoting them in rank, increasing their salaries, etc. In return, Asad was 'certified' as a Muslim by Sunni Muslim leaders (the 'Ulama) including the Mufti of Damascus. He also succeeded in obtaining, from the Shi'i religious leader in Lebanon, confirmation that the 'Alawis are Shi'is and therefore belong to the Muslim community.

These efforts have been obviously directed to emphasise Asad's recognition of Islam as the majority religion and, as such, a basic notion shared by most of the Syrian population. Toward the same end, Asad has endeavoured to blur the differences between the various Muslim communities in Syria – the Sunnis, and non-Sunnis – to stress that

Islam is their common faith and way of life.

At the same time, Asad continued to strengthen another central notion which also serves as a common denominator for the great majority of the population: Arab nationalism and culture. He has harnessed all the media toward this goal, particularly utilising the Syrian school system which is expanding at an impressive rate and providing a national Arab education for the youth.

The Arab nationalist image of the Asad government has also been strengthened by his pan-Arab policy. In contrast to Salah Jadid, whose policies led to Syria's isolation in the Arab world, Asad has sought a closer cooperation with most, if not all, Arab states and particularly Egypt. In November 1970, immediately after Asad came to power, Syria joined the Federation of Arab Republics - Egypt, Libya, and Sudan. Subsequently, Asad has worked steadily to improve or renew relations with the conservative Arab states - Saudi Arabia, Kuwait, and Jordan.

The October 1973 war won full approval of all Arabs for Asad's government; his participation in the war together with Egypt raised his personal prestige and strengthened his position in the Arab world.

And finally his vigorous policy against Israel - the enemy of the Arab nation - since 1973 has rendered him the image of a great pan-Arab leader.

V CONCLUSIONS

In conclusion it can be stated that the major source of intergroup conflict in the Middle East has been the conception of Arab and Islamic uniformity and domination professed and practised by the majority Arab-Muslim population; and combined with this, its intolerant attitudes towards the national and cultural aspirations of the non-Arab and non-Muslim minority groups. It has been argued by Muslims and Arabs that Islam always stood for tolerance of the 'people of the book' - both Christians and Jews; and that these tolerant attitudes were manifested by the *millet* system which granted autonomy to the Christian and Jewish communities under Islamic rule - in matters of religious worship and education and jurisdiction of personal status. This *millet* system, it has been said, provided for centuries a solid basis for accommodation between Muslims and non-Muslims. However, as has been shown in this paper, the intergroup accommodation under Islamic rule was dictated by the Muslims and carried out on their terms only. Christian and Jewish groups were treated as second or third-class subjects in the Muslim state and were neither accepted as equal citizens in the political community, nor allowed to enjoy autonomous political rights in the Muslim state. And when they insisted on obtaining these rights they were exposed to violent attacks. As for the heterodox groups, they were not allowed even to practise their religion, being officially subject to oppression or alternatively to conversion to Islam by force.

It has been also argued by Arabs that Arab nationalism and the modern Arab states could not grant political autonomy or independence to non-Arab national minorities, lest these entities undermine the political fabric of the Arab states and the Arab world.

Instead, it is said, the modern Arab states have worked to create new political communities, whereby all citizens are equal members and enjoy full political cultural and religious rights. In fact, however, most Arab states declare Islam as their official religion and accordingly discriminate against or persecute their non-Sunni Muslim citizens. Even in Syria, where a substantial measure of political integration was achieved, the non-Sunni 'Alawi elite has been bound to adjust its constitution and policies in accordance with the Orthodox Islamic conceptions.

Regarding the non-Arab groups in the Arab states, they have normally not enjoyed full cultural rights, let alone full political privileges; nor were they allowed to form politico-national entities even in areas where they constituted a majority.

It is true that several Arab leaders suggested plans to avoid or solve the grave intergroup conflicts in the Fertile Crescent by means of federal systems which would comprise non-Arab or non-Muslim autonomous entities within Arab states. However, these plans were either rejected by the bulk of Arab leadership and population because of their deviationism from the norms of Arab nationalism; or were unacceptable to the non-Arab groups because they did not provide for real politico-national autonomy. Even those programmes which provided for such autonomy were not implemented, as was the case with all other plans to settle the intergroup conflicts by way of compromise. Thus for example in 1919 Amir Faysal, the ruler of Syria, and a delegation of nationalist leaders from Syria each suggested the creation of a Jewish entity in Palestine to be linked with the Arab state of Syria. According to the Faysal-Weizmann agreement Jewish Palestine was to become an independent state and to be in close cooperation with the Arab state in Syria. Faysal later on clarified that in (Greater) Syria

Islamic-Arabism versus Pluralism

there was room for the two nationalist movements, i.e. the Arab and the Jewish. The Syrian delegation to the Paris Peace Conference stated that Palestine constituted the southern part of Syria and that it should become an autonomous Jewish region linked with Syria by federal ties. Yet it should be indicated that these suggestions were made at a time when the Arabs themselves sought their independence and needed the support of Britain and American Jewry to achieve their goals. At any rate the Arab nationalist movement in Syria and Palestine overwhelmingly rejected these suggestions and emphasised that Palestine was wholly Arab and Muslim.

The idea of a Jewish autonomous region, or canton, in Palestine, within a Greater Syria Federation or unity – was carried on into the interwar period by Prince, later King, Abdullah of Jordan. And in 1942 two Hashemite schemes – for a Greater Syria unity and for a Fertile Crescent Federation – were issued by King Abdullah of Jordan and Premier Nuri Sa'id of Iraq respectively. The latter plan, for example, provided for 'semi-autonomy' for the Jews in Palestine, i.e. 'the right to their own rural and urban district administration including schools, health institutes and police, subject to general supervision by the Syrian state'.[26] Regarding the Maronites this plan stated: 'that if they demand it, the Maronites in the Lebanon shall be granted a privileged regime such as they possessed during the last years of the Ottoman Empire.'[27]

To the Maronites in Lebanon and the Jews in Palestine these suggestions were unacceptable since they did not go far enough to meet their national expectations. But even the Arab nationalists in Syria, Lebanon, Iraq and Palestine vehemently rejected these schemes as going too far in granting concessions to both the Jews and Maronites, and as having been allegedly initiated by British 'imperialism'.

If this was the attitude towards these federation schemes, it is not surprising that the Arab nationalists in the Middle East strongly opposed the Palestine Partition Schemes in 1937 and 1947 which were accepted by the League of Nations and the United Nations respectively. These schemes provided for the establishment of a Jewish State in parts of Palestine, whereas the other parts were to be incorporated into Transjordan as an independent Arab state (1937) or to become a separate Palestinian state (1947). The Arab Palestinian Leaders – both nationalist and 'moderate' – likewise rejected Jewish or British proposals to establish an Arab-Jewish bi-national state in Palestine, based on a cantonal federal system. They were uncompromisingly opposed to any form of Jewish national autonomy in Palestine, which they regarded as a serious danger to Arabism and Islam.

By the same token the Arab nationalists, particularly in Syria and Lebanon, acted against the establishment of an independent Lebanese state which would be multi-communal. Christian-dominated and 'dismembered' from Arab-Muslim Syria. Even when Lebanon became an independent multi-religious state in 1943 Arab nationalist leaders, especially those of Syria, did not abandon their aim to annex Lebanon to Syria or turn it into a Muslim-dominated state. They tried to achieve both of these goals by violent means in 1958 and again in 1975-76. And although in 1958 these attempts failed, it seems now that Lebanon is fast losing its plural character and is likely to become a Syrian-dominated Muslim-oriented uniform Arab state.

A similar development has been taking place in yet another multi-ethnic Middle Eastern society – the Iraqi society. Here again, the Arab Sunni group which constituted only about 20 per cent of the total population has strongly objected for the last half-century to the formation of an Arab-Kurdish bi-national state, or to granting a national and cultural autonomy to the Iraqi Kurds.[28] During the last two years the ruling Arab group has been able violently to crush the virtual autonomy of the Kurds and forcibly impose upon them measures of Arabisation.

Finally, in the case of Syria the tendencies to promote Muslim-oriented Arab uniformity have not ceased even under the domination of the 'Alawi non-Sunni minority group, which for generations itself struggled for religious autonomy and for a multi-communal society – *vis-à-vis* the attempts of the Sunni Muslim majority at Arab-Muslim homogeneity.

Indeed, since the 'Alawi leaders seized control of the country, they have worked systematically to blur the differences between the various groups and to emphasise the Arab character of the society, and lately also, its Islamic way of life. The 'Alawi elite has carried out this policy of Muslim-oriented Arab cultural and ideological uniformity not for the sake of national integration *per se*, but also in order to sustain its domination in Syria. To achieve this goal a minority such as the 'Alawi group is bound to do away with religious and ethnic pluralism and ride upon the powerful tides of Arab-Islamic cultural-national uniformity. At present the only ethnic and religious groups which carry on their struggle against the powerful forces of Arab-Islamic homogeneity are the Jews of Israel and the Christians of Lebanon. These two groups still represent the surviving elements of pluralism in the Middle East.

NOTES

1. For definitions and divisions of the religious and ethnic groups in the Middle East see A. H. Hourani, *Minorities in the Arab World* (OUP, 1947) pp. 1–14; P. Rondot, 'Minorities in the Arab Orient Today', *Middle Eastern Affairs*, June–July 1959.
2. On the status of the non-Muslim subjects see G. E. von Gruenbaum, *Medieval Islam* (Chicago, 1953) ch. 6.
3. See R. H. Davison, 'Turkish Attitudes Concerning Christian-Muslim Equality in the Nineteenth Century', *American Historical Review* (July 1954) pp. 844–64.
4. See for example M. Ma'oz, *Ottoman Reform in Syria and Palestine* (Oxford 1968) pp. 200ff.
5. See for example ibid., pp. 108ff.
6. See Salman Falah, 'A History of the Druze Settlements in Palestine during the Ottoman period', in M. Ma'oz (ed.), *Studies on Palestine During the Ottoman Period* (Jerusalem, 1975) p. 12.
7. On pan-Arabian and its Islamic elements see H. E. Tutsch, *Facets of Arab Nationalism* (Detroit, 1965).
8. S. Lavan, 'Four Christian Arab Nationalists: A Comparative Study', *The Muslim World*, vol. 57 (1967) pp. 114–15.
9. See G. Wakin, 'The Copts in Egypt', *Middle Eastern Affairs*, vol. 12 (1961) pp. 198–208.
10. See E. Sivan, 'The Kurds: Another Perspective', in W. A. Veenhoven (ed.), *Case Studies on Human rights and Fundamental Freedoms* (The Hague, 1975) vol II, p. 144.
11. For details see ibid.
12. *Le Monde*, 29 July 1952.
13. See Sivan, op. cit., p. 155.
14. See K. S. Salibi, *The Modern History of Lebanon* (London, 1965) pp. 106ff.
15. For studies on various aspects of confessionalism in Lebanon, see L. Binder (ed.), *Politics in Lebanon* (New York, 1966).
16. For an account of the Lebanese Civil War, see M. Ma'oz, 'Homogeneity and Pluralism in the Middle East – The Case of Lebanon' in W. A. Veenhoven (ed.), *Case Studies on Human Rights and Fundamental Freedoms* (The Hague, 1976) vol. 3, pp. 181–208.
17. I. Burton, *The Inner Life of Syria* (London, 1875) pp. 105–6.
18. See M. Ma'oz, *Ottoman Reform in Syria*, op. cit., pp. 108–28.
19. S. H. Longrigg, *Syria and Lebanon under French Mandate* (London, 1958) pp. 123ff., 207ff.
20. See M. Ma'oz, 'Society and State in Modern Syria', in M. Milson (ed.), *Society and Political Structure in the Arab World* (New York, 1973) pp. 57–8.
21. For details see ibid., pp. 68ff.
22. For details and reference see M. Ma'oz, ''Alawi Military Officers in Syrian Politics, 1966–1974', in H. Z. Schiffrin (ed.), *Military and State in Modern Asia* (Jerusalem, 1976) pp. 214ff.

23. For an elaborated study on this conception see M. Ma'oz, 'Attempts at Creating a Political Community in Modern Syria', *Middle East Journal* (avtumn 1972) pp. 389–404.
24. M. Seymour, 'The Dynamics of Power in Syria Since the Break with Egypt', *Middle Eastern Studies*, vol. IV (1970) p. 39.
25. For more details see M. Ma'oz, 'The Background of the Struggle over the Role of Islam in Syria', *New Outlook*, vol. XVI (May 1973) pp. 13–18.
26. General Nuri al-Sa'id, 'Fertile Crescent Scheme' in J. C. Hurewitz (ed.), *Diplomacy in the Near and Middle East* (Princeton 1956) II, pp. 236–7.
27. Ibid.
28. D. Kinnane, *The Kurds and Kurdistan* (London, 1964), pp. 35ff., 54ff.

FURTHER REFERENCES

A. J. Arberry (ed.), *Religion in the Middle East* (Cambridge University Press, 1969).
H. Arfa, *The Kurds*, (Oxford University Press, 1966).
G. Baer, *Population and Society in the Arab World* (London, 1964).
M. Berger, *The Arab World Today* (New York, 1964).
R. B. Betts, *Christians in the Arab East* (Athens, 1975).
L. Binder (ed.), *Politics in Lebanon* (New York, 1966).
R. H. Davison, 'Turkish Attitudes Concerning Christian-Muslim Equality in the Nineteenth Century', *American Historical Review* (1953–4) pp. 344–862.
S. C. Dodd, *Social Relations in the Near East* (Beirut, 1940).
A. R. Ghassemlou, *Kurdistan and the Kurds* (Prague, 1965).
S. D. Goitein, *Jews and Arabs* (New York, 1955).
R. M. Haddad, *Syrian Christians in Muslim Society* (Princeton, 1970).
J. Joseph, *The Nestorians and their Muslim Neighbours* (Princeton, 1961).
J. M. Landau, *The Arabs in Israel* (London, 1969).
S. Landshut, *Jewish Communities in the Muslim Countries of the Middle East* (London, 1950).
W. Z. Laquer, *The Arab-Israel Reader* (London, 1968).
S. U. Longrigg, *The Middle East: A Social Geography* (London, 1963).
L. M. Meo, *Lebanon, Improbable Nation* (Bloomington, 1965).
B. Nikitine, *Les Kurds* (Paris, 1965).
N. Safran, *From War to War, The Arab-Israeli Confrontation 1948–1967* (New York, 1969).
A. K. Sanjian, *The Armenian Communities in Syria under Ottoman Dominion* (Mass., 1965).
F. Tassud, *The Cry of Egypt's Copts* (New York, 1951).
I. C. Vanly, *Le Kurdistan Irakies entite nationale* (Neuchatel, 1970).
E. Wakin, *A Lonely Minority: The Modern History of Egypt's Copts* (New York, 1963).

7 Patterns of Intergroup Accommodation in Southeast Asia: Is Democratic Pluralism Possible?

Justus M. van der Kroef
Charles Anderson Dana Professor of Political Science and Chairman of the Department of Political Science in the University of Bridport, Connecticut

I THE COMMUNIST PARTY OF MALAYA: AN EXAMPLE OF ACCOMMODATION

Today, and for the past two decades, a self-styled 'liberation army' of the Communist Party of Malaya (CPM) has waged a guerrilla campaign of ambushes and terrorist attacks along the Thai-Malaysian frontier, operating in the jungly crescent from North-eastern Kedah, across Perak, into Northern Kelantan. Integrating itself with the richly varied frontier population of the region, the CPM's 'regiments' have established something of an underground counter-government on both sides of the border, collecting 'taxes' from local rubber tappers and peasants, providing staff to and recruiting students from covert Chinese youth groups and 'Chinese culture' courses, encouraging a secessionist movement of dissident Muslims in such southern Thai provinces as Pattani and Yala, openly 'patrolling' (until recently) parts of the Thai border district of Betong which juts into Malaysia's Perak state, and so on. The CPM's own composition reflects the heterogeneity of the frontier population among which, despite party factional quarrels and despite the periodic intensification of a joint Thai-

Malaysian counter-insurgency campaign, it continues to operate with such relative ease.

At the beginning of 1976, the Malaysian Home Affairs Minister, Tan Sri Ghazali Shafie, with remarkable precision, pinpointed the total number of CPM insurgents at 2054, divided as follows: 732 'Malaysians of Chinese origin', 107 'Malaysians of Malay origin', 661 Thais 'of Chinese origin', 509 'Thai Muslims', 23 Malaysian Chinese 'claiming to be Muslim converts', two Malaysians of Indian origin, seven other ethnic Thais, 11 Malaysian *Orang Asli* (i.e. indigenous tribals), and two Japanese, both 'stragglers' from occupation forces in World War II.[1] One hastens to add that most other non-official estimates put the CPM's strength closer to three thousand, while the CPM's informal support network of sympathisers in the border villages – particularly important in providing intelligence and supplies – is believed to number an additional six to seven thousand.

It is however not so much the size of the CPM organisation that needs to be considered here but rather its heterogeneity. Not only have ethnic Chinese (both Thai and Malaysian), Malays, Indians, and even some indigenous tribals all apparently found it possible to join in a common political and violent action against their governments, but several hundred Muslims as well. Apart from the fact that in Southeast Asia cooperative ventures between adherents of Islam on the one hand, and of Marxism-Leninism and/or Maoism (the CPM is officially committed to 'Mao Tse-tung Thought') on the other have been rare and relatively tenuous, it is to be noted that to be a Muslim in the Thai-Malaysian border zone itself demands furtner categorisation because of the significant linguistic and cultural variations among this population group. Thus, Muslims in the Eastern Thai-Malaysian border zone (e.g. in the Malaysian state of Kelantan, and in the Thai provinces of Narathiwat and Yala) primarily speak Malay, while those in the Western border area (e.g. in the Thai province of Songkhla, and a little under 10 per cent of indigenous Muslims in the adjoining Malaysian state of Kedah) predominantly speak Thai. The latter tend to be perceived by other local Malaysian Muslims who are predominantly Malay-speaking as somehow of a more distinctively 'mixed blood' character, and hence are denigratingly dubbed '*Samsam*'.[2] Even so bilingualism, and among Chinese even trilingualism, is a frequent occurrence in this border area.

As a particular political microcosm of the very rich ethnic and racial mixtures common to many present-day Southeast Asian countries the CPM is perhaps representative, although few parties or movements, even among Communist organisations in this region, can match the diversity of background of the CPM's members. But it is of course not bi- or trilingual ability, or even relative uniformity of personal economic experience or, again, similarity of social status antecedents among CPM members that is the chief explanation of such intergroup accommodation that the party organisation shows. For example none of the presently known Politburo members or other leaders of the party have distinctively proletarian or peasant backgrounds. It is rather the CPM's ideology and its members' commitment to that ideology that constitute the major mechanism of mutual adjustment and which permits, for example, the operation of a distinctive 'regiment' within the CPM's 'liberation army' composed entirely of Malay Muslims, who have their own eating facilities (pork is forbidden them by Islam's dietary laws) separate from those of their Chinese comrades-in-arms (for whom pork is virtually a dietary staple).

In the Southeast Asian area ideology, whether religious or political, as well as language, race, ethnic background and economic activity (often a determinant of social class) are all so many variables in the intergroup accommodation process. Political systems in the region, whether at the local or national levels, exhibit a changing kaleidoscope of combinations, or of eventual dissolutions of combinations, of these variables, and no single one of them offers a clear avenue to understanding or improving intergroup relations.

II THE CHINESE IN SARAWAK AND MALAYSIA GENERALLY

Another Malaysian example, this one drawn from the Borneo state of Sarawak, but also representative of similar problems elsewhere in the region, may perhaps be offered as illustration. Of Sarawak's population of about 1.1 million, 33 per cent or the largest group consists of predominantly Sarawak-born ethnic Chinese. About 32 per cent are Ibans, 18 per cent or so Malays, 8 per cent Land Dayaks, and the remainder are of various smaller ethnic minorities.

As elsewhere in Southeast Asia, the Chinese in Sarawak have for many decades fought a dogged rearguard action to preserve the independence of their separate Chinese language schools. When this has proved increasingly difficult in the face of ever more government controls, standardisation of curricula and examinations and supervision over instructional facilities and staff functions, then their objective has been to retain a recognised place for the Chinese language as an instructional and examination medium. Considered first by both the colonial and later by the national Malaysian governments as hotbeds of subversive political indoctrination, it appeared often to be overlooked that the private Chinese schools in Sarawak, usually maintained at considerable cost by local Chinese associations, were deeply interwoven with the sense of ethnic identity and cultural pride of the Chinese community whose needs they served.[3] The increasing regulation and standardisation imposed by the Malaysian government on the private Chinese schools, along with the government's stress on the promotion of the formal *Bahasa Malaysia* or national language in all schools and in all aspects of public life, came to be viewed in much of the Sarawak Chinese community, and indeed among Malaysia's Chinese generally, as but yet another phase in the historic government 'attack on Chinese culture'. Already distrustful of the incorporation in 1963 of Sarawak in the new Malaysian Federation, which they considered to have been a British and American scheme to neutralise the influence of the Chinese in what could have been an independent Sarawak, the Chinese of Sarawak have continued to perceive the issue of Chinese language schools and instruction, and the place of Chinese in all of Malaysian public life, as a touchstone of their 'second class' citizenship status.

The backdrop of Sarawak's Chinese problem is, of course, the complex interplay of race, language, politics and economic activity in the Malaysian state as a whole. Though most adult Chinese in Malaysia are bilingual, in the sense that they speak Chinese as well as the *pasar* or 'bazaar' Malay (the common *lingua franca* before the advent of the Bahasa Malaysia), few ethnic Malays (who are familiar with 'bazaar' Malay, or with their local Malay dialect, and increasingly with the more formal *Bahasa Malaysia*) speak Chinese. Yet to foster the notion of an eventually officially bilingual Malaysia, or to take steps in that direction by according new recognition of Chinese as an equal medium of instruction and examination, would encounter not only the deepest opposition in virtually all layers of the politically influential ethnic Malay community and would undoubtedly add new insupportable strains to the delicate, already easily rent, fabric of ethnic Malay-Chinese parliamentary and political cooperation. It would also produce vociferous demands from the 1.2 million Malaysians of Indian-Pakistani origin that Tamil be granted official equal status as well. Then too it would require a *volte-face* in the government's established policy of creating a Malaysian national identity

Intergroup Accommodation in Southeast Asia   147

through a common national language (the *Bahasa Malaysia*), as distinguished from the more rudimentary 'bazaar' Malay, and through a common national ideology (the so-called *Rukunegara* or 'Pillars of the State'), the latter to be discussed presently. The acknowledged stability of the Malaysian state today, with its total population of 12 million inhabitants (about half of them ethnic Malays, 37 per cent Chinese, 10 per cent Indians, and 3 per cent other minorities) rests on what may perhaps be called Malaysia's own 'social contract', i.e. the *de facto* continuance of a primarily racial division of political and economic powers in the country. Although since 1969 new economic development policies have sought to bring changes, this racial division, in the main, has tended to persist until this day, so that the Malays have a preponderance in the political and public administrative spheres, while the Chinese dominate in economic life.[4] Indeed, in the private industrial and commercial sector of Malaysia, the Chinese have held a virtual monopoly, as 62 per cent of employees in this sector are Chinese, and only 28 per cent Malays and 9 per cent Indians.[5]

And so, when Malaysian Chinese press for bilingualism, or for further official recognition of their language along with the *Bahasa Malaysia*, a whole range of mutually enforcing antitheses that bear on the country's intergroup relations tend to come into play. Illustrative was the Sarawak government's reaction early in 1975 to what an editorial in a government monthly called 'a great deal of agitation among certain groups of people' for the reintroduction of the Chinese senior middle common examination in the state. The examination had been abolished by the government in 1969. The editorial, denying that there was a threat to Chinese languages education *per se*, not only termed it 'odd' that such 'agitation still exists' at a time when the state was moving toward making *Bahasa Malaysia* the main language of instruction in all schools, but also implied that those seeking the revival of the Chinese language examination were somehow disloyal: 'We would have expected all Malaysians to bring about the development of one country, one people and one language consciousness.'[6]

The predominantly Chinese-supported Sarawak United Peoples Party, a component of the ruling Alliance Party coalition both at the state and national Malaysian levels, has continued to call for freer and more extensive use and teaching of Chinese and Tamil. This demand comes at a time, however, when the Malaysian government is making determined efforts to enlarge the Malay population group's role in and benefits from the national economy, efforts popularised through publicity for the policy that by 1990 30 per cent of Malaysia's wealth must be in the hands of the Malays. The political consequences of such a Malay-oriented development policy immediately make the demand for greater equality for the Chinese language in school and public usage a part of the entire Malay-Chinese polarisation. Yet, enveloping the ever-present dynamics of this polarisation is the often deceptive atmosphere of relatively easy day-to-day interactions between individuals of the principal racial and ethnic groups in all walks of life, an atmosphere seemingly so socially salubrious as to persuade, on occasion, even seasoned specialists in Malaysian affairs to discount the dangers of racial communalism and to generalise that interrelationships are courteous and smooth; racial prejudices, if felt, are a personal thing and are scarcely a matter of issue'.[7]

III THE CHINESE IN THAILAND

Southeast Asian variations may sometimes lend credibility to impressions of smooth intergroup accommodation. For example, Thailand's five million Chinese (out of a population of over 42 million) probably exhibit a greater degree of cultural assimilation, political and economic integration, intermarriage and absorption into the indigenous population than anywhere else in the region. Outbursts of anti-Chinese racial hostility in Thailand are not historically unknown, but they were more characteristic of the late nineteenth and early twentieth century, before the Thai state developed mechanisms of modern representative government and a concomitant constitutional recognition of political diversities. There is nothing in recent Thai history comparable, for example, to the sudden, bloody violence of the 13 May 1969 anti-Chinese riots in Kuala Lumpur in which several scores of Chinese fell victim to enraged mobs of Malays. The gradual impact of these mechanisms on Thai political values, especially among the younger generation, along with the relative cultural homogeneity and popular sense of the historic continuity of Thailand (unlike Malaysia), the traditional religiously structured tolerance of the ethnic Thai, their historic ease in blending with all new influences in their midst, have all aided the accommodation process. Today, despite continuing resentment of sharp Chinese business and money-lending practices, the modern Thai urban elite's pragmatic recognition of the advantages of forging financial and commercial alliances with the Chinese, alliances which, in turn, find advantageous support in ruling Thai political and military circles, has positively affected the entire pattern of ethnic Thai-

Chinese relations. The days at the beginning of this century when a Thai monarch (King Rama VI) could write a series of hostile newspaper articles on the Chinese and on their alleged danger to his country and publish them under the title *The Jews of the East*[8] seem some considerable distance away, though suspicions over Chinese involvement in Thai Communism remain.

Noteworthy, too, is the comparative Thai tolerance of the Chinese language press and other media, so long as a minimally formal recognition is accorded in Chinese private schools and associations to Thai as the national language. Extensive Chinese bilingualism, however, has little counterpart among the ethnic Thai, whose preferred second language remains English. It may be noted that accommodation of the Chinese in Thailand is governed more by traditional Thai tolerance and acceptance patterns, combined with relative ease of integration for pragmatic reasons with the modern ethnic Thai elite, than by an uneasy and quickly ruptured Malaysian style 'social contract'.

IV INDONESIA: THE CHINESE AND OTHER ETHNIC GROUPS

On occasion, political mistrust so wholly pervades latent racial and economic antagonisms that the intergroup accommodation process is likely to be adversely affected, no matter what efforts toward assimilation are under way. In Indonesia the Chinese and also some East Indonesian ethnic groups afford examples. In the aftermath of the abortive coup attempt in Jakarta on 30 September 1965, in which Indonesian Communists as well as dissident Indonesian military were involved, the six million Indonesian Chinese community (out of a then total population of about 110 million) became the target of extensive and often bloody persecution by Indonesian mobs incited by a popular belief that Indonesian Chinese, as well as the government of People's China itself, had covertly known of or supported the coup attempt. The centuries-long history of uneasy Chinese adjustment in the Indonesian archipelago today pivots on this widely suspected link between Indonesian Chinese, People's China as a source of regional Southeast Asian subversion, and the 1965 coup attempt. So that today in popular Indonesian discussions about diplomatic relations with China (which were suspended, though not formally broken, in the coup's aftermath) the position of the Indonesian Chinese is an element, usually with a pejorative connotation. Typical of this is what one prominent Indonesian Islamic political leader was recently quoted as having said: 'We are not afraid of Mao's atom bomb; it is the overseas Chinese that worry us. The overseas Chinese are a Trojan horse'.[9]

The official Indonesian solution to this 'Trojan horse' problem has been to insist on complete assimilation: adoption of Indonesian names for all Chinese, exclusive use of the *Bahasa Indonesia* (Indonesia's national language) whether on shop signs or in the few private schools that remain, the virtual banning of all newspapers or books in Chinese, or of Chinese films, and so on. Characteristic of the official Indonesian attitude is the warning issued in 1975 by the then governor of Jakarta, a city which has some 300,000 Chinese residents. He warned the Chinese not to 'isolate' themselves, and to 'get rid' of the custom of living among themselves. At the same time Governor Ali Sadikin also attacked Chinese businessmen for continuing to prefer to employ Chinese workers, and he told Chinese parents to allow their daughters to marry ethnic Indonesians, because for so long many Chinese have married Indonesian women. Finally Sadikin told Jakarta Chinese to vary their interests in sports, instead of concentrating on basketball and volley ball in which Chinese have traditionally predominated.[10] It is unnecessary to stress the significance of Sadikin's warning, less, perhaps, in terms of what it may generally suggest of the difficulties of the position of the Indonesian Chinese today, and more as an index to the attitudes and racial grievances felt among even educated Indonesians toward the Chinese.

Amidst continuing official warnings of new and unspecified efforts at 'subversion' by the People's Republic of China against Indonesia, including supposedly several thousand returning Chinese who left Indonesia for People's China during the troubled aftermath of the 1965 coup, the government is now accelerating the controversy-ridden process whereby Chinese may obtain Indonesian citizenship.[11] This acceleration, presumably, will facilitate the Chinese adjustment process even further. But it may be emphasised that in the context of the *pembangunan* (development) and *ketahanan nasional* ('national resilience') policies of Indonesia's present Suharto government,[12] the price of survival is total assimilation (certainly for non-indigenous minorities like the Chinese) with the idea of monolithic national unity – not with a pluralistic entity that allows for a high degree of separate ethnic identification. Such separate ethnic consciousness, however, most assuredly continues to exist in the far-flung Indonesian archipelago where, after all, over 300 different ethnic groups, with their own usually distinctive legal, religious and other cultural traditions, as well as some

250 different languages, remain evident,[13] despite continuous erosion and absorption in a developing Javanese-dominated modernising national culture. Some of these other distinctively ethnic Indonesian subgroups, numerically smaller than the Javanese, have on various occasions in recent years projected their identity into political and even military opposition against the Javanese-dominated central Indonesian government in Jakarta. This problem is undoubtedly aggravated by common traditional hostility patterns toward resident Indonesians from other parts of the archipelago, or even from different parts of the same island: 'Many Indonesians of different regions are also resented while resident in other areas of the country – e.g. the West Javanese culture discriminates against citizens from East Java or Sumatra', and 'Violence often occurs against other Indonesians.'[14] Such inter-ethnic hostility in Indonesia, usually with anti-Javanese overtones, has on more than one occasion crystallised in political secessionist movements. In 1950–51, the inhabitants of the islands of Ambon, Seran, and Saparua proclaimed and fought for an independent 'Republic of the South Moluccas', and several thousands of their adherents, who eventually went to the Netherlands, continue to attempt to win international recognition for their cause, while, reportedly, in the South Moluccan islands themselves sporadic resistance also persists among a now largely quiescent population that still longs for greater autonomy from the Javanese officialdom sent by Jakarta to administer their region. Between 1957 and 1959 another secessionist 'Revolutionary Republic of Indonesia' functioned in some parts of West Sumatra and North Sulawesi, again as an expression of anti-Javanese political and ethnic sentiments among the respective Minangkabau and Minehassa population groups in those areas. Today, in Indonesian West New Guinea, local Papuan resentment of Jakarta's rule has spawned a secessionist and independence movement that has won semi-recognition or open support in Senegal, Benin and other African states.

In other Indonesian areas, e.g. Acheh in Northern Sumatra, the central Indonesian government, mindful of the fierce ethnic pride and past independence strivings of the Achehnese population, wisely has permitted a large measure of *de facto* political and judicial autonomy to come into existence. Almost everywhere in Indonesia, however, the balance between local ethnicity and national unity, whether in language, in the application of custom law (*adat*) in the courts, or in political life, remains to be achieved – an objective rendered the more difficult of attainment because of the archipelagic nature of and poorly developed communications system in the Indonesian Republic. A recent case study of just one administrative unit, the Regency of Simalungun, a component part of the province of North Sumatra, reveals separate residential and occupation patterns, as well as religious cleavages, between Javanese contract labourers, South Tapanuli traders, Simalungun Batak dry rice farmers, and the pork-eating North Tapanuli Batak (shunned by non-pork-eating Muslims), cleavages expressed further in separate partisan political orientations.[15]

In most of Indonesia, primary schools in the initial grades, as they did in the colonial era, still employ the local languages, and in Kalimantan (Borneo) and parts of Sumatra, no less than in Central Java, traditional literary forms remain part of the regional folklore, religion and culture. But while bilingualism (i.e. knowledge of the tongue of one's local ethnic group, as well as of *Bahasa Indonesia*) is observable everywhere, it is at best tolerated from a policy point of view; even more than in the Malaysian case, the present Indonesian government's interpretation of its recent political history (e.g. the 1965 coup attempt) and its perception of its security needs and national *pembangunan* (development) priorities, maximise emphasis on total identification by all inhabitants with national unity and common symbols. In this *gleichschaltung* process ethnic identity, custom law or bilingualism are conceded such official permission or application as a practical necessity on the road to eventually achieving the desired unity. Ideally, from this official vantage point whether one is an Indonesian of Chinese, Achehnese, Moluccan, or Papuan extraction should have significance only as a possible conversation piece.

In making such concessions to ethnic or religious consciousness as they must during the process of developing integrative national institutions and cultural identities, Southeast Asian nations do exhibit some variations. The Socialist Republic of Vietnam (SRV), Burma, and the Philippines may perhaps be offered as contrasting examples.

V THE SOCIALIST REPUBLIC OF VIETNAM

In the case of Vietnam the concessions to ethnicity are as limited as possible, a policy position in keeping both with Vietnamese nationalist priorities and with Marxist-Leninist ideology and practice. Some four million people of the SRV's 50 million population are officially considered 'minority peoples' as distinguished from what the Hanoi regime calls the 'majority people', the Viet or Kinh. The minorities vary greatly in size, ranging from nearly extinct groups like the high mountain-dwelling Lati of Ha Giang province, near the Chinese border, who probably number less than a hundred families today, to the horse-breeding and rice-cultivating Tho in Tuyen Quang and Ca Bang provinces, who aggregate some 400,000.[16] The Indochinese Communist Party in the 1930s originally promised the minorities the right to self-determination, including the right to proclaim a 'separate state'. But with the advent of Communist power after World War II, first in North Vietnam, and, since the mid-1976 proclamation of the new unified SRV, throughout the country, a policy of minority 'autonomy within the bloc of solidarity with Vietnam' has been proclaimed and reaffirmed.[17]

This has meant a concentrated effort at Vietnamisation through close, party-directed, educational and political training, and the provision for carefully supervised structured work experiences and economic development programmes in the so-called 'autonomous regions'. The Tay Bac and Viet Bac Autonomous Regions in the Northeast and Northwest of the SRV, during the two decades of their existence, have served as matrices of an intensive ideological assimilation process, comparable to that now being implemented in 'liberated' South Vietnam. In this process (1) some, if minimal, attention is paid to separate ethnic identity and language in the local judicial, administrative and educational systems, but the whole focus of party-directed policy is service to a new national state, and the promotion of the necessary 'socialist' consciousness to serve it; (2) explicit recognition and rewards, including party membership, are given to those minority group members who prove most adaptable in furthering nationally integrative aims; (3) all economic activity, whether it concerns the intensification of food production through cooperatives, or marketing, or the promotion of cottage industry, is wholly interlocked with party-approved national development plans, production quotas, transportation, and financing and distribution systems. A government assessment of educational policy in the minority areas describes schooling this way:[18]

> The school gives priority to civic training, aimed at turning the students into workers in the service of their own nationality and builders of their native land. It inculcates in them love of the fatherland and their native region, educates them in the spirit of unity, equality and mutual assistance with other brother peoples forming the great Vietnamese community. Besides the regular programme, teachers

help students study their own native regions: its geography, history, political and economic life, the customs and problems of its people ... Parallel to teaching general knowledge, the school disseminates new techniques of agriculture and forestry, struggles against superstitions, paves the way for a new way of life for the younger generation, and is in fact a scientific and cultural centre in each locality.

Bilingualism has in the SRV approximately the same significance as it has in Indonesia and Malaysia: whatever its reality for the évolués among the Tho, Meo, Nung, Muong and other minorities in the SRV today, officially it is at best accorded an obviously transient tolerence. As a policy instrument, bilingualism in the SRV is suitable for display on such occasions as local feastdays, exhibits of folk art, communication with children or the less educated, or whenever vestigial ethnic pride, wounded by some instance of Kinh overbearance, demands soothing promise of adjustment by a bilingual party spokesman or official. It is not viewed as a more lastingly and intrinsically desirable asset, a dimension of democratic pluralism that is, as a matter of policy, to be perpetuated and encouraged to grow, also as a possible dynamic in other facets of a minority culture. To a degree the SRV's official Marxist-Leninist perception of minority cultures as having until recently remained arrested in their social evolution at various stages of development 'ranging from disintegrating primitive community to feudality',[19] has obviously also influenced attitudes toward the minority languages.

VI THE UNION OF BURMA

The contrast in intergroup policy between the SRV and the Union of Burma today could not be more complete. Long before Burma formally attained its independence in 1948, it will be recalled, ethnic conflict and separatist political aspirations between ethnic Burmans (comprising about 58 per cent of Burma's total 32 million population) and such groups as the Shans (8 per cent), Karens (11 per cent), Kachins (4 per cent), Chins (2 per cent) and others, had gravely impeded the prospect of a unified nation state. Freedom from British colonial rule was ultimately achieved under a constitution formally giving the Shan State and the Kayah (Karenni) State the right to secede from the Union government after ten years of independence.[20] This fateful provision, alternately resisted, compromised with and quasi-reaffirmed or denied over the years by the Union government in Rangoon, spurred development of a myriad of secessionist groups throughout the country. Sometimes these groups allied themselves with, and, then again, confronted various Communist insurgent parties and organisations. Among the dissidents are, or have been, the Shan National Alliance, the Shan Independence Force, the Karen National Unity Organisation, the Karen National Progress Party, the New Mon National Party, the Arakanese Communist Party, the Burma Communist Party (White Flag), and others.[21]

The net effect of their separate and sometimes combined struggles which continue until this day has not only been to reduce the land area of Burma under effective central government control to 'perhaps only 40 percent', according to a US Senate Foreign Relations Committee staff report,[22] but also to promote a bewildering variety of political, judicial, educational and other accommodations between the hard-pressed capital and *de facto* quasi-independent or autonomous outlying states with their own governments and 'Presidents'. This is the case, for example, in Kayah state, where some 150,000 Karenni have been waging their independence struggle for the past 25 years against various Rangoon regimes generally not anxious (or logistically able) to press the matter to a definite military confrontation.[23] In the Shan State, a well-equipped 20,000 man 'Liberation Army' and local village militias guard the 'liberated zones' where an openly functioning counter-government, trading in rice and contraband merchandise, including opium, operates with its own officials. The latter include those of various Shan 'customs bureaux' established throughout the state, which collect taxes from the continuous caravan traffic.[24] Schools are maintained in the Shan 'liberated zones', comprising about 70 per cent of the Shan state area, where instruction is given in the Shan language. Shan is used extensively also in local media and local government announcements.

In this state of affairs, ethnic separatism, e.g. Shan or Kachin nationalism, clearly has more powerful adherents than the rather forlorn vision encountered among uneasy Rangoon officials that the Burmese state yet, somehow, can work out the mechanisms of intergroup adjustment, giving both democratic recognition to a plurality of deeply divergent ethnic interests, and still preserve itself as a single state. The price of this may be high: 'Burma survives because of its weakness, not because of its strength', one senior Foreign Ministry official told this author in Rangoon in June 1975. He was referring to the fact that so long as the relatively small, poorly equipped Burmese Army (about

170,000 men), and the corruption-ridden, stagnant central government make no real effort to crush the powerful ethnic separatists throughout the country, the stand-off persists and the *status quo* can probably continue. To be sure, members of all ethnic minorities are represented – if only in token fashion – in the national government structure, including the major Rangoon ministries, and the ruling Ne Win regime has its adherents even in the most determinedly secessionist areas of the country. Still, the accommodation often has a perfunctory and tentative character, and the Burmese political culture clearly is some distance away from providing meaningful national integrative mechanisms. Recent calls by the government-controlled Burmese press that more determined action must be taken against all manner of insurgents in the nation, because 'We, the people of this socialist republic, have vowed to live in weal and woe together, and to carry on with the tasks of socialist reconstruction',[25] are, at least for the time being, unlikely to persuade the wide spectrum of Burmese still determined to cast their ethnic identities into new, separate political moulds.

VII THE SOUTHERN PHILIPPINES

On 26 March 1977 President Ferdinand Marcos of the Philippines proclaimed the creation of an 'autonomous' regional government, comprising some 13 provinces in the Southern part of his country. The proclamation was in accordance with an agreement reached on 23 December, 1976 in Tripoli between Marcos and Libyan President Mu'ammad al-Qadhafi, whose government, reportedly, has assisted the Muslim dissidents of the 'Moro National Liberation Front' (MNFL) in the Philippines in their struggle for greater political freedom in, if not – as is widely believed – secession and independence from the Philippine Republic and establishment of a separate 'Moro' state. President Marcos, in explaining his 26 March proclamation, stressed that the proposed autonomy does not mean that the Southern provinces will break with the rest of the Philippines, and that the MNLF 'will never succeed in obtaining a separate state'.[26] Even at the time of the 26 March 1977 proclamation it was evident that many factions in the proposed autonomous region, which was to have its own 'provisional regional government' and assembly, after a popular referendum presumably was to have ratified the new arrangement, were already deeply dissatisfied with it. In the event, Moro rule was rejected by the popular referendum. And so the violent crisis between the 'Moros', the common, though incorrect appellation of all Philippine Muslims (and frequently resented by them), their Christian neighbours in the Southern provinces, and the Philippine government, which has already cost several hundred lives in the past five years, is likely to go on.

Numbering about 1.8 million in a total Philippine population of about 43 million, the *Bangsa Moro* (Moro people) are by no means homogeneous, being divided into ten ethno-linguistic groups (among them such major divisions as the Maranao of Lanao, the Tan Sug of Sulu, and the Maguindanao of Cotabato), as sharply different from each other as the Moro group as a whole is different from the Christian Philippine majority.[27] A similar cultural and ethnic variety, it may be recalled, exists among the earlier-noted Muslims of Southern Thailand. There are also wide occupational differences among the Moros, ranging from rice and coconut cultivation and brass and wood artisanship to fishing, urban trade and the major professions. The centuries-long and often bloody conflicts; with a Christianising Spain, and later with a distant Manila-centred Philippine national government, rightly or wrongly created the impression among the Moros that they were considered to be primitive provincials. As Gowing notes, among the Maranao the national Philippine government came to be characterised as *gobirno a sarwang tao*, i.e. 'the government of foreign people'. Such alienation came to be aggravated further in recent decades by conflicts over land tenure with the growing Christian element (now outnumbering the Muslims about two to one) in the Southern provinces. The Christians, often recent and better-educated immigrants in the region from the Northern and Central parts of the Philippines, had come to the Southern islands, particularly Mindanao, encouraged by the national government's development programmes. These provided them with lands which, though not then under cultivation, were regarded by Moro villagers as part of their communal reserve areas. The Christian presence sharpened an already deepening Filipinised Islamic consciousness, evident particularly in recent years in increased mosque attendance, proliferation of *madrasa* (Islamic religious schools) and Muslim colleges, in growing numbers of Philippine Muslims going on the *hadj* (pilgrimage to Mecca), in an influx of visiting Egyptians and other *Ulema* (religious scholars of the writ) into the Moro communities, and, in turn, in an increased attendance by young Moros at schools in Cairo.[28]

The new Islamic consciousness also accentuated Moro traditional ethnic loyalty patterns, perceived as being interwoven with the Muslim faith, its laws and historic institutions. Thus, among the Maranao, the profound pride in and identification with the clan (a value experience called *maratabat*) is the basis for political loyalty to the clan head or *datu*, which, in turn, interacts with loyalty to the old Sultanates of the region.[29] In the degree that the Philippine political party and public administrative systems of the last few decades established linkages with traditional Moro loyalties, intergroup adjustments between Moro groups and the national government were readily made. Yet, paradoxically, such linkage, and the emergence of a younger Moro elite, graduates of the University of Mindanao and other institutions of public education, also augmented the Muslims' sense of grievance. The belief that the Philippine political system and Manila politicians somehow were not dealing fairly with Moro grievances seemed to increase in proportion precisely as (1) that system's political accommodation, if not cooptation of the Moro, slowly became more visible, but also (2) as the economic development and exploitation of Mindanao's land, timber and other resources seemed to benefit primarily the non-Moro population groups. The impression that the Moro remained a kind of outcast was given yet further and powerful impetus through a Moro identification with the problems of the Palestinian refugees. As a former Philippine Commissioner of National Integration has put it:[30]

> The sad condition of Palestinian refugees dramatised to Philippine Muslims how a people can be gradually driven out of their lands. Many of those now with the Bangsa Moro have lived as students in the Middle East and have 'jumped the gun', so to speak, in order to prevent their people from falling into the same fate as the Palestinians.

It may be, as one Philippine anthropologist has stressed, that the current Christian-Muslim dichotomy, which lumps all Moros together, unduly minimises their diverse ethnic backgrounds, notwithstanding the fact that in the Philippines 'the blood of ethnicity is thicker than the water of belief'.[31] Some Philippino observers feel, however, that probably only a cornucopia of economic development benefits for the Southern region, as well as vastly accelerated political integration, not now evident, could begin to mitigate the aggrieved sense of Moro self-consciousness. In the absence of these, Muslim secessionism, and confrontation with the Christian element (which has its own anti-Muslim militants) as well as with the Philippine armed forces, is likely to continue: indeed the MNLF boycotted the government-sponsored referendum on the proposed autonomy, although other Muslims in the region approved it. *Inter alia,* one may speculate that such autonomy as eventually may be won by, or become acceptable to, the Moros will not go unnoticed among Muslim secessionists in other areas of Southeast Asia, e.g. in Southern Thailand, as noted earlier, while it also may give encouragement to other rebellious ethnic separatists, e.g. in Burma or Eastern Indonesia.

One point to be made in connection with the Moro rebellion, however, is that existing bi- or trilingualism in the region has thus far not been sufficient to overcome intergroup hostilities. In the Southern Philippine provinces, although local languages and dialects still tend to predominate, inhabitants are rapidly becoming bilingual, i.e. having knowledge not only of ethnic or local tongues, but also of a basic vocabulary of Tagalog, the *lingua franca* being promoted as the national Philippine language. In 1975 the teaching of Tagalog as the national language, along with English, was made mandatory in all primary schools in the country, and special instruction for adults is being widely touted. Additionally, a kind of Philippinised English (a mixture of English, American slang, Tagalog and local dialect) is becoming more common, especially in the towns and among the educated. Arabic is taught in *madrasa* and the Muslim colleges, and, though not as common, provides a linguistic bond among the more than nominal believers. There is, therefore, no linguistic communications problem among antagonistic factions in the Southern Philippines, and, as in the previously-cited case of inhabitants of the Thai-Malaysian border area, familiarity with more than one language does not significantly bridge prevailing ideological cleavages, reinforced by ethnic self-consciousness.

VIII NATIONAL IDEOLOGY: 'CIVIL RELIGION'

If Burmese centrifugalism may be placed at one end of the spectrum of intergroup accommodation, and the SRV's controlled and directed assimilation is representative (although not the only instance) of the other end, then the remaining Southeast Asian states, including the Philippines, can be placed somewhere in between, depending on time and variations in the status of particular groups under consideration. Yet all states of the area, with varying degrees of intensity and success, appear to be committed to the encouragement of a central, overcapping national ideology, a kind of 'civil religion', so to speak. This is not the place to consider the controversy over the analytical utility of the 'civil religion' concept;[32] what is suggested here is exemplified by a variety of a central regime's 'nation-building' political appeals and symbols, commitment to which, in a nationalistic spirit, and sometimes to the point of unquestioning devotion, is expected of all citizens. A formal religious element is usually present in these symbols, an element cast in such broad terms as to accommodate presumably most religious groups in the nation. Examples are the so-called *Rukunegara* ('Pillars of the State') of Malaysia, and the *Pantjasila* ('Five Pillars') of Indonesia, which comprise the following:

Rukunegara	*Pantjasila*
1. Belief in God	1. Belief in God
2. Loyalty to King and Country	2. Nationalism
3. Support for the Constitution	3. Internationalism (or Humanism)
4. Devotion to the Law (or Rule of Law)	4. Democracy (or Rule by Consent)
5. Proper Conduct and Moral Behaviour	5. Social Justice (or Social Prosperity)

Certainly as regards *Pantjasila* there exists by now a small library of varying Indonesian commentaries, interpretations, and (cautious!) criticisms, and the corpus of literature on the much more recently promulgated *Rukunegara* is growing as well. It is, however, not just the divisions of opinion as to the meaning of the 'Five Pillars', apparent in this literature, that is of note. For the division has not been confined merely to books and pamphlets. Rather, throughout the nearly thirty-two years of their existence as an independent nation, Indonesians have seen *Pantjasila* used as a weapon in the conflict between hotly contending factions, for example to denounce Communists as 'atheists' and to defend them, to attack supporters of the creation of an Islamic state in Indonesia and to argue that Islam can thrive in a modern secular state, to justify Sukarno's 'guided' democracy and to berate it as lacking popular 'consent', and so on. If its propagation was and is intended as a means of mutually adjusting divergent interest groups, then *Pantjasila* cannot be said to have been an unqualified success, even though some Indonesian and other observers have suggested that any process of modern national integration, with or without symbols like *Pantjasila*, is likely to be long and arduous.

In respect of *Rukunegara* it is, perhaps, noteworthy that official Malaysian explanations of the doctrine stress its purpose, among others, to be the promotion of a sense of national unity among all different population groups, based on a broadly 'liberal' attitude toward existing cultural traditions. Explicit in the *Rukunegara* doctrine, therefore, is the government's commitment to intergroup accommodation by recognising the worth of each Malaysian community – ethnic, racial, religious, or otherwise. All the same, however, Chinese Malaysians, when confronted by government imposed quotas favouring employment of Malays in trade and industry, cannot but wonder whether, in Orwell's trenchant observation, 'all are equal, but some are more equal than others'. Like *Rukunegara, Pantjasila* is perhaps best viewed, therefore, as an appeal to a national identity still *in statu nascendi*, and the obvious artificiality that clings to such symbols should be considered in terms of the pervasive competitive claims on individual and group loyalties in the heterogeneous Southeast Asian world. It is as if someone dedicated to the establishment of a new nation carefully considered the divergent but primary appeals of ethnicity, race, language, religion or even social class all around, and found that these appeals frequently are expressed in or experienced through a distinctive value terminology for the individual. Examples of such terminology are the earlier noted *maratabat*, of the Maranao Moros in the Philippines, or the 'Five Pillars of Faith' of the practising Muslim. The new nation state, therefore, according to such thinking, is to have its *maratabat*, its 'Five Pillars', too. Inevitably the question of the relationship of this new national *maratabat* to the other 'primordial' ones arises, especially in terms of whether the new relationship does not, in fact, displace the others. If democratic adjustments among groups, in a word 'democratic pluralism', is to mean anything in Southeast Asia, it would seem to have to rest on a maturing, though not necessarily always explicitly formulated, mutual acceptance of these relationships.

For the promoter of a new national ideology, when confronted by the long-haul process of intergroup adjustment, there may be virtue in not being too specific and in not overloading the process of accommodation with too many separate or distinctive symbolisms and nomenclatures. The Union of Burma, now formally describing itself as a 'Socialist' state, has not only left the details of that 'Socialism' carefully unspecified – which is perhaps a boon to Burma's already badly overregulated stagnant economy. But government spokesmen, historically, have been wont to argue that Buddhism, the country's dominant religion and belief system, is, in fact, the fount of the state's official concepts of social justice and common prosperity, i.e. the 'Burmese Way to Socialism', which rejects the allegedly 'vulgar materialism' of the Marxists. Attainment of *Pyidawtha*, or the 'Burmese Welfare State', has been described by Burmese publicists as based on the proposition that Buddhism long ago anticipated Marxism, and in any case is a more perfect path to modern 'people's democracy' than contemporary ideologies.[33] Thus the symbolism of the modern state may disclaim originality and bow to the older, more pervasive religious value system, instead of contesting it as a separate mechanism of intergroup adjustment in the same society. Ironically, even this concession has not been enough to stifle the secessionist aspirations of ethnic groups like the Shans, Kachins, and others, as we have seen. In Burma the ethnicity of minorities, for the moment, overrides even the unity of the Buddhist experience, certainly of the 'Burmese way' to a common welfare state presumably based on that experience.

On the other hand, there is the sloganless, culturally more diffused, assimilation programme being implemented by the Thai government among the so-called 'hill tribes' in the northern part of the Kingdom – a process similar in intensity, perhaps, but without the formal ideologically strongly focused component evident among the tribal minorities in the SRV, discussed earlier. There are approximately 500,000 members in the Thai 'hill tribes' category (out of a total Thai population of about 42 million), typically resident in the mountainous Northern Thai provinces of Chiang Mai, Lumphun and Chiang Rai, and involving such major groups as the Meo, Karen, Yao, Lisu, Kha Mu, Htin, and others.[34] Migratory and given to shifting cultivation, the hill tribes' destruction of forests and headwater lands, their illegal opium-growing, and their susceptibility to the blandishments of proselytisers of the underground Thai Communist Party and its 'people's army' insurgents who promise 'independence' have increasingly compelled the Thai government to bring the hill tribes more firmly under government supervision and control.

The decision to establish such control, and to encourage the hill tribes to take up a more sedentary agriculture and existence, in itself was something of a *volte-face* of policy on the part of the Thai government. The original Thai government policy of the 1950s was that the hill tribes were a less developed people, who preferred to live separately from the lowland Thais, and who, apart from cautious government welfare measures, should not be strongly interfered with. This policy was the result of anthropological and sociological experts, usually from abroad, who were hired by the government. The result was a 'non-integration' approach to the hill tribes, largely committed to preserving a *status quo* which proved, in any case, to be increasingly difficult if not impossible to maintain because of the adverse ecological

Intergroup Accommodation in Southeast Asia

effects of hill tribe cultivation methods, and because of the opium and security problems. By the late sixties a significant policy alteration was being implemented, aimed at changing drastically the residential and economic styles of living of the hill tribes. Moving the hill tribes (not without occasional resistance) to permanent new village settlements, e.g. in Tak province, the Thai government now commenced an 'accelerated integration' programme providing new medical, educational and other social services to the relocated groups, as well as farm land, credit, and equipment.[35]

Integrated now as units of the regular Thai local government and administrative structure, the hill tribe villagers are in effect asked to 'Thai-ise' themselves, by identification with the mainstream political culture of Thailand, i.e. veneration of the King and the ruling dynasty, and of the Buddhist value system and the Buddhist temple and monastic establishment, adoption of the Thai language and use of Thai media, and so on. There is, however, no single political symbol, philosophy, '-ism', creed or slogan that exemplifies the national culture of the dominant lowland Thai and which the hill tribes are now expected to adopt: the adjustment process sought is a diffused one, it is to take place through the pores, so to speak. It is complex, yet is to be achieved with all deliberate speed, and is dependent heavily on local administrative leadership. Bilingualism in this context is viewed only as a transition to complete mastery of and ultimately primary reliance on Thai in the context of accelerated integration.

Apart from the ideological difference, clearly what the Hill Tribe Welfare Division of the Thai government's ministry of the Interior, as well as local military commanders and provincial and local civil administrators, are committed to is an objective of integrative adjustment not basically at variance from what party cadres and officials in the 'Autonomous Regions' of the SRV are seeking. But in keeping with the relative tolerance and behavioural flexibilities that characterise Thai culture, the visible signs of the compliance demanded of the hill tribes as evidence of their 'Thai-isation' is less likely to be as doctrinically elaborate, specific, or even politically oriented as that now expected of a Tho évolué in the SRV.

IX THE MARXIST-LENINIST (MAOIST) ROUTE TO ACCOMMODATION

In a category by itself is the Marxist-Leninist (including 'Maoist') ideology as a means of promoting intergroup accommodation. Leaving aside Laos and Cambodia there is but one state in Southeast Asia officially dominated by such an ideology, i.e. the SRV. It is too soon to tell whether in the SRV such accommodation between the majority Viet or Kinh, and the 'autonomous' minorities described earlier, will be any easier or more complete, than in the rest of the region where other ideologies prevail. Considering their state of inter-ethnic tensions, the record of other Communist Asian or partly Asian states (e.g. the USSR and People's China) in this regard is unpersuasive. On the other hand, there is the instance of the ethnically heterogeneous CPM and its 'liberation army', cited at the beginning of this paper, in which traditional intergroup antagonisms seem to a significant degree at least to have been submerged. One might suggest, however, that the relative smallness of the CPM band (and of other similar 'Maoist' guerrilla forces, like the 'New People's Army' insurgents in the Philippines) may facilitate a lessening of ethnic or other intergroup tensions that might not be evident in larger Communist organisational settings. Prior to 1965, for example, the Indonesian Communist Party was one of the largest such parties outside the Communist bloc, having some 2.5 million members from many different ethnic communities, as well as additional hundreds of thousands in various front or satellite organisations. Even a few Muslim leaders were nominally affiliated with the party. As its involvement in the abortive 1965 coup attempt in Indonesia demonstrated, however, ideological control and organisational efficiency over this large party complex turned out to be far weaker than was originally believed, and this was, indeed, a major reason for the party's swift demise after the coup's failure. Party leaders themselves, even before the coup, had stressed the need for fuller theoretical training and indoctrination. In any case, as yet no certain or significant advantage can be accorded to Marxism-Leninism as an integrative ideology in the Southeast Asian environment.

X THE SOCIAL CONSEQUENCES OF ECONOMIC ACTIVITY

What, finally, of economic activity, and its potential social class corollaries, as mechanisms of intergroup accommodation and adjustment? Does a Malay smallholder, sensitive to the buffetings of the international rubber market, feel less ethnic self-consciousness today when made aware of the similar problems of his Chinese counterpart in one of the 'new villages' along the Thai-Malaysian border? Can a Shan schoolteacher, by virtue of his profession and the status it brings, empathise more readily nowadays with a colleague who happens to be lowland Burman? Does a Protestant assembler in one of Java's new factories sense a proletarian solidarity with his Muslim co-worker on the production line? Probably only the most doctrinaire Marxist analysist of the Southeast Asian scene would confidently answer yes to these questions. This is not to say, however, that traditional ethnic, racial, or religious bonds *within a group* may not be eroding as new economic interests begin to predominate. Even in remote areas of Southeast Asia today a new intragroup class consciousness, reflecting educational and employment differences, can be discerned. One recent view of this process, virtually a lament, describes conditions in the up-river Dayak tribal society of Sarawak:[36]

> In the past the Ulu folks were a close-knit tribal society. They practised the same religious rites, spoke the same language and lived very much the same kind of life in every sense of the word. Today this is no longer true of these same folks. Formal education and the influence of Western cultures have torn apart the warp and woof of social unity.... Despite the underlying pivotal force of their racial unity, the Ulu folks are merely superficially one ...
>
> With education has come economic classes. Those who have managed it to the top fare better and become economically different from their next-door neighbours. Many families who have passed several rungs up the economic ladder no longer remain on friendly terms with their next of kin of former days. The competition to make it to the top has made the educated folks unmindful of their relatives and neighbours of bygone days.

In the rest of Malaysia, too, differences in wealth are splitting ethnic in-group feelings, even to the point that the Malaysian premier has felt compelled to warn the rich not to be conspicuous in displaying their assets. The one-time belief that even poorer Malays would derive a kind of vicarious pleasure from seeing 'rich Malays being driven around in luxury' has been abandoned with growing understanding that resentment rather than vicarious pleasure would be the likely reaction of the Malay poor.[37] More to the point perhaps, is the contention of some observers that the economic development process in Malaysia and some other countries of the region today is likely to accentuate rather than mitigate existing disparities of wealth and a class polarisation within ethnic groups because of the absence of structural changes in the economy. The second Malaysia national development plan (1971–5), for example, though stressing the necessity of assisting the Malay population to achieve a greater share of the national wealth and increased participation in trade and industry, has been criticised because of (1) the retention of traditional Malay monarchical, aristocratic and conservative religious institutions and values; (2) the encouragement of a rapid Malay urbanisation without much indication as to how the modern corporate economic structure can accommodate the impact of a rising Malay proletariat; (3) the official promotion of broad rural development schemes that do not alleviate the polarisations of wealth and class already apparent in the Malay peasant society, and so on.[38] These criticisms may equally be applied to the Third Malaysia Plan (which began in 1976) because the Third Plan continues unchanged the 'New Economic Policy' of the Second Plan by which Malays presumably were to acquire a greater share of the country's wealth.

Certainly in the Indonesian case, grandiose national development schemes and huge injections of foreign capital investment and credits have benefited most Indonesians only to a minimal degree. Meanwhile, an Indonesian entrepreneurial elite, with its ancillaries in the military and political establishments, has reaped many advantages, and amidst spectacular business scandals and reports of corruption, has sharpened the social distance between itself and the mass of Indonesians, to the point that a proletarianised sense of class grievance, particularly in the urban areas, may certainly be said to be widening.[39] Whether such class consciousness necessarily will have exploitable value in Marxist or other ideological terms (the Communist party is outlawed in Indonesia, and the study of Marxism, except in an academic context, is forbidden), or can become a basis for new political action, remains very much in doubt, however.

For to Indonesia, Malaysia, and other areas of Southeast Asia (although admittedly less so in the SRV) can be applied at least to some degree Norman Jacobs' concept of 'modernisation without development', which he applied to Thailand. This concept is based on the overriding strength of traditional values of spiritual primacy and social hierarchy in the conduct of economic and political life.[40] The forms and even the processes of economic organisation may change and 'modernise', but the human value system that pervades them does so much more slowly.[41] This is not to say that economic interest is unable to overcome traditional communal barriers. Robert Shaplen, among the most astute observers of the Southeast Asian scene today, recently has noted that a new Malay elite and middle class, benefiting from the preferments of Malaysia's 'New Economic Policy', and enjoying a significantly improved standard of living, now 'tend to identify themselves with the better-off Chinese'.[42] Similar identifications of interest, also through common life-styles, are apparent among younger ethnic Thai and Thai Chinese in Bangkok. And in Indonesia the upper military establishment and the trade unions demonstrate internal erosion of ethnicity through realisation of common functional status. Nevertheless these instances are relatively rare. For most of the region such inter-ethnic identification processes are not now decisive in group adjustments, although their significance undoubtedly is growing. For Southeast Asia intragroup polarisation, e.g. between 'rich Malays being driven around in luxury' and the poor Malay worker or farmer, is one thing. It remains altogether another thing (the confident prognoses of Marxist analysts notwithstanding) to move from such intragroup polarisation to a new intergroup, class-based, self-awareness and empathy, let alone political solidarity.

XI CONCLUSIONS: ATTITUDES TO DEMOCRATIC PLURALISM

In Southeast Asia no single group or institutional variable, whether race, ethnicity, religion, class-consciousness or method of production, nor any one mechanism such as the promotion of bilingualism in diverse societies, can be counted on as a preferential approach to intergroup accommodation. Bilingualism is a fact in much of the area, and while from the present writer's personal observation Shaplen's middle-class Malays and their better-off Chinese friends and neighbours may converse in English or the *Bahasa Malaysia* (not in Chinese!), and while today even Moro schoolchildren, next to their own ethnic languages, are gradually learning to think in and use Tagalog in their primary schools because it is the Philippines' new national language, the racial or religious loyalties of the individuals involved in such bilingual experiences remain potent and, probably, still primary. With the qualified exception of Singapore, no national government in Southeast Asia is presently encouraging, or is likely to encourage in the future, bilingualism as a matter of policy. On the contrary, promotion of a single national language, however inadequate, remains *de rigueur*.

Sometimes racial or religious identity in Southeast Asia may appear to be submerged in a new political ideology (as the purveyors of various national policies from Hanoi and Rangoon to Jakarta and Manila stoutly insist is happening), sometimes economic stress may lessen the effects of ethnic in-group feelings, and thus, as in Malaysia, the government warns wealthy Malays not to flaunt their riches; and then again, as in Burma, a common, generally revered religion (Buddhism) is unable to mitigate ethnic secessionist aspirations. The kaleidoscopic variations possible in the patterns of group or institutional variables render both objective analysis and the formulation of consistent public policy rather hazardous. A case can be made for the desirability of almost any single rationale of intergroup accommodation in Southeast Asia, but rarely if ever as the definitive one. Thus some observers, addressing themselves to the solution of what is perhaps Southeast Asia's most intractable problem of minority adjustment, i.e. that of the *hua ch'iao* or 'Overseas Chinese', can and do emphasise the importance of the centuries-long assimilation of some Chinese groups in certain host Southeast Asian environments.[43] The Thai case has already been noted. Sometimes, as in the ports of Peninsular Malaya, and in Manila, distinctive well-established Sino-indigenous hybrid cultures and lifestyles developed, neither wholly Chinese nor indigenous, but drawing on the traits of both and reinforced by continuous formal or informal intermarriage or relations between Chinese males and native women, or, eventually, between members of the established Sino-Malayan and Sino-Filippino mixed-blood communities. Common modern educational and corporate work experiences further facilitate the assimilation today. Who, considering such a centuries-long process, and the absorption of the members of such assimilated or mixed-blood communities into the political and business establishments of the host countries, would not come to agree with the earlier-cited observations (p. 148 above) concerning the 'smoothness' of intergroup relations, and the relative insignificance of racial prejudice – until a bloody racial riot, like the one on 13 May 1969 in Kuala Lumpur, pulls one sharply back into reality.

Assimilation or intergroup adjustment because of mixed marriage patterns can, in any case, be deceptive. Intermarriage (in the sense of the Chinese male espousing an indigenous wife) is a common fact. But former Jakarta Governor Ali Sadikin's above-cited exhortation to local Indonesian Chinese to stop 'ghetto-ising' themselves and encourage their daughters to marry Indonesian males (p. 150 above) hit a nerve in the local Chinese community: historically, among the Chinese of Indonesia not even the oldest *peranakan* ('child of the country' i.e.

long-settled in the country) families have been especially eager for such marriages. One hastens to add that such Chinese reluctance still has indigenous counterparts in most of the Southeast Asian region, although less so perhaps in Thailand. Malay dislike of formal interracial marriage is, in part, structured by traditional preference for one's first cousin or other relative as ideal spouse. Such traditional family inbreeding over a period of time, especially among rural Malays, has led, in the delicate phraseology of one astute Malay observer, to 'the propagation of the poorer characteristics, whether dominant or recessive, originally found in the brothers and sisters who were parents of the married couple'.[44] With such deeply rooted marriage preferences and aversions, the psychological roots of which remain to be analysed, the vaunted Sino-Malaysian assimilation, or other forms of intergroup adjustment, obviously require considerable qualification.

There is, on the whole, a remarkable similarity of policies among the nations of the Southeast Asian region toward the idea of democratic pluralism and the means to attain it. On the one hand there is general, explicit, yet superficial acceptance of the concept of *bhineka tunggal ika* ('One out of Many'), as the motto on Indonesia's national seal puts it. This means official acceptance of the existence of a plural society in the nation state, in which the relationships of distinctive groups are considered to be the product of a centuries-long development. These relationships were given a particular and essentially undesirable form, it is believed, because of the common colonial experience, which none but Thailand escaped in the region. The colonial experience is considered to have compartmentalised and rigidified the various racial, ethnic, and religious groups in the Southeast Asian countries, because such compartmentalisation was to the advantage of the alleged 'divide and rule' policy by which colonial regimes maintained themselves in power. This whole process is said also to have 'distorted' the socio-economy of the region, e.g. by racially stratifying economic relationships. As Indonesian nationalists, for example, as well as some scholarly observers, have been wont to argue, because of the colonial era the mass of Indonesians became essentially coolies and peasants, the Chinese and Arab minorities in the Indies were relegated to the 'middle level' operations of the retail trade, small industries and money-lending, while the Dutch elite were the managers/owners of the major enterprises. Administrative decentralisation in the colonial era, retention in the colonial administration of traditional chiefs and 'indirect rule', establishment of separate schools with separate dialects or languages of instruction (e.g. including Chinese) for different population groups, application of ethnic custom or folklore in local jurisprudence – these were some of the ways of colonialism, all designed, it was said to prevent meaningful intergroup accommodation, let alone emergence of a feeling of national unity.

With the passing of the colonial era, even if accomplished as, e.g. in Malaya, the Philippines or Burma, without a major revolution against colonial authority, and even as colonial administrative practices (e.g. application of ethnic custom or folklore in the judicial process) were retained, the new states of the Southeast Asian region and the nationalism of their leaders demanded as far as possible formal rejection of the colonial past. Nationhood was apt to be stressed by these leaders in terms of the overriding priority of unity of territory and people, an emphasis likely to be voiced with vehemence in the measure that it was well understood that such unity was in fact far from accomplished and hence needed to be constantly reiterated in all national policies and political symbolism. 'Pluralism', i.e. group diversity, no less than the means – democratic or otherwise – to accommodate it, thus were not, from the start, favourite objects of contemplation or of policy concern among the Sukarnos, Ho Chi Minhs, or Rahmans of the Southeast Asian region. On the contrary, to the degree that the vestiges of colonialism, whether economically or politically, were still felt to be a reality even after independence was won, public policy could only stress and, indeed, overstress the imperatives of transcendent common nationhood.

The consequences of all this were not long in making themselves felt. After – and sometimes even before – the first glow of having achieved national independence had worn off, local, often ethnic-based, resistance and secession began plaguing the Southeast Asian politics, from the Shan state of Burma, to the Papuans of Indonesia's Irian Jaya (West New Guinea) province. In groping for solutions produced by these crises, however, no national government developed a comprehensive policy of intergroup adjustment, sensitive to diverse language and cultural needs, ethnic pride or racial fears. Adjustments, rather, have tended to be grudgingly *ad hoc*, being usually informal stand-offs between the national government and rebellious ethnics, as in Burma, or more formal, sweeping but ineffective promises, like the recent grant of autonomy to the Philippines' southern provinces.

In any case, the lodestar of official national policy has remained much the same: assimilation and the national 'recycling' of separate group interests as far, and as rapidly, as possible. Local literature and the arts, ethnic law and crafts – these can all be 'accommodated', in a relatively harmless, cultural sense. But as soon as they might become politically or administratively significant, e.g. as soon as the local pride in one's folk literature would translate itself into a concerted effort for bilingualism in the schools, or in the public utterances of officials, or as soon as the residual application of custom law would become an organised demand for equality in the national codes, then the call for accommodation takes on a different, and to the wielders of national power symbols, a more menacing form.

Is democratic pluralism possible in Southeast Asia? Beyond the thousand and one ways in which the daily round, through the centuries, forces the rough and ready practice of such pluralism in any heterogeneous society, priorities of a national *gleichschaltung* to the contrary notwithstanding, the answer must be: for the moment, no. But seeing the rate of social change in the Southeast Asian world, and the growing policy flexibility of its governments (resulting in no small measure from the disillusionments of the region's post-independence experience) may well suggest the advisability of a more qualified answer, and a perhaps more promising, perspective on the problem in the future.

NOTES

1. *Malaysian Digest* (Kuala Lumpur), 15 Feb 1976, p. 8.
2. See the letter of Professor David J. Banks in *Far Eastern Economic Review*, 23 July 1976, p. 6.
3. On the background of Chinese education in Sarawak see especially Michael B. Leigh, *The Rising Moon. Political Change in Sarawak* (Sydney University Press, 1974) pp. 10–12, and J. M. van der Kroef, 'Chinese Minority Aspirations and Problems in Sarawak', *Pacific Affairs*, spring-summer 1966, pp. 64–82.
4. R. S. Milne, 'The Politics of Malaysia's New Economic Policy', *Pacific Affairs*, summer 1976, pp. 235–62.
5. J. P. Arlès, 'Ethnic and Socio-Economic Patterns in Malaysia', *International Labour Review*, Dec 1971, p. 540.
6. *The Sarawak Tribune* (Kuching), 8 Jan 1975.
7. K. G. Tregonning, *Malaysia* (University of British Columbia Press, Vancouver, 1965) p. 11.
8. On this document see Kenneth P. Landon, *The Chinese in Thailand* (London and New York: Oxford University Press, 1941) pp. 34–43, and Victor Purcell, *The Chinese in Southeast Asia* (London and New York: Oxford University Press, 1951) pp. 153–5.
9. Franklin B. Weinstein, 'World Politics and World Powers: The View from Djakarta', *Asia* (New York) no. 27 (autumn 1972) p. 52.
10. *Empat Lima* (Jakarta), 10 Nov 1975, p. 2, and *Antara Despatch* (Jakarta) 10 Nov 1975.
11. On the Indonesian Chinese citizenship problem see especially David

Mozingo, *Chinese Policy Toward Indonesia, 1949–1967* (Cornell University Press, Ithaca, N.Y., 1967).
12. On these policies see Justus M. van der Kroef, 'National Security Defense Strategy and Foreign Policy Perceptions in Indonesia', *Orbis*, summer 1976, pp. 461–96.
13. Hildred Geertz, 'Indonesian Cultures and Communities', pp. 24–96 in R. T. McVey (ed.), *Indonesia* (Human Relations Area Files, New Haven, Conn., 1963).
14. David W. Chang, 'Current Status of Chinese Minorities in Southeast Asia', *Asian Survey*, June 1973, p. 590.
15. R. William Liddle, 'Ethnicity and Political Organisation: Three Sumatran Cases', p. 137, in Claire Holt (ed.), *Culture and Politics in Indonesia* (Cornell University Press, Ithaca and London, 1972).
16. On these minorities see J. L. Schrock *et al.*, *Minority Groups in North Vietnam* (Ethnographic Studies, Headquarters US Department of the Army, Government Printing Office, Washington, DC, 1972), esp. pp. 93–102 and 449–78.
17. J. M. van der Kroef, 'Religion, Ethnicity, and Communist Tactics in Southeast Asia's Plural Societies', *Plural Societies*, winter 1976.
18. Nhat Hung, 'Education in the Service of the National Minorities', *Vietnamese Studies* (Hanoi), no. 15 (1968) p. 115.
19. Viet Chung, 'National Minorities and Nationality Policy in the D.R.V.', *Vietnamese Studies*, no. 15 (1968) p. 5.
20. Klaus Fleischmann, 'Problems of Contemporary Burma', *Asia Quarterly*, no. 1, (1973) pp. 73–4; Tan Boo Hock, 'Burma's Insurgency Problem', *Journal of the Historical Society* (University of Singapore), Dec 1971, pp. 77–83; and Hugh Tinker, *The Union of Burma* (Oxford University Press, London, 1957), provide useful insights into the background of the ethnic separatist problem in Burma.
21. Mya Maung, 'Burma's Surpluses of Rice and Rebels', *Pacific Community*, Oct 1972, p. 140.
22. *Economic and Political Developments in the Far East. Report by Senator Charles H. Percy to the Committee on Foreign Relations, U.S. Senate, on a Study Mission to the Far East* (US Government Printing Office, Washington, DC, 1973) p. 8.
23. See e.g. Chris Mullin, 'Burma – An Enduring Struggle for Independence', *Far Eastern Economic Review*, 1 Apr 1974, p. 22.
24. See the articles by Catherine Lamour in *Le Soir* (Brussels), 27 and 30 Dec 1975, reprinted as 'Asia's Burmese Timebomb', *Atlas World Press Review* (New York), Apr 1976, pp. 13–15.
25. Editorial, *The Guardian* (Rangoon), 28 Dec 1976.
26. Radio Manila, domestic service in English, 29 Mar 1977 (Foreign Broadcast Information Service Bulletin, hereafter FBIS, 30 Mar 1977).
27. Peter G. Gowing, *Mosque and Moro. A Study of Muslims in the Philippines* (Manila: Philippine Federation of Christian Churches, 1964), and the same author's 'Kris and Crescent', *Aramco World*, July–Aug 1965, p. 6.
28. Peter G. Gowing, 'Kris and Crescent, Dar al-Islam in the Philippines', *Studies in Islam*, Jan 1966, p. 15.
29. Aprodicio A. Laguian, 'The Political Integration of Muslim Filipinos',

Philippine Journal of Public Administration, Oct 1969, pp. 366–9.
30. Mamintal A. Tamano, 'The Expectations of Muslims as Philippine Citizens', *Solidarity* (Manila), July–Aug 1975, p. 32.
31. Eric S. Casino, 'Structuralism in Philippine Cultural Diversities', *Solidarity*, July–Aug 1975, p. 27.
32. See, in this connection, Daniel Regan, 'Islam, Intellectuals and Civil Religion in Malaysia', *Sociological Analysis*, summer 1976, pp. 95–110.
33. Government of Burma, Ministry of Information, *The Burmese Way to Socialism. Policy Declaration of the Revolutionary Council* (Rangoon, 1962), and J. M. van der Kroef, 'Communal and Individual Property Rights: Patterns of Transition in Southeast Asia', *Solidarity* (Manila), Jan–Feb 1975, pp. 20–34.
34. On the hill tribes in Thailand see, generally, John E. de Young, *Village Life in Modern Thailand* (Berkeley: University of California Press, 1955); Gordon Young, *The Hill Tribes of Northern Thailand* (Bangkok: USOM, 1962); Peter Kunstadter, *Southeast Asian Tribes, Minorities and Nations* (Princeton, N.J.: Princeton University Press, 1967), and Thomas A. Marks, 'The Meo Hill Tribe Problem in Northern Thailand', *Asian Survey*, Oct 1973, esp. pp. 933, 938 and 941.
35. On changing Thai government policy toward the hill tribes see Krachang Bhanthumnavin, 'Overcoming the Problems of Resettling Hill tribes', *Southeast Asian Spectrum* (Bangkok), Oct 1972, pp. 23–34. See also Government of Thailand, Ministry of the Interior, *Hill Tribe and Welfare in Thailand* (Bangkok, Department of Public Welfare, Ministry of the Interior, 1971).
36. Joachim Ulok Laeng, 'Divisive Factors in theUlu', *Sarawak Gazette*, 31 Oct 1976, p. 197.
37. R. S. Milne, 'The Politics of Malaysia's New Economic Policy', *Pacific Affairs*, summer 1976, p. 260.
38. Michael Stenson, 'Class and Race in West Malaysia', *Bulletin of Concerned Asian Scholars*, Apr–June 1976, pp. 45–54, and M. J. Esman, *Administration and Development in Malaysia* (Cornell University Press, Ithaca, N.Y., 1972), especially pp. 54–5.
39. J. M. van der Kroef, 'Suharto's Indonesië: Vernieuwing Zonder Verandering?', *Internationale Spectator* (The Hague), April 1977.
40. Norman Jacobs, *Modernisation Without Development: Thailand as an Asian Case Study* (New York: Praeger, 1971).
41. For a controversial illustration of this contention in the case of Indonesia see Allen M. Sievers, *The Mystical World of Indonesia. Culture and Economic Development in Conflict* (Baltimore: The Johns Hopkins University Press, 1974).
42. Robert Shaplen, 'Letter from Malaysia', *New Yorker* 18 Apr 1977, p. 119.
43. See e.g. Go Gien Tjwan, 'The Changing Trade Position of the Chinese in Southeast Asia', *International Social Science Journal*, vol. 23, no. 4 (1971) p. 568.
44. Mahathir Bin Mohamad, *The Malay Dilemma* (Singapore: Donald Moore Publishers, 1970) p. 29. See also Jusoff bin Haji Hanifah, 'Malay Proverbs – Codes of Malay Behaviour Patterns', *Sarawak Gazette*, 31 Aug 1974, p. 166.

8 The Public Services in a Plural Society

William Gutteridge
Professor of International Studies, University of Aston, Birmingham, England

I A COMMUNITY OF DIVERSE ETHNIC GROUPS

The presumed objective of constitutional arrangements in a plural society is ultimately to create a community out of diverse ethnic groups. It is, however, unlikely that a genuine political consensus will be attained in one step: there will probably be an intermediate stage of what may be termed political acquiescence. A period of more or less passive acceptance of an evolving pattern is to be expected, during which there will be many uncertainties and a widespread feeling that the recognition of the interests of particular groups is less than adequate – whether they are minorities or the majority. Indeed, this may be the best that can be expected and it is particularly important that at this stage the management of fears and grievances should be such that the whole operation is not soured.

The assumption on which this short paper is based is that in a plural society – as probably in any other – the organisation, composition and conduct of the key public services are at least as important as the constitutional arrangements for policy-making and representation. The cynical view that the main purpose of a democratic electoral system is at intervals to involve each citizen formally in the process of government has something to be said for it. Universal suffrage or one man, one vote, can be seen in this context simply as the most convenient means of establishing the legitimacy of the government and giving it a mandate to rule. The implication is that for the majority who do not choose or cannot be involved in the political process except at the time of an election what matters is the quality of their experience at the hands of the public services in their bureaucratic, welfare, judicial and security functions.

II ORGANISATION OF THE PUBLIC SERVICES

Any federal or confederal state has to face the fundamental problem of deciding which services are to be provided entirely at a regional or territorial level, which are to be shared between regional and central authority and which are to be in the hands exclusively of an overriding central authority. This should depend to some extent on the degree of ethnic or perhaps linguistic and religious homogeneity prevailing in each of the smaller units. Federations, confederations and international communities around the world provide a range of models. Perhaps for the purposes of this discussion the national situations of Nigeria, Canada and India are the most relevant, and in spite of its recent disintegration there are useful lessons to be learned from the East African Community – the title 'East African Common Services Organisation' is itself suggestive of one method of approach to the question, i.e. a decision about the optimum range of services to be provided on a collective rather than a discrete basis.

The original East African High Commission established in 1948 had legislative authority over
(a) Customs and Excise but not rates of duty.
(b) Income Tax on terms similar to (a).
(c) Defence (including the East African Navy).
(d) Railways and Harbours.
(e) Civil Aviation.
(f) Research.
(g) Posts and Telegraphs – telephone and radio communication.
(h) Appropriations for expenditure and staff matters relating to the services provided.
(i) The University College at Makerere in Uganda.

This organisation fell well short of federation in a number of important respects. All essential authority over social and economic policy, e.g. agriculture and education, was left to the constituent units and there were no police force and no courts to enforce the laws. In the event the achievement of separate independence by the three territories quickly reduced the level of cooperation, and defence became a matter for each separately and the East African Navy was disbanded at the time of

Kenya's achievement of independence.

The East African case provides, however, a useful check-list of areas of integration which might apply in the South African situation. All aspects of communications and transport, customs and excise, currency and immigration are obvious candidates. Common taxes are not essential to the maintenance of such common services, which can be financially managed by territorial contributions. In the end, however, there is no escape from the difficulties arising from the need to man such services. The powers and composition of a Public Service Commission responsible for terms of service, entrance qualifications and recruitment have in themselves obviously to attract the confidence of the population of the constituent territories if the Commission's operation is not to become a source of grievance.

The security forces, however, constitute the most sensitive area. Any confederation or federation which does not consolidate its external relations on the basis of a common foreign policy and an associated defence posture can scarcely be said to exist. The composition of the regular armed forces has been shown in a number of plural societies to be a critical factor. The survival of India, for example, as a state may be at least partly attributed to the care which has been devoted to balance in the composition of its military regiments and formations, partly a legacy of imperial rule. It has even been claimed that military professionalism has tended to make the Indian army a 'national melting pot'. In Nigeria, on the contrary, the army reflected and even magnified the country's divisions which led to the coups of 1966 and the civil war which followed. In the present circumstances there may be more important lessons to be learned from the Nigerian than the Indian situation.

The powers and organisation of the police, however, constitute a peculiarly complex problem. The question as to whether there should be separate regional forces and if so whether the central and regional governments should have concurrent or distinct responsibilities for law and order throughout the whole country is critical, as is the political responsibility for police matters at both levels. Whatever arrangement is adopted clear-cut policies with regard to recruitment and the postings of personnel need to be evolved. Should policemen serve principally in their own home localities because they are intimate with its problems, or be deliberately posted to other areas because of this intimacy and the consequent possibilities of corruption and political influence? The choice with regard to organisation may depend substantially on the powers to be exercised and what are perceived to be the central functions of the police. A shift of emphasis away from the prevention and detection of crime to the maintenance of law and order and the control of public meetings and political events raises a number of issues. Multi-ethnic communities are liable, as both Nigeria and India have shown, to raise particular problems in this respect. What is to be the official police response to a 'strong-arm group' of supporters of the government in a territory which obviously intends to use force to intimidate political opponents? The confidence of minorities in government may well, in practice, depend upon the answer. Whether there is one comprehensive police force or several there is a dilemma for the officers, who may be torn because of a dual allegiance. Federal (a term used for the sake of convenience in this context) and regional police forces, separate and under separate control, would not appear to provide a stable solution.

The Police and the Armed Forces depend for adequate performance on a consciousness of unity and an awareness of their constitutional role and limits of action. These qualities must permeate the forces at all levels: hence the quality and loyalty (however defined) of the officers and other personnel is the central question. How can they be selected and recruited to this end?

III COMPOSITION OF THE PUBLIC SERVICES, PARTICULARLY THE POLICE AND THE ARMY

The diversification of the officer corps in forces which have previously been drawn exclusively from a minority group, ethnically and educationally distinctive, constitutes an especially difficult problem. In the first place, as the experience of Nigeria has shown, careers in the armed forces have to become politically respectable in the eyes of those who require to be recruited. Then there is the question of standards – and not only of education, which may in fact provide the least of the difficulties. Concepts of leadership qualities are, for example, inevitably culturally derived. It is not surprising that officers in armed and police forces (as in other occupations) tend to look for people in their own image and to attempt to identify the qualities which they suppose to be essential.The progressive invalidation of the British notions of 'martial races' and 'worthwhileness as soldiers' applied in India and East Africa since independence is a useful pointer to the difficulties here.

At the same time the application of double standards – essentially the lowering of accepted educational and other standards – to facilitate recruitment of people from other ethnic groups is liable to have undesirable effects which will almost certainly be counter-productive in terms of communal harmony. The pressures from Northern Nigerian rulers for expansion of the Hausa-Fulani element in the Nigerian army officer corps to 'compensate' for the initial Ibo predominance illustrates this point effectively.

Quota systems for recruitment based on ethnic group or region may themselves lead to the adoption of double standards. In any case the consequences of determining quotas presumably eventually proportionate to population would pose enormous questions in South Africa on which it is not necessary to elaborate here.

IV SOME CONSTRUCTIVE APPROACHES

If, as seems logical, the objective is intergroup accommodation and co-participation of ethnic groups in a plural society, then access to employment in the public services on merit has a claim to be regarded as a civil right. Where the groups are starting from very different cultures, levels of development and education, then success depends on anticipation of the problems briefly referred to above. A case for establishing special 'crash' programmes of training for different types of public employment can be made. Properly conducted they can go far to avoiding the divisive charge of 'double standards'. Again it is no coincidence that the most useful reference points seem to be in the transition from colonial rule: the Institute of Administration in Zaria in Northern Nigeria, subsequently reproduced in similar form in what is now Malawi, helped to resolve cultural differences and instal in successful careers individuals who would otherwise have been handicapped from becoming civil servants at an appropriate level. The establishment of a viable democratic social system in a complex plural society could well depend on the early establishment of training schools for different kinds of public servants or the recasting of those which already exist to meet the needs of a rapidly changing situation. In their turn, however, such institutions will not fulfil a useful function unless steps are taken throughout the educational system of the country to prepare young people of all races for the opportunities and responsibilities presenting themselves.

9 Prescriptions for the Plural Society: Theory and Practice in the South African Context

Alvin Rabushka
Senior Fellow of the Hoover Institute on War, Revolution and Peace, Stanford University, California

Is the resolution of intense but conflicting preferences in the plural society manageable in a democratic framework? We think not.[1]

In 1972 Kenneth A. Shepsle and I published a book entitled *Politics in Plural Societies: A Theory of Democratic Instability.*[2] The object of that book was twofold: first, to develop a formal model of politics in the plural society and, second, to test that model against the historical evidence of eighteen plural societies. In the concluding chapter we proposed a set of theoretically informed prescriptions to cope with the inherent problem of democratic instability in the plural society. The object of this paper is to apply those logically derived prescriptions to contemporary South Africa, to test both their theoretical soundness and political workability.

My approach to the study of plural societies had to date been largely theoretical and comparative, save for a detailed case study of Malaysia.[3] Thus I am not a specialist on South Africa but have only previously discussed its political history in a comparative analysis of democratic practices in 18 plural societies.

We organised our analysis of politics in plural societies along four demographic arrangements:

(1) *the competitive configuration*, in which two, or at best three, major ethnic groups monopolise electoral politics (Guyana, Belgium, Trinidad and Tobago, Malaysia, Surinam);
(2) *majority domination*, in which one ethnic group is an overwhelming political majority (Ceylon, Cyprus, Mauritius, Rwanda, Zanzibar);
(3) *the dominant minority*, in which electoral politics is limited to a minority of the population (South Africa, Rhodesia, Burundi); and
(4) *fragmentation*, which consists of the presence of many culturally distinct communities and the failure of any one of them to dominate the political process (Lebanon, the Congo, Nigeria, the Sudan, Yugoslavia).

The general theme which organised my analysis of recent electoral politics in these plural societies was that one-man, one-vote democracy was an inherently unstable arrangement.

How has this analysis held up since publication? Of the 18 countries virtually none has shown an increase in democratic practices. Several, however, have undergone serious deterioration and suffered widespread conflict, including civil wars. Belgium remains democratic, but linguistic regionalism increasingly predominates. Trinidad and Malaysia are dominated by one-party, one-race regimes. Cyprus has endured a full-scale civil war that culminated in Turkish invasion and occupation of one-third of the island. South Africa itself witnessed two serious racial disturbances in the past year and the political climate in Rhodesia has become more intense and violent. In Burundi, the minority Tutsi have killed off a very large segment of the educated Hutu. In Lebanon, Muslims and Christians have fought a full-scale civil war, thus ending Lebanese democracy. Since April 1977, exiled Katangans have invaded Shaba Province, revivifying an earlier secessionist attempt of a decade ago. Subsequent to the book's publication, East Pakistan was violently transformed into Bangladesh, Indians were expelled from Uganda, and tribal rivalries have intensified in some very new African states. That a plural society is not a conducive environment to the practice of democratic competitive party politics is no longer under dispute; still it is interesting to consider what solutions might prevent, in South Africa, the dramatic and often violent developments which characterise the history of so many post-war plural societies.

I A PARADIGM OF POLITICS IN THE PLURAL SOCIETY

For the purposes of this paper, I define a plural society by (1) cultural diversity, (2) politically organised cultural communities, and (3) the salience of ethnicity. A cursory glance at the social composition and organisation of nearly all extant countries suggests that the first feature is simply the reflection of a social truism; rarely are modern societies culturally homogeneous. It is the latter two features (ethnic politics), however, that distinguish the *plural* society from its *pluralistic* counterpart. When the values of these separate cultural communities conflict in the political arena, compromise solutions rarely emerge. *Ethnic preferences are intense and are not negotiable.* To promise less for one's group in the name of harmony and accommodation is to betray that group's interest.

Politics in Plural Societies sets forth a theory of democratic instability.[4] Using the tools of decision theory, I show in plural societies that stable democratic institutions invariably and *inevitably* give way to authoritarian institutions; compromise and bargaining among different ethnic groups is replaced by authoritarian rule of one group over another. Once the dynamics of ethnic politics are set in motion, toleration and conciliation can no longer contain inter-ethnic animosities. Ethnic politics and democratic decline are rooted in logic, not in immoral and pernicious politicians. Let me trace out the main dimensions of this logic.

Sooner or later, ethnicity emerges as the dominant political consideration in plural societies. A broad-based multi-ethnic political leadership may temporarily suppress an ethnic definition of politics, but it cannot alter individual ethnic identities nor entirely remove ethnic considerations. Loyalty in the plural society is *communal*, not *national*. And communal preferences are intense.

What sparks the manifestation of communalism and the increased salience of ethnicity? The answer is obviously complex, and ultimately depends on historical happenstance. Yet an investigation of political motives, that is, the incentives which confront political leaders in the plural society, reveals an important regularity. Politics is an inherently redistributive activity; control of government often carries with it the power to allocate economic resources to one's own supporters. Multi-ethnic coalitions that often emerge in the formative stages of nation-building are inherently unstable, being vulnerable to the political demands of ethnic chauvinism.

To gain increased support, ambitious politicians not included in the governing coalition have incentives to stress ethnic issues. As the salience of ethnic issues increases, the prospects for the ethnic politician correspondingly brighten. Ethnically based political entrepreneurs thus seek to increase the salience of communal issues and then to outbid those politicians who hold office on the moderate platform of inter-ethnic harmony and cooperation. When all issues are finally interpreted in ethnic terms, the rhetoric of cooperation and mutual trust sounds painfully weak and is strategically vulnerable to the politics of ethnic outbidding.

Let me highlight the main features of politics in plural societies, recognising that each society may yield a slight variant of the general pattern. One typically observes the formation of a broad-based multi-ethnic coalition during the formative period of a nation; its survival through the post-independence period, fostered by ambiguous pronouncements on divisive ethnic issues; the emergence of ambitious politicians (political entrepreneurs) whose quest for the perquisites of political office provokes appeals to ethnic passions; the consequent dominance of ethnicity as the salient dimension of political competition; the disappearance of the multi-ethnic coalition and the concomitant ineffectuality of moderate elements; and, finally, the decline of democratic competition, a result of electoral machinations and political violence. The reason that democracy cannot be sustained under conditions of intense ethnic preferences is because outcomes are valued more than procedural norms.

II RACE AND POLITICS IN SOUTH AFRICA[5]

In mid-1975, the population of the Republic was estimated to have been about 25.5 million persons: of these Whites number 4.2 million, Africans 18.1 million, coloured people 2.5 million, and Asians about 700,000.[6] Nor is the White population homogeneous: the relationship between the two major White groups, the Afrikaners and those of British descent, has comprised one of the major themes of twentieth-century political debate, a debate that has gone hand-in-hand with the policies to be pursued towards South Africa's non-White groups – the Africans, Coloureds, and Indians. Although such other issues have arisen as labour disputes, the gold standard, and so forth, the two foregoing themes have structured partisan debate and party competition.

It is not necessary here to reconstruct in full detail the history of South African politics, save to note that it conforms with the paradigm of politics set forth in *Politics in Plural Societies* for the 'dominant minority configuration'.[7] We may classify the first stage of South African history from 1652 to 1910 as dominated by Afrikaner-English competition for control of Southern Africa, especially following British arrival in 1806 and their establishment of a permanent governorship over the Cape Province. As a consequence of British rule in the Cape Province, the second phase of South African history, known as the 'Great Trek', began in 1836 for the purpose of establishing Boer Republics in the interior, free of British domination. These movements led to the establishment of the Transvaal and the Orange Free State.

From the days of the Great Trek until the establishment of the Union of South Africa as a self-governing state in 1910, the British-Boer division was of especial political salience, and sparked several instances of overt warfare. The South Africa Act of 1909, which created an independent South Africa in the British Commonwealth in 1910, restored pre-war political arrangements, and the original South African Party, led by Botha and Smuts, was primarily committed to the healing of wounds left by the Anglo-Boer War.

We may classify the second major chronological period of 1910–1948 as one of Afrikaner-English cooperation and the resurgence of Afrikaner nationalism. Louis Botha (1910–19) and Jan Smuts (1919–24), the first two Prime Ministers, each maintained the spirit of compromise reflected in the South Africa Act of 1909. Each resisted extremist Afrikaner elements and chose, instead, to cooperate with the British. But Hertzog's government (1923–33) began to reflect the successful rise of Afrikaner nationalism and his government displayed a more explicit Afrikaner orientation. A temporary rapprochement between Hertzog and Smuts from 1933 meant that the new government was less disposed to accept extremist Afrikaner demands. As a result of Hertzog's new moderate stance, the militant wing of the Nationalist Party split off and officially sought the creation of an Afrikaner Republic coupled with South African withdrawal from the British Commonwealth of Nations.

The 1948 election is the crucial turning point in South Africa's modern history. On 29 March 1948 Dr D. F. Malan made a campaign speech proposing apartheid – separate development of the races – as a policy of race relations. The United Party badly underestimated the appeal of this issue and was shockingly defeated by Malan's Nationalist Party.

This Nationalist Party victory takes us into the third phase of South African politics: minority domination and the politics of outbidding. Since their rise to power in 1948, Afrikaners have totally monopolised the decision processes of government. Control of Parliament since 1948 has enabled the Afrikaner-based Nationalist Party to impose on non-Whites a series of measures that include (1) the 1949 Prohibition of Mixed Marriages Act, (2) further amendments to the Immorality Act, (3) abolition of the Cape Coloureds from the common electoral role in 1956, (4) abolition of token representation of Africans by White members of Parliament in 1960, (5) a series of amendments to the Group Areas Act of 1950 that restrict physical movement and area of residence, (6) labour and educational legislation to place non-Whites at a serious disadvantage both in employment and in universities by prohibiting African workers from competing with Whites in many occupations and forbidding non-Whites from attending English-speaking universities, (7) 'pass laws' and numerous other measures that give the government wide powers of perquisition, confiscation of property, banning of organisations, exile, extradition, arrest, and detention without trial.

October 1976, the month in which the Transkei received its political independence from South Africa, marks the start of the fourth phase of South African political development.[8] The policy of separate development consists in giving independence to a group of eight or nine homelands (the Transkei, Basotho, Qwaqwa, Bophuthatswana, Ciskei, Banzankulu, Kwa Zulu, Lebowa and Venda). Put briefly, the theory of separate development argues that all Black Africans trace their origin to a particular ethnic group, whose language they speak, that these ethnic units have homelands, which have for decades been preserved by law from White purchase and ownership, and that the proper evolution of these tribal homelands is towards nationhood. Once a traditional homeland has become an independent nation, its citizens may remain in White South Africa, but only as 'guest workers' and citizens of their own new country. Thus Xhosas born and bred in Soweto, a township outside Johannesburg, would exercise their political rights in the Transkei, the Xhosa homeland, and not in the White Republic. In time South Africa would give birth to eight or nine Black nation-states within its own present territory. Everyone would enjoy political rights except that Blacks who live outside the homelands would work in one country and vote in another. Under this arrangement, Whites would comprise a numerical majority in the remaining White area of South Africa and could thus practise one-man, one-vote democracy without fear of Black majority rule. In the last fifteen years, South Africa has devoted considerable resources to building up the economies of the homelands in pursuit of this policy of separate development.

We might raise three questions about the homelands policy: what will be the character of the new states?; will separate development actually solve South Africa's dilemma?; and what will be the political effects of the new states? Only the middle question bears on this paper. We explore that question in the context of the main theme of this paper, the prescriptions for the plural society outlined in *Politics in Plural Societies*.

To this point, my treatment of South African politics fits in with what I term the dominant minority classification. Suppose that South Africa were immediately to grant universal franchise to all within its borders. I would then analyse South Africa in the context of ethnic fragmentation: Coloureds, Asians, nine major distinct African tribes, the English, and the Afrikaners. The reasoning presented in *Politics in Plural Societies* would forecast that Black tribal leaders would form a temporary coalition and attain a majority in Parliament, which would, in turn, lead to the exclusion of Whites and perhaps Coloureds from the political process. However, the oversized multi-tribal coalition would be unstable and give way to extremist pressures arising within each tribal group and lead, sooner or later, to the collapse of democratic institutions and the establishment of authoritarian rule by the most powerful tribe over all other South Africans, a pattern typical of several new African nations. The logic of electoral competition in plural societies suggest that immediate establishment of one-man, one-vote democracy would ensure the collapse of democratic institutions; it might even abort in civil war between Whites and Blacks in South Africa.

This situation is purely hypothetical and thus I resume analysis of South Africa as a dominant minority regime. Let us turn, then, to the prescriptions for South Africa's racial dilemma.

III PRESCRIPTIONS FOR THE PLURAL SOCIETY: THE CASE OF SOUTH AFRICA

A formula to guarantee democratic stability in plural societies is difficult to construct. Proportional representation, federalism, ideology, assimilation and expatriation have not been effective solutions. In so far as protection of minorities and equitable representation of multiple communities in one society has been investigated, no one electoral system has been found preferable to another and fair representation still eludes political theorists.

Politics in Plural Societies derived six solutions to cope with democratic instability. Although these solutions are grounded in theory, we may none the less question their feasibility in any specific context. As it turns out, only two solutions apply in the South African context.

A recurring feature of politics in plural societies is the breakdown of the multi-ethnic coalition shortly after independence is won from colonial or foreign rule. Refusal to grant independence thus represents a *first* solution for the problem of ethnic conflict that so often disturbs the peace in plural societies. Since independence provides the prize of decision-making authority over which ethnic groups inevitably fight, continued colonial rule precludes the crystallisation of ethnic hostility. In some instances, however, colonial rule creates more conflict than it precludes. Witness, for example, Portuguese involvement in Angola. Current conflict in Angola rests, in part, on inter-tribal rivalry, albeit masked somewhat by ideological rhetoric, an outcome forecast in *Politics in Plural Societies*; that is, the breakdown of a united nationalist movement into sectional rivalries. In any event, this first solution is not applicable to South Africa; it applies today only in Bermuda, Hong Kong, and Gibraltar, in which multiracial populations live peacefully under colonial rule, and in French overseas territories.

The *second* prescription calls for constitutional limitations on the powers of central governments. Confederation in Switzerland has confined divisive linguistic and religious issues to selected local cantons and democratic stability at the national level continues undiminished. Decentralisation relegates important issues for resolution to local administrative levels and thus prevents the aggregation of ethnic preferences on a national basis, with its possible harmful consequences.

But Switzerland developed as a nation from a series of alliances among independent cantons that joined together for mutual gains and protection from a common enemy. Loyalties in Switzerland are cantonal, not national. My guess is that it would be virtually impossible to superimpose a decentralised form of government on a plural society that has no tradition of such rule nor any institutions to cope with salient issues at a local level of government. Federalism in Nigeria, Malaya, Uganda, Burma, and the West Indies has not met with success.

A *third* approach to resolving democratic instability is the practice of elite accommodation to head off potential ethnic disputes. Elites must command widespread support and deference from their respective blocs of followers, and be able to strike and enforce bargains on potentially disruptive issues. To date, only the Netherlands seems to have managed successfully the politics of accommodation. In most plural societies, elites have been completely unable to accommodate the vociferous conflicting demands of their respective communities.

A *fourth* solution envisages the creation of permanent external enemies. While successful in the short term, when the public recognises a clear and present danger, this solution breaks down when the external threat is no longer credible.

Taking stock, these first four solutions are of little interest in the South African context. The remaining two, however, merit careful consideration. Let us examine each in turn.

1. Creation of homogeneous societies. The division of a plural society into its constituent ethnic components, each as a sovereign society, would certainly (by definition) eliminate cultural diversity and ethnic conflict. Though such a partitioning does not guarantee the disappearance of conflict, it does ensure that conflict will no longer follow ethnic lines.

We might raise three general questions about this policy. First, will the new states be economically viable? Second, are the ethnic groups concentrated in specific regions? Without ethnic residential concentration, it will be difficult to draw new political boundaries to give mutual satisfaction and costs of resettlement may become prohibitively high. Third, why should a dominant community, majority or minority, surrender its position of advantage and privilege?

The 'Independent Homelands Policy' of the South African government closely resembles this prescription to create homogeneous societies. On theoretical grounds, the solution is sound.[9] The question we must raise is its long-term feasibility in South Africa.

We may answer the first of these general questions with a qualified 'yes'. Although the new states will be poor, they will be comparatively well-off by African standards. The Transkei's annual per capita income of US $220 makes it richer than all but a handful of African states. Even though only 13 per cent of South African territory has been alloted to the homelands, nearly half of its fertile land is homeland territory. The success of the Transkei depends less on the morality of South African motives, or the failure of South Africa to provide budgetary grants-in-aid or technical assistance, than it does on altering native conservatism and traditional tribal forms of ownership which discourage efficient production. Lack of local jobs means that between a quarter and a half of all economically active males in the homelands must live as migrant labourers in White South Africa; present restrictions on the investment of White capital in the homelands, to stimulate an African business class, must surely reduce employment opportunities in the homelands. It is easy to give sound economic advice to the Chief Ministers of the homelands, viz., to adopt policies of unfettered economic liberalism. It is not so easy to get the Chief Ministers to follow this advice. If the Transkei cannot show any economic progress in the next decade, the policy of separate development may be throttled by recalcitrance within the other homelands. I am not optimistic that the Transkei leadership will adopt sound economic policies and, in the fashion of Hong Kong, move from a virtually resourceless, very poor economy to a centre for investment, manufacturing, and trade. The leaders in the Transkei may prefer to call for everlasting assistance from White South Africa, recognising that an economically and politically viable Transkei is essential to successful implementation of the independent homelands policy. It may be easier and politically more attractive to hold Pretoria to ransom than put liberal economic policies into place and disrupt traditional social and economic institutions.

A second question which emerges in the creation of homogeneous societies entails patterns of ethnic concentration: here we confront a major stumbling-block in the path of successful implementation of homelands policy. A successful policy of separate development requires that the majority of Africans living outside their homelands feel both loyalty and belonging to their designated nation. Without that sentiment, homeland citizenship is simply a legal manoeuvre to declare Africans non-citizens of South Africa. Some urban Africans in the townships of White South Africa have no direct tribal connection with their alloted homelands. They may be the children of a mixed marriage with no clearly defined tribal identity; many, indeed, may never have seen their putative homeland. Forced homelands citizenship for these urban Africans may provoke anger and irritation, rather than acceptance.

Nor does the homelands policy resolve the political problem of the Asian or Coloured communities, who have no tribal homelands. To demarcate one would cast doubt on the much-prized ethnographic validity of the existing homelands. Of course, if all Africans were citizens of the homelands, Asians and Coloureds would jointly constitute a numerical minority in White South Africa and could be fully enfranchised without risk to White rule.

Recall the third general question which attends the creation of homogeneous societies. Why should the dominant community give up its privileges? The answer is that Whites increasingly believe that a restrictive racial franchise is not a viable long-term policy. The motive underlying the independent homelands policy is that it is essential to create a South African state in which Whites are a numerical majority in order to preserve the European way of life. In economic terms, the discounted present value of segregation, in the eyes of a growing number of Whites, may soon become negative.

To summarise, the independent homelands policy rests on a firm theoretical footing. Whether the new homeland-states can make an economic go of things and whether the Black urban majority will passively accept homeland citizenship are the as yet unanswered questions. Separate development requires that each answer be in the affirmative; but only time and research will tell if this policy succeeds.

2. *Restrictions on the scope of government.* Jobs, housing, education, and other public services often become the preserve of the advantaged political community. Since the provision of public goods by the state is one of its primary motives for existence, regime legitimacy often suffers when public funds are used to provide benefits for a narrow ruling community. Thus, to tone down the invidious quality of ethnic politics in the plural society, government economic activity should be minimised and reliance on a *free market* economy maximised.

D. Hobart Houghton, a South African economist, argues in his text on *The South African Economy* that society must allow members of all racial groups an equitable share of the national income on the basis of individual effort and ability, *unhampered* by racially restrictive devices.[10] Only when all individuals realise promising economic opportunities irrespective of race will each person see positive benefits from supporting rather than opposing existing institutions. Houghton defines the government's basic economic policy up to the 1920s as essentially that of free trade. Since the 1920s, state intervention has prevailed in the form of protective duties, substantial government contracts, and the establishment of government-managed firms, that preferentially hire white workers. Thus the free play of market forces has been increasingly replaced by state intervention.[11] White voters have used a monopoly of political power to entrench their economic position by restrictions on the economic and educational opportunities of African workers; that is, contriving labour scarcity to ensure above-market wages for White workers.

William H. Hutt has specifically advocated the free-market solution to South Africa's racial dilemma.[12] For Hutt, a bloodless solution presumes that Black and White workers share access to the labour market on equal terms; only disinterested market pressures, under the profit motive, can dissolve traditional barriers and offer opportunities irrespective of race or colour. Note that neither author analyses the realities of Nationalist Party politics to see if this is a feasible solution. Classical economic analysis may have little to say about ethnic politics.

I recognise that politics is a complex subject in South Africa, and that radical policy initiatives are unlikely to emerge from a government that alienates the main stream of Nationalist Party support. Economic liberalism may be indeed the solution to racial problems in South Africa, but Whites must be persuaded of this belief. It may be possible to increase the number of non-Whites with a stake in the existing order if these individuals are afforded greater economic opportunities. To do this in a manner that does not threaten White rule requires that the government deftly defuse race as a political issue. It must de-emphasize talk about political evolution and political solutions; it must refocus both its talk and efforts for enlarging economic opportunities for non-Whites. To repeat, non-Whites as individuals must be accorded greater economic opportunity even as White political institutions remain intact. Nationalist Party supporters can accede to increasing economic gains for Africans, Asians and Coloureds only if they remain confident of stable White political rule. Leaders among non-Whites must perceive economic incentives that make individual gain in the market-place a more attractive prospect than investment in group (racial) political activity.

IV THEORY OF RACIAL HARMONY

In an earlier work, I have set forth a theory of racial harmony. The theory can be put in quite straightforward terms. Under conditions of voluntary exchange in free markets, racial tensions and conflict are kept to a minimum. Individuals, as members of specific racial groups, stand to gain or lose on the basis of their marginal value of productivity (which may be conditioned by genetic, historical, political or cultural reasons). Groups of individuals with low marginal values of productivity attempt to compensate by gaining public control over resources, thereby using political power and the decision-making authority of government to reallocate wealth to their own advantage. The public activities of government in the multiracial environment thus convert private economic competition among individuals in markets into social and political conflict between races. When the economic well-being of groups is significantly affected by political activity, politics becomes a fight between groups (or races) for survival. Thus, in a society where race is politically salient, the greater the extent of the public use of resources (i.e., the greater the extent of government economic activity), the greater the likelihood of racial conflict. Hence, governments should be seen as a chief cause of racial conflict, rather than as a promoter of racial harmony.

The logic of racial harmony. It is the assertion of the free-market approach to race relations that *racial tensions and conflict are kept to a minimum under conditions of voluntary exchange in free markets.* Or, from another standpoint, government intervention in or control over market activities harms racial minorities and exacerbates racial tension and conflict, especially when race is invoked as a political issue. What are the characteristics of market exchange that confirm this conclusion?

1. In free markets, the imposition of costs or the receiving of benefits is largely an *individual*, and impersonal, affair. Individual labour is rewarded or compensated on the basis of its marginal value of productivity, which is, in my opinion, the only equitable and simultaneously efficient method of payment. Any other method requires discrimination against productive persons. The two key aspects of market exchange are voluntariness and unanimity. No rational individual contracts to make himself worse off. Nor is any individual forced into choosing that which he does not wish to buy in a free market.

Contrast market choice with various political choice devices such as national polls, elections, committees, or legislatures. Political choice entials a group decision. The group agreement required of political decisions precludes action from being taken individually. And, when we begin to think of individuals in terms of groups, race becomes a natural basis of political appeal and group voting. Political competition requires the aggregation of individuals into winning coalitions; markets do not.

2. Markets permit individuals to express intensity of preference. Depending on his resources, a person may consume a variable amount of any given item consonant with his preference for it. In politics, on the other hand, a voter generally has only one vote to cast (and many do not have even one) and cannot vary the intensity of his convictions issue by issue. Minorities thus have appropriate representations in the market-place: the number of their votes is related to their proportional productivity. In politics, they may represent an inefficacious community, contributing taxes but receiving few or no benefits of their own.

3. Economic power and choice in markets are distributed thinly among decision-makers in most cases, unless wealth is extremely concentrated in a few hands. Each individual is as economically powerful as the amount of resources he commands. In politics, on the contrary, power is extremely concentrated and the power-holders can forcibly reallocate resources even more to the self-interest of their own community.

4. Free markets separate economic efficiency from other irrelevant characteristics. A businessman, entrepreneur, or a consumer who expresses preferences that are not related to cost or productive efficiency is at a disadvantage compared with other individuals who do not. The economic incentives of free markets encourage a maximum return on investment; those who choose to discriminate, and in the process fail to meet the competition, will ultimately be forced out of business, unless they can rely upon the power of government to protect them from competition or to enforce discriminatory social customs. The economic incentives in competitive markets should cause discriminatory conditions to disappear over time. By and large, discrimination against groups of particular colour or religion is least in those areas where there is the greatest freedom of competition.

5. Note also the differences between private firms and government-directed or regulated economic activities. In free markets, the right of entry is guaranteed and any individual, regardless of race, can begin production without fear or coercion or restraint, assuming the state performs its minimal tasks of maintaining law and order. The same is not true when government holds or grants economic monopolies, especially when the members of one race exclusively dictate public policy. Free entry is then often denied by government.

Additionally, government regulatory agencies can allow prices to be raised to cover higher costs in regulated industries. A private firm that hires exclusively its own kind must pay the costs of forgone additional profits if its employees have below average marginal values of productivity. Thus, non-competitive public firms have a distinct advantage over private firms: they can satisfy economic preferences and prejudice against political minorities without the cost of losing out to the competition. Clearly, *the most effective market power is that which can be enforced by the police power of government.*

But the most important of these characteristics of markets was the first, the fact that *individuals* and not *groups* are the key participants. Individuals benefit or lose on the basis of their *own* marginal values of productivity, not on the basis of a group property such as race. So long as all interpersonal interaction is confined to the market-place, conflict is purely economic and between private individuals. But when conflict becomes public, the need to form winning coalitions, whether by ballot or by guns, converts, communities of individuals into well defined groups: in the multi-racial environment these invariably are synonymous with races. Political competition thus becomes racial competition for control over the power that government alone commands. The impersonal market is replaced by a directly coercive political relationship in which race, rather than marginal productivity, becomes the basis for resource allocation. This in inequitable, illegitimate, and often politically unstable.[13]

The free-market solution to South Africa's political future, restricting the scope of government economic activity, rests on the same sound theoretical footing as the independent homelands policy. Can this solution mesh with the government's perception of political realities? That is, will the White contituents of the Nationalist Party agree to compete with Black workers on equal terms in the near future, or will they resist any efforts that erode White economic privileges? A free-market economy may allow the regime to co-opt the African middle class, who may choose and attain personal economic advancement in the market-place. Maintaining present discriminatory economic arrangements is likely to encourage Africans to invest in group political activity.

Other nations illustrate that a free-market economy is conducive to racial harmony and political stability. Chinese and Europeans live in harmony in Hong Kong's free-market economy (although China has indicated that Hong Kong will not be permitted to become independent and thus there is no political prize over which to fight). Singapore and Bermuda also enjoy considerable racial harmony. Economic opportunities are open to members of all races on equal terms and the governments of Singapore and Bermuda are multiracial in composition. In Singapore, the Chinese comprise 75 per cent of the population and a universal franchise does not threaten Chinese predominance – perhaps the Chinese can afford to offer liberal economic opportunities to their less productive Malay and Indian countrymen. Bermuda is thus a more interesting and relevant example.

Bermuda seems to have watched political events in the neighbouring Bahamas with great interest. A predominantly Black Progressive Liberal Party gained control of the Bahamian government in the 1972 elections and thus Britain agreed to schedule independence of the Bahamas on 10 July 1973. Whites in Bermuda make up only 40 per cent of the population and thus one-man, one-vote democracy implies Black majority rule at some future date.

Up to 1963, when the Parliamentary Franchise Act was implemented, the franchise had been restricted to owners of real estate to a modest stated value who would therefore presumably have a stake in the territory's well-being.[14] Bermuda was then a white paternalistic oligarchy. The new Act and its subsequent amendment provided universal suffrage to all British subjects aged 21 years and over who had resided in the Colony for at least three years. The General Election of May 1968 was the first conducted on political party lines. The result was a bi-racial vote of confidence in the United Bermuda Party, which won 30 out of 40 seats, the remaining 10 going to the chiefly Black Progressive Labour Party. A segment of the Black middle class was invited to join the White oligarchy in a multiracial party to give them a stake in the existing order. Since the May 1968 election and the new Constitution of 8 June 1968, which brought responsible internal government to Bermuda, vast changes have taken place in integration in education, housing, and social services.

Blacks and Whites enjoy equal economic opportunity under law. Unemployment is virtually non-existent and wages are high. Since 1968, strides have been made in Race Relation laws, Race Relation Councils, Advisory Committees, and integration of schools, all of which permit a multiracial United Bermuda Party to provide a climate of political stability so conducive to economic prosperity. Bermudian Blacks do better by competing as individuals in the market-place than as leaders of political groups competing for political power. Political instability and/or racial tensions in Bermuda would devastate social institutions in the island's small area and cripple both the tourist business and the continued establishment of exempted international companies. The United Bermuda Party still enjoys multiracial support and Bermuda seems well on its way to resolving what might have been an intractable racial problem. The keystone on which the Bermudian solution rests is the free market-place which treats Blacks and Whites on a colour-blind basis. Of course, South Africa is a more complex society than Bermuda, but the principles of this discussion may hold for both societies.

Can these two theoretically sound solutions – independent homelands and free-market economic institutions – be applied simultaneously? The key word here is *voluntary*. Those homelands that seek independence should so emerge and it would be greatly in their interest to rely on free market institutions. At the same time, South Africa should put into practice liberal economic policies to defuse political life. The outcome depends both on the skill of the government and the acquiescence of the politically active White population.

NOTES

1. Alvin Rabushka and Kenneth A. Shepsle, *Politics in Plural Societies: A Theory of Democratic Instability* (Columbus: Charles E. Merrill, 1972) p. 217.
2. Ibid.
3. Alvin Rabushka, *Race and Politics in Urban Malaya* (Stanford: Hoover Institution Press, 1973). See also my more general book, *A Theory of Racial Harmony* (Columbia: University of South Carolina Press, 1974).
4. (Columbus: Charles E. Merrill, 1972) ch. 3, pp. 74–88.
5. I have briefly tried to apply the paradigm developed in Chapter 3 of *Politics in Plural Societies* to the example of South Africa (see pp. 158–69). This application incorporates a portion of the very extensive literature in the fields of politics and race relations in Southern Africa, but is in no way a comprehensive and complete account of South African political history. One very useful, comprehensive study of electoral politics in South Africa is found in the work of Kenneth A. Heard, *General Elections in South Africa, 1943–1970* (London and Cape Town: Oxford University Press, 1974).
6. D. Hobart Houghton, *The South African Economy* (Cape Town: Oxford University Press, 1976) p. 32.
7. See note 5.
8. These few paragraphs follow John O'Sullivan, 'The Transkei and the Independent Homelands Policy', in Robert L. Schuettinger (ed.), *South Africa – The Vital Link* (Washington, DC: Council on American Affairs, 1976) pp. 63–4. For an earlier and more detailed treatment of separate

development as an appropriate solution to the racial dilemma in South Africa see N. J. Rhoodie, *Apartheid and Racial Partnership in Southern Africa* (Pretoria/Cape Town: Academica, 1969) pp. 336–84.
9. See note 4.
10. See note 6.
11. Ibid., pp. 250–1.
12. William H. Hutt, *The Economics of the Colour Bar* (London: published for the Institute of Economic Affairs by Andre Deutsch, 1964).
13. Some evidence on a number of multi-ethnic countries can be found in Alvin Rabushka, *A Theory of Racial Harmony*, pp. 74–83.
14. For a discussion of post-war Bermudian political history, see Terry Tucker, *Bermuda, Today and Yesterday (1503–1973)* (New York: St. Martin's Press, 1975) pp. 158–71.

10 Some Educational Imperatives regarding the Peaceful Pursuit of Intergroup Accommodation in a Plural Society

Edward Fort
Chancellor of University of Wisconsin Center System, Madison, Wisconsin

I BACKGROUND OVERVIEW

When one begins discussing the various options which are open to the plural societies in relationship to the pursuing of peaceful intergroup accommodation it becomes increasingly apparent that the mere listing of a plethora of options is, probably, not appropriate. It is not the intent of this paper to pursue a massively designed multiple-option approach. Instead this writer's thrust is designed to place keen emphasis upon the critical issue of *education* as the principal option which must be aggressively dealt with by the pluralistic society, as it seeks to accommodate the needs, longings and even demands of various subgroups within the matrix. In effect, it is suggested that education becomes the central pivot upon which all plural societies must platform their endeavours as designed to deal with the goal of peaceful intergroup accommodation. It becomes the keystone of the arch. It becomes one, if not the overriding consideration. This is not to say that education is proposed to the exclusion of political decision-making freedom, economic opportunity equality, social intermingling equality, and/or freedom of movement equality. Instead it is merely presented as one of the principal ingredients in whatever thrusts are designed by plural societies as a means of ensuring some semblance of progress toward an announced goal of peaceful intergroup accommodation.

Before one can begin the examination of the means whereby attention must be given to the ingredient of education as a principal option in this struggle, it is perhaps appropriate that we briefly examine agreed definitions in relationship to what happens in a pluralist society when inter-racial and/or inter-ethnic contact materialises. In that regard Smith and Preston[1] in their research on this topic indicate that these inter-racial/inter-ethnic contacts historically have resulted in a variety of conditions, including the following:

(1) *Segregation* implies a stringent separation between ethnic or racial groups with no group necessarily considered superior. The separation may be largely voluntary as in the case of the Mennonites, a religious sect concentrated in the United States mainly in Pennsylvania and Ohio. It may be clearly non-voluntary as with 'apartheid', the system of racial separation in South Africa. Or segregation may be accommodation of the two, as is the current reality for the Americans.

What we must keep in mind is that true segregation – separate or equal – seldom exists.

(2) *Stratification*, in the context of race and ethnicity, means the enforced separation of racial or ethnic groups with one group being clearly dominant. Two examples are the relations of Blacks and Whites in South Africa and of the American Indians in the dominant society in the United States during much of our history.

Like stratification in social classes, stratification by race and ethnicity is supported by an elaborate system of beliefs and ideas. These are usually expressed in the form of racial and ethnic stereotypes – i.e., the dumb Pole, the shuffling Darkie, the thieving Mexican, the drunken Irishman, etc.

(3) *Assimilation* is defined as a cultural blending of two or more previously distinct peoples. People who would pass take on cultural characteristics of the dominant group and consciously attempt to become a part of that group. Immigrants in the United States have often found the process of assimilation difficult. Yet for many there has been little choice about leaving their old homeland.

(4) *Pluralism* means relationship among racial or ethnic groups [where] none of the groups dominate. There is interaction among and

free movement between the groups, and the groups maintain their racial and/or ethnic identity. This seemingly utopian relationship does exist, though understandably it is relatively rare. While there are some elements of racial and ethnic pluralism in the United States, most notably in Hawaii, we could hardly say we have a pluralistic system; far too much segregation and stratification exist. Switzerland and Fiji offer better examples of pluralistic societies.

(5) *Expulsion* involves the forceful removal of one group by another. Most of us are able to think of numerous instances of expulsion. Two of the more notorious examples in American history involve Indians and Japanese Americans.

During the 1830s Federal troops removed the prosperous Cherokee nation from its homeland in the southeastern United States and herded it into what is now Oklahoma. Cherokees had suffered the misfortune of having gold discovered on their tribal land. Only half of the 10,000 tribal members who began the journey known as the 'Trail of Tears' survived it.

The forced removal of first, second and third generations of Japanese Americans from their communities during World War II was a shameful episode in American history. It was racism in its most virulent form. . . . The 'relocation', as it was euphemistically designated, succeeded in removing 120,000 Japanese Americans, mainly from the west coast, to ten camps established in isolated inland areas. The rationale for the removal was 'national security' during World War II.

(6) *Annihilation* as a sixth possible outcome of inter-racial and inter-ethnic contact [exists] when one group attempts to eliminate another racial or ethnic group. For example, White Americans annihilated a number of Indian tribes during the development of this country. . . . The island of Tasmania, located off the southern coast of Australia, witnessed the complete annihilation of its aborigines within 73 years. . . . The attempted extermination of Jews by Nazi Germany during World War II is more widely known and was so monstrous that a new word was coined to describe it – 'genocide'.

(7) *Amalgamation*: the physical blending of previously distinct groups. This is the 'mongrelisation', so much feared by the Klu Klux Klan and other similar groups. Much of the world's population has obviously resulted from racial and ethnic amalgamation.

II THE CHALLENGE OF CULTURAL PLURALISM

One of the most successful examples of cultural pluralism is the Republic of Switzerland. It is based on the arrangement whereby Swiss of Protestant or Catholic beliefs and of German French and Italian descent live in districts which are, to a great extent, ethnically homogeneous, but which are united in a Federal Republic that proclaims a respect for the cultures of all its ethnic groups without insisting on the dominance of any.[2]

Kurt Mayer also suggests that:

> The phenomenon of Swiss harmony, however, is often only imperfectly understood. Historically, the Swiss nation has originated from the desire of a group of heterogeneous communities to preserve their local independence through a system of mutual defence alliances. As a result of this long and often stormy historical process, the Swiss have finally learned to blend their cultural differences into national equilibrium. Today they no longer regard their cultural heterogeneity as an obstacle to the perpetuation of national unity and political stability. To a large extent this national equilibrium rests on an underlying balance of demographic factors which is not always perceived. ... The two most important ingredients of Swiss cultural pluralism are the ethnic-linguistic and the religious structure of the Swiss population. ... The national languages of Switzerland are German, French, Italian and Romansch, all of which are expressly recognised as equal in the Federal constitution.... In general, there is a widespread misconception abroad that every Swiss speaks all national languages and possibly English as well. In fact, most Swiss know only one language well, although it is true that the proportion of those who have a more or less extensive command of other languages than their own is much greater in Switzerland than in most other countries of the world. ... The facts, then, are that although Switzerland maintains more than one official language, the four national languages are spoken in clearly defined territorial areas. ... The individual Swiss are no more bilingual and multilingual than are people in other countries, although it is true that a good many of them have a good working knowledge of several languages in addition to their own.[3]

The apparent success with regard to intergroup accommodation in the pluralistic society of Switzerland (notwithstanding the cleavages existing) and in Canada are of historical importance in this entire question. As observed by Porter:

> In the United States a highly visible deprived minority was not

sharing in the affluence the society was supposed to have produced. In Canada, similarly, the French had been denied much of the opportunity and had carried a great deal of the cost in less education and lower-paid jobs – lower, that is, than some immigrant groups that were coming in near the bottom – of Canada's take-off as an industrial society. The demand by some intellectuals in French Canada that something be done about this inequality led to the establishment in 1963 of the Royal Commission on Bilingualism and Biculturalism. . . . The longstanding hostility of so many of the English in Canada to learning French is analogous to the hostilities toward Blackness that has marked Black–White relations. In both bases, psychological elements are deep layered, all the more so because Anglicans, like Whites in the United States, are the dominant majority in both numbers and power. Occasionally, the psychological tensions of colour may be invoked by referring to the French as 'les nègres blancs d'Amérique'. . . .

In response to the recommendation of the Royal Commission for 'equal partnership' and 'institutional bilingualism' the Federal Government embarked on a series of policies to improve the position of the French and the French language in those agencies and institutions within its jurisdiction. Bilingualism within the Federal public service improved. The French became better represented than formerly within the higher levels of the bureaucracy. Ottawa began slowly taking on the aspect of a bilingual national capital. Much money was spent on language training and grants made to Provincial governments to improve their provision of second language education. The Federal Government saw itself as constitutionally responsible for safeguarding the two official languages even though language, because it is the principal means of cultural expression, would normally be considered a provincial responsibility.[4]

Given the above examples, relative to (1) Switzerland's ability to accommodate, on a peaceful basis, intergroup needs, and (2) Canada's attempt, on the basis of nationally developed legislation, to accommodate the French-speaking minority, these represent thrusts in the area of options taken by pluralistic societies as designed to enhance the living of diverse groups on a peaceful basis side by side. Nothwithstanding the above, the history of the United States is such that efforts designed to move in the direction of peaceable accommodation have been slow, though some gains are being made on meaningful fronts. We are talking about a nation which has grown from a population of

2.9 million at the time of the first census in 1790 to a population approaching 207 million according to the 1970 census, with an addition of two million residents each year. As suggested by the literature, more than 45 million people immigrated to the United States between 1820 and 1970, with approximately 80 per cent of that number coming from Europe. In addition, several million Blacks were brought forcefully to this country, mostly from the African continent, as slaves, all prior to the 1820s. History tells us, as indicated by historians Wolfinger, Shapiro and Greenstein, that:

> The first generation of immigrants usually was desperately poor. But even when their children went to school and maintained some measure of prosperity, they often continued to experience discrimination from Americans of English-speaking Protestant stock. In many instances, these children maintained ancestral memories of their rejection, and in turn passed these memories on to their children. The consequences of these experiences has been to maintain to this day a strong sense of national group consciousness among many millions of Americans. Their national ancestry is what psychologists call a 'reference group' – i.e., a collectivity with which people identified and whose existence helps its members define themselves at least in some circumstances.... Members of almost all European ethnic groups have attained extraordinary progress in the last twenty years. If we look at the people aged sixty or more we see that Americans of Italian, Polish and other Slavic ancestry are well below the national average in income and education. The members of the same ethnic groups below the age of thirty rank above the national average in these categories.[5]

III BLACK AMERICANS, A RISE OF NEO-ETHNICITY, ABSENCE OF TOTAL ASSIMILATION

Given the circumstances under which the Black man came to America, and given the critical examples of a refusal on the part of that racial group to be continually subjugated by the happenstance of institutionalised racism, one becomes more and more suspicious of those sociological theories which would suggest that the ultimate solution of the Black problem, on the American scene, is that concerned with total Black assimilation from a sociological point of view, as suggested, for example, by sociologist Paul Metzger:

The belief that racial assimilation constitutes the only democratic solution to the racial problem in the United States should be relinquished by sociologists. Beyond committing them to a value premise which comprises their claim to value neutrality, the assimilationist strategy overlooks the functions which ethnic pluralism may perform in a democratic society. Suggestions as to these functions are found in the writings of Gordon, Greeley and Etzioni. The application of this perspective to the racial problem should result in the recognition that the Black Power and the Black National movements, to the extent that they aim at the creation of a unified and coherent Black community which generates a sense of common peoplehood and interest, are necessarily contrary neither to the experience of other American minorities nor to the interest of Black people. The potential of racial divisiveness – and in the extreme case, revolutionary confrontation – which resides in such movements should be recognised but the source of this 'pathological' potential should be seen as resting primarily within the racism of the wider society rather than in the 'extremism' response to it on the part of the victimised minority. . . . To abandon the notion that assimilation is a self-completing process will make it possible to study the forces (especially at the level of cultural and social structure) which facilitate or hinder assimilation or, conversely, the forces which generate the sense of ethnic and racial identity even within the homogenising confines of modern society. On the basis of an assessment of such forces, it is certainly within the province of sociological analysts to point to the possibilities of conscious intervention in the social process (either the majority or the minority group) to achieve given ends and to weigh the costs and consequences of various policy alternatives. The functions of the sociological analysis, however, should be informed by an awareness that *any* form of intervention will take place in a political context – that intervention itself is, in fact, a political act – and that the likelihood of its success will be conditioned by the configuration of political forces in the society at large. Without this awareness, which is nothing more than the awareness of the total societal context within which a given minority problem has its meaning, sociological analysis runs a very real risk of spinning surrealistic fantasies about a world which is tacitly believed to be the best of all possible worlds. Whether the call of the sociologists for racial assimilation in American Society, as it is currently organised, will fall victim to such a judgment remains to be seen.[6]

Given the absence of the almost utopia-like set of circumstances surrounding the earlier definition of pluralism, it becomes readily apparent that peaceful intergroup accommodation – at least in relationship to the model which I have selected, i.e., Blacks in America and elsewhere – awaits full birth. The author does not disagree with Smith and Preston's definition of pluralism. Their suggestion that pluralism comes in interaction among and free movement between groups – with the groups concurrently maintaining their racial and/or ethnic identity – is the Mecca to which many societies seek to move.

Given this definition, it is readily apparent that, like the earlier suggested problems surrounding the French in Canada, intergroup accommodation in the United States and elsewhere has not become a total reality. Hence, true cultural pluralism is yet to be attained. For example, it might be useful for us to review quickly the research of Martin Kilson, as pertains to the characterisation of what he defines as 'neo-ethnicity' in American life. For this model can well serve as platform from which the writer will briefly then focus on the area of education, as a vehicle whereby, on an equality of opportunity basis, greater movement toward intergroup accommodation can be effected.

As asserted by Kilson:

Negro Americans initiated the current flurry of neo-ethnicity in American political life. They did so, ironically, in a period when, for the White majority, the traditional pattern of ethnicity was attenuating. Compared with two generations ago, all major White ethnic groups are experiencing a significant attenuation of their ethnic cohesiveness. More Jews marry Gentiles, more Protestants marry Catholics, more Irish marry Italians, and more Whites marry Orientals and Negroes than in any period of modern American history. Religion, a central attribute in the hold of ethnic constraints upon individual choice, has likewise weakened.

For Afro-Americans, the formal attributes of their distinctive cultural patterns, such as religion, have also been in decline. But the salient factor in negro (Black) behaviour is rather the historical refusal by White supremist American society to accord Blacks equality of ethnic characterisation comparable to that accorded White ethnic groups. The new Black ethnicity is, then, initially an effort to redress this inferior ethnic characterisation. What is more – and what lends a special force to Black neo-ethnicity – Blacks themselves share the belief that in some way they do not possess a measure of full ethnic attributes. This given Black neo-ethnicity, as an ethnocentric revitalisation movement, a complex dynamic, both within the Afro-American sub-system and between Blacks and Whites.[7]

Kilson then goes on to note:

> The conflict surrounding the movements of ethnocentric revitalisation is highly contentious and not infrequently bloody. This is especially true of movements whose 'cultural indigene' is ideologically diffused or poorly differentiated from an adversary (often the dominant) culture. The Afro-American sub-culture is of this variety; so much of what it means to be Black in America is intricately linked to White society, and the formation of Black ideas, values and institutions occurs in complex dialectical interaction with this society. . . .
> Americans, after twenty-five years of extraordinary societal shifts, yearn for connections with the past – the moorings of identity. For both Blacks and Whites, neo-ethnicity has become the medium of such retrieval of the traditional sources of identity and thus a greater sense of personal worth. Paradoxically, the new Black ethnicity is reformist in thrust while the new White ethnicity is conservative. But both, alas, are militant; for as an instrument of political mobilisation ethnicity is curiously metapolitical, something more than politics.
> . . . The ultimate paradox surrounding neo-ethnicity in American political life today might well be that as White neo-ethnicity evolves into multi-faceted neo-conservatism, carefully orchestrated at the national level by the Republican Party, the politics of Black ethnicity is de-emphasising the militancy in anti-White orientation.[8]

Given the realities depicted by Kilson's observation that notwithstanding the rise in neo-ethnicity, not only on the part of American Blacks but also other ethnic and/or racial groups within this country, the movement towards intensification of conservatism on the part of the Whites has been accompanied by an apparent de-emphasis upon White orientation as far as the Black constituency is concerned. It might very well be that research will later discern the extent to which that same phenomenon is true as pertains to the linguistic problems of the nation of Canada, or the separation of races confrontation which currently exists on the African continent. Or for that matter, a similar phenomenon might very well occur in relationship to the schisms which exist between Jews and Arabs in the Middle East. But, at this juncture, it is appropriate now to examine the kinds of options which must be available to all the participating groups in a pluralistic society, given the need for a move toward cultural pluralism. It is the assertion of this writer that the education posture of a given society forms a platform upon which intergroup accommodation can rest.

As indicated by the former American Black Superintendent of Schools in the nation's capital of Washington, DC, Hugh Scott:

> Quality education has to do with the products of those educational institutions whose policies and practices contribute significantly to the intellectual, physical and psychological preparation of individuals for effective and satisfying participation in society. When applied specifically to Black Americans, such education designates the qualitative efforts of those institutions which provide assistance to Black people in altering (in legitimate ways) those elements of the social structure which will promote equal opportunity for all.[9]

IV RACISM AND EDUCATION AND THE CHALLENGE INTERNATIONALLY

The great and gnawing question before us, in the light of the Scott thesis, is the extent to which state school education, whether in Britain, America, Canada or South Africa, has really followed through with the above-mentioned definition. It would appear, particularly since the 1960s when, for example, the United States, certain European countries and portions of Canada began to categorise many Blacks as supposedly the inevitable product of slums, living in overcrowded apartments, dilapidated housing, maintaining high rates of unemployment, controlled by female-headed households, massive recipients of welfare, and persons living in homes with no fathers, no books, too much noise and distraction, loud music, dirty streets, poor health, high infant mortality rate, all sorts of disease, disorganised families and all other manner of denigration. Then, with the appearance of such literature as Reisman's *The Culturally Deprived Child* and Deutsch's *The Disadvantaged Child*, the cult of cultural deprivation made its appearance on the scene in American and other countries, particularly in the Western world. As suggested, for example, by Kenneth Clark:

> All the social and pathological arguments were defined in clear and precise terms. Blaming the victim became the name of the game.[10]

From this emphasis upon the deviant and deficient child grew a new justification for self-hatred and negative self-concept. Soon many minority youngsters, particularly Blacks in America, Canada and Great Britain, for example, were seen to possess a negative view of themselves with no power to control their own lives or destiny.

The writer's own experience as an urban school superintendent in America, a member of the faculty and currently a University System Chancellor, have led him to conclude that professional education has become all too accustomed to assuming that the majority of Black students, whether in Great Britain, Western Europe or America, who enter the school setting, have done so as pioneers from supposed slum-ridden environments. For example, the United States President's panel on urban education of a decade ago tended to validate this contention when it suggested that on the basis of its observations, these minority children have come from settings which have produced a pulsating tangle of academic retardation, pupil and staff transiency, ethnic imbalance, school rights, alienation, personnel and staff shortages and general inadequacy of resources.

There can be no doubt that there is an interrelatedness between environment and intelligence; that environmental stimuli have much to do with the creation of intelligence. And yet, somewhere along the academic line, usually at eight or nine, many of these children who have been exposed to the educational offerings of some so-called inner-city schools in America, in Brazil, Great Britain and Canada lost interest, and to all intents and purposes became psychological drop-outs. The Haryou Study, as researched in the Black section of New York City (Harlem), depicted a situation wherein youngsters, coming to school for the first time as kindergarten students, were observed to be 'bright-eyed and bushy-tailed', eager to learn, ready to accept the challenge of a brave new world. Within one calendar year many of them became dull, uninterested, listless and unwilling to go to school.

The question becomes one of why? To what extent had the school cultivated the apathy, the lack of self-confidence, the absence of persistent effort, the evasions, the suspicions, the defensiveness and the hostility of alleged slow learners? Were the attitudes and biases of professional educators, conscious or not, responsible for the inferior attainments and expressions of problems in inner-city schools, or were teachers being made scapegoats for the ills of society and the school, whether that school happened to be in America, Great Britain or Canada?

As previously indicated, research tends to demonstrate the reality that youngsters from so-called inner-city backgrounds bring, in some cases, to the all-majority setting a group of experiences which are completely different from those of their majority peers, particularly if those peers are caucasian. The fact of the matter is that many of these kids enter the new setting with a sense of powerlessness and alienation. Because of rumours, life in the minority ghettos, parental discussions concerning the evils of the majority White and visible signs of institutionalised racism, as well as economic discrimination, these kids appear in that classroom with a sense of defeat, with the proverbial chip on the hardened shoulder.

The American psychologist Kenneth Clark describes the situation from an American point of view, by suggesting that a clash of cultures exists in the classroom:

> A class war, a socio-economic warfare is being waged in the battleground of our schools, with middle-class and middle-class aspiring teachers provided with a powerful arsenal of half-truths, prejudices and rationalisations, arrayed against hopefully outclassed working-class youngsters. This is an uneven balance, particularly since, like most battles, it comes under the guise of righteousness.[11]

It is within this setting that the instructor, be he from the continent of North America, South America or Africa, is most susceptible to the dangers inherent in the syndrome which I refer to as 'attitudinal predetermination'. It is hypothesised herein that this predeterministic syndrome is a phenomenon which is inclusive of these indices:

Hypothesis 1: *The prevailing attitude that dictates the thought that all Black and minority children entering the all majority (White-European) setting are, by virtue of the alleged socio-economic and ethnic background, intellectually inferior.... One cannot expect children who come from culturally different homes to compete in an environment which reflects middle-class aspirations.*

This hypothesis is generally supported by such suppositions as the following:

(a) They have apparently come from homes in which there is no stimulation for educational achievement, i.e., there was an absence of books in the home and also lack of discussion that would stimulate intellectual curiosity. (Here Clark notes that:

> It is assumed that in homes in which there are books these books are read or that the resource of books in some other manner influences

the child in a way relevant to his ability to learn to read in the primary grades.)[12]

(b) The still held-to belief by a small band of 'research psychologists' that Blacks and other minorities are biologically inferior. For example, in the monograph *Race and Reason*, Putnam states that:

> Any man with two eyes in his head can observe a Black settlement in the Congo, can study the pure blooded African in his native habitat as he exists when left on his own resources, can compare this settlement with London or Paris and can draw his own conclusions regarding relative levels of character and intelligence.... Finally he can enquire as to the number of pure blooded Blacks who have made their contributions to great literature or engineering or medicine or philosophy or abstract science.[13]

(c) They (Blacks, other minorities) bring to the classroom, due to the alleged lower socio-economic backgrounds, certain psychological problems peculiar to that status which interferes with the educational process in the classroom.... Here the supposition is one wherein the rate of development is in substantial part, but certainly not wholly, a function of environmental circumstances, i.e., the greater the variety of situations to which the child must accommodate his behavioural structures, the more differentiated and mobile they become.... Thus the more new things a child has seen and the more he has heard, the more things he is interested in seeing and hearing. In addition, the more variation in reality with which he has coped, the greater will be his capacity for coping.

Thus the emphasis in point (c) above is on the suggestion that if variety in environment is important, then there are detrimental effects, supposedly, inherent in lack of variety. This leads, therefore (as Martin Deutsch suggests), to 'stimulus deprivation which ultimately leads to cognitive deficit'.

Rejection of Hypothesis 1
(a) The fact of the matter is, according to Clark and others, Hypothesis 1(a) is in reality a 'self-fulfilling prophecy', i.e., the common belief pervades certain school situations in America and abroad to the extent that the feeling tends to be one in which

> there is no point in their having high academic aspiration if, in reality, because of low IQ and low academic achievement, these

youngsters will be restricted to menial jobs for the bulk of their lives.

Living, as it were, in the slums of Birmingham, England, or São Paulo, Brazil, or Washington, DC. For example, as psychologist Ken Clark notes in the aforementioned Haryou Study, caucasian teachers admitted to caucasian interviewers that Black children in their classes were inherently intellectually inferior, and that, therefore, they could not be expected to learn as much or as readily as their caucasian counterparts. Furthermore, if one, as a teacher, tried to teach them as if they could learn, one would be running the risk of developing in them (the Black students) serious emotional disturbances, frustrations and anxieties. Therefore, the humanitarian thing to do with these children is to develop and provide schools which are essentially *custodian* institutions rather than educational institutions.

The same psychologist completely tears asunder this hypothesis (i.e. hypothesis 1) by discussing the fallacy of 'special programmes' designed to meet the so-called needs of Black children. The use of IQ test scores as a means of grouping youngsters homogeneously once they enter school is really a devious device for propagating the myth of inherently inferior culturally different children. The children, the psychologist continues, are really socially rejected students:

> They have been systematically humiliated, categorised, classified, relegated to groups in terms of slow learners, untrainables, track A, track B, the 'pussycats', the 'bunnies', the 'green giants', etc. But it all adds up to the fact that they are not being taught; and not being taught, they fail. They have a sense of personal humiliation and unworthiness.[14]

Furthermore, it would appear that this hypothesis has failed the most basic question of all, i.e., to what extent do these theories of cognitive deficit, biological predeterminism and stimulus deprivation obscure the more basic reasons for the alleged educational retardation of certain segments of a pluralistic society? To what extent, instead, do they offer acceptable and desirable alibis for educational default – or a representation of institutionalised racism, therefore thwarting the possibility for intergroup accommodation – with the use of education as a basic option through which such accommodation could be effected?

(*b*) As far as those who would continue to adhere to the doctrine still preached by that small band of 'race-oriented' biological inferiority group are concerned, it will suffice to refer them to some of the research accomplished by Harvard sociologist Thomas Pettigrew. Pettigrew points out that:

> Studies repeatedly cited by the scientific racists in defence of their position are not, upon closer scrutiny, critical tests of their contentions.[15]

For example, relative to T. A. Tauder's 1939 investigation of intelligence among Black and White children in Kent County, Ontario, wherein he found that the White sample obtained a higher IQ than the Black sample, it was later proven that the 'social and economic conditions were not equal'.[16]

As a matter of fact Tauder later admitted that this sample of Black children had not attended school on as regular a basis as had the White children. Moreover, there can be no doubt but that Southern Ontario, at that point in time, was not free of racial discrimination.

(c) As related to the contention that 'stimulus deprivation' results in academic retardation, one could refer merely to the question raised by a number of American and British psychologists thus:

> Specifically in what way does cognitive deficit actually interfere with the ability of a child to learn to read or to do arithmetic in elementary grades? What is really meant by 'cognitive deficit'? If it is remediable, how? Is it merely a jargon which says that which everyone knows already, i.e., that these children are not learning? The critical issue is why? Can the child be blamed?

In summary, it would seem then that this facet of the attitudinal predeterministic syndrome is really a self-fulfilling prophecy'. The brutality of this reality is rather succinctly captured by the researcher Dr Allen Wilson regarding his study of the effects of social stratification and segregation on the academic attainments of elementary children in one United States community, i.e. Berkeley, California:

> Students from the hills (more favoured) schools tend to be assigned to the academic streams while those from the flats (least favoured) schools are assigned, almost automatically, to the general or vocational programmes. ... Although many of the working class, and especially Black, entered the so-called open-door junior colleges, even at this late point they were 'counselled or cooled out' into terminal vocational training.[17]

Hypothesis 2: *The second major facet of the additudinal predetermination syndrome refers to the assumption that these youngsters, because of their allegedly different backgrounds, need not only a different approach in the educational process, but a different type of education than children from the majority group already in the school setting.*

This facet of the syndome suggests that, overcome by the cult of cultural deprivation, the teacher or administrator is convinced, even in the pluralistic setting, that these youngsters, because of their supposedly underprivileged environments, tend to come to school with a qualitatively 'different' preparation for the demands of that educational arena. Hence, their only salvation is one wherein there is a lowering of levels of expectations so as to compensate for their academic deficiencies.

This hypothesis is rejected easily on discernible grounds. As indicated by Henderson, the real problem in this situation is that of teacher alienation;

> Much of the plight of the middle income teachers [White and Black] assigned to teach [supposedly different Black youth] stems from their inability to understand the educational needs of Black students.... A closer analysis of their behaviour shows that it is not the classroom adjustment patterns of lower income Black students that are abnormal, but their opportunities to behave as 'normal students'.... [allegedly] culturally different incoming students do not need misplaced kindness.... Instead, they need fair guidance; no matter how well intended, social promotions and watered down curricula cause additional problems. With so much emphasis currently placed upon understanding and assisting culturally different students, it is easy to fall victim to the urge to engage in overcompensatory actions. These may well lead to the culturally deprived syndrome.[18]

The tragedy of this reality, as noted by Henderson, is that many of the minority students, in this case in an American setting, were using the system, and its adherence to this attitudinal predeterministic syndrome, as a means of 'sliding by'. In effect, school became a game. If the child won, he still lost. Making it easy for the youngster to succeed in school did nothing more, in the final analysis, than make it easy for him to fail later in the world of work.

Again here, racism combined with instructional naïvety, thwarts the possibility for intergroup accommodation in the pluralistic setting. As more and more youngsters treated in this way leave the school ill-prepared, alienation against the society which has spawned this setting arises and intergroup conflict is clearly perpetuated.

V BLACK STUDENTS IN A WHITE UNIVERSITY SETTING

Certainly even the casual historian of higher education in America, Great Britain and Canada is aware of the fact that institutionalised racism has doubtless determined, to a large degree, the historical delimitation of Black student enrolments in predominantly caucasian university settings. If one takes, for example, the Western world scene, as related to this reality, it becomes apparent that:

> The entrance of Black students on to predominantly White campuses posed a direct threat to the basic value systems of the University. The University viewed itself, despite a multiplicity of relationships with industry and government, as a collection of books and scholars devoted to an unswerving search for truth and knowledge. The Berkeley revolt [University of California, USA] signalled the beginning of the end of this traditional view and resulted in some cracks in the ivory tower.[19]

It we can turn for a moment to the American university setting as a model for depicting the problem, we note the following. Predominantly White colleges had little notion of the conflict and turmoil which would cripple some of them when they first began in the 1960s to demonstrate a commitment to the beefing-up of Black enrolments on all White campuses. The fact of the matter is that, historically paying little attention to the fate of Black people in this country, the University, according to Mr Ballard, was ill-prepared to face the three hundred years of pent-up feeling that the students brought with them to the campus; and thus one can really make little sense of the actions and attitudes of Black students as they entered colleges during these past few years without having some clear understanding as to the forces exerted upon them by the outside world. These forces could be summarised thus, and could very readily be applicable to other portions of the Western world as well as those in Africa, Asia and South America:

(1) Beginning with the Black revolt of the 1960s, the central thrust of

the Black movement in the United States was one of an assertion on the part of the Black people that they were going to demand the same kinds of economic, social and political benefits as those enjoyed by the majority of their caucasian counterparts. These demands came at a time when the poor, the disenfranchised and the ghettoed in the pluralistic societies worldwide were making the same kind of demands, particularly in the slums of Great Britain, the provinces of Canada and the ghettos of South America.

(2) Followed by the evangelical leadership of Dr Martin Luther King, American Blacks began to move, to an increased degree, into the urbanised North and South; thence the university loomed ahead as a means of salvation. At this point in history, in the mid-1960s, cities were on fire with racial revolt, including Bedford Stuyvesant, Watts, Hough, Rochester and Detroit.

(3) The newly urbanised Black male, often unemployed, was victimised by poor education, rat-infested housing and White-controlled narcotics traffic. He faced the same kind of deprivation as his minority counterparts in Hong Kong, Vietnam, Birmingham (England) and Toronto (Canada). Coupled with this, the national presence of Carmichael, Malcolm X, Jesse Jackson, the Black Moslems and others were all combined with the advent of internationalised pan-Africanism, Black Pantherism and the conversion of Cassius Clay to Muhammud Ali. Finally, with the appearance of Afros, Dashikis, the Third World Movement and growing Black uneasiness in Rhodesia and the Republic of South Africa, these, and other events, all whirled at the same time that Blacks began to enter, in increasingly large numbers, predominantly caucasian universities in the United States.

(4) Concurrently, in the mid-1960s, one witnessed the theatrics of Che Guevara, Castro, the Viet Cong and ultimately Frantz Fanon. Fanon, of course, popularised the internationalised thesis of 'decolonialisation' which would, some assert, somewhat neutralise the non-violent thesis which the American evangelist, Martin Luther King, had fought to continue promoting until his untimely assassination. It was this same Fanon, the Black Martinique psychiatrist, who indicated that:

> Non-violence is an attempt to settle the colonial problem around a green baize table, before any regrettable act has been performed or irreparable gesture made, before any blood has been shed. But if the masses, without waiting for the chairs to be arranged around the baize table, listen to their own voice and begin committing outrages and setting fire to buildings, the elite and the nationalist bourgeois

Some Educational Imperatives 215

parties will be seen rushing to the colonists to exclaim, 'This is very serious. We do not know how it will end; we must find a solution – some sort of compromise.'[20]

(5) The post-1964 upheavals on campuses, as led by American and some Canadian caucasian students, intensified the sense of need for struggle on the part of Black students. Caucasian-controlled student uprisings centered around issues concerned with campus-initiated recruitment by the American CIA, the presence of ROTC on campus, links between the university and defence establishments, the military-industrial complex controversy and the general breakdown of calm between professonial and student participation in campus life.

These and other forces were thus operating at the time that significant numbers of predominantly caucasian American universities began the thrust designed to increase the number of Black and other minority students on campuses in the 1960s and 1970s.

VI BARRIERS TO BLACK EQUAL OPPORTUNITY ON WHITE CAMPUSES

A. INSENSITIVITY OF COLLEGE ADMINISTRATORS AND STAFF

With the advent of the sixties and the increased influx of Black students on White campuses, the researcher Allen Ballard observes:

> Few had any Black faculty members, few had been sensitive to the spiritual anguish that affected those Black students in colleges – grateful for education, but full of grievances that were seldom voiced. These were colleges that accepted with a sense of normalcy, such conditions as all White fraternities, Newman Clubs, Hillel Societies, all White clerical and administrative staffs and professors whose sole academic concern was White America. The colleges, moreover, were operating on the premise that they were doing Black students a favour by permitting them to enter their institutions. The sentiment has been voiced to me [the researcher] by dozens of college administrators, 'Why do *they* act this way when we are permitting *them* entry into the mainstream of American society?' Acting on the assumption that admitting Black students was somewhat akin to divine dispensation, universities felt no particular pressure to make

special arrangements for the newcomers. On the other hand, the limited pool of 'academically qualified' Black youngsters meant that the colleges increasingly brought on to their campuses Black youth who not only had experienced deprivation and White scorn, but were also sensitive to every conscious or unconscious manifestation of racism. The problem lay in the fact that the colleges had failed to do what their professors daily preached to their classes: conceptualise. Thus, with few exceptions, every demand of the Black students burst upon them like a concussion grenade. . . . The root causes of hostility which Black students expressed frequently ran deep, in the tumult gripping both Black communities and the campuses. . . . That basic hostility was reinforced by myriad petty and grand insults paid the Black youth by the university. At Columbia, where Blacks in 1968 occupied a building demanding that the University cease efforts to construct a gymnasium in Harlem, the Cox Commission reported: 'At Columbia, the security guards were long allowed to follow the unforgivable practice of inspecting Black students' identification cards when they entered college buildings, although the White students passed without notice.' . . . Black applicants for assistance were often treated like welfare clients by bursars and financial officers. Most professors, teaching as they had always taught, would interject into discussions their own middle-class bias about poor people, never thinking that the children of those persons sat in front of them.[21]

B. THE ACADEMICANS' ASSAULT ON OPEN ADMISSIONS IN HIGHER EDUCATION

The academic grapevine would suggest that the 'best students' go to Universities such as Harvard, Berkeley, Oxford, Cambridge, Vassar, and University of Michigan and McGill University. Therefore, it stands to reason that the 'best' faculty teach at these institutions and on that basis one measures the prestige of an academic appointment by correlating with the average standards of the entering freshmen class. Hence, it seems perhaps inevitable, as asserted by some, that professional status is directly linked to that university's admissions criteria. With this as an assumption, it is then not difficult for one to hypothesise that the academicians, in the worldwide higher education arena, have long assumed the sacrosanctity of educational 'standards'. In the pre-campus-warfare days in America, Canada and elsewhere, the universities in which faculty operated were generally viewed as stable institutions with a well-established arrangement of internal checks and balances. Original appointments were rigidly controlled by departments – with heavy emphasis upon faculty input as being paramount; and the system was protective of faculty rights and prerogatives – weighted towards the *status quo* and apparently incapable of rapid change.

Then came the revolt. Concurrent with the advent of demonstrations by the students for a democratic society (in the United States and Canada), combined with the massive participation of students, from Simon Frazer University in British Columbia to Kent State University in the United States, universities were faced to an increased degree with the noticeable influx of Black students.

From an historical point of view, it is apparent that the admission of a large number of Black students to many of these institutions meant a suggested 'lowering' of entrance requirements and this position posed a threat to the status of professors and to the 'academic quality' of the colleges. For example:

> A survey of college professors, with 60,000 respondents, conducted by Professor Martin A. Trow of the University of California at Berkeley, determined the fact that less than half of the faculty members felt that more minority students should be admitted even if it meant relaxing admission standards.[22]

With regard to the open admissions concept, as popularised by the American City University of New York, one observes that the Columbia University sociologist Amitai Etzioni has suggested that:

> Open enrolment creates a mass education system inferior in quality to a selective system. Increases in the budget for higher education, a larger teaching staff and intensive compensatory education can reduce the loss of quality, but there remains, nevertheless, an unavoidable loss. Diluted standards often lead to almost automatic promotion from grade to grade and to almost automatic graduation. Thus, in such a system, advancement in the educational process is diassociated from any measure of achievement. Pressure is now on colleges and universities to emulate public high schools and provide a truly mass education. . . . Assuming that higher education would be provided to all who seek it, there still remains the question, how much? Should open enrolment, universal education, the legitimate

right of every man to be educated be carried out through undergraduate education? Graduate education? Post-graduate education? Is there a limit?[23]

The assault on open admissions even has an international flavour. Sir Eric Ashby, former Vice-Chancellor of Cambridge University and a member of the Carnegie Commission, makes these assumptions quite explicit by observing that:

> All civilised countries . . . depend upon a clear thin stream of excellence to provide new ideas, new techniques and the statesman-like treatment of complex social and political problems. Without the renewal of this excellence, a nation can drop to mediocrity in a generation. . . . The highly gifted student needs to be treated as an elite.[24]

Here there might be those who would assert that the elitists' view prevails as accompanied by the assumption that contact between the elite (presumably White, European, Protestant) and the masses is relatively unimportant. By its very nature elitism precludes a social mix in higher education, and thus represents a thwarting of equality of educational opportunity for all within a pluralistic society. Indeed, many of those proponents of the elitist view perhaps would suggest that a campus where students ranged widely in ability would, in the final analysis, constitute an unwholesome climate for the supposed elite. The implication seems to be one wherein their (i.e. the elite) progress would be impeded by the presence of the allegedly less academically prepared youth.

The problem with the attack upon the open admissions, particularly in a pluralistic society, is that which is related to the elitist attitude of the academician who is convinced that standards must apply, on an equal basis, for all students. When one criticises, as did one researcher, the Black students in a given Canadian institution as finding the syllabus 'over their heads', one immediately steps into the quicksand of over-generalisation, through the vehicle of seeking to extrapolate from a single example a suggestion which is then made applicable to all situations in many universities throughout the Western world.

In the final analysis, as observed by Karabel:

> Open admissions has aroused controversy precisely because it carries within it the seeds of an attack on the *meritocracy*. The system of

higher education is a bulwark of the meritocracy in that it not only allocates people to the upper positions, but also provides simultaneous legitimation of that placement. Open admissions, based on the assumption that everyone is entitled to a fair share of society's higher educational resources, suggests that colleges and universities (in the Americas, Europe, Africa and Asia) exist to educate people, not to put them in their proper slots in the meritocratic structure. Moreover, by abandoning merit as a criterion for determining who receives society's educational resources, it casts doubt on the meritocracy's means of distributing resources in general. Finally, open admissions implies that, thus far, universities have served mainly to transmit from parent to child an upper middle class status that entitles the child to disproportionate amounts of wealth and power.[25]

C. ASSAULT ON BLACK STUDIES

From an historical perspective the surge in the sixties occurred in the aftermath of the murder of the American Civil Rights leader Dr Martin Luther King, when there was in evidence a sufficiently critical mass of Black students on White campuses to permit an effective rejection of traditional educational practices. These practices, in effect, minimised the Black experience and accomplishments in the curriculum and permitted, even in the best situations, only limited amounts of Black participation on faculties and certainly on supporting staffs. One recalls that Black student demands escalated relative to an end to racism in the ivory tower. So-called under-prepared Black students, some of them sixteen and seventeen years of age, were coming from all-Black ghettos on to largely White campuses, in need of assistance, in need of Black adult advisers. Thus, by 1971, according to the managing editor of *Black Scholar*, approximately five hundred schools provided full-scale Black studies programmes. In some cases the results of these programmes in higher education were disappointing. As indicated, for example, by one Black scholar:

> We had planned to develop a comprehensive multi-disciplinary examination of the current condition in history of Blacks in this country, throughout the hemisphere and *especially in Africa*. It would have run the whole gamut: politics, sociology, art, history,

culture, economics and contemporary Black urban life, the whole range. The work would have been done in one centre, but we have drawn on the resources of the whole university. . . . What exists on that campus now bears no relationship to the plan implemented six years ago. There is no Black Studies programme. The Ethnic Studies Centre which grew instead is less and less hospitable to Blacks and enjoys virtually no academic respect. What happened is that White academics and administrators who were hostile to Blacks and Black Studies proposals in the first place picked up an academic hustler in a Dashiki to head the programme, gave him a lot of money to provide for himself and his incompetent friends, and that was the end of Black Studies around here. They knew exactly what they were doing when they picked him.[26]

One thing is certain, Black Studies will continue to remain controversial, not only in America but also in European and African universities, as the educational option is pursued as a design for accommodating intergroup relations on a positive basis.

D. SLOWNESS OF TRUE AFFIRMATIVE ACTION

As recently indicated in the *New York Times*:

A majority commitment to increase the number of Blacks in the nation's colleges and campuses made during the Civil Rights era of the 1960s appears to have ended. . . . 'The commitment has gone, it's not there any more, it's all over,' remarked Lawrence Barkley, the Minority Affairs officer for the college entrance examination board in New York. Black enrolment at institutions of higher learning has been going down for the last two years as efforts to recruit more Blacks and programmes to help them once they are enrolled are being cut back and scuttled at many colleges and universities. . . . With aggressive recruiting on the part of the White colleges, Black enrolment began to rise dramatically in the latter part of the last decade, according to the annual survey by Alexander Astin, Professor of Higher Education at UCLA. The percentage hovered between two and three per cent in the early and mid sixties. . . . The figure rose to six point three per cent in 1971 and peaked the following year at eight point seven per cent.

But in 1973 Black enrolment dropped to seven point eight per cent and to seven point four per cent at the beginning of this school year.... Ten years ago Vassar College could claim not more than a handful of Black students. This year there are a hundred and forty-five, fifteen down from last year.... In 1968 Blacks made up two point five per cent of the student body at the University of California at Berkeley, a figure that rose to five point five per cent in 1971, but was cut down to four per cent in the current school year.[27]

The same concern has been expressed by Walter Leonard, the Assistant to the President at Harvard University, who indicates, as part of his annual report to the Harvard community, that in the fall of 1970, the Business School reported that there were a hundred and twenty-eight Black students enrolled. In 1972 that number had dropped to one hundred and in the fall of 1974 it dropped again to fifty-three. In the past four years the Business School has lost a total of seventy-five Black students.

It should be noted that this movement away from affirmative action thrust to the degree once operational, in the 1960s and early 1970s, is not specific to the United States. Apparently it is an international phenomenon. As far as the American scene is concerned, factors which have contributed to this decline are apparently these:

(a) Retrenchment mandates have eliminated programmes designed to provide special services for incoming minority students, including counselling, tutorial services, financial aids.

(b) Officials of some institutions and funding agencies have indicated that they have kept their commitments: that the number of Blacks in most schools has increased, and that it is now time to move on to 'other priorities'.

(c) Pressures from community organisations and Black housing areas have declined.

(d) Alleged dissatisfaction among some caucasian academic liberals, relative to the 'calibre of minority students coming into the university from the ghetto'.

(e) Increasing numbers of Black and other minority students feel that they are not wanted anyway, despite the pluralistic posture of the nation.

This attitude, therefore, leads to a drastic drop in the numbers of Blacks and other minorities applying for admission to predominantly caucasian schools.

VII CONCLUSION ON THE HIGHER EDUCATION SCENE

Given the major option of education as *the* thrust in concert with a design affected to thwart the incidence of intergroup conflict, it becomes increasingly apparent that at the higher education level, the barriers to equal opportunity for Black and other minority students in predominantly white institutions continue. This phenomenon, as witnessed in the United States, on the African continent, in South America, in the rest of the North American continent and in Europe and Asia, is a representation of the same kinds of bureaucratic manipulation, institutionalised racism, excuses and denigration which exist at the pre-post secondary education level. If opportunities for Blacks and other minorities who represent a part of a pluralistic society are to be equalised, and thus enhanced, concerted efforts will have to be increased on the basis of plans designed by internationally thinking universities, their student bodies, their faculties, their administrations and by those who support their continued operation.

VIII ORGANISATIONAL IMPERATIVES FOR DROPPING THE BARRIERS TO EQUAL EDUCATIONAL OPPORTUNITIES FOR BLACK AND OTHER MINORITY STUDENTS IN PLURALISTIC SOCIETIES

A. THE PRE-HIGHER EDUCATION SCENE

(1) Somehow the institutions of pre-higher education, i.e., the elementary and secondary schools of these countries, are going to have to disavow the sacrosanctity of such documents as the Coleman Report and the United States Civil Rights Commission Report on *Racial Isolation in the United States*. As we are aware, these reports have suggested, on the basis of statistical evidence, that for Black and other minority students achievement is enhanced in a desegregated setting. As suggested by the researcher Donald Smith:

> Increasing the control factor, Coleman and his associates contend, increases achievement. Yet, the same Coleman Report also claims that while achievement increases in the integrated school, the self-

concept of Black pupils has diminished. I am not surprised that young Black children feel a sense of diminished self-esteem in integrated schools. Picture yourself being bused across town to the White school. Obviously your school wasn't good enough for you to learn there or for White children to come to join you, so for your own good you had to be herded off to buses to the good school. Once there you might have had to wade through jeering pickets to reach the building. Or if not that, you encounter hostile teachers, some overtly, some subtly so. Most White students will ignore you, a few well meaning ones will patronise you. Under such circumstances, I find highly questionable Professor Coleman's assertion that Black students do, indeed, achieve more because of a newly acquired sense of control. I would assert that a more logical explanation for the increased achievement is a combination of the following:

(a) The schools to which Black pupils are bused are middle class White schools where there is considerable academic pressure. White middle class parents demand that teachers teach. They accept no nonsense about missing library books and cognitive deficits.

(b) Faculties in these schools are stable. They are permanent rather than substitutes. Children in these schools expect to have continuity.

(c) Black pupils learn because of the above factors and because the teachers expect their pupils to learn and teach accordingly.

Because the control factor is alleged to be critical, and I believe that it is, let us look at the matter of control in terms of the ghetto school. It is hardly conceivable that any but a few children could feel a sense of control in a Black school where the principal is White and the assistant principal and the counsellors are White, the school engineer is White, the window washers are White, and when the windows are broken, glaziers are White. And so is the superintendent of schools, even in Detroit, Michigan, where the Black population exceeds sixty per cent. [Recently a Black was appointed.] It is virtually impossible for Black pupils or Black teachers to feel a sense of potency when from the top of the school system right to the boilerroom they are administrated, supervised and manipulated by the White power structure. The pattern of White dominance of Black welfare and Black interests is omnipresent and pervasive in all areas of Black existence.[28]

(2) The disavowal of attitudinal predeterministic syndrome becomes

obvious. Here we are talking about the elimination of those indices which would suggest that Black and other minority students from the pluralistic milieu cannot learn.

(3) Curricular relevance becomes an unavoidable mandate for Black students as well as White in the pre-higher education arena. If one is interacting in a school setting which contains Blacks, Chicanos, Asians, native Americans, Latinos, as well as Whites, then one can no longer assert that we are operating in an 'all majority' setting. The very essence of this fact is captured in an incident which occurred during the course of an American conference in July 1966 concerned for the education of the disadvantaged. One of the consultants at that conference described a situation which he referred to as the Ming dynasty syndrome. He pictured a history teacher in a Canadian secondary school (Halifax, Nova Scotia) who, while in the midst of an ancient history lesson, noticed an increase of noise in the courtyard below. As the noise grew louder, subsequent investigation revealed that a massive group of demonstrators had convened, spilling over from the street, as part of a drive on the part of minority students in the high schools of that Canadian city. The teacher, not to be disturbed, ordered those students nearest the windows to close them and lower the shades. He then proceeded to drill his students in the intricacies of ancient Chinese history.

(4) The operationalising of built-in mechanisms for accountability becomes imperative. Professional accountability is a simple concept in the pre-higher educational arena. It simply means that principals, headmasters, teachers and other professionals ought to be held accountable for the achievement or lack of it by their students. It means that if a non-majority child's reading score is at grade level in September, he should not still be reading at the same grade level next June. It suggests that the teacher or administrator who cannot demonstrate competency should not remain in that classroom or in that school system. Nor should that school system transfer that person to another school, as a reward for his performance. Accountability is the concept that makes it very clear that schools have educational standards which are going to be met by administrators, teachers and students alike, whether they are on the European continent or North America.

It would appear with respect to the issue of professional accountability that some attention might be given to the suggestions rendered by one psychologist, who asserted:

Let's get off our sentimental self righteous basis for rejecting and denying these children [Black] and look at them for what they really are, human beings who can learn, because there is evidence that their lower class predecessors (if in fact they are lower class) of a generation or two ago learned. They can learn if they are respected. They can learn if it is communicated to them that those who are responsible for teaching them believe that they can learn. And above all these children can learn if they are taught, and if they are taught with precisely the same standards and quality of instruction as those given to other privileged children; and if they are taught with whatever impirical evidence demonstrates what they need by way of extra attention. ... These children can learn if those required to teach them are held accountable and responsible for an effective job of teaching. ... The day when results without standards of judgment of their personal effectiveness must come to an end. Public educational systems must fill in effective supervision accountability and standards for determining effectiveness of teaching, if the discussion of so-called culturally disadvantaged children is going to be moved from the level of words to the level of social action. Teachers can no longer be permitted (nor administrators) to get away with the cruel and sophisticated alibis for their failure to teach the children.[29]

B. THE HIGHER EDUCATION SCENE

(1) The intellectualised assault on the open admissions model, as promulgated in university settings internationally, is one which must be thwarted. The rationale submitted by the egalitarian elite is one which probably should have no place in the higher education scene. As indicated earlier, what open admissions will do is to give every high school graduate a chance to pursue a college education, irrespective of cultural and/or ethnic background. One possible side-effect is that admissions tests will be used for diagnostic rather than exclusionary purposes. Another is that the conception of the university as an institution whose primary social responsibility is to serve as a training ground for the academic, socially elite, will gradually vanish. No longer will thousands of potentially educated students – particularly if they are Black and/or from other minority groups – be excluded from the stream of higher education, if educational systems on the continent, in the Americas and in Africa and Asia move even more aggressively.

Somehow concerned educators, even in an era of international fiscal retrenchment, are going to have to recognise the fact that the philosophical rationale for open admissions is one wherein the educational mission of an institution is not to select winners or to serve as a talent scout for future employers, but rather to foster growth in the student. Value added, not high grade point averages, should be the mark of the successful institution.

One anonymous observer said:

> There is no such thing as an unfit or unqualified seeker after education. Open admissions, at long last, will end that peculiar arrogance which has led many colleges and universities to say to many aspiring entrants, 'Shift for yourself if you want an education – you are not worth our time.'

There is one caution. As adequately observed by Karabel:

> Open admissions is not a panacea; no educational reform is more than a limited means of attacking vast political, social and economic ills. It will bring with it a plethora of problems and its long range effects remain unclear. Yet, as indicated by the proliferation of state master plans for universal access and by the vast growth of free access institutions, it is fast becoming a national reality. The question now is not whether there will be open admissions, but rather what form it will take and how can it best be made to work. These are the topics to which attention and energy must now be directed.[30]

(2) Two years ago the University of California, one of the most prestigious institutions in the world, was cautioned by federal officials that unless certain deficiencies in the institution's affirmative action programme were remedied, the government would issue a 'show cause' notice providing the institution with thirty days to show why it should not have its earlier committed dollars in contracts terminated, or be barred from receiving future ones. The rest is history. The institution produced a four-inch-thick document which, when made public, indicated the outline of plans designed to eliminate discriminatory hiring practices during the next thirty years by filling at least a hundred and seventy-eight faculty positions with women and members of minorities. The plan itself analyses the sexual and ethnic make-up of each of

the institution's seventy-five academic departments and proceeds to establish goals and timetables extending up to thirty years for reaching equality of opportunity, department by department. According to the complicated projection which has been worked out by the Berkeley staff, a hundred and seventy-eight positions now held by White males and a total staff of one thousand four hundred and eighty-nine must be replaced in the next thirty years by women and members of minorities in order to eliminate discrimination in the employment situation in Berkeley.

The Berkeley plan cannot be viewed as an instant panacea. As a matter of fact one member of the institution's administration admitted the fact that women and minorities are objecting to the plan because it does not call for preferential hiring on the basis of ethnicity and sex. This fact to the contrary notwithstanding, this is a plan which has national implications in relationship to the issue of affirmative action.

(3) The relevancy of Black studies must be effected. Perhaps one of the most viable alternatives present on the higher education scene in America today is that operating on the campus of Michigan State University, under the astute leadership of Dr Robert Greene, Professor of Educational Psychology. Greene is the Dean of the College of Urban Development – a unique inter-disciplinary college which has been established for purposes of approaching the problems of unemployment, inadequate housing, internationalised hunger, educational denigration, political insufficiency, urban morality, student self-interest and the economics of school finance. These areas are all encountered on an inter-departmental/multi-disciplinary basis. Professional scholars in the college of Urban Development have, on such a basis, grappled with the wide range of problems inclusive of public school finance, public school community control, problems of the poor, the politics of the ghetto, management training in the urban political arena, and the economy of urban life. Here, on the basis of this approach, the Black experience in America becomes an integral part of the entire urban scene, as exemplified by Michigan State University's College of Urban Development.

If this is an effort designed to find a means of ameliorating differences between the purists who insist upon Black studies as a separately defined entity, and those who would insist upon integrating Black culture into the main stream of existing academic pursuits within an institution, then perhaps the model defined above meets the test of such an attempt.

IX CONCLUSION

Education, of course, is only one option which must be looked at more searchingly in relationship to the design for ensuring peaceful intergroup accommodation. There are others, and they clearly include:

(1) the institutionalisation of a politicised decision-making process;
(2) the opening up of dialogue between differing religious groups;
(3) the elimination of geopolitical cleavages which threaten to rend asunder the uneasy peace which exists in the Middle East and elsewhere;
(4) the opening up of serious dialogue between competing groups on the African continent as that segment of the world moves towards potential crisis in race relationships in the decade ahead.

This writer's primary attention has been devoted to that of the educational option because, if pluralism does in fact appear to be more of a concern now than was the case even twenty years ago, means must be found for ensuring the accommodation of needs, desires and concerns of those segments of the pluralistic society which are not identified as 'majority' as far as political, educational or economic control is concerned. As indicated at the beginning of this paper, the relationships between varying ethnic and/or racial groups range from segregation to annihilation. Cultural pluralism is a Mecca which has been realised in few societies and/or institutions internationally. Our responsibility as educators, as organisational leaders and as theoreticians, is that concerned with the development and promulgation of methodologies which can enhance the possibility for meaningful inter-ethnic and inter-racial contact, devoid of forced assimilation, forced separate but 'unequal' status, and the inevitability of racial and/or ethnic confrontation. It would appear that equality of educational opportunity plays a pivotal role in the acquisition of peaceful intergroup accommodation in plural societies.

NOTES

1. Ronald W. Smith and Frederick W. Preston, *Sociology, An Introduction* (New York: St. Martin's Press, 1977) pp. 359–67.
2. Chester L. Hunt and Lewis Walker, *Ethnic Dynamics, Patterns of Inter-*

Some Educational Imperatives 229

    Group Relations in Various Societies (Homewood, Ill.: The Dorsey Press, 1974) p. 15.
3. Kurt Mayer, 'Cultural Pluralism and Linguistic Equilibrium in Switzerland', in *Inter-Group Relations*, ed. Pierre van den Berghe (New York: Basic Books, Inc., 1972) pp. 71–9.
4. John Porter, 'Ethnic Pluralism in Canadian Perspective', in *Ethnicity*, ed. Nathan Glazer and Daniel P. Moynihan (Cambridge, Mass.: Harvard University Press, 1975) pp. 266–71.
5. Raymond E. Wolfinger, Martin Shapiro and Fred I. Greenstein, *Dynamics of American Politics* (Englewood Cliffs: Prentice-Hall, 1976) pp. 25–6.
6. Paul Metzger, 'American Sociology and Assimilation: Conflicting Perspectives', in *Majority and Minority*, ed. Norman R. Yetman and C. Hoy Steele (Boston: Allyn & Bacon, Inc., 1975) pp. 326–7.
7. Martin Kilson, 'Blacks and Neo-Ethnicity in American Political Life', in *Ethnicity Theory and Experience*, ed. Nathan Glazer and Daniel P. Moynihan (Cambridge, Mass.: Harvard University Press, 1975) pp. 236–7.
8. Ibid., pp. 251–64.
9. Hugh Scott, 'Reflections on Issues and Conditions Related to Public Education for Black Students', *Journal of Negro Education*, vol. XLII, 3 (summer 1973) 418.
10. Kenneth B. Clark, *Dark Ghetto* (New York: Harper & Row, 1965) ch. 6.
11. Ibid.
12. Kenneth B. Clark, 'Education in the Ghetto', *Christianity and Crises*, XXV, 17 May 1965.
13. C. Putnam, *Race and Reason: A Yankee View* (Washington: Public Affairs Press, 1961).
14. Kenneth B. Clark, 'Clash of Cultures in the Classroom', in *Learning Together*, ed. Meyer Weinberg (Chicago: Integrated Education Associates, 1964).
15. Thomas Pettigrew, *A Profile of the Negro American* (Princeton: D. van Nostrand Company, Inc., 1964) pp. 102–3.
16. Ibid.
17. Allen B. Wilson, 'Social Stratification and Academic Achievement', in *Education in Depressed Areas*, ed. A. Harry Passow (New York: Teachers College Press, 1963) pp. 217–36.
18. George Henderson, 'Pupil Integration in Public Schools: Some Reflections', *Teachers' College Record*, 67, no: 4 (Jan 1966) 278–9.
19. Allen Ballard, *The Education of Black Folk* (New York: Harper & Row, 1973) p. 81.
20. Frantz Fanon, *The Wretched of the Earth* (New York: Grove Press, Inc., 1965) pp. 61–2.
21. Allen Ballard, op. cit., pp. 70–3.
22. *New York Times*, 23 Apr 1970.
23. Amitai Etzioni, 'A Sociological Perspective on Black Students', *Educational Record*, winter 1970, p. 70.
24. Eric Ashby, *Any Person, Any Study* (New York: McGraw-Hill, 1971) p. 101.
25. Jerome Karabel, 'Perspectives on Open Admissions', *Educational Record*, winter 1972, p. 42.

26. *New York Times*, 16 June 1975, p. 20E.
27. *New York Times*, 26 Mar 1975.
28. Donald H. Smith, 'Imperative Issues in Urban Education', address before Annual Meeting of American Association of Colleges for Teachers' Education, Chicago, 15 Feb 1968.
29. Kenneth B. Clark, 'Clash of Cultures in the Classroom', in *Learning Together* (1964) pp. 22-3.
30. Jerome Karabel, op. cit., p. 44.

11 The Special Role of the Mass News Media in a Plural Society

Leonard R. Sussman
Executive Director of Freedom House, New York City

The free press and broadcast media are under attack in many countries. Domestic news media are government-run or, if independent of the regime, harshly controlled or censored in most nations today. The South African Parliament recently considered a bill that would create a press code, council and penalties for certain acts by journalists. Transnational Western news services face unprecedented challenges from the developing nations of Africa, Asia and Latin America. These charge that four Western services dominate the news and culture of their countries, and hamper their economic development. The Soviet Union and other Marxist nations readily exploit Third World complaints to advance their own nationalistic and ideological objectives: absolute governmental control of international and national news media. The United Nations Educational, Scientific and Cultural Organisation (UNESCO), the new press pool of the non-aligned countries and other recently formed consortia advance diverse forms of governmental controls over the news media. For, indeed, there are as many rationales for restricting journalists as there are regimes which fear that their – or their national – interests will suffer if the press is free.

One argument for press control is based upon the fear of regimes in plural societies that uncontrolled dissemination of news and views will somehow lead to communal strife. For example, Malaysia's plural population is served by newspapers published in English, Chinese,

Jawi, Bahasa Malaysia, Tamil and Punjabi. The constitution of Malaysia does not guarantee press freedom though it pledges freedom of speech (customarily considered to cover the press). Yet there are ordinances and regulations restricting press freedom. These require annual licensing of presses and penalties for endangering the security of the nation by journalism considered detrimental to the state. In the face of such penalties and restrictions, news of racial and religious issues is generally withheld by the editors themselves. Since the communist disturbances of 1969, reports of racial and religious issues have been forbidden by the government. The *China Press* was banned for fourteen days for disobedience of this ruling. The Prime Minister of Malaysia defended the press ban and extended the attack to the 'foreign press'. Their 'irresponsible reporting', he said, 'purposely played to the advantage of the enemy.'[1] There is a clear challenge to the free press from those countries which fear violence stemming from ethnic differences and communal strife.

The issue of *whether* to permit the press to publish freely in plural societies may be restated: should the news media be permitted freedom in the interest of ameliorating the communal tensions in plural societies? Or, put differently, how early should the press in plural societies be free to exercise mature responsibility and also serve as a bridge between differing racial, religious or national-origin groups? To examine plural societies whose press has faced the challenge of explaining potential communal strife before it occurred we could discuss the United Kingdom, several northern European countries which have had a great influx of southern Europeans, or South Africa. We shall examine the experience in the United States of the reporting by its news media during the past three decades of the relationship between Negroes and whites.

I AMERICAN MINORITIES

The United States is second only to the Soviet Union in the size and diversity of groups of citizens retaining distinctive ethnic[2] affiliations based upon national, religious or racial identities. The Soviet constitution, while recognising the large geo-nationality blocs, grants *de facto* power only to the political units organised pragmatically by the Communist Party. In the absence of political, social or economic freedoms, the Soviet Union's ethnic groups are effectively submerged. The American Constitutional commitment has been to the citizen as an individual. As that gurantee is fulfilled, it, in turn, permits widening latitude for the development of ethnic groups. There are recognised ethnic groups such as Negroes, American Indians, and Spanish-speaking Americans. These may have territorial bases (Indians, Puerto Ricans). The much larger set of less readily defined ethnics includes national-origin groups such as the Irish, Italians and Poles; religious groups – the Catholics and Jews; and, in a certain sense, Southerners and New Englanders. America is composed of so many minorities that together they form the majority. These ethnic groups have grown or diminished at different paces in American history. There has always been a tension between the juridical basis for individual rights and responsibilities, and the correlative right of ethnic-group development. For at the points at which individual and group rights intersect, there are the possibilities for the individual citizen to be regarded – socially if not juridically – as an 'ethnic' whose group affiliations (involuntary, by definition) exceed his individualistic and voluntary choices. Through most of its first 150 years, America relied on structured ethnic affiliations to help the nation integrate the massive flow of immigrants. A great variety of social, linguistic, economic, recreational, political and even burial societies were developed by many national, religious and racial groups from the earliest days of the republic. These ethnic affiliations helped the American multiple melting-pot acculturate groups beyond the first generation of immigrants. Only the Negroes, until the 1950s, seemed frozen into a separate status. The system has not sought the elimination of ethnicity or indeed the value conflict based upon ethnicity. It has developed – as in many other areas of American life – a tension between differing constitutional rights. The checks and balances, here, derive from the commitments to both individual rights and voluntary group affiliations. The latter, proliferating in many directions, providing cradle-to-grave activities for members of their groups, have developed 'structural pluralism',[3] Milton Gordon's term for the dominant American sociological condition.

Gordon recognised significant exceptions to the continuing role of ethnicity for second and third generations of Americans and beyond. These exceptions are the intellectuals. They draw their numbers from all ethnic groups and provide them with 'an institutional setting for primary group relationships', once they have found ethnic communality personally uncongenial. Ethnicity is not ignored in the intellectual subsociety, Gordon holds. Instead 'ethnicity becomes an interesting but subsidiary issue rather than one which colors and dominates the rest of life.' With 'neutral ground' open to them; indeed with the freedom to opt out of any ethnic milieu, the juridical right to individuality is strengthened.

Bernard Ostry, formerly head of the Citizenship Branch of Canada's Department of the Secretary of State, maintains:

> We have come to see that a policy of multiculturalism is nothing more or less than a policy of cultural freedom – personal freedom to choose and explore one's identity. And because the stress is on freedom, every Canadian must also be at liberty to move about in our society, a liberty that can come only from familiarity with one of the languages in which our country conducts its business and politics: French and English.
>
> Everyone is free to choose his ethnic attachment as a positive value, but he is not to be locked into a particular ethnic group against his wishes, which might well follow if he remained ignorant of the official languages. A policy of multiculturalism can lead to freedom only if it is applied within the bilingual framework.[4]

A fundamental question raised by Gordon's analysis is the definition of the intellectuals as the prototype of the still developing US society. Clearly, Gordon does not limit his 'intellectuals' to a narrow group. He includes people in the professions, research, journalism, the arts and 'to a lesser degree, law and medicine'. He points out that in three US cities alone there are 43,000 college and university teachers. There are as many more in several enclaves in the field of mass communications. Obviously, they do not speak, write or teach solely to one another. The intellectual 'ethnics', I would argue, are the transmitters of the new American ethnicity, whatever that may be at any moment.

The central conveyors of this ethnicity are the media of mass communication. These are the same media which, for all the 200 years of America's national life, have served to integrate widely disparate groups into a national polity. It may be useful to examine one important aspect of this American experience: the special role of the mass news media in a plural society.

II HOW WELL DID THE NEWS MEDIA EXPLAIN THE BLACK AND WHITE GROUPS TO ONE ANOTHER?

Under the First Amendment to the US Constitution, nothing shall be done legislatively to limit the freedom of the press (taken to mean the broadcast as well as print media, including the ethnic and other specialised journals and broadcast outlets.) Yet the overweening fact of slavery as a common antecedent for most blacks – coupled with ensuing social and juridical limitations on educational, economic and interpersonal advancement – placed a special responsibility upon the mass news media: a social if not a Constitutional commitment to serve as a communication channel between the black and white populations. Except during the most severe crises (the Civil War and the postbellum era) the press widely ignored the black population, comprising nearly 10 per cent of the American people. This neglect by the general press of the condition of life of one large group of Americans had two aspects: the press failed generally to acquaint white people with the normative conditions, problems and complaints of black people; and the press reported exaggeratedly and without ample perspective the aberrational aspects of black society (the crime, 'quaintness' and critical differences). Most journalists in southern as well as northern cities of the country now accept this evaluation of American journalism prior to the changes effected in the sixties. These journalists may differ widely on the reasons for this failure of communication. And their differences may reflect their own southern or northern origins. But from a distance of eight years it is likely that most thoughtful journalists accept one conclusion of the US National Commission on the Causes and Prevention of Violence. The 1969 staff report on *Violence and the Media*, prepared under the direction of Dr Milton S. Eisenhower, brother of the late President, declared:

> A communication gap stretches wide between the black and white communities. Insulated from each other geographically, socially and politically, they have primarily the mass media as a medium of intergroup communications. The news media did not request this job, but when the need for communication became critical, they were the one institution in society equipped to do the most about it.[5]

The government report documented the understanding gap that existed for generations prior to the race riots of the sixties. Forty-five per cent of the whites but only 10 per cent of the Negroes believed that 'outside agitation' was a major cause of the riots of the sixties. Blacks cited inadequate housing and education as a major cause (68 and 61 per cent respectively) but whites regarded these factors as much less important (39 and 46 per cent). Police brutality, in the view of 49 per cent of the blacks, was an element in sparking the riots. Only 8 per cent of the whites agreed.[6] Obviously, whatever the objective factors (if they can indeed be separated from the *beliefs* of the respective populations), the perceptions of blacks and whites differed dramatically. The government study observed, 'If blacks and whites cannot agree even on the basic facts underlying the racial crisis in this country, there is little likelihood that we will be able to make any significant progress toward a final resolution of the American dilemma, and any resolution unilaterally imposed will most probably be violent.'[7]

An explanation for this faulty understanding was suggested by the Commission. One analysis of 100 motion pictures involving Negro characters made during the forties found that in 75 cases the portrayal was a disparaging stereotype. In only twelve films was the Negro favourably shown as a human being.[8] Mass circulation magazines paid little attention to the Negro. Fictional pieces were largely negative stereotypes. Most news coverage, until the late fifties, was limited to blacks involved in crime, sports or entertainment.

The performance of the southern press has been summarised by a leading southern white editor, Hodding Carter, of the Greenville (Miss.) *Delta Democrat-Times*:

> The obvious errors, the obvious omissions, the obvious commisions by the southern press are monumental. In the past it has been said that the church is the most segregated aspect of contemporary American life. I could say that for years the southern press was as segregated as the church ever dreamed of being.[9]

Thus, when Oliver Brown in 1951 sued the Topeka Board of Education for violating the Fourteenth Amendment by running a segregated school system, America was totally unprepared for the outcome. On 17 January 1954 at 12.52 p.m. the Supreme Court reversed the separate-but-equal principle that had been reaffirmed six times since 1899. This 'unpreparedness', writes George P. Hunt, 'was reflected in the press.' Looking back, he adds, 'one must admit that the existence of an intelligently prepared readership and audience would have helped the country weather those years with less agony.'[10]

Instead, race questions had been reported in the press mainly when a crisis arose and what was not readily made visual was not televised. The news media responded all too readily to the conflicts and controversies of the race-relations story; seldom, in the fifties and sixties, to the underlying sociological, economic, political and historical issues. Yet by the very nature of the mass news media in a large industrialised society, the news judgements of reporters, editors and news managers directly and indirectly affected the racial relationship of an entire nation. 'Thus, in becoming an arbiter of racial controversy, the editor has become a participant. He has taken a role in shaping the news as well as in reporting it', write Fisher and Lowenstein.[11] The principal dilemma which the editor faces in playing this role has been summed up by James Reston, columnist of the *New York Times*: 'How to keep the extremist minority from dominating the moderate majority in a country where the extremists tend to capture the headlines – this is the problem.' Reston saw this as the problem for newspapers, radio and television stations. In racial questions, he said, 'both extremes – those who shout "now" and those who shout "never" – have a ready audience, and much depends on the leadership of the moderates who say "neither".'

In the United States, in the fifties and sixties, the leadership of the moderates faltered, and the day was won by the extremists among blacks and whites who dominated the mass news media. That interaction could be foreseen as likely to produce violent confrontation. It was predicted accurately in some responsible journals. The *Los Angeles Times*, a half-decade before the August 1965 rioting began in the Watts section of Los Angeles, published pages of carefully documented reports by Gene Sherman on the mounting racial problems. The Pulitzer-Prize-winning writer concluded that 'although peacefully integrated on the surface, Los Angeles nevertheless has an undercurrent of racial antagonism running through its daily history.' Though less apparent than in some other large northern cities, warned Sherman, 'it is there.'

This warning was not heeded. And such warnings, in Watts or elsewhere in America during the fifties, were few in number and almost totally without impact. A communications system that had expanded widely in recent decades had somehow missed the most important domestic news development since the Civil War a century earlier. Sherman recognised this after the Watts riots had left 34 dead and 933 injured (including 85 policemen, 88 firemen, 10 national guardsmen and the remainder civilians). Immediately after the tragic disorders, Sherman wrote these notes for his own record:

> Obduracy, refusal to recognize that a problem exists (for whatever reason), simply crystallizes the danger. Another riot can be put down with force – but at what cost to lives and property! It's in Los Angeles' economic and humanitarian interest to find the answers.

This paper [the *Times*] must consult with Negro as well as white leaders, consistently and continually. Sometimes in the absence of officialdom. As the primary medium of mass communications, we *must* take primary responsibility for keeping the lines open.

We have a daily role to play, reporting the news and interpreting it. But we also have a longer-range duty, that of helping gear the community for intelligent action through careful delineation of the problem, through in-depth surveys, through our multiple good offices.

In the absence of enlightened press leadership, the rabble-rousers may take over. It is a truce now. It could be war.

Two years later, in the early summer of 1967, riots erupted during a two-week period in Newark, Detroit and other cities.

President Johnson immediately created by Executive Order the National Advisory Commission on Civil Disorders. The President sought answers to three questions: What happened? Why did it happen? What can be done to prevent its happening again?

The Commission examined the role played by the news media prior to and during the disorders. The President had specifically asked, 'What effect do the mass media have on the riots?' The Commission answered with the prefatory declaration that 'Freedom of the press is not the issue. A free press is indispensable to the preservation of the other freedoms this nation cherishes. . . . only a press unhindered by government can contribute to freedom.' The riots report continued:

> The Commission . . . determined, very early, that the answer to the President's question did not lie solely in the performance of the press and broadcasters in reporting the riots proper. Our analysis had to consider also the overall treatment by the media of the Negro ghettos, community relations, racial attitudes, urban and rural poverty – day by day and month by month, year in and year out.
>
> On this basis, we have reached three conclusions: First, that despite incidents of sensationalism, inaccuracies, and distortions, newspapers, radio and television, on the whole, made a real effort to give a balanced, factual account of the 1967 disorders.
>
> Second, despite this effort, the portrayal of the violence that occurred last summer failed to reflect accurately its scale and character. The overall effect was, we believe, an exaggeration of both mood and event.
>
> Third, and ultimately most important, we believe that the media

The Special Role of the Mass News Media

have thus far failed to report adequately on the causes and consequences of civil disorders and the underlying problems of race relations.[12]

For the future, the third finding was indeed most important. The Commission decided that the plight of the Negro population was not 'just another story', and should not be treated as one. Said the federal Commission:

> Our second and fundamental criticism is that the news media have failed to analyze and report adequately on racial problems in the United States and, as a related matter, to meet the Negro's legitimate expectations in journalism. By and large, news organizations have failed to communicate to both their black and white audiences a sense of the problems America faces and the sources of potential solutions. The media report and write from the standpoint of a white man's world. The ills of the ghetto, the difficulties of life there, the Negro's burning sense of grievance, are seldom conveyed. Slights and indignities are part of the Negro's daily life, and many of them come from what he now calls 'the white press' - a press that repeatedly, if unconsciously, reflects the biases, the paternalism, the indifference of white America. This may be understandable, but it is not excusable in an institution that has the mission to inform and educate the whole of our society.[13]

The Commission concluded that 'the failings of the media must be corrected and the improvement must come from within the media. A society that values and relies on a free press as intensely as ours, is entitled to demand in return responsibility from the press and conscientious attention by the press to its own deficiencies.'[14]

Specifically, the Commission said its major concern with the news media was not in riot reporting as such, 'but in the failure to report adequately on race problems and ghetto problems and to bring more Negroes into journalism.'[15]

III CHANGES IN THE ROLE OF THE PRESS

For the first 190 years of the republic - North and South - the press reported ethnic developments mainly as a series of detached crises. Not only the Negroes in the South but the waves of white immigrants in the

North, particularly during the nineteenth century, changed the social, economic and political patterns of major cities, entire states and the nation as a whole. The resulting socio-economic factors greatly affected the religious, cultural and educational patterns. These, in turn, strongly influenced developments in commerce, industrialisation and technology. Except for coverage of the exclusionary laws of the 1920s, the mass news media tended to miss the ethnic story throughout the half-century. Not until the academic explosion of the nineteen-fifties, with its great emphasis on sociological analysis, did the popularisation of social-scientific research begin, even haltingly, to enter the mass news media.

The St Patrick's Day parade was a perennial feature, but the problem that brought the Irish to American shores was seldom recalled. The difficulties they faced in employment, education and housing were just as infrequently noted. And the channel of advancement they took was seldom chronicled until John F. Kennedy made it to the White House. Even then, the history of the Irish immigrants was generally romanticised. During a century of immigration and the enlargement of ethnic structures serving every phase of pluralist life in America, only the superficial aspects were generally reported in the press.

To be sure, a broad spectrum of ethnic newspapers and magazines served the special interests of ethnic groups. There are 266 ethnic newspapers published in 36 different languages in the United States. There are another 307 Negro newspapers published in 38 states.[16] The first Negro newspaper was created in New York in 1827. It sought mainly to oppose slavery. It lasted only three years, succumbing perhaps to the single-mindedness of its proposed alternative: the back-to-Africa movement for American blacks. They apparently wanted a solution closer to what had become their national home. Their fuller accommodation would require better understanding by both blacks and whites of the realities of bi-racial life in America.

For the general press to accept that, and other responsibilities flowing from it, would require the balancing of two distinct obligations: in the words of Martin S. Hayden, editor-in-chief of the Detroit *News*, 'first, to report the news; second, to preserve the peace.'[17] American journalists had almost unanimously maintained, before the racial disturbances of the sixties, that their sole function was reporting (and only secondarily analysing) the news. Editors denied they had or should have a social responsibility beyond that of reporting the news as objectively as possible. Some insisted that to accept any responsibility beyond that of balanced and objective reporting was to invite, ultimately, governmental policing of a social responsibility of the press. And that has always been regarded by the press as the first step toward breaching the First Amendment guarantee of press freedom. The Supreme Court, on the relatively few occasions it has decided free-press issues, supports the 'clear and present danger' doctrine set forth by Mr Justice Holmes in 1919. In *Schenck vs. United States* the Court held that the time and place of an act may justify government regulation of free speech and press. 'The most stringent protection of free speech should not protect a man in falsely shouting fire in a theater and causing panic,' wrote Justice Holmes. 'It does not even protect a man from an injunction against uttering words that may have all the effect of force', he added. The test in every case is whether the words 'create a clear and present danger'. But the Court is consistently reluctant to apply this doctrine.

Hayden described the relationship between the obligation to report the news and that to preserve the peace:

> In general, the first obligation takes precedence, but under the rules of responsibility to which we try to adhere the second can be and is served by constant care in several areas – care in how stories are played, in avoiding exaggeration in both copy and headlines, in the checking of questionable details. Again, there is careful attention to coverage of both sides of a story and concentration on adequate follow-up of developments after the first day's headlines.
>
> As we cover the news we also try to provide readers with adequate understanding of what has happened or is happening, though editorials, depth pieces, and thoughtful columns based on the general assumption that our predominantly white readership may not be prejudiced so much as simply unaware of what a Negro's life is like and what disturbs him.[18]

IV THE IMPORTANCE OF PRESS CREDIBILITY IN COVERAGE OF CIVIL DISORDERS

The non-governmental Commission for a Free and Responsible Press in 1947 set forth these objectives for the journalist in fulfilling his or her obligations to provide the information the public has the right to know:

1. A truthful, comprehensive, and intelligent account of the day's

events in a context which gives them meaning.
2. A forum for the exchange of comment and criticism.
3. A means of projecting the opinions and attitudes of the groups in the society to one another.
4. A method of presenting and clarifying the goals and values of society.
5. Full access to the day's intelligence.[19]

These criteria, sound as they appear thirty years later, were never widely accepted by the American press. The Hutchins Commission report was generally regarded by the press as outside interference in the journalists' domain. Most of the Commission's researchers and authors had never been journalists. The report seemed to recommend objectives, and indeed responsibilities, for the news media far beyond those previously accepted by them. A 'forum' sounded like a series of special-interest discussions rather than the reporting of news. The projecting of opinions of differing groups appeared to be another vehicle for special pleading. The clarifying of goals of the society seemed to convert journalism into a sociological or political laboratory. Professional journalists, by and large, would have none of it.

American journalism in the fifties and sixties therefore reflected approaches and objectives little altered since the era of sensationalism ended in the thirties. The civil rights demonstrations, college disorders and Vietnam dissent of the sixties made a severe impact on the credibility of the press, as on most other institutions in American life. The American people in a large majority[20] seemed to question whether the mass news media had been telling the truth about major developments at home and abroad. It was not surprising. Coverage of racial questions had indeed suffered from what the Hutchins Commission, twenty years earlier, termed lack of competence 'at doing the kind of analysis necessary to place the event in context and give it significance'.[21] The news organisations, before the Civil Rights demonstrations, had not regularly covered the black community. The reporters seldom ventured into the black ghetto and rarely understood its aspirations. Few reporters and fewer editors were themselves black (many black journalists wanted to 'make it' on their own skills, covering general news, without being stereotyped mainly as reporters of black news). Inevitably, too, the white press accepted as black 'leaders' some whose only credentials were that they shouted outrageously. Such misperceptions were bound to disappear as Negroes became active reporters, editors and telecasters in the US mass news media.

Whereas in the mid-1950s 'it was difficult to find a black face in the American press corps',[22] by the 1970s blacks are employed before and behind the cameras in all TV network newsrooms, and in many independent stations across the country, including the deep South. It is estimated that 1500 Negroes in 1977 serve in television and newspaper city rooms across the country.[23]

The presence of black journalists – qualified both in the skills of the reportorial profession and in the human experience of inter-race relations – might have significantly improved the perceptions which white Americans had of the events leading up to the disorders of the sixties.

Once disorders begin, the most important function the news media serve is communication of accurate information. 'Almost invariably', said the Eisenhower study, 'if a modicum of journalistic responsibility is exercised, the information relayed by the news media will be more conservative than the rumors that would circulate in its absence. When suggesting non-coverage, most critics overlook the possibility that the information that will dominate is more likely to escalate violence than media coverage.' The report added, 'The decision to bar media coverage is a dangerous one, and the substitution of governmental news sources is undesirable.' In explanation, the report declared, 'Although the latter alternative [government-controlled information] might provide information that most white adults believe, in many communities the majority of young blacks and important segments of the young white population would not.'[24]

V THE DEVELOPMENT OF PRESS GUIDELINES FOR THE COVERAGE OF CIVIL DISORDERS

The American press since the days of the Hutchins Commission has been loath to commit to paper guidelines or criteria for general journalistic coverage. Numerous efforts to create a canon of journalism have faltered. The national associations of both publishers and editors considered and rejected the development of broad standards of practice such as physicians and attorneys maintain. In several cities the bar associations and/or judiciaries, in company with journalists, have developed informal guidelines covering the most controversial aspects of reporting and commenting on judicial processes. These are generally known as free press/fair trial codes. They are voluntary efforts by the legal and journalistic professions to deal fairly with situations in which there is a clash of Constitutional rights: that of the public to know and the defendant to secure a fair trial, untainted by press coverage or any other potential biasing of his or her case.

The Eisenhower report recommended that despite the general reluctance of the press to set guidelines, there should be voluntary, advance efforts by news organisations to devise their own guidelines on the press coverage of civil disorders. 'Although no set of guidelines will cover all eventualities, the more specific they are, and the more they are discussed within the news organisation, the greater probability that the reporter or correspondent under stress will adhere to them.'[25]

The Commission also strongly recommended meeting the problems created by unequal access to ethnic-group intelligence by

1. Hiring and training more newsmen from minority groups.
2. Applying the same surveillance to ethnic groups it provides for other segments of the population.
3. Using 'ghetto' reporters.
4. Covering members of ethnic groups in day-to-day news such as births, deaths, weddings, business promotions, social functions, etc. – in brief, humanizing those groups.
5. Providing more background on the social issues of which the general population has little experience.[26]

All these innovations would be voluntarily undertaken by the press and broadcasters.

This government report, written at a time of great social stress, concluded: 'The government can no more legislate good journalism than it can legislate good manners.'

VI ATTEMPTS BY THE THIRD WORLD TO CREATE A UNIVERSAL STANDARD OF GOVERNMENT-IMPOSED PRESS GUIDELINES AND IMPLEMENTATION

Over the past seven years, the facilities of UNESCO have been widely used to develop a new universal standard to determine the transnational exchange of information. These efforts have been based on the premise that the new International Economic Order supported by the UN can only be advanced if the major transnational news media, now headquartered in Western countries, significantly alter the content and procedures of news transmissions. These changes would correct what

The Special Role of the Mass News Media

is said by Third World leaders to be an imbalance in the flow of news, distortion of Third World events and personalities reported to the developed world, and inadequate coverage of news – particularly that affecting economic development – within and between the developing countries. All this adds up to 'cultural imperialism', a charge frequently made by the Soviet Union and other Marxist states in exploiting Third World complaints for ideological gains.

The Soviet Union in 1972 introduced a draft resolution (19 C/91) at the biennial general conference of UNESCO which called for the 'use' of the mass news media for a variety of purposes. The operative paragraph, Article XII, declared that

> States are responsible for the activities in the international sphere of all mass media under their jurisdiction.

Clearly, this would alter the status of every correspondent for a free press wherever in the world he serves. This dictum would justify the most repressive governments in clamping down on their domestic press. It would also provide the support of an inter-governmental organisation for the most retrogressive actions taken against foreign journalists within the borders of repressive states.

Alongside this declaration, also moving through UNESCO channels since 1972, have been a series of inter-governmental and expert conferences on the mass news media. In preparation for a conference at San José, Costa Rica, July 1976, experts recommended a series of governmental regulations and controls over the press. These included:

> The creation of national communications policies in each country; the establishment of national communications councils to supervise the press and broadcasters;
> the development of a code of ethics for journalists to be prepared by UNESCO and submitted for the possible implementation by member-states;
> creation of national and regional news agencies; compilation of statutes affecting the mass news media; etc.

All of these recommendations were placed before governmental delegates and, at San José, generally approved. These recommendations, in turn, were 'noted' at UNESCO's biennial in Nairobi in November 1976. Many of these projects will be examined in greater detail by UNESCO's experts or initiated as operative programmes during the next two years. The Soviet draft declaration was deferred at Nairobi and, though scheduled to be reconsidered in 1978, may be rendered relatively innocuous by then. Not so, the other programmatic efforts to support government control or regulation of the mass news by governments. These efforts continue.

VII THE SPECIAL ROLE OF THE MASS NEWS MEDIA

In both developing and developed countries where ethnic differences persist, the UNESCO model of a government-run council to enforce an official press code is attractive. Though UNESCO insists it has no particular 'communications policy' to recommend to governments it nevertheless maintains that its news media programme is committed to advancing economic development and balancing the North-South flow of information. 'Balancing' would be accomplished, in most of the projected plans, by governmental actions. UNESCO also maintains it would not harm the free press but would simply modify the 'free flow' doctrine of UNESCO's 1945 constitution by adding the element of 'balance' – balancing by governments.

President Carlos Andrés Pérez of Venezuela, a strong supporter of UNESCO's news media policies, maintains that his country is a 'democratic nation governed by a constitutional system'. It is. Yet he nevertheless affirms that 'international regulation of communication is required to ensure the sacred right to information by guaranteeing that *only the truth* will be reported . . .' [my emphasis].

Despite his democratic commitment, the UNESCO plan thus draws Pérez into ideological association with some of the most repressive countries in his hemisphere. And, as Venezuela and 84 other nations plan the Third World news agencies pool, they join as well with the most authoritarian nations in Africa and Asia.

In the face of government-control proposals, official disclaimers professing no harm to the free press provide little consolation for a journalist presently serving a free country that has a relatively free press. The news media are a vulnerable target for impatient government officials. For the mass media *do* have a special and important role in a free society. They comprise the non-governmental communication system for the nation. They are a check on the policies of the regime and a watchdog over the functioning of the governmental bureaucracy. They are a catalyst for reforms in all the institutions – private as well as public – of the society. The mass news media provide the primary channels of communication among the ethnic groups. Whatever the degree of integration, communication is vital for the creation and maintenance of a functionally free society with mutually acceptable cultural pluralism and the absence of ethnic conflict. President Johnson's Riot Commission determined:

> This is our basic conclusion: Our nation is moving toward two societies, one black, one white – separate and unequal.
> The alternative is not blind repression or capitulation to lawlessness. It is the realization of common opportunities for all within a single society.
> The alternative will require a commitment to national action – compassionate, massive and sustained, backed by the resources of the most powerful and the richest nation on this earth. From every American it will require new attitudes, new understanding, and, above all, new will.[27]

That 'new will' has been demonstrated, often haltingly, in many areas of American life. The mass news media have made major structural, editorial and personnel changes. Some are briefly described earlier in this paper. But the most fundamental decisions have been made by both the government and the mass news media. They have rejected governmental regulation, supervision or any other form of interference in the performance of the US mass news media. And the media have come to accept, voluntarily, a far more sophisticated set of standards – standards almost univerally *not* committed to formal publication – governing the daily functioning of the print and broadcast press in this highly plural society.

NOTES

1. Tan Peng Siew, *The Asian Newspapers' Reluctant Revolution*, John A. Lent, ed. (Ames: Iowa State University Press, 1971), p. 187.
2. The ethnic group is defined here as composed of individuals from common religious, national-origin, racial and other backgrounds. Within the group there is a network of organisations and unorganised social relationships deriving from the common antecedents. These enable and encourage the group's members to engage in all of their lifetime's primary and some of their secondary relationship through the facilities of the ethnic group.
3. Milton M. Gordon, *Assimilation in American Life*; (New York: Oxford University Press, 1964), p. 235.
4. Bernard Ostry, 'The Unmeltables: The Canadian Experience', in *The New*

Immigration and the New Ethnicity: Social Policy and Social Theory in the 1970s (New York: American Immigration and Citizenship Conference, 1974) p. 41.
5. David L. Lange, Robert K. Baker, Sandra J. Bull, *Mass Media and Violence*, a report to the National Commission on the Causes and Prevention of Violence (Washington: US Government Printing Office, Nov 1969) vol. 9, p. 44. The Eisenhower Commission was created by President Johnson after the assassinations of Senator Robert F. Kennedy and the Rev. Martin Luther King.
6. Poll conducted 1-8 Oct 1968 by Louis Harris and Associates, Inc. for the National Commission on the Causes and Prevention of Violence. Sampling instruments and procedures appear as Appendix III-I of the study.
7. *Mass Media and Violence*, p. 44.
8. Gordon Allport, *The Nature of Prejudice* (Cambridge, Mass.: Wesley Publishing Co., 1954).
9. In *The Black American and the Press*, Jack Lyle, ed. (Los Angeles: Ward Ritchie Press, 1968) p. 38.
10. George P. Hunt, 'The Racial Crisis and the News Media', in *Race and News Media*, Paul Fisher and Ralph L. Lowenstein, eds (New York: Praeger, 1967) p. 14.
11. Ibid., p. 6.
12. *Report of the National Advisory Commission on Civil Disorders* (New York: Bantam edition) p. 363.
13. Ibid., p. 366.
14. Ibid., p. 367.
15. Ibid., p. 382.
16. *Editor and Publisher International Yearbook* (New York, 1976) pp. 335ff. and 538ff.
17. Martin S. Hayden, 'Reporting the Racial Story in Detroit', in *Race and the News Media*, ibid., p. 28.
18. Ibid.
19. Robert M. Hutchins, chairman, *A Free and Responsible Press* (Chicago: University of Chicago Press, 1947) pp. 20–1.
20. A Roper Organization poll in Oct 1976 drew only 10 per cent of respondents who agreed that they are confident they can depend on what they are told by the press. Forty-six per cent were only fairly confident. In 1975 the very confident figure was 9 per cent; in 1974, 11; and 1973, 8.
21. *Mass Media and Violence*, p. 52.
22. Ibid., p. 58.
23. Estimate of Chuck Stone of the National Association of Black Journalists.
24. *Mass Media*, p. 104.
25. Ibid., p. 118.
26. Ibid., p. 160.
27. *Report of the National Advisory Commission on Civil Disorders*, ibid., pp. 1–2.

12 The Problems of Intergroup Accommodation and Pluralism in the Politics of Pakistan

Khalil A. Nasir
Director, International Studies Institute, C.W. Post Center, Long Island University, New York

I POLITICS OF PLURALISM IN THE FORMATIVE YEARS OF PAKISTAN

On 14 August 1947 two of the most populous independent states, India and Pakistan, were born in South Asia. On that day, the last British Viceroy of the Indian sub-continent, Lord Mountbatten, first flew from Delhi to Karachi to proclaim, and to participate in the celebrations of, the birth of Pakistan. A few hours later, he flew back to Delhi to preside over the independence ceremonies of India, a nation inhabited by the second largest population in the world.

It was truly one of the most historic and momentous days in the middle of the twentieth century. It started the inexorable process of the disintegration of the vast British *colonial* empire. In fact, it heralded the decline of the entire colonial period of the European powers which continued to gain momentum in the quarter of a century that followed. On the global scene, it founded the nucleus of a steadily rising group of the Third World nations now claiming more than one hundred seats in the United Nations organisation.

More specifically, for a majority of the Muslims of the Indian sub-continent, on the one hand, it ushered in an era of cherished hopes, of utopian dreams and of promising prospects. Yet, on the other hand, almost immediately after its foundation, Pakistan began to suffer from an unending series of major crises which have not only shattered the early hopes and dreams but have also considerably weakened and effectively damaged the stability of Pakistan as a nation.

This study is an endeavour to explore and analyse the causes and the background of these agonising crises. It aims to evaluate the writer's hypothesis that Pakistan, throughout its entire history of thirty years, has been plagued with the extremely serious problems of a highly complex pluralistic society. It is contended that the pluralist structure of Pakistan suffers from a diversity of major dimensions. Behind the facade of the unifying force of religion, which ostensibly provided the character of homogeneity to this newly born state, Pakistan has been suffering from cultural and social differentiations based on ethnicity, race, region and several other factors. Furthermore, this paper pursues the premise that Islam, which became the rallying cry for the Muslims of the sub-continent, has been used and manipulated as a potent instrument of divisiveness and disunity.

This study traces the major problems of intergroup accommodation in Pakistan in their historical context, from 1947 to the present.

The credit for the dream of Pakistan is often given to the vision and concepts of the leading Muslim philosopher-poet of the Indian sub-continent, Dr Muhammad Iqbal. His nationalistic writings sparked intense feelings among the Muslims that, as a people so basically different from the overwhelming majority of the Hindus, they had a right to exist as a separate sovereign nation in those parts of India where they constituted a majority, even though those areas were separated by several hundreds of miles.

The origin of the word Pakistan is attributed to the ingenuity of a young Punjabi Muslim, Rahmat Ali Chaudhry, who introduced the word in a pamphlet he wrote in the 1930s, when he was a student in England. The word literally means 'land of the pure' or 'the holy land' in Urdu. However, its letters also signify the initials of the parts of India (p for Punjab and North West Frontier Province, a for Afghan areas, k for Kashmir, s for Sind and tan for Baluchistan) which were, in earlier stages of the dream, expected to be incorporated in a Muslim sovereign state.

It must be noted, however, that if, in the process of the implementation of the Government of India Act of 1935, the two communities of India, the Hindus and the Muslims, could develop a working relationship based on mutual understanding, harmony and trust, most probably the movement toward Pakistan would have never materialised. The leading political party, the All India National Congress, even though secular in its commitment, was overwhelmingly oriented toward the safeguard of Hindu interests. The Muslim League, the principal voice of the Indian Muslims, became fully convinced that the events of the last half of the 1930s, when the two communities engaged in an experiment of working together, effectively proved that it was impossible for them to protect their rights in a united India.

Clearly, it is beyond the scope of the present study to offer a detailed account of the political developments of this critical period which could have changed the entire course of the history of the Indian sub-continent. Had the Hindus and the Muslims learned to live together with a reasonable respect for each other and to safeguard their respective rights and interests, today's India could have been a federated but undivided and unpartitioned single state. Instead, it was unalterably led toward the creation of two, and by 1971, of three separate nations.

As the Second World War became imminent, the Muslim leaders of both northeast and northwest India (later to be known respectively as East Pakistan and West Pakistan) began to convince the masses that they had no alternative but to struggle for the creation of Pakistan if they were to survive. They were told that Islam provides its adherents a homogenising and unifying force which can effectively and successfully transcend all other differentiations. Thus, the sub-continent was set on the inevitable course of a partition.

In the northwest of India, the movement toward the creation of a Muslim state started to spread with remarkable speed. Even more impressive was the way it electrified the imagination of the Bengali Muslims. In a special session of the Muslim League, held in Calcutta on 17 April 1938, the leader of the Krishak Praja Party, Fazlul Huq, perhaps the most popular Bengali Muslim politician of the period, reflected the Muslim's feelings as follows:

> We are passing through times which are extremely critical for the Muslims of India. On the one side, we find the Congress with all its might, on the other side, we find the Hindu Mahasabha [an extreme right wing orthodox Hindu organisation] with all its communal bigotry characteristic intolerance, narrow political outlook, and unholy intentions, devoting its energies to the frustration of Muslim hopes and the suppression of the legitimate rights and liberties of the

Muslim community.... Let us fight on a double front and with our backs to the wall. If Panipat and Thaneswar must repeat themselves, let the Muslims prepare to give us as glorious an account of themselves as did their forebears.... May the all-merciful God guide the deliberations on the right lines and may your decisions bring nearer the day of the Islam's deliverance in India.[1]

In less than two years after Fazlul Huq's foregoing observations, the movement toward the creation of a separate Muslim state had spread like a forest fire all over Muslim north India. By 22 March 1940, introducing a resolution demanding the creation of Pakistan, its founder, and later the first governor-general of the new state, Mohammed Ali Jinnah, observed in the historic Muslim League session held at Lahore:

The problem of India is not of an intercommunal character, but manifestly of an international one, and it must be treated as such.... The only course open to us all is to allow the major nations separate homelands by dividing India into autonomous national states.[2]

On 14 August 1947 Pakistan's birth was greeted with unbounded joy in both eastern and western regions. Jinnah and other Muslim League leaders had successfully capitalised upon the uniqueness of Islam to infuse among its followers the spirit that bound them together. He believed that Islam was a strong enough force to provide the Indian Muslims with all the basic characteristics of a nation.

Jinnah considered that adherence to the faith of Islam was a strong enough force to have a pervasive influence over all other cultural, social and regional differentiations. Later events painfully demonstrated the errors of this judgement. The religion did not prove to be an effective unifying force. In fact, some of the most violent massacres took place in the following years from the attempt of the politically manipulated majority not only to brand a minority sect as non-Muslims but to demand total exclusion of its members from public life.

Nor did the adherence to Islam succeed in eliminating the bases of other intergroup pluralism between East and West Pakistan. Some detailed account of the bloody and tragic events leading toward a horrible civil war and the emergence of Bangladesh as a separate independent nation will follow later.

At the very outset, it must be noted that the Pakistan which actually emerged in 1947 was at least territorially nowhere near the full materialisation of the dreams of the founders of the new state. In addition to leaving behind a substantial minority of the Muslims in India, the Muslim League leaders reconciled themselves to what Jinnah called a 'mutilated, moth-eaten, truncated Pakistan'. East Pakistan was composed of only a part of the former British province of Bengal and only two districts of Assam. In West Pakistan, Sind, Buluchistan and North West Frontier Province and a partitioned Punjab were included. David Loshak, a former correspondent of the London *Daily Telegraph*, called it a partition within partition.[3] More specifically, he took note of Pakistan's inherent pluralism even at that stage:

> Pakistan was a nation in a hurry ... in crisis and carnage. It was an ill-fated nation. ... [The Indian sub-continent] was a land of enormous diversity. It had a multiplicity of languages and customs, deep poverty and immense wealth, people of every kind and degree, and most crucial of all, two dominant and utterly contrasting religions.[4]

Except for the observation about two contrasting religions, what Loshak remarked about the sub-continent in general also applied to Pakistan. As A. Tayyeb observes, the disruptive forces in Pakistan have been operating both 'vertically, in the form of rivalries between classes, and horizontally, in the form of rivalries between the areas'.[5]

Added to the already existing groupings of Pakistan was a huge number of Indian Muslims who became a major part of an unprecedented flow of refugees from both sides of the border. It is estimated that close to eight million people poured into West Pakistan alone within a few months of the partition.[6] This, of course, proved to be an almost unbearable burden for the state in the early stages of its infancy. A hidden blessing, however, in the case of at least a sizeable minority of the refugees, emerged by their adding to the manifestly small numbers of the intelligentsia and private entrepreneurs. In the long run, a large number of these immigrant refugees, who found it more practical to settle in the urban areas, constituted an additional class in a large array of widely divergent and discrepant groups.

Thus the new state of Pakistan was born, which was, from the very outset, considered by many to be an anachronism in a twentieth-century world dominated by secular ideologies, its very existence offensive ... to many in the neighbouring India Union'.[7] Like many other Third World nations, it was, in the words of Rupert Emerson, more a 'nation in hope' than in actuality. He remarked:

Of the more recently created nations, the most striking and extraordinary case is that of Pakistan where a nation which almost no one had foreseen and few could credit in advance as even a possibility came into being virtually overnight through its own assertion (or that of a small number of leaders) that a nation existed which had not been there yesterday morning.[8]

With the emergence of Pakistan in 1947, at least for a temporary period, religious affinities had drowned out all other diversities of her social stratification. In spite of the pains of her birth and other related woes in her infancy, she asserted her nationhood rather strongly in the first few years. It took less than ten years before the first of the major problems of the intergroup political accommodation started seriously to threaten its existence. By 1958, the gulf between East and West Pakistan was already a major headache for the young nation.

II THE PROBLEMS OF PLURALISM IN THE CONSTITUTION-MAKING PROCESS

The process of nation-building relies heavily on the formulation of a reasonably workable constitution. It provides a direction for the state, regulates the political institutions, defines the rights, obligations and duties of its citizens, spells out the relationship of various groups within its people and lays out the framework in which the basic organs of the state can operate and interact. In relatively homogeneous societies, the constitution-making process is manifestly less difficult. In newly-born states, the accomplishment of framing a constitution as early as possible underlines a wide consensus among its people.

In Pakistan, the quest for a constitution has encompassed twenty-five long, agonising years. The latest endeavours resulted in the 1973 constitution, drafted only after East Pakistan, the larger sub-grouping within the original Pakistan, had already seceded. Many scholars of Pakistani politics observe that even the present venture will prove to be still another failure considering the unrelenting pressure of a highly complex pluralist society. Just for comparison, one can look at neighbouring India which succeeded in drafting and promulgating a constitution as early as 1950.

One must, however, make due allowance for the monumental problems of Pakistan's very survival. As Khalid Sayeed states, 'Very few states in the world started with greater handicaps than Pakistan did on

August 14, 1947.'[9] It is appreciated that the first five years of Pakistan's independence were, in the words of Wilcox, 'years of emergency government, near-famine, and disorder'. He correctly observes,

> The institutions which existed in the Pakistan provinces before independence were not strong and partition pulverized their remains. The new government had to fill every need, and its frantic totalitarianism was the sole barrier between oblivion and existence.[10]

What the foregoing statement does not say is that, simultaneously with their survival problems, the Pakistanis became preoccupied with the immediate question of exactly what kind of 'Islamic' state they wanted to build. Was she going to be a strictly theocratic state applying her religious laws to the Muslims and non-Muslims alike? Or was she being shaped as a completely secular state in the modern sense of the word? And, in that case, would this be in line with the original goals of the struggle for Pakistan? The pendulum of Pakistani opinion swung all the way from the ultra-right orthodox views to the extreme leftist ideas which find their expressions so frequently among the Third World nations. This situation was, of course, only symptomatic of the basic political, religious, social and economic disparities of Pakistani society. On 12 March 1949, her Constituent Assembly passed the famous Objectives Resolution. In part it read:

> This Constituent Assembly, representing the people of Pakistan, resolves to frame a Constitution for the sovereign independent state of Pakistan; ...
> Wherein the Muslims shall be enabled to order their lives in the individual and collective spheres in accord with the teachings and requirements of Islam as set out in the Holy Quran and the Sunna....[11]

It should be noted that nowhere in the Objectives Resolution was there any mention of an 'Islamic state' or an Islamic republic. The text was left deliberately vague to accommodate all shades of views. The underlying tensions, however, continued to delay the drafting of a constitution in the light of these Objectives. However, it eloquently underscored the vast diversity of religious pluralism. *The Jamiat-ul-Ulama-i-Islam*, one of the orthodox religious groups, for example, envisioned a return to the practices of a 'mythical Golden Age' in which 'an invisible supernational community would be presided over by a *Khalifa* and defended by strict adherence to the traditional schools of law.'[12]

Another formidable barrier in the way of drafting a resolution was the question of an equitable distribution of powers between the central authority and the provinces on the one hand and the voice of each zone of the country on the other. It was clear that, in spite of some expressions of merging all zones in West Pakistan into one unit, the regional, ethnic and linguistic groupings continued to guard their separate entities. The common bond of Islam which originally brought about Pakistan's existence could not serve the role of harmonising other diversities.

It was not until March 1956 that a constitution was finally adopted. It did not, however, succeed in stopping the disruptive forces inherent in the pluralist society of Pakistan. By 7 October 1958, President Iskander Mirza abrogated this short-lived constitution and declared a state of martial law. Three weeks later, he was on his way out of Pakistan, exiled by the new ruler, General Mohammad Ayub Khan, the former commander-in-chief of the country's armed forces. The task of the consolidation of the nation against the awesome complexities of a multitude of its diversities proved to be insurmountable for this frail constitution. It failed to satisfy the orthodox religious leaders, the *mullahs*, who continued to demand the establishment of a theocratic state. Equally important were the respective dissatifactions of East Pakistan and various regions within West Pakistan.

With the beginning of the rule of Ayub, the short-lived parliamentary democracy, which was not too strong even at the outset, had miserably collapsed. Martial law became the supreme law of the land for the next four years. It was not until June 1962 that another constitution was promulgated. At the time when General Ayub decided to take the reins of the nation into his hands, Pakistan seemed to be at the point of imminent disintegration. As General Ayub later wrote:

> ... I could not convince myself that we had become a nation in the real sense of the word; the whole spectacle was one of disunity and disintegration. We were divided in two halves, each half dominated by a distinct linguistic and cultural pattern. The geographical distance between the two halves was in itself a divisive factor which could be exploited to create all kinds of doubts and suspicions among the people. We had inherited a deep antagonism which separated the people in the countryside from the urban classes. The

latter represented a small minority of the total population, but it was a vocal minority and the people in the villages suffered from a sense of domination and exploitation by the elite of the towns.[13]

Founded on the concept of 'Basic Democracies', the new constitution of 1962 introduced a type of presidential democracy. A former prime minister of the country, Chaudhri Muhammad Ali, labelled it as a government of the President, by the President, and for the President.[14] President Ayub, on the other hand, claimed that the new constitution was designed to bring forth national unity combined with local autonomy but without the 'disruptive' presence of political parties.[15]

Soon after the promulgation of the 1962 constitution and subsequent legislative elections, Pakistan made another return to the introduction of the political party system. The Political Parties Act, however, defined the limits within which parties could function legitimately.[16] This was obviously a tacit recognition of the tragic problems inherent in Pakistan's hopelessly divergent society. Within a very short time, several parties appeared on the political horizons of the country, again signifying the highly diversified stratification of her society.[17]

By 25 March 1969, President Ayub was forced to resign as a result of public reaction against some scandals of corruption in high circles. His successor, General Agha Mohammad Yahya Khan, in turn resigned in December 1971, thus making way for the leadership of Zulfikar Ali Bhutto. On 14 August 1973, exactly 26 years after the birth of the nation, yet another constitution went into effect reintroducing the parliamentary type of democracy. Pakistan had again gone full circle.

An evaluation of the new 1973 constitution will follow in another context. The formulation and abrogation of the former constitutions decisively underscores the problems of Pakistan's pluralist society. One wonders how long the present constitution will last, in view of the unsuccessful record of the earlier ventures.

III THE POLITICS OF REGIONAL PLURALISM: THE FAILURE OF CONSOLIDATION AND THE EMERGENCE OF BANGLADESH

Today's Pakistan, known as West Pakistan until the emergence of East Pakistan as the independent state of Bangladesh, is composed of four provinces (Punjab, Sind, Baluchistan and North West Frontier Province) and the former princely states of Dir, Swat, Chitral, Khairpur, Kalat and Las Bela. Each one of these provinces has at least one major language of its own, quite distinct from other languages of the area. The literate Pakistanis communicate with people of other linguistic groups, generally in Urdu. College-educated people often use English as the *lingua franca*. Although Urdu is spoken as a mother tongue by less than 10 per cent of Pakistanis, it is expected to become the only official language of the whole of Pakistan in a few years. At present, Urdu shares the status of an official language with English.

The provincial division of Pakistan is a legacy of the British rule. It was done for administrative purposes, of course keeping in view other factors as well. However, a consequence of the provincial division is the addition of another factor to the already quite complicated picture of the population's diversity. Differences of tradition, ethnic background, population strength, a variety of languages and economic potential have been further accentuated after Partition.[18]

The Punjab, even after losing its substantial territory to India, remains both the most populous and the most prosperous province. It provides the bulk of the armed forces as well as civil service personnel to the central government, thus automatically gaining a dominant position among other provinces. It was only natural that Punjab's prominence should lead to deep-rooted resentment and bitter rivalries. Consequently, conflicting demands and pressures from each group started to produce a climate of confusion and instability of provincial governments. In the early 1950s, therefore, the central government started considering a merger of all provinces into one unit, just as East Pakistan had been a single unit from 1947 until it emerged as Bangladesh.

It is worth noting that, even during the British rule, schemes of a merger of some of these provinces was the subject of occasional serious consideration. Feldman observes that one such scheme was discussed as early as 1866. Furthermore, he remarks that as far back as 1948 Jinnah wanted to implement a 'One Unit' plan for West Pakistan.[19]

In spite of the diverse plural character of what was then West Pakistan, the desirability of the merger into one unit had been lucidly discussed by President Ayub. He commented:

> The population in West Pakistan . . . is probably the greatest mixture of races found anywhere in the world. Lying on the gateways to the Indian sub-continent, it is inevitable that each successive conquering race should have left its traces here. Consequently, this

forced mixture of races has brought about fusion of ideas, outlook and culture, despite the linguistic variety that it obtained. Strategically and economically, too, this area is destined to stand or fall as a whole. Lying as it does in the basin of the Indus river and its tributaries, its future economic development must be considered as a whole to achieve the maximum results. All this indicates, therefore, that West Pakistan, in order to develop properly and prove a bulwark of defence from the North or the South, must be welded into one unit and all artificial provincial boundaries be removed, regardless of any prejudices to the contrary which are more the creation of politicians than real.[20]

It was not until 1953, however, that the proposal for one unit started to gain momentum after the central government and the government of the province of Punjab developed a serious policy conflict over the issue of widespread communal disturbances. It was argued that under a structure of a fragmented administrative system, it was possible that what might be legal in Sind could be illegal in the Punjab, or what might be taxable in the Punjab could be tax-exempt in North West Frontier Province. Furthermore, each one of the provinces could conceivably create custom barriers between themselves. It could, perhaps, adversely affect the implementation of the badly needed irrigation projects.[21]

Consequently, the Prime Minister announced on 22 November 1954 that a unified West Pakistan would be established. The dismissed governments of the provinces vigorously opposed the action. They brought a case before the court questioning the Governor General's jurisdiction. The central government argued that the action was both necessary and legal, since the security and stability of the country was held to be of the utmost importance. The Supreme Court decided to uphold the central government's action.

It was vainly and perhaps wishfully hoped that the integration plan would effectively curb provincial rivalries. Representation of various former provinces in the One Unit legislature, as well as in the cabinet, was allocated, with Punjab getting less than her proportional share. This drastic action, notwithstanding the strong opposition from diverse quarters, was considered so necessary that, even as late as 1970, when the question was being reconsidered, it was defended even on religious grounds. It was argued that regionalism is repugnant to the idea of Pakistan nationhood.[22] It must be observed, however, that in the final analysis it remained to be nothing more than a forced integration. It was considered doubtful by many if it could succeed in eradicating the internal separations.

By 1970, it became quite clear that the concept of One Unit had proved to be a failure. The people of the projected new unit did not share homogeneity in language, culture, or way of life. Opposition to the One Unit Plan never ceased. By 1967, the agitation against One Unit had assumed new proportions. In some areas, like Baluchistan, troops had to be engaged to suppress the opposition.[23]

By March 1969, the protest against the rule of President Ayub finally forced him to resign. It was left for his successor, General Agha Mohammad Yahya Khan, to unscramble and abolish the One Unit Plan in July 1970. Four original provinces were re-established. Just as in the case of her constitution-making ventures, Pakistan had again gone full circle in her plans to consolidate various parts of West Pakistan.

The concept of creating an independent state with two distinctly dissimilar and distant areas had been received with criticism, astonishment and even contempt by the outside world, even before the actual emergence of Pakistan. As early as 1936, Pandit Nehru ridiculed the whole idea, commenting that

> the Muslim nation in India, a nation within a nation, not even compact but vague, spread out, indeterminate; politically the idea is absurd, economically it is fantastic; it is hardly worth considering.[24]

Some others called it a queer state, even a monstrosity. Those who were emotionally attached to the goal of carving a Muslim state, on the other hand, considered it a political miracle. In spite of numerous glaring disparities, it was forcefully advocated by the proponents of the concept that the common bond of Islam was bound to transcend all disparities within the duality of Pakistan. Obviously, in the context of the Indian independence struggle, as Crawford Young observes,

> the dialectic of conflict placed the religious identity in the dominant role, leading the Bengalis to accept the idea of Pakistan, even with joy, enthusiasm and excitement.[25]

The duality of East and West Pakistan can be brought into sharper focus by even an initial study of their geographical and demographic factors. East Pakistan, or today's Bangladesh, has an area of some 54,000 square miles. West Pakistan is almost six times as large, with an approximate area of more than 300,000 square miles. On the other hand, the population of Bangladesh was roughly 70 million at the time of the civil war; that of West Pakistan only about 60 million – almost ten million less than the eastern region, even though its area was much larger.

In general, the East is flat. The soil of its delta area is alluvial and subject to frequent inundations. In sharp contrast, West Pakistan contains a desert, some of the highest mountains in the world and a plateau of rather low altitude. The climate of the East is hot and humid, that of the West hot and dry. The West gets about three or four months of frosty winter, while the East never gets very cold.[26]

In addition to the geographical differences, the two regions gave an image of bi-cultural state, in which people's language, customs, manners, dress, art, economy and outlook – everything – differed. There was always the suspicion, real or exaggerated, of the economic and political advantages enjoyed by the 'other' group. G. W. Choudhury observes that when the Muslims of the Indian sub-continent were struggling for a separate state of their own in the 1940s, they put all emphasis on one 'R': religion. However, they forgot the second 'R': region, and the third 'R': realities.[27]

The issue of the imposition of a foreign language can be an extremely emotional one. The Pakistani leaders in the centre were, of course, keenly anxious to bring about a cultural and, if possible, a linguistic uniformity in both regions. The Bengalis reacted sharply against this 'threat' to their cherished culture. As early as 1952, violent agitation on the issue of language broke out in East Pakistan, leading to the death of three university students. Clearly, an attempt to develop cultural uniformity based solely on the Islamic affinities led only to a number of unfortunate consequences.

Of course, additional factors contributed to intensify the tensions. The administrative capital of the newly born state was established in the West, in the city of Karachi. This step by itself resulted in a preponderance of West Pakistan's representation on the staff of the central departments at the lower levels. Needless to say, the West Pakistanis already enjoyed a virtual monopoly at the higher levels. In addition, the armed forces were, in the early years, drawn almost wholly from the West.

Perhaps the most important factor in the widening gulf between East and West Pakistan was that of economic disparity. In 1947 East Pakistan, to begin with, was much poorer. During the first decade, compared to West Pakistan, the East's economy remained relatively stagnant. The economic gap continued to widen at least until the beginning of the Ayub rule in 1958. West Pakistan, in this first decade of the nation's existence, was further helped by the influx of migrant entrepreneurs, leading to more rapid industrialisation. The allocation of foreign aid and other developmental and non-developmental funds became another source of tangible disparity. The Bengalis felt particularly incensed by what they considered to be the deliberate transfer of resources from East to West through the diversion to the West of the foreign exchange earned from East Pakistan's main asset, the export of jute. In the formative years of Pakistan, all of these factors were mere complaints of being neglected. By the end of the first decade, the Bangalis started to look at the situation as a systematic exploitation.[28]

While, on the one hand, the Ayub regime started to make a determined effort to bridge the economic and political gap, the central government, on the other, strongly defended its record of doing everything possible to alleviate the economic woes and to eliminate the disparities of the two regions. It was argued, for example, that between 1948 and 1970 the Government of Pakistan allocated 8419 million rupees to the much larger West. Particularly, from 1960 to 1969, out of 8051 million rupees contributed to central revenues by East Pakistan, 3884 million rupees (48 per cent) was refunded to it as its share of provincial allocation. On the other hand, West Pakistan contributed 22,371 million rupees but she received back only 4000 million rupees, which constituted only 18 per cent.

Furthermore, it was emphasised that the government-owned East Pakistan Industrial Development Corporation invested nearly a billion rupees in the East toward a number of industrial projects, resulting in the only steel mill and the only newspaper plant of the entire nation being located in East Pakistan. Another major step was to declare Dacca as the second capital of the nation where the Pakistani parliament started to hold its sessions alternately.[29]

That the Ayub regime made a sincere effort to meet the complaints of the Bengalis and win their confidence is accepted widely both by the critics and the defenders of the case of the central government. After Ayub's resignation, General Yahya continued this policy and made a number of gestures in order to win the trust and confidence of the East Pakistanis. He should be given due credit for carrying out free and fair elections on the basis of 'one man, one vote'. It is also admitted that Ayub's economic policies helped swell the number of the 'counter-elite' in the government, and it succeeded in increasing the tempo of economic development and modernisation in East Pakistan.[30]

What is generally considered as the major mistake of the Ayub regime is not its economic policies, but its failure to integrate East Pakistan politically. It is argued that 'Ayub's political institutions limited the Bengali counter-elite's participation in the system.' The emphasis on economic growth did not, it is contended, correspond with simultaneous development of political institutions. Consequently, Bengali separation, based upon its wide range of cultural and social disparities, intensified. Mass Bengali support for the cause of autonomy received new momentum.[31]

Evidently, stronger ties and wider affinities than those of religion were needed to heal the emotional wounds caused to the East Pakistanis. Certainly, the contiguity of the two regions could have provided a better atmosphere for a dialogue. Instead, a distance of more than one thousand miles, particularly with India between the two regions, made it increasingly difficult, if not almost impossible, to communicate at a level where better sense could prevail. Inexorably, the divergencies of the two peoples took the upper hand. Pakistan was inadvertently led to a bloody, traumatic and shameful civil war. The tragic events in Pakistan began on 25 March 1971. The end came with the triumphant march of the Indian Army into Dacca, the capital of Bangladesh, on 16 December 1971.[32] The divergent pluralism of Pakistan, with profound and fundamental disparities, had taken its toll in the form of the disintegration and dismemberment of a state less than a quarter of a century old.

Looking back at the tragic events of 1971, one concludes that it would have been in the interest of Pakistan to let East Pakistan go voluntarily, and to spare the horrible calamity of a civil war. Some lone voices of sincere well-wishers of Pakistan had started to advise in this direction. Reflecting on the ominous situation as early as 8 March 1971, Sir Muhammad Zafrulla Khan, then the President of the International Court of Justice, wrote to a friend:

> East Pakistan is determined upon separation. West Pakistan has no decisive argument to offer in opposition to their demand; even if it had, East Pakistan is not prepared to reflect upon it.
>
> History bears witness that coercion is not only futile but it is suicidal. If, God forbid, blood is shed, this will create an unbridgeable gulf between the two. Material loss can be made up, loss of life cannot; and the bitterness and the gloating of our neighbour over our misfortune are inevitable.
>
> Even assuming that through coercion the partnership could be pro-

longed for a while, there is little chance of any real accord. Therefore, willingly or unwillingly, the only possible course left is separation in a beneficient way.... The present situation is fraught with peril and we are already incurring the mirth of the world and the glee of our neighbours.[33]

The capitulation of the Pakistani Army was completed on 16 December 1971. The new nation of Bangladesh was born.

IV THE ROLE OF RELIGIOUS PLURALISM IN PAKISTANI POLITICS

As discussed earlier, Pakistan's very existence was justified and defended on the basis of an independent and separate identity of the Muslims in the context of the Indian sub-continent. Yet it is rather ironic that, after her creation, religion has been ruthlessly exploited by the various parties toward their respective political goals. This underlines the paradoxical role of religion which, at the same time, has served as a basis of social identity as well as a major cause of cultural conflict. The interaction of religion and politics, therefore, is very relevant to the study of the pluralistic character of Pakistani society.[34] As Crawford Young correctly points out:

> The determinant role of religion in the dismantling of the British empire in India has meant that attention to the religious factor is unavoidable for all students of Indian or Pakistani politics.[35]

The proponents of the nationalist movement toward the creation of an 'Islamic state' found it relatively much easier to identify Islam as a distinct basis for nationhood. However, no attention was given in the years of the struggle for the creation of Pakistan to the very thorny and complex questions of defining: (*a*) What is Islam? and (*b*) What is the role of religion in modern society?

The question of a clear definition of the part religion should play in Pakistan, in view of the widely divergent beliefs of a large number of the Islamic sects found in Pakistan, is extremely complex. As Hoebel observes:

> Given the fact that there are significant basic differences between the Sunni and Shia Muslim sects and their associated laws in Pakistan,

plus the fact that Sunni Law has been interpreted and expanded by four major schools of Islamic jurisprudence, dating from the great Muslim expansion during the centuries immediately following Muhammad, it is clear that the finding of any authoritative body of Islamic postulates from the doctrinal literature is hopeless.[36]

Hoebel reports an observation by a Pakistani during the course of a conversation with him. He said:

> Everyone has his say as to what is and what is not Islamic. And, indeed, there are fundamentalists, maybe two thousand *ulama* [theologians], who have no modern education but considerable influence among the young people. Which view will prevail? Who can say?[37]

The varying degree of emphasis on religion in the three constitutions Pakistani governments have promulgated since 1947 offer an excellent picture of the dilemmas Pakistani governments have continued to face. As discussed earlier, the Objectives Resolution of 1949 evaded the use of the words 'Islamic state'. However, in the later constitutions, Pakistan was declared to be an Islamic republic. All three constitutions emphasise the equality of all citizens, regardless of their religious affiliations, yet the President and Prime Minister of the country are required in the 1973 constitution not only to be Muslims, but to declare in the oath of office their belief in certain doctrines of the faith. While this requirement may be questioned as discriminatory by many observers, the latest constitution is clearly emphatic about the religious freedom. As Article 20 says:

> Subject to law, public order and morality ... (a) every citizen shall have ther right to profess, practise and propagate his religion; and (b) every religious denomination and every sect thereof shall have the right to establish, maintain and manage its religious institutions.[38]

These and other constitutional guarantees have not proved to be effective deterrents against frequent and widespread exploitation of the masses by the *ulama*, often for ulterior political motives. This has led to sectarian riots resulting in tragic loss of lives and property, sometimes even resignations and the ousting of provincial and central governments. Richard Nyrop observes that:

Communal clashes have at times involved the entire membership of a religious group in a given locality. Religious holidays and the accompanying parades and festivals are potentially inflammable occasions.[39]

He cites, for example, the violent clashes between the *Shia* and *Sunni* Muslims in June 1963 in Khairpur and Lahore, leading to the police firing on the rioters, imposition of curfew and the call for troops to assist the civil authorities.

The unsavoury politics of a religious war have been particularly manifest in opposition to a small minority of the Ahmadiyya Muslims. It assumed ugly and violent dimensions first in 1953, when approximately 2000 people were killed. The situation was finally brought under control through the imposition of martial law, underlining the ineffectiveness of the civil authorities against the unchecked influence of the *mullahs*.[40]

The Ahmadiyya Movement is one of the small but well-organised reformist communities among the Muslims. Its world centre is in Rabwah, Pakistan. Its founder, Mirza Ghulam Ahmad, was born in 1835 in a small village called Qadian in the Punjab province of the Indian sub-continent. The Movement was founded in 1890 and, at present, it is led by Ahmad's third successor.

Ahmad believed that he was divinely ordained to revive Islam, to re-unify the Muslims around the world, to lead them out of their defeatist attitudes resulting from their general spiritual, economic, political and social decline and to propagate Islam around the world as a positive answer to the problems of our times. He claimed to be a reformer and a recipient of the divine revelation.

Of course, he was violently opposed by many *mullahs* and *ulamas* (Muslim divines and religious leaders). He was equally respected and admired by others for his services to the Muslims and for some fourscore books that he wrote to explain and interpret the teachings of Islam. To brand the leader or the members of another sect as heretics has been used as an effective weapon by the religious leaders of the opposing sects. In the case of Mirza Ghulam Ahmad, it was alleged that he falsely claimed to be a prophet and thus violated their particular interpretation of the doctrine of the finality of the prophethood of Muhammad. Nyrop observes that in this respect Ahmadiyyas are 'no more heretical than the Ismailis – the followers and devotees of the Aga Khan – and the members of that religious group must wonder if their turn is next. He concludes that:

Many folk religious leaders behave religiously in ways prescribed by the Quran, and the orthodox *ulama*, encouraged by their victory over the Ahmadiyya, might attempt to curb their activities. They would contribute additional strong divisiveness in a society that is already under considerable stress.[41]

By the time of the birth of Pakistan, the Ahmadiyya Movement had already spread around the world with more than fifty centres established in all continents. The Ahmadiyyas built mosques, established schools, colleges and hospitals, published translations of the Quran, the scripture of Islam, in several languages and produced hundreds of publications on various aspects of the teachings of Islam.

Due to their efficient organisation and a spirit of sacrifice and dedication, they presented a record of spectacular accomplishments in a relatively very short period. Nyrop observes that the Ahmadiyyas 'are known for their vigorous and able proselytising both in Pakistan and abroad.' He comments that the movement 'combined a spirit of orthodox reform, some modern liberalism, a mystic irrationalism, the infallible authority of a new revelation, and the enthusiasm of a small and self-conscious group.'[42]

While Nyrop's description of the Ahmadiyyas needs some modification, it is true that the Ahmadiyyas did invoke strong feelings in some Muslim quarters. Consequently, they became the subject of envy and victims of persecution instigated by the orthodox *mullahs* and politicians who found the anti-Ahmadiyya agitation an easy means of gaining popularity and support of the religiously-oriented masses.

To add to the ironies of these communal strifes, the initial instigators of the anti-Ahmadiyya agitation were the *Ahrar*, who were formerly an anti-Muslim League group and therefore violent opponents of the concept of Pakistan. The government circles in Pakistan felt that the aim of the *Ahrar* group, in trying to exploit religious feelings, was 'to discredit the Muslim League Government in the eyes of the people'.[43] Khalid Sayeed remarks that 'in West Pakistan, masses can be stirred out of their apathy only when strong religious or ideological issues are raised'.[44]

Levak describes the Ahmadiyyas as a 'well-disciplined and close-knit community which has its own mosques and practises a rigid adherence to endogamy'. He observes that some Ahmadiyya 'occupy influential economic social positions in the country far beyond the numerical strength of the sect.'[45]

At present, the numbers of the Ahmadiyyas are approximately between five to ten million in the world. In Pakistan, there may be about two million of their followers, although some estimates go as high as four million.

The Ahmadiyyas suffered along with the rest of the Muslim refugees when they too were a part of the millions of people displaced during the widespread upheaval at the time of the partition of the Indian sub-continent. They were forced to leave their original centre, Qadian, back in India, where they had established valuable educational and spiritual institutions and built vast commercial and economic assets.

They moved to Pakistan to start a new life. Through their hard work, perseverance and well-knit organisation, they re-established themselves within a few years, even though they had lost almost everything in the tragic mass migrations of 1947.

They purchased a tract of arid, uncultivated land from the government and started resolutely to build a new centre. Within a few years, it emerged as an active, bustling small town, with educational institutes, research laboratories, weekly and monthly journals and a daily newspaper.

As Lewis Simmons of the *Washington Post* reported:

> They [the Ahmadiyyas] leveled sand dunes, leached salt out of the ground, installed irrigation systems from the nearby Chenab River, and planted gardens, trees, rice and wheat. They laid out a relatively modern city of bricked streets, curving bazaars, dozens of mosques, a 30,000 volume library, schools and one of the finest universities [college] in Pakistan.[46]

One member, who became the subject of persistent heated controversy, was Sir Muhammad Zafrulla Khan, who led the case of Pakistan before the Boundary Commission in 1947. Soon after, Mr Jinnah, the Founder of Pakistan, appointed him as the first foreign minister of the nation. Sir Zafrulla led the Pakistan delegation to the United Nations General Assembly for more than a decade. Another prominent figure, Mr M. M. Ahmad, retired as Chief Economic Advisor to the President of Pakistan. Several others held some of the highest ranks in the country's armed forces. The opposition demanded that all Ahmadiyyas be immediately removed from any key positions in the economic life of Pakistan.[47]

One must give credit to the Pakistan central government of the time which brought the 1953 massacre under control. It appointed a blue-ribbon commission, led by Justice Munir of the High Court, to conduct a comprehensive inquiry into the causes of the disturbances. The hostile *ulama* argued before the Commission that Ahmadiyyas are heretics and, therefore, they should be declared as a non-Muslim minority. The Commission's findings, later known as the Munir Report, observed that:

> Keeping in view the several definitions given by the *ulama* [the religious scholars], need we make any comment except that no two learned divines agree on this fundamental? If we attempt our own definition, as each learned divine has done, and that definition differs from that given by all others, we unanimously go out of the fold of Islam. And, if we adopt the definition given by one of the *ulama*, we remain Muslims according the the view of the *alim* [religious scholar] but *Kafirs* [unbelievers] according to the definition of everyone else.[48]

For almost two decades since the 1953 upheaval, hostilities against the Ahmadiyyas did not assume any widespread, violent proportions, even though the orthodox divines and some politicians did manage to continue to exploit the inherent emotions of the masses. They instigated them to carry on their agitation toward declaring Ahmadiyyas as non-Muslims, to expel them from all government, civil and military jobs and to boycott them socially and economically. At the very least, the issue was always kept alive. The situation, in general, remained relatively less tense and largely under control.

The latest episode of the persecutions of the Ahmadiyyas was triggered in May 1974, when a group of non-Ahmadiyya students travelling by train from Peshawar to Multan got off at Rabwah, the Ahmadiyya world centre, and shouted filthy slogans and abusive epithets against the founder and other leaders of the Movement. They were confronted by some Ahmadiyya youths. A minor riot ensued. Its impact could have been easily contained had the Punjab's provincial government been alert and willing to take prompt, firm and effective action. Instead, like the flash of lightning, almost overnight, as *The Times* of London and many newspapers around the world reported, violence flared all over the country.[49] In the words of *Blitz* of India, Pakistan turned into a Belsen for the Ahmadiyyas, who were 'subjected to plunder, arson and rape, all with the active connivance of the Pakistan authorities'.[50]

For weeks to come, small Ahmadiyya communities were driven out of their homes, their properties and businesses destroyed and looted, even their bodies thrown out of cemeteries, and their places of worship burned down.

The politicians exploited the situation to the utmost. A campaign was launched challenging the government to declare the Ahmadiyyas as non-Muslims. The implications of this kind of action could be disastrously far-reaching in the 'Islamic state' of Pakistan. Reason demanded that the government follow the example of the Munir Commission of 1953 and reject surrender to such obviously repressive action. Instead, Prime Minister Bhutto decided to acquiesce to these demands even though in a deviously political way. He announced that he was submitting this question for a 'final solution' to the legislative body of the country.

Up to this time, the policies of the government in regard to providing protection for Ahmadiyya lives and properties had been variously interpreted. The government contended that they had succeeded in defusing the situation through the Prime Minister's decision to submit this issue to the National Assembly. The Ahmadiyyas complained bitterly about the government's apathetic attitude and its sheer indifference if not outright encouragement of the anti-Ahmadiyya agitation. They considered the Prime Minister's declaration as only a political manoeuver to gain more popularity.[51]

From the Ahmadiyya point of view, it was nothing but a political ploy to gain personal popularity with the masses. It was beyond Ahmadiyya comprehension that any legislature in modern times could presume to be legally, intellectually and theologically qualified to pass judgement on the religious beliefs and convictions of any people and thus to expose them to further persecution. It was nothing less than a flagrant violation of the fundamental rights guaranteed in the constitution of Pakistan to all of her citizens.

The National Assembly of Pakistan continued its deliberations on the issue, described by Prime Minister Bhutto as the 'question whether or not the followers of the Ahmadiyya sect are Muslims',[52] for almost three months. To dispense with the usually followed procedural regulations, the legislature turned itself into 'The Special Committee of the Whole House'.

Some rather bizarre and peculiar procedures were adopted toward the settlement of the so-called Ahmadiyya question. The entire proceedings were held in camera. The entire testimony was taken in strictest secrecy. No part of the text of the debate which followed was ever brought to public knowledge. And yet, here was a legislature introducing amendments to the constitution which flagrantly infringed the very basic rights of approximately two million citizens of the state. The considerations of the Pakistani legislature were concluded on 7 September 1974. Two amendments were passed. A new clause was added to Article 260 which excluded 'from the fold of Islam all those who do not believe in the absolute and unqualified Finality of the Prophethood of Muhammad'.[53]

The amendments state that a person who 'claims to be a Prophet in any sense of the word or of any description whatsoever after Muhammed . . . or recognises such a claimant as a Prophet, or a religious reformer, is not a Muslim for the purpose of the constitution or law.'[54]

Another resolution passed by the Pakistani legislature, to be added to Section 295-A of the Penal Code, stipulates that any Muslim professing, practising or propagating against the 'Finality of the Prophethood of Muhammad as set out in Clause III of Article 260 of the constitution shall be punishable under this section'.[55] In other words, as Nyrop comments, 'the legislature excommunicated the sect.'[56]

The ramifications of this kind of unprecedented action by government are immeasurably far-reaching. One must be fair to the Pakistani government by observing that, along with these discriminating provisions added to the constitution, the Pakistani legislature also resolved that 'life, liberty and fundamental rights of all the citizens of Pakistan, irrespective of the communities to which they belong, shall be fully protected and safeguarded'.[57] However, this assurance cannot conceal the fact that the government of Pakistan has been instrumental in reducing the Ahmadiyyas to second-class citizenship. Of course, this action helped Prime Minister Bhutto gain momentary popularity.

Addressing the National Assembly on the very same day that the foregoing amendments were passed, Prime Minister Bhutto declared that 'every Pakistani has a right to profess his religion, proudly, with confidence and without fear.' In practice, this assurance is flagrantly contradictory to the newly-legislated provision which makes certain beliefs punishable. The revised contents of Section 295 of the Penal Code put restrictions not only on the propagation and practice of some convictions, but also on their belief.

In fact, the whole matter of one's beliefs in certain tenets of one's faith has assumed inconsistent and unrealistic proportions. For example, it is now illegal for a Pakistani Muslim to convert to some beliefs allegedly embraced by the Ahmadiyyas, but it will be perfectly legal if he converted to any other faith, Christianity, Judaism, Hinduism, etc. Hypothetically, there can be a situation where a non-Ahmadiyya Pakistani Muslim could first join a faith other than Islam and then embrace the Ahmadiyya beliefs, in order to be sure that he is not violating any Pakistani laws.[58]

It is this wholesale discrimination, as a direct result of this peculiar legislation, which causes grave apprehension to the Pakistani Ahmadiyyas. Many government officers across the country, for example, have been conducting surveys, singling out Ahmadiyyas. Obviously, their jobs, both in the civil and military administration, have lost the normal security, their promotions have been endangered and new recruitment has become vulnerable to discrimination. In their economic activities, the businesses of many Ahmadiyyas have already been adversely affected. Socially, they are being isolated. In some villages, it becomes impossible, at times, for the Ahmadiyyas to purchase even the basic necessities for their sustenance.

It is obvious that, if religious pluralism in Pakistan is permitted to pursue its own unrestrained course, other minority Islamic sects may also become the victims of the wrath of the inflamed masses, exploited by the *mullahs* and encouraged by the recently adopted amendments to the constitution.

V THE POLITICAL DYNAMICS OF CULTURAL DIVERSITIES IN PAKISTAN

The dream of Pakistan was fulfilled in 1947, supported by the dominant force of the universalism of Islam. As the dust settled and the Pakistanis started the monumental task of consolidation and nation-building, they were jolted by the rude shock that it was far easier to create a country than to accomplish the goal of building and consolidating the nation on the foundations of a deep sense of belonging. The adoption of the Objectives Resolution in 1949 was the first major admission of underlying highly complex diversity. Tragically, thirty years later, the enduring challenge of diversity is even more severe than at the time of Pakistan's emergence. The divergence of its geography and culture continues to have its relentless impact upon the nation's politics. In fact, in some ways, the earlier differentiations of ethnicity might have developed even deeper roots.[59]

Crawford Young states that the defining attributes of ethnic communality may include language, territory, political unit, or common cultural values or symbols.[60] Pakistan seems to have a preponderance of the problems of diversity on virtually all of the foregoing factors.

To begin with, language, which is considered by many scholars to be the most powerful binding factor toward nationhood, has so far only served to be a source of tension and divisiveness in Pakistan. The official language has been declared as Urdu and yet it is spoken only by approximately 8 per cent of the people. It developed as the result of a mixture of Arabic and Persian, the languages of religion and culture introduced to the Indian sub-continent through the immigration of the Muslim conquerors, with the indigenous languages. But, the centre of Urdu-speaking population was Delhi, the capital, and those regions east of Delhi where the Muslim political power was concentrated during the centuries of their rule. In what is today's Pakistan, regional languages continued to be spoken, although Urdu gained a position of prestige. Thus, while languages of the daily conversation remained the languages indigenous to various areas, Urdu became the language of literature and an instrument of virtually all written communication. It is estimated that, at present, Punjabi is spoken by about 63 per cent of the Pakistanis, and Sindhi by about 12 per cent. The Pashtu, Brahui and Baluchi-speaking population is estimated to be another 16 per cent.[61]

It is not surprising, therefore, that Pakistan has frequently experienced the strains of linguistic strife. On the one hand are the regional languages interposed in a rivalry of their own. On the other hand is Urdu, the language of a prestigious and influential but small minority. Yet another complicating factor is that of the refugees who predominantly speak Urdu and who are mostly settled in urban areas. It may be noted that, due to overwhelming illiteracy, organised political activity is generally concentrated in the cities and towns of Pakistan, rather than in the villages.

One manifestation of the linguistic conflict took place in 1972 in the province of Sind. More than half of the population of Karachi, the largest city in Pakistan, speak Sindhi. However, Karachi has also witnessed the influx of the Muslim immigrants from India, as well as Pathans, Baluchis and Punjabis attracted by the expectations of job and business opportunities.[62] Unlike the other three provinces, early in 1972 Sind demonstrated her regional loyalties to the indigenous language by opting for Sindhi as its sole official language at the provincial level. This action caused concern among the 'new Sindhis', leading to the eruption of bloody riots in July 1972, first in Karachi and subsequently spreading to other parts of Sind. The situation was brought under control only after some fifty people were reported to have been killed.[63]

The people of Pakistan are diversified not only on the basis of language but also regional and ethnic backgrounds. The Punjabis form the bulk of the population, followed by substantial and formidable minorities of the Sindhis, Pathans, Baluchis, Brahuis and others. Wilber points out that this rather broad classification is further subdivided into functional and occupational castes.[64] Although the Pakistani social structure is in no way nearly as rigid and immobile as in orthodox Hindu society, yet many castes guard their 'ethnic purity'. As far as possible, inter-caste marriages, particularly in rural society, are limited to the minimum. Although, as Levak observes, 'as Pakistan moves through the process of modernisation, some of the rigidity will disappear', nevertheless modernisation has not yet reached the tribal regions of the nation.[65]

Levak's views are generally shared by Wilber, who writes:

> The egalitarian ideal, however strongly it is believed in by its proponents, is far from being practiced or accepted at all levels of the society. In villages and towns, in government and the army, in business and education, it is evident that the society still bears the stamp of pre-partition India and that, while Moslems are no longer second-class citizens, much remains of class and caste and of inherited differences in rank and privileges.
>
> The cultural diversity within Pakistan permits only approximate description of the total social structure. There is not one system of social organisation and ranking, but several, and the ranking of the self and social group depends upon the frame of reference and values of the individual.[66]

It is only logical, therefore, that this type of social stratification should lead to complex economic inequalities. The origins of the agrarian economic class divisions, of course, go back to several centuries of the area's history, while the classes of factory owners and workers in industries are only a recent development. There are significant signs of discontent among the underprivileged classes. This, of course, does not imply that Pakistan's economic growth has not been considerably impressive. She can take legitimate pride in her industrial and agricultural development accomplishments, considering the myriad difficulties she has continued to suffer throughout her entire history. The workers are, no doubt, earning significantly better wages and enjoying a higher standard of living than they did in the 1950s. Never-

Pluralism in the Politics of Pakistan 275

theless, they have developed increasing awareness of what they consider to be their legitimate share in the national growth. As Angus Maddison observed:

> The main beneficiaries of independence have been (a) the bureaucracy and military themselves, who have enjoyed lavish perquisites and have grown considerably in number, (b) the new class of industrial capitalists, (c) professional people whose numbers have grown rapidly, and (d) landlords in West Pakistan.[67]

It may be further noted that the government of Pakistan has made some efforts to introduce land reforms in order to curb the political and economic dominance of the landlords over their submissive and ignorant tenants. However, the impact of these reforms has been disappointingly below expectations. In President Ayub's evaluation:

> The main purpose of the so-called reforms introduced in West Pakistan before the Revolution [1958] was to preserve the privileges of the Zamindars [landlords] and not to secure the rights of the tenants. The landlords subverted all attempts at a more rational distribution of land through the influence they exercised over the political parties.... Apart from its social and economic consequences, such concentration of power naturally hampered the free exercise of political institutions. Democracy could never have a chance, so long as the big landlords enjoyed protected constituencies immune to any pressure of public opinion.[68]

In short, the diversities of the Pakistani society are painfully complex in their nature. The gaps of ethnicity, languages, regions, social stratification, caste, religion and economic inequities all combine to tax the consolidation and integration of Pakistan. The history of the nation-building process indicates that nations need at least one overall strong and enduring basis of a common affinity. In the absence of this vital factor, the impact of hostile disruptive forces may push this nation toward a catastrophic future.

Unless Pakistani leadership can unite, in commitment and in action, to develop such all-pervasive bonds, the future of the nation in the face of the disruptive and divisive forces may be tragically bleak. Unfortunately, so far the performance of the politicians and political parties has not been much help to the goals of unification. In fact, the campaign, the results and the aftermath of the elections held in early

1977, at both the central and provincial levels, have even more eloquently reflected all the complex problems of Pakistan's pluralism and diversities. A brief review of the political developments in the country in the 1970s should prove to be of particular interest in this context.

At the end of 1971, Pakistan received the most stunning blow of her entire history of 30 years in the secession of East Pakistan and her humiliating defeat in the 1971 civil war. The general elections held prior to these fateful events had already indicated that the country was ready for a new leadership. On 20 December 1971, General Yahya stepped down as President and martial law administrator. The reins of the nation were handed over to Zulfikar Ali Bhutto, the leader of the Pakistan Peoples Party which had won a decisive victory in the general election held a few months earlier.

Bhutto, all through his election campaign, had committed himself to the drafting of a new constitution. The traumatic impact of the dismemberment of Pakistan underscored the urgency of a fundamental revision of the 1962 Constitution under which the country was being governed. In April 1972 the National Assembly assumed the role of a Constituent Assembly.

The heated and tense debates on the topic of drafting a new constitution, both inside and outside the Constituent Assembly, clearly demonstrated that almost all the old controversial issues, reflecting the acute problems of Pakistan's pluralist diversity, still continued to plague her politics. Among the major questions to be resolved were:

> The degree of power to be accorded to the executive; the measure of regional autonomy to be assigned to the provinces; the relationship between the centre and the provinces; and the relationship between the state and religion.[69]

Specifically, the political party dominating in Northwest Frontier Province and Baluchistan, the Nationalist Awami Party, was strongly opposed to yielding much power to the central government, thus reflecting the fears of these regions over the preponderant positions of the other regions. Bhutto resolved this problem by dismissing the governments of these two provinces and placing them under presidential rule. In the following weeks, the political factions managed to reach a compromise. The third, and current, constitution thus came into effect on 14 August 1973.

The new constitution defines Pakistan as a federal and an Islamic republic. Fazlur Rahman observes that, at the opening of the

Preamble, it declares, on the one hand, the Sovereignty of Allah in the Universe – a compromise with the traditionalists; but, on the other hand, obviously as a conciliatory gesture to the modernists, it links this directly with the 'delegated sovereignty of the people of Pakistan'. Other such compromises between the divergent positions of the religious factions can be observed in the definition of 'Islamic Socialism', social provisions concerning the participation of women in public life and professional careers and the role of Islam in the structure of the State.[70]

Perhaps the most formidable task before the Constituent Assembly was to resolve the sensitive issue of the location of sovereignty. Mawdudi, the leader of one of the traditionalist parties, the *Jamaat-i-Islami*, advocated the view that since the Quran declares God as 'sovereign in heaven and earth' and, therefore, the real source of law, the people could not be considered as lawmakers.[71] The new consitution compromised with this position by declaring in the Preamble, 'whereas sovereignty over the entire universe belongs to Almighty Allah alone', but incorporating the modernist view by adding, 'and the authority to be exercised by the People of Pakistan, within the limits prescribed by Him, is a sacred trust.'

As further evidence of the accommodation of diverse religious elements, a new Article was added. It declares Islam as the State religion of Pakistan. Another Article stresses the 'preservation and strengthening of fraternal relations among Muslim countries based on Islamic Unity'. The constitution states that the individual freedoms otherwise enumerated in the Fundamental Rights are subject to the overall consideration of the 'glory of Islam'.

Fazlur Rahman attributes this problem of religious divisiveness to the phenomenon of the Pakistan masses being so attached to Islam, on the one hand, and on the other to the widely diverse developments and distortions of the past fourteen centuries 'of such sectarian character that masses blindly follow these forms'. He observes that Mr Bhutto, 'with his eyes ever fixed on the emotions of the masses' considered an explicit mention of such phrases as the 'glory of Islam' apparently necessary.[72]

It may be observed that while the first, as well as the second, constitution had declared that the President of the State shall be a Muslim, the oath to be administered did not explicitly mention adherence to the faith of Islam. The new constitution provided that the President and the Prime Minister profess in the oath their belief in God, in the Holy Books, of which the last is the Quran, in the Prophets, of whom the final one is Muhammad, and in the Last Day. Obviously, this is another attempt to appease the extremist *mullahs* who were determined to close all doors to the possibility, however remote, of an Ahmadiyya Muslim assuming the top leadership of the nation. As if these restrictions were not enough, the Pakistani legislature later took another unseemly and unprecedented step in excommunicating the Ahmadiyyas from the fold of Islam. Many scholars of Pakistani politics continue to wonder as to who gave the authority to a country's legislature to declare what Islam is or is not.

In March 1977, much-delayed elections for the National Assembly were held. While in the 1970 elections nine different parties of religio-political and right-left views had participated, thus reflecting the wide range of Pakistan's political pluralism, the recent elections became the battleground of ten factions. The major difference between the two elections, of course, was that of the formation of a united front of all parties other than Bhutto's Pakistan People's Party, named as Pakistan National Alliance, based solely on the common interest of defeating the Prime Minister and his party. Mr Bhutto branded his opponents as 'nine cats tied together by their tails'.[73]

A look at the whole panorama of the participant parties in the Pakistan National Alliance makes interesting reading. At least three parties, *Jamiat-ul-Ulama-i-Islam*, *Jamaat-i-Islam*, and *Jamait-ul-Ulama-i-Pakistan*, present predominantly divergent religious views as to how Islam should be defined and how much of the faith should be implemented by the state. It may be interesting to note that the former two parties had, earlier in 1947, vigorously opposed even the creation of Pakistan. Another two, *Tahrik-i-Khaksar* and the Muslim League, were basically the legacies of the pre-partition politics. Another three, *Tahrik-i-Istiqlal*, the National Democratic Party and the Pakistan Jamhoori Party, were varied expressions of discontent with the predominantly social and economic course the country was following. Yet another, the Jammu and Kashmir Muslim Conference, represented strictly regional interests of one area.

On the eve of election day, the Opposition had high hopes of either defeating Bhutto or coming very close to it. However, the results proved to be stunningly different. The ruling party conceded only 38 out of 200 seats to its rivals. The leaders of the Opposition immediately challenged the results as a farce. They boycotted the provincial elections which followed a few days later. This gave, in the words of *The Dawn*, one of the leading English daily newspapers of Pakistan, a virtual walkover to the government party, which bagged 435 out of 460 provincial seats.[74]

The National Alliance claimed that widespread and very flagrant violations of the election rules were committed by Mr Bhutto's party. They have served notice that they would not settle for anything less than a re-run of the General Election. The confrontation turned into ugly violence in several parts of the country. The Opposition declared a boycott of the National Assembly, called for strikes and held demonstrations and rallies to press their demands. The Prime Minister declared a state of emergency, imposed martial law and ordered a curfew in several cities. The country was virtually paralysed. Several hundred people were killed, many more injured, becoming the victims of this latest manifestation of the problems of Pakistan's complex pluralist society.

Many foreign correspondents agreed with the Opposition's allegations of the elections having been rigged by the ruling party. However, some of them have observed that the Opposition was equally guilty of the same kind of violation. They too engaged in illegal practices wherever they could get an opportunity. In this context, one Pakistani correspondent's interview, a few days before election day, with Professor Ghafoor Ahmad, Head of the ultra-conservative *Jamaat-i-Islam* in Karachi and Secretary-General of the Pakistan National Alliance of the Opposition, is of particular significance. To a question, 'In the event that you do lose the elections, what happens?', Professor Ghafoor Ahmad replied:

> The whole country is with us and not with PPP [Pakistan People's Party] . . . so, if any result contrary to the situation is announced, it will not be accepted by us. We just cannot lose the election. It is just out of the question.[75]

After several months of wrangling and bitter discussions, the negotiations between Prime Minister Bhutto and the Opposition came to a complete standstill. On 4 July 1977, the Pakistan Armed Forces finally decided to step in. The civilian government was deposed and the country returned once more to rule by marial law.

A survey of this agonising period of the latest elections makes it manifestly clear that, given the strains and complexities of Pakistan's pluralist society, any fair, legal, honest and peaceful determination of the popular will, under the present situation, is virtually impossible.

VI CONCLUSION

A survey of the problems of intergroup accommodation in Pakistan during the last three decades leads us to the conclusion that the complexities of Pakistan's pluralism have created deep-rooted and enduring tensions of both a vertical and a horizontal nature. On the contemporary scene, there is violent divisiveness within a myriad of social, economic and religious groupings. Added to these are the rivalries, fears and distrust stemming from Pakistan's regional divisions.

The problems of Pakistan's diversities can be traced from her very birth. It was a nation conceived on the basis of common affinities of a religious nature. However, neither the ideology nor the goals of the envisioned nation were clearly defined, other than the desire to save a part of the Indian Muslim community from political subjugation by the overwhelming Hindu population. The concept of creating a country of two distant regions so far apart physically, as well as emotionally and culturally, proved to be a catastrophic folly which finally resulted in the disintegration of the two regions after a disastrous and rather shameful civil war.

In the religious context, the Pakistani leadership has thus far failed to take a decisive and firm stand against the rigid traditionalist and bigoted *mullahs* and ultra-orthodox religio-political parties, who are interested more in the social and economic destruction of the adherents of any religious beliefs not in accord with their own brand of Islam.

Pakistan's unending quest for a reasonably functional constitution has conclusively demonstrated the intricate problems of the diverse character of her regions afflicted with profound differences of ethnicity, languages, disproportionate demographic distributions, diversity of castes and classes and inequality in economic resources. The third and current constitution is but one clear example of the failure of Pakistan toward her national consolidation. The federal and provincial elections of March 1977 further emphasised the fact that Pakistan is hopelessly plagued with an agonising divisiveness of the most complex nature.

Unless the leadership of Pakistan embarks upon a programme of a thorough orientation of the nation which can triumph over most of the current diversities, the prospects for her stability and solidarity do not seem to be very hopeful and bright. In the meantime, after thirty years, Pakistan is still groping for a clear and well-defined direction which

Pluralism in the Politics of Pakistan 281

can successfully and effectively overwhelm all other weakening diversities.

NOTES

1. Mitra, N. N. (ed.), *The Indian Annual Register, Calcutta. 1921–1947*, quoted in Bloomfield, J. H., *The Conflict in a Plural Society* (Los Angeles: University of California Press, 1968).
2. Mitra, N. N. (ed.), *The Annual Indian Register*, vol. I, p. 46.
3. Loshak, David, *Pakistan Crisis* (New York: McGraw-Hill, 1971) p. 6.
4. Loshak, David, *Pakistan Crisis*, p. 1.
5. Tayyeb, A., *Pakistan: A Political Geography* (London: Oxford University Press, 1966) p. 167.
6. Schechtman, J. B., *Population Transfers in Asia* (Philadelphia: University of Pennsylvania Press) pp. 1–50.
7. Wheeler, Richard S., *The Politics of Pakistan: A Constitutional Quest* (Ithaca: Cornell University Press, 1970) p. 1.
8. Emerson, Rupert, *From Empire to Nation: The Rise to Self-Assertion of Asian and African Peoples* (Boston: Beacon Press, 1960) p. 92.
9. Sayeed, Khalid B., *The Political System of Pakistan* (Boston: Houghton Mifflin, 1967) p. 60.
10. Wilcox, Wayne A., *Pakistan: The Constitution of a Nation* (New York: Columbia University Press, 1963) p. 108.
11. For full text of the Objective Resolution, see, among other sources, *The Muslim Sunrise Quarterly*, vol. XXI, no. 2, p. 27, or *Constituent Assembly of Pakistan, Debates*, v, no. 1 (7 March 1949) p. 1.
12. Wheeler, Richard S., *The Politics of Pakistan*, op. cit., p. 93. For a detailed discussion of the traditionalist, fundamentalist, and modern approaches to Islam, see Binder, Leonard, *Religion and Politics in Pakistan* (Berkeley: University of California Press, 1961).
13. Ayub Khan, General Mohammad, *Friends Not Masters* (New York: Oxford University Press, 1967).
14. *The Dawn Daily*, Karachi, 2 Apr 1963.
15. Wheeler, Richard S., *The Politics of Pakistan*, op. cit., p. 233.
16. Anwar, Muhammad Rafi, *Presidential Government in Pakistan* (Lahore, 1967) App. 1, pp. 332–4.
17. For a discussion of the platforms and viewpoints of the political parties of the 1960s, see Wheeler, *The Politics of Pakistan*, op. cit., pp. 233–83.
18. Tayyeb, A., *Pakistan: A Political Geography*, p. 175.
19. Feldman, Herbert, *From Crisis to Crisis: Pakistan 1962–1969* (London: Oxford University Press, 1972) pp. 192–212.
20. Ayub Khan, Mohammad, *Friends Not Masters*, op. cit., p. 187.
21. Feldman, Herbert, *From Crisis to Crisis*, p. 197.
22. *Pakistan Times* (quoted in Levak, *Case Studies on Human Rights and Fundamental Freedoms*: A World Survey, Vol. I, p. 286).
23. Feldman, Herbert, *From Crisis to Crisis*, op. cit., p. 209.

24. Nehru, Jawahar Lal, *An Autobiography* (London: John Lane, 1936) p. 469.
25. Young, Crawford, *The Politics of Cultural Pluralism* (Madison: University of Wisconsin Press, 1976) p. 6.
26. For a detailed discussion of the geographical contrast of East and West Pakistan, see Tayyeb A., *Pakistan: A Political Geography*, op. cit., pp. 3–9.
27. Choudhury, G. W., *The Last Days of United Pakistan* (Bloomington: Indiana University Press, 1974) pp. 1–3.
28. Jahan, Rounaq, *Pakistan: Failure in National Integration* (New York: Columbia University Press, 1972) pp. 9–49.
29. For a reasoned and well-balanced account of the disparities of the two regions as well as the steps taken to remedy it, see Khan, Sir Mohammad Zafrulla, *The Agony of Pakistan* (London: Kent Publications, 1974). Sir Zafrulla was the first Foreign Minister of Pakistan and later President of the International Court of Justice.
30. Jahan, Rounaq, *Pakistan: Failure in National Integration*, op. cit., p. 180.
31. The Bengali case for the 'dilemmas of political development' is argued in detail in Jahan's *Pakistan: Failure in National Integration*.
32. Choudhury, *The Last Days of United Pakistan*, op. cit., p. 202.
33. Khan, Sir Muhammad Zafrulla, *The Agony of Pakistan*, op. cit., pp. 151–2.
34. For an excellent discussion of the involvement of religion in the Indo-Pakistan sub-continent see Smith, Donald, *South Asian Politics and Religion* (Princeton: Princeton University Press, 1966).
35. Young, Crawford, *The Politics of Cultural Pluralism*, op. cit., p. 20.
36. Hoebel, E., 'Fundamental Cultural Postulates in Judicial Lawmaking in Pakistan', in *American Anthropologist*, vol. 67, no. 6, pt. 2.
37. Hoebel, quoted by Levak, Albert E., in *Case Studies on Human Rights and Fundamental Freedoms: A World Survey*, vol. I, p. 285.
38. Ahmad, Q., *The Constitution of the Islamic Republic of Pakistan*, Karachi: 1974, East and West Publishing Company.
39. Nyrop, Richard F., *Area Handbook for Pakistan* (Washington: US Government Printing Office, 1975).
40. For further discussion see Nyrop, Richard, *Area Handbook for Pakistan*, p. 6, or Wheeler, Richard, *The Politics of Pakistan*, op. cit. The *New York Times*, 4 July 1974, recalled the 1953 riots in the context of its story on the 1974 atrocities.
41. Nyrop, Richard, *Area Handbook for Pakistan*, p. 7.
42. Ibid., p. 135.
43. Sayeed, Khalid, *The Political System of Pakistan*, p. 70.
44. Ibid., p. 194.
45. Levak, Albert, in *Case Studies on Human Rights and Fundamental Freedoms: A World Survey*, vol. I, p. 302.
46. *Washington Post*, 23 Sep 1974.
47. Sayeed, Khalid B., *The Political System of Pakistan*, op. cit., p. 179. Also, see Williams, L. F. Rushbrooks, *The State of Pakistan* (London: Faber, 1962).
48. *Report of the Court of Inquiry Constituted Under Punjab Act II of 1954 to Inquire into the Punjab Disturbances of 1953* (Lahore: 1954) p. 218. This report is popularly known as the *Munir Report* after Justice M. Munir who was the president of the Court of Inquiry.

Pluralism in the Politics of Pakistan 283

49. *The Times* (London), 31 May 1974.
50. *Blitz* (Bombay), 27 July 1974.
51. *Christian Science Monitor* (Boston), 25 June 1974.
52. Ibid., 25 June 1974.
53. *Pakistan Times* (Karachi), 8 Sep 1974. This amendment is entitled *The Constitution Second Amendment Act* (1974). The full text reads as follows: Whereas it is expedient further to amend the Constitution of the Islamic Republic of Pakistan for the purposes hereinafter appearing; it is hereby enacted as follows: 1) Short Title: & Commencement (1) This act may be called the Constitution (Second Amendment) Act 1974. (2) It shall come into force at once. 2) Amendment of Article 106 of the Constitution: – In the Constitution of the Islamic Republic of Pakistan, hereinafter referred to as the Constitution, in Article 106 in clause (3) after the word communities, the words and brackets and persons of the Qadiani group or the Lahori group (who call themselves Ahmadis) shall be inserted. 3) Amendment of Article 260 of the Constitution: – In the Constitution, in Article 260 after clause (2) following new clause shall be added, namely: – A person who does not believe in the absolute and unqualified finality of the prophethood of MUHAMMAD the last of the Prophets or claims to be a prophet, in any sense of the word or any description whatsoever, after Muhammad or recognises such a claimant as a prophet or a religious reformer, is not a Muslim for the purposes of the Constitution or law.
54. Ibid., 8 Sep 1974.
55. *The Crescent* (Toronto), 15 Sep 1974.
56. Nyrop, Richard F., *Area Handbook for Pakistan*, op. cit., p. 7.
57. *National Assembly's Verdict on Finality of Prophethood* (Islamahad: Ministry of Information and Broadcasting, 1974).
58. Lavan, Spencer, *The Ahmadiyyas in Crisis, 1974: Old Fires Rekindled in Punjab*, a research study manuscript. The author is on the faculty of Tufts University, Medford, Mass.
59. Wheeler, Richard, *The Politics of Pakistan: A Constitutional Quest*, opp. cit., pp. 119–20.
60. Young, Crawford, *The Politics of Cultural Pluralism*, op. cit., pp. 47–8.
61. Nyrop, Richard F., *Area Handbook for Pakistan*, op. cit., p. 111.
62. Latest census in Pakistan was taken in 1972. Provisional Tables of this census were issued by the Interior Organisation in 1974. It was reported that within ten years the population of Karachi had grown from 1.9 million to 3.5 million.
63. Nyrop, *Area Handbook for Pakistan*, p. 116.
64. Wilber, Donald N., *Pakistan: Its People, Its Society, Its Culture* (New Haven: Human Relations Area Files, 1964) pp. 44–6.
65. Levak, Albert E., in *Case Studies on Human Rights and Fundamental Freedoms: A World Survey*, op. cit., vol. 1, p. 297.
66. Wilber, *Pakistan*, op. cit., p. 117.
67. Maddison, Angus, *Class Structure and Economic Growth: India and Pakistan Since the Moghuls* (London: Allen & Unwin, 1971) p. 136.
68. Ayub Khan, M., *Friends Not Masters*, op. cit., p. 87.
69. Nyrop, *Area Handbook for Pakistan*, op. cit., p. 204.

70. Rahman, Fazlur, in 'Islam and the New Constitution of Pakistan', in Korson, J. Henry (ed.), *Contemporary Problems of Pakistan* (Leiden: E. J. Brill, 1974) pp. 30–44.
71. Mawdudi, Abul Ala, *The Political Theory of Islam*, translated into English by M. Siddiqui (Lahore).
72. Rahman, Fazlur, in Korson, *Contemporary Problems of Pakistan*, op. cit., p. 43.
73. *Time Magazine*, 11 Apr 1977.
74. *The Dawn* (overseas weekly, Karachi), 20 Mar 1977.
75. *Herald* (monthly, Karachi), Mar 1977.

13 The Protection of Minority Rights in Africa

W. J. Breytenbach
Chief Researcher, Africa Institute of South Africa

I THE PROBLEM OF MINORITY PROTECTION

An analysis of the constitutions of the world reveals that the vast majority of states profess to guarantee fundamental freedoms and civil and human rights. Yet, according to Professor Max Lamberty of Brussels these rights pertain to individuals ('the rights of man') rather than to groups ('the rights of community'). He claims that there is no charter to which groups, minority groups, in any constitutional system, can appeal directly for the protection of their subjective rights and interests (see Max Lamberty, 1971, p. 30). This is the typical pattern followed in the Western liberal-democratic tradition. The socialistic tradition, on the other hand, refers to the rights of the state and/or party and the interests of the working classes. It is interesting to note that neither the Covenant of the League of Nations nor the Charter of the United Nations refer to the 'rights' or 'interests' of minorities. The Covenant of the League referred to the 'sacred trust of the civilization' of 'those peoples not yet able to stand by themselves'. The Charter of the UN again enshrines the principle of the 'self-determination of peoples'. So both these documents refer to 'peoples', in other words to groups, but do not attempt to define the concept of 'people', whether it be a homogeneous or plural entity. The well-known authority on international law, J. G. Starke, QC, submits that aspects such as common territory, common language, and common political aims may be considered (see

J. G. Starke, 1967, p. 120). Starke therefore looks at 'people' from a homogeneous point of view. This is in line with anthropological thinking as well. This type of anthropological approach to 'people' is broadly synonymous with the views of some authors who have tried to define 'minority groups'.

It is not argued here that the concepts 'people' and 'minority group' (or for that matter 'classes' and 'factions' – see later) are identical, because they are not necessarily. It is only submitted that since international law supports the right of peoples to self-determination, this principle could also under certain circumstances be extended to those minorities whose attempts to achieve equality with or assimilation into the privileged majority of any given society are constantly being frustrated by the privileged and the powerful. The reactions that set in at such a stage could cause minority demands for secession. This, and other less dramatic 'solutions' to minority problems will be dealt with later on. The factors responsible for the violation of minority rights and interests will be looked at first.

II THE INTERNATIONAL PATTERN

Although the mandatory system of the League of Nations referred to the 'sacred trust' of certain dependent peoples, it did not take their rights and interests specifically into account with the exception of the various League Mandates. Under the UN trusteeship system the principle of self-determination of peoples was enshrined. All these did not apply to minorities *within* states. This is perhaps a manifestation of the liberal democratic pattern of (personal) fundamental freedoms and civil and human rights which were, as mentioned before, not 'group'-orientated but 'individual'-orientated. Moreover, the territorial integrity of states became an international principle as well, so minorities within states had to abide by this rule.

One must admit, however, that 'group' rights are not easily separable from 'individual' rights. For instance, the 14th Amendment in the USA stipulates that one cannot discriminate against race groups or religious groups although the phraseology refers to individual members of such groups. Group rights could therefore in some circumstances in fact be protected under the individualistic approach, provided of course that an independent judiciary and the rule of law exist. In only one other case are group rights specifically protected. The constitution of the Federal Republic of (West) Germany refers to the protection of minority (group) rights. The liberal democratic approach therefore seems to be almost a universal pattern. Even the socialistic approach to the interests of the working classes cannot be regarded as the protection of group rights, which were, at least in the case of Marxist states, superseded by state or party rights.

The individualistic approach stems perhaps from the 'guidelines' set out by the UN Declaration of Human Rights of 1948, which is concerned about human and fundamental rights and does not protect group rights or even refer to things such as minorities. Almost all the new African states adopted this approach as reflected in their constitutions. This implies that Africa as a whole shows little concern for the constitutional acknowledgement of groups within the state, despite the fact that most African states have intensely plural societies that have so far shown a high propensity for conflict. In fact most states look down upon any kind of ethnic expression. The same applies to minorities, both of which tend to become informal groupings as a consequence of this.

Interestingly, the United Nations at one time showed some concern about minority rights. In 1946, just after the United Nations was formed, the Economic and Social Council (Ecosoc) agreed, *inter alia*, to deal with the violations of group rights, for which purpose it established the Commission on Human Rights which subsequently formed the Sub-Commission on the Prevention of Discrimination and the Protection of Minorities. But unfortunately for minorities who were the victims of discrimination, both the Economic and Social Council and the Commission on Human Rights declared that the Sub-Commission had no power to take any actions in regard to complaints concerning human rights. The Sub-Commission then became virtually powerless, and so was the United Nations for the time being. However, renewed attention was paid to (individual) human rights as opposed to (group) minority rights in 1968. In that year a resolution was passed that requested the Commission on Human Rights, not the Sub-Commission, to deal henceforth with all situations that reveal a 'constant pattern of gross violations of human rights and fundamental freedoms', as exemplified especially by 'the policy of apartheid in South Africa and racial discrimination in Rhodesia'.

Violations elsewhere were to be largely ignored. This biased approach gave rise to the application of double standards in dealing with the problems of human rights (see W. Weinstein, 1976, pp. 16–17). The application of double standards was ostensibly the result of the fact that the Sub-Commission on the Prevention of Discrimination and the Protection of Minorities was not disestablished by the resolution of 1968, but its membership was in fact enlarged from 18 to 26 members, who mostly included representatives of the Afro-Asian block at the UN. This institution continues to play a very important advisory role to the Commission on Human Rights which, since then, had unfortunately developed its own kind of racialism, a sort of anti-White racialism.

III MINORITIES AND FACTORS RESPONSIBLE FOR MINORITY SITUATIONS

The definition of 'minority groups' (whether it refers to certain 'peoples', 'classes', or 'factions') is problematical, because the factors that create minorities differ from one situation to another. Yet, authoritative writers are in agreement on a number of intrinsic points of reference which seem to be either physical, cultural, socio-economic, political or a combination of some of these. For instance, Professor Leo Kuper stresses the importance of race and ethnicity as intrinsic points of reference (see Leo Kuper, 1970, p. 378), whereas Professor Eugen Lemberg again stresses the importance of language (a facet of culture) as the decisive factor in group formation. However, he and other writers also mention the importance of other facets of culture like religion and tradition (see Eugen Lemberg, 1974, p. 48). One may therefore so far infer that minorities are groups that display particular physical (racial and ethnic) and/or cultural (ethnic, linguistic and religious) characteristics which distinguish them from other groups in the same society. These characteristics are important in the sense that they become the visible signals for the differential and unequal treatment of minorities. This factor was stressed by Louis Wirth who also maintained that minorities normally become the objects of collective discrimination, that they enjoy lower status, have lesser privileges and are denied full participation in all the aspects of society life (see his article in Ralph Linton's book, 1945, p. 347).

This description by Wirth is interesting because it covertly focuses attention on class and power. Wirth's references to 'lower status' and 'lesser privilege' have definite class connotations, not in the sense that minorities are necessarily classes, only that certain minorities may perceive their status and role *vis-à-vis* the privileged in the same light as would lower classes in stratified class societies. However, some classes could still be minorities. But there are normally big differences between minorities and classes: most minorities are due to their intrinsic physical and cultural points of reference referred to earlier, almost like hereditary castes and ethnic groups, whereas classes tend to be far less rigid and depend on dynamics such as socio-economic and educational criteria. Social mobility thus exists within class societies. And this is the same in cultural and socio-economic minorities, as will be explained below.

Minorities may therefore also accommodate their own classes. Yet the crucial point is that most (if not all) minorities display certain lower-class values in their relationships towards the 'higher' groups within the same society. This adds up to the complexities of minority problems. But in Africa, with its not too well developed class structures, minorities are almost like castes and ethnic groups and not like typical classes (the socio-economic ingredient is largely absent in rural areas). Most of Africa's minorities therefore tend to have their roots in pre-class or rural conditions based mainly on kinship and descent factors or in some cases on religion as well. Yet classes do exist in Africa's industrial complexes, and in these cases lower classes with lesser privileges behave or respond in the same way as would minorities. That is where trade unions normally express class interests. The other aspect mentioned by Louis Wirth is that minorities are denied full participation in all aspects of society life. This implies, *inter alia*, discrimination or deprivation in the field of power relations, in other words, minorities then start to resemble 'factions' that must be relevant to the power structure, otherwise their existence becomes of 'academic interest' only.

This – their lack (and awareness of that) of effective political power – leads to another characteristic of minorities, namely that 'we' (the minority) are exploited by 'them' (the privileged and powerful). And because of this, all minorities invariably claim equality with the others. Some groups even strive for assimilation into the privileged 'majority' who might even represent a numerical minority. However, according to Professor Eugen Lemberg (see p. 48 of his quoted article) many minority groups that initially strove for both equality with and assimilation into the dominant group eventually abandoned their attempts in the face of continual rejection by the privileged 'majority'. These frustrated minorities then turn more and more towards self-examination and self-preservation, as was the case with Garveyism in the USA, Black Power in the USA and South Africa and Zionism in Europe. Other minority groups, probably most of them, however, do not strive for assimilation but only for equality in opportunities (such as perhaps the Asians in South Africa). These groups tend to preserve their autonomous identities with regard to language, religion, tradition and so on. This is a form of self-preservation and parochial nationalism which could, in extreme cases, such as in the cases of the Ibos of Biafra and the Eritreans of Ethiopia, lead to demands for secession. This is not the case with the South African Asian but is nevertheless a phenomenon not unknown in both Europe and Africa. European examples are for instance the Basques, Catalans, Corsicans, Scots, etc.

IV FACTORS RESPONSIBLE FOR THE VIOLATION OF MINORITY RIGHTS

Most African nations have plural societies, owing their heterogeneous population structures to the fact that colonial powers drew colonial boundaries arbitrarily at the time of the scramble for Africa, notably at the Conference of Berlin. These boundaries, almost without exception, laid the territorial foundations for the 'artificial' nations that came into being later during the era of decolonisation.

The newly independent regimes accepted constitutions that were dictated by London or Paris and were not fully compatible with the pluralities of Africa's population structures, especially as far as ethnic heterogeneity is concerned, a factor which has subsequently been referred to as the 'scourge' of Africa (see Kwame Nkrumah, 1961, p. 167). It was a 'scourge' because it bedevilled attempts at nation-building, and also because it was the cause and the result of competitions and conflicts over limited opportunities (see Ali Mazrui, 1970, p. 5). These political actions were primarily not caused by ethnic groups but were structured along ethnic and other primary lines in the quest for limited opportunities. This is the point when ethnicity becomes a factor. The ethnic quest for wealth should therefore not be underestimated, especially if the deprivation of wealth concerns not only individuals, but regions and communities of individuals. The lesser opportunities and wealth allocated and available to these groups – a frustration of their claim for equality of opportunities – are major factors causing the politisation of minority aspirations. This stimulates their informal action whether it be along ethnic, class or factional lines.

Ethnic, class and factional power struggles (whether over the control over scarce resources or not) therefore seldom result in 'winner-takes-all' or zero-sum power games where compromise solutions are seldom contemplated by the contesting parties. Take Angola for example, where the various ethnic factions competed intensely for the control over the power structures of the regime. Without reaching compromise, the winners (MPLA) assigned some kind of minority status on the (ethnic) losers, depriving them of power and privileges. The Ovimbundu supporters of Unita and the Bakongo supporters of FNLA were relegated to almost the status of 'wealthless classes' in Angolan society.

This leads to another point which is *per se* not a violation of minority rights, but bears causal relevance to the eventual denial of wealth, power and privilege to the hapless losers of power games. This is the phenomenon of pluralism which tends, in Africa at least, to be conflict-producing in the face of the scramble for limited opportunities, and not conflict-reducing as is apparently the case in some Latin-American and some Caribbean states (see, Sammy Smooha, 1975, pp. 73–80). So, in Africa each and every 'winner-takes-all' encounter produced an ethnic, class or factional loser which was assigned minority status by the rulers to be. The implications of this have already been spelt out. The relations between the rulers and the minorities (who might represent the popular majority) invariably tended to radicalise the situation, which resulted in extreme actions on both sides. Fanaticism became part of the power game. This is a reflection on the general quality of leadership in Africa. Leaders, and their parochial supporters are responsible for so many recorded instances of the violations of those rights enlisted under the Convention for the Protection of Human Rights and Fundamental Freedoms (1950). It is impossible to discuss all of them. Suffice to state that certain items listed in this Convention, such as its condemnation of political purges, political trials, political detentions and political convictions are commonplace treatments meted out to individual opponents and recalcitrant self-preserving minorities who sometimes make too excessive demands for equality of opportunities and full participation in the affairs of the state.

Constitutions and declarations on human rights are, as pointed out earlier, of little legal avail to deprived minorities anywhere who, in the absence of enshrined rights, have no constitutional means of appeal. In fact, only three of the 51 African constitutions refer to the guarantee of some or other minority rights. These are the constitutions of Libya (where reference is made in the constitution to the rights of the non-Moslems), Chad (where reference is made in the constitution to the prohibition of oppression by one section of the people), and Senegal (where reference is made in the constitution to the guarantee of the liberties and rights of local groups). There is only one other case, albeit not of an independent state, that refers explicitly and overtly to the protection of the rights of minority groups, and that is the Declaration of Fundamental Rights adopted by the Turnhalle Conference (1976) on the future constitutional dispensation of SWA/Namibia. This has been modelled on the West German example. Furthermore, the political tendency in Africa is to challenge the doctrine of the supremacy of constitutions.

Leaderships, that is a combination of presidents, soldiers and party executives, tend to assume supreme positions. They amend and suspend constitutions with the greatest of ease and speed, depending on their needs and preferences. So a great factor in Africa once again seems to be the problem of leadership. For example, in four of Africa's 51 independent states the constitutions are currently under suspension. These are in Swaziland, Comoro, Lesotho and Sychelles. And in another four cases the current constitutions make no reference whatsoever to either civil or human rights, for instance in Ghana and Sudan. In 24 of the 43 remaining states explicit and overt references are made to the protection of civil rights while in the 19 other constitutions acceptance is pledged of the Universal Declaration of Human Rights.

Another important reason for the violation of minority rights and interests is to be found in the political policy of regimes in respect to nation-building. These goals imply the destruction of group loyalties and interest in order to foster the integration, assimilation and coalesence of the various racial, ethnic and cultural (local) groups into one single nation-state. So far these aims are still far from being accomplished (see Mazrui, op. cit.). In fact, greater fissure has occurred recently on many occasions, and this phenomenon was described by Dov Ronen of the Hebrew University in Jerusalem as the post-colonial era of 'ethnoseparatism' (see Dov Ronen, 1975). This reality of growing group consciousness is not always reflected in nation-building policies which implies that the protection of minorities would be tantamount to integration policies. State policies in this regard tend to be assimilationist rather than pluralistic, in other words diversities are discouraged. The emphasis is on communal rather than on functional integration. And this quest for unity is rather intolerant. The methods are varied, and include the following: deliberate non-recognition of separate racial, ethnic, cultural, socio-economic and political minorities; the expulsion of unassimilable groups such as the Asians in East Africa and the Goans in Malawi; the institutionalised subjugation of minorities through, *inter alia*, the perpetuation of the subjugated statuses of opposition groups, especially in Africa's oligarchical minority regimes – according to Peter Enahoro (see his article in *Africa*, 1976, p. 30) methods applied in terms of this approach are, *inter alia*, imprisonment of opposition elements and even their physical elimination. The most publicised examples of physical elimination are the persecutions, not of groups – because groups are not recognised – but of 'disloyal elements', such as the Tutsi tribesmen in Rwanda, Hutu tribesmen in Burundi, Negroid southerners in Sudan, Ibo tribesmen in Nigeria, and the elimination of disloyal opposition elements among the Ganda, Lango, Lugbara and Acholi tribes in Uganda. And finally, there is also very little tolerance towards the Jehovah Witnesses and Watchtower Sects in Zambia and particularly in Malawi. All these examples are in total conflict with the contents of the above-mentioned Convention of 1950.

These intolerant nation-building policies could be counter-productive because inadequate cognisance of ethnic and other minority groups threatens the existence of these groups, who then become more and more aware of their presumed common interests which they begin to regard as their subjective rights. This leads to faction formation on informal lines. Subsequent rivalries imply the conflict of ethnicities and other groups as well as the impossibility of compromising their interests. There can be a compromise of principles (e.g. on leadership) but not of peoples or factions. And this is precisely what some nation-building policies are demanding. So somebody's 'rights' have to suffer. Hopefully, compromise on leadership will be followed lower down the hierarchy, and include 'issues' as well.

A by-product of the collective discrimination against minorities is the fact that minorities are the objects of collective discrimination and unequal treatment – the victims of favouratism – either in the allocation of resources and opportunities or in the field of political recruitment. This is when minorities complain about being denied full participation and/or proportional representation at the national level of the political hierarchies of the systems concerned. A basis of recruitment consonant with minority demands would be 'meritocratic' or 'realistic' in proportion to their developmental achievement or merits and *not* necessarily as a product of their numbers. (This is one big weakness of the one-man-one-vote approach.) Examples of the deprivation of power-sharing are to be found in Botswana, where representatives of the Kalaka, Mbukushu and Koba tribes have never been appointed to powerful executive positions. Maybe these tribes, who live in the remote and less developed areas of Botswana, do not merit meaningful proportional representation on account of their achievements. The same applies perhaps to the Tlokwa of Lesotho, also a tribe that has never tasted power in that country. So, from a meritocratic point of view, discrimination against members of these tribes is perhaps not such a serious negation of their 'rights' to be represented. But it is indeed the case with the vanguards of Moçambican Liberation, the Makonde of the far north, who spearheaded Frelimo attacks for many years. The Makua tribe, the largest and one of the most educated and wealthiest tribes in that country, has constantly been denied participation in the power structure ever since the new Frelimo rulers took over in Moçambique. The new Frelimo rulers represent mostly southern interests and tribes. It is the same with the numerically large and wealthy Bakongo and Ovimbundu tribes in Angola who have also become the objects of collective discrimination. The leaders of these groups failed to reach a compromise, after which their ethnic followers resorted to ethnicism and factionalism in the pursuit of their aspirations, which included the right to power-sharing.

V HOW MINORITIES COULD BE PROTECTED AND/OR ARE INDEED PROTECTED IN SOME CASES

The power to protect minorities lies within the scope of the state, and not in the so-called universality of the norms and values of the Universal Declaration of Human Rights of 1948. Firstly, this Declaration is not an enforceable Convention and is, as mentioned before, concerned with the individual rights of man and not with the communal rights of groups. It therefore offers little legal protection to minorities that cannot appeal to this Declaration for the protection of their rights. And, secondly, states cannot be forced by either their citizens or, say, the ICJ in the Hague to follow the prescriptions on human rights and fundamental freedoms contained in their own constitutions. The Carter Administration is championing this right now. Yet it is entirely a matter for the state, or the judiciary, to decide upon the scope and the application of these prescriptions. These rights remain paper-rights unless they are enforced by higher authorities. African constitutional law is quite comprehensive as far as the guaranteeing of fundamental freedoms and human rights are concerned. Unfortunately, however, African practice has so far lacked sadly in this respect. The culprits are the politicians. But even if individual rights were adequately protected, the problem of minority rights still remained. African constitutional law is, as demonstrated earlier, completely inadequate for the protection of minority rights. Thus, great leeway for the improvement of the situation lies in the remaking of constitutions in order to include the protection of the rights of Africa's numerous minorities. But this seems unlikely in terms of African concerns with 'nation-building', the demise of the 'rule of law' and tendency towards centralised power structures.

The second alternative concerns the modification of nation-building policies. This does not necessarily require the remaking of constitutions, say, in the direction of federal structures. It has already been pointed out that current nation-building policies are essentially intolerant towards the preservation of group loyalties and the protection of (minority) group rights and interests. Nation-building policies should not discourage diversities, otherwise they could easily become so politicised as a result of the perceived threats to their existence. Policy-makers should realise this and rather try to foster cross-cutting alliances, whether they be aggregated in political parties (preferably mass parties) or in all-embracing middle-classes which share in so many common interests. Middle-class activities may eventually push participating minorities towards more meaningful participation, equality and even assimilation. The 'mass party' and 'middle-class' approaches are much to be preferred to the methods of alienation, expulsion and elimination practised so often in Africa today. This is perhaps again a reflection on the state of political leadership in Africa.

The third alternative concerns the decentralisation of Africa's unitary regimes into federal structures. Theoretically, this type of structure seems to offer a practical solution for the coexistence of plural elements within a single state – provided, of course, that all the constituent societal elements have the real desire to manage their own local affairs. If this desire is absent, or if the tendency is towards a greater centralisation of power and authority in the hands of the party, the executive, or the army, then it would be wishful thinking considering 'Bills of Rights' and federal structures as solutions to minority problems. This is exactly what is happening in Africa. At present there is only one federal state in Africa and that is Nigeria, but even in this case there is not much tolerance and/or decentralisation of powers because the state is ruled by a centralised Supreme Military Council, which really makes a mockery of the values of federalism.

An exercise in federalism, however, does not necessarily cater for the protection of minority rights. It is rather concerned with special and/or regional interests. The problem of rights is usually catered for in Bills of Rights that form part of so many federal constitutions. But in order to enforce them (otherwise they remain paper-rights) one needs an independent judiciary. This hardly exists in Black Africa, where politicians reign supreme. Again, the problem of leadership.

The fourth alternative is purely political and concerns leadership more than anything else. Wise, tolerant and benevolent leadership is required. It is a political variable that could flourish in almost any type of state, regime or system. It implies the protection of interests as well as rights, depending on the style and attitudes of the leadership concerned. In more precise terms, the prerogatives for political recruitment rest mainly on the preferences of political leadership – this could range from oligarchal to widely representative systems. The latter should be manifested in the type of proportionalism referred to earlier, in other words, power should be allocated fairly, preferably on the basis of merit, to as many *group* representatives as possible. Admittedly, this involves interests, rather than rights, but these representatives could then keep a close check on, for instance, his/her group's language, religious and other special rights. It must be reiterated that this does not require constitutional amendments or the adoption of new systems, only that these *group* representatives check the possible abuse of the constitutional prescriptions on fundamental freedoms and human *rights* in the interests of their own groups. Admittedly again, this argument has one fundamental weakness, and that is the general powerlessness of the so-called independent judiciary. The enforcement of the 'rule of law' involves the question of rational leadership, amongst other things.

Nevertheless, by extending the possibility of full participation to minority groups, the onus is theirs to attempt to eradicate institutionalised discrimination, to try to elevate their status and to legislate if necessary, the possibility of greater privileges for all. The universal claim of all minorities – equality – could then be realised along democratic and evolutionary lines. The 'mass party' and 'middle-class' approaches, referred to earlier, could also serve as additional instruments in the hands of leadership to protect minorities or even to eradicate the inequalities and discriminations against their existence.

The fifth alternative is the most extreme and should only be contemplated in uncompromising cases. This concerns geo-ethnic secession in terms of which existing state boundaries are redrawn. Both the United Nations and the Organisation of African Unity are not favourably disposed towards this approach, probably because it so often results in unilateral declarations of independence which are deemed to violate the 'integrity' of the mother country. Territorial integrity is regarded as more important than self-determination for breakaway peoples which have so far not been accorded international recognition, e.g. Rhodesia and Cabinda. Other examples of abortive attempts at secession were made by the Anyanya rebels of the Southern Sudan, the Ibo tribesmen of Biafra, who wanted to break away from Nigeria, the Eritrean Liberation Front, which is still engaged in a breakaway struggle from Ethiopia, the Polisario Front which is still engaged in attempts to restore the integrity of the Western Sahara and, therefore, tries to break away from Morocco and Mauritania (which now control the former Spanish Sahara), the ongoing attempts of the people of the island of Mayotte to break away from the Comoros in the Indian Ocean, and, lastly, the recent attempts of the Katangese exiles to re-establish themselves in the Shaba Province of Zaïre.

VI EVALUATION

Africa has numerous minorities, yet these are not protected by constitutions and politicians. Assimilationist nation-building policies are also not conducive to their protection. Secession is discouraged. A pragmatic approach therefore seems to lie in the structuring of states into federal systems which guarantee minority interests and minority rights in a 'Bill of Rights'. Unfortunately this is incompatible with the tendencies towards greater centralisation of power and authority in the hands of the executive and the party and the military, which tend to overrule the rule of law and thereby nullify the potential role of a declaration of human rights and fundamental freedoms. The most promising approach is, lastly, the re-education of leadership to resort to proportional recruitment of (other) group leaders, according to the merited proportions of their respective groups, which should also be afforded desired levels of local autonomy. These group representatives should act as watchdogs over the interests of their groups as well as the enforcement of individual and group rights. This approach does not require ill-fated declarations or incompatible federal systems. It only calls for responsible and tolerant leadership, and not necessarily for unity in leadership. (This is not yet possible in Africa's plural states.) It requires the kind of leadership structures that are compatible with the concept of unity-in-diversity. Unfortunately not many African states pursue this approach. Yet there are positive signs to this effect, albeit in an informal sense, already appearing in some of the multi-party and also in some of the one-party-participatory-democracy regimes.
(The author wishes to express his gratitude towards Professor D. A.

Kotzé and Mr Pierre Hugo, both of the University of South Africa, for their valuable comments on the first draft of this paper).

REFERENCES

Enahoro, Peter, 1976. 'Opposition in the One-party System', *Africa* (London), no. 53 (Jan 1976).
Kuper, Leo, 1970. 'Continuities and Discontinuities in Race Relations: Evolutionary and Revolutionary Change', *Cahiers d'Etudes Africaines*, vol. 10(3).
Lamberty, Max, 1971. 'The Rights of Minority Groups, People and the State', *Journal for Plural Societies* (The Hague), autumn 1971.
Lemberg, Eugen, 1974. 'Ideology and Minority Conflict', *Journal of Plural Societies* (The Hague), vol. 5, no. 3 (1974).
Linton, Ralph (ed.), 1945. *The Science of Man in the World Crises* (Columbia).
Mazrui, Ali, 1970. *Post Imperial Fragmentation: the Legacy of Ethnic and Racial Conflict* (Denver).
Nkrumah, Kwame, 1961. *I speak of Freedom* (New York).
Ronen, D., 1975. *The Wilsonian Principles of African Self-determination* (African Studies Association, San Francisco).
Smooha, Sammy, 1975. 'Pluralism and Conflict: A Theoretical Exploration', *Journal of Plural Societies* (The Hague), vol. 6, no. 3 (1975).
Starke, J. G., 1967. *An Introduction to International Law* (6th ed., London, Butterworth).
Weinstein, Warren, 1976. 'Africa's Approach to Human Rights at the United Nations', *Issue* (Ann Arbor, Mich.), vol. VI, no. 4.

14 What is the Lesson of Swiss Solutions to Pluralist Problems for South Africa?

Christopher Hughes
Professor of Politics at the University of Leicester, England

I STYLE AND FORM OF GOVERNMENT

It is a commonplace that the style of a government may diverge from its form, and that the form may contain contrasting elements. Thus the form of British government contains a contrast of monarchical and republican elements, while the style (Prime Minister, party, consensus etc.) bears only a loose connection with either of the contrasting elements of the form.

The 'form' of Swiss government links two divergent ideas: the unfettered sovereignty of the majority on the one hand, and ideas connected with the Rule of Law (*Rechtsstaat*) on the other hand. Within these latter I include minority rights, individual liberties, federalism, the separation of powers, and so on. One can term this form 'democracy'. The 'style' of Swiss government is typically somewhat different from the expectations aroused by the form. It is somewhat elitist, somewhat decisive, authoritative but not authoritarian, and somewhat oligarchical. Although the federal style of government is different from the cantonal (i.e. provincial) style, I would apply this generalisation to both levels.

Swiss government is by general assent adjudged a success. Switzerland is a plural society, most conspicuously in the two spheres of language (German, French, Italian, etc.), and religion (Protestant, Roman Catholic). It seems reasonable, therefore, to ask Switzerland, and political science, for lessons about how to cope with a pluralist social and cultural predicament. Ulster, and South Africa, for example, might reasonably ask 'What are Switzerland's lessons for us?'

But is it the form (democracy, etc.), or is it the style (oligarchy, etc.) that should be copied? The two lessons are very different.

The consensus of Swiss opinion is that it is the form which should be copied, democracy, federalism, good language laws, good laws concerning the practice of religion and the right of association, and so on. Foreign opinion on Swiss affairs is content to follow the Swiss lead, but it is a rather tenuous body of thought. My own belief is the eccentric one that it is the style (oligarchy, decisiveness, etc.) which should be imitated. This opinion of mine may be due to my personal ideological blinkers (Plato, Hegel, and Machiavelli and Locke interpreted in the light of Hegel, with an indirect Thomist coloration derived from my religious commitments), but some of these positions were themselves entered into in consequence of my readings in British, Swiss and German history. The substance of my paper is a warning; 'Do not be too sure what the Swiss lesson is.'

The fixed point in my argument is Swiss success, outside the Bernese Jura. But Switzerland has changed a great deal in the last ten years. After around 1965 traditional Switzerland began to fall apart and to reconstitute itself anew. It was a process that had been somewhat delayed by non-belligerency and the incapsulation imposed by voluntary neutrality in two world wars. This *aggiornamento* is still going on, and it is too soon to say whether it is a success or not: it probably will be, but not assuredly so. So I am confining the first part of this paper to the time before 1970. The chief modern changes are: the extent to which religion has lost its hold as a source of discord, and the dissolution of the natural incapsulation of the country by free personal movement. Much of the historic life-blood of federalism has recently ceased to flow.

II RELIGION

Historically (but not now) religion has been the source of discord and civil war in Switzerland. Under the old regime (before 1798, but to some extent up till 1848) religious difficulties were accommodated by the 'geographical principle'. That is to say, as a general rule, in a

Protestant canton only the state cult of Protestantism was permitted within the cantonal boundaries, while in a Catholic canton only Roman Catholicism was permitted. Between 1515 and 1798 there were four civil (inter-cantonal) wars, which arose from conflicts derived from religious differences. The important practice of Neutrality in the foreign relations of the Confederacy was imposed by the religious split.

III LANGUAGE

Under the old regime, language was insignificant as a cause of fissure. Language difficulties were accommodated on the 'personal principle'; each person (roughly speaking) took his own language with him. In confederative affairs, German was the official language. In cantonal affairs, the rulers of bilingual cantons, aristocrats, learnt French; they sometimes spoke it at home, and could normally speak it to their subjects. Italian Switzerland had its own problems: the Ticino was subject territory, and the Grisons must be left out of our generalisation.

IV LANGUAGE AND RELIGION COMBINED

After 1848 (and to some extent in the years before then) the position of language and religion was reversed. Since 1848, *language* has been treated on the 'geographical principle', so that the language boundary once established is in principle treated as unalterable, and therefore a person moving over that boundary does not take his language with him but is held to speak the language of his new 'homeland' area. But religion is treated as strictly personal. A Protestant moving into a (formerly) Catholic area takes his religion with him, and *vice versa*. This is the opposite principle to that of the old regime, but it works equally successfully. I hold, therefore, that it is the decisiveness and rationality with which the formula is applied which accounts for its success, as much as the formula itself.

A further paradox may be noted. The policing of the language problem falls almost entirely on the four cantons through which the language frontier runs (Berne, Fribourg, Valais, and Grisons). Although the stability of the Confederation depends on the acceptance of an immovable language frontier – in principle, but not quite in detail – the matter is almost entirely left to the cantons concerned. On the other hand the policing of the religious settlement has been largely done by the central government, under the Constitution, in derogation of the cantonal sovereignty which otherwise would prevail in religious matters: church and education are matters of cantonal sovereignty, subject to federal protection of the religious liberty of the individual against the cantonal authorities.

However, the *combined* religious and linguistic settlement is the most important of all. The two frontiers do not coincide. The religious map is the patchwork of sovereignties of the old regime (which by and large, but not in detail, coincide with modern cantonal boundaries). But the language frontier is the meeting of Germanic and Roman civilisations, and is approximately where it was around the year AD 500, when the age of great tribal treks stopped. In principle, but not in detail, the language frontier is an unbroken line that pays little heed to the feudal sovereignties that became superimposed upon it. The Confederation is traditionally about two-thirds German-speaking, and two-thirds Protestant. But both the German and non-German areas are themselves divided as to religion in the same proportions as the whole Confederation. And the language minority and the religious minority combined have, in effect, a blocking vote in federal matters. This is secured by federalism. The federal referendum for constitutional amendment requires the double majority of 'people and cantons' to alter the basic law. And the federal legislature has two chambers, in one of which the cantons are equally represented. The effect of both these institutions is to give a blocking vote to the two minorities *taken together*. Confident of this protection, they can relax.

I have mentioned the decline of religious tension. This is partly due to decline in religious passion generally, partly to the spirit of Vatican II and a general tendency to separate religion from politics, but partly to a more interesting and paradoxical development. Between 1870 and 1914, the Catholics 'withdrew into a ghetto' of their own construction. They drew apart from the political parties, pressure groups, workers' unions and voluntary societies which were either non-confessional or Protestant, and formed their own. In their own political and social environment they cultivated their own separate identity – this is not only a Swiss phenomenon, but can be seen in Germany, and Holland, and probably elsewhere. In recent years, they have 'returned from the ghetto'. It has been asserted (but not fully argued) that without this period of separate development they would not have acquired the confidence and self-respect to return, to treat the dominant Protestant groups as equals. Are there South African parallels here?

V THE LESSON

Is the lesson then to be found in a decisive style, in oligarchy rather than in democracy? At first sight, there is much to support this. The problems of language, and some nineteenth-century elements of the problem of religion, only appeared when democratisation was imminent, and can be considered as accompaniments of democratisation. But though I would argue that democracy instigated the problems of language (and to some extent, of religion) in their nineteenth-century form, yet it did also provide their solution – or rather, their transmutation into other, more bearable, problems. Swiss cantonal history is more revealing than Swiss federal history: time and time again one sees cantons on the brink of civil war, itself caused by democracy, solving their problems by a massive further injection of democracy. In particular, proportional representation on the cantonal level, and on the federal level also, had an extraordinary, sedative, effect on political strife – while introducing problems of its own. My readers will remember that there is no legal possibility of *intra*-cantonal federalism in Swiss law. The cantons must be unitary states within their boundaries.

VI SINCE 1970

The characteristic modern Swiss problem of pluralism derives from the presence on Swiss soil of nearly one million foreign workers, and their dependants; many are of southern Italian origin, and they are for the greater part Catholic. Their position is rather like the position of foreign workers in West Germany, described in vol. 1, ch. 5 of *Case Studies on Human Rights and Fundamental Freedoms* (I had always heard that West German practice was more liberal than Swiss, but I see it is not). These tolerated immigrants are nearly completely devoid of political rights, and in practice I suspect even slightly underprivileged in the courts of law, since they may face administrative expulsion. The cases reported in newspapers sometimes suggest an uncharacteristic severity towards them in the (cantonal) criminal courts. Whether there is any parallel in South Africa, I do not know. The difficulties put in the path of those seeking Swiss citizenship suggest an idea of the status of Swiss citizen which has almost racial implications, a status that can neither be gained nor lost but only inherited, implications which are nonsensical in the case of so agreeably mixed a population. As an English conservative who disapproves of the ease with which non-

Europeans have acquired British citizenship, I find much to admire in the Swiss clarity and decisiveness, but, more to the point, I see more harmony in Switzerland as a result of this uncompromising course of action than I find in Britain, where the criminal law is required to be brought into play against the native English to persuade them to accept negroes and Indians as full fellow-citizens. Once again, there is the paradox that a decisive style of action produces greater overt harmony than liberal equivocation.

VII CONCLUSION

On the negative side, I do not see any *clear* parallel between any Swiss phenomenon and any South African phenomenon. Historically, I see quite a number of 5 per cent, 10 per cent and even 20 per cent parallels, sometimes to British/Dutch relations, sometimes to white/coloured/black relations. Some of these parallels are to very remote times, and of no current political application. I have only suggested a few here. My pessimism, however, may be due to my characteristic national ignorance concerning South Africa, concerning which I am only in possession of the ordinary British stereotypes, even though they be imprinted on a sceptical and cautious mind.

The lines of inquiry from which a more positive approach could start would, in my view be like this: just as there is a conservatism based on a reluctant approach to democracy and (on the Swiss model) a conservatism on the 'far side of democracy', based on referendums and meta-democratic institutions generally, so there is a pluralism based on acceptance and entrenchment of differences as well as the pluralism based on an attempt to ignore differences. 'Accommodation by entrenchment' is *prima facie* a plausible interpretation of the Swiss language and religious-confession experience. But it is an interpretation that needs more documentation and buttressing than it has received, and it needs consideration of the cantonal as well as the federal level. Such an interpretation might easily degenerate into a chicken and egg argument. Furthermore, the whole of this enquiry raises questions concerning the proper 'use' of history, and the status of Politics as predictive science.

15 Plural Societies and the Application of Democracy

Mburumba Kerina
President of the Namibia Patriotic Coalition

I INTRODUCTION

The theme of my paper is an extremely wide-ranging one, which, if not approached carefully, could lapse into a virtually theoretical discussion. I do not think that is the purpose of our being here today. Fortunately most of the concepts which are relevant to my theme have been included in previous papers. Consequently, I shall connect the basic concepts inherent in the present discussion to practical and concrete realities. That situation is inevitably the one existing in Namibia today. This is done for good reason. Apart from the fact that I would be on safe ground talking about my own country, it is today also an extremely important issue, being one of Africa's unique plural societies, currently engaged in the difficult search for true power-sharing, and also very much in the spotlight of international attention due to its history.

In my analysis I shall outline a general framework to serve as a guideline for the analysis of the problems involved in trying to apply democratic practices and structures in plural societies in general, but in Namibia in particular. This second task should provide some basis for optimism that socio-political accommodation is possible, not only in Namibia, but also in the large number of plural societies existing in the troubled world of today.

II INTERGROUP CONFLICT AND ACCOMMODATION IN PLURAL SOCIETIES

Without attempting to join the queue of those countless sociologists who have been, and still are, trying to define *society*, I would like to describe it as a particular group of people, occupying some territorial area, substantially independent of other societies, capable of self-perpetuation through reproduction, and which possesses a distinct culture and institutional structure. In political terms this might be equated to a state or a nation. In essence this description boils down to one of a homogeneous society, but it must be clear to any observer of the contemporary world that there are few, if any, truly homogeneous societies or states. This might sound surprising to some of the world leaders of today, but the problem of group conflict in states is not the exclusive right of the states of Southern Africa! The majority of states and societies are plural societies, and the majority of them face the problems that the countries of our troubled continent face.

The term *pluralism* can be widely interpreted. In political terms it is the belief that power is, or should be, distributed among many groups and interests in society, in contrast to the belief in monism. Edward Shils (*Torment of Secrecy*, 1956) has used the term *pluralistic society* to refer to one in which there is a plurality of centres of power and where there are many areas of privacy together with tendencies for mutual adaptation among the several parts.

In sociological terms pluralism denotes the social condition in which a variety of ethnic groups and subcultures maintain autonomy and develop their cultural traditions within a single complex society. A society can therefore be pluralistic in terms of the existence of cultural differences between different groups, and also in terms of the presence of a number of ethnic groups. Often the cultural and ethnic grouping coincides. In Namibia, for instance, there are eleven ethnic groups each with its own culture, although overlapping and development is taking place. These groups do not only share certain common religious, cultural, racial or tribal characteristics, but they often use these differences to justify claims to superiority, demands for territory, and, in the case of those in subordinate positions, to demand freedom from oppression by the dominant group or groups. Today this is often wrongly seen as a white/black group conflict, but the history of Africa contradicts this assumption, or rather exposes the biased nature of this superficial view.

As a result of basic human nature it is a truism that some degree of *conflict* is universally present within and between all societies. Often the more diverse the society, the greater are the chances and opportunity for conflict. A plural society, whether cultural, ethnic or both, is therefore a born victim to social and often physical conflict. It is consequently a challenge to the leaders of dominating elites to minimise or attempt the cessation of conflict and strive towards a harmonious situation or complex of relationships. A major stumbling-block in the process of harmonising relationships is that of ethnocentrism, i.e. man's sense of superiority and prejudice to others, and his inclination to use his own cultural standards to judge others as inferior. Again this is not something unique to Southern Africa, but it is a phenomenon which I have often encountered in the United States despite its present official policy of moralism. Prejudice is to my mind probably the biggest single cause of group conflict in plural societies, and the one element which has to be eradicated totally in the search for harmony in a complex and diverse society.

Conflict is a general feature of human activity, and must be related to the basic needs and goals of the parties involved. In a plural society these needs and goals of the various groups are often inconsistent or incompatible. These conflicts may be resolved when some set of mutually consistent or compatible positions can be worked out, *which stresses the need for peaceful social change.* Namibia is a case in point. Here I would like to quote Hans Morgenthau (*Politics Among Nations*):

> The vital function of peaceful change within the state is performed, not by any particular agency acting in isolation, but by domestic society as an integrated whole. The moral consensus of society, supported by the authority and material power of the government, will avail itself of all social and political agencies to bring about a state of affairs in conformity with its conception of justice.

This is important: *the moral consensus of society and its conception of justice.*

Conflict resolution or minimisation in plural societies can basically take two courses: assimilation and accommodation. *Assimilation* is the process by which different groups lose their distinctness and indentities, both culturally and ethnically, and are absorbed into the dominant group or a new group formed from the component parts. If we look at the American society, which is often presented to us as the classical model, we see that the process of assimilation is under way for some *cultural* groups into American society. But this is clearly not the case with *racial* groups in that country, where groups like the Black and Indian movements, and leaders such as the late Malcolm X, have maintained that assimilation of Blacks and Indians into the mainstream of American society would result in the loss of their identities and cultures. Rather than favouring assimilation, these people call for accommodation for liberation of Black and Indian people from oppression, and for Blacks, Indians and Whites to retain distinct cultures. Nevertheless, the process of assimilation has started, but very slowly and only peripherally.

Accommodation is the process through which people belonging to different subcultures and ethnic groups can co-operate for mutual benefit in spite of differences or latent hostility. Among different races or ethnic groups accommodation can be achieved by the mutual adjustment of the sources of societal or intergroup conflict, so that each group can enjoy reasonable freedom and security without necessarily surrendering all differences. Accommodation can be *informal*, i.e. achieved by common and non-coercive actions and agreement to alleviate stress. It can also be *formal* and cast in laws regulating relations among groups, e.g. among the Walloons and Flemish in Belgium, or the Chinese, Indians and Malays in Singapore.

I believe that at the moment the eleven Namibian delegations are already actively and voluntarily engaged in the process of informal accommodation, which is probably unique in Africa, as well as in most plural societies of the Third World. Following a long struggle of adjustment between the blacks of the country, the Germans came, and the conflict assumed a new dimension, that of white against black based on the perceived superiority of the whites. This situation has been perpetuated and probably aggravated since the start of the Mandate Period under the SA administration, particularly with the application in the territory of the institutionalised system of apartheid. This system of enforced separatism has, however, introduced relative forward movement, and could probably be seen as the basis of the present process of informal accommodation. *Formal accommodation* in Namibia has to do with the hard reality of politics, which brings me to the next facet of my address, namely the application of *democarcy* and the sharing of power in plural societies.

III. COMPLEX POLITICAL STRUCTURES FOR PLURAL SOCIETIES

Today everybody from Washington to Moscow, from London to

Maputo and Kampala, is talking about democracy. There are probably as many definitions of democracy as there are talkers, not to mention political scientists, philosophers and UN ambassadors. Democracy can be seen as a system of government in which ultimate political authority is vested in the people, and a form of rule in which the members of a society are represented by a smaller number to make policy on their behalf. In the modern pluralistic political system, power is exercised by groups or institutions in a complex system of interaction that involves compromises and bargaining in the process of decision-making. To function effectively, democracy requires a decision-making system based on majority rule, while effective guarantees of freedom for minorities should be indispensable.

Relating all this to the plural societies of Africa, we are faced with a number of difficult problems:

(a) the complexity of the democratic machinery and the democratic state;
(b) different levels of political cognisance, skill and knowledge among diverse groups in such societies;
(c) different forms and development of political culture among the various groups, some completely alien to Western concepts of political life;
(d) the existence of centralised authoritative or monistic perceptions of political power; leading to
(e) the ignoring of minority rights or the physical destruction of minorities in such societies as Uganda where virtual genocide is being conducted by the government.

These are all problems existing in Africa today. Probably the major problem is that connected to the concept of majority rule, which some of the prominent Western nations are today trying to ram down the throats of some selective and selected African states. As far back as the nineteenth century Alexis de Tocqueville commented about the tendency toward a *tyranny of the majority,* emerging from democratic structures. We have to remember that minority status groups, whether ethnic or cultural, exist in most societies. Their minority interests cannot be entirely served by the functioning of ordinary democratic procedures. They will always be undermined by the mere fact of a lack of numerical strength, which could easily lead to *institutionalised discrimination* against minorities. Viewed from this angle, Namibia today is not the only country in which political discrimination exists. It is a phenomenon to be found in every country in the world.

In trying to apply democratic structures, principles and procedures to the complexities of plural societies, the above problems must be kept in mind. This has been done in a profound way in Namibia over the past eighteen months, and the structure of government which has been devised for a projected interim period of rule in my country, must be seen as unique in the history of constitutionalism.

IV ETHNICITY AND DEMOCRACY

In the Middle East, the Arabs and Jews are engaged in a war now in its third decade; in Guyana in South America, Africans and East Indians far removed from their native lands are struggling to gain control of the land; Nigeria's Civil War; in Uganda the Indians were first scapegoats to be removed from the country, while now General Idi Amin is conducting genocide against other African ethnic groups. The common theme in all of these situations is intergroup conflict based on ethnic differences. *Ethnicity* means the degree to which ethnic identity is held to be important by individuals, groups or societies – a potent force pregnant with volcanic power of construction or destruction.

We have by now gathered sufficient experience of events in Africa and the world to take serious cognisance of the volcanic nature of 'ethnicity' in a newly independent African state. Namibia is part of Africa. Its problems are infinitely linked to the larger problems of African history, culture and politics. Realism dictates, however, that though we are all Namibians, we must recognise the diversity of our people with a view to blending it into our new legal institutions, national character and image.

In seeking solutions to social and political problems on the African continent, we must take cognisance of ethnicity. Admittedly, it is not very easy to define 'ethnicity' and its role in a modern structure of government. But it would be tragic for us in Namibia simply to ignore the existence of various national groups in our country and to label their recognition as a mere 'Bantustan' design. The questions that confront us in this connection are of tremendous importance to our future as an independent nation.

Would tribal, linguistic, racial and political identities submerge themselves automatically in a new national identity? Or would these ethnic identities emerge as future problems threatening Namibia's unity and territorial integrity? Would the various Namibian ethnic groups demand their separate political identity and recognition, with a possible claim to the right of secession as has been the case in many African states? Or would they seek future independence as separate groups united with their kith and kin across the borders of Namibia? In Africa we have witnessed the rise of new ethnic states amid serious conflicts of old ethnic identities. The causes of suffering and massive population dislocation in many African states are 'ethnicity' or 'tribalism'. Those states in Africa which are effectively entrenched in their newly achieved independence are those with single ethnic groups or nationalities, such as Somalia.

Regardless of our attitude towards the problem of 'ethnicity', there is the need in the individual for some kind of personalised identity – smaller than the national government, larger than his immediate family; something related to a 'familistic allegiance'. Hence, our efforts in Namibia must be to produce a national constitution blending the multi-ethnic groups of nationalities of our country into a unitary nation in a secure and viable future Republic. The creation of a homogeneous society out of a heterogeneous population united through peaceful constitutional negotiations will indeed be a great step forward, not only for the people of Namibia, but equally for Africa and the international community.

V THE PROPOSED FORMULA FOR NAMIBIA

I believe that Namibia is one of Africa's plural societies which can reach great heights, through its own efforts and energy due to its unique geography and temperament.

The highway to peaceful constitutional change in Namibia will not be found or chartered for Namibians by foreign governments, the United Nations, the Organisation of African Unity or the South African Government. Support from these agencies must only be complementary to the initiatives of Namibians within the Territory. Ultimately, it will be the quality of Namibians at home that will determine their destiny.

The Turnhalle Constitutional Conference, regardless of reservations abroad, has created a tranquil atmosphere in which all the people of Namibia are re-examining legal, socio-political, cultural, educational and economic institutions of the Territory at a round-table conference of equals mutually dedicated to coexistence and survival. This historic development is in conformity with major resolutions of the United

Nations, the Advisory Opinions of the International Court of Justice, and the Lusaka Manifesto, which among other things states:

> As an aftermath of the present policies, it is likely that different groups within these societies will be self-conscious and fearful. The initial political and economical organisations may well take account of these fears, and this group self-consciousness. But how this is to be done must be a matter exclusively for the peoples of the country concerned, working together. No other nation will have the right to interfere in such affairs. All that the rest of the world has a right to demand is just what we are now asserting, that the arrangements within any State which wishes to be accepted into the community of nations must be based on an acceptance of the principles of human dignity and equality. On the objectives of liberation as defined, we can neither surrender nor compromise. We have always preferred, and we still prefer, to achieve it without physical violence. We would prefer to negotiate rather than destroy, to talk rather than kill. We do not advocate an end to the violence against human dignity. If peaceful progress to emancipation were possible, or if changed circumstances were to make it possible in the future, we would urge our brothers in the resistance movements to use peaceful methods of struggle even at the cost of some compromise on the timing of change.

VI THE TURNHALLE CONSTITUTIONAL CONFERENCE AND THE CRAFT OF DIPLOMACY: POLITICS OF REALISM VERSUS POLITICS OF FRUSTRATION

There comes a moment in the affairs of mankind when honour requires an unequivocal affirmation of a people's right to freedom with dignity and peace with justice. This is such a moment for us in Namibia.

The age in which we live has variously been called the 'Age of Revolution', the 'Age of Anguish', the 'Age of the Dusk before the Darkness'. But even after the last criticism of our Time has been made, no one can honestly deny that it is also an 'Age of Unprecedented and Creative Challenges' in the history of Namibia.

Amongst the more creative and challenging crisis is the opportunity to witness the difficult transition of the people of Namibia now undergoing an extraordinary political transformation of involvement and awareness destined to give birth to a dynamic Namibian nation.

With particular reference to the African continent, and especially to those countries in Southern Africa, there are many heroic patriots who have sacrificed their lives for the freedom of their countries. In addition, there are the names of our youth who have sacrificed the comforts of home, health and family in order to pursue education abroad in alien lands far from their native shores, only to find themselves victims of deceit and international fund-raising campaigns at their expense.

The international climate of our time, the concentrations of powers and the determinants that direct these concentrations impose certain limitations on the effectiveness of those who have exclusively preoccupied themselves with struggle from outside the boundaries of our country.

At the central stage of this extraterritorial campaigning, there is a glamour that attaches to leading deputations to foreign governments, to appearing as petitioners or in any other capacity before international tribunals, and in delivering speeches on the need for independence for one's own country. Unfortunately, the glamour is entirely superficial, soon rubs off and more often than not is eventually substituted by frustration and desperation when gradual realisation of the fruitlessness of these exercises develop. The cold, hard, incontrovertible reality is that regardless of qualified reservations the Turnhalle Constitutional Conference ushered in a new era in the politics of Namibia by moving the country closer to independence through peaceful negotiations. The very existence of the Turnhalle created a dynamic basis for major international negotiations between the Western Powers, South Africa and the United Nations.

One is tempted in the face of these promising developments to praise the far-sightedness of the Turnhalle participants and the manner in which they contributed constructively to the negotiations which paved the way for free election to the Constituent Assembly, the involvement of the United Nations and the creation of a proper international jurists' agency for the processing of political prisoners within Namibia and outside. The establishment of an Administrator-General is indeed a great victory. No single political group in Namibia has created such dynamic political developments in the history of Namibia.

If there be anything to which the Organisation of African Unity and the United Nations should give their unqualified support, it is the present agreement that has emerged from the crucial negotiations in Cape Town and Windhoek. Therein lies the future solution of the problem of Namibia. Today, the negative force of mutual recrimination which rent the political atmosphere among black political groups in the past is being channelled into positive directions to prevent the recurrence of political catastrophe that has ruined many promising African States.

The lesson of our two decades of extraterritorial activity would have been in vain if we had not yet drawn the moral from it all. And that moral is this – that in the last analysis, there is *no substitute* for the hard, unspectacular labour of working within Namibia, for politicising the masses, for organising scattered and desperate groups of our peoples and welding them into a truly representative coalition movement which alone will be able to reclaim the precious gems of freedom and independence in peace and tranquillity.

Not even the most eloquent pleas to foreign governments, the African States or the United Nations, however friendly they may be, can be an alternative to organisation and hard work inside Namibia.

The philosopher George Santayana once said that those who do not remember the past are doomed to repeat it. I urge our people in Namibia to respect their historical lessons and to prepare themselves for the victorious internal liberation struggle that alone opens the entrance to the highways of peace, freedom, independence and human dignity. There is no doubt that they have found their first victory in solidifying their unity through their participation in the Turnhalle Constitutional Conference over the past eighteen months. Unity is our insurance premium for a secure future. Consequently, I strongly emphasise the need by all parties concerned to pursue a flexible, imaginative and dynamic diplomacy of a kind associated with the recently stated five Western Powers and South African policy dedicated to successful 'peaceful negotiations' for the independence of Namibia. We were encouraged by the declaration of the five Western Powers submitted to the Maputo Conference on Namibia and Rhodesia and the reservations contained in that declaration with regard to the 'Maputo Programme of Action' on Namibia.

If, in a continent where 'peace' has become an expensive commodity, we in Namibia can succeed in strengthening the cause of peaceful negotiations for the independence of our country, as has already been demonstrated, an extraordinary achievement would have been attained in the African sub-continent, giving immense weight to continued catalytic diplomatic initiatives in the region and the opportunity of diplomatic success rather than violent racial confrontation.

Our strategy should be devoted to the achievement of concrete results through diplomatic negotiations in the Namibia problem. Hence, it is imperative to harmonise our respective objectives. The aim should be to achieve agreement on ultimate goals, regardless of disagreement on the modalities. In the case of Namibia there is already agreement by all parties concerned on an independent, viable and politically stable Namibian government. The Five Western Powers' Settlement package contains positive and constructive achievements which cannot be brushed aside unless one is a lover of headhunting in Africa.

It is true that in war there is no substitute for victory. However, in the changing geopolitics of Southern Africa there is no substitute for talking to each other if the fragile structure of peace is still to be salvaged in our region for the preservation of world peace in general. Peace is precious in Southern Africa today, and for that reason the problem of Namibia must not be allowed to become a pawn in the hands of Big Powers, thus plunging Africa into a state of perpetual strife and transforming our people into permanent refugees in the continent of their birth. Namibia must be a humanising ingredient in the organisation of a NEW AFRICAN ORDER.

The recent positions of the Five Western Powers and several African States welcoming the 'settlement package' regarding Namibia is an encouraging development.

Dr David Owen, Secretary for Foreign Affairs of the United Kingdom told the Commonwealth Press Union on 20 June 1977 that:

> the change in the SWA/Namibian situation was a formidable demonstration of what could be achieved in Southern Africa by pursuation and negotiation when Western Powers stood together. There has been a profound change for the better in SWA/Namibia in the last three months as a result of the Five Western Powers' initiative.

It is obvious that though it has been the object of criticisms, the Constitutional Conference in Windhoek, Namibia, has accomplished major objectives which are fundamentally in accordance not only with relevant resolutions and requirements of the United Nations, the International Court of Justice, the Organisation of African Unity and the Lusaka Manifesto, but also the broader principles of human dignities, rights and freedoms.

These historic accomplishments are:

1. Acceptance for the first time by the Government of South Africa of the principle of self-determination as prescribed by the United Nations Charter;

2. Acceptance by the Government of South Africa of a target date for the total independence of Namibia as a unitary state – 31 December 1978;
3. Appointment of an Administrator-General;
4. Ending of instituionalised apartheid in Namibia.

In February, 1972, the Security Council requested Secretary-General Waldheim to initiate contacts with the parties (South Africa) involved in the dispute, and in March 1972, Waldheim visited Namibia. He was then told by the South African Government that its policy was in agreement with the UN aims for the Territory, namely *self-determination and independence of SWA*. Later in 1972 Waldheim appointed Dr Alfred Escher as his personal representative, and in October Escher and two aides arrived for a 17-day visit to the Territory. Following his visit the South African Government reiterated its acceptance of self-determination for the peoples of Namibia in accordance with the UN Charter. On 6 December 1972, the Security Council passed a resolution which approved continued contact with South Africa and stressed that this contact must be conducted in the light of UN insistence on independence for Namibia as a whole. Exactly one year later the Security Council *reversed* this decision, due to pressure by several African States in the Security Council. This was the beginning of an encouraging and exciting new era in the long and troubled history of Namibia, leading to the Constitutional Conference at the Turnhalle in Windhoek, where the representatives of all the people of Namibia gathered to draw up a blueprint for a new constitutional formula that will ensure a peaceful transition to self-determination and independence on 31 December 1978.

Had the Security Council continued the contacts of the UN Secretary-General with the South African Government the problem of United Nations involvement in the independence negotiations in the Territory could not have become a controversial issue. However, the United Nations' disengagement from further contacts with South Africa did not deter the people of Namibia from seizing the negotiation initiatives which resulted in the Turnhalle Constitutional Conference.

As of this moment, the leaders and representatives of the people of Namibia inside the Territory have demonstrated their flexibility on several major issues, such as open elections in which all parties will be involved and some form of international presence during the electoral process.

We are fully aware that we are confronted by great difficulties as we search for a peaceful solution to the problem of Namibia. Nevertheless, we are optimistic that pragmatic diplomacy will triumph. We are determined through constructive diplomacy to defuse the threat to 'peace', thus averting a major holocaust in Southern Africa.

It must be stated in no uncertain terms that while we appreciate the involvement of the United Nations on one hand, the Namibian people will not procrastinate in the process of decolonisation. It is rather unfortunate for us to be pressured to remain under colonialism when South Africa is ready to vacate our country. The United Nations has been seized of the problem of Namibia for the past thirty years. It should have developed its blueprints for the Territory in the course of its thirty years' involvement.

The strategic geography and mineral resources of Namibia will continue to play a major role in the ultimate solution of the Territory's problem. While the Sahara Desert yields oil, the desert lands of Namibia contain mineral riches that can assist in the transformation of Southern Africa. Of all the countries of Africa, Namibia continues to be least known and understood. The peaceful constitutional negotiations in the Territory have provided a constructive vehicle for the emergence in Namibia of a viable independent government.

Namibia produces the highest grade of uranium in the world. In addition, our country is a producer of copper, lead, zinc, arsenic, silver, cadmium and germanium. Germanium makes Namibia tremendously important to the Western military system. This rare metal is essential for transistors because it dissipates heat and facilitates the transfer from AC to DC current. And transistors are essential to rockets, missiles and all the electronic apparatus of the Western defence establishment. There are only two major sources of germanium available to the Western world – a mine in Katanga, Zaire, and the Tsumeb mine in Namibia. Namibia's strategic position provides air and seapower mobility to the South Atlantic and Indian Oceans. Given understanding and time to complete the peaceful road to independence, Namibia could become a positive catalyst in the restructuring of Southern Africa.

There is no question that in the foreseeable future, the world will see that the nations of Southern Africa, pivoting around Namibia, developing into an economic union and political community more in symmetry with the exigencies of the African sub-continent. Africa will herald these developments in the near future as the most decisive events in the history of Southern Africa.

POSTSCRIPT

The following article by Professor Kerina was published in *To The Point*, 23 December 1977, p. 20. It brings the situation in SWA/Namibia up to date.

UNITY IS NAMIBIA'S PRESSING NEED

The most pressing need for SWA/Namibia is operational unity based on trust and confidence. Since the proposals of the Turnhalle Constitutional Conference were shelved, the necessity for a single coalition or an alliance cannot be overstressed.

It must be a national organisation capable of charting and implementing both short- and long-range strategies for the realisation of Namibia's independence. There is a serious need for a massive mobilisation of the nation's energies and resources.

It we are to pursue this policy we must all discipline ourselves, no matter of what race or colour, towards leading Namibia to a peaceful independence. It would be wrong to continue to accuse each other over incidents of the past, as a single wrong move at this moment at the crossroads of the nation's history could cost all of us our heritage.

The intervention of the five Western Powers recently has provided us with a tremendous leverage both nationally and internationally. And the wisdom with which South Africa's Prime Minister, John Vorster, and Foreign Affairs Minister 'Pik' Botha have conducted delicate negotiations on Namibia are important factors we must bear in mind as we usher our country into an era of the most creative challenges.

The appointment by the South African government of an Administrator-General and the far-reaching changes introduced by that office have already set up new political and economic patterns. These are of importance not only to Namibia, but equally to the African states generally and the international community. The changes make possible an orderly and peaceful constitutional settlement.

But this possibility could be threatened by hasty political manoeuvres designed to achieve short-range objectives at the expense of both Namibia and southern Africa generally. The confidence of African states must be strengthened in what is being done in Namibia and the current diplomatic moves by the five Western members of the UN Security Council contain many elements of hope and optimism for the future.

It is therefore imperative that we in Namibia pursue flexible, imaginative and dynamic politics to disarm our enemies and to win friends in Africa and the United Nations. And the formation of the Democratic Turnhalle Alliance is a positive political development.

There is already agreement by all parties, including the South African government, on:

(*a*) Holding a general election;
(*b*) Establishing a constituent assembly charged with the formulation of the independence constitution;
(*c*) Self-determination for Namibia as a unitary state and in accordance with the United Nations Charter;
(*d*) Target date for Namibia's independence – 31 December, 1978.

The South African government has already acquiesced, in the best interests of Namibia, to the five Western Powers' requests to:

(*a*) The appointment of an Administrator General;
(*b*) The presence of a representative of the UN Secretary-General in Namibia to monitor the transitional process to independence;
(*c*) The gradual phasing out of the SA military presence in Namibia;
(*d*) Negotiation with a Namibian independent government on the future status of Walvis Bay.

The experience of neutralist nations with a temporary limited foreign presence on their soil does not render independence any less meritorious than for a country without that foreign presence. For instance, the People's Republic of China is baby-sitting with British Hong Kong and Portuguese Macao, Cuba has its own contradiction in the American base at Guantanamo, Algeria is content with the French base of Mers-el-Kebir and Tunisia inherited the burden of Bizerta.

These are graphic examples bequeathed to us by recent political events and the exaggeration of the Walvis Bay issue by those opposed to a peaceful transition is merely a device to detour Namibians from concentrating on a peaceful constitutional solution by democratic election.

British Secretary of State for Foreign Affairs, Dr David Owen, told the Commonwealth Press Union on 20 June:

The change in the SWA/Namibia situation was a formidable demonstration of what could be achieved in southern Africa by persuasion and negotiation when Western Powers stood together. There has been a profound change for the better in SWA/Namibia in the last three months as a result of the five Western Powers' initiatives.

It is true that in war there is no substitute for victory. However, in the changing geopolitics of southern Africa there is no substitute for dialogue if the delicate structure of peace is still to be salvaged.

As Andrew Young recently stated:

> Too often the armed struggle is advocated most vigorously by those who are thousands of miles away and whose only contribution to the struggle is the rhetoric of bitterness and frustration.

It is difficult to know where the external SWAPO differs from the Democratic Turnhalle Alliance. For instance:

(a) SWAPO agreed to accept a South African as Administrator-General during the transition to Namibia's full independence. Previously, SWAPO had insisted the appointment be made by the UN and not South Africa;
(b) SWAPO also agreed to accept the principle of a general election for a constituent assembly. Until recently it had insisted that it alone should take over power because of its recognition by the UN and the Organisation of African States;
(c) SWAPO agreed to the proposed gradual SA military withdrawal – that has now been substituted with the Walvis Bay issue.

In fairness to all Namibian political groups, they all support total independence and avoidance of a Rhodesian-like fiasco.

There is no doubt that a free and independent Namibia will seek to exert its identity nationally and internationally and formulate a foreign policy dictated by national interests and not those of South Africa and other countries.

In the not-too-distant future the world will see the nations of southern Africa pivoting around a free dynamic Namibia and developing into an economic and political community more in symmetry with the exigencies of Africa. Let us pledge our determination, through the Democratic Turnhalle Alliance, to cooperate with every group in Namibia committed to a peaceful constitutional change in our struggle to preserve those noble ideals to which we have dedicated ourselves. We shall employ every possible measure to achieve this purpose and to overcome every political, economic and cultural stumbling-block, internally and externally, that hinders the march towards our independence on 31 December 1978.

16 A Comparative Perspective on Metropolitan Areas as Laboratories for Community-oriented Local Government Reorganisation in South Africa

W. B. Vosloo
Head of Department of Political Science and Public Administration, University of Stellenbosch

One of the most striking features of the pattern of urbanisation around the world is the enormous growth of metropolitanisation – the increasing centring of the urban population in the small percentage of land area occupied by what is usually called 'metropolitan areas'. Although the statistical criteria for the definition of metropolitan areas vary from country to country, the general concept of a metropolitan area is one of a large concentration of urban dwellers – in one city or several contiguous cities, together with surrounding or adjacent towns or suburbs – with a high degree of economic interdependence and social interaction.

I THE SCOPE OF METROPOLITISATION

In terms of the 'standard metropolitan statistical area' (SMSA) definition used by the US Census Bureau, metropolitan areas contained 140 million or 69 per cent of the US population in 1970, encompassing 11 per cent of the nation's land area.[1] As metropolitan areas expanded and began to touch each other the term 'megalopolis' was introduced to refer to an extended area of contiguous urban and suburban territory such as the 'Atlantic Urban Seaboard' in the US, containing about 25 per cent of the total US population.[2] In Japan 70 per cent of the total population lived in cities in 1970 with a concentration of 58 per cent in three cities: Tokyo, Osaka and Nagoya.[3]

In South Africa, as in other countries, the bulk of the process of urbanisation takes place in a limited number of towns and cities. There are four major metropolitan areas: the Pretoria-Witwatersrand-Vereniging region, the Cape Peninsula, the Durban-Pinetown region and the Port Elizabeth-Uitenhage region. In 1970 close to a third of the total South African population and approximately 75 per cent of the total urban population were concentrated in these four metropolitan areas, which together account for only about 4 per cent of the total area of the country.[4] Smaller urban concentrations have developed at the Orange Free State goldfields, East London, Bloemfontein and Klerksdorp.

II METROPOLITAN PROBLEM AND APPROACHES TO METROPOLITAN REFORM

Metropolitan areas usually emerge from a combination of two kinds of urban expansion. The first is a gradual concentric expansion of a single urban core. The second is the convergence of two or more urban areas. Historically, most urban growth has been concentrated on the fringes of cities where there has been vacant land. Many cities grew in population and area by annexing these new neighbourhoods. In other instances new neighbourhoods were incorporated into new independent municipalities.

In most countries the proliferation of new municipalities produced a very complicated local government structure in metropolitan areas. This pattern is characterised by:

(1) existence of many different local governments in a single metropolitan area;

(2) smallness in population and geographic size of a great majority of these local governments; and
(3) multiple layering, i.e. the geographic overlapping of several local governments.

Most residents of metropolitan areas are served by several governmental units. This fragmentation of the local government structure not only created problems in terms of economy and efficiency considerations, but serious consequences also arose from the splintering of the tax base and political decision-making.

Many scholars over the years have insisted that the 'metropolitan problem' was essentially the problem of 'fragmented' government – that is, the proliferation of governments in metropolitan areas and the lack of coordination of public programmes. To put it another way, a common cliché is that the metropolitan problem is one of 'big problems and little governments' due to the fact that in metropolitan areas the entire area is economically and socially integrated to a large degree, but politically divided into many separate governmental units. The objective of the metropolitan reform movement of the last thirty years was to rid metropolitan areas of ineffective multiple local jurisdictions and to establish metropolitan-wide governmental arrangements. In recent years three different approaches have emerged: the *consolidation* approach, the *federation* approach and the *cooperation* approach.[5]

Consolidation. The consolidationist approach calls for the creation of a single municipal-type government for an entire metropolitan area.[6] Contending that fractionated government is the root of the problem, consolidationists agree that governmental unification will produce

(1) economy and efficiency,
(2) greater service integration and coordination,
(3) greater popular control over service delivery,
(4) an end to uneven or inadequate service levels throughout the metropolitan area,
(5) an end to inequalities in financial burdens, and
(6) a simplification of the local government structure.

The one-government plan could be put into effect through annexation or amalgamation, or through the creation of an urban county government with jurisdiction throughout the entire metropolitan area. In abstract terms the idea has an obvious attraction, but because of popular resistance to the plan, there has been little experience with it in actual operation. There are, however, numerous examples where the annexation of unincorporated areas around city borders has been successfully used.[7] The most important variable in annexation success, and probably other efforts at metropolitan consolidation, seems to be the differential in status between the central cities and its surrounding suburbs. Consolidation appears to be more successful where there are only minor social, cultural or political differences between the communities constituting the metropolitan area.

Federation. Known as the two-level or two-tier scheme, this plan seeks to provide a general-purpose metropolitan government with jurisdiction over the entire area while at the same time permitting existing local governments to exercise local jurisdiction within their own boundaries.[8] Essentially, this is the application of federal principles to metropolitan government and the basic problem is the allocation of powers between the two levels of government.

The idea of metropolitan federation has been tried in Toronto, Greater Miami (Dade Country), Rochester, Greater London and in a limited degree within the Minneapolis-St. Paul region.[9] In all these experiments with two-tier arrangements, the area-wide jurisdictions have assumed public service responsibilities that previously were only inadequately met at the local level. The main functional asset of this arrangement appears to be that it provides an area-wide servicing unit which has an extensive fiscal base from which to support essential regional programmes, particularly those of a redistributive nature.

Cooperation. The cooperative approach advocates the retention of decentralised units of local government in metropolitan areas whilst at the same time calling for cooperative agreements between the existing governmental units on an *ad hoc* basis.[10] The extolled virtues of polycentricity, in the sense of retaining separate and independent community-oriented units of local government, include the following:

(1) its role in developing and maintaining a sense of community identity and an escape from the anonymity of a mass urban culture;
(2) its protection of grass-roots democracy in providing the individual with a sense of personal effectiveness in public affairs;
(3) its creation of an open system of multiple access in offering a larger number of groups the opportunity to exercise influence over government policy – e.g. groups that would be minorities in the metropolitan area as a whole;
(4) its creation of an opportunity to the suburbanite to protect his

cultural homogeneity and to insulate himself from those standards and way of life he does not share;
(5) its creation of instruments for the resolution of intergroup conflict, particularly in heterogeneous societies.

The cooperative efforts between the separate, independent units of local government within a metropolitan area may take several forms, e.g.:

(1) the creation of *special districts* or authorities charged with administering a particular function or service on a metropolitan-wide or at least an inter-municipal level (e.g. sewage, transit, water, electricity, etc.);
(2) the development of functional cooperation based on *interjurisdictional agreements* e.g. between a county and urban units or a central city and suburban municipalities for performing a service or providing a facility on a contractual basis, or between two or more units agreeing to assist and supply mutual aid in emergency situations; and
(3) the creation of voluntary associations of governmental units or officials that provide opportunities for study, discussion and recommendations regarding common metropolitan problems (e.g. numerous councils of governments in the United States and the Cape Metropolitan Planning Commitee).

The cooperative approach is by far the most commonly used method of metropolitan decision-making. Most metropolitan areas have developed a complex network of interjurisdictional relationships. Cooperative arrangements embrace a broad sweep of local services and facilities including law enforcement, library services, planning, street maintenance, refuse disposal, sewage disposal, ambulance services, water, electricity, fire protection, clinics, tax assessment and collection, welfare activities, cemeteries and abbatoirs. One of the main attractions of interjurisdictional agreements is that they provide a means for dealing with metropolitan problems on a voluntary basis while retaining local determination and control. They do not threaten the existence of communities, units of local government, or the jobs of incumbent public officials. Yet at the same time they enable governments to achieve the economies and provide the specialised services that only a larger jurisdiction can make possible.

III THE CHARACTERISTICS OF THE SOUTH AFRICAN METROPOLIS

As major centres of population, industry and employment, South African metropolitan areas reflect most of the problems that typically face the urban complexes of the modern world: pollution, poverty, inadequate housing and health care, crime, unemployment, juvenile delinquency, drug addiction, traffic congestion, transportation, financial crises, fast population growth, an insatiable demand for public services, overlapping jurisdictions, fiscal disparities and governmental fragmentation. In addition, however, they are in a sense miniature models of the society of which they are part, for within their geographic and jurisdictional bounds are all the problems which are unique to the unusually intricate plural structure of the South African population.[11]

The distinguishing characteristics of metropolitan life in South Africa are the heterogeneity, physical separation and interdependence of the various communities constituting the metropolitan areas. These characteristics reflect the segmented population structure, the convoluted history of intergroup relations and the peculiar pattern of settlement of the various population groups in South Africa. In addition, an important role must be assigned to the impact of official policies of separate development, as manifested by segregated land-use patterns under group areas and related legislation as well as separate governmental structures for the various population groups.

The heterogeneity of the four major metropolitan areas is illustrated by Table 16.1. These metropolitan areas include amongst its population all the major South African racial groups: Whites, Coloureds, Asians and Bantu. Each of these major racial groups comprises various linguistic or ethnic sub-cultures.

The physical separation of the various urban communities is chiefly regulated by the *Group Areas Act* (1950), as amended. In terms of this Act, the Group Areas Board is authorised to assign certain urban areas for the exclusive ownership and/or occupation of members of specified population groups. The outcome of this measure is the emergence of a network of separate residential areas for Whites, Coloureds, Indians and Blacks in most South African cities and towns. Most central business districts and industrial areas are situated within the limits of group areas assigned to Whites.

Despite the physical separation of the various population groups,

TABLE 16.1 Population in Major Metropolitan Areas

	1960					1970				
	Whites	Coloureds	Asians	Bantu	Total	Whites	Coloureds	Asians	Bantu	Total
Pretoria-Witwatersrand-Vereeniging	1 043 885	89 858	49 091	1 646 141	2 828 975	1 394 398	130 735	67 053	2 060 818	3 653 004
Cape Town (Peninsula)	305 155	417 881	8 975	75 200	807 211	381 775	606 075	11 086	108 827	1 107 763
Durban	195 114	26 990	234 772	196 926	653 802	256 836	45 189	321 204	227 717	850 946
Port Elizabeth	94 931	68 332	4 247	123 183	290 693	150 710	114 879	5 225	205 055	475 869
Total	1 639 085	603 061	297 085	2 041 450	4 580 681	2 183 719	896 878	404 568	2 602 417	6 087 582
Percentage of urban population in the Republic	63,5	58,5	74,8	58,8	61,22	66,7	59,0	74,0	51,3	58,5
Percentage of total population in the Republic	53,1	39,9	62,3	18,7	28,6	57,8	42,4	64,3	16,9	27,9
Urban population in Republic	2 582 000	1 031 000	397 000	3 471 000	7 481 000	3 274 000	1 520 000	547 000	5 070 000	10 410 000
Total population in Republic	3 088 000	1 509 000	477 000	10 928 000	16 003 000	3 773 000	2 051 000	630 000	15 340 000	21 794 000

Source: Republic of South Africa, Department of Statistics, *South African Statistics 1976*, pp. 1.8, 1.23.

Comparative Perspective on Metropolitan Areas

interdependence is also a fundamental characteristic of metropolitan areas. The typical urban dweller is dependent upon the larger metropolitan community for employment, goods and services. This interdependence involves an intricate web of economic and social relationships, a considerable degree of communication, and a great deal of daily interchange among residents, groups and firms in a metropolitan area.

IV GOVERNMENTAL ORGANISATION IN METROPOLITAN AREAS

Metropolitan areas do not have one single governmental organisation which functions for the entire area. On the contrary, they abound with units of local government and reflect the complex network of local government institutions in South Africa.[12] This situation is mainly due to the following factors:

(i) The divergent Dutch and British traditions dating from the early colonial period;
(ii) the constitutional arrangement adopted at the formation of the Union of South Africa in 1910, in terms of which local government matters fall mainly under the four provincial councils so that each province can decide on its own system in accordance with its traditions and needs;
(iii) the particular pattern of settlement of the various components of the population, which has led to the concentration of certain population groups in certain provinces and regions; and
(iv) the divergent local government arrangements made for the various population groups in terms of official government policy.

The practical result of these divergent local government arrangements is *inter alia* that in each province there are a variety of local government institutions which have different names and vary greatly as regards size and density of population, extent of their areas, composition, and their functions and powers.

The typical South African city, town or village consists of a central area inhabited by Whites and one or more non-White residential areas (usually on the outskirts of the municipal area), e.g. areas for the Bantu, for the Coloureds, and for the Indians. There are divergent local government arrangements for the various population groups.

Whites. A common feature of the urban local government system for Whites is that every urban community with a sufficient number of citizens has its own municipal council of elected members. The provincial council or the Administrator of the province concerned has the power to confer a specific kind of municipal status – the differentiation between city, town or village, depending on the size of the community – on any urban area. For very small rural communities local boards (Cape Province) and health committees (Natal and Transvaal) are appointed by the Administrator concerned. All municipal councils, as well as local boards and health committees, are empowered by provincial ordinance to make by-laws. These local authorities fulfil two basic functions in the life of the community. The first is a *service* function, i.e. to supply services such as sanitation, streets, water, electricity, housing for low-income groups, parks and recreation facilities, health services, etc. The second is *regulatory*, i.e. to order and regulate the life of the community within the scope of powers granted, by determining priorities in connection with the supply of services, township layout, licensing, the provision of community services, the appointment of personnel and the procuring and spending of funds.

For peri-urban or rural areas different arrangements have been made in the various provinces. In the Cape Province a system of divisional councils was introduced to provide local community services in areas outside the boundaries of municipalities. In the Transvaal this function is performed by an appointed Board for the Development of Peri-Urban Areas. In Natal a Board for Development and Services was appointed for this purpose and in the Orange Free State this function is performed by the Small-Holding Areas Control Board. When peri-urban areas served by these institutions have reached a sufficient stage of development, they may apply to the Provincial Administrator for the powers of one or other of the regular municipal authorities.

Coloureds and Indians. All Coloured or Indian group areas are currently serviced and controlled in one of the following manners:[13]

(a) by the White local authority having jurisdiction over the area in which such a group area falls, but acting with the advice of a management or local affairs committees consisting of elected Coloured or Indian members;
(b) by an independent elected Coloured or Indian municipal council.

In terms of government policy all the advisory management or local affairs committees are considered as the first step towards independent municipal status. These committees exercise such powers and functions as may be conferred on them under the supervision and control of the adjacent 'parent' municipality, subject to the conditions prescribed by the Administrator of the Province concerned. The only examples of independent municipal councils are Verulam (Indian), Isipingo (Indian) and Pacaltsdorp (Coloured).

Bantu. Originally the municipal services in the Bantu areas were provided by the White municipal councils acting as agents of the Department of Bantu Administration and Development of the central government. Since 1973, the administration of Bantu urban areas outside the Bantu homelands is the responsibility of Bantu Affairs Administration Boards. The Republic is divided into 22 administration areas with a board for each. Each such area comprises a number of Bantu residential areas previously administered by White local authorities. The members of the boards are appointed by the Minister of Bantu Administration and Development. Urban Bantu Councils consisting of elected members have been established for residential sections in the larger administration areas. The provision of specified local community services have been delegated to these councils. Examples of such councils in existence are Atteridgeville, Daveyton, Mamelodi, Natalspruit and Soweto.[14]

V THE CHALLENGE OF METROPOLITAN REORGANISATION IN SOUTH AFRICA

The challenge of metropolitan reorganisation inevitably forms part and parcel of the broader challenge of constitutional change in South Africa: to develop suitable governmental arrangements for the accommodation and reconciliation of the interests and aspirations of its various population groups. Metropolitan areas contain a large and rapidly growing proportion of the population and are therefore destined to exert a major influence on the future pattern of government in South Africa. All the major social, economic and political problems facing society are ultimately metropolitan problems because they occur principally in metropolitan areas. Metropolitan areas are therefore important laboratories for future developments.

At the heart of the metropolitan problem in South Africa lies the socio-economic, racial and ethnic differences of the people living in the major cities and suburbs and the inadequacy of existing governmental arrangements to accommodate and reconcile the various community interests and aspirations. Since metropolitan areas consist of large numbers of different kinds of people the problems of regulating conflict, maintaining order and providing adequate public services assume tremendous proportions.

The heterogeneity of the metropolitan areas is manifested by various forms of socio-cultural distance existing between the component communities. People with different social, economic, racial and life-style characteristics generally live in different parts of a metropolitan area. These differences are reflected in different views on a wide variety of public issues such as planning and zoning, housing policy, welfare programmes, the provision of public facilities, the distribution of tax burdens and a host of other problems. The failure to achieve consensus on these public policy questions also explains the failure to develop integrated government institutions at all levels of government.

The inadequacy of existing governmental arrangements in the urban areas is chiefly manifested by the underdeveloped nature of representative institutions for local self-government in the Coloured, Indian and Black urban communities. The unsatisfactory development of adequate representative institutions for self-government is largely responsible for what can be described as an 'institutional vacuum' in many urban areas. The existing institutions for self-determination at the local level have not as yet made satisfactory progress in the sense of creating the necessary capacities to provide adequately for the needs of the various Coloured, Indian and Black communities.

But what about the future? It would seem that metropolitan areas will have to find a formula that is geared to two distinct though interrelated levels of urban government: an area-wide (common) level and a neighbourhood (community) level. Metropolitan areas must find a system of government that is capable – administratively, fiscally and politically – of responding not only to problems of metropolitan-wide concern, but to those of local communities within metropolitan areas. It must meet both *efficiency* and *civic* considerations. All governmental functions throughout the metropolitan area should be analysed against two principal yardsticks – efficiency and community control – in order to decide whether they should be performed on a regional level, the community level, or shared between the two. The underlying philosophy of this approach is that it is of crucial importance in South Africa to reconcile *common* interests and *community* interests.

Amongst the major practical implications of this direction of change are the following:

1. The accelerated conversion of community councils in Coloured, Indian and Black neighbourhoods into incorporated municipalities.
2. The drastic revision and adjustment of the boundaries (jurisdictional areas) of existing local government units in order to diminish the jurisdictional fragmentation of adjacent neighbourhoods forming integrated socio-economic units.
3. The development of formulas for the equitable allocation and distribution of fiscal resources (revenue sharing) on a metropolitan-wide basis – particularly revenues derived from central business districts and industrial areas.
4. The regionalisation of services by means of regional service corporations and interjurisdictional agreements (interlocal contracting and joint enterprise).
5. Increased subsidies from the central and provincial governments to raise the standard of services at the community level and to supplement the revenue of community governments as and when required.
6. The creation of voluntary metropolitan councils of governments is a first step towards more coordinated metropolitan governmental arrangements.

VI CONCLUSION

From a comparative perspective it appears that the deep cleavages which exist in large urban areas cannot be made to disappear simply by encompassing all the urban communities under a single governmental umbrella. Divisions of race, income, ethnic background, and social class tend to persist and may even become more intense when brought within a single governmental structure. For this reason the solution to the vexed question of jurisdictional fragmentation is increasingly sought in the reconciliation of functional and community-oriented considerations: functional cooperation in the interests of greater efficiency and community-oriented representation in the interests of promoting local self-determination and autonomy.

In the South African setting metropolitan areas appear to be crucial laboratories for the development of viable local government institutions for Coloured, Indian and Black urban communities. The success or failure of this venture towards responsible self-government and administration will ultimately determine the capability of the South African political system to absorb peaceful change.

NOTES

1. Regional Plan Association, New York: *Growth and Settlement in the U.S. - Past trends and future issues* (June 1975) p. 27.
2. Jean Gottman, *Megalopolis: The Urbanized Northeastern Seaboard of the United States* (New York: Twentieth Century Fund, 1962).
3. Japan Information Service, *Land and People of Japan* (1972).
4. South African Department of Information, *South Africa 1974 - Official Yearbook of the Republic of South Africa*, pp. 76–7.
5. See L. Gulick, *The Metropolitan Problem and American Ideas* (New York: Knopf, 1962); Committee for Economic Development, *Reshaping Government in Metropolitan Areas* (New York, 1970); L. Wingo (ed.), *Reform of Metropolitan Governments* (Washington, DC: Resources for the Future, 1972); Advisory Commission on Intergovernmental Relations, *Alternative Approaches to Governmental Reorganization in Metropolitan Areas* (Washington, DC: US Government Printing Office, 1962).
6. See L. Gulick, op. cit.; Victor Jones, *Metropolitan Government* (Chicago: University of Chicago Press, 1942); Committee for Economic Development, *Modernizing Local Government* (New York, 1966) pp. 11–13.
7. Some of the best-known examples include Jacksonville, Nashville, Indianapolis and the Baton Rouge Area.
8. See Advisory Commission on Intergovernmental Relations, *The Challenge of Local Governmental Reorganization* (Washington, DC: US Government Printing Office, 1974) ch. v.
9. See M. Mogulof, *Five Metropolitan Governments* (Washington, DC: The Urban Institute, 1972) and A. Rose, *Governing Metropolitan Toronto* (Berkeley: University of California Press, 1972).
10. See R. Bish and V. Ostrom, *Understanding Urban Government: Metropolitan Reform Reconsidered* (Washington, DC: American Enterprise Institute for Public Policy Research, 1973); A. Hawley and B. Zimmer, *The Metropolitan Community: Its People and Government* (Beverley Hills: Sage Publications, 1970) ch. IV; and R. Warren, *Government in Metropolitan Areas: A Reappraisal of Fractionated Political Organization* (Davis, California: Institute of Governmental Affairs, 1966).
11. See W. B. Vosloo, Jeppe and Kotze, *Local Government in Southern Africa* (Cape Town: Academica, 1974) ch. 1.
12. See Vosloo *et al.*, op. cit.
13. For a more elaborate description and appraisal of the local governmental arrangements created for the Coloured population group see Republic of South Africa, *Report of the Commission of Inquiry into Matters Relating to the Coloured Population Group* (Pretoria: Government Printing Office, R.G. 38/1976) ch. 19.
14. A new system of elected community councils with expanded powers of local self-government was introduced in May 1977.

17 Plural Accommodation in South Africa: Problems, Perspectives and Solutions

G. C. Olivier
Department of Political Science and International Politics, University of Pretoria

There is only one crisis in South Africa today. It is the crisis of transformation. At present South Africa is in the throes of a great historical transition towards a new order of things. What the precise nature of this new order will be is unclear. Owing to the storm of crisis problems our decision-makers face at the moment, present South African society is like Pandora's box. This calls for fundamental thinking, planning and action if we are not to be overhauled by the sequence of events and the pressures of time. We need a clearer picture of the South African society of tomorrow. The clearer our view of the future, the more objectively we will be able to imagine it and the more decisively and responsibly we will be able to act.

Fortunately, fundamental changes in thinking seem to prevail among a broad spectrum of elite-groups in South Africa at the moment. Events over the last three years have removed all doubt that, if we are to survive, the ideal of just political and social structures for all the people of South Africa can no longer be postponed nor be subject to the approval of the lowest common denominator in the ranks of the ruling party.

In the past number of years scores of paradigms or scenarios have been suggested by academics, social research institutions, publicists, etc. However, these seem to have had little noticeable effect on government policy-making. The impression is created that people outside the ruling party hierarchy producing policy alternatives are 'heard' but not 'listened to' by government policy-makers. It might be said of academics that 'ever since Plato advocated the ideal of a philosopher king, the intellectual has sought to guide the destinies of the State.' However, it is equally valid to say that there is hardly room for intellectual chauvinism in South African politics at the moment. Politicians, community leaders and academics should start a meaningful communication if we are to overcome the impasse in which our society currently finds itself.

If the process of intellectual fermentation on South Africa is to produce wine and not vinegar, it is also important that academics should come forward with alternatives based on relevant research and make 'yes-able' propositions to the policy-makers which maximise options for action. In short, research must concentrate heavily on 'actionables'. Also, advocacy in pursuit of alternative policies instead of opposition to established ones is more likely to make for a receptive government audience even though advocacy might involve a degree of dissent from present policy. If opposition becomes a substitute for advocacy, the impact of dissent is weakened.

The point I wish to emphasise is that suggestions for adaptation and change in South Africa should incorporate, and not exclude, whatever positive tenets in present government policy there might be. A complete and immediate restructuring of the South African political system, by constitutional means of reform, is totally impracticable. The existing value and institutional framework by which the ruling Nationalist Party operates must be incorporated in any blueprint for change in South Africa. What we should concern ourselves with is how the existing framework can be adapted, augmented, modernised and legitimised in order to bring about just social-political structures in our country.

Right from the outset we must admit that both discriminatory apartheid and liberal constitutionalism have become unacceptable as political alternatives in South Africa. South Africa's political alternatives can no longer be dichotomised on this basis. A third alternative, a new constitutional mix, must be contemplated. In doing this we will have to relate the different constitutional options as directly and concretely as possible to the total South African configuration including the prevailing political system.

I THE FAILURE OF LIBERAL CONSTITUTIONALISM IN SOUTH AFRICA

As long ago as 1842 Lord Stanley warned against the introduction of representative government for the Cape Colony, because

it had been found to be a task of insuperable difficulty to reconcile the principles of free institutions with the legal equality between races. At the Cape of Good Hope, more than in almost any other possession of the British Crown, the elements of society were more heterogeneous and dissimilar and, in addition, these elements were separated from each other by distinctions almost indelible.[1]

In the same vein Settler leader Robert Godlonton wrote that

the universal suffrage in a colony like this is a reckless and dangerous experiment, involving a great wrong to European inhabitants, jeopardising property, and fraught with future mischief.[2]

While the ideal of liberal constitutionalism was never really abandoned in subsequent years it made little headway in South African politics. The reason for this failure is clear: the liberal tradition is ultimately linked with the social and economic structures as well as secular beliefs and mores of the European countries of origin. This tradition is based on elements of individualism, the mechanistic views of the role of the state; basic opposition between the individual and the state; protection of individual liberties, etc. These conditions constitute the opposite pole to plural accommodation. To this way of thinking the group basis of politics is seen as an obstacle which must be eliminated rather than accommodated.[3]

In South Africa the group basis of politics is an undeniable fact. Therefore, devices such as Bills of Rights, civilised tests for qualified franchise, electoral reforms of the senate will not, it would seem to me, assist the transition from a divided plural society, characterised by domination, to a free and open pluralistic society. In short, a constitutional setttlement whose viability depends on the prior disappearance of white and black nationalisms and cultural cleavages does not seem to hold the answer to our problem. Leo Kuper states that 'The parliamentary system in racially divided societies is calculated to intensify the politics of race.'[4] However, the possibility must not be ruled out that liberal constitutionalism can be fused with other political strategies in South Africa once an open plural society is finally achieved.

II THE FAILURE OF APARTHEID

As regards the failure of apartheid, no further confirmation is needed than the repeated pledges by senior government officials that colour discrimination will be phased out. In an article in the *Transvaler* of 5 May 1977 Deputy Minister Louis le Grange gave an inventory of about 40 instances where discrimination previously applied in South Africa has had to be removed in the immediate past. The actual effect of these may be negligible, but it points to a definite direction of change in government policy. A conclusion one might draw is that while the maintenance of cultural diversity and group identity remains a firm policy objective, the government seems to realise that this ideal should exclude domination.

This is where the crux of the matter lies. The nature of South African society is extremely complex and there is no ready-made recipe or model we can opt for. Especially two salient aspects stand in the way of our society becoming an 'open' democratic society. They are firstly that in its totality South African society is a *transitional society*, and secondly that in South Africa one finds one of the most *extreme cases of plurality* anywhere in the world. Both these conditions have an overwhelming impact on constitutional change in South Africa. To adopt a strategy for national development is as Dahl said 'a little bit like deciding how to look for a fuse box in a strange house on a dark night after all the lights have blown'. As for the present, the possibility that separate development or plural devolution of power, applied in its most liberal terms of interpretation, might provide a way out of the dilemma of domination in a divided plural society by facilitating the transition to an open pluralistic society must be given serious thought.

III SOUTH AFRICA AS A TRANSITIONAL SOCIETY

One can assume that political change in South Africa is a particular instance of political development. Such an assumption implies, *inter alia*, an open-ended process towards some kind of end-product. More specifically Coleman describes political development as that open-ended increase in the capacity of political man to initiate and institutionalise new structures, and supporting cultures, to cope with or resolve problems to absorb and adapt to continuous change, and to strive purposively and creatively for the attainment of new Societal goals.[5]

The process described in Coleman's definition is not a smooth one. Actually all political systems pass through certain crises in the developmental process. Briefly, these consist of (1) the *identity* crisis, wherein the citizens search for a national identity; (2) the *legitimacy* crisis, which arises whenever there is conflict over the appropriate form which political decision-making should take in a society; (3) the *penetration* crisis, which grows out of the desire on the part of the central government to extend authority and jurisdiction into previously untouched areas of national political life; (4) the *participation* crisis, covering the multitude of ways in which citizens can demand access to and influence over the modes of power; (5) the *distribution* crisis, involving a dissatisfaction with the ways in which goods and values are allocated in the system.[6]

The history of South African society as a whole reveals that while these crises have by and large been solved for the white group, the various non-white groups by and large are still to emerge from all five of these crises. While these crises are inevitable in the political development of any society, they need not necessarily involve revolution. They can be evolutionised or orchestrated by intelligent and skilful leadership. A leader of a relatively inert society can mobilise it to those issues which he feels ready to handle, at the time he desires. For instance, if a political system can meet and perhaps temporarily solve the identity crisis first, other crises need not be quite as severe as anticipated. Further, a resolution of the identity crisis makes it easier to move on to the legitimacy issue, and so on.[7]

It is a fair statement to make that White leadership in South Africa is currently engaged in an effort to evolutionise and stabilise the forces of change in the country. Actually they are fulfilling what may be called an important refereeing function without which our society will not progress in a stable manner. Elsewhere in the Third World, and particularly in Africa, this very same function is being performed largely by one-party regimes, military juntas and dictatorships. These arrangements of course fail to meet the standards set by parochial Western values and norms. However, the development of a political order essentially means increasing the capacity, or the capability, of that order to do things. In the developing areas of the world power or capacity of this nature is a scarce resource. This phenomenon is not always understood by adherents of liberal constitutionalism. Huntington points out very succinctly that:

> When an American thinks about the problem of government-building, he directs himself not to the creation of authority and the accumulation of power but rather to the limitation of authority and the division of power. Asked to design a government he comes up with a written constitution, bill of rights, separation of powers, checks and balances, federalism, regular elections, competitive parties – all excellent devices for limiting government.... Confronted with a need to design a political system which will maximize power and authority, he has no ready answer. His general formula is that governments should be based on free and fair elections. In many modernising societies this is irrelevant.... The problem is not to hold elections but to create organisations. In many modernising countries ... the primary problem is not liberty but the creation of a legitimate public order. Men may, of course, have order without liberty, but they cannot have liberty without order. Authority has to exist before it can be limited....[8]

One can conclude from this that it is in the public interest for a government to be able to govern. With this capability entrenched, the system can develop in the capability to assimilate the new social forces which are created and drawn into politics by modernisation and industrialisation.[9]

As far as South Africa is concerned, it seems completely justifyable to explain at least some aspects of change in terms of modernisation theory. Separate or plural development (the term *plural development* seems to be preferable) may be regarded as a particular example of transitional politics. In terms of this explanation it is quite in order to regard the whites as the modernising elite inducing change towards an intended goal, e.g. the creation of separate areas of liberty. However, in South Africa there is not clear consensus as regards, firstly, the merits of this specific goal, or, secondly, the decision-making structure and process leading towards this goal. The major reason for this is of course the divided plural nature of South African society and the zero-sum tendency of cross-cultural politics in the country.

IV SOUTH AFRICA AS A PLURAL SOCIETY

The term plural society refers to 'societies with sharp cleavages between different population groups brought together within the same political unit'.[10] Plural societies are divided by tribal, religious, linguistic, cultural, economic and regional differences. The implications of these conditions for building a stable democracy are manifold. Most important is the question of conflict management. The principal ways in which such conflict are dealt with are (1) violence and repression, (2) secession or separation, (3) mutual veto, (4) autonomy, (5) proportional representation, and (6) assimilation. The first, second, and last of these alternatives are the outcomes predicted by the majority of the theories of political integration.[11] Leo Kuper's generalisation is more specific:

> Integration rests on common values. . . . It presupposes cultural homogeneity. Cultural diversity or pluralism automatically imposes the strictest necessity for domination by one of the cultural sections. It excludes the possibility of consensus . . . and necessitates non-democratic regulation of group relationships.[12]

The 'Baasskap' era in South African politics (1948–59) coincides specifically with Kuper's conflict model of plural accommodation. The government's policy of Separate Development, introduced by the Promotion of Bantu Self-Government Act of 1959 brought into being separation or partition as a mode of plural accommodation for the Black section of the population. However, only a portion of the Black population group is being effected by the above arrangement, with the result that domination is still prevailing in the South African political system.

As yet, no comprehensive policy exists whereby this domination can be eliminated. While both geographical partition and integration are being rejected by the government for non-whites in the 'common area' a third alternative must be devised for these people. In considering a third alternative cognisance should be taken of the deep and mutually reinforcing cleavages, and the lack of cross-cutting or overlapping affiliations characterising South African Society. Viewed from another angle, Seymour M. Lipset states that

> the chances for stable democracy are enhanced to the extent that

groups and individuals have a number of cross-cutting, politically relevant affiliations.[13]

It should of course be remembered that there are some major exceptions to the above-mentioned consensus among a school of integration theorists concerning the link between cultural homogeneity and political integration: the theories developed by Haas and Etzioni and the theories of federalism.[14] Haas states for instance that many cultural characteristics may not be politically relevant. Etzioni suggests that 'sharing culture is not required for unification nor does the lack of a shared culture prevent it; it simply has little effect on political unification.' He admits however, that shared culture may not be a 'prerequisite for unification but a requirement that has to be fulfilled before the process can be advanced'. Federal theorist K. C. Wheare argues in similar vein to Haas and Etzioni when stating that community of language, religion, race and nationality cannot be regarded as 'essential prerequisites of the desire for union'.[15]

The latter arguments seem convincing enough when applied to plural societies where there is some 'mutual compatability of main values' as Deutsch puts it, or, using F. S. C. Northrop's terminology, in societies where a 'common living law' prevails.[16] Morgenthau speaks of a common intellectual and moral climate as prerequisites for peace in a plural state system.[17] Although, as pointed out earlier, cultural cleavages are very profound in South African society and cross-cutting affiliation are limited, such a 'common living law' can be nurtured if cultural obstacles which at present cause polarisation between White and Black can be depoliticised.

In this context it is important to realise firstly that there are various degrees of plurality between the Whites and other population groups in South Africa and secondly that the Coloureds, Asians, Urban Blacks and Homeland Blacks have differing mass cultures. This of course calls for differential accommodation strategies. For the Coloureds and Indians differential policies already apply in contrast to the policy for the Blacks. Likewise it is important that the Homeland and Urban Blacks, respectively, should also be subjected to different patterns of accommodation. They should not, and cannot, be regarded as one cultural mass any longer. At the same time, while we accept that assimilation is not the answer to South Africa's problems of pluralism, we should be careful not to neglect beliefs, norms and values that are held in common.

For even if shared values occupy only a small fraction of the total cultural sphere, they tend to be among the most highly relevant values for political action. To focus on the extent to which common values are lacking is often to obscure the slender threads of consensus that may form the basis of political action. To emphasise the separateness of the cultural sections and the divergence of their institutions may entail a high cost of neglecting emerging patterns of interaction.[18]

In South Africa we have already achieved a significant degree of depoliticisation in Afrikaner/English relations. Currently the degree of pluralism between these two sections of the population is relatively small. It is lamentable that while the degree of plurality between the Coloureds and the Indians on the one hand, and the Whites on the other hand, is not maximal in empirical terms, it is constantly being artificially forced in this direction. It may be justifiable to report that equal conditions are being created for these people. To this no better answer can be given than that of de Tocqueville, namely,

If men are to remain civilised or to become so, the art of associating together must grow and improve in the same ratio in which the equality of conditions is increased.[19]

V PATTERNS AND DIRECTIONS OF CHANGE IN SOUTH AFRICA

It is clear from the foregoing analysis that political change in South Africa, owing to the specific nature of the political system, calls for various separate, yet interrelated, strategies. The over-arching ideal, perhaps, remains the creation of separate areas of liberty as expounded some 40 years ago by Alfred Hoerhlé. However, practical conditions prescribe variation not only of the strategy whereby this goal is striven for, but also in the structural configurations and constitutional progress of these areas of liberty.

In an important sense this type of approach is implicit in the race policies of the present government. At the same time, however, one cannot fail to detect a tendency in the overall application of these policies pointing at the strong penetration of the philosophy and policy underlying White/Black politics into the other areas of non-

White politics. In other words, there is some degree of contamination between White/Black, White/Brown and White/Asian politics, with White/Black politics dominating. In view of the variegated degree of plurality and modernity of these groups, each one should of course be treated on its own merits and performance. Above all, the tempo of development and the degree of 'emancipation' of one group should be decided on merit and not be determined by the lowest common denominator in the entire cluster of groups. It is a gross anomaly and an element of great asymmetry in South African politics that the Coloureds and Indians should still clamour for a place in the sun while Transkeians have reached the top of the ladder.

VI A STRATEGY FOR CHANGE: SOME PRACTICAL SUGGESTIONS

1. *The Homeland Blacks.* Partition still seems to be the most logical policy to follow for at least some of the homelands. Transkei is already independent and Bophuthatswana is on the verge of becoming so. Independence may also be considered for Kwazulu and Lebowa, provided drastic consolidation, coupled with dramatic economic and infrastructural development can take place. As for the rest of the homelands, I seriously doubt the practicality and wisdom of their excision from South African territory. They are too small, too underdeveloped, too fragmented and too dependent on the Republic of South Africa. It would really be somewhat absurd to grant independence to them because I do not think they can exist in a hostile world as independent states. These homelands may of course receive maximal internal autonomy and as such serve the purpose of being separate areas of freedom. At most they may develop into fully-fledged provinces in a union or federation or regions in South Africa. Above all, such a dispensation will be much more saleable to the outside world than total independence. Transkei's negative reception in the arena of world politics should not be lost sight of and future independent homelands will do no better.

2. *The Urban Blacks.* To regard the Urban Blacks as a distinct group is empirically justifiable. However, should this empirical reality become policy, it will necessarily hamper the complete execution of the homeland policy. Of course, once the major homelands are independent, or internally autonomous, the government will enjoy greater latitude in regard to policy alternatives for the Urban Blacks, and a new

deal for these people may become possible. At the same time, their political future cannot be subjected entirely to the time-scale set for homeland independence or internal autonomy. The recent urban unrests in South Africa clearly reminded us of the type of crisis we may expect if the political and social aspirations of the Urban Blacks are not acted upon seriously and expeditiously. Municipal autonomy coupled with large-scale improvements in the social conditions of these people is undoubtedly a short-term necessity. Eventually, however, the status of these Blacks will have to be divorced from that of the homeland Blacks. Once this becomes policy, internal autonomy on the same basis as that of the smaller homelands, with participation in the South African body politic, seems to be a logical option.

3. *Coloureds and Asians.* There is probably not much wrong with the policy of parallelism but for the lack of, *firstly*, parity in the existing parallel institutions; and, *secondly*, the absence of adequate consensus structures. The problem of parity can be overcome only by the elevation of the status of the Indian and Coloured Representative Councils in time to come to the same level as that of the present White Parliament. Further up in the decision-making hierarchy one can envisage a plural Executive Council of State, consisting of representatives of all existing Parliaments, with a President with real powers as chief executive. For the moment the essential character or detail of these suprastructures is perhaps of lesser importance than the creation and fascilitating of over-arching cooperation of some kind or other, which would tend to decrease the intensity of conflict and improve conditions for consensus decision-making which are absent at present.

In respect of all the non-White groups for which independent homelands are not feasible, serious thought could be given to consociational engineering in South Africa. Consociational theory (also referred to as 'pacification' democracy or *proporzdemokratie*) draws an explicit distinction between 'elite political culture and mass political culture', which means 'that political stability can be maintained in culturally fragmented systems if the leaders of the subcultures engage in co-operative efforts to counteract the centrifugal tendencies of cultural fragmentation'.[20] To quote Lijphart further:

> Consociational theory differs from other theories of integration not only in its refutation of the thesis that cultural fragmentation necessarily leads to conflict, but also in its insistence that distinct lines of cleavage among subcultures may actually help rather than hinder peaceful relations among them. Because good social fences may

make good political neighbours, a kind of voluntary *apartheid* policy may be the most appropriate solution for a divided society. Political autonomy for the different subcultures is a crucially important element of a consociational system, because it reduces contacts, and hence strain and hostility among the subcultures at mass level.[21]

Albeit in embryonic form, consociational engineering is clearly discernible in South African politics. Here I particularly refer to the Cabinet Council for the Coloureds and the Indians, the restriction of direct popular involvement, the growing emphasis on consultation between incumbents of positions of leadership, the creation of subsystems of representative government, and so on. These no doubt decrease the intensity of conflict and improve the conditions for rational negotiation not provided by the prevailing Westminster model. The latter has a competitive and centralised structure and the majority of the population has no direct access to it. Its replacement by a structural device more directly and concretely related to the unique pluralistic South African situation is a matter which cannot be delayed any longer. In consociational engineering we seem to have an option which offers in important respects a continuation of constitutional development on the basis of the positive, non-discriminatory elements in existing government policy. In the long run, these consociational structures may come into being not only for the Whites, Coloureds and Indians, but also the Urban Blacks and the semi-autonomous homelands may cooperate under these structures. These arrangements may not provide the final answer, but through them we will learn to master the 'art of associating together'. Once this is achieved parliamentary democracy for entire South Africa may become a reality. This in turn may make possible the ideal of over-arching, broad South Africanism and loyalty which is so important for combating the external threats to our security which we face at the moment.

NOTES

1. As quoted by Haasbroek, D. J. P., 'Political liberalism and the rise of differential development (apartheid) in South Africa', *Inaugural address*, University College of Zululand (no. 6) June 1966, p. 7.
2. As quoted ibid., p. 10.
3. Cf arguments put forward by the Report of Spro-cas Commission (no. 10) entitled *South Africa's Political Alternatives* (Raven Press, Johannesburg, 1973) chs 9 and 10.

4. Kuper, L., and M. G. Smith, *Pluralism in Africa* (University of California Press, Berkeley, 1969) p. 188.
5. Coleman, James, 'The Development Syndrome: Differentiation-Equality-Capacity' in Binder, L., et al., *Crisis and Sequences in Political Development* (Princeton University Press, 1971) p. 73.
6. Cf. Clark, R. P., *Development and Instability; Political Change in the Non-Western World* (The Dryden Press, Hinsdale, Ill., 1974) p. 206.
7. Ibid.
8. Huntington, S. P., *Political Order in Changing Societies* (Yale University Press, 1968) pp. 7–8.
9. Cf. Clark, R. P., op. cit., p. 227.
10. Kuper, L., and M. G. Smith, op. cit., p. 3.
11. Cf. Lijphart, A., 'Cultural Diversity and Theories of Political Integration', *Canadian Journal of Political Science*, vol. IV (1971) p. 10.
12. Kuper, L., and Smith, M. G., op. cit., p. 14.
13. As Quoted in Lijphart, A., op. cit., p. 5.
14. Ibid., pp. 6–9.
15. Ibid., p. 8.
16. Ibid., pp. 4–5.
17. Morgenthau, H. J., *Politics Among Nations; The Struggle For Power and Peace* (Knopf, New York, 1967) p. 213.
18. Horowitz, D. L., 'Multiracial Politics in the New States', in Jackson, R. J., and M. B. Stein, *Issues In Comparative Politics* (Macmillan, London, 1971) pp. 165–6.
19. As quoted in Huntington, S. P., op. cit., pp. 4–5.
20. Lijphart, A., op. cit., p. 9.
21. Ibid., p. 11.

18 Deriving Policy for South Africa

Anthony de Crespigny
Head of Department of Political Science, University of Cape Town

This essay explores the question of how one sets about the *rational* derivation of policy for our complex and divided society. The word 'rational' is stressed since the policies which are currently enforced, or which appear in the programmes of opposition parties, seem so rarely to be logically derived from assumptions that are openly stated, clarified and justified. Indeed, it is often far from clear what the underlying assumptions of these policies are, so that the task of evaluating them becomes difficult or impossible.

The problems of our country are becoming increasingly serious and they are not going to be resolved through self-indulgent posturing, casual attributions of motive, deliberate misunderstanding and misrepresentation, the politics of envy and prejudice, the belief that people with opposing views are necessarily stupid or wicked, resort to naked power, and so on. They will be resolved, if at all, only through reason and compassion – qualities which *in combination* are so little evident in our politics that one wonders whether substantial progress is possible. We confront instead a widespread insensitivity to human suffering and, at the opposite extreme, an apparently prevalent view that the conspicuous merit of the heart compensates for the muddles of the head.

Rational policy-making is usefully viewed as a triadic process which involves (*a*) factual assumptions, (*b*) value assumptions, and (*c*) policy derivations. If the assumptions are made explicit they can be critically inspected, as can the relations between assumptions and derivations. I shall therefore proceed by stating some assumptions and by then considering what policies are rationally derivable from them.

I FACTUAL ASSUMPTIONS (FAs)

FA 1. The major groups – national or ethnic groups, social classes – which comprise South African society will as a matter of fact pursue their own interests as they perceive them.

A group is a collection of people who have a common objective or end. What makes a group is the fact that each member is conscious of himself and acts as a member of that group, whether it be a class, a church, a social club, or a football team. The group is held together, and therefore constituted, by an awareness of common purposes. A group may survive elements of division within it provided that the bonds which bind its members together are stronger than disuniting influences.

To say that a policy, for example, is in a group's interests is to say that it puts its members in a better position to satisfy their settled preferences and ambitions, whatever these may be. Mistakes may, of course, occur since people may think that a policy will enhance group opportunities when in fact it will accomplish the reverse.

That groups, usually through their representatives, pursue their own perceived interests is hardly a contentious proposition. Nevertheless, I shall support it by reference to the writings of David Hume, Reinhold Niebuhr and Bertrand Russell. It could equally well, though perhaps less interestingly, be supported by reference to empirical literature in sociology and political science, particularly to studies of voting behaviour in democratic countries.

In one of his essays Hume writes:

> It is . . . a just *political* maxim, *that every man must be supposed a knave*; though, at the same time, it appears somewhat strange that a maxim should be true in *politics*, which is false in *fact*. . . . Honour is a great check upon mankind; but where a considerable body of men act together, this check is in a great measure removed, since a man is sure to be approved of by his own party for what promotes the common interest, and he soon learns to despise the clamours of adversaries.[1]

Hume rightly believed that people are capable of sympathy and that Hobbes was wrong in supposing that sympathy is a refined form of egoism. (We suffer at the sight of *another's* suffering, and not at the thought of *ourselves* suffering as he does.) But Hume's *political* theory assumes that we are predominantly selfish and frequently foolish, the latter because of a marked tendency to prefer a lesser immediate good to a greater but more remote one. Men are genuinely sympathetic and benevolent in the context of their families and friends but their sympathy is typically not strong enough to have a wider operation. Moreover, men are *partisans* in their political behaviour, and their egoism is consequently less liable to restraint. Those who share a common interest will applaud a man whenever he promotes it, and this applause will render him indifferent to the opinions of others. 'Honour' is a strong restraint on individual man in his personal and private relationships but not on the partisan in his dealings with members of competing groups.

A similar view was expressed, among others, by the Protestant theologian Reinhold Niebuhr, who advanced the thesis that 'a sharp distinction must be drawn between the moral and social behaviour of individuals and of social groups, national, racial and economic....'[2] He continues:

> Individual men may be moral in the sense that they are able to consider interests other than their own in resolving problems of conduct, and are capable, on occasion, of preferring the advantages of others to their own. They are endowed by nature with a measure of sympathy and consideration for their kind.... But all these achievements are more difficult, if not impossible, for human societies and social groups. In every human group there is less reason to guide and to check impulse, less capacity for self-transcendence, less ability to comprehend the needs of others and therefore more unrestrained egoism than the individuals, who compose the group, reveal in their personal relationships.[3]

Niebuhr is particularly concerned to attack the facile talk about intergroup accommodation which is so frequently to be found in the writings of social scientists and modern religious idealists:

> What is lacking among all these moralists, whether religious or rational, is an understanding of the brutal character of the behaviour of all human collectives, and the power of self-interest and collective egoism in all inter-group relations.[4]

Let me turn finally to Bertrand Russell and to the conclusion of a lecture which he gave on the occasion of receiving the Nobel Prize for Literature.

I do not wish to end upon a note of cynicism. I do not deny that there are better things than selfishness, and that some people achieve these things. I maintain, however, on the one hand, that there are few occasions upon which large bodies of men, such as politics is concerned with, can rise above selfishness, while, on the other hand, there are a very great many circumstances in which populations will fall below selfishness, if selfishness is interpreted as enlightened self-interest.[5]

It may not unnaturally be wondered why I have sought to buttress my initial statement by quotations from eminent authorities, particularly after describing it as 'hardly... contentious'. I have done this because after long experience of students here and elsewhere, and on recollecting my own opinions as a young man, I have come to the not very original conclusion that, among the young in particular, there is a widespread and deep resistance to the view that in their political behaviour men are predominantly selfish. One suspects that this resistance is sometimes due to an unconscious and illicit transition from 'ought' to 'is', from views about how people *ought* to behave to views about how they *do* behave. But more commonly, I suppose, the resistance is due to a conviction that, never mind how things have been in the past, they could be quite otherwise in the future, and would indeed *be* different if only the old immoral world were destroyed by sufficiently resolute endeavour – a conviction that has survived many generations of disappointment and which will no doubt survive many more. Whatever the explanation, however, the resistance is manifest, and in anticipating it I have felt a need to bring up some heavy intellectual artillery.[6]

FA 2. In current and foreseeable circumstances many of the (*actual and perceived*) *critical interests of Whites and Blacks* (*i.e. Africans*) *are and will remain irreconcilable within a common society.*

In a common society and assuming White rule, Whites will therefore fail to secure many of the critical interests of Blacks. In a common society and assuming Black rule, Blacks would therefore fail to secure many of the critical interests of Whites. Irreconcilable critical interests here include the protection of personal identity and dignity.

But there is an obvious need to clarify and justify this assumption. What are *critical* interests? What are *irreconcilable* critical interests? And why are *many* of the critical interests of Whites and Blacks irreconcilable within a common South Africa?

Crucial to the promotion of a group's interests are generalised means to numerous and important ends. Obvious examples are power and money because they are clearly means to the achievement of a very wide range of ends, including ends which are central to our lives – such as physical survival, a sense of identity and the development of abilities. This brings us to 'critical' interests. They are the things that people generally would prefer more of rather than less, since with more of them we are more likely to get whatever we may finally seek. They have been called 'primary goods' and are taken to include 'rights and liberties, powers and opportunities, income and wealth'.[7]

Interests are irreconcilable only when *two* things are true: (1) when the demands of the relevant parties are incompatible, and (2) when they cannot reach a settlement which seems just by standards common to them. To be irreconcilable it is not enough that interests should conflict; it is also necessary that there should be no possibility of a settlement which seems just to those involved. One further point: demands and standards of justice may change, so that interests which are irreconcilable at one point in time may cease to be so at another.

Let us now look at our own society and provide justification for the statement that *many* of the critical interests of Whites and Blacks are irreconcilable within a common South Africa.[8] This raises what is surely the most important question in our politics. But it must first be noted that (1) our statement is *factual*, not evaluative, (2) we are not making predictions about the unforeseeable future and (3) to say there are irreconcilable interests is not to deny that there are common interests. Avoiding galloping inflation, for example, is in everyone's interests.

It is not difficult to see why, as we have defined them, many of the critical interests of Whites and Blacks are irreconcilable within the 'common area'. Whites seek to maintain their economic standards, their freedoms, their power, their cultural identities, their status. They believe they are entitled to these things partly because they are accustomed to them and have come to expect them and to depend on them. Blacks, on the other hand, seek the dominant political position to which they think their numbers entitle them, the land and opportunities of which they feel deprived, a status more conducive to a sense of their own worth. If they get much of what they most of all want the Whites cannot get much of what they most of all want; and the contrary is also true. Many important claims of Blacks and Whites are therefore incompatible and in the foreseeable future there is no possibility of a settlement which would seem just to both groups. In brief, many of their critical interests are irreconcilable.

FA 3. In respect of the protection or promotion of critical interests which are irreconcilable, political power cannot be shared.

This statement is true by definition, for to describe interests as irreconcilable simply *means* that with respect to them power cannot be shared. It may be wondered why if the statement is definitionally true – true by virtue of logic and the meanings of its terms – I bother to make it. The answer is simply that it is a useful tautology, reminding us that power can be shared only to the extent that interests *are* reconcilable, or bargainable.

But what do people mean when they speak of sharing power in our society? I take it that they usually have in mind such institutional devices as elections, enfranchisement and parliamentary representation. Yet if political power is understood as an ability to influence legislative and executive decisions, especially 'important' ones, then it is clearly possible for a person to have a vote, to be represented in Parliament, even to be in Parliament, and at the same time to be without power in any substantial sense. This is obviously the situation of many white South Africans. Equally it is possible for people to be voteless, etc., but nevertheless to have influence in the sense and to the extent that a government, in framing policy or planning legislative measures, feels it necessary to take account of their possible or likely reactions to anything it does. Black industrial workers have a measure of power in this sense, as do some foreign governments.

I don't at all wish to deny that enfranchisement at free elections can be crucial to the protection or promotion of critical interests. I wish only to make the elementary point that votes don't necessarily confer power and that votelessness cannot simply be equated with powerlessness.

To return to our original proposition, however, political power, when viewed as the capacity to affect 'significant' political outcomes, cannot be shared in respect of critical interests which are irreconcilable and for as long as they remain so. The word 'cannot' here is a *logical* cannot.

FA 4. The critical interests of Whites on the one hand and Coloureds and Asians on the other are not *irreconcilable within a common polity.*

In connection with this statement a critical though obvious distinction to make is between the interests of the National Party and the interests of Afrikaners, or Whites in general. It is not difficult to understand why the National Party is likely to continue to be opposed to the unqualified, or even qualified, enfranchisement of Coloureds and Asians on a common roll. Ruling parties in countries where elections are free are the world over not keen on strengthening the position of opposition parties, even when they may not be seriously threatened by doing so.

On the other hand, it is an obvious mistake simply to equate the interests of the National Party with the interests of Afrikanerdom, or Whites in general. It is clear that in the past this party has done a great deal to promote the interests of Afrikaners and has thereby gained the solid support of most members of the group. It also seems clear that the interests of Afrikaners are on the whole likely to be best served by the continuance in office of the National Party. But this does not mean that this party is incapable of making serious errors of judgement about how best to secure the interests it tends to represent, or of succumbing on occasion to the temptation to promote the narrow party interest at the expense of the broader interests of Afrikanerdom. My own view is that the interests of Whites in general, as of Coloureds and Asians, would best be served by enfranchising the latter groups on a qualified or universal basis.

However, I also think that this is at best a distant prospect. What is much more likely is the slow establishment of genuine community legislative bodies for Coloureds and Asians with some representation on a joint cabinet council which is more than merely consultative. Whether this will be done in such a way as to give these groups real control over their own affairs and real influence in matters of common concern seems doubtful. It is also unlikely that any such arrangements would for long satisfy these groups, the bulk of whose members, the Coloureds particularly, wish to avoid the stigma of enforced separateness and to participate on an equal basis in a common society and polity. As for the establishment of independent states for Coloureds and Asians, this idea scarcely makes any sense given the fragmented character and geographical dispersion of these communities.

It may be argued that my view that White, Coloured and Asian interests are reconcilable within a common polity is rendered invalid by the higher average population increase rates of Coloureds and Asians. According to the most recent projections they will together outnumber the Whites by 2020. But in present circumstances and given the urgent need to come to an accommodation with the Coloureds especially, it would be foolish to permit such long-range and uncertain considerations to have any significant influence on decisions to be taken in the present. In any event, if Coloureds were to constitute a majority of the electorate, there is no reason to believe that they would act so as to threaten vital White interests by seeking to accommodate

Black political demands. Indeed, considerations of self-interest and self-protection would be likely to lead them to resist Black rule as vigorously as it is currently resisted by the vast majority of Whites. (And the same applies with even more obvious force in the case of the Asians.) It may sound cynical, though it is not, to say that while they remain similarly treated, Coloureds will increasingly make common cause with the Blacks and even identify themselves as Black, but that if they were to enjoy the same legal rights as Whites, they would soon become rather less concerned to advance the interests of non-Homeland Africans.

But there remains the key question of whether in fact the partial or full enfranchisement of Coloureds and Asians on a common roll is consonant with the interests of the National Party. Suffice it to say that with so large a parliamentary majority, it is difficult to believe it impossible for the ruling party to contrive means of greatly improving the political position of Coloureds and Asians without seriously risking electoral defeat. However, in embarking on such a course, there may be possibly adverse consequences for party unity and for the positions of particular leaders about which I have not sufficient knowledge.

FA 5. In current and foreseeable circumstances liberalism in the classical English sense is in our society wholly incompatible with universal adult suffrage in a common polity, whatever constitutional safeguards may exist.

The first question to take up is what is meant by 'liberalism in the classical English sense'. We shall then go on to examine the relations between universal adult suffrage and classical English liberalism, dealing first with the problem in general terms and then within the context of South Africa.

To say that a person is a liberal is not very illuminating since there are different sorts of liberalism just as there are different conceptions of liberty. For the classical English liberal, our social and political freedom consists in the absence of deliberately imposed obstacles to our actual and potential choices, and liberalism is a doctrine which emphasises the restriction to a minimum of the coercive powers of government. He tends to distinguish carefully between *his* conception of liberty – liberty as non-interference – and the conception of liberty as the *ability* to satisfy our desires. A person may be able to do what he is not free to do because a law prohibits him from doing it, or he may be unable to do what he is free to do because nobody is trying to stop him from doing it.

The dislike of the English liberal for the conception of freedom as ability or power is primarily due to his determination that the cardinal value of liberty should not be exploited by collectivists to justify large amounts of state intervention. If liberty is viewed as power, there is no end to the number of legislative measures which can be justified as extending the range of choice of persons, or their effective power to do whatever they may wish. The result could be the destruction of individual liberty in the name of a spurious notion of liberty. It must be emphasised, however, that classical English liberals are not committed to denying that the limited provision by government of skills and opportunities is desirable; they are only saying that such enabling activities should not be represented as promoting freedom.

English liberalism, then, is the doctrine of the minimal state. The English liberal has sought freedom for the individual from the constraints of government because he has viewed the individual as the final repository of ethical values, and the state as merely an instrument for the protection of the interests of individuals. But he is not, of course, an anarchist and has always qualified his demand for freedom from the constraints of government by recognising that there are limits to the extent to which such constraints can be reduced, if people are to be sufficiently protected against being harmed by one another.

The possibility of conflict between liberalism as the doctrine of the minimal state and universal adult suffrage has often been stressed – for example, by Benjamin Constant, John Stuart Mill, Alexis de Tocqueville and (among contemporaries) Isaiah Berlin. While it is recognised that universal adult suffrage, in given societal contexts and when combined with freedom of election, provides the best guarantee of individual liberty, it is also understood that in other societies it may be deeply inimical to the promotion or protection of such liberty. Thus Berlin writes:

> ... there is no necessary connexion between individual liberty and democratic rule. The answer to the question 'Who governs me?' is logically distinct from the question 'How far does government interfere with me.' ... The connexion between democracy and individual liberty is a good deal more tenuous than it seemed to many advocates of both.[9]

For those who believe that governments should consider all interests equally, the main value of democracy is as a means of producing sensitivity to the widest possible range of interests. This is for the obvious reason that with universal adult suffrage and freedom of election, governments have a strong inducement to attend to claims made by large numbers of people, since otherwise they may find themselves voted out of office. On the other hand, universal adult suffrage will not produce wide sensitivity to interests where elections are unfree, or where there are distinct permanent minorities whose interests can be safely disregarded.

Let us now turn to South Africa mindful of the fact that when we conjecture about the likely effect in our society of universal adult suffrage on personal liberty, we don't start from a position of minimum government, or maximum individual liberty. Indeed, there is clearly a great deal of governmental intervention both in our private lives and in the workings of our economy. We are therefore not concerned with the preservation of a liberal social order, which does not exist, but with the question whether in respect of individual liberty, universal adult suffrage may be expected to lead to its further diminution.[10] This question is critical for those who value individual freedom whether for its own sake or as an instrument of social progress or both.

It would seem to be of a high order of probability that the full enfranchisement of Blacks in a common polity would bring about the destruction of most of the limited freedom that currently exists. If the establishment of a Black government were preceded by a free and fair election, it is probable that this would be the last free and fair election for many years. And even if *per impossibile* freedom of election were to persist, the policy preferences of distinct permanent minorities – Whites, Coloureds and Asians – would consistently be voted down by the Black electorate, in so far as they regarded them as contrary to their interests or in retribution for the past.

It is frequently argued that the qualified enfranchisement of Blacks would obviate the worst effects of one-man-one-vote, including the further curtailment of social freedom. But Blacks would hardly settle for long for limited voting rights in a common polity and it is therefore a reasonable assumption that a qualified franchise would soon lead to mounting pressure, domestic and foreign, for universal suffrage. It is sufficiently evident that Blacks are finally interested only in the *transference* of power to themselves, not in *sharing* power with minority groups, whatever that might mean in practice. This would appear to be a simple and undeniable fact thinly concealed beneath the reassuring rhetoric of some Black leaders, and yet there is among many White 'liberals' a chronic refusal to admit it.

It is also argued that the possibly adverse consequences for freedom (among other social values) of Black rule could be avoided through constitutional devices of one kind or another that are designed to protect individual and minority rights – an entrenched bill of rights, a written and rigid constitution, a system of judicial review, etc. But constitutional arrangements, like democratic institutions, normally work only in so far as there is a pervasive will to make them work and such a will exists only where there is a strong tradition of constitutionalism. A Black regime in South Africa, lacking a constitutional tradition which might protect individual rights, is hardly likely to respect a constitution which imposes restraints or fetters upon the free expression of its will. After all, what ultimately matters in politics is the actual distribution of power and, particularly where power is narrowly concentrated, the ends pursued by those who are powerful.

Universal adult suffrage in South Africa is often equated with 'Black majority rule'. But like 'White minority rule' the phrase is ambiguous. It is possible – indeed, a standard situation – to have Black majority rule in a society in the sense that Blacks are in a majority and that those whole rule are Black, without its being the case that the Black majority indirectly controls or even significantly influences the use of the supreme legislative and executive powers. What typically happens is that effective control falls into the hands of a well-organised minority within the Black majority, a minority which then simply imposes its will on society. It has been argued that any machinery of majority rule is bound to put effective control into the hands of a minority, even in the mature 'Western' democracies. Be that as it may, however, the real choice before South Africa lies not between 'White minority rule' and 'Black majority rule', but between one form of minority rule or another. 'Black majority rule' in any substantial sense is in South Africa a spurious alternative, and doubt about the truth of this proposition should not be induced by the frequency with which the phrase is employed. The phrase is a slogan which does not survive analytical probing but which nevertheless serves the rather obvious purposes of those who use it.

FA 6. The creation of wealth and the long-term improvement of living standards are greatly assisted by the maintenance of a free enterprise economy.

This statement is, of course, disputable and leads to the raising of questions which form the subject-matter of weighty tomes and international conferences. I shall have to justify it in rather cursory fashion and shall do so by briefly summarising the essentials of Hayek's position as a liberal economist, a position with which I am in substantial agreement.[11] Hayek writes:

Liberalism ... derives from the discovery of a self-generating or spontaneous order in social affairs ..., an order which [makes] it possible to utilize the knowledge and skill of all members of society to a much greater extent than would be possible in any order created by central direction, and [reflects] the consequent desire to make as full use of these powerful spontaneous ordering forces as possible.[12]

Crucial to Hayek's argument is the irremediable ignorance of individual persons concerning many of the factors on which the attainment of their ends depends, an ignorance that increases with the growth of knowledge: for the larger the sum total of human knowledge, the smaller the share that any one individual can absorb.[13] If we wish to make the best use of our incomplete, dispersed knowledge, we need an impersonal mechanism to integrate our individual actions. It is this mechanism that the spontaneous order provides.

An 'arrangement' designed to serve particular human purposes requires an organiser and is therefore more restricted in respect of the use of knowledge than a spontaneous mechanism. It is necessarily confined by what can be known to the organiser. But where it is a matter of employing limited resources known to an organiser in the service of a unitary hierarchy of ends, an arrangement will be the more successful method. On the other hand, where the task involves the use of knowledge scattered among and available only to thousands or millions of separate individuals, the use of spontaneous ordering forces will be more effective.[14]

To its radical or socialist critics, the prime defect of the end-independent, spontaneous order is that it does not ensure that for society as a whole the more important comes before the less important. Hayek's answer is that, save in limited contexts, we are not in agreement about specific ends, and we cannot settle disputes by reference to some unitary conception of relative 'merits' or 'needs'.

... it is due to the fact that we do not enforce a unitary scale of concrete ends, nor attempt to secure that some particular view about what is more and what is less important governs the whole of society, that the members of ... a free society have as good a chance successfully to use their individual knowledge for the achievement of their individual purposes as they in fact have.[15]

The difference between what is called a national or world 'economy' and a firm, a household, or a farm, illustrates Hayek's distinction between a spontaneous mechanism and an organisation. The small purpose-governed organisation is an 'economy' properly so-called because it is a deliberate arrangement of a given stock of resources in the service of a unitary hierarchy of specific ends. On the other hand, so fundamentally different are organisations serving individual purposes from the spontaneous order of the market that Hayek thinks it highly unfortunate that the same word 'economy' has come to be applied to both. Hayek proposes that the word 'catalaxy' be used to describe the market order. This confusion of terminology has obscured the vital difference between the two and has led to the view that the market ought to be made to serve a unitary scale of particular ends. But this is impossible as well as undesirable. Since the spontaneous order of the market, resulting from many interacting economies, rests on reciprocity or mutual benefits rather than on common purposes, it 'cannot be judged in terms of a sum of particular results'.[16] What can be said, however, is that through *competition* the spontaneous order tends to minimise the cost of production.

Hayek's belief in the efficiency of the impersonal mechanism should not be taken to imply any acceptance of the doctrine of *laissez-faire*.[17] A liberal state will do a great deal to promote competition by voiding all agreements in restraint of trade and by exposing to damages all actions designed to enforce them. Hayek is opposed to all measures of economic control which cannot be enforced by general rules because they are by their very nature discretionary and arbitrary. The most important of these are 'measures designed to control the access to different trades and occupations, the terms of sale, and the amounts to be produced or sold.'[18] Controls over prices and quantities are necessarily arbitrary, and they make it impossible for the market to function properly. But this does not at all mean that Hayek is an advocate of non-intervention in economic affairs. Provided it claims no exclusive rights in what it does, a government can do much to assist the spontaneous forces of a market order by providing an efficient monetary system, by supplying useful information, by supporting education, by preventing fraud, by enforcing contracts, by protecting property, by controlling pollution, and so on. There is, however, a presumption against state enterprises since it is very difficult to ensure that they enjoy no special advantages as against private business, such as subsidies or tax concessions. But if they compete on equal terms with private enterprise, there is room for some state enterprise in a free economy.

One final point before we leave Hayek's impressive defence of the

Deriving Policy for South Africa 361

free enterprise economy, He emphasises repeatedly the importance of the *service* functions of government. The market mechanism does not provide, or provide adequately, for all needs; and government, to the extent that the overall level of wealth permits, should intervene in order to help those who cannot earn a minimum income through it. But there are some important provisos: namely, that government should not possess a monopoly in the provision of welfare and that it should not try to make the market itself serve some ideal of distributive justice. If government does this, it will simply reduce the total wealth in which all can share.

II VALUE ASSUMPTIONS (VAs)

It would be possible to list a host of value assumptions but I shall be as parsimonious as possible. After all, I am primarily concerned with a rational procedure for deriving policy prescriptions in critical issue-areas. I should add that while I shall be applying my value assumptions in the South African context, the values themselves are applicable in all contexts.

I assume that it is morally desirable for a government to promote:
VA 1. Maximum individual freedom
By 'freedom' I mean absence of restraint. In social and political discussion, a man is said to be free in so far as he is not restrained by others from doing what he chooses, or might choose, to do. By 'maximum individual freedom' I mean that individuals should be as little restrained as is compatible with the prevention of harm to others.
VA 2. Equality and justice
By 'equality' I mean that people ought not to be treated differently unless there are sufficient reasons for doing so. The principle is therefore compatible with inequalities of treatment, provided they are based on relevant differences among the people who are differently treated. Thus differences in treatment based on differences in need or desert or ability may well in given contexts be compatible with equality as a social ideal.

'Justice' may be defined in terms of equality. It exists in a society to the extent that all inequalities of treatment are susceptible of sufficient justification.
VA 3. Maximum national wealth and minimum civilised conditions of life
The USA has the highest average living standards in the world but a great deal of poverty. The countries of Western Europe have lower

average living standards but very little poverty. Hence the need to maintain a minimum as well as to maximise the average.

VA 4. Internal and external security

This value assumption needs little elucidation. But in case of possible misunderstanding, it should perhaps be said that promoting domestic peace means minimising violence both within and between all sections of a society.

VA 5. Protection of identity and self-respect

People do not typically develop a sense either of personal identity or of self-respect apart from their group identifications.[19] In so far, therefore, as they have a right to preserve their identity and self-respect, and they do, they have a right to protect group identities. I take it, for example, that Afrikaners and Jews have a right to protect their group identities, a right which extends far beyond mere physical survival and includes the survival of Afrikanerdom and Jewry as cultural and identity-conferring phenomena.

III POLICY DERIVATIONS (PDs)

This brings me to the critical task of deriving policy prescriptions from my assumptions. But before doing this, I must make a few preliminary points:

1. *Social principles compete.* More equality may mean less liberty, more liberty less security, more security less national wealth. Consequently one may have to weigh principles against one another in making judgements about desirable policy in concrete situations. One cannot rank social principles so that one is always preferred to another. If we could place them in an ordered list, so that each principle had a unique weighting in a hierarchy of moral importance, then the problem of conflict between competing principles would never arise. No such ordering, however, is possible.

2. There is the possibility of conflict *within* as well as *between* some of my social principles, as they are stated above. What promotes one man's identity may damage another's self-respect, what promotes internal security may endanger external security (and conversely), what promotes minimum civilised conditions of life may fail to secure maximum national wealth (and conversely). This problem could be resolved by breaking up my last three principles, but this would be tedious and also unnecessary provided one is aware of the possibilities of conflict within them.

3. The logical relations between assumptions and derivations vary greatly in their strictness from entailment through inference to intimation. When social values have to be weighed against one another in concrete situations, one may be looking for no more than intimations in deciding what policies to adopt.
4. When I come to the derivation of policies it will become clear that I often leave obvious and hardly contestable factual assumptions unstated. Thus it is hardly necessary to state that there is such a practice as 'petty' *apartheid* before stating that it should be eliminated.
5. After stating my policy derivations I shall indicate symbolically what the underlying assumptions are, and where there are assumptions that might be thought to run counter to derivations, I shall also indicate what these are. Where the bearing of assumptions on derivations may be unclear, I shall say what I think it is.
6. The policy derivations are not listed in order of assumed importance.

PD 1. State intervention in the economy should be substantially reduced.
This policy prescription is derived from FA 6, VA 1 and VA 3.

PD 2. All laws which treat Coloured and Asian differently from Whites should be repealed.
This is derived from FA 4, FA 6, VA 1, VA 2, VA 3, VA 4 and VA 5. I include FA 6 and VA 3 because differential treatment here impedes material progress. I include VA 4 because differential treatment is an obvious cause of civil disturbance and also because our external security will be strengthened if Coloured and Asians wish to join in promoting it. I include VA 5 because legal equality would not here threaten anyone's personal identity and would at the same time promote dignity.

PD 3. 'Petty' apartheid should be eliminated.
This is derived partly from VA 1, VA 2 and VA 3. VA 3 is mentioned because the cost of 'petty' *apartheid* substantially reduces national wealth. But what about VA 4 and VA 5? It is often argued that by reducing inter-racial contact 'petty' *apartheid* reduces the likelihood of racial conflict. But whatever the merits of this argument may be – and I don't think much of it – it must be clear that on balance at any rate 'petty' *apartheid* is subversive of internal and external security. It engenders frustrations, indignities and hostile reactions which are potent sources of trouble both from within and from without our society. In respect of VA 5, 'petty' *apartheid* does little to protect identity and does much to undermine self-respect.

PD 4. The Mixed Marriages Act and the section of the Immorality Act

which prohibits miscegenation should be repealed.
This is derived from VA 1 and VA 2. But what about VA 5? It can hardly be argued that there is something inherently damaging to self-respect about marital or sexual relations between members of different ethnic groups. However, it is often claimed that this legislation is necessary to protect group identities. In this connection it is worth noticing that there are very few 'mixed' marriages in the USA, where they are not prevented by law, and that in our society there is no evidence that miscegenation has decreased since it was made illegal.

PD 5. Job reservation should be abolished.
This is derived from FA 6, VA 1, VA 3 and VA 5. FA 6 and VA 3 are included because job reservation restricts free competition and thereby hinders material progress. VA 5 is included because reserving jobs on a racial basis is incompatible with dignity or self-respect.

PD 6. Blacks (Africans) should be denied voting rights in parliamentary elections in the 'common area'.
This no doubt highly controversial policy prescription comes from FA 1, FA 2, FA 3, FA 5 and VA 5. But what about VA 1, VA 2, VA 3 and VA 4? Assuming full enfranchisement of Blacks and with respect to VA 1 and VA 3, I would say that under Black rule our society as a whole would probably have substantially less freedom and less wealth than it has now. (Partial enfranchisement, on the other hand, would serve only to intensify pressure for universal franchise.) As for VA 2 and VA 4 and assuming full enfranchisement, I would say that under Black rule our society would become more equal, but that the equality would be one of oppression, and we would be likely to be torn for many years by civil strife.

PD 7. Local governments in Black urban residential areas should be given greatly increased powers and functions and should be 'Africanised'.
This is derived from VA 2, VA 4 and VA 5. VA 4 is mentioned because there is more likely to be peace in Black urban areas if these areas are policed by Blacks working under their own elected authorities.

PD 8. The Black 'homelands' should be fully consolidated and encouraged to become independent and every effort should be made to help them become economically viable societies.
This is derived primarily from VA 2 and VA 5.

PD 9. The position of permanent urban Blacks should be officially recognised and they should enjoy freehold rights in respect of the ownership of property.
This is derivable from all the value assumptions when fully elab-

orated. VA 3, VA 4 and VA 5 are relevant because a stable urban Black population enjoying family life and their own homes would be conducive to dignity, domestic peace and minimum civilised conditions of life.

PD 10. Civil liberties and the rule of law should be vigorously promoted.
This is derived primarily from VA 1. But there is obviously the unstated premiss that in the present situation the operation of these values is highly circumscribed.

PD 11. There should be equal pay for equal work.
I derive this from VA 2, VA 4 and VA 5. VA 4 and VA 5 are relevant because unequal pay for equal work is clearly a prime source of anger and humiliation.

PD 12. People should have equal opportunities to achieve success in the careers of their choice.
I derive this from FA 6 and from all my value assumptions. FA 6 is relevant because through the most efficient mobilisation of talent, equality of opportunity promotes wealth and the improvement of living standards.

PD 13. Provision should be made for much more adequate welfare services.
I derive this from VA 3, VA 4 and VA 5.

PD 14. The security of all people in their persons and possessions should be more adequately protected by improving the capacities of law-enforcement agencies.
I derive this from VA 1 and VA 4. The issue is of particular urgency for urban Blacks. VA 1 is included because people cannot enjoy liberty unless others are prevented from harming them. One man's freedom may be another's unfreedom; freedom for the pike is unfreedom for the minnow.

PD 15. Defence expenditure should be sufficient to provide us with a capability adequate for dealing with the most likely forms of internal and external war.
I derive this primarily from VA 4, but, given my assumptions about the probable consequences of Black rule in a common society were it to occur, VA 1, VA 3 and VA 5 are also relevant. (Against conventional attack by a major communist power, there is scarcely any defence, but such an attack is in the foreseeable future very unlikely to occur.)

It is obvious that many critical policy-areas have had to be left unconsidered, such as residential segregation, freedom of movement, decentralisation, education and foreign policy. But I hope I have succeeded in disclosing what I believe to be the best framework within which issues of public policy can be fruitfully approached.

NOTES

1. David Hume, 'One the Independence of Parliament', in *Essays, Moral, Political and Literary*.
2. Reinhold Niebuhr, *Moral Man and Immoral Society* (New York and London, 1934) p. xi.
3. Ibid.
4. Ibid., p. xx.
5. Bertrand Russell, *Human Society in Ethics and Politics* (London, 1954) p. 174.
6. Concerning the capacity of the young to understand politics Michael Oakeshott has written:

   ... politics is an activity unsuited to the young, not on account of their vices but on account of what I at least consider to be their virtues.... Everybody's young days are a dream, a delightful insanity, a sweet solipsism. Nothing in them has a fixed shape, nothing a fixed price; everything is a possibility, and we live happily on credit. There are no obligations to be observed; there are no accounts to be kept. Nothing is specified in advance; everything is what can be made of it. The world is a mirror in which we seek the reflection of our own desires. The allure of violent emotions is irresistible. When we are young we are not disposed to make concessions to the world; we never feel the balance of a thing in our hands.... We are not apt to distinguish between our liking and our esteem; urgency is the criterion of importance; and we do not easily understand that what is humdrum need not be despicable. We are impatient of restraint; and we readily believe ... that to have contracted a habit is to have failed.... (See *Rationalism in Politics* (London, 1962) pp. 195–6.)

   There is a profundity in this statement in spite of the elements of exaggeration and parochialism. We were not all Cambridge undergraduates and some young people have to endure harsh circumstances of life.
7. See John Rawls, *A Theory of Justice* (Oxford, 1972) p. 62. Rawls also includes self-respect as a primary good.
8. In response to an earlier and much shorter version of this essay, Dr van Zyl Slabbert questions 'whether it is possible to have an agreed "rational policy derivation" between two groups with "irreconcilable interests"' (White and Black). But I didn't say that *all* or even *most* of the critical interests of White and Black are irreconcilable. What I did say was that 'in current and foreseeable circumstances *many* of the (actual and perceived) critical interests of White and Black ... are and will remain irreconcilable

within a common society' (my italics). The prime purpose of this article was to get at policies which would promote the vital interests of Blacks, while at the same time being compatible with, or conducive to, the protection of vital White interests. (See Dr Slabbert's article and my rejoinder in *The Argus*, 5 May and 10 May 1977.)

9. Isaiah Berlin, *Four Essays on Liberty* (London and New York, 1969) pp. 130–1.
10. But it becomes clear later, when we have disclosed our value as well as factual assumptions, that we are concerned with the *promotion* of a liberal social order.
11. I have already done this in Anthony de Crespigny and Kenneth Minogue (eds), *Contemporary Political Philosophers* (New York, 1975) pp. 52ff.
12. F. A. Hayek, *Studies in Philosophy, Politics and Economics* (London, 1967) p. 162.
13. F. A. Hayek, *The Constitution of Liberty* (Chicago, 1960) p. 26.
14. F. A. Hayek, *The Confusion of Language in Political Thought* (London, 1968) p. 14.
15. *Studies in Philosophy, Politics and Economics*, op. cit., p. 165.
16. *The Confusion of Language in Political Thought*, op. cit., p. 29.
17. In *The Road to Serfdom* Hayek writes:

> There is ... all the difference between deliberately creating a system within which competition will work as beneficially as possible, and passively accepting institutions as they are. Probably nothing has done so much harm to the liberal cause as the wooden insistence of some liberals on certain rough rules of thumb, above all the principle of *laisser-faire*.

See *The Road to Serfdom* (London, 1944) p. 13.

18. *The Constitution of Liberty*, op. cit., p. 227.
19. In this connection it is interesting to note a statement by Sigmund Freud:

> Whenever I felt an inclination to national enthusiasm I strove to suppress it as being harmful and wrong. ... But plenty of other things remained over to make the attraction of Jewry and Jews irresistible – many obscure emotional forces, which were the more powerful the less they could be expressed in words, as well as a clear consciousness of inner identity, the safe privacy of a common mental construction.

See Erik H. Erikson, *Identity, Youth and Crisis* (New York, 1968) p. 20.

19 South Africa – a Black Viewpoint

Percy Qoboza
Editor, The World

I SEPARATE DEVELOPMENT UNACCEPTABLE AND UNWORKABLE

Events of the past few months have served to confirm what Blacks have been telling White South Africa over the years – that the policy of separate development is unacceptable and unworkable. This is probably one of the most significant developments in the entire history of the country.

We all know that we have come a long way from the undisguised racism of the apartheid era of Dr D. F. Malan and his 'pure race' policies. These were followed by Dr H. F. Verwoerd's dream of separate freedoms and these, in turn, by Mr B. J. Vorster's policy of multi-national development which he sees as differentiation, not discrimination. The state has now been reached where the political semantics of the day centre on 'plural democracy', a term first attributed to Dr Connie Mulder, leader of the National Party in the Transvaal.

II CONSULTATION ESSENTIAL FOR DERIVING NEW POLICIES

On each of these occasions, when the policy in its current form came to a dead end and circumstances demanded that it be revamped, only Whites went back to the drawing-board. There were no consultations whatever with Blacks. The implication always was, and still is, that the White man, the defender of civilisation and Christianity, knows best. He has been vested by the Creator with the sacred duty of upholding decent standards against the barbarism of the uncivilised hordes of Blacks.

This is how Blacks have been expected to perceive themselves over the decades, and this is how they are expected to perceive themselves to this day. But after the civil unrest of last year this is no longer a feasible proposition. The Black man is no longer prepared to play a passive role in his own country. People are beginning to realise that the Black man has no intention of allowing these popular myths about him to dominate political thinking and the ordering of South African society.

Last year, through the death of 600 of their brothers, Blacks throughout the country finally said to their White compatriots, 'We are sick and tired of being told what is good for us'. Indeed, they were saying that the time for negotiating alternative policies had arrived, that the White man's policies were his own creation and quite unacceptable to Blacks.

III HOMELANDS, TOWNSHIPS AND BLACK LEADERS

What is particularly galling is that Blacks in the White areas of South Africa are there simply to minister to the needs and comforts of their White masters. If they demand a say in the way their country is being run, they are told to go to the homelands where they can have all the say they want! Eventually, to compensate for this state of affairs, the government decided to grant the urban Blacks what they call Urban Bantu Councils but which the Black masses in the townships have dubbed 'Useless Boys Clubs'. This name is very apt, because these councils have only advisory powers: the real power with regard to the administration of urban Blacks remains in the hands of government agencies called Bantu Administration Boards. But since we regard ourselves as neither Bantu nor 'urban Blacks', but South African Blacks, these bodies have been of only marginal significance in our lives. Indeed, in a city such as Soweto, with more than a million people, only 11 per cent bothered to vote in the last elections called to elect members of these bodies. More significantly, the present chairman of the Soweto Urban Bantu Council, Mr David Thebehali, whom White South Africans fondly call the 'mayor' of Soweto, drew only 68 votes in a constituency in which almost 10,000 people were entitled to vote! Yet he won, beating his opponent by one vote. This is the man who, the world is glibly told, represents the people of Soweto. Hardly a week passes without him appearing on the South African Broadcasting Corporation's radio or TV programmes where he is presented as the 'true voice of Soweto'.

Most of the homeland leaders fall within the same category. None of them, with the possible exception of Chief Gatsha Buthelezi, would ever have occupied a position of leadership in the Black community if they had not been created by the apartheid system. Until comparatively recently, the leaders of these Bantustans still dared to venture into Soweto for regular public meetings. During the past year none has dared to show his face in Soweto. Surely, this must be indicative of the mood and attitude of the people.

Transkei, the illegitimate child of separate development, is a monumental joke. Not a single country in the world has agreed to recognise the 'independence' of Transkei. In this attitude the world enjoys the support of millions of Black South Africans who will consider it an unfriendly act on the part of any country to recognise Transkei. As far as we are concerned, Transkei is part and parcel of South Africa and we believe the day will come when the people of Transkei will take their rightful place in a united South Africa.

All this should serve to underscore the growing division between the White establishment and Black South Africans. This alienation and its accompanying tensions will persist as long as White South Africans insist that they alone have the ability and the divine right to formulate a policy for coexistence in South Africa. The current crisis in South Africa will continue to simmer for as long as we have this unilateral system of government in which the White powers-that-be insist on consulting only those Blacks that are acceptable to them.

IV SOME QUESTIONS AND ANSWERS

In all my years I have never once come across any responsible Black leader holding the view that the Whites of South Africa are expendable or that they should be driven into the sea, as the saying goes. On the contrary, we have always stated that Whites are South Africans and that they have the right to coexist with us in a common fatherland. At the same time, however, we have insisted that all of us, both White and Black, must meet around a conference table to devise a formula for coexistence which will be acceptable to all of us. And yet, many noble Black men have been silenced by the country's security laws for saying exactly this. Today, many are called communists simply because they believe in the dignity of man. Many have been labelled agitators simply because they have advocated a society in which merit, not colour, will be the criterion for a man's advancement and rewards. Indeed, those Blacks who have been subjected to all sorts of punitive measures are precisely the leaders to whom the government should now be talking. The real danger inherent in the South African situation is that when the time comes when the White establishment is compelled to talk to Black leaders, there will be no one to talk to. And, believe me, our troubles will really start on the day that happens.

In the light of all this, I can but express my concern and alarm that once again Blacks are excluded from the current debate and deliberations on the future of the country, which are the order of the day not only in government but also in academic and business circles. Instead of talking to the people of Soweto, the government insists on going to Vienna, London and Washington to talk to representatives of the governments of Europe and the US. All these expeditions are an exercise in futility because the policies of South Africa are not saleable. They will only be saleable when they have the support of the Black people of South Africa, and they will only have that support if they are devised in consultation with the Black people. Indeed, we will continue to be isolated from the rest of the world until such time as we convince the world that both Black and White South Africans together are engaged in devising a new dispensation for the country.

We are a house tragically divided against itself at a time when the dangerous world we live in demands that we be united. Who among us cannot but be distressed when White South Africans regard Andy Young as an enemy while Black South Africans welcome him as a friend? Or when White South Africans are angry and disgusted at attacks on South Africa at the United Nations while Blacks in the same country rejoice at them?

Once again the cry is going up that overseas countries should maintain or even increase their investments in South Africa so that they may help generate an economic revival, for such a revival will permit South Africa to discharge its obligations to the Black peoples of this country. But how valid is this argument? A few years ago, the Black people helped the Whites to achieve an unprecedented economic boom. Who benefited? Only the Whites. They built luxurious homes with swimming pools while the Blacks, whose labour fuelled the boom, suffered poverty. What confidence can my people have in the free enterprise system if that system merely means White privilege and Black denigration?

These are the questions Blacks are asking at the moment.

We are told we should be patriotic, we should work for our country. But how can the Black people be expected to develop patriotism in a country that denies them even the most fundamental right – that of owning their own property in urban areas, a place to call home? Throughout history men have been inspired to take up arms and defend with their very lives what is their own – their own homes. But the Black people in the urban areas of South Africa have nothing they can call their own, nothing that they will defend with their lives. They have no stake in the country. How can you build patriotism in these circumstances?

V BLACK AND WHITE LOVE FOR OUR COUNTRY: HOPES FOR THE FUTURE

South Africans often tell of how they defended democracy in the Second World War, and even died for their country. What they conveniently forget is that hundreds of Blacks fought alongside them and that many of these Blacks laid down their lives to eradicate once and for all Hitler's brand of racism. Two of my uncles were among those who lost their lives. They made the supreme sacrifice to destroy racism once and for all. Yet it seems that their sacrifice may have been in vain, for I their nephew have become the victim of a new brand of racism. What kind of patriotism is expected of us?

Let me hasten to assure you that our people love South Africa. The last thing we would like to see destroyed by strife and confrontation is this beautiful country so richly endowed with resources sufficient for the happiness and prosperity of all her people. This accounts for the patience which we have shown over the years. We have always hoped and believed that the authorities would realise the folly of their ways. So, despite the extreme indignities inflicted on us, we still managed to smile and extend a hand of friendship. One day historians will conclude that the human endurance of Blacks in South Africa was peerless and without precedent. Once General J. C. Smuts said that Blacks in South Africa had the patience of a donkey. Unfortunately, the goodwill behind that patience is being frittered away.

And yet I still believe that we have not gone beyond the point of no return. I still believe that we can turn frustration into hope. We can still douse the flames of anger and bitterness that have been raging through Soweto and other parts of South Africa. There is still time to establish genuine understanding among all the peoples of South Africa. For it is never too late to do the right thing. It is never too late to try to transform South Africa into a country with justice and dignity for all. It is never too late to try to build a country in which people of all races can live together in peace and mutual respect.

We have the power and the resources to transform this unjust and racial society into a just and non-racial society. There is no short cut to such a dispensation. It will not be easy to achieve, for it will not be easy to dismantle three hundred years of White domination and substitute a free society which attaches no value to the colour of a man's skin. We do not even begin to do this if, as we are still doing today, we insist on identifying those things that divide us. What we should be doing is to identify and emphasise those things that unite us. Some people continue to harp on the cultural differences which they profess to detect between Black and White in this country. Now, I would like to know from you, have you today noticed any cultural differences between you and me that could possibly justify my being relegated to the ghettos of South Africa? Those who habitually postulate these alleged differences are merely compounding our problems and eventually they will have to suffer the most severe judgement of history, for in the course of the ages they will become known as the men who let South Africa down in her hour of need.

Finally, I must confess that I cannot pretend that I have answers to all South Africa's problems. I do not. But I do know that if we could sit down at that conference table, we would find the solutions to the problems facing the nation today. Together we have built South Africa to what she is today. Together we have the responsibility to ensure that she survives to become a truly great nation.

20 The Restoration of Human Rights: a Means Towards Achieving Social Justice in South Africa

B. G. Ranchod
Dean of the Faculty of Law, University of Durban-Westville

Never before has our legal system been exposed to such organised international and internal pressure for social justice. Fundamental and wide-ranging changes in the economic, social and political spheres are being demanded. It is a challenge to our system which I believe can no longer be ignored even if there are some who are foolhardy enough to believe it possible.

We in South Africa have lived side by side for centuries and are interdependent. To achieve social justice and develop a truly democratic society is something worth achieving but it is not free of obstacles. The obstacles that stand in the way of achieving social justice should, however, not be regarded as arguments against it.

What are the changes necessary to effect social justice and how can these be effected?

The former question is much easier to answer than the latter. Cosmetic changes alone will merely polarise our society further and so threaten peace and order. But a pragmatic two-pronged strategy should be devised to deal with the following matters:

1. Eliminate statutory race discrimination.

2. Restore fundamental human rights.
3. Create channels which enable the unenfranchised to have the opportunity to participate in the decision-making processes.
4. Ensure that all citizens are treated alike before the law, have the essential needs of life provided by the society and enjoy the same opportunities.
5. Enshrine these in a Bill of Rights to be embodied in the new constitution.
6. Create a special Constitutional Court which will have the power to pronounce on the validity of legislation in conflict with the Bill of Rights.

Unless these changes are effected speedily through the law, totalitarianism will triumph over democracy. Admittedly, it will be necessary to introduce systematic and radical reforms to our Constitution.

I AIM 1: ELIMINATE RACIAL DISCRIMINATION (STATUTORY)

Racial discrimination is not unique to South Africa but whilst an earnest attempt has been made in the rest of the world to eliminate it, the official government policy of apartheid has institutionalised the separation of the races. In terms of this policy the Coloureds were disenfranchised, representation of Blacks in Parliament removed and an arsenal of legislative measures introduced which entrenched White privilege and was essentially discriminatory in effect. As a result, the social climate in our land is conducive to racial discrimination, exploitation and injustice. Prejudice feeds upon injustice.

It is not a simple matter to repeal legislation enacted in terms of the apartheid policy nor can any individual or Court challenge the validity of such blatantly discriminatory laws. Our present constitution is based on the Westminster model. The powers of Parliament are practically absolute and unlimited. This is no longer acceptable in our society, as only a minority (Whites) enjoy the franchise and are solely represented in this, the most important decision-making institution.

The absence of any legal limitation on the powers of Parliament results in discriminatory legislation being beyond challenge. Our Courts attach great significance to the protection of individual rights, when the language of the statute leaves doubt as to the real intent of the Legislature, the Courts have tended to allow the interpretation which affords broader protection to individual freedom to prevail. But where the language is clear, effect has to be given to the intention of Parliament, regardless of the hardship caused.

The dilemma which confronts our Courts in matters involving important moral, social and political issues is reflected in the following passage from Mr Justice Diemont's (now Judge of the Appeal Court) address to law students.

> ... the controversial political legislation. This type of legislation obviously comes before the Court frequently. When it does, the judges find they have to deal with cases of hardship and they do make some new law. The rules of interpretation are elastic, one sugars the pill, and says politely that Parliament could never have intended to create an injustice of that nature. What is the result? The Act goes back to Parliament, and Parliament and the Bench become involved in a sort of legal ping-pong. In the next session, Parliament patches up the loopholes and fills the gaps. Soon after the Courts face another case of hardship and they find a further ambiguity and back the Bill goes to Parliament again. And so after a few years the original piece of legislation is hardly recognisable. ...

An accurate description of the position today is that 'once the courts are confronted with an Act of Parliament, all they can do is to ascertain its meaning if they can and then apply it as justly and mercifully as the language of the law permits.' The Courts can no longer be described as the guardians of civil liberties and the mainstay of the individual against governmental abuse of power.

The need to place legal limitations on the powers of Parliament will be discussed below in connection with the protection of human rights. Suffice it to mention, at this juncture, that in my Inaugural address delivered in 1975 I called for the introduction of a constitutional check on the legislative supremacy of Parliament. I argued that our judges need some standard, some durable and unyielding ideal which will compel them to rise above the prevailing prejudice, and this could take the form of an entrenched Bill of Rights.

For the present, Parliament alone can repeal discriminatory legislation. Several members of the Cabinet have publicly committed the Government to move away from discrimination, and in our present conditions the absolute powers of Parliament are largely vested in the Cabinet.

Before the outside world and, more important, the local population will accept that the Government is sincere in moving away from racial discrimination, there must be tangible evidence of a shift in policy. I would suggest that legislation in the following areas be amended or repealed without undue delay:

1. the abolition of all forms of petty apartheid,
2. repeal of the Prohibition of Mixed Marriages Act No. 55 of 1949 and the Immorality Act (Sec. 16) Act No. 23 of 1957,
3. the opening of private schools to all race groups,
4. the opening of all universities at the undergraduate level, subject to the sole decision of their respective Councils,
5. the acceptance of urban black representation on the Cabinet Council,
6. the restoration of the municipal franchise in metropolitan areas to all citizens,
7. the repeal of all legislation which hinders the operation of our free enterprise economy, such as job reservation, unequal pay, etc.

In addition there is an urgent need to train as many Indians, Coloureds and Africans as possible for the top positions in the Civil Service. In recent years there has been an immense flow of delegated legislation accompanied by a vast area of government operating outside Parliament being entrusted to statutory boards. A more equitable representation of all groups on such Boards can be achieved without this resulting in disorder.

Furthermore, the introduction of an independent radio and television service, which would have a Board of Governors representative of all racial groups, is needed to educate our people and encourage harmonious relationships between the races. As I have indicated earlier, the social climate in our country is conducive to racial discrimination. The media, by making available particular kinds of information and by the range of perspective which they present, by what they emphasise and what they play down, may help to influence public consciousness. Too often, the news coverage of race has been irresponsible. Men of colour are not always presented in news items as ordinary members of society, e.g., in reporting crime, where the offender is black, this is usally specifically mentioned and invariably included in the headline. Negative stories about black people have a real potential for harm because the distorted picture presented may be the only source of information available to the members of the dominant group.

The changes I have suggested should be embarked upon without delay, otherwise democratic change might not be possible. If the Cabinet agreed to such reforms, the West would, at this stage, still support South Africa and may well agree to invest in South Africa and probably be prepared to guarantee the protection of minorities in South Africa.

II RESTORATION OF FUNDAMENTAL HUMAN RIGHTS

In his address to the Conference on Plural Societies (May 1977) a senior member of the Cabinet stated that

> We in South Africa recognise that we have to do much towards the restoration of human rights. . . . South Africa openly committed herself, even in the United Nations Organisation, towards restoration of human rights, and by doing so we recognise the fact that the present society still has much scope for improvement in this respect.

Human rights can be broadly divided into two classes – civil and political on the one hand, and social and economic on the other. Rather than catalogue the rights men should enjoy (these can be conveniently found in the Universal Declaration of Human Rights) it will be more useful to focus our attention on those rights which should be regarded as fundamental and capable of immediate recognition and protection.

The protection of civil liberties is essential in a modern state. The law has a major role to play in achieving equal opportunity in our society, but for the law to be effective changes in our social and political fabric will be essential. After all, the belief in human rights is an ideology. What we should strive for are the following:

(*a*) curtail racism – there should be no gradation in legal status based on the circumstances of birth;
(*b*) equal protection before the law;
(*c*) the essential needs of life should be provided by the society – this will entail major changes in the economic sphere;
(*d*) freedom to enjoy all the advantages and opportunities conducive to human well-being;
(*e*) every citizen should be given the opportunity to participate in the decision-making process. If we aim to achieve a democratic

The Restoration of Human Rights

society some formal arrangements through which the individual may effectively participate in the affairs of his community will have to be devised. Rather than take fright at the idea of extending political rights to the black majority and be bogged down by a catalogue of fearsome problems which will be encountered, let us apply our minds to a solution. We must recognise that fundamental human rights are not adequately protected under our law and it is high time we did something about it!

A new constitutional structure modelled on the Swiss cantonal system as proposed by Mr Koornhof deserves consideration.

All the race groups should be involved in deciding on the future constitution of South Africa rather than the Whites alone deciding what is best for all.

A few thoughts which I have for such a constitution are:

(i) Major decentralisation of power in all matters of 'local' rather than national interest to the cantons.

(ii) Cantons should be organised on a territorial and not on an ethnic or race basis. Provision for 'city' cantons such as Soweto, Johannesburg and Durban should be made. All citizens residing in a canton should enjoy the franchise and be free to participate in the decision-making process. The rights of minorities should be protected by law.

(iii) Self-governing homelands which have not opted for independence could form part of this constitutional structure.

(iv) Each canton will have its own Canton Council which will provide the formal arrangement through which all citizens may effectively participate in the affairs of the group/community.

(v) From the ranks of the Canton Councils will come the representatives for a two-chamber Parliament having a Lower House, which will be widely representative of all the race groups on a proportional basis, and a Senate (Upper House) which will have an equal number of representatives from each canton. Parliament will only deal with matters of national interest such as foreign affairs, defence, communications, economic affairs, etc. The Senate will be empowered to reject legislation passed by the House of Representatives.

(vi) The premiership may rotate from canton representatives on the Senate.

(vii) Human Rights and the rights of minorities should be entrenched in a Bill of Rights. The Bill should be amended only by special majorities of Parliament which should be difficult to achieve.

Discrimination on the grounds of sex, race, religion and political beliefs should be prohibited.

The Rights listed in the European Convention on Human Rights could provide a useful guide on the other rights which should be included.

(viii) All rights in the Bill should be justiciable – i.e., capable of enforcement in a court of law.

(ix) A Constitutional Court for Southern Africa should be established. The creation of such a Court would have the following advantages:

(*a*) ensure that rights cannot be taken away or disregarded by the majority in Parliament. The Court should have the power to test the validity of legislation to ensure that it conforms with the Bill of Rights.

(*b*) The Court would be able to adapt the Constitution to changing circumstances and standards as in the United States of America.

The composition of the Court should broadly represent the various interest/canton groups.

21 The Devolution of Power in South Africa: Problems and Prospects

Lawrence Schlemmer
Director of the Institute for Social Research, University of Natal

I PLURAL DEVOLUTION OF POWER

By now it is fairly commonplace to hear or read of political commentators on South Africa predicting a 'plural' devolution of power for the country. One of the first major statements of this alternative came from the SPRO-CAS Politics Commission (Randall, 1973), and the theme has been reappearing ever since, among the most recent references to it is in a paper by Welsh at the 1976 Annual Council Meeting of the South African Institute of Race Relations (Welsh, 1976). The concept, in very broad, perhaps very vague, terms, has also been creeping into party political nomenclature – the Minister of the Interior recently referred to South Africa as a 'plural democracy', and currently an internal commission appointed by the South African Cabinet is considering ways of 'moving away' from the Westminster model of government. This development follows a rejection by the Cabinet of a recommendation in the report of the Theron Commission that the franchise on the South African parliamentary voters' roll be restored to the Coloured people.

In examining this development in South African politics, I will proceed in two ways. Firstly I will consider some of the fundamental political assumptions and motivations bearing upon the issue of a 'plural' devolution of power, in order to assess the degree to which it is compatible with some of the dominant underlying political imperatives; and secondly I will examine the practical feasibility of such developments in the light of the characteristics of the South African political arena.

Before proceeding, it is necessary to offer a broad, neutral definition of what we may mean by a 'plural' devolution of power. By this term I understand a process wherein effective political participation and decision-making power is progressively extended to groups other than the present White oligarchy by allowing political institutions and leadership in these groups, which currently exist separately from White parliamentary institutions, access to decision-making authority in regard to both their own 'communal' affairs and to major national resources and national affairs of common importance to all. It will be noted immediately that I have not included in this definition the granting of self-government or independence to territories which are referred to as homeland areas. While this development undoubtedly constitutes a devolution of power of a type, the powers extended cannot be claimed to represent a share in the control of major national resources. I need not convince anyone that the homelands are underdeveloped territories, small in size and without the relatively advanced infrastructural development which is characteristic of the common area of the country. Once independent, these territories will inevitably constitute economic 'dependencies' of South Africa, in the sense of major dependence on South African aid and employment for their citizens within the Republic. Such 'dependency' produces a variety of critical distortions in development which tend to maintain or deepen relative underdevelopment among the masses, as well as tending to encourage the emergence of local elites who are fundamentally supportive of the economic and political interests of the 'metropolitan' power (in this case South Africa). Since debate on this issue of dependency has waxed fast and furious in international forums in recent years, it is highly unlikely that the granting of independence to Bantustans will be accepted by the international community or by local critics as a true devolution of power. In this sense, the Transkei experiment has come 15 to 20 years too late to do South Africa much good in terms of international approval of 'internal' decolonisation. The policy is likely to be seen as the creation of 'hostage' states on the economic periphery of South Africa, functioning as labour pools for the central economy, and lacking bargaining power to redress inequality.

If, however, the granting of independence follows or accompanies the transfer of significant resources (in land, infrastructure and productive plant), then, of course, power over national resources would in effect be extended, and then the definition I have given may be qualified accordingly.

II REFORM WITHIN THE INSTITUTIONS OF THE COMMON SOCIETY

A suitable introduction to the first part of my argument is to ask why a 'plural' devolution of power? Why not reform within the institutions of the common society? The reason for posing these questions will become apparent in due course. In attempting to answer the questions some of the basic assumptions regarding political change in South Africa have to be explored briefly.

The viewpoint of the present government on the issue of political development has been stated and restated myriad times, i.e. that South Africa is a multinational society, thereby implying the presence of more than one national identity, and a variety of languages and cultures so diverse that absorption of all into a common society is impossible or undesirable. Inasmuch as this principle stands in super-prominence at the base of current policy-formulation, it represents an *ideology*, in the sense of being a more or less coherent set of ideas 'actively concerned with the establishment and defence of patterns of belief and value' (Geertz, 1973: 231).

Recourse to argument about culture and cultural diversity as justification for race policy has a long history in South Africa, as careful historical analysis by Welsh ably demonstrates (Welsh, 1972). He concludes that despite these arguments, 'segregation was *not* a response to "diversity", rather it was a response to the assumed threat posed by a growing class of acculturated Africans' (p. 52). No major African political movement, whether it be the African National Congress, the Pan African Congress, recent movements like the various organisations associated with the Black Consciousness movement, or even the Zulu-based 'Inkatha' movement, has accorded any relevance to the ethnic diversity *within* the African community, and all have laid claim to a stake in the common society and to South African nationhood. The Coloured people, for example, have a culture which is synonymous with 'White' culture (unless one misleadingly takes aspects of a 'culture of poverty' as one's reference). Numerous other arguments gainsaying the multinational assumption from the Black point of view may be adduced, for which space in this essay is inadequate.[1]

For these reasons one must assume that the policy principle of multinationalism is primarily an ideology which is rooted in White, or more exactly, Afrikaner political sensitivities and motives. In other words it *may* reflect a dominant concern with the maintenance and protection of national identity (*volksidentiteit*) among Afrikaners, who by virtue of superior numbers (among Whites) and superior political organisation as a corporate group, can afford a form of loose non-party political coalition with English-speaking South Africans without sacrificing identity. Adam (1976), however, rejects this view very firmly. He argues, following Dickie-Clark, Moodie, and de Klerk, that the ideology of multinationalism is but a shallow set of justifications for the maintenance of White and Afrikaner political hegemony in the common area: 'a tactical device, invented as a response to pressure, almost a last resort of token decolonisation....' (pp. 84/85). Hermann Giliomee (1974) largely supports the view that the 'ideologies of identity' among Afrikaners are closely bound up with the maintenance of power and privilege, even though their content has been shaped by historical threats to Afrikaner identity and socio-religious views on race. Identity, power and privilege are inextricably interwoven.

Adam makes the point that much of the literature on ideology fails to take account of the *degree of conviction* underlying the proposed claims and rhetoric (Adam, 1976: 84). My own research can shed some light on the extent of popular support for the goal of maintenance of cultural identity. In one study (Schlemmer, 1973) we found that, among Afrikaners generally, concern with identity and concern with privilege were completely interwoven. Among a minority of Afrikaans-speaking White subjects (< 20 per cent), however, a concern with group integrity and identity seemed to be a considerable degree unconnected with discriminatory attitudes. In a large nation-wide study among Afrikaans-speaking Whites[2] we found evidence of a great deal of pride in language and traditions (e.g., 86 per cent felt it important to safeguard and maintain language and traditions; 65 per cent were proudest of all of their language and culture when asked to give sources of pride and satisfaction). When comparisons were made, however, between the importance for respondents of advancing Afrikaans culture, serving the Afrikaans community and safeguarding the use of Afrikaans, on the one hand, and issues relating to the maintenance of stability on the other (unity and loyalty among all groups, justice for all groups), the latter issues emerged as a shade more important. Finally, when asked what the feared consequences of Black rule in South Africa might be, only 20 per cent mentioned threats to language and culture; the vast majority referred to threats to privilege and law and order.

My tentative conclusion, therefore, must be similar to that of Adam in the sense that it does not seem that there is a strong majority conviction underlying those ideological justifications which relate purely to Afrikaner identity. The policies may enjoy far stronger support as they bear upon the issue of *White* identity, but then this cannot validly be presented in the guise of 'cultural' identity; there is far greater cultural differentiation within the White group than there is between the White and Coloured Afrikaans-speaking South Africans, for example, and for that matter between middle-class English-speaking Whites and middle-class English-speaking Indians or Africans.

III PLURAL DEVOLUTION ON THE BASIS OF RACE AND PRIVILEGE

The point of this rather lengthy diversion is to attempt to show that we have to consider the possibilities of a 'plural' devolution of power not primarily on the basis of the empirical validity of the ideology of multinationalism, but rather more so on the basis of race and privilege. (This does not mean to say that a very sincere and committed concern with Afrikaans cultural identity does not exist as a motivation for policy. It is probably true to say that sincere ethnicism has played a key role in shaping the symbols of the ideology. I fear, however, that this orientation is dominant mainly among idealists and ideologues.) This conclusion is very important in considering the prospects of a devolution of power along separatist lines. It means, firstly, that the costs of the policy in material terms cannot be too great, and that any such policy cannot be based on the assumption of 'intrinsic support' from either Whites or Blacks. It will succeed or fail on the basis of the resources it can offer and the resources it can protect, and on the basis of the kind of negotiation which will take place as any such policy is implemented. (For an excellent discussion of the problems of a cultural interpretation of Separate Development see Van Zyl Slabbert, 1971.)

Stated bluntly, we have to consider the prospects for a devolution of power along plural lines because up to this point the politically dominant White leadership as well as very substantial proportions of the White rank and file would not countenance integration as a means of securing stability. Since 1948 the entire trend in legislation has been in a diametrically opposed direction, notwithstanding certain recent modifications to laws discriminating against access by Blacks to a limited range of social facilities. The government would be the first to argue that these moves do not represent structural integration or any moves in that direction.

Adam in his analysis (1976) as well as in earlier works has concluded that the lack of a widely supported 'ideology of dedication' (the phrase he uses in contrast to policies of expedience) among the Afrikaans corporate group may imply that there will be a responsiveness to pressure and a pragmatic accommodation of longer-term political realities in the future, even extending to alliances across the colour line. I would tend to agree with him if his conclusions (and my own tentative conclusion stated above) about the partly expedient nature of White ideology are correct, and if by alliances across the colour line he does not mean a reversion to political and social integration at rank-and-file level. Elsewhere I have argued (Schlemmer, 1976) that the White interests which are most potent as far as generating political expectations is concerned are a form of 'elaborated popular materialism'. These interests are centrally served by segregation, which secures for Whites a privileged life-style as regards access to a very wide range of amenities, opportunities and services. If one wishes to term the conflict in South Africa a class-conflict then in the modern South Africa it is at its most acute between an artificially inflated White lower-middle and middle class and Black proletarian and subsistence classes. My concurrence with Adam is therefore qualified by the proviso that alliances across the colour line are not seen by rank-and-file White voters as prejudicial to the interests I have described; and in this sense one should bear in mind that interests of this nature are short-term. I am very uncertain about how willingly White voters will be prepared to sacrifice popular privileges for the sake of longer-term stability – Adam places specific emphasis on a realistic calculation of longer-term interests.

One further qualification of Adam's argument that I would make is that the identity-based ideological justifications are not quite as shallow as he suggests. Identity concerns of an intrinsic kind are present among Whites, particularly Afrikaners – see my empirical results quoted earlier. Although their influence may not have been sufficiently strong to inject idealism into the implementation of policy, there is a rich and compelling symbolism in these perceptions of identity which may come powerfully to the fore in informing behaviour under conditions of severe threat to group interests.

This, then is the background against which I must attempt to assess the possibilities of a 'plural' devolution of power, or as it is more commonly referred to, a 'consociational accommodation'.

IV CONSOCIATIONAL ACCOMMODATION

Arend Lijphart (1974) observes that a plural society tends to be either democratic and unstable or not fully democratic and stable, unless the society has been stabilised by a substantial measure of agreement among the leaders of the various segments – in other words a consociational accommodation. Potentially disruptive conflicts in a deeply divided society are defused by the incorporation of leader groups into what Lijphart terms a 'grand coalition'. I believe that this is the kind of goal that many political observers and government politicians are setting for South Africa. Considerable optimism surrounds this type of thinking. Politicians at ministerial level have made reference to 'rule by consensus'. Others outside of the National Party framework (mainly within the centre parties) see this basic idea taking the form of various kinds of federal or confederal arrangements, with race rather than geographic units making up the federal divisions. The details of this thinking need not delay us at this point, because as I understand the situation one probably has to await the recommendations of the cabinet commission before details become apparent of the kind of forward thinking that is taking place. It is more appropriate, therefore, that one consider the difficulties and challenges which lie in the path of any moves toward an equitable consociational arrangement in South Africa.

Lijphart (1974) gives an excellent summary of the kind of preconditions which need to exist in a society if consociational accommodation is to prosper. He would be the first to agree that the requirements he mentions are not absolutes. Nevertheless, a brief consideration of the points he lists will assist us in assessing the probabilities of a successful devolution of power along these lines in South Africa. It is perhaps relevant to note that Lijphart, in the article referred to, discusses these requirements in the light of the problems in Northern Ireland, a country which must surely rank with South Africa as being among the more problematic of plural situations.

The first factor mentioned by Lijphart as being conducive to the establishment and success of consociational democracy is a *multiple balance of power*. South Africa, like Ulster, obviously does not possess this; in fact it has a very great racial disequilibrium. Attempts by the present government, through the policy of Separate Development, to divide the African majority into ethnic segments appears to have failed in so far as acceptance of tribalism as a category of political organisation is concerned (Mayer, 1974). In fact, 'Multinational Development' has probably generated more unity among the unenfranchised groups than would otherwise have been the case. While it has failed as an imposed mobilising ideology, ethnic organisation may creep in at the back door, however, simply as a result of the African people being deprived of any alternative focus of political identification (Mayer, 1972; Schlemmer, 1972). This has certainly not occurred to such an extent that ethnic political organisation has become rooted in the political culture of Africans, and in places like Soweto a determined value-informed resistance to fragmentation is maintained. At some future stage, it is possible that Whites, Coloureds, urban Africans and those non-urban Africans in homelands which have not taken independence could potentially provide a rough demographic equilibrium. Under the circumstances leaders may be willing to enter into the kind of association required. Further speculation is impossible, however.

Secondly, Lijphart mentions the need for *acceptance of the consociational model as a normative concept*. He points out that the Westminster pattern of government, with one party in power and a large opposition, is fundamentally competitive, whereas the consociational model is 'coalescent'. White politics in South Africa are markedly competitive, with almost a fetish being made of party affiliation. African politics, however, need not be in this mode. Recently Chief Gatsha Buthelezi, Chief Minister of the KwaZulu Homeland, has denounced the competitive Westminster system as being incompatible with African traditions. Certainly, traditional politics among Africans were not competitive, and the notion of debate among elders until consensus was achieved was fully entrenched. The picture in this regard, then, is somewhat mixed. One concern, however, is whether the examples set by independent Black Africa will produce a new normative model or not; this model being the non-competitive one-party system. It already has its adherents among Blacks in South Africa (cf. Bengu, 1976). It may be non-competitive but it is also authoritarian in most instances; a system totally different from the European multi-party model which has produced coalition government as a basis for accommodation in certain plural societies like Austria, the Netherlands, Belgium, etc.

The third condition mentioned by Lijphart is that some degree of over-arching national solidarity should be present. Here the picture is gloomy. The policies of the present government, reinforced by an ideology of fragmentation, have, to my mind, eroded goodwill towards Whites and loyalty to the system among Blacks down to the bedrock. A study by Worrall and Bertelsmann (*Rapport*, 14 Mar 71) and one of my own (Schlemmer, 1976b) amply demonstrate this.

Furthermore, as African opposition in South Africa hardens over time, the possible grounds for consensus that existed earlier in regard to the basic economic system in South Africa are being steadily weakened. Criticism of the capitalist system at a fundamental level is being expressed by more and more African opinion-leaders and organisations, including the Black People's Convention and Chief Gatsha Buthelezi. The proposed alternatives at this stage are still compatible with the dominant mode of production in South Africa, but thinking seems likely to polarise. A Marxist-capitalist ideological conflict cannot be ruled out for South Africa in the future.

Fourthly, Lijphart mentions the desirability of small size in relation to the availability of talented, prudent leadership; consociational arrangements in his view make heavy demands on leaders and talent. He concludes that Northern Ireland, for example, has an advantage in being a small country (1.5 million people) and hence reasonably simple to administer. However, he also suggests that the population may be below a certain minimum threshold for the supply of the necessary talent to manage the delicate tasks of leadership in a consociational setting. South Africa has even greater problems in this regard. It has a very large territory, an extremely complex administrative system, and a very small pool of educated people from which to draw talent for leadership. The emergence of leadership among Blacks has been inhibited, more particularly in the urban areas, and even White leadership has for decades functioned within a tradition of grass-roots 'mobilisation' rather than within a tradition of negotiation and sophisticated conflict-management. In South Africa, in my view, we have taken too speedy a recourse to repressive legislation as a means of controlling conflict. Our society has a notable lack of institutional channels for the resolution of conflict and tension.

Next, Lijphart observes that where lines of cleavage are particularly clear-cut and if there is little contact between members of different segments then the 'good fences make good neighbours' principle may apply, facilitating the kind of orientations appropriate to consociational accommodation. In South Africa, while lines of cleavage are very sharp due to the history of race conflict and differentiation, and legally entrenched in a very rigid form in recent years, other conditions do not apply. There is a very great deal of contact between the races in the economic sphere, and what is more, the contact involves superordinate-subordinate relations for Whites and Blacks in almost every sphere of employment. Hence, the South African situation is so structured to produce a maximum of day-to-day tensions between the segments in the plural society. The superimposition of racial status and employment status produces in fact a superimposition of race and class, a feature which, according to Lijphart's paradigm, is a distinct counter-indication as far as a consociational accommodation is concerned. Added to this we must take account of the fact that South Africa is a heavily bureaucratised society, and that at present in all Black urban areas the 'soulless bureaucracy' is represented by Whites (certainly as far as senior positions are concerned).

A point associated with the one just discussed is the extent to which the leaders of the various segments have the necessary leeway, as far as their own support is concerned, to enter into cooperation and make compromises with other leaders. Lijphart points out that very distinct lines of cleavage between subcultures often produce the kind of internal cohesion within subcultural segments which gives the leaders room for manoeuvre. In South Africa the position is very mixed. There is a great deal of factionalism in Black politics; note for example the tremendous cross-pressures on leader figures like Chief Buthelezi and Mr Sonny Leon. In urban areas there are great numbers of self-appointed Black leaders of varying legitimacy ever ready to challenge the stance of anyone ready to cooperate with the regime. This, *inter alia*, is a function of the extent to which the emergence of 'constituency politics' has been discouraged in South Africa: legitimate, effective leadership and political cohesion within communities are only possible if leaders are allowed to compete reasonably freely with one another for constituency support.

It is often assumed that the Afrikaans Nationalist leaders have more-or-less automatic support from their constituencies and hence have the leeway to negotiate and compromise. One powerful indication of this is the extent to which the very large National Party has been able to retain overwhelming support for two decades despite large differences of opinion and cleavages in interest in its own ranks. These observations suggest that the present regime leadership is potentially fairly free to enter into the kind of compromises that consociational accommodation requires. We must bear in mind, however, that internal cohesion within Afrikaans Nationalist ranks has had to be very carefully nurtured, and the past decades have seen a very judicious balancing of the self-interest of the various groups within the party. On the other hand, however, White opposition to the party is weak, and although the leadership has to remain very cautious, it probably does have the freedom to act.

Another point made by Lijphart is that external threat can often serve to impress on quarrelling elites the need for unity and cooperation. He finds this not to be the case in Northern Ireland, however, due to linkages outside the society itself. The same conclusion applies broadly to South Africa. The external threat, channelled through neighbouring Black states, is not uniformly viewed in South Africa – many Blacks have covert sympathies for the aims of militant expatriate organisations and for the Black states ready to support them. Our external threat can cleave our society even more deeply. Already, in my view, we have seen how events in Southern Africa have lead to rising political expectations and a climate of deepening militancy, as manifested in the recent disturbances.

V ALTERNATIVES TO DEVOLUTION OF POWER

The prospects for a successful process of consociational accommodation in South Africa, via the cooptation of leader elites on to decision-making bodies which over-arch the corporate segments, do not appear to be very favourable. The discussion in this paper has suggested that the basic dynamics of corporate group competition are not intrinsically culture-based, as it were (or at least not exclusively so). If maintenance of group identity were a pervasive and deeply imbedded motive, then there would be a substantial basis for consensus within the system. Our politics, however, are in large measure *interest-based*, and, due to a fully integrated economy, the various segments are fundamentally in competition with one another. The integrated economy brings with it the inevitability of geographic overlaps which set the scene for competition for social and residential amenities.

The emphasis on culture as a means of attempting to legitimate the policies of segregation, far from building an alternative focus of political motivation for South Africa's peoples, generates reaction. Note for example the growth of a Black consciousness ideology in opposition to the cultural prescriptions of the White regime, an ideology which above all rejects any form of ethnic separation apart from an inclusive Black separatism necessary to enable Blacks to consolidate in order to strengthen their position within the whole system.

Culturally-based justifications for policy are also counter-productive in that they tend to draw attention away from the real difficulties in reconciling material interests, and in promoting a false sense of altruistic mission among White policy-makers and administrators.

This discussion has also suggested that there is an absence of the values of moderation and compromise necessary to facilitate consociational accommodation. Originating in frontier wars and competition for land, our society has throughout its development been characterised by profound conflicts and hostilities, kept under cover by the very strictest of security measures. The only accommodation which South Africa has accomplished hitherto is that between English and Afrikaans-speaking Whites, and, even this has turned out to be more than somewhat one-sided.

Another way in which our history of conflict is likely to impede consociational accommodation is seen in the underdevelopment of Black political leadership, and cohesion within constituencies. Attempts at establishing a framework for intergroup negotiation are likely to have to *coincide* with the emergence of local Black political leadership struggles. If anything will be generally counter-productive of constructive negotiation this will. This is particularly true if the framework is to include urban Africans as a separate entity, as it will have to if it is to be attuned to the real imperatives in the situation.

A cardinal problem is that of material inequality. At present there is only a very slight overlap between the Whites and Africans with regard to their material conditions. Perceptions of relative deprivation are a key basis of conflict in the society (Schlemmer, 1976b). There are at present few effective institutions for regulating economic conflict in ways which are perceived to be legitimate; i.e. no recognised African trade unions operating within the system, etc.

As a consequence of these conclusions I would be irresponsible to rate the prospects of success for inter-elite negotiation very highly. We have already seen in the Coloured Persons' Representative Council how readily such a system could degenerate into an arena of bitter and unyielding conflict; and inevitably so bearing in mind the inauspicious preconditions existing in the society at large.

There are two theoretically feasible alternatives to a devolution of power along consociational lines. The one would be the progressive extension of voting rights to Blacks on an individual basis. There is support for this in opposition policies which propose a qualified franchise and full social and political incorporation of those Blacks who meet the franchise requirements. A policy like this probably would have the effect of dramatically promoting a cooperative and 'moderate' Black middle class as a node of consensus in the society. This is a policy which *in one way* is best suited to defusing the conflict in South Africa. The disadvantages of this policy, as ably spelt out by the SPRO-CAS Politics Commission Report (Randall, 1973) are that the opening up of opportunities for higher-status Black people would produce powerful demands for participation and privileges from the categories excluded from the full franchise. Whites would be presented with more immediate threats to their interests than ever before, and could react by demanding closure of the franchise or more stringent qualifications. The extension of a qualified franchise would probably be accompanied by an unaltered level of repressive legislation in order to control the conflicts of transition. Some would argue that these types of conflicts are bound to arise sooner or later in any case and hence claim that a policy of qualified franchise is the most effective means of securing stability, simply because it would create a middle-class consensus across the colour line. I think this argument is valid – this policy boils down to being a more effective cooptive strategy than consociational accommodation. Its adherents constitute a small minority of the White electorate, however, and therefore at this stage there seems little point in teasing out the complexities of this alternative.

The other alternative is a transformation of the homeland policy into a radical partition, involving the transfer of a great deal of land, developed economic infrastructure and urban development. This, if sufficiently far-reaching, is theoretically the most appropriate solution, apart from the possibility that the African states emerging out of the partition would persist in their claims to the remaining non-African 'homeland'. There seems to be much militating against this type of development. The transfer of resources will deeply affect the interests of a range of powerful lobbies and interest groups; it is difficult to imagine that the regime will have the courage to implement it. Yet, it may be the kind of last-resort policy adaptation that a regime which refuses to make meaningful 'internal' concessions will have to accept.

Since both these alternatives seem unlikely in the short to medium-range future, we are brought back to the alternative of a consociational accommodation. If one assumes great pressure on the system (which already exists and is likely to intensify) then there is one incentive for consociational accommodation, which Lijphart (1971) refers to as the 'self-denying prophecy' – 'elites cooperate in spite of sharp and reinforcing cleavages because to do otherwise would be to call forth the prophesied consequences of such cleavages' (p. 49). The South African Prime Minister has spoken of consequences too ghastly to contemplate. The very depth and urgency of the conflicts in South Africa may themselves force the contending segments into compromise.

If this is to be so, then the following developments seem to be an *immediate* necessity to secure some hope of successful negotiation in South Africa, and the present government may have the leeway to act:

1. The recognition of the urban Africans as representing an important separate segment of interests which cannot be accommodated within the homeland orbit.
2. The encouragement of a range of institutional developments and devices for dealing with conflict within the system – recognition and registration of African trade unions, real powers for urban Black councils, the removal of centrally-dominated White-controlled bureaucracies from Black areas and the crash-training of Black administrators to take their place.
3. The encouragement of a rapid development of socio-economic 'overlap' between Blacks and Whites by improving training and the ending of all controls on job-mobility for Blacks.
4. A significant increase in the number of Blacks appointed to all the various boards of control, commissions, etc., which make up an intermediate level of authority.
5. The recognition that without a more vigorous political development in Black areas, neither the effective leadership nor the coherence can emerge to enable successful negotiation to take place.
6. The encouragement of attempts at interracial negotiation by local metropolitan and provincial councils as a precursor to higher-level dealings.
7. The establishment of the 'Inter-Cabinet Council' as a genuine decision-making body, with fiscal powers, as opposed to a consultative body.
8. The appointment of Blacks, Coloureds and Indians to senior positions in government departments dealing with the respective communities.
9. The correction of inequalities in resources, such as differential expenditure on education, differential quality and quantity of group areas, etc., and opening up possibilities for the voluntary sharing of resources and amenities; mixed universities, 'open' residential areas, and the like. The point here is that since complete separation with equality is impossible it is imperative for opportunities to be created

for shared use of facilities in areas where it really counts.

Adaptations such as these, in the light of the 'self-denying prophecy' referred to earlier, may yet make consociational accommodation feasible in South Africa.

NOTES

1. The recent Black Consciousness movement, which sets a value upon the rejection of many White norms and standards, is essentially based on an ideology of protest, self-assertion and mobilisation – it makes no claim to being a nationalism.
2. As yet unpublished: sample size 700+ in major urban areas (1974).

REFERENCES

Adam, Heribert, 1976. 'Ideologies of Dedication versus Blueprints of Expedience', *Social Dynamics*, vol. 2, no. 2, pp. 83–91.
Bengu, S. M. Address given at the 1976 Annual Council Meeting of the South African Institute of Race Relations (no full title available). Enquiries to author, c/o the University of Zululand.
Geertz, Clifford, 1973. *The Interpretation of Cultures* (New York: Basic Books).
Giliomee, Hermann, 1975. 'The Development of the Afrikaner's Self-concept', in van der Merwe, H. W. (ed.), *Looking at the Afrikaner Today* (Cape Town: Tafelberg).
Lijphart, Arend, 1971. 'Cleavages in Consociational Democracies: A Four-Country Comparison', presented at the *Symposium on Comparative Analysis of Highly Industrialised Societies*, Bellagio, Italy, 1–7 Aug.
Lijphart, Arend, 1974. 'The Northern Ireland Problem: Cases, Theories, and Solutions', *British Journal of Political Science*, vol. 5, pp. 83–106.
Mayer, Philip, 1972. *Urban Africans and the Bantustans*, Hoernlé Memorial Lecture (Johannesburg: South African Institute of Race Relations).
Mayer, Philip, 1974. 'Class, Status and Ethnicity as Perceived by Johannesburg Africans', in Thompson, L., and Butler, J., *Change in Contemporary South Africa*, (Berkeley and Los Angeles: University of California Press).
Randall, Peter (ed.), 1973. *South Africa's Political Alternatives* (Johannesburg: Ravan Press).
Schlemmer, Lawrence, 1972 'City or Rural "Homeland": A Study of Patterns of Identification Among Africans in South Africa's Divided Society', *Social Forces*, vol. 51, no. 2, pp. 154–64.
Schlemmer, Lawrence, 1973. *Privilege, Prejudice and Parties* (Johannesburg: South African Institute of Race Relations).
Schlemmer, Lawrence, 1976. 'Theories of the Plural Society and Change in

South Africa' in *Social Dynamics* (forthcoming) and in *Proceedings of the 1976 Annual Meeting of the African Studies Association, Boston, U.S.A.*
Schlemmer, Lawrence, 1976b. 'Political Adaptation and Reaction Among Urban Africans in South Africa', *Social Dynamics*, vol. 2, no. 1.
van Zyl Slabbert, F., 1971. 'Cultural and Ethnic Politics', in Randall, P. (ed.), *Towards Social Change* (Johannesburg: Ravan Press).
Welsh, David, 1972. 'The Cultural Dimension of Apartheid', *African Affairs*, vol. 71, Jan, pp. 35–53.
Welsh, David, 1976. 'The Need for Urgent Fundamental Political Change', Proceedings of the 1976 Council Meeting of the South African Institute of Race Relations (Johannesburg: South African Institute of Race Relations).

22 South Africa's Domestic Politics: Key Questions and Options

W. J. de Klerk

Editor, Die Transvaler. *The paper was read at the Congress of the Political Science Association of South Africa, 30 September 1977, and subsequently published in* Politikon, *official journal of PSASA, December 1977.*

I MULTINATIONALISM

The key problem of South Africa's domestic politics is how multinationalism is to be accommodated in a political and social dispensation which will be acceptable to all concerned.

It is an undisputed fact that the basic premiss is multinationalism. It is also a fact that multinational communities create problems for government. These problems may be summarised in the term *accommodation*.

> How does one accommodate a multinational society politically?
> How does one accommodate various cultures with their distinctive traditions and value systems?
> How, in a multinational society, does one guarantee basic human rights, group identities, principles such as equality, freedom, non-discrimination, etc., and how does one accommodate various even conflicting demands, ideals and ideologies?
> Is there a secret way in which all can be joined in a sort of unanimity, concord in national loyalty?

Each multinational society is beset by its own distinctive problems which demand unique solutions. The distinctive features of the South African multinational problem are indicated here in broad outline only.

(i) *The imbalance in numbers of South Africa's pluralism.* According to an authoritative projection of the Human Sciences Research Council, South Africa's population will be composed as follows in the year 2000: Whites (6,826,900), Coloureds (4,217,100), Asians (1,178,400) and Blacks (33,707,300). According to the same projection, the population will number 62.8 million in the year 2020 and of these 31.4 million will be living and working in the White areas. These figures tell the story of an almost overwhelming problem.

(ii) *The ethnicity of South Africa's pluralism.* This is not merely a matter of a White group and a Black group. Put in its simplest form (for it is very much more complicated), the problem concerns three groups who are not Black (Whites, Coloureds and Asians) and ten Black peoples, each of which has its own ethnic identity, in addition to a common ethnicity shared by all.

(iii) *The racial element in South Africa's pluralism.* It is a universal fact, long since established and from time to time underscored in many countries, that the racial element of a multinational situation adds a much more difficult dimension to pluralism. It has far greater potential for conflict than pluralism in which the components are of the same race. Also, there is a tendency to polarise and form solidarity blocks. The infrastructure is an ideological, cultural and traditional confrontation. Moreover, if the race element largely coincides with other divisions, such as class distinctions, economic and educational differentials, as is the case in South Africa, this pluralism becomes a powder keg. This racial element, particularly in view of the numerical imbalance, rules out assimilation completely, maximises the problems of mutual accommodation and even casts an ever-lengthening shadow on mutual association.

(iv) *The 'people' (Volk) element of South Africa's pluralism.* This is not the same dimension as race. Despite their mutual bond of Black consciousness, the various Black peoples have traditional feuds, mutual differences in tradition, jealousies and national aspirations. This makes our pluralism extremely difficult to accommodate.

Nor is the Coloured community as homogeneous as is often alleged. They have sharp differences in political aspirations. The White community is also divided against itself. To a large extent, political groupings are still based on the old division between Boer and Briton.

Despite various processes that have been set in motion here – assimilation, acculturation, growing solidarity in the face of a common threat, political regroupings, etc. – there are still many unburied hatchets which cause one White group to be suspicious of the other. This tension in our politics may be unnecessary, yet it is very real. The tension caused by differences in outlook on life, political ideals and style, economic power and various other differences in emphasis is delaying if not obstructing the development of a homogeneous White political profile.

It is true that old divisions are being blurred and that political groupings are increasingly taking place in the context of various policy directions which straddle the old language barrier, but it is equally true that liberalist integrationist politics are associated with the English-speaking section and the conservative politics of separation with the Afrikaans-speaking section.

Nor is this the end. Within Afrikaner politics there are various currents and sub-currents which introduce a certain hesitancy into the articulation of political objectives. A delayed tempo, equivocal objectives and various differences of emphasis in respect of the future political and social dispensation sometimes lead to a situation where apparently there is no clear-cut plan for the political and social development of our multinationalism.

II AGGRESSIVE HETEROGENEITY

I can summarise my basic argument as follows: the key problem of South Africa's domestic policies is how multinationalism is to be accommodated in a political and social dispensation which will be acceptable to all concerned.

This problem is complicated and compounded by the fact that the components of South Africa's multinationalism have the image of an *aggressive heterogeneity*. These components are:

(i) The aggressive heterogeneity of mutual threat. For the White identity and the survival of the Afrikaner people, the very numbers of the Blacks hold the threat of being ousted and losing both a power base and room for development. For Black identity, White political and social control threatens their national aspirations and their so-called political liberation.

(ii) The aggressive heterogeneity of racial polarisation and all the emotion associated with it;

(iii) The aggressive heterogeneity of conflict in formulating political ideals;
(iv) The aggressive heterogeneity of socio-economic and educational class differentials;
(v) The aggressive heterogeneity of historical experience, traditional patterns and ethnic self-consciouness.

All this gives South Africa's domestic politics the dimension of intensity, almost indigestibility, which makes the task of accommodating multinationalism so much more difficult.

III MULTINATIONALISM AND INTERNATIONAL POLITICS

This agressive heterogeneity which marks our multinationalism is further complicated by the dynamics of international politics. Africa and the Western world see our current policies as relics of the colonial era, albeit a little camouflaged, but nevertheless in conflict with their recipe for a political dispensation in South Africa. However much euphemised by expressions such as 'gradual evolution towards the ideal', the essence of what the current Western leaders demand of South Africa is the following, no less:

(i) One man, one vote; Black majority government; a completely open society and a common voters roll.
(ii) A new constitution devised by a national convention of all races which would ditch the current political dispensation and start from scratch.
(iii) Anything resembling camouflaged separateness or entrenched ethnicity is quite unacceptable to them. This would include Turnhalle-type dispensations or a federal system.

These demands originate in the United States and from there they are taken up by all Western countries which support them with varying emphasis. Moreover, they back up these demands with the threat of economic and other sanctions against South Africa. Support for these demands has become part and parcel of their foreign policy. They believe that the more they dissociate themselves from the White regime in South Africa and the more they associate themselves with Black Power aggression against the White regime, the more they will ingratiate themselves with Black Africa. They argue that by consolidating their power base in Africa in this way they will be able to neutralise Red China's and Russia's influence in this part of the world. Meanwhile South Africa is left to hold the baby.

This attitude on the part of the West raises expectations among South African Blacks that the great anti-White utopia is about to dawn for them. The result was that it caused the emergence within the domestic Black leadership of revolutionary Black Power elements which are reluctant to negotiate for solutions. Instead, they make unrealistic demands and await the coming crisis.

This, together with what has happened in Angola, Mozambique, Rhodesia and perhaps also in South-West Africa, has made both Blacks and Whites apathetic towards a multinational solution. Many are of the opinion that the time for negotiation is past, that we are already engaged in a war of confrontation. Consequently, South Africa is faced with an increase in subversive elements whose aim it is to destroy law and order and prepare the way for the revolution. This has the effect of blurring the dividing line between positive Black nationalism and revolutionary Black consciousness. In practical politics it is becoming ever more difficult to distinguish between the two.

The key problem of South Africa's domestic politics is that the aggressive heterogeneity is fired by aggressive demands from abroad that a homogeneous political dispensation be introduced in which the Black majority will be in control.

It is in this atmosphere that South Africa has to try to accommodate its multinationalism.

IV FOUR OPTIONS

Against this background, what are the options open to South Africa?

I do not wish to give an academic answer by stating and analysing all options. Instead I will highlight the following four points:

1. *The Model Foreign Countries Would Impose*

The model which foreign countries are trying to impose on us for our domestic policies does not take multinationalism into account.

We must not prostrate ourselves – we must reject this out of hand for such a model will get us nowhere. We still have much bargaining power with which to resist the outside world – our natural resources, strategic position, the stabilising effect of the White government, sympathy for our cause on the part of important individuals and groups in the electorate of every Western country, and many other similar assets which can be utilised to moderate foreign pressures.

The only circumstance, however, that will at least partially normalise our international relations is significant support by both Whites and non-Whites for a new political and social dispensation. We must devise a domestic settlement which will command such support by White, Brown and Black that, for a time at least, it will defuse foreign impatience with us and spike their guns.

Despite my diagnosis of aggressive heterogeneity, South Africa is still fortunate in having a large middle group of Whites, Coloureds and Blacks whose ideal is cooperation and consensus on fundamental issues. But their numbers are gradually diminishing. It is still possible for the current generation of adults to clasp hands across the divide. But we shall have to accelerate the pace so that the current generation does not pass from the scene without a settlement having been reached. As quickly as possible we must identify the leaders who are prepared to cooperate in a system based on multinationalism, and we must provide them with sufficient arguments to make followers of their people. I will return to this problem in my fourth statement.

What I wish to emphasise now is that, if we tackle the job with enthusiasm, there is still room and time to achieve a dispensation based on multinationalism which, to say the least, will change the tune of most overseas countries.

2. *Three Options Within a Settlement Plan*

The settlement plan can be in one of three directions only. The separation model, the integration model and the multinational model.

In this, my second statement, I would like to reject both the separation and the integration models.

(i) *The separation model* is based on the old apartheid concept of White hegemony in the Republic of South Africa. The Coloureds and Asians are minority groups which are treated as such. Their aspirations are accommodated only at the local level – with a certain degree of autonomy in respect of the affairs of their own communities.

Blacks are citizens of Black states or homelands yet to be established, and those residing and working in the Republic of South Africa are *gastarbeiter* with the rights and restrictions of *gastarbeiter*. The societies and their structures of White and non-White are strictly separate: each is hived off into his own world where he must undergo the usual evolutionary processes until, eventually, he reaches the level of development which is his fate in all walks of life. To a great extent, this model has landed in a cul-de-sac. The need for separation (segregation?) is still there, but not in the way envisaged in the distant past. Of course, those who know the South African situation do not need elaborate motivations for my rejection of this model. The following will suffice:

(a) The development of the homelands has not been dynamic. I shall pass over the reasons. The fact of the matter is that they have been unable to absorb Blacks. The demand for Black labour in South Africa has caused a tremendous increase in the influx of Blacks to the White urban areas. Territorial separation could neither eliminate nor reduce the physical presence of Black people in White areas. Economic integration is a fact.

(b) Meanwhile, the leaders of some homelands have tended to reject independence. They claim that they are part and parcel of greater South Africa.

(c) Owing to consolidation problems, capital shortages, and resistance among Blacks in the homelands themselves, often finding expression in a lack of enthusiasm, development of the homelands has become a long-term evolutionary process, far too slow for the new Africa and the new world.

(d) Nor could adequate and equitable facilities for Blacks be provided everywhere. Meanwhile, a large middle class has emerged among Blacks. Not only have they developed the usual needs of civilisation, but their numbers and national aspirations are increasing every day. There are increasing demands for equality, human rights in the Western pattern, a voice in the political future of the country, a dispensation free of all discrimination, and all the other twentieth-century political slogans.

(e) The degree to which the urbanised Black man in White areas identifies himself with his homeland has decreased instead of increased. Culturally, they are still very much aware of their ethnic origins, but at the political level they have begun to develop their own identity, with their own demands in respect of their South African civil rights.

(f) The traditional policy for urban Blacks has been torpedoed by sheer numbers – 31.4 million *gastarbeiter* as against 12 million citizens of South Africa by the year 2020. This will always be a major threat to the political authorities trying to govern these 31.4 million people as temporary sojourners.

(g) Both the Coloureds and Asians have discarded the yoke of minority groups; their minimum demand is a share in the politics of the common fatherland.

The separation model failed to accommodate South Africa's multi-nationalism in all its implications, at either the political or social level.

The model will always be a source of conflict and, unless adjustments are made, its relevance to the country's problems will decrease even further.

(ii) *The integration model.* The liberalist concept of the integration model is much the same age as the watertight separation model. Its basic ingredients are the following.

In South Africa there must be one integrated parliament elected by all population groups. All voters should be placed on a common voters roll. Suffrage may be qualified by predetermined economic and educational qualifications. The pattern of integrated government must be extended from the national level right down to the regional and local level. The new constitution must be devised by a national convention representative of all racial groups. Certain guarantees for minorities must be entrenched in the constitution by a 'Bill of Rights'. Society must be freed of all forced differentiation based on ethnicity so that the various races may associate freely in integrated groups according to the usual socio-economic norms.

These conditions or requirements find expression in various types of the integration model. The one would create the integrated state by way of revolution. The other would decentralise the country into three types of province – White-dominated, Black-dominated and mixed. In this way the large Black vote would be divided and White sovereignty protected at a regional level. The White vote would then have much more bargaining power in respect of the composition of the central government. A third type of integration model would have a race federation as an interim phase to prepare the way for an integrated unitary state.

The Achilles heel of the integration model is the following:

(*a*) It underrates the importance of the imbalance in numbers in the South African situation. Despite the inherent conflicts, integration would still be acceptable if the numbers involved guaranteed some sort of power balance. But if the preponderance of numbers and, therefore, power, is on one side, power sharing will inevitably lead to a situation where minority groups relinquish power to the majority groups who will simply usurp it.

(*b*) It underrates the current political mood of Black Africa, which is relentlessly set upon a complete *coup d'état*. Black racism is absolute and will not be thwarted by the bits of paper on which constitutions are written.

In South Africa, a multiracial political dispensation would inevitably be a uniracial Black dispensation.

3. *Multinational Model*
In my third statement I would like briefly to discuss what in my view is South Africa's only option – the *multinational model*. The *facts* on which this model is based are South Africa's multinational population, described earlier.

The philosophy underlying this model is that in a multinational country, two poles must be accommodated in the political dispensation. I would term them separateness or distinctiveness, and community of destiny or communality. These two poles are manifest at all levels. Thus, as a model multinationalism would create a dispensation wherein the distinctive interests of the various groups are upheld in all walks of life. This I would term the aspect of distinctiveness of multinationalism.

Simultaneously and in equal measure, multinationalism would create a dispensation in which community of interests, co-partnership and interaction are guaranteed at all levels of human endeavour. This I would term the communality aspect of multinationalism. The heart of the matter is that multinationalism places equal emphasis on the distinctive world of each group and the communal world that all groups have to share. The dimensions of multinationalism must be manifest and realised in all walks of life. In the church, in business and industry, in education, science and sport, in our social life and wherever society is organised – in all these spheres full recognition must be given both to that which is peculiar to each group and that which is common to all groups.

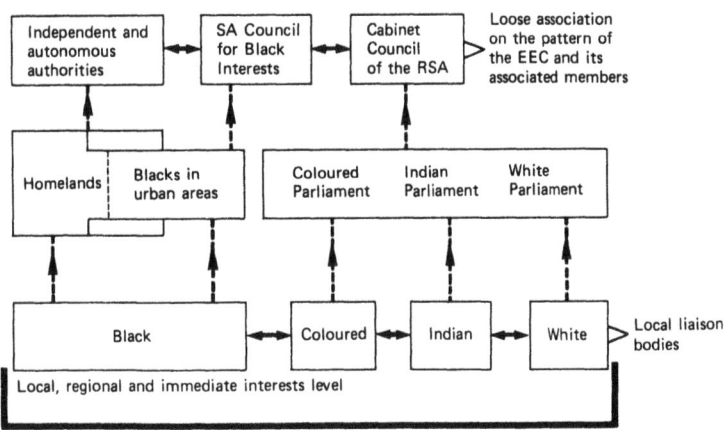

I could discuss them one by one and lay down a few guidelines, but the political sphere remains the most important. The various levels of multinationalism are indicated here and a few observations added on multinationalism at the social level. At all levels it must be manifest that each group has an existence of its own – that it exists next to and coexists with all other groups.

(i) In South Africa political multinationalism has *three components*: (*a*) Black states (homelands), either independent (such as Transkei) or with internal self-government (such as KwaZulu): (*b*) Blacks in urban areas who are recognised as a distinctive group: (*c*) Whites, Coloureds and Indians with their own institutions of authority, linked by a Cabinet Council and President's Council (the Senate of today).

The distinctiveness of the various groups is reflected in the fact that they have their own authorities from the local to the national level: independent homeland authorities and self-governing homeland authorities; a distinctive umbrella institution of authority (SA Council for Black Interests) for urban Blacks, comprising representatives from local Black municipalities; autonomous White, Coloured and Indian parliaments with unfettered control over their own affairs; local authorites for each group.

Communality is realised as follows. At the local and regional levels there are various liaison bodies with a joint voice in matters of common interest. At the national level, there are various bodies each with its own competency in joint control. For Coloureds, Indians and Whites there is a firm umbrella institution of authority – the Cabinet Council – with the competency of joint government in matters of common concern. Urban Blacks are represented in a council which promotes their interests in negotiation with both the homeland governments and the authorities of the Republic of South Africa. Where Black interests in the Republic are concerned, they have access to the Cabinet Council of the RSA, but they also have representation in the homeland parliaments to safeguard their interests *vis-à-vis* the homeland policy.

At the highest level there will be a representative consultative body, an association of homelands, urban Blacks and the Republic of South Africa, which will deliberate on matters of common interest in the widest sense.

Footnotes to the model

1. One is immediately aware that this is a most complex system. There is, however, no simple solution to a complex multinationalism. But perhaps it is not quite as complex as the first cursory glance seems to

indicate. In reality, the whole system comprises no more than distinctive and communal structures. I suggest there is no reason why it should not work.
2. I have not attempted to give details on composition, powers and functions or the mechanics of these. That is a job for politicians, jurists and political scientists.
3. The entire model must be kept flexible, for in the process of application it could evolve further. It is a point of departure, a direction, and certainly not the omega of political dispensation in South Africa.
4. Urban Blacks are recognised as a separate group, without severing their ties with their respective homelands. They are citizens of another country but live and work in South Africa; therefore they must have a voice in both spheres. In the Republic of South Africa, in addition to their own local government institutions they must also have a share in decision-making on matters affecting them directly. As citizens of their own state they have a strong vested interest in the government of that state. Similarly, their state must be given an increasing share of responsibility for the ordering of their affairs. For these reasons, they must be well represented in the governments of their homelands.
5. There are also various other possible models for urban Blacks. In terms of one of these, frontiers could be redrawn so that many Black townships in White South Africa would be included in the homelands. Another, that Blacks in the Witwatersrand-Vereeniging complex should be incorporated in a city state, also has much potential.
6. In order to persuade the homelands to become partners in this model, much attention will have to be given to further consolidation and concerted development programmes. And in order to make urban Blacks, Coloureds and Indians partners of good will, it is imperative that the quality of life in their communities be improved at all levels.

(ii) *Multinationalism in the Social Field*

Official policy is separate public facilities for the various race groups. That is the ideal and the rule. As far as possible, these facilities should be equal. The National Party, however, is unable to implement its present policy of separate but equal facilities. There are various reasons for this: a shortage of funds; limited demand by the vast majority of Blacks for certain types of facilities; and the difficulties in providing separate facilities for Blacks in White areas.

Current policy keeps running into discrimination. If there are not enough equal facilities and one group with few facilities is forbidden to share the many facilities of another group, then we have discrimination in its most obvious form.

In order to save the situation, the authorities are handing down *ad hoc* decisions on situations involving more than one race group. These rulings are hedged about by all sorts of provisos, some of which are humiliating and others simply silly. The overall impression is one of back-pedalling after concessions in response to pressure.

It has become fashionable to say that something should be normalised, but that is exactly what should be done here, for in a multinational country it is perfectly normal to have many multinational times, places and occasions.

What is more, we have already shown the way with the introduction of international hotels. And in future we are bound to have increasing difficulties with, for instance, Black citizens of neighbouring states (such as Transkei) who in South Africa will demand treatment different from that meted out to South African Blacks. This will obviously lead to much confusion.

We should start by acknowledging that there are – and should be – three levels in our society – White, Black and Grey. To a great extent, the first two have already been established by tradition and by implementation of official policy. The two separate worlds have been created. The time has now come to create the grey areas on a more or less permanent basis – quite apart from facilities shared on a temporary or *ad hoc* basis. This implies that certain public facilities should be declared grey facilities – open to all race groups. They include certain hotels, theatres, cinemas, restaurants, holiday resorts, specific private schools, specific courses at certain universities, and recreational facilities. The real needs in this respect can be determined from time to time. These 'mixed' facilities may still be controlled by, for instance, a permit renewable every year.

In large measure we already have this kind of dispensation, even at government level where Whites and non-Whites serve together on the Cabinet Council and various other boards and councils. This, too, needs to be normalised and developed further.

What are the risks? Perhaps a little friction at first, but that will come to an end as soon as the novelty has worn off. Appropriate action can always be taken in those cases where friction is serious. Loss of identity and integration? Surely not in these circumscribed and limited 'mixed' situations. Won't Blacks step up their demands? Perhaps yes, but they are doing so in any event, and we can always set some sort of ceiling. What of Whites being crowded from their own facilities, and what about one's right to reserve something for oneself? Surely, enough of one's own facilities will remain intact, and one has a choice whether or not to use 'mixed' facilities.

There are many advantages to such a new dispensation. Establishing and maintaining such grey areas on a permanent basis will eliminate discrimination in a visible and meaningful manner. In this way we shall be able to accommodate the Black and Coloured middle class. In certain areas we shall no longer have enforced racial segregation, for in virtually all areas there will be, apart from segregated facilities, those shared by all races as the need arises. Finally, in this way we will remove a major source of irritation and reproach, both inside and outside South Africa.

4. *Marketing the Multinational Model*

My fourth statement is that this multinational model, discussed in my third statement, should be properly marketed among Whites and non-Whites, both in South Africa and overseas. All interested parties should know that this is a new concept and that there is much potential for evolutionary progress in this programme. Above all, they should understand and accept that this is not merely window-dressing. I would suggest a powerful information programme, perhaps to be undertaken by an institute specially established for the purpose, and by other communication media.

There is a most important proviso, however. We won't be able to market this model successfully unless all the various groups are fully involved at every stage in the design of the new programme.

Instead of a national convention which will score a line through the existing constitution to start afresh, thereby introducing an unacceptable degree of uncertainty, we should rather consider a multinational advisory committee to act as consultative body to the government and to undertake various studies and surveys as the need arises.

V CONCLUSION

In summary, the essence of my argument is as follows:
(i) The key problem of South Africa's domestic politics is how multinationalism is to be accommodated in a political and social dispensation which will be acceptable to all concerned.
(ii) In South Africa, multinationalism is beset by serious problems, because we have to cope with an aggressive heterogeneity. In fact, our multinationalism has been given a crisis dimension, particularly by racial polarisation and socio-economic and educational class differentials, coupled with the demands by Africa and the rest of the world.

(iii) The only option open to South Africa is to develop the multinational model in such a way that equal emphasis is put on guarantees for distinctive group interests and self-realisation, and on communal interests and joint decision-making.

The various national and racial groups in this great country of ours have a common destiny. If, with the grace of God and, on our part, purposefulness we set about developing programmes to accommodate that destiny, we may very well succeed in changing that aggressive heterogeneity into a co-operative heterogeneity.

The policy of multinationalism is not the final answer, but it is at least a signpost away from disaster for all the peoples of South Africa.

23 Individual Economic Responsibility: a Necessary Condition for a Stable Order in South Africa

J. A. Lombard and P. J. van der Merwe
Professors in the Department of Economics, University of Pretoria

I SOUTH AFRICA ON THE THRESHOLD

There can be no doubt that people living in South Africa are on the threshold of a new experience in interpersonal association. Until very recently the social structure of Southern Africa was strongly characterised by what is known in economic literature as 'dualism'. Historically, this dualism manifested itself in the form of a highly developed and economically dynamic core, functionally closely tied to the European economy, but geographically surrounded by a numerically preponderant but economically backward population. Functionally the economic growth, cyclical fluctuations, institutional arrangements, technological processes, etc., of this core were dependent upon conditions in Europe. In fact this core was no more and no less than an integral part of the traditional Western international economy. To the managers and other important decision-makers in this core, Europe and the United States of America were spiritually much nearer than was the Africa around them.

The economically backward domestic peoples around this growth core were affected by it mainly through the opportunities for unskilled labour. A lively pattern of trade in commodities never developed. The ease of physical movement was too great to turn anyone's economic ingenuity towards trade. This movement took a number of forms, namely (1) structural migration (which continued until about 1950); (2) oscillatory migration which existed from the early days of mining, but increased in importance as structural migration was officially constrained; and (3) a system of commuting between traditional settlements and places of employment in the core economy. But, whatever the form, the substance of the relationship was largely restricted to the exchange of labour for income.

This kind of dualism is changing with dramatic rapidity. The underdeveloped African periphery is inexorably moving on to the European core in many ways. The most important forces inspiring both the tempo and the character of this movement are the awakened nationalism or statism embodied in the emergence of independent national states like Botswana, Lesotho, Swaziland, Transkei, Mocambique and the advent of a rapidly growing urban Black population with certain articulate political aspirations within the European core area. A strong characteristic of this movement is its insistence on functional equality for Blacks in the economy of the core area. The demand is for 'full participation' in both the market economy and its political management.

In short these forces are about to shatter the framework of the traditional dualistic economic order in Southern Africa. The old idea of the Republic of South Africa as an extension of Europe is making room for a new idea of the Republic as the mainspring of economic development in Southern Africa at large.

A tremendously important question is what the guiding principles of the new economic order of the future will be? Is it to be the kind of integration normally found in a common society? Or must it be a system of economic cooperation in a plural society, to some extent even organised in politically independent states? Is it possible that a viable new kind of isolation may develop out of ideas about a 'White Homeland'? To what extent is the new society to be governed by the disciplines of the market economy or by those of central planning? In all these questions, answers for the economic system depend very largely upon acceptable patterns of political accommodation of the peoples of Africa, both Black and White.

Let us examine the socio-economic implications of the necessary conditions for a stable political order in South Africa, assuming that the economic implications of an unstable order are in themselves unstable and undesirable. But before doing so, let us examine the outstanding features of the socio-economic problem as they have unfolded themselves in recent years.

II THE SOCIO-ECONOMIC DIMENSIONS

In view of the limitations on this paper, we shall focus only upon what we regard as the most important social and economic dimensions of the emerging South African society – important in the sense of having a direct bearing upon the necessity and feasibility of the kind of institutional reform referred to earlier.

It is, rather surprisingly, still necessary to record that this South African society is a plural one. The development of programmes for institutional reform and policy principles on the assumption that the people of South Africa constitutes a 'common society', must, at best, be regarded as hypothetical political theorising. Moreover, there are no circumstances and experiences in real life supporting such a sociologically powerful hypothesis for South Africa. It is, of course, an easy intellectual escape from the reality of South Africa, and consequently attractive to both superficial observers as well as politicians who do not expect to be saddled with the responsibilities of government over this territory.

The fact remains that the people of South Africa find themselves governed in their behaviour by several different cultural orders. On the basis of such an important cultural element as language, for example, at least fourteen distinct groups identify themselves – and are determined to protect this identity through their social and political institutions. At the same time, however, these academic exercises in differentiation, although sociologically probably more realistic than 'common society models', can also be carried to such extremes that it would become impracticable to give constitutional content to them. Like politics itself, political programming remains the 'art of the possible'.

As far as the Blacks are concerned, their geographic location in the sub-continent makes it possible to retain their ethnic identity to a very high degree. For example, the core of the Xhosa nation still inhabits, to the virtual exclusion of all other peoples, their traditional homeland north of the Kei river. Much the same applies to most of the other Black nations. The fact that large numbers of these peoples now find themselves living elsewhere, mostly for economic reasons, does not detract from the fact that in these homelands the symbols and institutions of each Black nation are still preserved. The programme to vitalise these homelands politically and economically may at present attract a great deal of criticism, but under certain conditions, for example the redrawing of borders, this programme may well hold the key to many issues at present confronting the sub-continent.

Even with a very positive attitude towards the politico-economic development of acceptable Black states, it has to be recognised that the real problems of plural socio-economic policy manifest themselves *outside* these socially homogeneous areas of the several Black nations. It is in the Republic of South Africa proper that the plural society exists. It is in such growth areas as Pretoria/Witwatersrand/Vereeniging that the problem of the convergence of the African periphery on the European core has to be handled. From the point of view of the Republic of South Africa the programmes for the development of the several Black homelands must be seen as contributing to the solution of this problem. The contribution expected of these area development programmes is (*a*) to put the problem of political associations between Black Africa and the European core into a proper framework of international relationships, and (*b*) to decentralise economic activity in order to prevent a further convergence of people on to the core area.

Quantitatively this economic core, under the political authority of the Republic of South Africa, employs about 6.3 million people. On the basis of the admittedly misleading criterion of colour only, the total number is made up of 1.5 million Whites, 0.7 million Coloureds, 0.2 million Asians and 3.9 million Blacks. The latter figure includes 632,000 contract workers (oscillatory migrants) from the Homelands, 431,000 from the rest of Southern Africa, 560,000 commuters and 2.3 million workers socially established in the Republic (about evenly divided between urban and rural areas).

The patterns of socio-economic association on farms still differ very greatly from those in urban areas. It is clearly in the Republican urban areas where institutional change is most urgently demanded. Of the 4.8 million economically active people in urban areas, about 1.3 million belong to the White groups, 0.6 million to the Coloureds, 0.2 million to the Asians and about 2.7 million to the various Black ethnic groups, again including most of the 1.1 million contract workers and 560,000 commuters. The latter figure reflects mainly the contiguity of homeland townships to Republican areas of employment such as Umlazi in the greater Durban area, Garankua near Pretoria and Mdantsane near East London. Similar trends are developing near New

Castle, Richards Bay, the Western Transvaal, etc. This means that at present there are slightly more than 1.0 million Black workers in the Republic permanently established in urban areas outside the jurisdiction of their own governments, while about 0.5 million are already accommodated in urban areas within the jurisdiction of their own homelands, a figure which is rapidly growing.

This paper is mainly addressed to the situation in the Republican towns, particularly the large concentrations. Consequently the erosion of the development potential of homelands caused by oscillatory migration, and even by commuting, cannot be discussed. It should be stated, however, that these methods of obtaining employment involve a drain of economic dynamism among the population, while the income generated contributes little towards domestic development as it is mostly spent outside the homeland.

Within this demographic context, the central problem of institutional change in the urban economy of the Republic must find a solution. To fix ideas, we are basically dealing with 1.0 million Black workers, 0.7 million Coloureds, 0.2 million Asians and 1.5 million Whites who are permanently settled in these urban areas. As far as participation in political processes are at issue, these are the numbers of workers concerned. As far as economic processes are concerned, another 1.2 million should be added to the purely numerical dimensions of the problem.

The economics of the new urban society will cut across these colour classifications. This will happen, not only for reasons of basic justice, but also for reasons of political stability and economic productivity in the system. But what is to take the place of this dualism based upon colour? The socialistic formula is obviously out of the question.

The only sound approach to the problem is to build up from the first principles of individual freedom and welfare, our best conception of the kind of institutional framework within which economic cooperation can proceed into the future. This involves us in a sharp focus upon the individual, his basic rights and particularly his basic responsibilities. We have to remind ourselves constantly that the system of competitive democracy as conceived by the classical philosophers, and to a large extent implemented in the constitutions of the United States of America and many other Western Democracies, *makes a very important assumption about the characteristics of the people concerned.* The following views of two of the greatest classical liberals, Lord Robbins of our own day, and John Stuart Mill, a century earlier, should command our deepest attention. As put by Robbins:

The case for liberty as I have presented it involves an assumption that so far I have not made very explicit – the assumption, namely, that the citizens are sufficiently mature to know their own interest or to be guided towards it by reason and persuasion. Even in the most advanced society, the argument for freedom cannot sensibly be applied to the case of children or imbeciles. It would be fairly generally conceded that it does not apply in full rigour to backward adult societies. This point was well put by John Stuart Mill in his classical statement of the case for liberty, who said: 'It is, perhaps, hardly necessary to say, that this doctrine is meant to apply to human beings in the maturity of their faculties. We are not speaking of children, or of young persons below the age which the law may fix as that of manhood or of womanhood. Those who are still in a state to require being taken care of by others, must be protected against their own actions as well as against external injury. For the same reason we may leave out of consideration those backward states of society in which the race itself may be considered in its nonage ... Liberty, as a principle, has no application to any state of things anterior to the time when mankind has become capable of being improved by free and equal discussion. Until then, there is nothing for them but implicit obedience to an Akbar or a Charlemagne, if they are so fortunate as to find one.'[1]

What is the state of affairs in this respect among the 3.7 million urban workers? Will they be able to support this edifice of competitive democracy? What are the performance requirements expected of the adult individual and in what functional areas? Answers to these questions have been clearly formulated in a report of an 'Adult performance level project' recently conducted at the University of Texas. Six basic skills were identified as necessary for five separate areas of performance, namely, occupation, consumption, preservation of health, participation in community activities and participation in government and law. The skills required were reading, writing, computation, speaking-listening, problem-solving and interpersonal relations. From extensive field surveys of 7500 adults in thirty states, an impression was obtained of the ranking of the population in respect of these performance requirements. Three competency levels were defined, adults who functioned with difficulty, functional adults and proficient adults.

On the whole American adult society was found to be about 46.3 per cent proficient while only 19.7 per cent functioned with difficulty. Performance was positively correlated with education, income, job status and negatively with size of family. Striking ethnic differences were found, with the Spanish group showing the lowest average performance level, followed by Blacks, other groups and finally Whites. Since some auto-correlation may be present in these profiles, we may perhaps assume that one circumstance such as education could be vital to all the others. Looking at this element one finds that 85 per cent of persons with an education of 0–3 years fell into the class who functioned with difficulty. Even among persons with an educational level of 6–7 years, 49 per cent functioned with difficulty.

Looking at the South African urban scene in the light of the above findings, it is disturbing to find that in 1970 40 per cent of the economically active Black males had no educational qualification at all, while another 17 per cent had an education of less than four years, and another 25 per cent had an education of less than seven years. In rural areas, whence contract workers (oscillatory migrants) are drawn, the position is even worse, since 94.3 per cent of the economically active male population had an educational qualification below the level of standard 6 of whom 65.4 per cent had no educational qualification at all. The position in regard to economically active Black females is roughly similar.

This means that by these American criteria the adult performance level in a sophisticated mixed economy of a very small percentage of Blacks is high while 70 per cent is low – preventing them from functioning in the system with ease.

In the case of Coloureds, 68.0 per cent of the economically active male population and 67.0 per cent of the corresponding Coloured female population had an educational qualification below the level of standard 6. The corresponding percentages for Whites were 4.4 and 2.8 respectively.

III THE WAY AHEAD

It is clear from the above statistics that on the criterion of educational level alone the great majority of Black and Coloured workers in the urban areas of the Republic lack the ability to use skills and knowledge with the functional competence needed for meeting the requirements of adult living as *responsible* and *free* citizens of a *democratic* society.

By the standards of students of the liberal principles, the South African plural urban society is in need of a great deal of reform before it could be expected to function in an orderly manner. We have quoted the economists, but an even stronger argument, in more operational detail, is put forward by the well-known British proponent of adult education, Professor Robert Peers. In emphasising the need for ongoing general education throughout the adult life of members of society, as against the narrow functional training for a specific job, Peers takes the following position:

> For the exercise of the duties and privileges of citizenship in a free and progressive society are needed breadth of vision, balanced judgement, understanding of the problems confronting other individuals and groups and the whole society, tolerance, and a sense of the values which give meaning and purpose to all the rest. This is the case for insisting on the need for liberal adult education to supplement, not to replace, the specialized training which must now dominate to an increasing extent the earlier years of our adult lives. And it is this aspect of education which belongs necessarily to the succeeding adult stage in the life of the individual, first because there is not enough time for all that it involves at any earlier stage, but also because this kind of education demands the background of experience and the maturity of mind which come only with adult years. We have now reached a stage in the development of advanced societies when adult education, no longer merely a substitute in later life for missed earlier opportunities, has come to be an essential part of the educational system of a democratic state.[2]

In other words, even in a 'common society' democracy cannot prevail without this fundamental precondition of civilisation. Peers stresses the tremendous dangers emerging from the complex social relationships in dense urban concentrations.

> Specialization in the applications of knowledge to the business of living and getting a living has resulted in great complexity of social grouping, and common interests are more difficult to see and to define. Failure at any point in these complicated relationships threatens the stability of the whole, and the promised gains may be lost through failure in our ability to control the colossus which we have created. This problem of control goes to the heart of what we are trying to do in maintaining the ideal of democracy in the face of growing difficulties.[3]

For these reasons there should be complete consensus among all views in South Africa about the priority of general education in the ideas and values of responsibility in a complex society. Perhaps one of the basic reasons for the urban frictions in Soweto and elsewhere may be found in the communication gap between children and their less articulate parents.

In the context of a plural society, additional problems of democratic order remain, even if most members of society are educationally sophisticated. In this connection we are confining our remarks simply to government in the economic system and the problem of economic policy. Most economists are familiar with the famous Arrow theorem that

> if there are at least three choices that the members of society are free to order in any possible way, then there can be no social welfare function that always meets both the doctrine of voters' sovereignty and the minimum conditions of collective rationality. The dangers that democracy cannot be economically rational are large even in theory.[4]

In practice, as Richard Musgrave, a famous authority on Public Finance remarks,

> democracy works well where considerable similarity in preference patterns exists – furnishing the necessary degree of cohesion.[5]

Where such close similarity in preference patterns is absent, simple majority rule becomes highly arbitrary. In a plural society simple majority rule cannot claim much support from the principles of justice, and efficiency.

In such circumstances the classical formula of integration is inherently dangerous, especially if it leads to the situation where each cultural group tends to specialise in separate economic functions, but they are expected to combine indiscriminately in the process of government. Exactly the reverse seems to be necessary in a plural society, i.e. a movement towards diversification of each actual group in all the functions of the economy, and a decentralisation of government or political control down to culturally homogeneous groups as far as possible.

Finally, it would appear to be necessary to place a heavy emphasis on the principles of limited government – in order to allow as many choice problems to be solved by the more effective and less conflicting processes of the market mechanism, where individual preferences are exercised in an infinitely more articulate manner and where the dignity and sovereignty of minorities may be safeguarded.

These, we believe, are the most important issues to be faced on the road towards the removal of discriminatory institutions in the urban economic society of the Republic: education, functional differentiation, institutional decentralisation, including the basic idea of limited government.

NOTES

1. Robbins, Lord, *Politics and Economics*, (London: Macmillan, 1963) pp. 30–1.
2. Peers, R., *Adult education*, (London: Routledge & Kegan Paul, 1972) p. 350.
3. Ibid, p. 348.
4. Musgrave, R., *The Theory of Public Finance* (New York: McGraw-Hill, 1959) p. 126.
5. Loc. cit.

24 Internal Security and External Support – the South African Dilemma

Peter Janke
Senior Researcher at the Institute for the Study of Conflict, London

This paper examines briefly an entirely new complex of political factors in Africa – the Soviet interest – and considers some aspects of the security situation in southern Africa arising from this, with particular reference to the Republic of South Africa (RSA). Specific developments which have contributed to this change were the crystallisation of Marxist-Leninist parties in Angola and Mozambique and the widest-ranging treaties, enduring for twenty years, that were concluded with the USSR. These and concomitant incidents can be accounted detrimental to the Republic. But the reaction to the Soviet African interest from individual Western and Arab states may redound to its benefit if the Republic, by meeting demands on human rights issues, is prepared to take advantage of recent Western anxiety to safeguard its own security through attending to dimensions other than overtly military ones in the Northern Atlantic sphere.

Behind the creation of a Russian sphere of interest in black Africa lay a number of related interests: the development of a global naval strategy, the search for food (particularly fish), interest in specific minerals such as bauxite, a desire to have a hand in controlling Western mineral supplies, and a need to strengthen its voice in the Third World, especially at the expense of China. But the opportunity for the USSR to establish itself arose through a series of local circumstances which the Soviet Union daringly exploited to its own advantage when it prompted Cuban intervention in the Angolan Civil War. Without this military aid, which still sustains MPLA government, and particularly President Agostinho Neto, Angola would not be aligned with Moscow.

I USSR AND MOZAMBIQUE

Weakness, too, drove FRELIMO into the protective shelter of the Socialist world order. Carried to power in the wake of a revolution in Lisbon, the infant Mozambican movement of some 15,000 guerrilla fighters, lacking any administrative experience, had little hope of governing successfully a country which was economically dependent upon neighbouring, hostile, white states and two-thirds of whose population of eight million people had never seen a guerrilla action. The need for a state philosophy became suddenly indispensable, where it had not been during the struggle. Moreover the Soviet Union offered the long-term political and economic underwriting which Western countries, bedevilled by changing governments and variable market forces, could not offer.

Compelled by this constellation of local factors, FRELIMO adopted the tenets of 'scientific socialism' at its third congress held during the first week of February 1977, when FRELIMO formally emerged as a Marxist-Leninist party.

> The hard class battles demand that the working class, in close alliance with the peasants, its fundamental ally, and the progressive elements from other workers' classes, have a vanguard party, directed by the scientific ideology of the proletariat. The setting-up of the party arises as a need of the development of the revolution.[1]

The language used at this congress was remarkable: it bore for the first time the stultifying phraseology familiar to Eastern Europe but quite new to FRELIMO. The leadership extolled the cardinal precepts of old-fashioned Communist orthodoxy, amongst others the 'destruction of capitalism', 'the dictatorship of the proletariat', 'democratic centralism', 'class struggle', and the 'decadent values of the bourgeoisie', concepts many of which the popular European Communist parties have abandoned.

> The final objectives in the constitution of the People's Republic of Mozambique are, basically, the construction of the political, ideological, scientific, and cultural basis of the socialist society. The consti-

tution establishes that the land and natural resources of our country are the property of the state. It stresses the value of the collective form of production and defends the interests of the working masses . . . The constitution gives particular emphasis to internationalism – a gain of our struggle and a constant factor in FRELIMO policy. It defines as fundamental features of the foreign policy of our state, the unity of the African peoples and states, the natural alliance with socialist countries, support for and solidarity with the struggle of the peoples for liberation, the struggle against colonialism, neo-colonialism, and imperialism, the fight for peace and general and univeral disarmament. . . .²

These developments in Mozambique did not take place in isolation. President Nyerere, who for years had adopted an independent socialist path chose this moment to set up a single revolutionary party – the *Chama Cha Mapinduzi*. It was described by Moscow as 'the vehicle to implement the principles of scientific socialism'.³ President Nyerere however preferred to see in it the means to exercise authority for the benefit of the individual. In the People's Republic of the Congo too President Ngouabi, at the Central Committee session held on 5 November 1976, was determined to set up a single structure based upon Marxist theory, recognising that 'men pass away whilst the revolution continues'. 'The new leadership must include only elements capable of advancing the revolution on the basis of the class struggle. . . .' Since his assassination on 18 March 1977 there has been no indication to make one believe that the system will change although in June 1977 the country re-established diplomatic relations with the USA.

II USSR AND ANGOLA

Angola declared its intention to formalise its vanguard party in October 1977, strengthening in the meantime its links with the Soviet Union on 14 March, when both countries ratified a 20-year treaty of friendship and cooperation. This provided the long-term legal basis for the all-round development of political, economic, commercial, scientific, technical, cultural and other cooperation between the two countries. But the treaty not only regulated bilateral relations, it created a framework for the expansion of Soviet foreign policy objectives. As President Podgorny explained, 'the treaty mirrored in essence our country's policy in its relations with peoples struggling for national and social liberation and with developing countries in Africa and on other continents who have won independence.' Both countries solemnly pledged to continue the struggle against 'the forces of imperialism and to uproot colonialism and neo-colonialism, racialism and *apartheid*'. Furthermore, the military dimension was added with a reference to the declaration adopted in November 1976 by the Warsaw Treaty Member states, which 'reaffirmed their readiness to continue their aid and support to the people of Zimbabwe, Namibia, and South Africa. . . .'

In essence the formula to 'continue the struggle against the forces of imperialism and to uproot colonialism and neo-colonialism, racialism and *apartheid*' is one which provides for the setting up of Moscow-line Socialist states not only in Rhodesia, Namibia and South Africa but also in Zambia, Zaire and even Tanzania. Indeed one might add in all those African states which have not chosen 'scientific socialism' as a development model. Even President Neto made it very clear in an interview in *Afrique Asie* in November 1976 that this philosophy alone could deliver the world from exploitation and the terrible injustice of the capitalist system.

A similar treaty was signed by President Podgorny on 31 March 1977 in Mozambique. The two countries agreed 'to co-operate in every way in creating evermore favourable conditions for preserving and deepening social and economic gains of the peoples of the USSR and Mozambique.' To achieve this, trade and shipping would be expanded on most favoured nation treatment and cooperation would be deepened in industry, transport, agriculture, fisheries, mining and the training of national cadres. Similar contacts will be promoted in the sporting, cultural and educational spheres.

Of great importance was the determination to continue developing cooperation in the military sphere. Both parties undertook not to enter any alliance whatever which might be directed against the other nor to conclude any international agreements incompatible with the new treaty. In addition Mozambique would support the Soviet view on how to proceed with nuclear disarmament. There is a clear alignment of interests on this point, bearing in mind South African nuclear development. The implementation of the idea of turning the African continent into a nuclear-free zone would in President Podgorny's opinion undoubtedly be useful for the cause of relaxation of internal tensions. This issue is likely to receive a lot of attention in the future.

According to Article 9 of the treaty, if situations arise that threaten peace or break the peace the two countries will immediately contact one another so as to coordinate their positions in the interest of eliminating the arising threat or of restoring peace. There seems little doubt that this article could be invoked were South Africa to engage in pre-emptive strikes on guerrilla bases in Mozambique, as the Rhodesians have done.

It is worth detailing the common foreign policy objectives of both Angola and Mozambique with the Soviet Union. These include an Indian Ocean zone of peace free of Western bases; support for the 1975 Helsinki détente agreements; an Israeli withdrawal to pre-1967 boundaries and the creation of a Palestinian state; Vietnam membership of the UN; the peaceful unification of Korea and the withdrawal of US troops; a restructuring of international economic relations and support in the UN for the Third World and non-alignment movement. To these objectives can be added support for the withdrawal of US control of the Panama Canal and even a condemnation of the 'occupation' of Puerto Rico, pledged earlier to Cuba on the occasion of Castro's visit to Mozambique. Of these considerations far and away the most important to the Russians is that of the Indian Ocean peace zone, for, as President Podgorny reminded the Tanzanians in a speech on 24 March 1977, the communication routes linking European Russia with the Soviet Far East passed through the Indian Ocean. The argument follows that the Soviet Union therefore has legitimate interests in the Indian Ocean, unlike China, the US or Europe, and that these should be defended. This claim obviously affects the security of the Republic, whilst the military clauses go further than anything India or Egypt had agreed to in earlier treaties signed with the USSR.

III USSR AND THE LIBERATION MOVEMENTS

With the establishment of two Marxist-Leninist states to the north, committed to expanding scientific socialism in Africa, came the development of vehicles for this process: the ideological satellisation of the Rhodesian *Patriotic Front*, and *South West African Peoples Organisation* (SWAPO) and the South African ANC. As with Angola and Mozambique the adoption of a pro-Moscow stand by the *Patriotic Front* and SWAPO was a recognition of political realities most likely to favour the accomplishment of their political aims. (In the case of the ANC the ideological alignment dated back to a long relationship with the Moscow-line South African Communist Party.) The new political alignment provided these movements with secure base areas contiguous to their military targets as well as the assurance of logistical back-up and aid prior and after their assumption of power.

The *Patriotic Front's* new allegiance had its origins in statements from Robert Mugabe and ZANU spokesmen working through the guerrillas then known as the Zimbabwe People's Army (ZIPA). This was only later taken up by Joshua Nkomo with the emergence in October 1976 of the *Patriotic Front* and during the abortive settlement talks with Geneva. Indeed, the early ZANU statements specifically excluded Nkomo:

> the guerrillas are fighting for more – for a new kind of society in Zimbabwe. The far aim is to establish a socialist society. Of course we realise this cannot be achieved overnight – it will mean a protracted struggle. If Nkomo and Muzorewa came to power such a chance would not be available. If independence is achieved through the barrel of a gun the country will be ruled not by civilian politicians but by political soldiers, the freedom fighters. In the new Zimbabwe there will be no parliamentary democracy, no voting and no canvassing.[4]

On 22 September 1976 ZIPA made its first public utterance on Radio Maputo. It said moves were being made to 'transform this organisation into a revolutionary vanguard for the people's struggle'. A spokesman in London confirmed that the war would continue and demanded the immediate arrest of the heads of the Rhodesian Government, including the Army and Police Chiefs to stand trial for war crimes. This intransigent attitude developed in a context of new hardline Marxist propaganda put out from Maputo on behalf of the guerrillas.

> Workers and peasants of Zimbabwe: It is not your fellow worker or peasant who is responsible for your unbearable economic condition, it is not your fellow worker who is responsible for your poverty and the bad conditions you are forced to work under, it is the capitalists.

When in December 1976 ZIPA sent a delegation to Geneva it did so in the conviction that it alone represented 'the people's revolution' and was responsible for ensuring that the 'imperialist initiated' conference did not 'sabotage' or 'hijack' the achievements of the armed struggle and impose neo-colonialism on Zimbabwe.[5]

Although this process of ideological alignment has not yet been completed within SWAPO the movement's constitution speaks in Article 7 of

> insuring that the people's government exercises effective control over the means of production and distribution and pursues a policy which facilitates the way to social ownership of the resources of the country.

It is also true that SWAPO leader Sam Nujoma visited Cuba and Moscow seeking arms in 1976. SWAPO thinks of itself as forming a

> vanguard party of progressive intellectuals uniting the working class and the peasantry and building a classless non-exploitive society based on scientific socialist ideals and principles.[6]

Furthermore, foreign policy objectives are clearly aligned with Moscow. Both President Neto and Samora Machel felt strongly that it was their duty to give 'concrete form' to joint 'internationalist help' on Namibia and Rhodesia so as to extend the revolutionary base in Africa from the Indian Ocean to the Atlantic Ocean.[7]

The Soviet Union is aware that a new and exciting dawn has risen for it in Africa. The trends described above represent a new historical period in the development of the continent. President Podgorny's tour in March 1976 of Tanzania, Zambia and Mozambique clinched the relationship. Whilst in Zambia he visited the Victoria Falls and gazed south into Rhodesia, a gesture which, following the aborted conference held on the Falls Bridge in 1975, history will recall. Whilst in Lusaka the leaders of three liberation movements, Sam Nujoma (SWAPO), Joshua Nkomo (ZAPU) and Oliver Tambo (South African ANC) were presented to the Soviet President on 28 March. The following day at a welcoming dinner in Maputo President Podgorny spoke of 'the wind of freedom blowing from Mozambique and Angola and inspiring the patriots of all Southern Africa'. Such an historical allusion confirmed for black Africans Soviet intentions to pursue a forward foreign policy in the area: this meant the subversion of South Africa itself.

> Invariable solidarity with the peoples fighting against colonialism for national independence and progressive transformation is a key principle of the Leninist foreign policy of the Soviet Union.[8]

Soviet foreign policy in Southern Africa derives overwhelming advantages from the clarity of its 'anti-colonial' and 'anti-racist' stance.

428   *Intergroup Accommodation in Plural Societies*

Unlike South East Asia there is no large and secure Communist base which affords Soviet expansionist efforts an ideological and logistical hinterland. Communist ideology is strange in the mouths of black Africans. It must contend with forces it has never encountered elsewhere – tribalism and the most complete savagery and primitive conditions juxtaposed with pockets of great intellectual sophistication, and immense raw material wealth and strategic importance valued by the West.

IV   CAN THE SOVIET THREAT BE CONTAINED?

To maintain the initiative undoubtedly seized in 1976 the USSR must be able to count on at least two factors: firstly, that internal change in the region does not occur quickly enough either to forestall revolutionary demands from being formulated or, having been formulated, from spreading; secondly, that Western Europe and the US are satisfied with the results of the Helsinki Agreements on détente and become increasingly less concerned with the Soviet threat.

The first condition lies almost entirely within the sphere of the Republic of South Africa: it can pursue reform or not. The nature of the threat is clear. The state is confronted by a combination of a foreign ideology backed by a super-power which is exploiting an internal numbers problem to its own advantage. The state's safety therefore lies in tackling quickly and radically the problem of separating the foreign element from the internal element. In other words the issue of human rights for blacks and coloureds must be attended to. Legislation in this direction will not halt this subversive drive, to which the whole free world is subjected, but it will blunt its impact and open to the Republic the moral assistance of African states fearful of Soviet domination as well as Western support generally.

So far as the second condition is concerned there exists in Europe a much more realistic appraisal of Soviet intentions now than twelve months ago. Furthermore, the issues of geography and resources play a greater part in strategic debate,[9] and have moved some elements in NATO to considering deploying limited conventional offensives outside traditionally conceived operational theatres in defence of vital raw material supplies.[10]

French reactions to an incursion by former Katangese gendarmes from Angola into Zaire on 8 March 1977 demonstrated that France was prepared, if asked, to resist Communist encroachment in the score of French-speaking African states. Although other countries opposed, the prompt French airlift of 1500 Moroccan troops to Shaba significantly attracted West German support within the EEC. More to the point, it had considerable African backing, including that of Nigeria, which allowed the French to refuel. The UK made no comment on the French action, but Prime Minister Callaghan was moved at a meeting of Socialist leaders in Amsterdam on 17 April 1977 to warn the Russians that an anti-Western policy in Africa was incompatible with détente. It is probable that France would have acted in this way without regard to US opinion, which in this case was favourable, itself supplying non-military provisions to Zaire.

Perhaps the most unexpected Soviet denunciation came from President Sadat whilst visiting the United States in early April. Egypt had had experience of close Russian cooperation before breaking with the USSR in 1972 and more recently Sadat had strongly opposed Soviet influence in the Sudan and Ethiopia. Both Egypt and South Africa are well placed to contain this new presence and might cooperate were there not the moral objection to racial discrimination in the Republic. To take advantage of this new strategic perception by non-Communist forces South Africa would do well to remove swiftly and imaginatively this element from the apartheid system.

NOTES

1. Samora Machel, 1 February 1977, in Maputo.
2. Ibid.
3. Moscow Home Service, 7 January 1977.
4. Austin Chakaodza, ZANU London representative, in exclusive interview with *Rhodesia Herald*, 10 June 1976.
5. ZIPA statement, 29 November 1976.
6. *Namibia News*, September 1976.
7. Joint speeches at rally on 11 November 1977 in Luanda and Machel's opening speech on 1 February 1977 at FRELIMO'S third congress.
8. President Podgorny's speech, 29 March 1976, Maputo.
9. See for instance *New Dimensions of Security in Europe* (ISC, London, 1975) and *The New Strategic Map*, by Geoffrey Kemp in *Survival*, March/April 1977 (IISS, London).
10. Air Chief Marshall Sir Neil Cameron, quoted by Eric de Mornay 'World in Focus', BBC Radio 4, 20 April 1977.

25 Citizenship and Intergroup Accommodation in Plural Societies

Marinus Wiechers
Professor of Constitutional and International Law, University of South Africa

I CITIZENSHIP AND DISTRIBUTION OF POWER

For the purposes of a discussion of the way in which citizenship can play a significant part in the accommodation of various population groups within the same state, it will be accepted that a plural society is one in which people of differing race, colour, descent and national or ethnic origin live, each group possessing to a varying degree its own language, culture and identity. The scope of this enquiry will be the question whether citizenship affords a sound basis for the distribution of power between the various population groups so as to ensure that there will not be any domination of one group by the others and that discrimination will be eliminated. The reason why citizenship is considered a crucial factor in the equal distribution of power is that citizenship, as a juridical concept, contains within itself the three components which are supposed to comprise the sum total of a subject's public law competences, i.e. political, civil and social rights.[1] Therefore, if a citizen enjoys full citizenship, he should be able to exercise full rights and benefits in the political, social and civil spheres of life: on the other hand, if, in his capacity as a citizen, he is denied the fulfilment of these rights, he must of necessity be considered a second or even third-class citizen. This enquiry will be whether it is possible to have various kinds of citizens, all having the same nationality, in order to construe a plural structure in society in such a way that diversity does not become a means of 'divide and rule' but of safeguarding the rights and privileges of all citizens.

Citizenship is closely linked with nationality in the sense that a national of a country will at the same time be a citizen of that country. But it is generally accepted that nationality and citizenship may, legally, have two connotations: in the realm of international law, nationality simply means the link which exists between a state-subject and its subjects, whereas in the constitutional law context, citizenship means the legal status which a person acquires as a result of his being a national of that particular country.[2] Briefly stated, it may be said that the concept of nationality as it exists in international law has at its roots the relationship of allegiance as it existed between monarch and subject (which eventually developed into the relationship of state-subject and member of that state community); citizenship will then rest on the legal tie which binds government and subject within a particular state.[3] Citizenship in the sense of a legal status implies that the citizen has certain rights and privileges *vis-à-vis* the government, but that at the same time he also has certain responsibilities which flow from the state's right to demand loyalty and obedience.

II NATIONALITY AND NATIONAL AND INTERNATIONAL LAW

It is interesting to note that nationality, i.e. the legal relationship of international law between state-subject and its members, is of comparatively recent origin; it was only during the nineteenth century that nationality became a subject for state legislation since, up to then, there had been in most states a diversity of groups and classes, the members of each having their own particular status without an overriding or inclusive state nationality.[4] In that respect, it may be said that citizenship, meaning a person's public law status within a given community, preceded nationality. As a result of the growth of national states and the strong insistence on state sovereignty in international law, the position has become reversed and it is now the state-subject who decides who are its nationals. The acceptance of the principle that it is within the sovereign power of a state to decide for itself whom it will consider to be its nationals is reflected in Article 1(3) of the International Convention on the Elimination of All Forms of Racial Discrimination:

> Nothing in this Convention may be interpreted as affecting in any way the legal provisions of State Parties concerning nationality, citizenship or naturalisation, provided that such provisions do not discriminate against any particular community.

Nationality and citizenship usually go hand in hand. In other words, if a person is a national of a particular state, he is at the same time also a citizen of that state in the public law meaning of the word. But this is not always so: In the German Reich there was a Reich nationality which was not the same as, and did not coincide with, citizenship of the component parts of the Reich, and in the British Commonwealth there is an umbrella international law nationality which provides for citizenship of the various Commonwealth countries even though the citizenship laws of these individual countries differ.[5]

There are very few rules of international law governing the granting of nationality. In general, it is left to each state on whom and under which conditions it will grant nationality. But it has become more and more accepted in international law that no state has the right to compel foreigners to take up its nationality against their wishes, and furthermore that the deprivation of nationality is also not allowed against the will of the national concerned – in this respect, the right to possess the nationality of some state or other is considered as a fundamental human right.[6]

As regards citizenship, i.e. the constitutional law status which nationals of a state possess within that state, it is significant that modern international law with its strong insistence on the promotion of human rights has increasingly come to occupy itself with the position of the citizen and his political, social and civil rights. Not long ago, the idea of a 'citoyen actif' and a 'citoyen passif' was well-recognised and accepted in constitutional law, in the sense that there are in every state some citizens who have the capacity to exercise all their civil, political and cultural rights but that at the same time there are other citizens who are restricted in or even denied the exercise of these rights.[7] Of course, it is perfectly understandable that in any state there will always be persons of unsound mind, minors, convicts or unrehabilitated insolvents who will be debarred from fully exercising their competences as citizens, and that such restrictions will not be considered unreasonable in the sense of Article 25 of the International Covenant on Civil and

Political Rights (16 December, 1966). But the old idea that citizens who are dependent on the charity of the state, who do not and cannot work, should lose their right to participate in the affairs of government, especially through the exercise of their voting rights, has definitely lapsed.[8]

III INTERNATIONAL HUMAN RIGHTS

For the purposes of this paper it is not intended to go into the question whether international organisations such as the United Nations can through its resolutions create new rules of international law, and more particularly, whether the various UN declarations, resolutions and covenants on human rights are to be seen as rules of international law. Suffice it to say that, over the past thirty years, the organised international community has, in the General Assembly of the United Nations, elaborated a whole set of rules in regard to what the content of citizenship should be – particularly in the light of the elimination of all forms of racial discrimination. To many states these rules created by the United Nations may constitute unauthorised interference in the domestic affairs of member states, but the fact remains that they have nevertheless become the normal standards by which state behaviour in the field of human rights is judged, and they form the basic principles for many international agreements for the promotion of human rights.[9] Perhaps the most explicit rules for state regulation of the rights and privileges to be granted to citizens, particularly in a pluralistic context, are to be found in *Article 5* of the International Convention on the Elimination of all Forms of Racial Discrimination of 21 December 1965, which reads as follows:

> ... State Parties undertake to prohibit and to eliminate racial discrimination in all its forms and to guarantee the right to everyone, without distinction as to race, colour, or national or ethnic origin, to equality before the law, notably in the enjoyment of the following rights:
> (a) ...
> (b) ...
> (c) *Political rights*, in particular the rights to participate in elections – and to vote and to stand for election – on the basis of universal and equal suffrage, to take part in the Government as well as in the conduct of public affairs at any level and to have equal access

to public service;
(d) Other *civil rights*, in particular:
  (i) The right to freedom of movement and residence within the border of the State;
  (ii) The right to leave any country, including one's own, and to return to one's country;
  (iii) The right to nationality;
  (iv) The right to marry and choice of spouse;
  (v) The right to own property alone as well as in association with others;
  (vi) The right to inherit;
  (vii) The right to freedom of thought, conscience and religion;
  (viii) The right of opinion and expression;
  (ix) The right to freedom of peaceful assembly and association;
(e) *Economic, social and cultural rights, in particular*:
  (i) The right to work, to free choice of employment, to just and favourable conditions of work, to protection against unemployment, to equal pay for equal work, to just and favourable remuneration;
  (ii) The right to form and join trade unions;
  (iii) The right to housing;
  (iv) The right to public health, medical care, social security and social services;
  (v) The right to education and training;
  (vi) The right to equal participation in cultural activities;
(f) The right to access to any place or service intended for use by the general public, such as transport, hotels, restaurants, cafés, theatres and parks.

It would be most difficult to classify the above-mentioned rights according to their intrinsic importance or to establish a hierarchy of rights which flow from citizenship. It must, however, be stated, that the political right to participate in elections and to be elected is a particularly important element of citizenship. The right to be represented and to represent has become for many authors a fundamental human right and a basic assertion of human dignity.[10] This is because it is in the process of being elected and in participation in elections that a citizen can effectively share in the business of government and ensure the effective bestowal by means of legislation and other governmental actions of civil and social rights on members of his particular group. Without the right to elect and to be elected, citizenship is divested of much of its material content. Thus it is said that only in the process of representation of the nation (through its electorate) does the nation (the subjects) acquire the quality of a nation with visible features and the capacity to speak for itself.[11]

In brief, therefore, it may be said that nationality in the international law sense of the word is a matter which falls within the scope of state sovereignty and that, apart from a few general directions, a state is free to bestow nationality on such persons and under such conditions as it may decide for itself – except for the clear provision that in bestowing nationality a state may not discriminate against any particular community.[12] Citizenship, on the other hand, meaning the constitutional law status of a subject within a particular state, must entail meaningful political, civil and social rights.

IV THE POSITION IN SOUTH AFRICA

As far as South African nationality is concerned, i.e. the legal tie that binds the Republic as a state with its subjects, the Citizenship Act 1949 is apparently colour-blind. On the face of it, anybody, notwithstanding his race, colour or origin, can acquire South African citizenship by birth, descent and naturalisation. On closer scrutiny, however, the position is not quite as simple: in some instances for the acquisition of South African citizenship by birth or descent and in all cases of acquisition of citizenship by naturalisation, the criterion of a 'prohibited immigrant' is of vital importance; the children of prohibited immigrants cannot by birth or descent acquire South African citizenship and a prohibited immigrant himself can never become a citizen by naturalisation. Now, a prohibited immigrant is someone who is a foreigner and who has no right to permanent residence in the Republic. One of the conditions for the granting of permanent residence is that the applicant must be 'likely to become readily assimilated with the European inhabitants' of the Republic.[13] Under this condition it simply means that a black or coloured alien is precluded from obtaining permanent residence in the Republic and cannot therefore apply for South African citizenship by naturalisation. Similarly, the child of black or coloured aliens born in South Africa and the child of a black or coloured alien father (even though the mother is a South African citizen) born outside the Republic cannot become a citizen by birth or descent. Another prohibition based on racial grounds is contained in sect. 6(2) of the Act, which prescribes that a person born outside the

Republic can never become a citizen by descent if the marriage of his natural parents would have been unlawful under the Prohibition of Mixed Marriages Act 55 of 1949 notwithstanding the fact that his father or both his parents are South African citizens.

Although the provisions of the Citizenship Act do not discriminate against *any particular nationality* in the sense of Article 1(3) of the International Convention on the Elimination of All Forms of Racial Discrimination, it has a very strong racial bias in so far as it requires permanent residence for the acquisition of nationality – a requirement which only a white person can fulfil. In short, it means that under the Aliens Act 1937 and the Citizenship Act 1949 black and coloured immigrants and the acquisition of citizenship by such persons are made impossible.

Looking at the material content of South African citizenship for blacks, coloureds and whites as far as political, civil and social rights are concerned, one finds still more obvious discrepancies. White citizens in the Republic enjoy many rights and privileges which are denied to coloured and black citizens. It can be said without fear of contradiction that white citizenship in South Africa entails a maximum of civil, political and social rights, whereas brown and black citizenship carries considerably fewer rights and privileges. In the case of the coloureds it has been found that under the present system they enjoy very few political rights and the government has been seriously urged to provide for the further and effective extension of their political rights at all levels of representative government.[14]

The position as far as black citizenship is concerned is even worse. Blacks born in the Republic have South African nationality under the Citizenship Act 1949. At the same time, under the Bantu Homelands Citizenship Act 26 of 1970, every black citizen is considered to have a 'double' citizenship, i.e. a South African citizenship which carries with it an absolute minimum of political, civil and social rights – to such an extent that it has been said that it would be 'justified to assert that Bantu citizens in the Republic possess almost nothing more than naked South African nationality'[15] – and a homeland citizenship which could be described as a 'narrower kind of citizenship which has the potentiality to grow into a citizenship of the widest meaning'.[16] The underlying ideology is namely that blacks, once they have become nationals of their respective independent homelands, will enjoy full citizenship with all its concomitant political, civil and political rights. Of course, this grand design will remain a mere fantasy if the millions of black nationals of the independent homelands remain living in the 'white' Republic and have to bear with the deprivation of all civil and social rights just as they do now. The policy of the government eventually to denationalise all blacks in 'white' South Africa so as to remove their political demands for representation and to escape a one-man-one-vote domination, may appeal to some hard-line ideologists, but may prove in the light of reality to be extremely dangerous and perhaps even disastrous. A black national of an independent homeland who lives and works permanently in the Republic is going to derive very little comfort from the idea that he enjoys full citizenship in his distant homeland if, under the conditions where he toils and sweats, he suffers all the injustices of possessing a minimum of political, civil and social rights.[17]

To conclude this brief survey of the present position in South Africa, it must be sadly stated that racialism and discrimination cast a dark shadow over our nationality and citizenship laws and that there is very little in the present system which can stand up in the face of internationally minimum standards as contained in the various conventions, declarations and covenants of the United Nations and other international bodies. Instead of employing nationality and citizenship as a means to achieve intergroup accommodation in a plural society, they have become the tools of a white government to promote exclusively white immigration and to create categories of first, second and even third-class South African citizens.

V DIFFERENT CITIZENSHIP STATUS

Is it not possible, however, to create a different citizenship status for the different communities in our plural society, which at the same time guarantees similar political, civil and social rights? In other words, would it not be feasible to have in South Africa one nationality in the international law sense of the word but a different public law citizenship status for the different population groups so as to prevent group domination?

The first possibility which springs to the mind is to have in the field of political rights, and especially the right to represent and be represented, a system of qualified franchise which will ensure that only the best-qualified members of each group will enjoy the benefit of representing and being represented by the members of their group. What is so attractive in such a system of meritocracy is that it is considered that vested interests will be safeguarded thereby and domination by a largely uneducated and poor majority will be prevented. In terms of citizenship this would mean that some citizens will qualify – but not on racial lines – for full political participation whereas other citizens will be disqualified until by their own industry and perseverance they attain the necessary qualifications. Ideally, this solution may seem to be attractive, but in a plural society such as South Africa where pluralism at the same time also implies a highly structured class society, this would in effect amount to domination by the privileged and promotion of 'closed shop' policies, and the greater arrogance and disregard for human dignity which such a system carries within itself. In this respect, one cannot but agree with the following observation:

> Now, the merits of a qualified franchise on a common roll no doubt deserve serious consideration as a proposal for constitutional reform, but they do not even begin to deal with the presence or lack of multiple membership and cross-cutting affiliations between a multiplicity of non-inclusive secondary groups. So far from providing a solution to the problem of democratic stability in a divided plural society, they are begging the very real questions of the social preconditions for their own successful implementation.[18]

It is my belief that in order to achieve full civil and social rights for the different population groups in a context of minority protection and the elimination of group domination, it will be necessary to solve the problem of political rights for all citizens, and more particularly, the right of representation. For this, the reform of the electoral system so as to contain the principle of a general franchise, whether with joint or separate voters' rolls, and representation in common legislatures and governmental bodies seem to be the most realistic. It is often said that one of the characteristics of the Westminster system is the principle of one-man-one-vote, which necessarily leads to majority domination of other groups. Without discussing the question whether one-man-one-vote is really so characteristic of the Westminster system, it must be pointed out that in England, as in South Africa, our system of constituency delimitation and a voters' quota, with its possibility of loading and unloading, is very far from being a simple one-man-one-vote system. In this way it was, for example, possible for the present government to obtain a majority of seats in parliament in 1948 without the support of the majority of the total number of voters. Would it not be possible to have a combined constituency or geographic representational system, coupled with proportional representation, in order to ensure that all population groups will be represented in both the central government and in other subordinate legislative bodies? And, once this group representation is achieved, then to elaborate a system of government whereby group interests and rights are protected?

Another possibility of employing citizenship as a means of intergroup accommodation could well be to have a decentralised union *inaequale iure* not on ethnic, homeland lines but on a geographic basis, such as regions and provinces, and to leave it to the different regions or provinces how the political, civil and social rights of their citizens would be regulated. In this way it could happen that one region or province opted for an open society (thus attracting the more *verligte* elements of the nation) and that another province opted for a greater degree of black, brown or white *verkramptheid*. Of course, apart from and including the regional or provincial citizenships, there must always be a South African citizenship which will allow all South African citizens – brown, black and white – to participate in the affairs of the central government.

VI POLITICAL REALITIES IN SOUTH AFRICA

Political realities in South Africa do not offer easy solutions to our problems. The granting of full political, civil and social rights to all South African nationals regardless of colour, creed or origin will immediately create fears of black majority rule and the ensuing suppression of minority rights and freedoms. In this respect Africa presents very little comfort to allay white fears and apprehensions.

From whatever perspective one views the present constitutional arrangement in the Republic, it is undoubtedly true that the white population contributed and still contributes much to the country's overall development and stability, factors which in turn are to the benefit of all its citizens. It would amount to extreme naïveté and shortsightedness to expect the white population group simply to abdicate its present dominant position and to accept, in the place thereof, majority dictatorship and the inevitable disasters concomitant therewith, such as economic and political instability and the ideological uprooting of existing political mores and traditions. If one considers how rapidly this happened after the lapse of colonial rule in Moçambique, it must be conceded that many of these fears (which are held not only by the whites) are well founded. It is also in this context that it is understandable why the Republic must adhere to a strict and rather selective immigration policy in order to protect less developed members of the community from being overrun by foreigners from poor neighbouring countries who have, except for their unskilled labour, very little to offer with which to combat the social hazards and economic demands which their presence will create. However, this in itself does not perhaps justify the insistence on an exclusively white immigration policy.

If these realities are taken into account, one must needs ask whether the granting of political, social and civil rights, i.e. the giving of full material and substantive content to South African citizenship for all the Republic's peoples on a basis of equality, cannot and must not be arranged in a different way. Far from creating a privileged and less privileged status for members of the different population groups, the feasibility of allowing a maximum of civil as well as social rights and privileges, meaning the elimination of all discrimination on a basis of colour or creed, must be considered; at the same time a system must be introduced whereby political rights on a collective or group basis are effectively safeguarded. As regards the question of franchise, it will be of particular importance to ensure that groups which are represented in joint decision-making bodies on local, provincial and national levels will have no fear of being deprived of their individual civil and social rights by sheer majority domination on the part of other groups. It is only by creating a solid representational system that plural democracy can attain full meaning and content and it is only from such a sound basis that responsible government can stem forth.

Of course, the distribution of political rights on a group basis within a plural democracy does not in itself solve the vexing question of where the ultimate power in the state is going to reside. If this ultimate power is to remain with the white population group, this will necessarily mean that, in the final analysis, the whites will always have to contend with the accusations and incriminations of other groups if government is not, in the opinion of the latter, conducted satisfactorily – thereby creating a fertile ground for constant polarisation and the fomenting of anti-white attitudes. The only way to deal with such an eventuality is to create effective intergroup consultation and action, especially in the executive branch of government, and of course, to provide for lively cross-cutting political affiliations among the different population groups. At present, the latter factor is dismally absent in South African political life as a result of the Act on the Prohibition of Political Interference 1967 which prevents the establishment of multiracial political parties.

Citizenship and Intergroup Accommodation

A discussion on citizenship in the present constitutional framework of the Republic is not a very happy task, since it urges one to underline many of the imperfections and, indeed, the harshness, of the existing system. But on the other hand, it does provide us with a key concept of how a pluralistic and yet truly democratic system of government can be achieved. Because it is only a system of government in which citizenship – in the sense of the sum total of a subject's individual and collective rights and liberties – acquires full meaning and content for all the different groups which is worthy to be called a democracy.

NOTES

1. Cf. The Marshall 'Citizenship and Social Class' as discussed by F. H. van der Berg in 'Mens en Burger', *De mens in het Recht*, essays in honour of Prof. W. F. Prins (1975) 47 at 53.
2. Alex. Makarov, 'Règles Générales du Droit de la Nationalité', 74 Rec. des Cours (1949 I) 269 at 279; JFH, 'A Transkeian Citizen of South African Nationality', 1963 THRHR 44.
3. Makarov, op. cit., 279.
4. Makarov, op. cit., 277.
5. J. P. verLoren van Themaat, *Staatsreg* (2nd edition 1966) 361: 'Imperial nationality should be world-wide and uniform, each dominion being left free to grant local nationality on such terms as its legislature should think fit'; Makarov, op. cit., 285.
6. George Dahm, *Völkerrecht* I (1958) at 461 and 491.
7. F. H. van der Berg, op. cit., at 49.
8. F. H. van der Berg, op. cit., at 55.
9. Jost Delbrück, *Die Rassenfrage als Problem des Völkerrechts und nationaler Rechtsordungen* (1971) at 67.
10. Johannes Messner, 'Die Idee der Menschenwürde im Rechsstaat der pluralistichen Gesellschaft' and Hans-Justus Rinck 'Allgemeinheit und Gleicheit der Wahl als wegbereiter su einem Zeitgemässen Verständnis der Menschenwürde', both in *Menschenwürde und freiheitliche Rechtsordnung*, festschrift for Willi Geiger (1974) at 221 and 676; H. J. M. Jeukens, 'Kiesrecht as Grondrecht' in *De Mens in het Recht* (1975) at 125.
11. A. M. Donner, 'Over Representatie' in *De Mens in het Recht* (1975) at 105.
12. Article 1(3) of the International Convention on the Elimination of All Forms of Racial Discrimination.
13. Sect. 4(3)(b) of the Aliens Act 1 of 1937.
14. Recommendation 178 at 512 of the Report of the Commission of Enquiry into Matters relating to the Coloured Population Group, RP/1976.
15. F. Venter, 'Bantoeburgerskap en Tuislandburgerskap', 1975 THRHR 239 at 250.
16. Ibid.
17. See sect. 6 of the Transkei Status Act 1976 and sect. 6 of the Bophuthatswana Status Act 1977 which promise that Transkei or Bophuthatswana

citizens will not lose any of their existing rights, privileges and benefits except those regarding citizenship, as a result of their becoming nationals of an independent homeland. These provisions are extremely ambiguous if it is taken into account that such nationals become prohibited immigrants in the Republic once their homelands gain independence.
18. *SA's Political Alternatives*, Spro-cas Publication no. 10 (1973) at 132.

26 The Structuring of Political Change in South Africa

C. F. Nieuwoudt

Professor of Political Science, University of Pretoria. The paper was read at the Congress of the Political Science Association of South Africa, 30 September 1977, and subsequently published in Politikon, *official journal of PSASA, December 1977.*

I CHANGE AND DEVELOPMENT

The recorded political history of states during the past 3000 years has underscored one major feature – a process of uninterrupted change. Of course, this springs from the very being of man himself. Man is for ever engaged in a dynamic process of intellectual growth and development which leads to a systematic increase in knowledge of the political systems which man has created for himself. Thus, political systems, embodied in political structures, are also subject to continuous change: they are transformed, reshaped and fashioned anew to meet the needs of a new age and its circumstances. These needs are derived from the various social phenomena encountered in human society, which have an ethnic, religious, territorial, economic, racial, class or national basis. The differentials between people are virtually limitless; therefore various groupings of people have emerged in the form of national states. But even within these various states, each of which has its own distinctive plural character, there is a wide variety of groupings. Such a state is South Africa. Formal institutional structures as well as conventions, customs and other forms of social and economic institutions are designed to create order and stability. Indeed, the purpose of these institutions is to exercise authority in order to eliminate conflict and reduce the impact of differences for the greatest common good. A society which is based on mutual interests and reflects a moral consensus is also vested with a special responsibility in respect of the individual as well as the various groups in the complex modern state. Such a responsibility can only be discharged through a process of institutionalisation by which values are established and upheld and stability achieved. Within their own context, however, these institutions must make provision for adjustment and change if continued development is to be possible.

In South Africa, meaningful political adjustment and change is feasible only if cognisance is taken of the unique realties of the South African society; the plurality of the composition of the South African population; the differing degrees of political, economic and social development of the various population groups; and the realities which the post-colonial history of Africa have brought home to the White man in Africa.

These realities demand a differential pattern of political accommodation for South Africa. It would naturally be quite futile to impose Western European or Anglo-American models on the political system of South Africa. At the same time, any programme for political accommodation in South Africa must be based on the willingness to accord each population group the greatest possible measure of social justice. South Africa must acquire moral legitimacy if it is to remain a home to all its population groups in the future. This is a matter of urgent national importance. After careful and responsible consideration, and in the light of current realities, South Africa must choose a strategy best suited to the achievement of the ultimate objective – a society with social justice. In this respect the following considerations are of vital importance: the solution of the South African problem does not lie in the polling booth – in the sense that all should be granted the vote in one common and undifferentiated society; differentiation has always been part and parcel of South Africa's history; therefore the solution must be found in structural changes in the traditional South African political system; in each of the various structures the leaders will have to be designated by their own people if they are to acquire legitimacy; during the period of transition, the Whites will have to play the role of umpire and effective political power must remain in their hands; in this respect, no final blueprint can be devised at this stage; it is important, however, that adjustments be made to improve options in future and to allow more room for manoeuvre; if structural changes are not made,

South Africa will irrevocably move in the direction of a 'military' or 'non-political' solution which will be catastrophic for the Whites and, in fact, for all groups concerned.

II POLITICAL INSTITUTIONS

There is a continuous interaction between human expectations and political institutions. 'Political machinery needs active participation, and must be adjusted to the capacities and qualities of such men as are available.' This interaction between form and content is the central feature of all political development, including that of South Africa. Therefore, it follows that any effort to solve political problems without due regard for the historical context would be relevant only in an ideological sense. Specifics and universalities are not identical but they certainly are correlated, and the South African tradition of political differentiation should be seen in this context: the reasons why this differentiation has degenerated into so-called discrimination are to be found in the realities of power of the South African situation. The inherent object of differentiation is identification, not evaluation: the South African political system makes sense only if it is seen as an effort to accommodate peoples, not classes. Consequently, there is a need to coordinate rather than integrate the various existing and potential groupings.

Each community has certain distinctive and typical features and characteristics which distinguish it not only from other communities within the same period of history, but also from communities which preceded it in time. These distinctive features are not only confined to material or biological characteristics or those ascertained by the senses. In fact, they are rather to be found in non-physical, abstract or spiritual values. Each political community has its own distinctive and spontaneous spiritual or cultural way of life. At this level, the individual citizen enjoys his deepest spiritual experiences and at this level his communication with his fellow-citizens is at its most profound, for here he is aware of shared convictions, values and norms. The values and norms which one member of a political community shares with all other members of the same community are not only a basis for contact and negotiation: they are at the same time the foundation and framework of the institutions of that community. Political institutions, official or unofficial, are not only the structural instruments by means of which a political community is ordered or governed, but much more; for they are also the physical embodiment of the values, ideals and interests of the citizens of the community. Thus, interaction between ideas and institutions is of the utmost importance.

Political institutions and techniques are dependent for their survival on the continued support and loyalty of the citizens of the community concerned. Such loyalty and support will, however, only be given to the extent to which these institutions are an expression of the spontaneous spiritual life of the people or nation. Therefore, whether or not institutional measures are effective depends in the first and last instance on the verdict of the citizenry, and their judgement is made against the normative background of national values, norms and interests.

Whenever institutional measures are introduced without this base or framework, they lead to misunderstanding and frustration in the community and – eventually – their own destruction, for in these circumstances they will have no value or validity, their potential will not be exploited to the full and the individual citizen will not feel obliged to ensure their success or survival by his co-operation. The history of Africa during the past two decades provides grim proof of the statement that, to be successful, institutional measures must exist for the sake of the citizens, not vice versa. If this is not the case, the institutional framework of the community will be destroyed and superseded by some other system of which the point of departure is the values and ideals of the community.

All forms of political association are complicated by questions as to the most desirable relation between authority and freedom. From time immemorial, the tensions between these elements – whether in a metaphysical, moral, social or political context – have been a major point of debate in Western philosophy. A review of this polemic would indeed be a review of civilisation itself. Similarly, a review of the development of the British parliamentary system would span the history of at least a thousand years The present-day system of government in Britain is, in liberal-democratic terms, one of the most successful products of the social technology in which these elements have been institutionalised in a functional relationship. In the light of the success of this development, the principles and practices of justice, democracy and free political association have been accepted and applied far beyond the borders of Britain.

We would probably all agree that the following are among the fundamental features of the British constitution: The rule of law is upheld and respected. This implies that there is no arbitrary exercise of power, that personal freedom is guaranteed and that all citizens are equal before the law as applied in impartial and independent courts. Parliament is sovereign and has absolute power to make or repeal any law. This principle also implies that no parliament may bind any future parliament to any particular course of action. The right of the judiciary to independent interpretation of legislation is jealously safeguarded. All Cabinet Ministers, under the leadership of the Prime Minister, are responsible to Parliament. Basic to the system is the concept of the constitutional state which is unitary in character and democratically orientated. British parliamentary government is therefore based on a head of state without political power and, immediately below, a government of ministers vested with all effective political power and accountable to the representatives of the people in Parliament – 'an irremovable but powerless Crown, and a powerful but removable Ministry'. Should the government lose the confidence of Parliament or should serious conflict arise, the government may dissolve Parliament and call an early election. This means that, in the final resort, the government appeals to the people to resolve the conflict.

In terms of the Westminster system, therefore, a new government is designated at every parliamentary election which determines the representation of the people in the House of Commons: the voters decide which will be the majority party and therefore also who will be the next Prime Minister. This is the effect in practice of the fact that political competition is largely confined to two main parties. This dominant two-party system is in fact further secured by the application of the principle of relative majorities based on constituencies which return only one member to Parliament. Inevitably, owing to the cultural heterogeneity of the South African community, this system has had to undergo some ajustments in South Africa.

III DEVELOPMENTS IN SOUTH AFRICA

A cursory glance at the South African situation reveals that the Westminster system has become part and parcel of the South African dispensation which shares the following features with the British system. South Africa is a unitary state comprising four provinces which are subordinate to the central government; the head of state, the State President, is vested with only nominal powers; the legislative authority is bicameral: real and effective power is vested in the House of Assembly while the Senate no longer plays an effective political role;

executive authority is parliamentary in nature, i.e. it is vested in the Prime Minister and a Cabinet who are all members of Parliament; and the courts may not adjudicate on the validity of any Act of Parliament. From this it is evident that the entire political system of South Africa is based on the Westminster system. In addition to these typically British institutions, the plural nature of the South African population has necessitated the development of several new and complementary institutions which can serve as an infrastructure for future political development. The Coloured community is an inseparable component of the South African population. Nevertheless, it is accepted that they will evolve and realise their political aspirations parallel to the Whites: they will promote their specific and distinctive interests through separate institutions, while interests common to both Whites and Coloureds will be promoted in joint institutions. An institutional base for future evolutionary development has already been established in the form of the Coloured Persons Representative Council, the consultative, management and community affairs committees and various advisory and management boards. In the case of the various local committees, the final power of decision-making is vested in the various local councils concerned. Similarly, the advisory and management councils are also subject to various restrictions. The Coloured Persons Representative Council is only partially elected and its competence is restricted by the fact that Bills may be tabled only with the permission of the Minister concerned. Furthermore, these Bills become law only after they have been assented to by the State President, and they are automatically *ultra vires* if they are repugnant to an Act of the Parliament of South Africa. The Minister may also take over all the functions of the Executive Committee or of the Chairman of the Executive Committee while the latter official may also be relieved of his office by the State President. The Minister also determines the sessions of the Council.

It is evident, therefore, that at this point in time the Coloured population is not vested with final powers of decision-making as far as their own distinctive interests are concerned. This state of affairs must of necessity put a damper on their political aspirations. If the Coloureds are accepted as a permanent part of the South African population, it is imperative that their political aspirations be fully realised within the South African political system. It must be accepted that no inflexible institutional framework may place a ceiling on these aspirations. It is envisaged that the Coloured Persons Representative Council will be a fully elected body from its third term. Should the subordinate position of this Council *vis-à-vis* the White decision-making structures be maintained, however, it would lead to much more frustration and dissatisfaction in that representatives would be given a mandate by the voters which they would not be able to carry out. Should the Coloured Persons Representative Council be permitted to develop into a full-fledged Coloured Parliament with sovereign legislative authority in respect of all Coloureds and the Executive Committee into a full-fledged Cabinet, a problem of jurisdiction would arise. The question would then arise whether Coloured voters should be subservient to White legislation or not, particularly in view of the fact that local instituions for Coloureds may also develop to full-fledged autonomous local authorities.

Despite certain agreements, some concluded as early as 1914, which prove the contrary, until the early sixties both Whites and Indians shared the view that the latter were not really part and parcel of the South African population. Confusion on this issue was finally eliminated in 1960 by the pronouncements of the Prime Minister of the time and by further statements by the Minister of Foreign Affairs in 1961. The official view today is that the Indians, like the Coloureds and Whites, are a permanent component of the South African popluation. In 1964 this view was given institutional embodiment when the first National Indian Council was appointed. In 1968 this Council was superseded by the South African Indian Council while various committees were launched at the local level. Today, most of the latter comprise elected members only, while some have already achieved the status of full-fledged independent municipalities.

At present, only 15 members of the South African Indian Council are elected but the government has made it clear that its ultimate objective is a council comprising only elected members and that this council will be vested with legislative authority in respect of Indian affairs. At the same time provision is being made for the transfer of certain responsibilities from the Minister of Indian Affairs to the Executive Committee of the South African Indian Council which, ultimately, will probably develop into a full-fledged Indian cabinet. Similarly, provision is being made for the appointment of Indians to statutory bodies which decide upon matters of importance to Indians in their daily lives. This means that the infrastructure for future constitutional development in respect of the Indian community has been established. Nevertheless, certain problems associated with this development, similar to those arising from constitutional development for the Coloureds, may be foreseen at this stage. Like the Coloured Persons Representative Council in its role of full-fledged Coloured Parliament, the South African Indian Council as a full-fledged Parliament for Indians will be confronted with the problem of its position *vis-à-vis* the White Parliament and other decision-making structures and, on the other hand, the problem of jurisdiction. Eventually it will be necessary to demarcate the authority of both the Indian and Coloured institutions of decision-making. This will lead to serious problems, large-scale confusion and uncertainty unless such a demarcation is given a territorial base.

About half the total Black population of 15 million reside in the White areas of South Africa (about 4.5 million in urban areas). By natural increase alone there will be some 16 million Blacks and six million Whites in 'White' South Africa by the year 2000. Inevitably, any discussion of the adaption of the Westminster system in South Africa must take cognisance of the implications of these ratios. In terms of current policy, Blacks will always be secondary to Whites in White areas, in the same way as Whites will remain secondary to Blacks in the Black homelands. Blacks in White areas must exercise their political rights in their respective homelands and are for ever denied direct participation in the political process in White areas. Nevertheless, urban Blacks have been vested with limited administrative powers in terms of legislation providing for advisory Black committees as well as elected urban Bantu councils which, in addition to their advisory function, may also perform certain specific functions on behalf of the Bantu Affairs Administration Boards. The fact of the matter, however, is that these urban Bantu councils cannot meet the political demands of urban Blacks, particularly in view of the expectation on their part that a new political dispensation, quite different from that introduced to an increasing extent in the homelands, might be envisaged for them. On the other hand, it is hardly possible to grant increased local powers without meeting the demand for participation in central government processes. There is also the anomaly that, unlike the homelands, the urban Bantu councils don't have the same ethnic associations, nor are they closely linked to the traditional institutions and figures of authority. At this stage, however, Blacks do not figure any further in this discussion because their development is closely associated with the development of the homelands.

The Cabinet Council of South Africa has been established to permit regular consultations between Whites, Indians and Coloureds at the highest level. Like the Cabinet, it functions on a basis of consensus and serves as a link between the Cabinet, Coloured Persons Representative Council and the South African Indian Council.

There are several issues which immediately arise from the concept of a Cabinet Council – whether it is acceptable or not to the Coloureds and Indians, the powers of this body and the relationship between the Cabinet, the Cabinet Council and Parliament. The Coloured Labour Party has already indicated that it will not serve in the Cabinet Council. This means that acceptance of the Cabinet Council by the Coloureds (or at least a large proportion of them) is in the balance. However, the Council may become more acceptable in proportion as its development gathers pace, provided that the powers of the Council and its relationship with the Cabinet and Parliament are put on an acceptable and effective footing.

As far as the powers of the Cabinet Council are concerned, it has been stated that while it is no super-parliament and will have no legislative authority, it is customary for the decisions of cabinets to become law. Thus, the functions of the Cabinet Council will not only be consultative: it will be able to take decisions which will be executed. Because most Bills are initiated by the Cabinet, which also plays the major role in determining the budget, it follows that membership of the Cabinet Council should be of greater significance to both Coloureds and Indians than representation in Parliament. The real problem, however, lies in the future relationship between the Cabinet Council, on the one hand, and the Cabinet and Parliament, on the other hand. The Cabinet, functioning on the principle of joint responsibility, closes ranks *vis-à-vis* the outside world, but it is conceivable that Coloured and Indian members of the Cabinet Council may differ from their White counterparts and refuse to compromise. This would exclude the possibility of consensus and deadlock would be the result.

The Cabinet Council as well as the Cabinet is accountable to Parliament, not to the Coloured Persons Representative Council or the Indian Council. Should Parliament refuse to accept the recommendations of the Cabinet Council, the Cabinet would have to accede to the wishes of the majority in Parliament. It is, of course, conceivable that this problem may be resolved in the parliamentary caucus, but it is nevertheless clear that the Cabinet will not compel the caucus to accept recommendations of the Cabinet Council if these are quite unacceptable to both the Cabinet and Parliament. Nevertheless, the Cabinet Council has a significant development potential and may serve as a base for such development.

IV PROBLEMS INHERENT IN DEVELOPMENT

As for the problems involved in the presence within the same territory of Whites, Coloureds and Indians, there are several fundamental theses which should be clearly formulated at this stage. Complete integration is not an acceptable alternative to the *status quo*, because each of the three groups would lose their identity; it would open up the possibility of polarisation of group interests; it would open up the possibility of a racial confrontation or an overt struggle for power; and the various groups cannot be represented in a single parliament. Independent homelands for the Coloureds and Indians are not a viable alternative because there is no single geographical unit; large-scale removals to create such a geographical unit would be virtually impossible; and it would lead to further fragmentation of the national territory. Therefore, solutions to current problems must be sought somewhere between these two extreme poles and within the framework of the *status quo*. The foundation of future constitutional development was laid in the past. Thus, future development could take place in an evolutionary manner. This would imply few really radical changes and very little socio-economic disruption. There are, however, certain specific requirements for this process of development which should be stated clearly.

(i) All planning for future political development must be such that further development will always be possible, i.e. options must always be kept open.

(ii) In a dynamic society there must always be a certain degree of constitutional flexibility so that adjustment and change will always be possible: political evolution may not be smothered.

(iii) The plurality of the South African population must always be a basic premise.

(iv) In the process of change, cognisance must always be taken of the deeply rooted democratic idea.

(v) Democracy is in large measure based on the concept of consensus; therefore, all planning must be such that constitutional procedures may be developed from consensus politics.

(vi) The plural nature of the population implies that the various population groups must be accommodated within the constitutional framework.

(vii) One of the most important requirements is that the ceiling on political development be raised so that leaders or potential leaders may emerge and develop to share in responsibility.

(viii) Naturally, the notion of discrimination must be rejected. Instead, the concept of a just society must be unequivocally adhered to and implemented.

(ix) Basic to all deliberations must be the fact that South Africa is an

The Structuring of Political Change

African state. This implies that a distinctive political structure must be created which will satisfy the requirements of local conditions.

(x) It is imperative that both the process of change and consultations with the various population groups take place within the existing constitutional framework. A national convention, often propagated by some, is unacceptable: it will serve no purpose and would indeed amount to a repudiation of existing institutions. If the *status quo* is accepted as the point of departure, it will serve to make all new developments far more readily acceptable to all groups; this, in turn, will ensure that the processes of institutionalisation runs much more smoothly. Two guidelines must be accepted as basis for the development process: one, the exercise of power and authority is meaningful only when it is based in a specific territory; and, two, sovereignty can be brought to finality only on a basis of consensus.

V INSTITUTIONAL FRAMEWORK

All interested parties accept that all population groups of South Africa are entitled to self-determination and that each group must exercise this right parallel to all the others, with full recognition of the rights and interests of the others. Officially, it has been repeatedly stated that the Coloured Persons Representative Council and the South African Indian Council are intended to develop into, respectively, a full-fledged Coloured and Indian Parliament, while the White Parliament will be retained intact. This implies that, eventually, each parliament will have jurisdiction over a specific population group and will be empowered to legislate on matters of interest only to that particular group.

Such a situation will not produce any insuperable problems as far as the Whites are concerned. If, however, the subordinate status of the Coloured Persons Representative Council and the South African Indian Council *vis-à-vis* the White decision-making structures were to be conferred on the future Indian and Coloured parliaments, there would be a surfeit of problems as a result of frustration, dissatisfaction, overlapping and confusion. Such a state of affairs can be avoided by granting the Coloured and Indian parliaments jurisdiction not only over specific groups of people but also over specific areas where the decision-making structures of no other population group will operate. The devolution of power to these parliaments can be readily accommodated within the framework for which legislative provision is being

made at present. In fact, only minor adjustments will be required.
Even now, the existing institutions at the local level for Coloureds and Indians may develop into fully autonomous local authorities. These local areas may eventually serve as bases for the territorial embodiment of the authority of the future Coloured and Indian parliaments. At the same time, the White Parliament will retain responsibility for the White area where the emphasis might be shifted from the current provincial dispensation to one providing for much smaller provinces or regions. In this, specific areas or regions with common interests could be amalgamated and administered far more effectively than can be done at present. This implies, however, that it will be imperative for more land to be added to certain territories of specific groups so that all these areas may become functional units. Various aspects and programmes, such as the decentralisation of industries and associated development, will have to be considered so that all units and groups have an equitable share in economic and other resources. This proposed system can be introduced gradually by, initially, effecting the necessary adjustment at the local level for which, in all cases, the institutional framework has already been established.

Those interests peculiar to a particular group will be promoted and protected by the legislative institution of the group concerned, but issues in other fields such as foreign policy, fiscal and economic policy, defence, etc., will have to be decided at a joint level, for not only are all groups affected by these issues but they must also bear the effects of all decisions on these matters. Therefore, none of the White, Indian or Coloured parliaments will be able to make a final decision in isolation on any one of these issues. These issues will have to be decided by a joint decision-making body for which a basis for future development has been established in the form of the recently inaugurated joint Cabinet Council. With the necessary willingness to cooperate and compromise on the part of the leaders of the various population groups, this institution can be developed – not into an umbrella multiracial parliament, but into an institution which in terms of the accepted practices of consensus politics will take decisions on matters delegated to it by the constitution. To avoid stalemate in the Cabinet Council, the constitution may provide that in respect of those matters on which the various groups are unable to reach consensus in the Council, the power to make the final decision will be vested in an executive head of state who will be elected and perform his duties in such a way that he will be acceptable to all population groups.

VI CONCLUSION

The whole system may be described as a decentralised system of differentiated political control; with a large measure of local autonomy for the various population groups; the utilisation of federal systems and methods within the framework of a unitary state; coupled with the preservation of the identity of the various cultures in a plural society.

Giving effect to the new dispensation will probably entail the following:
(i) the abolition of the Senate;
(ii) redrawing the provincial boundaries and transforming the provincial councils into regional or territorial councils or cantons;
(iii) the further development of local authorities for all population groups, based in substantive territories so that they may be viable units;
(iv) the development of the Cabinet Council, into a formal institutional body, such as a National Council, Constitutional Council or Council of State;
(v) the granting of parliamentary status to the Coloured Persons Representative Council and the South African Indian Council, each with a cabinet of its own;
(vi) consideration should be given to the development of existing councils, such as the Economic Advisory Council, to make provision for representation of all three population groups, as well as the establishment of new functional councils and boards to serve as advisory institutions so that as many issues as possible may be kept out of politics (i.e. depoliticising issues); and
(vii) it will probably be necessary to involve, by a system of nomination, experts in various fields, such as parliaments, territorial councils and local authorities. In conclusion it must be added that this system will be relatively expensive. On the other hand, money is not the only consideration when the survival of a people or nation is at stake.

I wish to express my gratitude towards the members of the Department of Political Science and International Politics of the University of Pretoria for their contributions in compiling this paper.

27 Cleavage and Conflict in Modern Type Societies

Talcott Parsons
Emeritus Professor of Sociology, Harvard University

I THE THEORETICAL PARADIGM AS APPLIED TO SOCIETY AS A WHOLE

There are two things I would like to do in this paper. The first is to develop in very brief outline a theoretical paradigm of the principal axes of potential cleavage and conflict in modern-type social systems, meaning to apply it to the society as a whole. The second will be to attempt to apply this to what I see to be the situation in the Republic of South Africa as of something close to the present time.

I think we can assume that there are two primary structural features of immediately pre-modern types of society. I use the terms modern and pre-modern in a rather broad and loose sense, but I think it will suffice for the present purpose. The first of these is a form of stratification based on the membership population being differentiated on the axis of relative superiority and inferiority of economic and political status. There are many criterial bases on which this can occur, but I suppose the commonest have to do with determinants of class such as property and wealth, including the famous relations of production in Marxian theory, and with forms of political power. The second structural feature concerns other bases of status differentiation, among which race and other aspects of ethnicity have historically figured widely. These ethno-racial indices of status ranking often coincided or were supported in various degrees by religion, language and other predominantly cultural factors which normally also serve as important criterial bases for social differentiation.

What we usually call modernisation involves the development of what are more or less new bases of differentiation, often on both these axes. They have tended to be on the one hand political and territorial, and on the other economic. In the Western world the first has been associated with the development of the nation-state, which on the whole has come first and been followed by the industrial revolution, which has been in the first instance a change in the organisation of economic production. Both these, of course, lie in the historic background as far as the main structure of Western societies is concerned, including its extra-European developments such as those in North America and Japan. There have, of course, been important repercussions in other areas. Many of them occurred in the aftermath of the great discoveries and the settlement of Europeans outside of Europe.

The national state crystallised around the establishment of sovereignty of a government over a territorial area. There has, however, been an ideal that the population subject to such a government should be ethnically homogeneous. In Europe this was the case to widely varying degrees of approximation. Of the larger European nations England and France came the closest to fulfilment of it. Austria-Hungary (see Chapter 3 by Friedrich Prinz) was at the opposite end of the range, mainly on the ethnic bases of four divisions, namely the German-culture Austrians, the Magyar Hungarians, and two Slavic groups, the Czechs in Bohemia and the Southern Slavs now called Yugoslavs. Not surprisingly, under the stress of the First World War Austria-Hungary broke up.

In the United States the fact that the earlier settlers were for the most part Anglo-Saxon Protestants and that massive immigration of other cultural elements did not arrive until well into the nineteenth century, is a very important factor, of course to be qualified by the earlier importation of African blacks as slaves which, however, was mainly confined to one section of the emerging new society, mainly 'the South'. Australia was another case where the originally indigenous population was almost completely driven out by the European settlers, as was the case for the continental United States. In New Zealand the Aboriginal group, the Maori, were much more highly organised than the Australian blacks, and have proved to present much more of a problem of integration. Canada was also interesting in that there were two European groups, the English and the French, and the problems of their relations to each other is still highly acute. South Africa differs from all of these in initially receiving two relatively large European groups, namely the original Dutch, French and Germans (the forebears of the present Afrikaners) and the later English settlers. Even more important, however, for South Africa was the fact that they soon established settlements in the midst of a large and socially highly organised black population. In the latter half of the nineteenth century a smaller in-migrant group, but of non-European origin, namely the Indians, arrived on the scene. Parallel to these settlements there also developed an equivalent of the Latin-American Mestizo group, namely the 'Cape Coloureds', who were the product of mainly White-Hottentot-Bushman-East Indian intermixture.

As has been indelibly imprinted in modern ideologies the industrial revolution produced a new emphasis on social cleavage on the basis of social stratification. We may take with a grain of salt the opening statement of the Communist Manifesto that all previous history is the history of class conflicts, but a division on the basis of the organisation of economic production into owning and managing components on the one hand and the so-called 'working class' on the other certainly did become a very prominent feature of the new economic organisation. Furthermore, this economic organisation in countries that underwent an important process of industrialisation became extremely prominent for the society as a whole. In particular the new economic bases of stratification tended to supersede previous status determinants in the older stratification systems or to reduce them to considerably lesser significance, for instance the hereditary aristocracies on the one hand, and those social structures rooted in agriculture rather than industry on the other hand.

The main basis of division in the less heterogeneous medieval society of Europe was narrowly political, so that it could be involved mainly in the power interest, in the first instance, of princes and dynasties and then the gradually evolving national states. Especially, however, so far as ethnicity came to be involved this tended to become the basis of solidarity and the interests which were mobilised in its name tended to become increasingly diffuse. In modern terms what we call nationalism is not only *raison d'état*, but comes to involve sentiments of solidarity, national prestige and so on which can involve whole populations. Similarly, in the case of recent developments around the structure of economic production, sentiments of identity can be generalised from the narrower references of specific economic interests to the basis which has often been called that of 'class solidarity'. This 'solidarity' has in the more extreme versions of Marxist theory been interpreted to involve the total existential interest of the relevant population group. It is notable in this case that in Marxist theory class involves not merely workers in their occupational roles, but also their families, including their descendants.

I should now like to note that these two axes of division are not by any means normally parallel to each other, but stand in something more like an orthogonal relationship. From one point of view the politico-ethnic division cuts social systems in a 'vertical' dimension whereas the class dimension cuts them in a lateral or horizontal way. The two axes (economic and political power in contradistinction to racial-ethnic differentiation) are often sharply divergent. In the original political theory of nationalism, of course, territorially based national units could be neatly cut off from each other by their political boundaries, and though they might have conflicting interests which often erupted into wars, internally no such line of division ideally existed at all. Correspondingly, in the earlier days of the socialist movement, class interest was supposed to take precedence over any national loyalties. It was thus a symbolic event when in 1914 the German social democratic party voted in favour of war credits for the government, thereby repudiating their solidarity with foreign working class socialist movements in favour of national loyalty.

The accompanying schema, *Paradigm of the Western politico-ideological spectrum*, attempts to show a number of different related associations of this distinction between the two predominant components or types of diffuse solidarity. The schema is meant to relate the political spectrum which has characterised the Western world for the past century or so to some sociological categorisations which are germane to the South African situation. It exploits the fact, which has

Homogenisation (De-differentiation)	Pluralistic Types of Socio-Political Organisation		Homogenisation (De-differentiation)
Radical Left	Liberalism	Conservatism	Radical Right

Agents of Action	Class	Party (in Democratic sense)	*Volk* (Nation)
Structural Matrix	*Gesellschaft*	Division of Labour	*Gemeinschaft*
Solidarity Type	Mechanical	Organic	Mechanical
Ethical Stance	*Gesinnung*	*Verantwortung*	*Gesinnung*

impressed many observers, that there are important elements in common between the two extremes of what has come to be called the Right and the Left, which come to be mitigated as we approach the middle range.

The top row, labelled 'Agents of Action' to which the qualifier 'collective' should be added, includes the 'politicised' structural categories on which I have dwelt, namely Class on the Left side and *Volk*, or nation or 'people' on the Right. I mean class in the sense of Marxian ideology. The Nazi movement was in my opinion the most extreme radical movement of the right in our times and hence I use the German word *Volk* which was the one the Nazis used. Both of these categories have become the basis of 'parties', namely the Communist and Nazi, or other Fascist, parties. But in the middle range we have the more usual conception of 'democratic' parties, which can roughly be divided into liberal and conservative.

The second row of categories is built about the very well-known dichotomy of Toennies, between *Gemeinschaft* and *Gesellschaft*. I think that its applicability in the present context is closer than has ordinarily been appreciated. In the middle, in which I conceive both sets of components to be pluralised, I have thought it appropriate to place the Division of Labour, specifically in Durkheim's sense as transcending the level of roles in economic production alone.

The third row, designating types of solidarity, again adopts a famous pair of categories from Durkheim, namely mechanical and organic solidarity. This way of looking at things clearly stresses what the two extreme wings have in common, whereas the first two rows stress their difference.

The similarity of the wings is true of the fourth row. These two categories were put forward by Max Weber, to distinguish two fundamental types of ethical orientation with which he was concerned. It has seemed best to leave them untranslated.

With respect to political organisation the appropriate symbolic agency is perhaps best referred to by the German concept *Volk*, which has been widely used to denote a more restricted and homogeneous political system than the English concept 'nation', and more recently the concept ethnicity has been so used. At the other extreme of the lateral division class is the dominant concept. In the middle, in pluralistic types of organisation, the term party in the democratic sense, which does not imply total identification with either of the other two (nation or class), is a common usage. This distinction also relates to the famous dichotomy of *Gemeinschaft* and *Gesellschaft*, which certainly

Cleavage and Conflict in Modern Type Societies 461

formed an important chapter in the historical scriptures of sociology. It does not seem worth while to attempt to translate the German words. Where neither *Gemeinschaft* nor *Gesellschaft* is predominant however, I should say that the society is characterised by a division of labour in Durkheim's sense.

If we then turn to the type of solidarity which is involved, it seems to me that the two more extreme emphases are predominantly cases of mechanical solidarity in Durkheim's sense. In the middle, which represents the pluralistic area, however, is the field in which Durkheim's concept of organic solidarity is applicable. Finally, I think that Durkheimian thinking is not alone relevant to this context, but I would like to suggest an association with some of Max Weber's thought. It will be remembered that Weber made an important distinction between two types of ethical orientation. One he called *Gesinnungsethik*. This is a view which I have sometimes translated as ethical absolutism. There is the domination of a single value component and the repudiation of responsibility for any consequences other than the direct implementation of the central value. The alternative which Weber proposed was *Verantwortungsethik*, where the actor took responsibility for the whole range of consequences of his action, including indirect and sometimes unanticipated consequences.

I would like to suggest that these four sets of categories constitute a kind of syndrome which has much to do with the structure of both national and class conflicts and their convergences in modern and modernising societies. I would like to suggest, and have included in the diagram, the way in which these themes in a combined version spell out in modern Western political ideologies the spectrum extending from the Radical Right through Conservatism and Liberalism to the Radical Left.

II THE SOUTH AFRICAN SITUATION

I should like in this section briefly to attempt to apply the above conceptual scheme to the situation of South Africa as I understand it. I hope it will be kept in mind that I am in no ordinary sense an expert on South African society, having been there only for a brief visit in May 1977, and having read very briefly and unsystematically about it.

One way of putting the problem as I see it is to state that South African society has been confronted with two starkly incompatible alternatives. These would constitute maximising the lines of cleavage and/or solidarity in each of the two directions the previous discussion has indicated. A radical alternative which has never been quite seriously considered would be the total separation of the black and white components. This would be much more radical than the apartheid idea of establishing 'homelands' for the black groups. It would mean the extrusion of the black elements from the white society altogether, and with the obvious enormous cost of dispensing with the services of the black labour force for the benefit of the white society. Few societies have attempted anything approximating to this mode. The so-called 'columnar' structures which in different versions have developed in Holland and Belgium certainly conform partially to this model. In the Dutch case, as I understand it, the main line of division has been on the religious axis as between Protestants and Catholics, but there has been a tendency in politics in all sorts of associational contexts and the like and to a high degree in occupational organisations to separate the society into a Protestant sector and a Catholic sector. It is important that this division has not been primarily geographical. The result would have been much more divisive had it been. In the case of Belgium the basis has not been religion, but primarily ethnic, as between Walloons, who are ethnically French, and Flemings, who are ethnically for most purposes Dutch. There have been also other crosscurrents in Belgium such as between religious and secularist orientations, for example the University of Brussels in a highly secularised university whereas some of the others are predominantly Catholic. In the Belgian case the division has also been importantly territorial. A third case is Canada, where the division is between English-speaking and French-speaking elements, and where there has been a great deal of territorial separateness with the French highly concentrated in the province of Quebec. The great difficulty there has been that the English-speaking minority in Quebec have on the whole been in class status and in economic status predominant, and the French separatist movement, though it plays with total political separation and national independence, is presumably more oriented in the columnar direction.

The apartheid policy of the national party in South Africa has allegedly tried to institutionalise the columnar model, but still retaining the national unity of the sub-republic of South Africa, namely its sovereignty over most of the black homelands as well as the white territories. It seems to me that this attempt not only has not yet succeeded, but seems to be quite unpromising. The basic reason for that is that the black homelands as presently structured do not have now or prospectively the resources which would enable them on their own to become viable as both ethnic and territorial sub divisions of some kind of a federal South Africa. A historical example which comes to mind is the place of Prussia in the nineteenth-century Germany down to the First World War. Especially after the annexation of the Rhineland to Prussia in the wake of the Napoleonic wars, Prussia had about two-thirds of the population of the imperial Germany established in 1871, and a good two-thirds of the wealth. This meant that even Bavaria could not be a genuinely independent federal unit, to say nothing of many of the smaller ones. I am afraid that the disparity in respect of people and resources in a federal South Africa would be even greater should the homelands retain anything like the present structural limitations which limit their growth potential and their economic and political bargaining power.

The consequences of industrialisation have come to play a major part, as was quite evident from many of the discussions in the Conference. I think it became quite clear that this came to focus on the fact that there was for most of the lower ranks of labour occupations a black working class which had come to be sharply segregated from even the white working class, to say nothing of the middle and upperclass elements of the white sector of society. The black working class, however, has developed to a point where the white society has come to be highly dependent on its economic contributions and simply cannot bring itself to face the consequences of the radical exclusion of the blacks and their relegation to their own homelands. What this seems to mean is that the two bases of diffuse solidarity, namely ethnicity and class, have come to be amalgamated in one aspect of cleavage, namely the white upper, to use the Marxist symbolism, capitalist class, and the black lower 'working' class. This does not fit exactly, but it has developed to a very sharp degree of accentuation. It seems to me that among the possibilities of relation of these cleavages to each other this is the most explosive of all.

The situation in the United States stands in very sharp contrast, and I hope it is not ethnocentric on my own part to stress this point. There was a time when American society could have been said to be clearly dominated by the so-called WASP group, standing for White Protestant Anglo-Saxon. This was the impression given by André Siegfried in his notable book, *America Comes of Age*, published in 1928. The European immigrant groups, however, who began arriving in large numbers before the mid-nineteenth century have now been largely integrated in the society, so apart from colour it certainly cannot be said to be any longer a WASP society. It seems to me that on the background of this integration and of widespread black migration from the rural South to the Northern and Western cities, the way was paved for a new wave of integration of the blacks. We are standing now in the middle of this process. It is far from complete, but it has in my opinion, which is not universally shared, gone far enough for its broad outcome to be no longer seriously in doubt. During my visit to South Africa the presence of Andrew Young, a black from Georgia, in the capacity in which he stood, was a symbol of this change, as was the election in 1976 of his superior, President Carter, a deep South Southerner, with 90 per cent of the black vote. This surely symbolises a major change in the structure of the situation.

The American situation I have barely outlined can I think legitimately be called pluralistic, though it is only one type of pluralism. The two modes of diffuse solidarity which I have discussed, however, have both in the American case been fragmented. It is sometimes forgotten that a substantial majority of those who in American discussion are classified as 'the poor' are white not black, and there has by now emerged a very substantial black middle and even upper middle class, so by no means all the blacks or even anything like the majority of them are inhabitants of the 'ghetto'. If this is true of white and blacks generally within the white community it is certainly true across many other ethnic lines. Just to take one example I think it is safe to say that the average socio-economic status of American Jews is substantially higher than that of those of Protestant Anglo-Saxon origin. This is to say that the ethnic lines of division no longer coincide with the class lines of division. Both ethnic status and class status have been pluralised and fragmented and cannot form the basis of lines of conflict which could lead to radical revolutionary-type consequences. Something like this has happened as between Afrikaners and English in South Africa.

If the class basis of solidarity is to be broken up in South Africa, it seems to me imperative that channels of opportunity for socio-economic advancement *within* the white society must be opened up to blacks. I think the most important mechanisms for that type of thing are things like trade union support, even greater access to education, including higher education, and a variety of different kinds of occupational opportunity. The more immediate pressures are on the political front with special reference to enfranchisement. The problems in this area are sufficiently complex, so I hesitate to enter into them. It seems to me that to say anything very sensible about them would require a knowledge of particular South African circumstances which I do not have.

I do, however, think that I have been able to present an outline frame of reference which may be valuable in considering the nature of the problems. To conclude then, it would seem to me that, short of the truly radical solution of extrusion of the blacks from participation in the white society, I do not see any other direction of development for South African society which would lead to a gradual mitigation of the built-in conflicts than pluralisation in the sense in which I have defined that concept above. There is no reason to believe that either the end-result or the process would have to have any very close resemblance to the experience and situation of the United States. I do, however, feel that the tendency for the two lines of cleavage, ethnic and class, to coincide in the South African situation does constitute a dangerously explosive situation.

Among the possible models of decentralisation, that of Switzerland, which was mentioned by the Minister of Education in his opening address to the Conference, certainly should be included. This suggests a theme not stressed above, which is the rather radical one, which the minister may or may not have had in mind, namely that a federalist/confederalist structure, if it were to advance pluralisation across the racial line, would have to break up what is now *white* South Africa into several federated units, each of which had a substantial degree of autonomy relative to the others and to a federal government. Without this, surely white South Africa as an unbroken entity would far too overwhelmingly predominate over other federal units. Perhaps this is a way in which the historic difference between certain regionally based communities, even between Afrikaans and English-oriented communities, could be accommodated. Inevitably, for a variety of reasons certain geopolitical units will be more developed and thus more influential than the rest. Thus two of the Swiss cantons clearly are much stronger than the rest, especially in economic respects, namely Vaud, which is French-speaking, centring in the city of Geneva, and Zürich, which is German-speaking.

A pluralist system based on federalism/confederalism would thus encompass more than one unit in which each identifiable politico-historical population group was a majority, namely the Whites, the Coloureds, the Indians and also the Black communities that cannot be accommodated in independent Black states. It also seems to me essential that there should be maximum freedom of movement and residence for all citizens, whichever groups they belong to, as between all these units.

If development should take this kind of course, with perhaps Johannesburg as the centre of one especially strong 'canton' and Durban that of another, it is probably important that the federal capital should not be too closely associated with one, as Pretoria now is. Thus Bern is in between Zürich and Geneva, and in the United States Washington is not part of such powerful complexes as New York or Chicago, or indeed Los Angeles.

If anything like federalisation turned out to be the course taken, it seems to me essential that its constitutional framework would have to be firmly established, setting sharp limits to the independence of action of any one or coalition of federal units, and of the federal government *vis-à-vis* them. The US Constitution has been such a framework, and only once has it been put to a supreme test, namely in the Civil War.

In any case, I think these points fit with my most general argument that the most dangerous feature of the recent and current South African situation lies in the structured coincidence of the two main axes of what is both in-group diffuse solidarity and, *vis-à-vis* the outgroup, cleavage and potential conflict, namely ethnicity (in your case mainly in the form of race) and social class, backed up by politically enforced white supremacy. Any changes, whether politically planned or not, which can put more blacks on the same side of the fence with whites in the social class will tend to be a mitigation of this coincidence. Thus it seems to me that both the Indians and the Coloureds can serve as important spearheads in promoting this process of pluralisation. This cannot, however, occur so long as they remain without political representation in the top institutions of power, for example a national legislature.

28 The Problems of Plural Societies with Special Reference of the Urban Blacks of South Africa

M. T. Moerane
President of the Soweto Residents Council

I HISTORICAL BACKGROUND

South Africa regards the South African problem as unique, but when one examines it as a sociological phenomenon it soon becomes apparent that in its genesis it is part and parcel of colonialism, the dominant feature of the recent history of the African continent. To a greater or lesser degree, all nations are ashamed of their colonial past. Vernon Bartlett, in his 'The colour of their skin', describes how, because of this sense of shame, Britain, France and Belgium with varying degrees of haste or dignity withdrew from Africa in the fifties and sixties of this century.

It is not surprising that White South Africans do not see their colonialist rule for what it is, inhibited as they are by this feeling of shame implicit in all forms of colonialism. Another reason is that the Afrikaners and most other South African Whites have been divorced from independence against colonialism in Africa. Indeed, their struggle against British colonialism is for them the most glorious feat of their people. There is also another consideration. For centuries, the Afrikaners and most other South African Whites have been divorced from their European ancestry: they are South Africans, no longer Europeans. For these reasons the South African White cannot or will not see himself as a colonialist.

Colonialism in Africa was reversed in the decade after the Bandung conference of 1955. This was the burden of the challenge of British Prime Minister Harold Macmillan's 'winds of change' address to the South African Parliament in February 1960. The speech articulated the demands of world opinion and the Black man's clamour for freedom in South Africa – just when independence and freedom were being achieved all over Africa, except in Southern Africa. Pressure against South Africa's policies mounted at the UN and at Commonwealth forums, and within South Africa the Blacks were in open revolt. The tragic shooting at Sharpeville took place in March 1960 and a year later South Africa's membership of the Commonwealth was terminated.

White South Africa, long ensconced in its privilege, did respond to the challenge. In his well-known 'Live and let live' address to the South Africa Club in London a day after South Africa had been expelled from the Commonwealth, Prime Minister Dr H. F. Verwoerd propounded the policy of 'separate development'. In essence, his statement accepted that it was right for every people to enjoy freedom and self-determination in their own land. In South Africa, he continued, the White man had not seized land from the Black man. Both the White and Black man were pioneer immigrants to this subcontinent and either group migrated to the areas of their preference. Separate development therefore was no more than a codification of these preferences, whereby each group would be given full self-determination in its own area.

This is the theory, but every schoolboy knows that in the course of the nine Frontier wars during the nineteenth century the Black man was relentlessly pushed ever further and dispossessed of his land until, finally, he was left only with what are the 'homelands' of today, while the White man, by conquest, ruled all of South Africa.

Thereafter, by various Acts of Parliament, notably the Bantu Land Act of 1913 and the Bantu Trust and Land Act of 1936, South Africa proceeded to set aside areas for Black occupation in the rural hinterland of South Africa which today comprise about 14 per cent of the total surface area.

This short excursion into history was essential to provide a context within which to discuss the problems of pluralism in South Africa.

In a sense Dr Verwoerd's 'homeland' plan was a commendable exercise in decentralisation of power and local self-determination. After all, in certain parts of the country the population is predominantly Black. Indeed, it was a progressive idea to recognise the right of these people

The Problems of the Urban Blacks 469

in these areas to self-determination and meaningful local adminstration. A case in point is Transkei, which is predominantly but not entirely Black: there has always been a minority of Whites, mostly traders and farmers.

II DR VERWOERD'S HOMELAND PLAN

South Africa's power structure comprises the central national government and a second echelon of four provincial councils. The 'homeland' areas, once known as reserves, could easily have been fitted into the second echelon: they could have been made provinces with their own provincial administrations. That would have been simple enough. But the major problem arises when the Black people have to be accommodated or represented in the top echelon of government, the central Parliament, the members of which have since the late fifties been elected solely by Whites. According to the census of 1970, South Africa's total population was 21,448,169 of whom 3,751,328 were White. Naturally, whenever the notion of universal suffrage to elect a common Parliament for the whole country is mooted, this imbalance in numbers raises in the minds of the Whites the spectre of Black majority rule which they find utterly unacceptable. They ask how the identity, security and rights of the Whites can be safeguarded in a common Parliament in a country such as South Africa whose population is predominantly Black. Providing an answer to that question may very well be the ultimate test for South Africa statesmanship, both Black and White. Certainly, it will not be easy to find the answer, but it had better be found fairly soon, for at present there is a growing and ominous polarisation between Black and White on these issues. The Whites and their government are firmly opposed to power-sharing between Black and White in a common government, while the Blacks demand just that. The most articulate Black exponents of this demand, the leaders of the Black Consciousness Movement, have all been silenced by detention.

III SHARED HOMELAND FOR ALL SOUTH AFRICANS

But these leaders are not alone in the view that all South Africa (not only the 'reserves' or 'homelands') is the homeland of the Black man and that this homeland is to be shared with the White man. Another proponent of majority rule (*Not* Black majority rule) in South Africa as a whole is Chief Minister Gatsha Buthelezi of KwaZulu. Similarly, in his inaugural address on 6 December President Lucas Mangope of the newly independent Bophuthatswana slated the discriminatory policies of South Africa and the inadequacy of the land allotted to his people. He added that independence for his country was a stepping-stone to a federation of states in South Africa.

Moreover, not only Blacks believe in power-sharing and participation by all in the national government. Both opposition parties in the White Parliament are committed to power-sharing on a federal basis. The prospects for this ideal will be discussed later. For the moment, we propose to examine the problems of South Africa as a plural society at the present point in time.

IV PRESENT STRUCTURE OF POWER

The South African Parliament is the supreme legislative authority of the country. It determines national policies and votes funds for services for all the people of the country. But because Parliament consists of Whites elected by Whites only, its first responsibility is towards the Whites. There is no guarantee that the interests of Blacks will be effectively promoted or safeguarded. They have to rely on the goodwill of the White legislators who are not their elected representatives. In these circumstances, it is not really surprising to find that the per capita expenditure for White children is ten times that for Black children and that often the ratio is even worse. Similarly, the rights of the voteless Black workers are disregarded if not actively thwarted. Black trades unions are not registered and Black workers may not strike. In addition, White workers are paid far better wages than Blacks for the same jobs.

In a post-election pledge on 1 December 1977 Prime Minister Vorster stated that his government would do everything in its power progressively to close the wage gap between Black and White workers.

There are many other indications that the national policies of South Africa are designed primarily to ensure the well-being of Whites. Some years ago South Africa's ambassador at the UN, Mr R. F. Botha, admitted that discrimination based on colour was unjustified, and committed his country to move away from discrimination. Indeed, this is one of the greatest challenges facing South Africa – moving away in a meaningful manner from discrimination based solely on colour. Tentative peripheral steps have been taken in this regard, but the desire for change is growing, even in some citadels of reactionary conservatism. If we advocate an accelerated tempo, it is not because we are unaware of the gravity of the obstacles in the way of change.

One moment Prime Minister Vorster raises hope by announcing that urban Blacks will be given the power to administer their own affairs by means of fully-fledged town councils. But the very next moment, as if suddenly reminded not to betray the sacred tenets of Afrikaner nationalism, he states that these concessions must not be taken as a stepping-stone in the direction of one-man one-vote representation in a national government – something the Blacks of South Africa have never demanded of him.

Inspired by a national vision, the Afrikaners, numerically a small people, have struggled valiantly for their ascendancy as a people in the land of their adoption, today the land of their birth. In order to achieve this, they closed their ranks, defended their identity at all costs, and at all times remained true to the tenets of Afrikanerdom. Certainly, that course yielded dividends. Today, at the pinnacle of his power, the Afrikaner fears that once he slackens in his resolve to preserve his security and identity, he will be overwhelmed and lose all he has so painstakingly built up over the years. The Afrikaner is, however, not alone in fearing change. All Whites do. For to be a White in South Africa is to be a most privileged person. Segregation or apartheid, separate development or multinational development – whatever you call the policy, it has secured and entrenched the White man's privileged position. No White man would relish losing that privilege, so he is afraid to take his chances in an egalitarian society. I would like to assure him that he will not lose privilege; he will merely exchange colour privilege for the privilege of merit, which is the only privilege worth having, for it is earned and therefore just and intrinsic.

V NEED FOR AN INCLUSIVE SOUTH AFRICANISM

The only way for the White man to safeguard the great values he has acquired and cherishes today, is to share them with his fellow-Africans, to become truly an Afrikaner (a man of Africa), to identify himself completely with Africa. That is the identity we need to cultivate today. South Africa's need today is for a new and greater patriotism including all the various peoples in their cultural and historical diversity. We need a national purpose big enough to command the allegiance of every South African, regardless of his ethnic identity. Indeed, if the purpose is big enough, we shall need one another, for it will certainly be too big to be accomplished by any one group on its own, and in that adventure we shall become comrades and brothers-in-arms. In this way the aspirations of each individual and group will be fulfilled. Our history is consistently propelling us towards this new type of South Africanism and this new dispensation. Together, Black and White have achieved a miracle of industrialisation. Look at our cities, our industries and roads, and above all, our people. Among the urban Blacks there are people of quality and sophistication who would be accepted as neighbours in any society. Much remains to be done, however, to improve the opportunities and life-style of our people in certain areas of our cities. This problem is being tackled with the assistance of institutions such as the Urban Foundation, whose purpose it is to improve the quality of Black urban life. And more recently there was the declaration of intent by eleven of the biggest employers of the country: they will seek to improve the employment conditions of their workers, follow fair employment policies eliminating discrimination, and assist their workers in acquiring adequate housing. It seems the nation is on the move, but this can be no more than a beginning.

As far as the urban plural society is concerned, the private sector has begun to accept that it will be in its interest if the Blacks, who constitute the backbone of the labour force of industry, commerce and the public services, are developed and trained to be a contented and well-placed segment of society. With the cooperation of social agencies as well as self-help organisations and the civic bodies of the people themselves, a social revolution may be set in motion which will mobilise the people into positive community development. The result will be a settled and productive urban Black community, an asset to themselves and to the nation; not merely cogs in the wheels of industry, but responsible citizens building a nation. In this way, the churches, educational agencies and trades unions will acquire new relevance, fulfilling their true functions.

VI THE WAY TO A TRULY NATIONAL GOVERNMENT

As mentioned earlier, the government has decided to introduce autonomous Black local authorities to adminster the civic affairs of urban Blacks. This is perhaps the opportune moment to return to the question posed earlier: how, in a heterogeneous society such as that of South Africa, do we fashion a national government which will promote the well-being of all inhabitants, so that no single group will dominate any other, by virtue of its numbers or economic prowess.

Naturally, Whites see this as a real problem, mainly because of the preponderance of Blacks and their relative backwardness and lack of experience of modern democratic government of the Westminster type. That is why Whites insist on preserving and safeguarding their group and ethnic identity and prefer to balkanise the country so that each group will have its own territory where it can develop fully and realise its political aspirations without endangering any other group. Unfortunately, however, the division of land has been imposed by the Whites. Thus, 86 per cent of the total surface area, including all the major cities and industrial regions, has been reserved for Whites who constitute no more than 15 per cent of the population, while only 14 per cent of the total area, comprising mostly rural land with little industrial potential, has been set aside for Blacks who account for 75 per cent of the total population. The Black man's view is that the modern industrial state that South Africa is has been built up jointly by Black and White who should also share the fruits of their labour together. Blacks do not share the enthusiasm of some Whites for the homelands policy as a solution to the country's problems. On the contrary, they regard it as little more than a manoeuvre designed to perpetuate White privilege in South Africa.

But let us suppose that the homelands policy is part of the answer to the problem, that it will give a modicum of political self-realisation to the rural Black people in 14 per cent of South Africa. But 55 per cent of all Blacks will still be living in so-called White South Africa where, at the moment, they are denied all rights to political self-expression. Recently, however, the government announced that these Blacks would be given local authority powers within their own residential areas. This is a positive move in the right direction, and one can only hope that these residential areas will be allowed to develop into real towns with full scope for commercial and industrial development. In time, these local authorities could constitute themselves into some extra-municipal 'front' or organisation to be representative of the views of all urban Blacks of the country. In addition, the Black people would have their own non-statutory national political and social organisations, such as the Black Social Workers Association and the African Chamber of Commerce.

At this point it would be as well to admit that we do not have a ready-made formula for an effective national government for South Africa as a whole. Nor do we believe that such a formula could ever be produced by the fiat of any one group – certainly not by the government which, as presently constituted, is not representative of all the people of the country.

As a first step the government, in consultation with the elected representatives of the non-homeland national Black organisations and those of the congress of the Black town councils, could mount an *ad hoc* campaign to 'move away from discrimination based on colour'. This should involve specific issues which lie at the heart of the current unrest in the country. These would include Bantu Education which should be superseded by free and compulsory education. Meanwhile, the efforts of the private sector to improve the quality of life of the Black urban population would have gathered momentum and the various newly established community centres would be hives of activity, entertaining and training the people.

This level of achievement and progress would be the ideal cue for launching the overall campaign in search of the big national purpose – to accentuate our unity in diversity and our common South African patriotism. This common commitment will enable us to make South Africa what it ought to be – a country for whose future all its citizens would care, where people would not only be doing their own thing but also mend their neighbours' fences, where opportunities would be opened up for everyone according to his ability and his needs. I believe that our young men and women at college and university, both Black and White, could have much fun working at this ideal, debunking the obsolete tribalist loyalties of the past and laying the foundations for the brave new world of a broad South Africanism.

In this way the tensions caused by Bantu Education and other discriminatory measures will be relaxed. This, coupled with the various tangible steps taken by the government and the community organisations to improve the social condition of the people, will create an atmosphere of confidence and trust in which the grave problem of national political representation for all could be tackled around a conference table.

I have no preconceived ready-made plan to offer such a round table conference. Indeed, such a plan would be counter-productive. What will need to be done is to define the purpose of such a conference – to evolve machinery that would make the well-being of all the people of South Africa the objective and determinant of all national policies of the country. The fears, doubts and misgivings of all participants would be freely aired and eventually reconciled with the basic aim in a spirit of accommodation. All the known options in systems of government would be expounded by experts, preferably independent guest jurists, and freely canvassed by the constitutent members of the convention until consensus is reached on a system suited to the South African situation.

At present a federal system of government seems to enjoy a considerable degree of public support in many quarters. Both White opposition parties favour such a system and one member of the Cabinet has suggested that the canton system used in Switzerland might be adapted to South African conditions. The plan is relatively simple. It incorporates current policy providing for seven to nine ethnic Black homelands, either independent or with an advanced degree of self-government, each with its own government and parliament. It also accepts the Coloured Persons Representative Council and the South African Indian Council, as well as the central Parliament – for Whites. On these various institutions of government would be superimposed a sort of super-parliament composed of representatives from all these institutions. The division of powers and legislative responsibility between the super-parliament and the various ethnic governments would be negotiable. The immediate obstacle to such an arrangement would be the unwillingness of Whites, as represented by the ruling National Party, to subjugate their Parliament to any super-government of multiracial composition.

Another option, recently reiterated by President Lucas Mangope of Bophuthatswana, is an economic union incorporating all the states of Southern Africa along the same lines as the European Economic Community. Yet another permutation of the plan is a commonwealth of nations, first mooted by Dr H. F. Verwoerd, father of the concept of multinational development.

All these options have one basic weakness in common. Any dispensation which would accept and incorporate the concept of 'homelands and their governments would be firmly opposed by urban Blacks in particular and by most Blacks in general, including the Coloureds and Indians.

VII CREATING THE RIGHT ATMOSPHERE FOR PROGRESS

Nevertheless, I am firmly convinced that if the elected representatives of all the peoples of South Africa were to sit down around a table they would certainly find a feasible and just solution to the impasse of the South African situation. Needless to say, it would be in the interest of all if South Africans found that solution. The sooner the better.

We have repeatedly stressed that the first prerequisite for success is that the right atmosphere should be created and advantage taken of the prevalent desire for change in order to initiate practical programmes which will involve all. This we have done because we are under no illusion as to the gravity of the problems and imponderables involved. It will take time, patience and goodwill to eliminate the age-old prejudices and resolve the carefully cultivated group interests, all of which have the potential for catastrophic confrontational conflict.

The potential of this country is so great that it would certainly be worthwhile to forfeit all the sectional prejudices and interests that have held our people in perilous bondage for so long. Our nation comprises virile sturdy people of 'selected' pioneer stock on either side of the 'colour' line – magnificent human material. In addition, we are blessed with a healthy climate and rich natural resources. Even now, our common enterprise, often unplanned and sometimes badly directed, has made of this land a vibrant modern state. But this is no more than a preview of what we can achieve as a nation if we accept that we are indeed a plural society, a single society in our diversity, and concentrate less on what divides us but more on what we have in common, particularly our common citizenship, with all the rights and obligations which that citizenship implies. Then, having shed our preoccupation with ethnic and tribal loyalties, we might glory in the advantages of a plural society rather than be obsessed by the problems of pluralism.

Index

Page numbers in italics indicate that the name appears in notes or references.

Abdullah, King of Jordan, 139
Adam, Herbert, 384–6, *395*
Aga Khan, 266
Agee, Philip, *112*
Ahmad, Ghafoor, 279
Ahmad, Mirza Ghulam, 266
Ahmad, M. M., 268
Ahmad, Q., *282*
Ali, Muhammud, 214
Allport, Gordon, 248
Allworth, Edward, *111*, *114*
Almond, Gabriel A., 32, 41, *42*
Althusius, Johannes, 27, *41*
Amin, Idi, 22
Anwar, Muhammad Rafi, *281*
Apter, David, 27, *41*
Arberry, A. J., *142*
Arfa, H., *142*
Arlès, J. P., *171*
Aron, Raymond, 18
Asad, Hafiz al-, 131–4
Ashby, Eric, 218, *229*
Assad, Hafeez, *see* Asad, Hafiz al-
Astin, Alexander, 220
Augustin, Saint, 14
Ayub Khan, Mohammad, 256–60, 275, *283*

Baer, G., *142*
Baker, Robert, K., *248*
Ballard, Allen, 213, 215, *229*
Banks, David, J., *171*
Barazani, Ahmad, 121
Barazani, Mahmud, 121
Barazini, Mustafa, 121–2

Barber, Benjamin, *114*
Barker, Ernest, 67–8, *81*
Barkley, Lawrence, 220
Barron, John, *112*
Barry, Brian, *43*
Bartlett, Vernon, 467
Bauer, P. T., 19, *26*
Bazzaz, Abd al-Rahman al-, 122
Benedict, Burton, *114*
Beneš, Edvard, 48, *52*
Bengu, S. M., 388, *395*
Berg, F. H. van der, *441*
Berger, M., *142*
Berlin, Sir Isaiah, 356, *367*
Bertelsmann, E., 389
Betts, R. B., *142*
Bhutto, Zulfikar Ali, 257, 270, 276–9
Binder, L., *141–4*, *281*, *347*
Bish, R., *334*
Bismark, 57
Bloomfield, J. H., *281*
Botha, Louis, 183
Botha, R. F., 318, 470
Bourguiba, Habib, *82*
Bozeman, Adda B., 20, *26*
Braestrup, Peter, xvii
Brandt, Conrad, 79
Brisk, William J., *114*
Brown, Oliver, 236
Bull, Sandra J., *248*
Burke, Edward, 101, *113*
Burton, I., *141*
Busch, Peter, *81*
Buthelezi, Gatsha, 370, 388–90, 470
Butler, J., *395*

477

Calhoun, John C., 34, *43*
Callaghan, James, 429
Calvin, John, 14
Cameron, Sir Neil, *429*
Carter, Hodding, 236
Casino, Eric S., *173*
Clay, Cassius, *see* Ali, Muhammud
Castro, Fidel, 23, 214
Chakaodza, Austin, *429*
Chang, David W., *172*
Chaudhri Muhammad Ali, 257
Chen, Lung-chu, 113
Choudhury, G. W., 261, *282*
Clark, Kenneth, 206, 208–10, *229–30*
Clark, R. P., *347*
Cobban, Alfred, 84, 104, *114*
Coleman, James, 338, *347*
Connor, Walker, 7, *11*, *111–12*
Constant, Benjamin, 356

Daalder, Hans, 40, *43*
Dahl, Robert, 7, *11*, *114*, 338
Dahm, George, *441*
Davison, R. H., *141–2*
Delbrück, Jost, *441*
Deutsch, Karl, 52, 55, *80–1*, 94, 206, 209, 342
Dickie-Clark, H. F., 384
Diemont, Justice, 376
Dierickx, Guido, *43*
Dodd, S. C., *142*
Donner, A. M., *441*
Dunn, James A., *113*
Durkheim, Emile, *113*, 460–1

Eisenhower, Milton S., 235, *248*
Emerson, Rupert, 68, 72, 78, *83*, *112–13*, 253, *281*
Enahoro, Peter, 293, *298*
Erikson, Erik H., *367*
Escher, Alfred, 316
Esman, Milton, 79, *173*
Etzioni, Amitai, 203, 217, *229*, 342
Evans-Pritchard, E. E., 89, *112*

Fairbank, John, 79
Falah, Salman, *141*
Fanon, Frantz, 214
Fazlul, Huq, 251

Faysal, Amir, 138
Feld, Werner, *82*
Feldman, Herbert, 258, *281*
Fisher, Paul, 237, *248*
Flanagan, Scott C., *43*
Fleischmann, Klaus, *172*
Foster, Philip J., *26*
Freud, Sigmund, *367*
Furnivall, J. S., 7, *11*, 31–2, *42*, 71, *82*

Galtung, Johan, *43*
Gastil, Raymond D., 9, *11*
Geertz, Clifford, 67–8, *81*, 383, *395*
Geertz, Hildred, *172*
Geiger, Willi, *441*
Ghassemlou, A. R., *142*
Ghazali Shafie, Tan Sri, 144
Giliomee, Hermann, 384, *395*
Glaser, Kurt, 46
Glassl, H., *52*
Glazer, Nathan, 5, *11*, 64, *81*, 229
Godlonton, Robert, 337
Go Gien Tjwan, *173*
Goiten, S. D., *142*
Goodman, Alan, *112*
Gordon, Milton M., 7, *11*, 203, 233–4, *247*
Gottman, Jean, *334*
Gowing, Peter G., *172*
Greeley, Andrew, 6, *11*, *114*, 203
Greene, Robert, 227
Greenstein, Fred I., 202, *229*
Gruenbaum, G. E. von, *141*
Guevara, Che, 214
Gulick, L., *334*
Gutmann, Emanuel, 30

Haas, E. B., *342*
Haasbroek, D. J. P., *346*
Haddad, R. M., *142*
Hafiz, Amin al-, 130
Halle, Louis J., *80*
Hallowell, John H., *42*
Harris, Louis, *248*
Hawley, A., *334*
Hayden, Martin S., 240–1, *248*
Hayek, F. A., 358–61, *367*
Hayes, Carleton, 68

Haywood, Jack, 82
Heard, Kenneth A., 195
Henderson, Conway W., 42
Henderson, George, 212, 229
Hertzog, J. B., 183
Hitler, Adolf, 60, 63
Hobbes, Thomas, 349
Hoebel, E., 282
Hoernlé, Alfred, 343
Holmes, Oliver Wendell, 241
Honigman, J. J., 113
Hook, Sidney, xxvii
Horowitz, D. L., 347
Houghton, D. Hobart, 189, 195
Hourani, A. H., 141
Hugo, Pierre, 298
Hume, David, 349, 366
Hunt, Chester L., 228
Hunt, George P., 236, 248
Huntington, Samuel P., 33, 42, 112 340, 347
Hurewitz, J. C., 142
Hutchins, Robert M., 242, 248
Hutt, William H., 190, 196

Iran, Shah of, 22

Jackson, R. J., 347
Jacobs, Norman, 166, 173
Jadid, Salah, 130-4
Jahan, Rounaq, 282
Jaszi, Oscar, 50, 52
Jeppe, Julius, 334
Jeukens, H. J. M., 441
Jinnah, Mohammad Ali, 252
Johnson, Lyndon B., 238, 247, 248
Jones, Victor, 334
Joseph, J., 142
Jusoff bin Haji Hanifah, 173

Kann, R. A., 52
Karabel, Jerome, 218, 226, 229, 230
Kemp, Geoffrey, 429
Kendall, Willmoore, 28, 41
Kennan, George F., 21, 26, 107, 114
Kennedy, John F., 240
Kennedy, Robert F., 248
Kilson, Martin, 204-5, 229
King, F. H. H., 82

King, Martin Luther, 214, 219, 248
Kinnane, D., 142
Kipling, Rudyard, 23
Klerk, W. J. de, 384
Kohn, Hans, 68
Koornhof, P. G., xiv, 379, 465
Korson, J. Henry, 284
Kossuth, Louis, 47
Kotzé, D. A., 297, 334
Krachang Bhanthumnavin, 173
Kriek, D. J., 42
Krislof, Ladis, 78, 83
Kuhn, Thomas S., 27, 30, 41-2
Kunstadter, Peter, 173
Kuper, Leo, 42, 288, 289, 337, 341, 347
Kwan, Kian, 81
Ky, Nguyen Cao, 93

Laeng, Joachim Ulok, 173
Laguian, Aprodicio A., 172
Lamberty, Max, 285, 298
Lamour, Catherine, 172
Landau, J. M., 142
Landon, Kenneth P., 171
Landshut, S., 142
Lange, David L., 248
Laquer, W. Z., 142
Lasswell, H., 113
Lavan, S., 141
Legters, Lyman, 114
Lehmbruch, Gerhard, 43
Leigh, Michael B., 171
Lemberg, Eugen, 288-9, 298
Lent, John A., 247
Leon, Sonny, 390
Leonard, Walter, 221
Levak, Albert E., 267, 281-3, 374
Lewis, Sir Arthur, 29, 31
Liddle, R. William, 172
Lijphart, Arend, 113, 345, 347, 387, 394, 395
Linton, Ralph, 288, 298
Lippman, Walter, 42
Lipset, Seymour M., 32, 42, 341, 347
Locke, John, 28, 41, 59
Longrigg, S. U., 142
Lorwin, Val R., 43
Loshak, David, 253, 281

Lowenstein, Ralph L., 237, 248
Lucas, Paul, 112
Luther, Martin, 14
Lyle, Jack, 248

Machel, Samora, 427, 429
McDougall, M., 113
Macmillan, Harold, 468
McRae, Kenneth, 43
McVey, T., 172
Maddison, Angus, 275, 283
Mahathir Bin Mohamad, 173
Makarov, Alex., 441
Malan, D. F., 184, 368
Malcolm X, 308
Mangope, Lucas, 470, 475
Marcos, Ferdinand, 156
Marks, Thomas A., 173
Mawdudi, Abul Ala, 277, 284
Mayer, Kurt, 200, 229
Mayer, Philip, 388, 395
Mazrui, Ali, 290, 292, 298
Melson, Robert, 82
Meo, L. M., 142
Merritt, R. L., 81
Messner, Johannes, 441
Metzger, Paul, 202, 229
Mill, John Stuart, 31, 42, 101–2, 105
  110–11, 113, 356, 415
Milne, R. S., 171, 173
Minogue, Kenneth, 367
Mirza, Iskander, 256
Mitra, N. N., 281
Mogulof, M., 334
Moodie, D., 384
Morgenthau, Hans, 307, 342, 347
Mornay, Eric de, 429
Morris, H. S., 81
Mountbatten, Lord, 249
Moynihan, Daniel P., 5, 11, 18, 65,
  81, 229
Mozingo, David, 171
Mugabe, Robert, 426
Muhammad Iqbal, 250
Mulder, Connie, 368
Muller, Hilgard, xiv
Mullin, Chris, 172
Mundt, Robert J., 43
Munir, Justice, 268

Musgrave, Richard, 419, 420
Muzorewa, Abel, 426
Mya Maung, 172
Myrdal, Gunnar, 18

Nanda, Ved P., 93–4, 112
Nasser, Gamal Abdul, 123
Nehru, Jawaharlal, 5, 260, 282
Neto, Agostinho, 422, 424, 427
Neuman, Stephanie, 112, 114
Ngouabi, M., 423
Nhat Hung, 172
Niebuhr, Reinhold, 349–50, 366
Nikitine, B., 142
Nkomo, Joshua, 426–7
Nkrumah, Kwame, 290, 298
Nordlinger, Eric A., 42–3
Northrop, F. S. C., 342
Novak, Michael, 26
Nujoma, Sam, 427
Nyerere, Julius, 423
Nyrop, Richard F., 265–7, 271, 282–3

Oakeshott, Michael, 366
Obler, Jeffrey, 43
O'Connell, D. P., 112–13
Olorunsola, Victor, 83
Olton, Roy, 79
Orwell, George, 161
Osgood, Robert, 112
Ostrom, V., 334
Ostry, Bernard, 234, 247
O'Sullivan, John, 195
Owen, David, 315, 319

Passow, A. Harry, 229
Peers, Robert, 418, 420
Percy, Charles H., 172
Pérez, Carlos Andrés, 246
Pettigrew, Thomas, 211, 229
Pipes, Richard, 112
Plano, Jack C., 79
Platt, John, 81
Podgorny, N. V., 423–7, 429
Pomerance, Michla, 113
Porter, John, 200, 229
Preston, Frederick W., 198, 204, 228
Prins, W. F., 441
Purcell, Victor, 171

Putnam, C., 209, *229*

Qadhafi, Mu'ammad al-, 156
Qassem, General, 121

Ra'ahan, Uri, 105, *114*
Rahman, Fazlur, 276–7, *284*
Rahmat Ali Chaudhry, 250
Rakowska-Harmstone, Teresa, *111*
Ramazani, Rouhollah, *114*
Ramsey, Paul, *113*
Randall, Peter, 381, 393, *395–6*
Rawls, John, *366*
Regan, Daniel, *173*
Reissman, L., 206
Renner, Karl, 46–51, *52*, 105–6
Reston, James, 237
Revesz, Laszlo, *112*
Rhoodie, N. J., *196*
Riklin, Alois, 109, *114*
Rinck, Hans-Justus, *441*
Robbins, Lord, 415, *420*
Rondot, P., *141*
Ronen, Dov, *113*, 292, *298*
Roper, Burns, W., xxvii
Rose, A., *334*
Roth, Guenther, *80*
Rousseau, Jean-Jacques, 29, *41*
Russell, Bertrand, 349–51, *367*
Russett, B., *81*
Rustow, Dankwart, *80*

Sadat, Anwar, 429
Sadikin, Ali, 150
Safran, N., *142*
Said, Abdul A., 6, *11*, 79
Sa'id, Nuri al-, 139, *142*
Salibi, K. S., *141*
Sanjian, A. K., *142*
Santayana, George, 314
Sauvigny, G. de Bertier de, 62, *80*
Sayeed, Khalid B., 254, 267, *281–2*
Schermerhorn, R. A., 7, *12*
Schiffrin, H. Z., *141*
Schlemmer, Lawrence, 7, *12*
Schnettinger, Robert, L., *195*
Schrock, J. L., *172*
Schwartz, Benjamin, *79*
Schwartz, John, *82*

Scott, Hugh, 206, *229*
Seiler, John, *43*
Selassie, Haile, 22
Senghaas, Diter, *81*
Seymour, M., *142*
Shapiro, Martin, 202, *229*
Shaplen, Robert, 166–7, *173*
Shepsle, Kenneth, *179*
Sherman, Gene, 237
Shibutani, Tomotshu, *81*
Shils, Edward, 31, *42*, 67, *306*
Shishakli, Adib, 127–8
Siddiqui, M., *284*
Siegfried, André, *463*
Sievers, Allen M., *173*
Silva, Milton da, *81*
Simmons, Lewis, 268
Simmons, Luis R., 6, *11*, 79
Sivan, E., *141*
Slabbert, van Zyl, *366*, 385
Smith, Donald, 222, *230*
Smith, M. G., 7, *12*, 32, *113*, *347*
Smith, R. W., 198, 204, *228*
Smock, David and Audrey, 6, *12*, *113*
Smooha, Sammy, 291, *298*
Smuts, Jan, 183, *372*
Spengler, J. J., *114*
Stanley, Edward Geoffrey, Lord, 337
Starke, J. G., 285, *298*
Steele, C. Hoy, *229*
Stein, M. B., *347*
Steiner, Jürg, 39, *43*
Stenson, Michael, *173*
Stone, Chuck, *248*
Suharto, 150
Sukarno, 160
Sureda, Rigo, 97, *112–13*
Swart, C. F., xxvi
Szporluk, Roman, *114*

Tamano, Mamintal A., *173*
Tambo, Oliver, 427
Tan Boo Hock, *172*
Tan Peng Siew, *247*
Tassud, F., *142*
Tauder, T. A., 211
Tayyeb, A., 253, *281–2*
Thant, U., 91
Thebehali, David, 369

Theodorson, Achilles and George, *81*
Thieu, Nguyen van, *93*
Thompson, L., *395*
Tinker, Hugh, *172*
Tocqueville, Alexis de, *309, 343, 356*
Tönnies, Ferdinand, *113, 460*
Touré, Sekou, *5*
Toynbee, Arnold, *52*
Tregonning, K. G., *171*
Trow, Martin A., *217*
Tucker, Robert, *112*
Tucker, Terry, *196*
Tufte, Edward, *114*
Tutsch, H. E., *141*
Tyrmand, Leopold, *26*

Urban, George, *114*

Van den Berghe, Pierre L., *7, 12, 113, 229*
Van der Merwe, H. W., *395*
Van Dyke, Vernon, *96–7, 113*
Vanly, I. C., *142*
Veenhoven, W. A., *141*
Venter, F., *144*
verLoren, van Themaat J. P., *441*

Wakin, G., *141–2*
Waldheim, Kurt, *316*
Walker, Lewis, *228*
Warren, R., *334*
Weber, Max, *66, 80–1, 460–1*
Weinberg, Meyer, *229*

Weinstein, Franklin B., *171*
Weinstein, W., *287, 298*
Welsh, David, *381, 396*
Wharton, Edith, *107*
Wheare, Sir Kenneth, *342*
Wheeler, Richard S., *281–3*
Wilber, Donald N., *274, 283*
Wilcox, Wayne A., *255, 281*
Williams, L. F. Rushbrooks, *282*
Williams, Raymond, *80*
Wilson, Allen B., *211, 229*
Wilson, Woodrow, *30–1, 42, 99*
Wingo, L., *334*
Winik, Charles, *81*
Wirth, Louis, *228–9*
Wittich, Claus, *80*
Wolfinger, Raymond E., *202, 229*
Wolpse, Howard, *82*
Worrall, Denis, *389*

Yahya Khan, Agha Mohammad, *257, 260, 262, 276*
Yeats, W. B., *19*
Yetman, Norman R., *229*
Young, Andrew, *320*
Young, Crawford, *5, 10, 12, 90, 111–13, 260, 272, 282–3*
Young, Gordon, *173*
Young, John E. de, *173*

Zafrulla Khan, Sir Muhammad, *263, 268*
Zimmer, B., *334*

GPSR Compliance
The European Union's (EU) General Product Safety Regulation (GPSR) is a set of rules that requires consumer products to be safe and our obligations to ensure this.

If you have any concerns about our products, you can contact us on

ProductSafety@springernature.com

In case Publisher is established outside the EU, the EU authorized representative is:

Springer Nature Customer Service Center GmbH
Europaplatz 3
69115 Heidelberg, Germany

www.ingramcontent.com/pod-product-compliance
Ingram Content Group UK Ltd.
Pitfield, Milton Keynes, MK11 3LW, UK
UKHW041952230426
12048UKWH00008B/282